Production and Operations Management

Production and Operations Management

SIXTH EDITION

Alan Muhlemann
John Oakland
Keith Lockyer
University of Bradford

PITMAN
PUBLISHING

Pitman Publishing
128 Long Acre, London WC2E 9AN

A Division of Longman Group UK Limited

© KG Lockyer 1962, 1969, 1974, 1983
© KG Lockyer, AP Muhlemann and JS Oakland 1988, 1992

First and second editions published under the title *Factory Management* 1962 and 1969; third edition published under the title *Factory and Production Management* 1974; fourth edition published under the title *Production Management* 1983.

This edition published in 1992.
Reprinted in 1993.

British Library Cataloguing in Publication Data

A catalogue record for this book can be obtained from the British Library.

ISBN 0 273 03235 6

Typeset, printed and bound in Great Britain

Contents

Preface to the Sixth Edition

'As all experienced operations managers know, there are but two simple devices necessary to run an operating unit – a crystal ball and a magic wand. In the absence of these, the present volume is offered to those engaged in that peculiar form of juggling, known as production or operations management (POM), in the hope that it will indicate some areas of knowledge which it may be of use to study. The text is not encyclopaedic, nor is it intended to be a training manual for any of the specialist disciplines, illumination is intended to be general rather than intense.'

The above, slightly modified, paragraph opened the previous five editions and as a statement of purpose it will serve to introduce this, the sixth edition, which has tried to take a more 'strategic' view of POM. The authors Alan Muhlemann John Oakland and Keith Lockyer have considerable POM teaching experience, and all have undertaken much research and consultancy 'at the coal face' both in the UK and internationally. This worldwide experience of the authors is reflected in the material incorporated in the book.

The authors' experience in a wide variety of industries and geographical locations has brought a realization that there are more similarities than differences in the management of the various types of transformation process, and that the management of non-manufacturing activities has only superficial differences from the management of those which create artefacts. For this reason the word 'operations' is included in the title.

The 5 Ps model of a transformation organization – Product, Plant, Processes, Programmes and People – fits teaching and fieldwork so well that it continues to be used as the structure for this edition as it was in the fifth edition. Thus, the text divides into six sections: Section 1 puts POM into perspective, Sections 2–6 deal with the 5 Ps. There is also a set of appendices.

As always there is the usual conflict between cost and length, and every attempt has been made to keep the increase in length of the text to a minimum. This has resulted in the abandoning of some material, particularly that which was of interest to a limited readership and the consolidation of some other material in existing chapters. Despite this, the present volume is one of the most comprehensive works dealing with production and operations management now available.

New chapters cover strategic issues in production/operations management and operations management in service (non-manufacturing) environments. Balanced discussions of the newer 'panaceas', 'TQM', 'OPT', 'JIT', 'MRP', 'MRP II', are included where appropriate. In addition to these major changes, the whole text has been carefully scrutinized and, where desirable, re-written. Readers of earlier editions will notice that in the present edition the lists of Recommended Reading are, in some cases, shorter than previously. This comes about because economic circumstances have dictated that many specialist texts have had to be taken out of publication and not replaced.

When the first edition was published in 1962 it was possible to identify with some precision the examinations whose syllabuses had helped determine the form of the work. The enormous increase in the teaching of management at all levels now makes this quite impossible. As previously, the book covers most of the 'production' and/or 'operation' work in the Masters in Business Administration (MBA), Diploma in Management Studies, and in the examination of many professional bodies, including the Institute of Industrial Managers. Equally, undergraduates taking management, business or administration in their degree studies, and MSc, and MTech students will find the text more than adequately covers the POM parts of their course. It is also anticipated that this edition will continue to be as useful to the practising production, operations and general manager or director as previous editions are known to be.

Our thanks are due to our wives for their forbearance, and to our friends and colleagues in industry and education who have helped us so much. Particular thanks go to Barbara Morris and John Dotchin for many discussions on non-manufacturing aspects of production and operations management and to Roy Followell and Geoff Marsland for their knowledge and experience in manufacturing. Probably the most helpful groups of all are the many and various students who have passed through our hands. They have been unsparing in their comments. In spite of the acknowledged thanks, the authors accept responsibility for any imperfections!

Alan Muhlemann · John Oakland · Keith Lockyer

SECTION 1

Strategy and Interfaces

Production/Operations Management (POM) cannot be viewed in a vacuum. This section examines the responsibilities of POM, and its role within the enterprise. Strategic issues and the relationships between POM and Marketing and Financial Management are explored. Similarities and differences between manufacturing and services are presented from a POM perspective.

1   The Production/Operations Function and the Organization
2   Production/Operations Strategy
3   Planning and Controlling the Operations
4   Production/Operations Management and Financial Management
5   Production/Operations Management in Manufacturing and Service Environments

Chapter 1

The Production/Operations Function and the Organization

Introduction

Organizations of whatever kind are viable only if they provide satisfaction to the 'customer'; this simple criterion is the only general condition for the continued existence of an organization. Such a statement, of course, raises as many questions as it produces solutions, but two things need to be clarified right at the outset:

1. That which satisfies may be either physical or intangible or both. In this book it will be called the product.
2. The customer may be either outside or inside the organization and may be a customer for the product or a user of the 'system'.

What is production/operations management (POM)?

Any organization can be represented by a hierarchy of input/output diagrams. At the base of the hierarchy is a simple diagram which shows that a customer's needs flow into the organization which then transforms them into that which satisfies the consumer (Fig. 1.1).

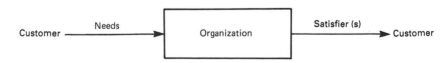

Fig. 1.1   The customer needs and satisfiers

Since the output returns to the origin, the input/output diagram can be represented as a closed loop (Fig. 1.2).

This basic diagram may be broken down into five sequential input/output diagrams. In the first the customer's needs are identified and translated into a statement of explicit forecasts (Fig. 1.3(i)), which in turn become the inputs to the second diagram

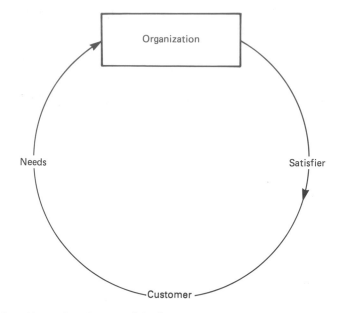

Fig. 1.2   The closed loop of customer satisfaction

where they are analysed and integrated to become a statement of resource plans (Fig. 1.3(ii)).

These resource plans are satisfied from suppliers, either internal or external, and generate the inputs which move into the transformation facility (Fig. 1.3(iii)), which produces outputs either physical or tangible (Fig. 1.3(iv)), which are then distributed to the customers providing the satisfaction originally required (Fig. 1.3(v)).

Since the output from any one diagram represents input to the next, and as the last output returns to the start, the total diagram can be represented as a closed loop (Fig. 1.4).

This diagram is, of course, grossly simplified. For example, when forecasts are analysed it may be found that within the facilities available they are unachievable. A reverse reaction should then cause the forecasts to be modified, and a second iteration will take place. Equally, distribution facilities may be inadequate for clearing the output from the transformation facility: this should cause a series of modifications in the preceding stages. A complete diagram, therefore, would not be a single circumferenced circle but a complex of interconnected stages. Eventually, however, when all signals have passed along all ganglia, a final impulse should flow around the circumference of Fig.1.4.

The production/operations management (POM) function is that which covers the second, third and fourth of these input/output diagrams, namely the analysis, supply and transformation facilities (Figs 1.3(ii)–(iv)). Since these are extremely closely linked it is not uncommon to regard them as one facility and the production/operations manager or director can then be regarded as the manager of the whole transformation process (Fig. 1.5).

Similarly, the identification and forecasting facility and the distribution facility are also very closely linked and may be regarded as a single one, called marketing. In some situations the distribution facility may be linked to production/operating rather

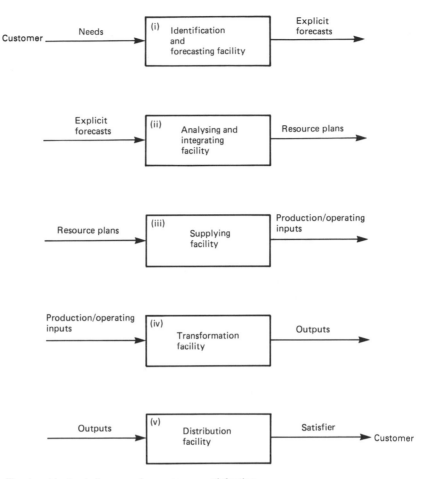

Fig. 1.3   Five input/output diagrams for customer satisfaction

than marketing; in others – for example retailing – the transformation facility may become vestigial or disappear altogether. Despite these possibilities, the fundamental tasks of any organization may be said to be 'Marketing' and 'Production/Operations', as shown by the two enclosing circles of Fig. 1.6

The relationship between these two major functions is crucial to the success – that is, the survival – of the whole organization. The closer together they approach, the greater the likelihood of success, and it is interesting to realize that at the beginning of any organization the marketing/operations functions are usually carried out by one and the same person. Separation of these two functions or a reduction of their inter-connections increases the likelihood of disaster (Fig. 1.7).

Is there a difference between production and operations? Earlier it was stated that some of the outputs from the transformation facility might in fact be intangible. Thus, instead of being artefacts they may be a service for the customer. An example of such a situation might be a club where the needs of the customer are that s(he) shall be entertained by providing an opportunity for social intercourse. Here the transformation process results in the provision of an ambience which will allow the

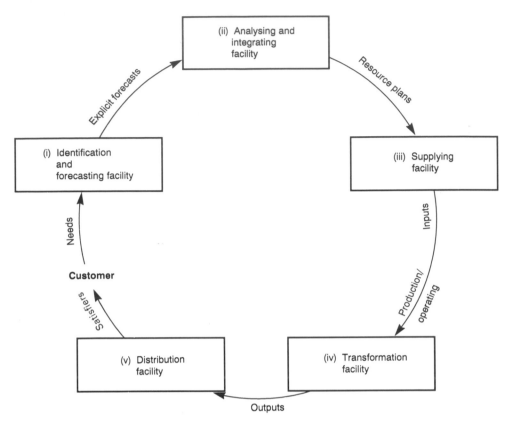

Fig. 1.4   From customer to customer — a closed loop

social intercourse to take place. The manager of such an enterprise conceptually carries out the same tasks as the manager of an enterprise producing artefacts. Equally, loading jobs on to a set of equipment is not significantly different from providing passenger accommodation on a range of train services. The replenishment of stock in a factory has many of the characteristics of the problems of replenishing staff in an aircraft. This co-existence of structure between tasks in parallel disparate organizations enables a useful study of POM to be carried out.

The interesting fact which has emerged over the last few years is that the well-established tools of the production manager, that is one who produces artefacts, are equally applicable to the manager of an 'intangible' enterprise. That is not to say that every technique is applicable in every circumstance, but that there is a 'tool kit' of techniques and methods which is available to operations/production managers, and which should be known in order to be able to choose the appropriate tool. A domestic

Fig. 1.5   Transformation — inputs to outputs

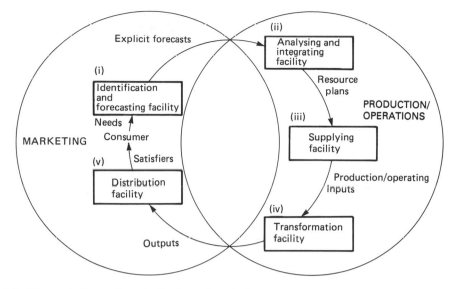

Fig. 1.6   The marketing and production/operations tasks

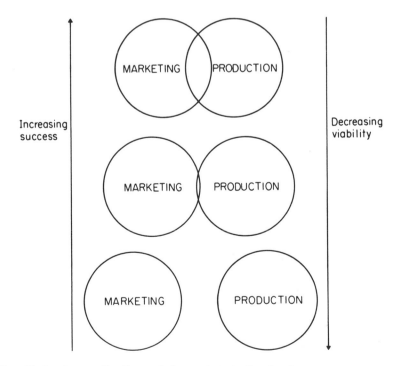

Fig. 1.7   The effects of separating the marketing and production functions

tool kit might very well contain a range of screwdrivers of different sizes. Depending on the circumstances, the appropriately sized screwdriver is chosen. Similarly in POM the tool kit will contain techniques which are not always used, but which are available to be used when appropriate.

Production/operations management: a framework

Of all managerial tasks the production/operations management function is the hardest to define since it incorporates so many diverse tasks that are interdependent. To divide it up, therefore, is to destroy it, but without such division it is impossible to discuss the work of the production/operations manager in anything but the most general terms. This problem of the whole and the parts is well known to the logicians, but nevertheless it is proposed here to consider the POM function under five separate headings. The division is arbitrary, but has been found to provide a useful conceptual framework for consideration of the work of the production/operations manager.

The five Ps

The product

The product is the most obvious embodiment of the interface between marketing and production, and it is not sufficient that the customer requires the product: the organization must be capable of producing it. Agreement, therefore, must be reached between all the business functions on such matters as:

    performance;
    aesthetics;
    quality;
    reliability;
    quantity;
    selling price or production/operating costs;
    delivery dates and/or times;

In reaching agreement on the above, cognisance must be taken of external factors, such as the needs of the market and the existing culture, the legal constraints, and the environmental demands. At the same time there are a number of internal considerations which must be examined: for example, the compatibility of a new product or service with the existing systems, facilities and traditions, and whether a new enterprise will excessively increase the variety of activities being undertaken within the organization. Variety, like entropy, tends to increase and as it does so it brings with it disorder and confusion. The temptation to increase variety is extremely great and, whilst it must not be resisted 'at all costs', the decision to increase it must be a conscious one. It is not possible for the POM alone to operate a variety control policy: this must be an essential part of the corporate strategy of the organization.

The plant

To make the product, plant of some kind, both in terms of buildings and equipment, is required. This plant, which accounts for the bulk of the fixed assets of the organization, must match the needs of the product, of the market, of the operator and of the organization, and it must continue to do so for as long as the consumer need can be foreseen. POM, therefore, will be concerned with questions such as:

> future possible demands;
> design and layout of buildings and offices;
> performance and reliability of equipment;
> maintenance of performance;
> safety of installation and operation;
> social responsibility.

These must be considered in conjunction with the financial, fiscal and political/cultural constraints imposed by the environment within which business is carried out.

The processes

The decision on product or service creation is made by bringing together the technical and organizational needs of the product and the organization and the people within the organization. It is extremely rare to discover that there is only one way to make something or to provide a particular service, and the ingenuity of man needs to be constrained if variety of methods is not to increase. At the same time, it is sensible to try to engage the skills, knowledge and intellect of those who are going to carry out the processes. If it were possible to harness the goodwill and good sense of *all* levels of employees, many organizations could be both more pleasant and more wealth-producing than they are today. The attitude 'we don't pay you to think but to do as you are told' may not be expressed in words, but it is often made painfully clear in behaviour.

In deciding upon a process it is necessary to examine such factors as:

> available capacity;
> available skills;
> type of production/operation;
> layout of plant and equipment;
> safety;
> maintenance requirements;
> costs to be achieved.

The programmes

Timetables setting down the dates/times of the transfer of products or services to the consumer are the other visible expression of the production/marketing interface, not merely setting down dates and/or times but also effectively determining cash-flow, that prime controller of organizational viability. If programmes are not appropriately agreed, then programming becomes 'the art of reconciling irresponsible promises with inadequate resources'.

Transfer timetables generate timetables for:

purchasing;
transforming
maintenance;
cash;
storage;
transport.

Although the problems of timetabling are simple to state, their resolution may be of immense complexity, involving not merely the solution of combinatorial problems, which are notoriously intractable, but also the simultaneous satisfying of multiple objectives, many of which are in conflict. Unfortunately the mathematical solution is often conceived to be a complete answer to the timetabling problem. In fact, of course, the behaviour of people, both within and without the organization, can disrupt the most elegant solution in an entirely unpredictable way. Conflict will inevitably arise between the need for discipline to achieve an effective solution, and the need for freedom to meet the personal expectations of employees and consumers.

The people

Production, from first to last, depends upon people. Like all other products of human beings, humans are variable – in intellect, in skill, in expectations. The work of the social scientist is continually enlarging our understanding of people and organizations and bringing home the fact that the 'simple' panaceas, better communications, small groups, worker participation, empowerment, industrial democracy, job enrichment . . . are rarely simple, since they usually involve fundamental rethinking of the whole organizational purpose. Despite the growth of specialized functions, the sharpest expression of personnel policy takes place within the production/operation unit itself, since it is here that the bulk of people are employed. Again, the need for the involvement of the POM in the determination of such policy is clear – again, separation and divorce increase the likelihood of disaster. The production or operations manager should, therefore, be involved in discussions on:

wages/salaries;
safety;
conditions of work;
motivation;
trade unions;
education and training.

POM is an amalgam of all the above aspects of work (Fig. 1.8), being that ill-defined area of interest where the five sub-areas overlap. Not merely is the area ill-defined, it is continually changing as external and internal pressures change. New legislation on, say, product liability may thrust the 'product area' into prominence while a strike at a supplier may cause the 'programme area' to be emphasized.

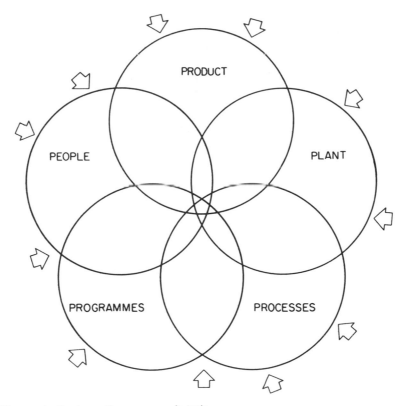

Fig. 1.8 The production/operations manager's task

POM and the 'mission' of the organization

Characteristically the transformation function will employ the bulk of the workforce, utilize the bulk of the physical assets and engage the bulk of the financial resources. Pressures for immediate solutions to transformation problems, therefore, are very great – a failure to deliver, an idle piece of equipment, a line of operators who are not producing, a breakdown in quality, an unsafe process or service – all *demand* attention. Without that understanding of the corporate strategy of the organization which derives from taking part in its determination, the POM will be forced to take short-term operating decisions which may generate unacceptable long-term actions by the whole organization.

The determinants of a successful and continuous operation of any organization include:

> quality
> reliability
> transfer   } of the product or service, and
> cost
> cash flow of the organization,

and it is clear that these are largely determined by the behaviour of the transformation function. To try to separate POM policy from the 'mission' of the organization, therefore, is an exercise which must be self-defeating. It must be an integral part of that mission and it may often be the most decisive part of corporate policy. It is not uncommon, however, to find that mission statements for the organization have been set down without adequate consideration of the abilities of the transformation function, and the consequential results frequently bring chaos and frustration. A policy on delivery (e.g. 'Company policy is to deliver within 24 hours of receipt of the order') can only have meaning if it is accompanied by policies on such matters as:

utilization of plant,
utilization of labour,
investment in stock,
cost,

and by an understanding of the technological imperatives of the product. Board decisions must not be taken in the absence of sound transformation information, as those decisions have to be executed through the transformation function.

POM policy

Assuming that an organization has a POM function, there will be the need for a POM *policy*, an integral part of corporate policy or mission statement.

POM policy is the term applied to those aspects of corporate policy which particularly concern the production or operations departments. Clearly this is an integral part of corporate policy and must act within, and not independently, of it. However, corporate policy cannot set down the operational details, and it is in making policies and taking operating decisions within the organizational capability that the production/operations manager effectively determines POM policy.

Failure to incorporate POM policy into corporate policy, or to include POM considerations in corporate policy will inevitably lead to the all-too-familiar conflicts with which the POM often has to deal. To be presented with policies which require

'a reduction in training costs . . . a substantial reduction in error rates'
'quicker delivery of special orders . . . less work-in-progress and lower material stocks'
'higher resource utilization . . . and greater flexibility'

can only result in frustration and malfunction. No set of policies can be wholly consistent, but to operate without too many changes of direction, the wilder inconsistencies must be moderated and some acceptable compromises effected.

CHAPTER 1 – HIGHLIGHTS

- Organizations are viable only if they provide satisfaction to their customers.
- Satisfying the customer can be broken down into five main activities: needs identification, leading to explicit forecasts; needs analysis and integration, leading to resource plans; supply of inputs; transformation of inputs by production or operations into outputs; distribution of outputs to satisfy the customer.
- The production/operations management (POM) function covers the analysis, supply and transformation activities, i.e. the whole transformation process.
- The identification and forecasting, and distribution facilities may be regarded as marketing.
- The close relationship between POM and marketing is crucial for survival and success.
- Many aspects of the management of the production of artefacts and the generation of services are similar.
- A good framework for thinking about the POM function is the 5Ps: Product, Plant, Processes, Programmes and People.
- A POM policy must exist and must be integrated into the corporate strategy and 'mission' of the organization.

Recommended reading

Journals

There are a large number of current journals of interest to the production/operations manager. These include:

Business Decisions
Business Management
Factory
The International Journal of Production and Operations Management
The International Journal of Production Research
The International Journal of Quality and Reliability Management
Management Services
Management Today
Operations Research
Purchasing and Supply Management
Production and Inventory Management
Quality and Reliability Engineering International
The Harvard Business Review

The Journal of Industrial Engineering
The Journal of the Operational Research Society
The Production Engineer
Total Quality Management
Works Management

British Standards Yearbook, British Standards Institution, London

It is sometimes assumed that the British Standards Institution is concerned only with specifications for physical products. This is not so; there is now a substantial number of specifications dealing with production/operations management topics. While individual specifications are identified later in the appropriate chapters, production/operations managers are well advised to check on the existence of standards before setting up new systems or projects.

Textbooks

Hill, T., *Production/Operations Management, Text and Cases*, 2nd edn, Prentice-Hall International (UK) Ltd, 1991

A British book which details the management perspective on the POM function in a business.

Murdick, R. G., Render, B., and Russell, R.S., *Service Operations Management*, Allyn and Bacon, 1990

An American textbook dealing exclusively with 'Services', such as MacDonalds, 'The Corner Drug Store', Red River Blood Store and The Palm Beach Institute of Sports Medicine.

Schmenner, R.W., *Production/Operations Management, Concepts and Situations*, 4th edn, Macmillan, 1990.

Another American text on POM which treats production of artefacts and services processes together.

Chapter 2

Production/Operations Strategy

Policies and objectives

Management at all levels is constantly required to take decisions and, in order that these will stand the test of time and advance the organization as a whole, it is necessary that they should be taken logically, not arbitrarily. This is as true of the decisions taken by the most junior supervisor as of those taken by the chief executive officer, and each in his/her own way requires to know:

1   The *objectives* or *mission* of the organization, that is the purpose for which the undertaking is in being.
2   The *policies* of the organization, that is the means whereby the mission or objectives are to be achieved.

In the absence of such knowledge, decisions can only be taken capriciously, and a short-term decision may determine some long-term action which is undesirable but inescapable. Without a clear understanding of objectives and policies a manager cannot, for example, embark upon a rational training programme, a maintenance programme, a recruitment campaign or a plant replacement scheme. In fact, no decisions can be sensibly taken which are of anything but immediate value.

Too often in the past, production/operations has been regarded as a self-contained, self-sufficient body, and its dependence upon integration with the rest of the system is recognized only when other parts of the enterprise change. The dangers of this tunnel-vision are great: for example, government legislation may force a marketing change which requires a service modification. In turn, this can alter processes in such a way that 'operators' are displaced, with consequent redundancy and retraining problems. Had the manager looked outside the four walls of his own unit, these problems could well have been foreseen and their effects mitigated. Similarly, a board decision to change from a selling policy, where orders are accepted *passively*, to a marketing policy, where orders are *actively* sought, will inevitably demand major changes in the whole transformation system and, again, these can be foreseen if the manager looks outwards as well as inwards.

The POM strategy must try to link the policy decisions associated with production and/or operations to the market place, the environment in which the organization operates and the overall objectives of the organization. This being so, the successful manager must plan, execute and control operations within the framework of the corporate plan. Indeed, unless the production/operations plan is part of the corporate plan, the total enterprise can only be a failure, or at best a partial success.

From the corporate policy of the organization, through its links into the market place, the POM function must then derive a POM strategy. These activities must not be separated, but linked in a two-way flow of information and decision making:

Corporate policy

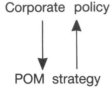

POM strategy

Strategies, guides and unities

It is only when POM is understood to be part of the whole organization – a sub-system within a system – that it can be truly successful. Organizations can succeed only by carrying on active transactions with their environment, and any production/operations unit stands within two identifiable, but not independent environments – the community at large and the parent corporation. The effects of either or both must always be considered. Furthermore, any production/operations unit itself provides the environment for its own constituent 'departments', and again the interaction of the parts among themselves and with the host environment must be realized. These interdependences produce two important consequences of high practical value:

(a)   changes in the environment impose changes on the organization;
(b)   changes within the organization affect the environment.

To survive, therefore, organizations must be prepared to *respond to change*, and no manager should believe that any decision is eternal. To construct an organization to be so rigid that it cannot accept change is to invite disaster, particularly since market and technological change is now accelerating at such a rate that continuous adaptation is essential for any sustained success. Clearly, change for the sake of change is wasteful and piecemeal change, 'tinkering with the parts', likely to be unproductive or counter-productive. All too often the installation of a new 'efficient' system has produced no effect on the *organization as a whole*, since the necessary accompanying changes elsewhere have not been put into effect. Where cost is measured, it is the *total cost to the enterprise* that is of importance, not the unit cost of a product, service or process.

It would be comforting to think that the setting of POM strategy is a matter which can be programmed ('. . . follow steps 1–10 and a strategy will emerge'). Unfortunately, such a routine can only be set down in specific cases: a routine for a small hand-knitwear organization would be quite different from that for a complex multi-occupier holiday hotel. Experience has shown, however that there are some useful aids to setting the POM strategy. These may be considered in the form of five guides and three unities.

Five guides

1 *Where multiple objectives exist, it is unwise to try to try to satisfy them all simultaneously.* A simple example will illustrate this. A public swimming bath can be designed to satisfy at least three objectives.

(a) to allow divers to practise;
(b) to enable serious swimmers to swim;
(c) to let 'fun' swimmers enjoy themselves.

These three objectives do not coincide: the divers will get in the way of the serious swimmers, who in turn will interfere with the 'fun' swimmers. To try to satisfy all three groups will inevitably result in dissatisfying them all. The local authority must decide which group of users it wishes to serve principally, and take action accordingly.

Similarly, an operations manager may identify a number of possible objectives:

(a) maximum customer satisfaction;
(b) minimum cash flow;
(c) minimum scrap and/or rework;
(d) minimum inventory;
(e) maximum resource utilization;
(f) maximum employee satisfaction . . .

Some of these are likely to be in direct conflict with each other. What is necessary is to identify the *key* objective and plan to satisfy this in the hope that the others will be 'acceptably' achieved. Customer satisfaction is usually the most important criterion.

2. *The greater the diversity the greater the difficulty.* The temptation to increase diversity is great: 'just one more of this, that or the other will solve all our problems'. One more product, one more machine, one more document . . . the process is insidious. Diversity must not be resisted at all costs, but the costs of diversity must be realized when taking the 'just one more' decision.

3. *Problems become easier if broken into parts.* Some problems when first viewed seem too vast to be dealt with. Breaking the problem up can result in solving the parts which can be resolved, and thence displaying the rest in a form which indicates how they may be dealt with.

4. *Organizations should be kept as small as the market and the technology permit.* We live in an age of change, which is more rapid than ever in man's history. The larger the organization the greater its inertia and hence the slower its response to change. It should be the market and the technology which dictates the size rather than an unsupported and outdated belief in the economies of scale.

5. *Organization structures should serve the needs of the customer.* Enterprises must create that which satisfies the consumer. It is from an analysis of the needs of the customers and those 'in the front line' that a structure should be built. Building 'from the top down' can result in meaningless and costly layers of hierarchy.

Guides to creating POM strategy

1. Identify the key objective.
2. Control diversity.
3. Break problems into parts.
4. Keep organizations small.
5. Structure serves customer needs.

Three unities

In addition to the above guides, there are three unities which should be obeyed:

1. *Unity of market position.* Whatever the technology, an attempt to satisfy two significantly different market positions is often doomed to failure. A restaurant renowned for its haute cuisine would be foolish to try to enter the fast food market. By doing so it would either change its haute cuisine to mauvaise cuisine or produce fast food at a high cost, or both. A common situation which arises is that there are idle resources. An attempt is made to use these by producing a 'cheaper' product or service, and the skills and judgements applicable to the main product or service are lost.
2. *Unity of volume.* To attempt to produce high and low volume through the same resources can result in considerable organizational difficulties. The shirt manufacturer who produces in very large volume for a retail chain has the technology to produce a special, non-standard shirt – but often at an excessive cost.
3. *Unity of complexity.* Simple products or services cannot readily be produced in organizations designed to make complex ones – the infrastructure of the organization will impose enormous burdens. Imagine a sophisticated aerospace organization being asked to make a clothes peg. The whole routine of estimations, competitive buying, work study, jig and tool design, planning, inspection standards, automatic testing . . . would swing into action. The result would probably be the finest clothes peg ever made – at a cost which could never be recouped.

Three unities

1. Unity of market position
2. Unity of volume
3. Unity of complexity

From a POM audit, the corporate policy, consideration of the five guides and three unities, a POM strategy will emerge. To put it into practice forecasts, systems and decisions are necessary.

Forecasting the requirements

To the operating manager there are two basic forecasts without which he/she can take only arbitrary decisions. These are:

1. The long-term market forecast, covering the expectations of the whole enterprise for the next five (or more) years.
2. The short-term sales forecast, covering the requirements of the market for, say, the next 12 months.

The long-term market forecast

The detail of the preparation of a long-term forecast is outside the scope of the present text, since the production/operations manager has little responsibility for it, although he/she must comment upon it, and eventually agree with it. It should be carried out by marketing people backed by economic, statistical, political and technical advisers, and will be based upon information on such matters as:

1. levels of activity, both national and international;
2. Government expenditure;
3. availability of human and other resources,
4. possible changes in price structures;
5. variations in living standards;
6. competition, both national and international;
7. possible new products and/or services;
8. marketing potentials;
9. technological changes;
10. resources of the organization;
11. history of the organization;
12. long-term objectives, policies and plans of the organization.

This forecast may take the form of a statement of anticipated output in monetary terms for the next five years, with notes on each year as amplification (see Fig.2.1). A long-term forecast is particularly necessary when considerable expansion is required and when heavy capital expenditure is contemplated. In exceptional cases – for example, the building of a new oil refinery or the construction of a new leisure complex – forecasts of up to 20 years are made, although some authorities believe that in view of political uncertainties there can be little usefulness in forecasts of any kind over periods of longer than five years.

The short-term sales forecast

The short-term forecast is the basis from which much transformation activity stems. It is a prediction covering the next budget period, usually 12 months, of:

1. the products/services to be sold, defined in as much detail as possible;
2. the prices which the market can bear,

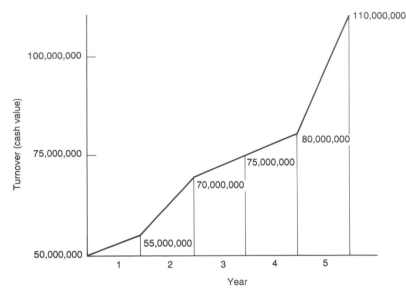

Fig. 2.1   Long-term forecast

3.   the quantity
4.   the quality   } of each product or service, and
5.   the reliability
6.   the required delivery dates/timings,

and will be in agreement with the general policy of the organization, as laid down by the top management, and the long-term forecasts previously made. Where a company is producing items for stock, for example, the statement of the short-term forecast is quite straightforward. However, a difficulty might appear to arise in the case of a company manufacturing to customers' designs, or a company offering a service rather than a product, for example plating, painting, repairing, travel, packaging or computer programming. In these cases it is necessary to assume that the work done is of a foreseeable nature – should it be purely random, no forecast is possible. Accepting this reservation it is then necessary to determine the product or service groups offered, defining a group as work offered having a stable and similar cost pattern. The short-term forecast will then detail:

(a)   the product/service groups offered;
(b)   the volume of business measured financially to be derived from each group;
(c)   the distribution of this business throughout the year.

The procedure for setting up a forecast may be as follows.

1.   A target figure for profit and/or volume for the forthcoming year is received from the senior management.
2.   The marketing people, using information on such matters as past sales, knowledge of present trends and market research information, will set a tentative forecast, which is submitted to the operating and finance people.

3. The feasibility of meeting the tentative forecast will be considered, having regard to the appropriate facilities available and obtainable. As a result of this scrutiny it might be found that one or more parts of the organization is overloaded while others are underloaded. Modification to the draft forecast will then be suggested.

4. The finance people will then examine the amended forecast to see if it will satisfactorily meet the company's policy on earnings and investment. This might reveal, for example, that the most readily sold product or service has the lowest contribution and that marketing, by suggesting a substantial increase in the sales of this product or service, has seriously affected the total profit yield. From considerations of this kind finance may propose further modifications to the forecast.

5. With the comments of the operations and finance people available, marketing will produce another forecast which again is scrutinized. Eventually, after a series of iterative processes, a forecast is generated which is acceptable to all concerned.

6. The final forecast is then submitted to the top management for approval.

This procedure, although apparently cumbersome, must be carried out effectively if the forecast is to be stable and useful. The forecast *must* have the support of the marketing, operations and finance people, and *must not* be produced by any one group in isolation. Equally, once a forecast has been agreed, everyone must work to it, preparing their own plans and carrying out their activities in order to achieve it.

The POM system

While recognizing that Production/Operations Management is a system within a system, it is worth repeating that it has characteristics which distinguish it from the rest of the organization. It generally employs the bulk of the people, utilizes the bulk of the physical assets, requires the bulk of the financial resources and is made up of many sub-systems in the organization. This is not to suggest that the production/operations function is more important than, say, the marketing function, but to indicate that its planning is likely to be of a *different kind* from that of other functions. In particular, the weight and size of the resources involved are such that the systems and planning must enable operating decisions to be made rapidly. The scale of resources deployed will often permit analyses within the function of a type which cannot be carried out elsewhere – but with this condition goes the danger that these analyses are carried out *for their own sake* and not for the results which flow from them.

The framework for the POM system has been set down in Chapter 1, in the form of the five Ps: Product (or Service), Plant (or Equipment), Processes, Programmes (or Timetables) and People. These will be discussed in Chapter 3 in terms of planning the operations and setting up the systems to manage the processes. The details of the methods and techniques involved in the management systems are the subject of the remainder of this book.

To set up and operate management systems is never simple, and to carry out this task with a multi-faceted function like production or operations is very difficult.

Before any system can be set up, developed or used, it is essential to audit the situation, discover what is extant and what is desirable. Corporate strategists have long suggested that in setting up a strategy it is useful to consider:

the strengths
the weaknesses } of the enterprise, and
the opportunities
the threats } offered to the enterprise

In considering a system for POM the authors have found that it is an invaluable discipline to combine the above four considerations with the five Ps of POM described in Chapter 1. This produces a grid (Fig. 2.2).

	Strengths?	*Weaknesses?*	*Opportunities?*	*Threats?*
Product				
Plant				
Processes				
Programmes				
People				

Fig. 2.2   POM system grid

To illustrate the use of the POM system grid, consider a proposal to use a computer for production control in place of an existing manual system. In this discussion only some of the cells are highlighted:

Plant – Opportunities? An effective computer system offers the chance of significantly increasing utilization of resources.
Processes – Strengths? All processes are well-defined for purposes of a quality system.
Programmes – Weaknesses? The present methods of production control will not easily transfer to a computerized system.
People – Threats? The existing staff believe that a computerized system will result in the loss of jobs and a reduction in status for those remaining.

Any significant POM system design problem can be presented to the grid for systematic analysis in this way so that every facet of operational behaviour is questioned, and in so answering a sensible strategy will emerge. In strategic and tactical matters the disciplines and illumination of a systematic question and answer method such as this can be extremely helpful.

Decision making

Whilst the life of the production/operations manager is exciting, challenging and worthwhile, it can never be said to be easy. Its multi-faceted nature, allied to the fact that the production/operations manager controls the bulk of the organization's physical and personnel resources, ensures a continual bombardment of problems which *have* to be resolved. Some method of simplifying the decisions which need to be made by the production/operations manager is essential.

Simon has made a seminal suggestion. He distinguished between *programmable* and *non-programmable* decisions, these being the extremes of decision types. Programmable decisions are repetitive and routine, so that a fixed procedure can be set down to solve them. Non-programmable decisions are moved, unstructured, and are often associated with people, their resolution depending upon the decision-maker's judgement, knowledge and experience. Clearly, the more problems which can be formulated so that their decisions can be programmed, the more time will be available for dealing with the non-programmable problems which are frequently the most important and subtle.

To simplify life, therefore, the production/operations manager should endeavour to set down procedures enabling programmable decisions to be made as a matter of routine. Areas of activity which lend themselves to this treatment include:

materials management;
methods and procedures;
timetabling;
preparation of estimates;
quality management;
safety procedures;
maintenance policies;
payment policies

In dealing with any one of these it might well be found that the programmed decision is not necessarily an 'ideal' or 'optimal' solution, but any apparent loss must be set against the benefits of releasing the manager to deal with the non-programmable problems. It is the aim of the present text to show how these programmable decisions can be made and to offer assistance in the handling of the non-programmable ones.

CHAPTER 2 – HIGHLIGHTS

- In order that sensible decisions can be made throughout any organization, it is necessary for any manager to know the objectives or mission, and the policies, of the organization.
- The POM strategy must link the production or service processes to the market place, within the framework of the corporate plan.
- To survive, organizations must respond to change – those caused by the environment and those which happen within.

- There is no stepwise process for developing POM strategy, but there are five useful 'guides': identify the key objective; control diversity; break problems into parts; keep 'organizations' small; serve the customer needs (through the structure).

- In addition to the five guides, three 'unities' should be obeyed: 'unity of market position; unity of volume; unity of complexity.

- To put into practice the POM strategy, forecasts, systems and decisions are necessary.

- There are two basic forecasts required – long-term and short-term. A procedure for setting up forecasts should be followed.

- The POM system generally employs the bulk of the people, utilizes the bulk of the physical assets, requires the bulk of the financial resources, and is made up of many sub-systems in the organization.

- It is essential to audit any POM situation before a system can be set up. A five Ps and SWOT matrix is useful in this task.

- There should be a distinction between programmable and non-programmable POM decisions. Systems and procedures should be developed to deal with the programmable ones, leaving more time for the more difficult non-programmable decisions.

Recommended reading

Hill, T., *Manufacturing Strategy: the Strategic Management of the Manufacturing Function*, Macmillan, 1985

Probably the best UK book devoted to a discussion of manufacturing strategy.

Jauch, L.R. and Glueck, W.F., *Business Policy and Strategic Management*, 5th Edition, McGraw-Hill International Editions, 1988

The fifth edition of a successful American book which is designed primarily to meet the needs of students of business policy and strategic management.

Luffman, G., Sanderson, S., Lea, E. and Kenny, B., *Business Policy – An Analytical Introduction*, Basil Blackwell, 1987

POM strategy has no meaning without reference to corporate strategy. This book is an excellent well-written introduction to the subject.

Primozic, K., Primozic, E. and Leben, J., *Strategic Choices*, McGraw-Hill, 1991

Presents a powerful tool for exploring the threats and opportunities for businesses in the 1990s and beyond.

Simon, H.A., *The New Sciences of Management Decision*, Prentice-Hall, 1977

A great book by a great man. Get it and read it.

Skinner, W., *Manufacturing: the Formidable Competitive Weapon*, John Wiley & Sons, 1985

A bringing together and amplification of a number of Skinner's articles. Well worth studying.

Thompson, J.L., *Strategic Management – Awareness and Change*, Chapman & Hall, 1990

Drawing on the writings of distinguished academics in strategic management and on the experience of a broad range of organizations, the author surveys the relevance of the various functional disciplines to the overall strategy of the business.

Chapter 3

Planning and Controlling the Operations

Product/service selection

Products and services must be developed from initial concepts to practical realities. Ideas for new offerings are not usually in short supply, but to convert these into products or services which perform successfully in the market place, in terms of the objectives of the organization, requires skills in their selection and management of their development through to full-scale operation.

Market research and research and development are clearly important activities in the selection of the product or service mix. These will enable customer requirements and attitudes to be understood and the ideas to be converted into practical products/services which can be transferred to the consumer.

In the early stages of product/service selection, feasibility studies and analyses will play an important role. These should collect all the information together and present it in a coherent statement which covers any necessary changes in existing products, services, process designs, marketing plans, and POM strategies and tactics. Proposed new products and services which survive the feasibility study may then enter the periods of start-up and growth.

Some products and services are market-driven, or pulled by the market from the supplying organization. This means that the output from the processes moves into the market place in response to an identified consumer need that is not being fulfilled. If the product or service is successful it finds its own niche and secures market share. Other products are R&D-driven or pushed into the market place by innovations which take place within the supplier. This usually leads to a special feature, such as additional programmable settings on a video recorder, a new toothpaste flavour, or a revolutionary packaging material.

Planning for the selection, development, introduction and maintenance of new or existing products and services requires the participation of all the functional areas. In particular good coordination is required between marketing and production/operations to ensure that their efforts are linked with those of research, development, finance and personnel to meet truly the needs of the customer.

Linking the production/operations with marketing

Marketing is the planning, implementation and analysis of the communication with the organization's target market. The marketing of services is just as vital as marketing devoted to physical products and, until recently, insufficient attention has been focused in this area. Marketing is needed to communicate new technologies, especially in information processing, and new service concepts across the supplier/customer interfaces. In many cases, the consumer must be educated on the value of new products and services and how to use them. This is clearly a challenge for marketing in all types of business activity.

In the interface between marketing and POM, neither should dominate. They should be in balance and support each other. *Undermarketing* is common in some service sectors, such as hospitals, consultancies, architecture and construction, information technology and many others. As a result, they fail to position themselves correctly in the market and try to run in several different directions at the same time. Market segmentation and concentration, portfolio analysis and market research are essential to effective and efficient POM in any environment.

Of course, some organizations make the mistake of *overmarketing* and spend too much effort, money and time on the marketing function. This can jeopardize the very operations on which the sale claims are based. There must be sufficient time and money devoted to the organization of resources, time to train and develop staff, etc., so that business or demand does not develop at a faster rate than the organization's ability to deliver quality outputs. Many organizations have declined, both in the manufacturing and service sectors, not because of adverse conditions in the market place, but by simply paying the penalty for a long-term emphasis on hard selling whilst neglecting the production or operations position.

The importance of marketing and production/operations being regarded as two sides of the same coin has been stressed in Chapter 1 and cannot be repeated often enough – there are many industrial and service sector success stories which provide evidence for this.

The scope of any marketing activities is set down by the basic concept of the *marketing mix*. This consists of all the variables that can be controlled in or by the organization in order to communicate with the target market. The traditional marketing mix has four basic elements – the four Ps of marketing:

product or service,
price,
place,
promotion.

In order to satisfy fully the needs of the service sector, to these may be added:

process (in which the consumer is often bound up);
people (employees and customers).

Detailed discussion of these issues, specifically addressed to marketing is outside the scope of this book. It is vital, however, for the management of all organizations to design and market services and/or products. This in turn requires good knowledge of the consumer requirements, decision processes and behaviour, and stresses the importance of the marketing mix for both services and products.

Planning the operations

Taken together, the objectives and policies of an organization should form a *plan* for its operations. Planning occupies a considerable portion of the manager's time, and it is worth while trying to identify those characteristics which should be found in a useful plan. A plan should be:

(a) *Explicit*. Lack of clarity usually indicates a lack of understanding, or knowledge or of purpose.

(b) *Understood*. The recipients of a plan may not have the same communication and technical skills as its originator, so that although it seems to be expressed quite explicitly, there is a barrier to understanding. This is most often found in plans drawn up by specialists for non-specialist colleagues.

(c) *Accepted*. Any plan should be accepted by all concerned in its execution – indeed, it is desirable that a plan should be drawn up by all those who will be held responsible for its execution. Inevitably, there will need to be tactical modifications during the operation of any plan, and if it has not been both understood and accepted, then there is a very real danger that these modifications may seriously affect the ultimate achievement of the purpose of the plan.

(d) *Capable of accepting change*. As mentioned above, circumstances may arise which require changes to be made. Any plan which is made or presented in an unnecessarily rigid form will be of limited value in times of change.

(e) *Compatible with the internal resources*. Cognizance must be taken of the internal limitations (e.g. people, materials, capital assets, and money).

(f) *Compatible with external constraints*. The plan must be practicable with the environment within which the organization is operating.

(g) *Capable of being monitored*. To be able to check on the execution of a plan, it should be cast in such a form that it can be monitored. This will usually involve expressing the plan in numerical terms where possible.

(h) *A spur to action*. Any plan which is not a very real stimulus to action is of limited value.

Questions to be asked of an operations plan

(a)   Is it *explicit?*
(b)   Is it *understood?*
(c)   Is it *accepted?*
(d)   Can it *accept change?*
(e)   Has the *external environment* been considered?
(f)   Are the *resources adequate?*
(g)   Can it be *monitored?*
(h)   Is the plan a *spur to action?*

To be successful in planning, the POM requires an unequivocal statement, which should be explicit and in writing, of the purpose of the operating unit and the means of achieving that purpose. The act of preparing such a statement must start from the top – the chief executive and 'board of directors' – and must spread downwards to each managerial level, gaining in detail as each succeeding level is reached. Thus, the top management should, after discussion, issue a broad directive to any manager indicating the objectives of his/her unit and the general policies to be carried out. This may lead to the identification of the 'Critical Success Factors' for the directive to be achieved.

From this the manager with his senior executives can derive critical processes or departmental requirements, and the further directives could be issued in terms of organization and operational responsibilities. These must, of course, be discussed and agreed between the appropriate departmental process or team managers and their associates. This procedure will be carried out at each level, so that all concerned know what is required and how it is expected that it will be achieved. The whole process is never 'one-way' as constraints at a lower level may require modification of requirements at a higher level. The availability of sound information concerning past performance can assist the planning process greatly, and the storage and easy retrieval abilities of computers can help to provide historical information, analysed in a wide variety of ways.

The most succinct expression of objectives is the *marketing forecast*, which can be considered as the quantitative statement of the corporate objectives of the company. In turn this forecast is translated into policy by an *operating budget*, the quantitative representation of corporate policy. Clearly there is a very real interdependence between objectives, policies, forecasts and budgets, and it is difficult – and possibly unnecessary – to try to decide where one ends and another begins. The important requirement is that they should all be self-consistent and this may mean that the examination of a forecast may require a re-examination of either objectives or policies, as the derived budget may demonstrate the impracticability of that forecast. The planning process is essentially an iterative one, and the planner will frequently need to travel up and down the chain

$$objectives \longleftrightarrow policies \longleftrightarrow forecasts \longleftrightarrow budgets$$

before a stable plan is achieved.

Setting up the production operations systems

The size, capabilities and complexities of modern organizations, even small ones, are such that management of the whole and of the parts must be an integral part of the organization. This is not to suggest that it is impossible to *direct* – i.e. determine the use of – an organization. Far from it: the important concept here is that an organization must have operating systems built as part of it, and that these must derive from the function of the organization itself. The *purpose* of a POM system is to assist in the setting *and achievement* of targets, which are in turn driven by customer requirements.

The essential features of a POM system

What, in essence, has had to be done in order that any activity is in accordance with requirements? In the first place, the whole operational system requirements have to be thoroughly examined, and an appropriate design developed. In the course of this examination any system initially proposed may then need to be modified and a 'model' system constructed. Should this model reveal that no choice of alternatives is ever possible, then no control can be exerted.

The system having been designed, it is necessary that it be set up that way and documented. When in operation, the system has to be measured. These measurements are then compared with the initial plan, and finally a report has to be fed back to the active portion of the system, in terms which are intelligible. Corrective action is then taken to restore the performance to that which was initially required.

The five Ps framework, set down in Chapter 1, provides a check-list of areas which must be considered when designing, developing, documenting and operating the management system. The authors are grateful to Alastair Nicholson for indicating two further Ps – procedures and paperwork.

Procedures

It is necessary to lay down procedures whereby programmable decisions can be carried out. In the absence of such procedures, decisions will largely cease to be programmable and will degenerate into a series of opportunistic statements which, sooner or later, will conflict with each other. Furthermore, the effort to make *ad hoc* decisions will reduce the effort available to deal with the really difficult non-programmable decisions, those requiring experience, judgement and personal sensitivity.

Paperwork

The formal mechanism by which a procedure is implemented is some form of paperwork (although it is recognized that the medium need not necessarily be paper, but may be some form of computer input or output). Frequently the existence of documentation is thought of as a form of bureaucracy existing solely to occupy the time of clerical workers. Indeed, in many cases this is so: the need for a procedure and the consequent paperwork may have disappeared with changing circumstances, but the documentation itself remains. A properly controlled paperwork system, however, is as useful as the rungs in a ladder, assisting the manager to climb from one situation to another.

All good management systems exhibit the same essential features. They are all capable of being

1. planned,
2. published (or documented),
3. measured,
4. compared,

5. reported,
6. corrected.

The tasks of *planning* (except in the most mechanical sense) and *correcting* should not be carried out by a separate 'control department' but should be considered to be the duties of the POM personnel. This causes any 'control department' to be part of the complete control system of the organization.

It is suggested here that the features isolated above are inherent in any system or mechanism for managing operations successfully. For example, consider a budgetary system. For satisfactory operation the following steps have to be taken.

1. *Planning*. A budget has to be prepared which takes into account the purpose, abilities, limitations and levels of activity of all departments to which it applies. It is this budget which forms the system control model, and which also sets down the objectives.
2. *Publishing*. Once agreed, the budget has to be distributed to all concerned. A well-founded budget which is never disclosed to those to whom it applies is of limited value – yet it is not uncommon.
3. *Measuring*. Measurements of activity have to be obtained by means of time sheets, material requisitions, account notes or any other appropriate means.
4. *Comparing*. The measurements obtained have to be compared with the levels agreed in the budget. It is probably necessary here to process the measurements in order to be able to carry out the comparison.
5. *Reporting*. Statements have to be fed back to the appropriate supervisors concerning any deviations from the budget.
6. *Corrective action*. Upon receipt of a report that performance is not in accordance with plan (that is, upon receipt of an error signal) the appropriate manager or supervisor needs to take corrective action – either by reducing expenditure or by initiating a new plan. Note here that (a) if there is no ability to choose between various courses of action, no control is possible, and (b) the taking of the corrective action is outside the usual terms of reference of the budgetary controller.

Similarly, in a quality system, precisely the same steps have to be taken:

1. *Planning*. Specifications ('models') have to be drawn up which take into account not only the purpose for which the product or service is required, but also the feasibility of meeting the specification and the cost of so doing.
2. *Publishing*. These specifications once agreed have to be incorporated in the operating information and hence communicated to the appropriate departments.
3. *Measuring*. The operator/inspector/checker/tester has to measure the characteristics appearing in the specification.
4. *Comparing*. These measurements are then compared with the specification. Again it may be necessary to process the measurements in order to carry out the comparison.
5. *Reporting*. Significant deviations (e.g. those which are outside 'limits' or those which appear, by their rate of change, to be drifting outside limits) are fed back to the responsible management.
6. *Corrective action*. The deviations will cause corrective action to be taken which will restore the performance to its desired level. In this case the initiation of this

action may take place within or without the POM function, depending upon local circumstances. In the process industries, for example, it is increasingly common to find that the corrective action is taken automatically upon receipt of the 'error signal'.

Controlling the production/operations

Tocher has pointed out that there are four necessary conditions for the existence of a control function:

1. There must be a specified set of times at which a choice of action is possible.
2. At each time there must be a specified set of actions from which to choose.
3. A model must exist which can predict the future of the system under every possible choice.
4. There must be a criterion or objective on which the choice of action is based by a comparison of the predicted behaviour of the system with the objective.

Ideally, decisions should only be taken if all possible actions and their outcomes are explored and the 'best' selected. In practice it is often not possible to do this as either the number of alternatives is too great or some factors are difficult to determine. Hence a decision which is probably sub-optimal may have to be accepted.

For the POM control system to function in the manner in which the originator or designer intended, it is necessary that attention should be directed towards a number of features. These include the following:

1. The purpose of the activity – its objectives – must be defined. Without such definition, effectiveness will be random.
2. Control is only possible if *choice* can be exerted. The greater the choice, the finer the possible control, but excessive choice can be expensive, so that it may be desirable to restrict choice by 'fixing' some parameters or boundaries. In scheduling, for example, the number of possible schedules is often so great that some restriction is vital.
3. Any measurements must be of an appropriate precision. Thus, in a quality control situation, if output is required to be held to ± 10 units, measurements to the nearest 25 units are of limited utility, whilst those to the nearest 1 unit, while useful, are perhaps more costly to obtain and process than necessary. Moreover, an oversensitive system may record minor deviations and generate unnecessary disturbances.
4. The information gathered needs to be pertinent – a material management, for example, rarely needs information on salesmen's expenses, although this would be appropriate to a budgetary system. Feeding unnecessary information into a system may well mask the effects which the system itself is designed to detect, just as noise may prevent the ear from discriminating between two musical notes.
5. Comparisons need to be made at intervals which allow useful action to be taken. The value of knowing that stocks have fallen below the level set for re-ordering is seriously diminished if that knowledge is obtained too late to permit material to be purchased in time for it to be available when required. Such tardy information

is usually termed historical – for example, historical costing – and it has use only as a guide for future action; it does not permit corrective action to be taken while the 'disturbed' situation is still in being. In some cases it is useful to use the rate of change of a characteristic as an action-sponsoring device. Thus, if the means of sets of measurements on the length of a bar being cut off were seen to rise rapidly, investigations would probably be justified even if the figures themselves were still within the specification limits required.

6. Reports must be fed back in a form acceptable to the active department. If a material control file is expressed in dozens of parts the information that so many standard hours' worth of parts have been produced is, at best, confusing and, at worst, useless. Care must be exercised here of course, since the processing of information may cause delays and/or distortions in the feedback.

7. The information collected by the system must be correct, or at least consistent. The non-observance of this particular requirement has often caused a POM system to be improperly discredited. Management systems do not *generate* information: they process it. An apparent shortage of material may arise from incorrect information entered on a requisition: a cost variance can derive from an inaccurate time sheet, and so on. The consequent errors do not arise from the system, although it is often improperly held to be at fault. It must be recognized that the way in which the information is collected may, by bad design, provoke the incorrect measurement or recording of data.

   Where an organization has a number of management systems working together, the effects of inaccuracy in any one of them should be reduced by the operation of the others: the interlinking of the various systems should cause them to act as a net in which one broken strand does not destroy the utility of the net. Moreover inaccuracies, if consistent, can be compensated for, and it may be cheaper and simpler to design a stable inaccurate system rather than one which is highly accurate.

8. The number of stages through which information is passed while being fed back from the output to the active portion of the system should be kept as low as possible. Each stage not only inevitably causes delay, but will also generate distortions, the correction of which may well be difficult, costly and time-consuming.

Requirements for the installation of a POM control system

1. Purpose must be defined.
2. Choice of action must be present.
3. Information should be appropriately precise.
4. Information should be pertinent.
5. Response of the system should be fast.
6. Information should be presented in acceptable form.
7. Reports should be accurate, or of consistent inaccuracy.
8. Stages in the feedback loop should be as few as possible.

Advantages of an explicitly designed POM control system

The above discussion suggests that at least one management system is inevitable in the running of an organization. This, of course, is not necessarily so: organizations can be 'regulated' by means of random ON–OFF switches, just as the temperature of a room can be regulated by arbitrarily switching the heater on and off by hand. This type of regulation is all too common, and possesses all the disadvantages of manual temperature control such as violent 'swings' in activity, irrational changes and lack of delicacy. It does, however provide a considerable element of surprise when results are obtained ('. . . after a year's trading we find we have made a loss').

It is sometimes argued that any situation will have within it a number of regulators, irrespective of the intention of the designer. While this may be so, it would seem likely that a control system explicitly designed to be an integral part of the situation has a number of very real advantages. These include the following:

1. The formulation of the plan itself, if carried out with due responsibility, will require the detailed consideration of the complete system. For example, when drawing up a budget, the objectives and the tasks to be performed must be clearly known and understood, and the material, plant and personnel to fulfil the tasks must be estimated. This will inevitably cause an examination both of the task itself (for example, is the sales forecast achievable?) and of the various resources (are ten supervisors necessary? – are more cashiers needed? – can another cleaner be afforded? – must cash be raised from the bank?). In the course of this examination, the tasks and the resources may require modification. Thus, the planned system itself is an organizational tool of considerable and unique value.
2. Once set up, the plan will give prior knowledge of the achievable performances of the system. This is obviously so with a budget, but may not appear to be so with other control systems, yet in all cases it applies with equal force. For example, if a quality system in operation requires a dimension to be held to $\pm$ 0.01 mm, then implicit in this is not only the statement that this precision is desirable, but also that it is economically achievable.
3. By deriving information from the system as it is functioning, it is possible to correct the behaviour of the system and modify the effects of any distortions. This is shown most spectacularly in the case of statistical process control, where the reductions in variation can be dramatic. Thus, control systems must be realized to be constructive, not restrictive.
4. By signalling deviations from a plan, management is released from the necessity of examining all data, and can examine those which require most urgent action.

Advantages of an explicitly designed POM control system.

1. The system is an organizational tool.
2. Prior knowledge of achievable performance is obtained.
3. Corrective action can be taken while such action is useful.
4. Only 'trouble' areas are examined.

CHAPTER 3 – HIGHLIGHTS

- Market research and R&D are important activities in the selection of the product or service mix, in order that customer requirements can be understood and met.
- Good communication links between marketing and POM arc vital. 'Undermarketing' and 'overmarketing' are both common and should be avoided by channelling resources accordingly.
- The marketing mix has four basic elements represented by the four Ps – Product (or service), Price, Place and Promotion. To these must be added process and people if the needs of the service sector are to be fulfilled.
- Planning production and operations should occupy sufficient time to ensure that the plan is explicit, understood, accepted, capable of accepting change, focused on the external environment, resourced adequately and monitored, and to act as a spur to action.
- The planning process is an iterative one and uses the reversible chain: objectives↔policies↔forecasts↔budgets.
- To the five Ps framework (products, plant, processes, programmes, people) must be added two further Ps: procedures and paperwork, in order to manage the P/O function effectively.
- Good management systems (procedures and paperwork) are planned, published (documented), measured, compared, reported and corrected. This is as true of, for example, budgetary systems as quality systems.
- There are four necessary conditions for the control of the POM function: specified times when choice of action is possible; specified actions; a model for predicting the future; criteria or objectives for comparison.
- The requirements for the installation of a POM control system include: defined purpose; choice of action; pertinent and precise information in acceptable form; fast response; consistent and accurate reports; few stages in the feedback loop.
- An explicitly designed POM control system has advantages including: it provides an organizational tool; prior knowledge of achievable performance is obtained; corrective action is in 'real time'; only the 'trouble' areas are examined.

Recommended reading

Wild, R., *Production and Operations Management*, 4th edn, Cassell, 1991

A good treatise on the planning aspects of POM. It sets a framework, provides definitions, and identifies critical problem areas in planning operation.

Chase, R.B. and Aquilan, N.J., *Production and Operations Management – a Life Cycle Approach*, 5th edn, Irwin, 1989

This text has been created to provide 'students' of POM with a powerful resource. The chapters on planning and control represent one of the best American treatments.

Chapter 4

Production/Operations Management and Financial Management

Understanding and using financial information involves several components:

Construction of accounts – how they are made.
Content of accounts – what they mean.
Analysis of accounts – how they are used.
Financial policies and business performance – how to plan for the future and measure.

The content of accounts in terms of how they are made, the principles involved in preparing them, what they say, what the words mean and how the figures are arrived at, is outside the scope of this book. There are many excellent texts on business accounting.

This chapter will be concerned with how the production/operations manager can plan and control the current performance of his/her unit or site and plan for improved performance in the future. It will be important for the P/O manager to understand profit/volume ratios and appreciate return on assets. He/she must also be able to develop and manage capital expenditure budgets and operational budgets, and understand costing systems.

When preparing and finalizing the forecasts for demand, it will have been necessary to examine the various constraints upon the organization to ensure that the forecast lies within these constraints. In so doing, all the data necessary for drawing up a budget will have been assembled – although possibly not in the form most appropriate to budgetary control. When these crude data are broken down into responsibility areas, then a budget will have been created, and the basis for budgetary control laid down. Similarly, if the information is grouped together in cost centres around products or services, then a cost control system can follow.

A budget is best considered as a statement of policy expressed in financial terms. An overall budget is, therefore, the corporate strategy of the organization, and from this strategy the production/operations manager must derive a POM policy.

Operational budgets and their preparation

One of the most powerful tools for planning and control available to any manager is the *budget* which, if properly prepared and used, has all the advantages of an explicitly designed control system. Furthermore, since most activities can be expressed and measured in financial terms, a *financial budget* can assist in displaying all the activities of an operating unit in a common language.

The preparation of a budget must start with a *forecast* of intended activity, and it may well be that the first forecast is modified several times when *intent* is offered to *ability*. The more closely the various functions can come together, the more rapidly will an agreed forecast and a subsequent agreed budget be prepared. It cannot be emphasized too strongly that unilateral decisions anywhere will result in stress and possibly dysfunction.

Given a forecast, the operations manager can use it as a basis from which to prepare the various budgets. These are usually expressed in financial terms so that a budget covering many different activities will be homogeneous. The method of preparing an operating budget may be as follows.

1. From the forecast an estimate is made of:
   (a) any material content;
   (b) the direct human resource content in person-hours of the required tasks.
2. From the direct human resource estimates, estimates are made of:
   (a) the direct resource requirements for each of the departments – i.e. the direct labour force required in each department;
   (b) the supervisory resource necessary to control the direct labour in each department;
   (c) the ancillary resource required to support the work of each department.
3. From the above estimates and the forecast the service and control staffs (for example, the maintenance, quality, wages, costing, accounting, technical, design and development, and managerial staffs) required to achieve the forecast are estimated.
4. From the long-range forecasts and the general objectives and policies of the organization an estimate is made of any other indirect staff (e.g. research and training) which may be required to be employed during the current financial year.
5. Calculations of general costs – rent, rates, insurance, tax, heating, lighting and so on – are made.
6. All the above are then consolidated into an estimate of what the total expenditure will be during the financial period under consideration.
7. The difference between the total estimated expenditure and the total revenue is any 'profit' which should be achieved.
8. This profit, added to the estimated expenditure, gives the operating budget for the financial year.

The budget is clearly a very complex statement, embodying both policy decisions (for example, those concerning the methods of depreciation to be used) and organizational assumptions (for example, those concerning the acceptable levels of support staffs). None of these can be justified except on pragmatic grounds, and it is therefore impossible to produce a budget which is clearly 'correct': what is required in an *acceptable* budget, i.e. which does not conflict with *any* of the organizational objectives. It is unlikely that such a document will be produced at a first attempt, and it is usually necessary to make a series of drafts, starting with one in fairly broad terms, and amending and refining it successively until acceptable results are obtained.

It must be stressed that the budget should be an *agreed* document representing a consensus of the views of all whom it directly concerns. The executive who co-ordinates the drawing up of the budget must actively involve the appropriate managers in the preparations, discussions and analyses required in preparing it. The budget is a *situation-displaying* document, and all managers need to recognize this.

The importance of the preparation of a budget cannot be stressed too greatly, since it results in management knowing *in advance* the activities to be undertaken in the budget period and their probable results. Beside this very obvious benefit, the act of preparation itself produces other gains – notably, it requires that the organizational structure and the staff required should be greatly considered. Without a budget a decision concerning, for example, the employment of extra staff can only be made on the grounds of immediate expediency. On the other hand, the budget will show immediately what effect the extra expenditure will have on the year's trading, and whether the benefits to be gained justify that expenditure. The structure discussed and agreed when preparing the budget will also result in a clarification of the duties of each individual so that each person can know what is expected of him. Furthermore, the act of being involved in the preparation of a budget – that is, in policy making – can be a potent motivating force; equally, the *imposition* of a budget can be inhibiting or destructive.

During the initial stages of an organization's existence, the preparation of a budget is difficult, and the results inaccurate. As information is accumulated, however, a budget becomes both easier to prepare and much more accurate. Thus, early difficulties must not be allowed to prevent the preparation of the budget – it is one of the most important weapons in the armoury of the manager. Furthermore, once the budget is prepared, it can be used as a very simple, yet accurate, means of monitoring activity by continually comparing budgeted with actual performance. Finally, should circumstances change during the year, the budget can be used to show what steps need to be taken to compensate for the altered circumstances.

The break-even chart

The derivation of a break-even chart from a budget enables rapid assessments of the variations in the budget factors to be made, and thus increases the overall value of the budget. In its simplest form it consists of the graphical representation of costs at varying levels of activity shown on the same chart as the variation of income with the same variation in activity. The point at which neither profit nor loss is made is known as the 'break-even' point, and is represented on the chart by the intersection of the two lines. On Fig. 4.1 the line OA represents the variation of income with output, and BC the variation of costs with output. At low output, costs are greater than income, while at high output, costs are less than income. At the point of intersection, P, costs are exactly equal to income, and hence neither profit nor loss is made. If the budget figure for output is below the break-even point (i.e. less than Q) then the organization is said to be budgeted for a loss. A more usual situation is for the budget figure to exceed the break-even figure (i.e. to exceed Q), when the organization will be budgeted for a 'profit'. Variations in either income (i.e. from

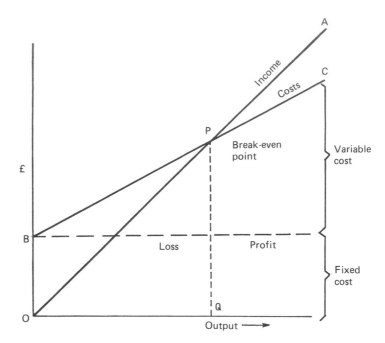

Fig. 4.1   Break-even chart

sales or revenues/or costs) will result in the slopes of the respective lines varying, causing the break-even point to slide up and down.

The margin of safety

In practice, it is clearly desirable for budgeted income to exceed break-even income by as large an amount as possible – working at or near the B/E point is very difficult as the ability to accept changes is small. A measure of this ability is given by the *margin of safety*: the ratio of the amount by which budgeted income exceeds B/E income to the budgeted income itself:

$$\text{Margin of safety} = \frac{\text{Budget income} - \text{B/E income}}{\text{Budgeted income}} \times 100$$

For example, if:

$$\text{Budgeted income} = \pounds 200{,}000$$
$$\text{Break-even income} = \pounds 160{,}000$$

then:

$$\text{Margin of safety} = \frac{(200{,}000 - 160{,}000)}{200{,}000} \times 100$$

$$= 20\%$$

Clearly, the smaller the percentage becomes, the more the organization is at risk.

Expenditure can be considered in the short term to be made up of two parts, the *fixed* costs and the *variable* costs. The fixed costs are those which do not change with variations in output within a relevant range and include such items as rent and rates. Variable costs, on the other hand, are the costs which do change in the short term, and within a relevant range, with variations in output: these include human resource and material costs, insurance, management and similar items. Together they form the total cost: the difference between the *income* and the *variable costs* is the *contribution*.

Profit/volume ratios and value added

In place of the B/E chart, a *profit graph* may be drawn which relates profit earned to output (see Fig. 4.2). At outputs below B/E costs exceed incomes, and negative profits, that is losses, are made, so that the profit graph is on the negative side of

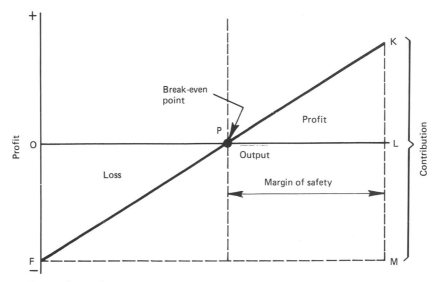

Fig. 4.2 The profit graph

the output axis, while at B/E neither profit nor loss is created, and the graph crosses the output axis. Above B/E, profit appears and the graph rises above the axis. The increase in profit for a unit increase in output is said to be the profit/volume ratio (P/V ratio), and is the slope of the profit graph; that is, it is the ratio:

$$P/V \text{ ratio} = \frac{KM}{FM}$$

where FM is the budgeted output. KM is the sum of KL (the profit generated at the budgeted output level) and LM, which is equal to OF, the loss at zero output, i.e. the fixed cost. Hence:

$$P/V \text{ ratio} = \frac{KL + LM}{FM}$$

$$= \frac{\text{Profit} + \text{Fixed costs}}{\text{Output}} \times 100$$

Alternatively:

$$P/V \text{ ratio} = \frac{KL}{PL} = \frac{\text{Profit}}{\text{Margin of safety}}$$

(expressed in £)

Whilst the profit/volume ratio is the increase in *profit* per unit increase in output, another useful concept is the *marginal cost*, which is the increase in *variable cost* per unit increase in output.

Value added

Contribution has been defined above as the difference between the income and the variable costs, that is that portion of the income which contributes to non-variable, non-assignable charges such as rent, rates, insurance, supervising and managerial salaries, design costs, taxation and disposable profit. A different relationship between income and expenditure is given by *value added*, the most generally accepted definition of which is:

Value added = Income – Expenditure on materials and services

Value added, therefore, represents the sum of money available to the organization from which its internally incurred costs (rent, rates, insurance, depreciation, design costs, taxation, disposable profits *and direct labour*) must be met.

Various VA ratios may be defined – for example, VA/employee, VA/£ paid in direct salaries – which have the advantage that they are free from any particular set of financial conventions. Clearly VA and the various VA ratios can be increased by:

1. increasing income, i.e. by increasing prices;
2. reducing expenditure on purchased materials and services

Changes in the key ratio

$$\frac{\text{Value added}}{\text{Wages and salaries}}$$

indicate the effectiveness with which human resources are being deployed *provided* that income and all other factors remain effectively constant. This ratio is sometimes used as the basis for financial incentive schemes.

Capital expenditure budgets, depreciation and DCF

From the preparation of the opening budget, and knowing the long-term requirements of the organization, the production/operations manager will build up a list of any new equipment required. This will be cast into the form of a capital expenditure budget which, when ratified by the executive or board, will permit the purchase of the new equipment. Subsequent purchasing will depend upon the cash resources of the organization, and the actual placing of an order for such items as may be authorized by the financial accountant, who will verify that the placing of the order at that time will not prove embarrassing. Depreciation of equipment is an important consideration in capital expenditure.

Depreciation

The Institute of Cost and Management Accountants lists nine different methods of calculating depreciation, and many others can be found. The choice of depreciation method depends largely upon convenience, and the effect of the prevailing tax laws. Two of the most common methods are as follows.

Straight-line or linear depreciation

In this method the same absolute value is deducted each year from the value: for example, if equipment is depreciated over five years, its value each year (as a percentage) will be: 100; 80; 60; 40; 20; and from the sixth year onwards it will have no book value.

Algebraically this is represented by:

$$\text{Value} = P - \frac{P(n-1)}{N}$$

where P is the initial price, N the number of years over which it is being depreciated and n the number of years at which the value is being calculated.

Reducing balance method of depreciation

In this a constant percentage of the book value is deducted each year from the book value. For example, if the depreciation each year were 50 per cent *of the remaining book value*, the value each year (stated as a percentage of the initial value) would be: 100; 50; 25; 12.5; 6.25; and in fact would never become zero, although when its value became negligible (say 1 per cent of initial cost) it would be 'written off'. Algebraically this is represented by:

$$\text{Value} = P(1-R)^{n-1}$$

where P and n have the same significance as previously and R represents the depreciation rate.

This method is simple to calculate, and provides heavier charges at the beginning of the equipment's life – when maintenance costs can reasonably be expected to be lighter – and lighter charges at the end of the equipment's life, when maintenance costs are likely to be heavier. Against these two advantages can be set the apparent disadvantage that, unless the sum of the depreciation and maintenance charge is constant each year, the apparent cost of operating a piece of equipment will change from one accounting period to the next.

Discounted cash flow (DCF)

The appraisal technique known as discounted cash flow (DCF) takes cognisance of the earnings made from the equipment and of the *time* at which they are made. Thus, the method recognizes that £1 now and £1 in a year's time have today quite different values, and that a profit of £1,000 obtained in a stream of £200 a year for five years has a different value from a stream of £100 a year for ten years.

The concept of present value
£1 available now, and invested to produce an income of 10 per cent a year (this income being immediately reinvested) would grow as follows:

	£	£
	£	£
Now, beginning of year 1	1	
End of year 1	1 + 0.1	= 1.1
End of year 2	1.1 + 0.11	= 1.21
End of year 3	1.21 + 0.121	= 1.331
End of year 4	1.331 + 0.1331	= 1.464

and so on. It is thus possible to say that £1.464 in four years' time, at an earning rate of 10 per cent, has a *present value* of £1. The figure of £1.464 in four years' time is an inconvenient one, and it is usually reduced to £1, which thus has a present value of £1/1.464 − £0.683, and the table above could be rewritten:

Present value of £1, at earning rate of 10 per cent

	£	£
Obtained one year hence	1/1.1	= 0.909
Obtained two years hence	1/1.21	= 0.826
Obtained three years hence	1/1.331	= 0.751
Obtained four years hence	1/1.464	= 0.683

and so on. The validity of the above table can be checked, and the meaning of present value underlined by taking the present value of £1 obtained four years hence and calculating backwards, that is, calculating the value to which £0.683 would increase in four years if invested in an enterprise continuously producing a 10 per cent return on income.

Had there been a steady stream of £1s received at the end of each year, then the following table could have been constructed:

Present value of £1 received annually at earning rate of 10 per cent

	£	£
For one year	0.909	
For two years	0.909 + 0.826	= 1.735
For three years	1.735 + 0.751	= 2.486
For four years	2.486 + 0.683	= 3.169

and so on. Thus £1 a year received annually for four years is equivalent to £3.169 available now, which is *invested in a project which produces a return of 10 per cent. Note:* it is assumed that the project earns at a rate of 10 per cent and that the earnings are immediately reinvested to earn at the same rate, the original capital investment remaining unchanged. If the capital had been invested in material at the rate of £1 each year, and the material had lain idle but still useful, then this would have had an earning rate of 0 per cent and a present value of £4.

If the annual £1 had been received in amounts of £1/12 at the end of each month, or continuously throughout the year, different tables of present value would have been constructed. Such tables are readily available commercially and, of course, programming a computer to carry out DCF calculations is quite simple.

Discounting

The act of taking a sum in the future and calculating its present value, assuming some particular rate of return, is called *discounting*, and it can be considered the inverse of compounding. To return to the original table, a single sum of £1 in four years' time is said to be discounted at a rate of 10 per cent to a value of £0.683. If there is a stream of £1s in cash, or a cash flow of £1 at the end of each year, then it can be said to form a *discounted cash flow* with a present value of £3.169 if the earning rate is 10 per cent. Clearly, different earning rates will produce different present values.

Present value of £1 received annually at earning rates of:

	1%	2%	4%	6%	10%	20%	50%
	£	£	£	£	£	£	£
For one year	0.990	0.980	0.962	0.963	0.909	0.833	0.667
For two years	1.970	1.942	1.886	1.833	1.735	1.528	1.111
For three years	2.941	2.884	2.775	2.673	2.486	2.106	1.407
For four years	3.902	3.808	3.630	3.465	3.169	2.589	1.605

Internal rate of return (IRR)

Any single project will generate a series of in- and out-flows of cash. It is possible to discover the earning rate which allows the present value of the inflows and the outflows to balance, This rate is the *internal rate of return* (IRR), the *time-adjusted return* or the *project rate of return* (PRR). Discovering this rate allows competing projects to be compared, the most desirable having the highest rate of return.

Budgetary control

Once a budget has been drawn up it can be used as an instrument of control by continually comparing actual with budgeted performance. Since all activities are ultimately capable of being expressed in financial terms, the breadth of control possible is very great. The comparison is known as *budgetary control*, and the essential features of this, like any other control system, are as follows.

1. *Planning*, i.e. the preparation of the budget. In general there is a master budget which summarizes a number of detailed or departmental budgets. The departmental budgets are produced first, then amalgamated into the master budget which will need to be compared with the directives issued by the board or executive. The reconciliation of master budget, departmental budgets and board directives may well require several iterations. Drawing up a budget in the absence of past information is difficult, but the act of preparation *forces* consideration of organization and potential.
2. *Publishing*, i.e. informing each executive of that which is expected of him/her. This is often done implicitly in the very act of planning a budget, but once the

whole budget is complete an explicit statement should be made. This 'selling' of the budget is most important, since no system is able to work unless the people concerned with it understand it and are prepared to make it work.

3. *Measuring* results. This is always a difficult task. It is necessary, of course, that the items being measured are those which appear in the budget, and that they are measured in the same units as those originally used.

4. *Comparing* the results with the budget. The measurements taken, while being significant in themselves, have a much greater significance when compared with a budget. The difference between actual and budgeted expense is sometimes called the variance, although this term is strictly applicable only to deviations from standard.

5. *Reporting* on the results of the above activity. This is done by means of budgetary control statements, which enable the manager, and such of his subordinates as are necessary, to know whether the objectives set out in the budget are being fulfilled and, if not, in which areas attention should be concentrated.

6. *Correcting* the behaviour of the system or modifying the plan itself. The responsibility for taking the corrective action often lies outside the 'control' department, being the responsibility of the departmental manager. The budget, and the budgetary control statements, must be *tools* to assist the manager, not *weapons* to assault him/her.

The essential features of budgetary control

1. Planning.
2. Publishing.
3. Measuring.
4. Comparing.
5. Reporting.
6. Correcting.

Preparation of budgetary control statements

The preparation of a budgetary control statement requires care, and the following points should be observed:

1. *Information should be accurate*, or at least of a known inaccuracy. If it is known that inaccuracies are present, then consistency of measurement may lead to incorrect action being taken, which will bring the whole scheme of budgetary control into disrepute. An unwarranted air of accuracy is sometimes given by quoting numbers to too many significant figures.

2. *Information should be pertinent*, and no information should be presented to an executive concerning matters over which he/she has no control. The simpler the control statement, the more use will be made of it. Two sources of useless information are: (a) the recording of expenditures which are fixed, such as rent and insurance; and (b) the presentation of information to one departmental executive of expenditure incurred in another department.

3. *Information should be adequate.* Nothing is more frustrating than the inability to make a decision because some information is missing. This can lead to the collection of excessive data, and a balance must be struck between 'too little' and 'too much'. Probably the only appropriate test which can be applied here is that of *usefulness*. Will the operating manager *use* the information? Clearly, the detail required varies with hierarchical level: information needed in one position will probably be excessive in a superior position and adequate – but too broad – in a subordinate one.

4. *Information should be up-to-date,* so that appropriate action, if required, can be taken. The presentation of data concerning matters over which, by virtue of the time which has elapsed, nobody has any control, is of little more than historical interest, and as such can only be useful as a guide to future action. The frequency with which statements should be issued depends very much on local circumstances: usually monthly statements are adequate in stable organizations although weekly ones, may be necessary in times of rapid change.

Information requirements for a budgetary control system

1. Accurate.
2. Pertinent.
3. Adequate,
4. Up-to-date.

Three points must be borne in mind when operating a budgetary control system:

(a) Budgets are only useful if the managers are *committed* to them, and commitment is best achieved by involving the manager concerned in the preparation of the budget. A budget imposed without discussion will be, at best, feared; at worst, ignored.

(b) Budgets, and the derived control documents, are *tools* of management, not punitive weapons. They should exist to help the manager, not to punish him/her.

(c) No budget should ever be considered to be fixed and immutable: differences between performance and budget (the cost accountant's 'variances') may arise from changes in external circumstances, and if these are significant, then the budget must be revised.

Costing and overheads

Whilst budgets and budgetary control apply to the organization as a whole, costing is the ascertainment of the amount of expenditure incurred on a single item or service, or group of items or services. There are two different types of costing: *historical costing*, where the costs are collected and analysed after the expenditure has taken place, and *standard costing*, where costs are compared as they occur with a predetermined cost, prepared in advance and usually known as the *standard cost*. Standard costing is particularly useful in repetitive operations and is a type of control (cost control) exhibiting exactly the same features as other managerial control, namely:

1. plan;
2. publish;
3. measure;
4. compare;
5. report;
6. correct.

In certain types of operations, the extraction of costs of individual projects may be more costly than the value of the results obtained. As with any other data-collecting project, consideration must always be given to the use to which the information obtained will be put. Unless there is an immediate need for data, it is probably unwise to collect them: too many files are filled with information which is awaiting analysis. 'The figures will come in useful one day' is heard all too frequently, particularly now that the computer makes the collection and analysis of data easy and relatively inexpensive.

Sources of costing information

No costing system can be more accurate than the information which is fed into it, although once a considerable amount of data is accumulated it is often possible to observe probable errors which can then be referred back to the originators. All information used originates somewhere, and it is important to realize this, as often criticisms of the costs being 'wrong' should in fact be aimed elsewhere. The cost accountant will require to know, when costing a job:

1. the time *spent* and by whom – human resource costs;
2. the material *used* – material costs;
3. the *overhead expenses* incurred – overhead costs.

Overheads are derived partly from the normal financial records and partly from returns from the operating departments. A policy decision is required on which items shall be recorded as direct costs and which as direct expenses. Those operations which constitute an inherent part of the product or service are usually considered as direct costs. No general rules can be laid down, however, each case being entirely dependent upon local circumstances.

Other indirect costs are those which arise from lost time and/or lost materials. These require very careful consideration. Analysis of both, particularly if reasons can be assigned to the costs, can be extremely helpful in pin-pointing weaknesses. One method of preparing such analyses is to set up a code of indirect costs, each common source bearing a number. These summaries will then indicate any weakness and also show its financial importance.

Location of costs

Data on costs are collected only in order to help the manager control his/her work. To do this, the figures need to be organized in a useful way, i.e. they need to be grouped around *cost centres*. A cost centre is a division, part or function of the whole enterprise wherein *responsibility* can be meaningfully located, for it is only when responsibility can be sensibly identified that control can be properly exerted.

There are no simple rules for identifying a cost centre beyond that of requiring an unambiguous definition of responsibility. Clearly the size and complexity of a cost centre will vary from organization to organization, although it is desirable to make it small enough to enable *rapid* action to be taken if the figures generated indicate a need for this.

The cost centre itself may well include the provision of a number of different activities or the production of a number of different products or services. It may also be useful to discover the cost of each of the various *cost units*. As with a cost centre, the definition of a cost unit is a matter of judgement and, again, the overriding requirement is that the results obtained should be *useful*. Each organization needs to define its own cost centres and units, although within any 'industry' common practices will probably have grown up and these are often usefully followed.

Recovery of overheads

Consideration of the budget will show that trading expenditure falls into three main categories:

1. Direct human resource costs, which can be allocated to specific jobs.
2. Direct material costs, which again can be allocated to specific jobs.
3. Those other costs which cannot be allocated to specific jobs, i.e. the aggregate of the indirect material cost, indirect people costs and indirect expenses. This aggregate is known as the overhead.

So that this overhead charge can be recovered, some method must be available for sharing it. The apportionment of overheads to particular products or services is a problem of some complexity, and reference needs to be made to a good modern textbook on costing for a full discussion of the alternatives available.

It must be noted that since the overhead cost contains elements which are the results of managerial decisions (a good example of this would be the rate of depreciation) then the operating cost too will be the result of a managerial decision; that is, cost is a matter of policy.

It is a common failing to assume that high overheads are a sign of inefficiency: this may of course be not so, and the relation between cost, direct people costs and overheads must be clearly understood. Any increase in direct human resource cost must always be accompanied by a reduction in overheads if the operating cost is to remain the same. There is little point in reducing overheads while at the same time causing the direct people charge to increase. It is not uncommon to find that a reduction in 'overhead' staff will throw more work – and hence greater costs – on to the 'direct' staff, giving an *increase* in total costs. This has given rise to the phrase 'the high cost of low overheads'.

Standard costing

Standard costing is analogous to budgetary control, but deals with cost units rather than the whole organization. Values for all the elements of cost are estimated prior to their commitment, and the actual cost is then shown as the standard cost plus or minus a difference, always known as the *variance*.

This method has the advantages of (a) giving price estimates of achievable costs, and (b) enabling management's attention to be directed to those places where effort is needed, i.e. to those places where performance differs significantly from plan.

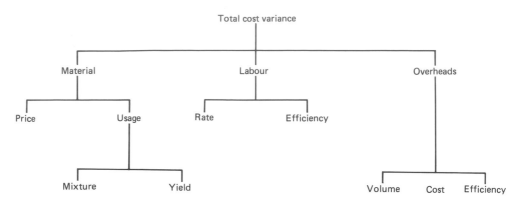

Fig. 4.3 Cost variance pyramid

The three principal variances (human resource, material, overheads) may arise from a number of causes, and the reduction of variances to their constituent parts, and the subsequent discovery of reasons for these variances, is known as *variance analysis*. Whilst it is based upon the classic variance pyramid (Fig. 4.3), a complete discussion of this topic is beyond the scope of this text, and recourse to one of the works shown at the end of this chapter is recommended.

CHAPTER 4 – HIGHLIGHTS

- The P/O manager must understand profit/volume ratios, return on assets and costing systems, and develop, manage and control capital expenditure budgets and operational budgets.

- Budgets are powerful tools for planning and control and can assist in displaying all the activities of an operating unit in a common agreed language.

- Budgets, which are complex statements, must start with a forecast of intended activity, which may be modified later. From the forecast an estimate is made of material, direct and indirect human resource, general costs and any 'profit'.

- Break-even charts may be derived from budgets and allow rapid assessment of the effect of variations. The 'break-even' point on the graph is where neither profit nor loss is made. The margin of safety measures the ability to accept changes.

- Expenditures (total costs) are made up of fixed and variable costs, Contribution is the difference between the income and variable costs.

- A profit graph relates profit earned to output. The increase in profit for a unit increase in output is the profit/volume ratio. The marginal cost is the increase in variable cost per unit increase in output.

- Value added (VA) is the income less expenditure on materials and services. Various VA ratios may be defined: VA/employee, VA/salary unit, etc.

- Capital expenditure budgets permit the purchase of new equipment. Depreciation is an important consideration and there is a choice of methods, including linear and reducing balance.
- Discounted cash flow (DCF) takes account of the earnings made from the equipment and of the time when they are made. DCF involves the concepts of present value and discounting.
- The internal rate of return (IRR) (or time-adjusted return or project rate of return, PRR) to the earnings rate allows the net present value (NPV) of the inflows and outflows to balance. It can be used to compare competing projects.
- Budgetary control is the comparison of actual and budgeted performance; its essential features are planning, publishing, measuring, comparing, reporting and correcting.
- In the preparation of budgetary control statements, care should be taken to ensure that the information is accurate, pertinent, adequate and up-to-date.
- Budgets are only useful if managers are committed to them, they are used as tools not weapons, and they are not fixed and immutable.
- Costing is the ascertainment of the amount of expenditure incurred on items of services. There are two principal types, historical and standard. Good information is essential to all costing systems.
- Overheads are costs which cannot be allocated to specific jobs and include indirect material, human resources and other expenses. A method must exist for recovering the overheads.

Recommended reading

Cowe, R. (ed.), *Handbook of Management Accounting*, Gower Publishing Company Ltd, 1987

A useful collection of papers by leading authorities in the field of costing. Expensive but worth obtaining from a library.

Drury, C., *Management and Cost Accounting*, 2nd edn, Chapman & Hall, 1988

An excellent wide-ranging text. Very well produced.

Drury, C., *Costing an Introduction*, 2nd edn, Chapman & Hall, 1990

The 2nd edition of this established text has been fully revised and updated. It retains, however, the optimal balance between theory and practice.

Dyson, J.R., *Accounting for Non-accounting Students*, 2nd edn, Pitman, London, 1991

Specifically written for those who are not accountants but need to use accounting techniques and conventions. Clear and up-to-date, it is wide ranging enough to be worth a place on every POM's shelf.

Mott, G., *Management Accounting for Decision Makers*, Pitman Books, 1991

Very useful, inexpensive, simple.

Owler, L. W. J. and Brown, J. L., *Wheldon's Cost Accounting*, Pitman Publishing Ltd, 1984

This is the sixteenth edition of the classic *Wheldon's Cost Accounting and Costing Methods*, a text tried and tested by time. Thorough and useful.

Pike, R. and Dobbins, R., *Investment Decisions and Financial Strategy*, Philip Allan, 1986

This is an established text which covers all aspects of the theory and practice of investment, including the use of the micro computer. There is also a student workbook to go with the text (with L. Chadwick, 1987).

Thom, D., *Finance for Managers*, Mercury, 1991

Well written general text on financial management for managers in other functional areas.

Production/Operations Management in Manufacturing and Service Environments

The spectrum from manufacturing to services

At first it appears relatively easy to agree a definition of what is an apparently 'straightforward' manufacturing or production environment, and illustrations quickly come to mind, especially if the range of retail products available to consumers is considered. There are component manufacturers; for example, for the car industry, tyres, batteries, starter motors; for the furniture industry, glue, screws, bolts, packaging; for the clothing industry, fabric, buttons, thread. It is then possible to go forwards in the chain and consider the car assembly plants, or the furniture manufacturers themselves, or to go backwards in the chain and consider the raw material manufacturers for these component supplies: metal manufacture, or chemical plants producing the ingredients for the glues. The list of manufacturing environments is never-ending and an indication of the range and length is given in the following list, adapted from Government statistical publications under the classification 'Production Industries':

Mining and quarrying
Food processing and manufacture
Food consumption
Drink and tobacco
Coal and petroleum products.
Chemical and allied industries.
Metal manufacture.
Mechanical engineering.
Instrumental and electrical engineering
Shipbuilding, vehicles and other metal goods.
Textiles, leather, leather goods and fur.
Clothing and footwear.
Bricks, pottery, glass, cement, etc.
Paper, printing and publishing.
Construction.
Gas, electricity and water.

It could be argued that all of these industries produce a tangible product required by a consumer or organization. However, this consumer might just be one individual in the chain. Consider the case of a customer who wants a dining table and chairs: these might be purchased from a retail outlet, which in turn was supplied by a furniture manufacturer. However in the manufacturing process the tables and chairs have to be assembled, which might be achieved using patented bolts and screws (especially if the products are to be supplied for self-assembly). The furniture manufacturer will be supplied with these fixings, by a component factory specializing in their manufacture, and itself supplied with the raw materials to make them by a metal producer. The retail store itself might have a 'do-it-yourself' section, and so might directly be supplied with screws, bolts and so on. Figure 5.1 illustrates these supply chains.

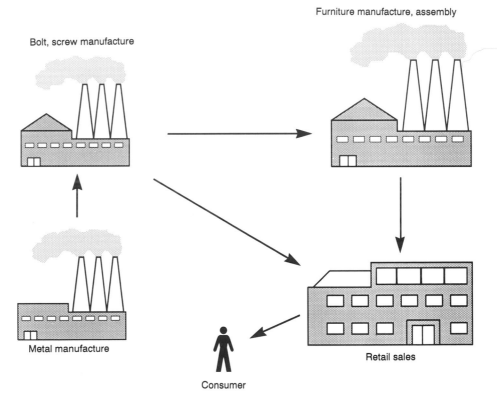

Fig. 5.1   Supply chains

The products or materials involved in this chain are all tangible in that they exist as artefacts. They are also functional in that they perform some specific function or purpose. The metal used to manufacture the screws and bolts will have a strict specification, and be supplied to conform to this; the same applies to the manufacture of the bolts and screws themselves. However, whilst the table and chairs provide a functionality, a surface on which to eat a meal, they also have an aesthetic quality, which is more difficult to specify and can be viewed differently by different individuals. If the meal itself is being served in a restaurant (in which the dining tables and chairs are to be used), again the meal is a tangible 'product', at least in part. However in 'judging the experience' of having the meal there is a multitude of other factors which contribute to the experience – a perfectly cooked and presented meal can be spoilt by a surly waiter providing bad service, or a table with one leg shorter than the others so that it wobbles throughout the meal. There are therefore other intangible aspects which come into play when examining whether the meal meets the customer's requirements (specification). One customer will not notice that the table leg wobbles while it will infuriate another.

It is possible to move on down the spectrum from the tangible towards the intangible. Figure 5.2 gives some examples of organizations and the products manufactured or the services provided in progressing from the one extreme (tangibility) to the other extreme (intangibility).

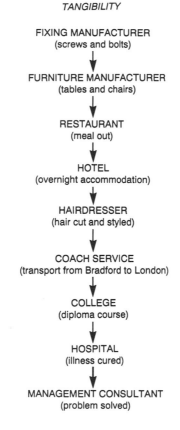

TANGIBILITY

FIXING MANUFACTURER
(screws and bolts)

FURNITURE MANUFACTURER
(tables and chairs)

RESTAURANT
(meal out)

HOTEL
(overnight accommodation)

HAIRDRESSER
(hair cut and styled)

COACH SERVICE
(transport from Bradford to London)

COLLEGE
(diploma course)

HOSPITAL
(illness cured)

MANAGEMENT CONSULTANT
(problem solved)

INTANGIBILITY

Fig. 5.2 The spectrum from manufacturing to services

It is worth pointing out also that as we move down the scale towards intangibility, quantification/measurement of the customer requirements appears to become more difficult. It is possible to prepare a detailed specification for a particular nut and bolt. It is more difficult to know exactly what a client staying overnight at a particular hotel requires or expects, and cost inevitably enters into this. Indeed, establishing a service strategy is crucial in identifying the target market and which aspects of the service experience are valued. A businessman staying at a hotel midweek on business will have different requirements from the same businessman spending the weekend at the hotel with his family.

There might be several 'classes' of customer involved. For the college, the students are clearly involved in the process and their needs should be considered in developing the 'product' (the course). However, business and commerce generally are 'customers' for the diploma holders, and are also therefore concerned with the product. All have expectations from the system; these might be in conflict, and might not be fully understood by the provider.

Comparisons and contrasts

Many authors have compared services and manufacturing (see recommended reading), and this section reviews some of these major points of comparison and difference.

There are a large number of similarities in terms of the management of the conversion process as we move along the spectrum from the tangible towards the intangible. The furniture manufacturer needs stocks of wood, screws and so on to allow manufacture and assembly to proceed, the restaurateur needs stocks of vegetables in order to prepare the meals, the hospital requires stocks of appropriate drugs to treat patients. All therefore need to try to predict requirements and to adopt a policy for managing the stocks of materials in order to be able to meet demand in the most cost-effective manner. All organizations need to plan and manage the availability of the human resources: the cooks need to be available to prepare and cook the meals when they are required by the diners at the restaurant, drivers must be available to drive the coaches according to the timetables (and must satisfy additional restrictions on maximum driving time), lecturers must be available to provide the courses within the college. It is also necessary to manage the physical resources, the kitchen equipment and ovens, the bedrooms in the hotel, the hairdriers in the hairdresser's, the coaches, the lecture room. Many of the topics and concepts covered later on in the text concerning these issues can be applied in many environments, provided allowance is made for specific constraints imposed.

It is tempting to claim that, as we go further down the path towards intangibility, there are fewer similarities and the concepts have much less to offer because of the idiosyncrasies of the service environment, However, this argument is not valid since it could be argued also that every manufacturing situation is unique, with its own set of constraints. One of the challenges of POM is the adoption of general concepts in a specific situation.

It has to be said, however, that there are some differences between 'pure manufacturing' and 'pure services', and that some of these should be recognized and can be exploited to advantage.

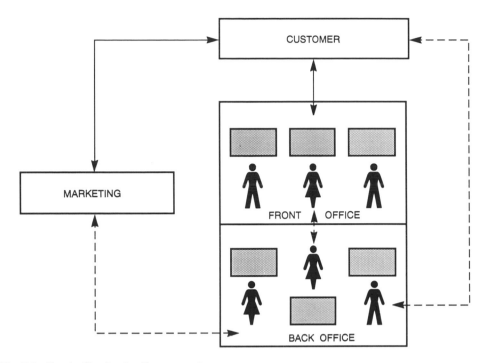

Fig. 5.3   Front office/back office concept

One concept which a number of authors have developed is that of the 'front and back office'. This is illustrated in Fig. 5.3. It is a structure which is found frequently in service operations. Specific illustrations are in banking, with counter staff in direct contact with the customers handling their transactions. They are supported by 'behind the-scenes' staff, processing the direct debits, checking account details, ordering and preparing foreign currency and performing other activities independent of the presence of the customer. A similar type of structure exists in building societies, with customer contact concerned with such issues as discussing mortgage requirements and account transactions, and back office activities involving arranging building surveys, checking and preparing documentation and so on. Other illustrations are insurance offices, retailing (e.g. in-store stock management and warehouse stock management), health care (e.g. taking an X-ray and processing it). The presence of the customer is 'accepted' in the front office (in fact *required* in some environments – try taking an X-ray without the patient!), but this acts as a buffer for the back office where the customer goes or makes contact less frequently. The presence of the customer in the front office is a 'disruptive' influence from the viewpoint of planning. The back office is more like a 'factory' (some authors have used this comparison more directly); activities can be more readily planned since it is a more predictable environment, and more amenable to many of the planning-related concepts described later in the text. The effect of the customer in the system will be discussed later.

A distinguishing feature of service operations is the general inability to hold stocks 'of the service' (not to be confused with holding stocks of materials required or consumed in producing the service). If the fixing manufacturer has no specific orders to fill, he can make screws for stock; if the management consultant has no clients then he is idle, he cannot solve problems in anticipation of future work. If the coach has only half the seats occupied, then it must still make the journey and the potential seat occupancy is lost for ever. This has implications for resource utilization, and capacity and demand management.

The presence of customers during the provision of the service can be a mixed blessing. They can be used as a resource, e.g. filling in forms in a bank, serving themselves in a supermarket. The entire concept of self-service in so many of today's activities provides many examples of this. However, there are negative aspects of customer presence which have to be balanced. Customers are often able to check directly the quality of the processes behind the service that is being provided, because they are present in the system. They will see the fork that is dropped on the floor while the table is being set, yet still used. Purchasers of a car are not generally aware that the steering wheel was a tight fit and had to be 'helped on' with a hammer since they are not present during the manufacturing process. Customers can also be used to control quality, in selecting their own fruit and vegetables, or checking their own bank statements for errors. In a supermarket it is easy to set up stock management systems in the warehouse to ensure the items are loaded on to the shelves in strict date rotations (first-in – first-out). This is far more difficult to ensure once the items are on the shelves, since customers will often search for the item with the latest sell-by date, leaving perfectly acceptable older items on the shelf. The customer also provides a degree of unpredictability which makes resource planning difficult. Will the next customer in the queue at the bank be paying in one cheque (a ten-second transaction) or the whole day's takings in small change from an ice-cream stall (which will occupy several minutes), and will that customer then take the opportunity to resolve some other problems (changing a standing order/direct debit, enquiring about a car loan or mortgage)?

In manufacturing it is easier to specify the bounds of responsibilities. In service operations the role of operations merges into marketing and there is some direct overlap; this is particularly true in the front office structure outlined earlier. The customer going to the building society for a cheque in favour of the credit card he holds through his bank is likely to be told that the building society also issues that type of credit card (on more favourable conditions) and be invited to apply for one. It is the presence of the customer which makes it possible to exploit the situation. Thus what was essentially an operations activity (a withdrawal) has been merged with a selling function. This also has implications for training, staff development and multi-skilled working.

Operations management within manufacturing

The distinction is made above between manufacturing and services. Frequently within services the phrase 'operations management' tends to be used, whereas in manufacturing the phrase 'production management' is adopted to describe the management of the conversion process. However, even within a manufacturing organization, operations management concepts can be used within the non-manufacturing aspects of the operations.

The administration manager has an inventory of office stationery to manage (copier paper, envelopes, preprinted invoices, and so on). Delay in invoicing the customer due to a lack of invoice forms can significantly affect cash flow. This can be just as important as a late delivery of raw materials in the factory. He is also responsible for office equipment – both its selection and maintenance.

The accountant has to establish procedures for handling invoices and payments. This is 'work' in the same sense as 'work' is done on the factory floor where the products are actually being made to be sold to customers. As such it should be carried out in the most efficient manner. There is no reason why it should not be studied in a similar manner to the shop floor work.

The procedures for handling customer queries should be free from errors in exactly the same way as the products manufactured should be free from defects. Quality management is important in both of these environments, and concepts from the common pool of approaches are appropriate.

CHAPTER 5 – HIGHLIGHTS

- There is a spectrum of environments for production/operations management: from tangible (e.g. watch manufacture) to intangible (e.g. estate agent).
- The main features of service operations are: inability to hold 'stocks' of the service; the front office/back office concept, which facilitates planning; possible integration of operations and marketing; participation of the customer.
- Operations management within manufacturing organizations occurs in the administration function, in accounting and in the marketing area.

Recommended reading

Harris, N.D., *Service Operations Management*, Cassell, 1989

A relatively new book, which claims to show how management techniques developed primarily within manufacturing industries can be effectively applied to the more customer orientated service sector.

Jones, P. (ed.), *Management in Service Industries*, Pitman, 1989

A collection of articles which provides an overview of current practice in this area.

Lovelock, C., *Managing Services*, Prentice-Hall, 1988

Includes substantial analysis of the operations functions in service businesses.

Moores, B. (ed.), *Are They Being Served*, Philip Allan, 1986

An interesting selection of cases in the field of service quality control, based on a range of companies which will be well known to readers, including travel, retailing, hospitality and health.

Murdick, R.G., Render, B. and Russell, R.S., *Service Operations Management*, Allyn and Bacon, 1990

One of the latest texts to focus on service operations, comprehensive, and well supported by case studies.

Sasser, W.R., Olsen, P. and Wycckoff, D.D., *Management of Service Operations: Text, Cases and Readings*, Allyn and Bacon, 1978

One of the original texts on service operations management, well worth reading.

Voss, C.A., Armistead, C., Johnston, B. and Morris, B., *Operations Management in Service Industries and the Public Sector*, Wiley, 1985

An interesting blend of concepts and case studies; many of the ideosyncrasies of 'service environments' are covered in detail.

SECTION 2

The Product or Service

One of the principal focuses of the organization is the product manufactured or the service provided. This section reviews the various issues associated with this aspect. Product/service design is examined, especially the inputs from marketing. This leads to a discussion of variety, and value. Finally quality and reliability are introduced, along with an analysis of the competitive advantages to be gained through sound POM practice.

Chapter 6

Marketing and Product/Service Design

Understanding and meeting customer requirements

The foundations for long-term success in any type of operation can be established only on the basis of a synergistic relationship between the marketing, design and operations functions of the organization. Good integration and iteration between these groups is essential.

Product or service development should be an interactive process whereby the customer, and marketing, sales (if any), product or service designers, purchasing, suppliers, and operations or production teams work together to develop a service or product that meets customer expectations and can be generated or produced economically.

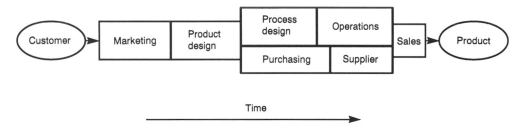

Fig. 6.1   Traditional sequential product development

A traditional product/service development process, used in many industries including automotives, involves barriers between pairs of functions, each member of which believes the other is incompetent. This is a sequential process (Fig. 6.1) divided into separate functions, whereby:

1. Marketing passes the requirements to the product/service designers.
2. The designers believe the requirements are unrealistic with regard to available technology or resources, alter the requirements and design a product or service to meet the *corrected* market analyses.
3. The designers pass the product or service design to the process designers and purchasing.

4. The process designers believe the product designers do not understand the real world – they find design flaws – and correct the product or service design so that they think it can be produced or offered. (By this time scheduling problems have developed and there is insufficient time to re-check the true requirements.)
5. The process designers pass the new product/service and process design to operations or production.
6. Purchasing interact with suppliers, who indicate problems with the design, and they work with the suppliers to correct it.
7. The suppliers are contracted to produce what will meet the needs of the *new* designs economically.
8. Operations receive the process design and the purchased materials, which all have to be corrected before anything can be sensibly produced.
9. Operations change the market analysis and product or service design, and have to rush into production while still designing the product or service.
10. In a manufacturing company, production pass the first few products (produced only by a series of quick fixes) to sales.
11. Sales receive, with the products, a suggested selling price and a forecast from marketing, but they are not happy with selling what the customer does not want – 'sub-standard' products.

Investigations then bounce from one barrier to another with responsibility and accountability for the product or service being denied, unrealistic demands being claimed, little or no feedback being given, and nothing but resentment is generated.

In theory this approach should have led to an understanding of the customer requirements, through the market analysis, but the customer is not *really* part of the traditional product/service development process. The length of time from the initial market analysis to the first sales is so long that the analysis is often invalid. It is not, therefore, surprising that the product does not meet the requirements. Moreover, the entire product/service development process is restarted at each phase, creating time-consuming and expensive duplication.

Changing this traditional approach to an integrated iterative one requires that each element is carried out in the context of the others and that there are excellent communications (Fig. 6.2). Representatives of the customer, marketing, sales, product design, process design, purchasing, suppliers, and operations need to work as a cohesive, flexible, supportive product or service development team.

Many organizations have found increased efficiency, simplification, faster response times, less politics and red tape, more focused expertise, and lower costs, by adopting this team approach. To facilitate manufacturing, this computer-aided design (CAD), computer-aided engineering (CAE), and electronic data interchange (EDI) have been important tools of design and communications.

The team approach to product or service development is usually implemented on a product-by-product basis. The team should be broad-based and the true customer requirements known to the entire team, which should 'live' with the project from preliminary concept through to successful operation or production.

Once the team has been formed it must assess the magnitude of the task, whether it is concerned with a completely new product/service or a minor modification of an existing one. All the customer requirements, product/service assumptions and any restrictions, production or operation requirements must be documented. Specific

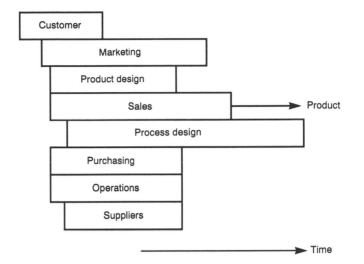

Fig. 6.2 An integrated iterative approach to product development

product goals must be established, accepted and embraced by the entire team and there must be commitment to these by top management.

Turning requirements into designs

Turning the requirements into designs may involve some research, development, and design activities. The following are working definitions:

1. *Research*. The discovery of novel products, services, techniques, ideas, information or systems. Market research is certainly part of research.
2. *Development*. The improvement of existing products, services, techniques, ideas or systems.
3. *Design*. The translation of the requirements into a form suitable for operation, production or use. It may include re-design to cater for ease of operation or changes in specification.

Accepting the above definitions, it will be seen that design may encompass both research and development, as these are creative activities.

The design function sits between the marketing and the operations functions. Its purpose is essentially to take the needs of the market, as determined by marketing, and translate them into such a form that they can be satisfied within the operating unit.

It is clear that the decisions taken during the design stage can have significant and very long-term effects upon the whole organization. A badly designed coat, for example, will never sell however well it is made; a poorly designed questionnaire which asks the wrong questions will never elicit the right information, however well it is presented and distributed; an 'extravagant' design will involve costs which can never be recovered in the market place. The importance of the design function can hardly be over-estimated.

The design processes and systems

In every project the design programme will pass through the following stages.

1. *Conception*, when a draft specification for the product or service is laid down incorporating the user requirements.
2. *Acceptance*, where the specification is shown to be achievable. It is here that the trade-offs between requirements and achievability are made explicit *and resolved*.
3. *Execution*, where a number of models or pilot runs are prepared from the work above. This applies equally to services and to products, since trial runs of new service offerings should be made.
4. *Translation*, where the project is put into such a form that it can be operated within the organization, and to the specification laid down at stage 2.
5. *Pre-operational*, where quantities are produced or services provided in numbers sufficient to check the design, personnel, equipment and specification. It is not until this stage that specifications can be 'frozen', i.e. considered to be final and not liable to change without authorization.

The above five steps are always present in some form, although in small organizations they may be telescoped, while for production in very small quantities or in infrequently operated services the trials often coincide with the first, and possibly the only, product or service. In projects where large articles – boilers, power plants – are being designed, the last three stages effectively coalesce with the actual production stage. It must be remembered that the decisions taken at each stage are never made in isolation: they all affect, in some degree, previous and succeeding stages and the activities of the marketing and operations functions (Fig. 6.3). Once a design is complete, steps must be taken to maintain it, or to amend it *formally*.

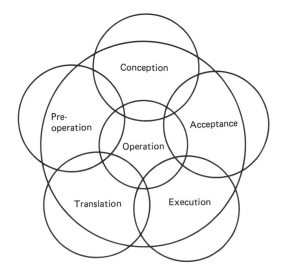

Fig. 6.3   The interaction of the five stages of design with marketing and operations

Conception

This first stage is most important in providing the basis for control of all subsequent design activity. A specification must be drawn up in as much detail as possible by marketing in discussion with the customer or representatives and the design group. Where highly technical and capital goods are concerned, discussions are often on an 'engineer-to-engineer' basis, as the technical requirements and consequences may be extremely taxing.

Time spent here will not only indicate to the designers exactly what is required, it will enable marketing to discuss the project with actual or potential customers, and it will enable some measure of the cost of changes in requirement upon the design effort to be made and charged to the appropriate source. In effect, this is a translation of a marketing requirement into terms intelligible to the designer.

The following minimum information should be given on a design specification:

1. The technical or performance requirements, including explicit statements on quality and reliability.
2. Any appearance or 'styling' requirements.
3. The intended selling price or operational cost. This can often only be in the form: 'Price not to exceed . . .'.
4. The date when output, that is the product or service, must be available.
5. The probable quantity or service usage that will be required. This quantity can substantially affect the design and, as a consequence, the first cost.
6. The maximum cost of designing which can be accepted, since the final product or service must bear the cost of the design.
7. Information concerning any special safety, legal or quality features required by current legislation.

Acceptance

This is essentially a 'back room' function carried out in the design group by designers and their associates. It is usually the first stage where costs for the design work will be assigned directly to the project, and is normally initiated by a formal instruction embodying the draft specification laid down at conception. The draft specification is tested and is then accepted, rejected as impracticable, or modified in conjunction with marketing. Sometimes, particularly in simple projects, this stage will coincide with the previous one, and may consist of only a meeting between all interested parties. At this stage it is particularly important for the designer to know the capability of the operating unit which will carry out the final design. Formal and frequent consultation between design and operations here and in all later stages can save much trouble and cost when producing the product or offering the service.

Execution

A working model or trial service run should be based on the ideas thrown up at stage 2 and on general design considerations, both theoretical and practical. These should, as far as possible, conform to the specification. Where this is not possible, the differences should be known and their effects considered. The differences usually arise either from the scale of the problem (for example, an oil refinery) or from the need for special parts or human resources whose cost cannot be justified until the design is finalized. Whilst cost considerations must not be overlooked, the technical appearance or service performance requirements are most important at this stage, and the trial runs or models made should indicate clearly the feasibility of the proposed design completely meeting the specification. The cost of the final product or service is a matter which must be accepted by the designers as a factor as important as any other, although subsequent development work can often produce significant reductions in cost.

Translation

At this stage the appropriate operations and after-sales service groups must be involved in the design work. It is quite common practice for the teams responsible for the original work and for the model or trials to hand over their task to a development team which, while appreciating the originality of the design, can also appreciate the problems involved in its execution. This development team should discuss at all stages the operating problems with the appropriate groups or departments. Detailed estimates will begin to be formed, and it will be possible to assign maximum acceptable costs to the various aspects of the service or product. Lack of co-operation at this time between designers and the operational people will prove very costly; the design finally placed upon the operating unit will be difficult to operate or produce, and emergency re-designs carried out will result in a debasing of the product or service. Too often a sense of economy on the part of the management, or of aloofness on the part of the designer, has resulted in this stage being omitted or made vestigial; in every case, an inferior product or service has eventually been offered.

Work will also be proceeding on preparing the final operating information summarizing all the design and development effort. Control of the amount of work put into obtaining this information is both important and difficult, and it must be remembered that the information is intended to aid operation, and not to be an end in itself.

Pre-operation

Once all the foregoing stages have been completed, it is desirable, particularly in high-volume operations, to carry out a pilot run or test marketing under normal operating conditions. In addition, tests to the customer specification should be carried out again under normal operating conditions. Both tasks should be done at some time before the start of delivery of the product or service offering, so that any faults or weaknesses which are shown up can be corrected. Such a pre-operation run will check:

(a)   operational information;
(b)   operational resources;

(c)   operational techniques and estimates;
(d)   specifications;

and only after such a run should the operational information be considered final.

The above outline of the processes of designing for satisfying the customer is an attempt to separate out the various stages of a creative act. In small organizations, one person might well carry out two or more of the above tasks and, indeed, it may then be impossible to analyse the work done. Nevertheless, it is suggested that some process similar to the above must be carried out whenever design is necessary.

Control of design

It is not possible to exert the same tight control on design effort as on operational effort, yet the cost involved and the time used are often substantial and both must appear somewhere within the organization's budget. Design must never be a task undertaken 'for its own sake'. The following points are worth considering.

1. No design will ever be 'complete' in the sense that, with effort, some modification (improvement?) can always be made.
2. Few designs are entirely novel. An examination of any 'new' product or service will almost certainly show that it largely employs existing techniques, components or systems to which have been added a comparatively small novel element. In most 'new' products or services the 'novel' design work rarely exceeds 10 per cent of the total design work, the rest being modifications to existing ideas, material, or constructions. The effort which must go into these modifications is likely to be reasonably predictable.
3. There appears to be a 'law of diminishing returns' on design effort. The longer the time which is spent on a design, the less the increase in the value of the design unless a technological breakthrough is achieved.
4. External and/or internal circumstances will impose limitations on design time and cost. It is as difficult to imagine a design project whose completion date is not implicitly fixed, either by a promise to a customer, the opening of a trade show or exhibition, a seasonal 'deadline', an operational or production schedule, or some other constraint, as it is to imagine an organization whose funds are unlimited, or a product or service whose price has no ceiling.

The use of critical path analysis in design

The most effective tool for the control of the design effort is critical path analysis (CPA). This will exert a discipline and enforce a degree of pre-planning upon the design effort which is invaluable. It will ensure that the sequence in which design tasks are undertaken is determined by need rather than by interest, and it will enable the supervisor concerned to compare the progress made with that planned.

A common difficulty in using CPA in design tasks is the belief that it is not possible to assign duration times to design activities. When dealing with this problem, the following steps are useful:

1. Determine the design specification as accurately and in as much detail as possible.
2. Involve the people concerned in the drawing of the network. (It will be found that the logical basis of CPA is appealing to most designers.)
3. Establish any fixed dates. If a fixed final date is not available, agree a reasonable one.
4. Assign duration times on non-contentious activities.
5. Break contentious activities into smaller parts, on some of which times can be readily agreed since past experience can be a guide.
6. Examine the remaining activities to see whether there are any historical precedents. If not, then assign to them as much time as possible without over-running the final date. It is then possible to pose the question, 'There are Y units of time in which to design X – is this possible?' which is often found to be more stimulating than the question 'How long will it take to design X?' If at this stage the design team will not, or cannot, accept the available time, then either the logic or the resources must be changed, or a re-negotiation of the completion date must take place.

Once a network has been completed and analysed it must be used as a control device; otherwise, much of its potential value will not be realized. This is probably done most simply by holding a regular meeting at which all those concerned report on progress. This meeting should be a progress meeting, not a design meeting to which problems are brought for solutions. Problem-solving is best treated separately. It will be found that the effectiveness of this meeting will depend almost entirely upon the manner in which it is run. A tradition of accepting the discipline of time is an invaluable asset to the design function.

Many design groups undertake a number of projects simultaneously, and the problem of sharing limited resources among these projects is an important one. Here it is probably simplest to draw a network for each project, to translate each of these into bar charts and to superimpose the various bar charts upon each other. From this superimposition it will be possible to read off the total resources of any type required at any time and, if these exceed the resources available, then some float manipulation must take place. It must be remembered that the more float is absorbed by resource allocation, the more critical the project becomes, and the effect of over-running of time becomes more serious. Float represents flexibility.

Design project costs

An estimated cost for design should be one of the figures submitted at the design acceptance stage. It must be recognized, however, that the calculation of this cost is not easy, and no general recommendations can be made since different situations will require entirely different systems. Thus, a design group set up to deal with one special project will need to be controlled more carefully, and in more detail, than a group which undertakes all the design tasks within a consumer product/service organization, and both need different treatment from a design function which exists to produce designs for other organizations to use.

The purpose of the costing system must be clearly established before any system is installed. Essentially the purpose must be to enable the design manager to manage; to extract figures 'because they would be interesting' is expensive and valueless. As with any other situation, detail should be minimized.

In setting up an estimate and subsequently using it for control, it must be remembered that human resource costs are derived from times, so that if times are controlled, the derived costs are also controlled. This means that using a network to control times will automatically control staff costs – and in design projects it is these which generally form by far the largest portion of the total costs. Consumable items are best dealt with as burden spread over all projects and included in the on-costs assigned to direct human resource costs, leaving the design manager to control these as items appearing on his budgetary control returns. Special items or expensive equipment purchased solely to meet the needs of particular tasks must, of course, be assigned to those tasks.

Buying design effort

Design effort is expensive; a qualified designer not only has a high basic pay but may attract considerable support staff and sometimes heavy capital equipment. It is frequently possible to avoid the heavy fixed costs of permanent staff by purchasing design effort. There are a number of sources:

1. *Research associations*. There are many of these, covering most sectors and industries. Their income is partly derived from government grants and partly from members' subscriptions. They offer information services, bulletins, and research/development facilities.
2. *Government research organizations*. These can often undertake development work for companies.
3. *Educational establishments*. Within colleges and universities there are substantial resources which can be tapped. Staff will sometimes undertake work at very low cost if it is academically interesting and capable of being published, or they will act as consultants charging a normal consultant's fee. Most academic and learned societies have extensive libraries which can be used at negligible cost.
4. *Private design organizations*. There is an increasing number of commercial design research companies which undertake fee-paid assignments. These include 'industrial designers' and, although most have specialist training, they will frequently bring to a task a fresh and uninhibited attack on function and cost. It is foolish to introduce a designer to a product when all the 'real' design is complete and expect him or her to carry out some painless cosmetic surgery. A designer should be involved in a design project from its inception. Frequently, the fee required by a commercial designer appears high, but it must be remembered that it does not involve the user company in the heavy fixed expense of employing its own staff.
5. *Licences to operate/manufacture*. It is often possible to buy the results of other companies' efforts by negotiating licences to manufacture new products or

provide new services. This is most commonly done with companies in other countries, and it should be remembered that conditions may be different in those countries, and that there will usually be a need to ensure that any drawings, specifications and methods are appropriate to the licensee.

Use of a computer

The tremendous speed and vast storage capacity of a computer can aid the designer in a number of ways:

1. A library of 'ready-made' designs can be easily stored and retrieved using a computer.
2. Frequently repeated, and long tedious calculations can be carried out rapidly. Without a computer, a designer will reduce the need for calculations by using tables or graphs of 'established standards' or 'good practice'. These, to become manageable, are the abbreviated results either of a few calculations or of a series of trials, and in either case contain ample 'safety' factors which usually over-compensate for the inadequacies of the calculations. As a result, the design produced may be unnecessarily costly in some way. The computer enables these calculations to be carried out as and when needed, reducing wasted effort.
3. Some calculations are so lengthy that they cannot be carried out by hand. A computer may perform these if appropriate software is available. A lengthy calculation by hand will produce an acceptable result, but the effort of examining the effect of changing one or other of the constituent parameters may be so great that no such examination is made. This may result in accepting a result which could be modified. Again, the computer's abilities could be used to check the effect of modification.
4. Quantities of data can be held in the computer's store and withdrawn with such ease that it becomes possible to refer readily to previous designs, experience and data.
5. Computer graphics may well permit a visual display of a design under various conditions, so that the effects of different requirements can be observed immediately.
6. The computer can store the results of the design process and issue it in a useful form, often obviating the need for the preparation and storage of hard copy specifications or drawings.

Specialization by designers

Concentration upon a limited field allows a designer to build up a body of knowledge which will permit the answering of questions within that field very much more rapidly than if interests ranged over a wide area. This again does not produce stagnation, since the concentration brings with it a deepening knowledge and a more fundamental understanding of the problems within that field of limited study. This is generally recognized so that there are now no individual designers responsible for, say, the complete design of an aeroplane; there are design teams, each member of which specializes upon a few aspects.

Families of products or services

When designing a product or service, it is frequently possible to do so in such a way that it can be scaled up or down as need arises. A company which organizes conferences is likely to have a basic conference 'design' which can be enlarged or reduced as required.

Use of a sound classification and coding system

The fewer the designs, the greater the productivity of the design group. It is frequently found that a product or service will be designed which could be identical to or is replaceable by an existing one. This wastes not only design effort, but all subsequent effort. Often minor modifications to an existing product or service will render it useful for a number of functions other than that for which it was first designed. At first this might appear to impose restrictions upon the designer which might inhibit his creative ability, yet in fact it will release him or her from the drudgery of detailed designing. While computer search techniques are available, a sound classification and coding system is invaluable.

Use of library and information services

Considerable savings in time and money can often be effected within a project by reference to published information. This is true of all departments, including research or development, but it is usual to house all technical sources, standards and codes of practice within one area which forms part of the design group.

In its simplest form, a library consists merely of a passive collection of books, but it should play a very positive function by being an information system, from which information can be requested. A librarian trained in searching and abstracting can rapidly and cheaply produce information from which problems can be solved or new developments advanced. With the present enormous flood of technical information being published each day, no scientist, technologist or manager can hope to be up-to-date with his subject except in a very narrow field. The librarian, by discriminating and abstracting, can assist by limiting any field of enquiry to that of immediate interest.

Within a small organization, it is probably more effective to employ an information officer than to start a library. The information officer would rapidly build up the comparatively small volume of essential reference books and would be able, by collaborating with local municipal libraries, national libraries, professional institutions, research associations, and the excellent lending libraries, to provide quickly any reference book needed. He or she would also be able to abstract appropriate journals and circulate bulletins of information to all who require them. This would enable the designers to assess their need for the information and save much wasted time in examining articles of little interest. Of course, journals should be available for inspection, as 'browsing' can be a very effective method of cross-fertilization. Various catalogues and data sheets can also be housed in the library rather than in the purchasing office. These will be readily accessible to all, and should be kept up-to-date as a matter of course. The collection of such catalogues by the librarian or information officer, rather than by the more directly interested persons, has the practical advantage that designers, for example, are insulated from the enthusiastic representatives of firms who will make a personal call upon receiving a request for a catalogue. Requests from librarians are not usually followed up so vigorously.

Properly organized, controlled and supported by management, an information system can be a very useful tool to a designer. It has been estimated that up to 30 per cent of the cost of a development project can be saved by an effective information department, and the savings in time can be equally great.

Ways of reducing design project costs

1. Buying-in design effort.
2. Computer-aided design.
3. Specialization by designers.
4. Families of products or services.
5. Classification and coding.
6. Library and information services.

Transition of designs to operations

The conveying of information to the operating unit is an essential part of the work of the design department. In some industries, 'drawings' may be used, in others these are replaced by product specifications or by service/process layouts.

The authority for publishing and amending finalized design information must be vested in one group only, which must also be responsible for ensuring that all the information held by that group is up-to-date and represents current practice in that organization. All the information necessary for the production of the article or for the generation of the service, either explicitly or by reference to published standards, specifications or codes of practice, should be available.

No information should be issued which has not been approved by an authorized person, since an error, even though apparently trivial, can have a profound effect upon operation. Some organizations require not only that the information be checked before issue but that it should be authorized by the designer responsible for the whole project. If this is done, care must be taken to avoid any very great reliance on the value of this 'authorizing' signature, because in a complex project the signature becomes a purely automatic device, since the authorizer has no time to check each information document personally.

Change systems

To control changes (or modifications) to design information a formalized change system is usually necessary. This can take a form similar to the following:

1. A change proposal is raised by any interested person but, to avoid any changes of a frivolous nature, this should be countersigned by the appropriate departmental supervisor. This proposal should state:
    (a)   the design concerned;
    (b)   the change required;
    (c)   the reason for the change;
    (d)   the degree of urgency – that is, whether 'retrospective', 'immediate', 'as convenient' or 'as from . . . date'.
2. Comments on this proposal must be made by departments concerned. Thus, the purchasing department might comment on the stock situation and the cost of reducing that stock; the industrial engineering department would discuss the changes in method; and so on.
3. Acceptance is given by a team which considers all the suggested changes and the comments arising from them.
4. A change document is originated if the change proposal is accepted, and this is published generally, being used by the design group as an authority to change the design concerned. The design itself will be changed, a note of the date of the change and a brief description of it made, and a new design issued, the number of the issue also being recorded. All old design specifications should be withdrawn and destroyed; new specifications are issued to departments with a request that all old ones be destroyed.

Once a change system is in effect it must be clearly understood that no person has the right to change a product or service design without recourse to a change proposal. At the design stage this can often be a considerable hindrance, and designs are often assumed to be free from the change system until they are 'frozen' at the completion of the 'consolidation' stage. Before they are so frozen it is unwise to engage in any substantial expenditure or action derived from them, and often designs are not published until they are frozen.

The design of services

The emergence of the services sector has been suggested by economists to be part of the natural progression in which economic dominance changes first from agriculture to manufacturing and then to services. It is argued that if income elasticity of demand is higher for services than it is for goods, then as incomes rise, resources will shift toward services. The continuing growth of services verifies this and is further explained by changes in culture, health, fitness, safety, demography and lifestyles.

In considering the design of services, it is important to consider the differences between goods and services. Some authors argue that the marketing and design of goods and services should conform to the same fundamental rules, whereas others claim that there is a need for a different approach to services because of the differences which can be recognized in the goods and services themselves.

In terms of design, it is possible to recognize three distinct elements in the service package, the physical elements or facilitating goods, the explicit service or sensual benefits, and the implicit service or psychological benefits. In addition, the particular characteristics of service delivery systems may be itemized; intangibility, perishability, simultaneity, and heterogeneity.

It is difficult, if not impossible, to design intangibility aspects of a service, since consumers must often use experience or the reputation of a service organization and its representatives to judge quality. Perishability is often an important issue in services since it is often impossible or undesirable to hold stocks of the explicit service element of the service package. This aspect often requires that service operation and service delivery must exist simultaneously.

Simultaneity occurs because the consumer must be present before many services can take place. Hence, services are often formed in small and dispersed units and it is difficult to take advantage of economies of scale. There is evidence that the emergence of computer and communications technologies is changing this in some sectors like banking, but contact continues to be necessary for the majority. Design considerations here include the environment and the systems used. Service facilities, procedures and systems should be designed with the customer in mind, as well as the 'product' and the human resources. Managers need a picture of the total span of the operation so that factors which are crucial to success are not neglected. This clearly means that the functions of marketing, design and operations cannot be separated in services, and this must be taken into account in the design of the operational controls, such as the diagnosis of individual customer expectations.

Heterogeneity of services occurs in consequence of explicit and implicit service elements relying on individual preferences and perceptions. Differences exist in the outputs of organizations generating the same service, within the same organization, and even in the same employee on different occasions. Clearly, unnecessary variation needs to be controlled but the variety attributed to estimating, and then matching, the consumer's requirements is essential to customer satisfaction and *must* be designed into the systems. This inherent variability does, however, make it difficult to set precise quantifiable standards for all the elements of the service.

Characteristics of service delivery systems

1. Intangibility.
2. Perishability.
3. Simultaneity.
4. Heterogeneity.

In the design of services it is useful to classify them in some way. Several literature sources help us to place services in one of five categories:

(a)   service factory;
(b)   service shop;
(c)   mass service;
(d)   professional service;
(e)   personal services.

Several service attributes have particular significance for the design of service operations:

1. *Labour intensity*. The ratio of labour costs incurred to the value of plant and equipment used (people-versus equipment-based services).
2. *Contact*. The proportion of the total time required to provide the service for which the consumer is present in the system.
3. *Interaction*. The extent to which the consumer actively intervenes in the service process to change the content of the service; this includes customer participation to provide information from which needs can be assessed, and customer feedback from which satisfaction levels can be inferred.
4. *Customization*. This includes:
    (a)   *fixed* – a single choice;
    (b)   *choice* – providing selections from a range of options;
    (c)   *adaptation* – the interaction process in which the requirement is decided, designed and delivered to match the need.
5. *Nature of the service act*. Either tangible, i.e. perceptible to touch and can be owned, or intangible, being insubstantial or touchable.
6. *Identity of the direct recipient*. Either people or things.

Attributes useful in the classification of services

1.   Labour intensity – high or low.
2.   Contact – high or low.
3.   Interaction – high or low.
4.   Customization – choice, fixed or adaptation.
5.   Nature of act – tangible or intangible.
6.   Recipient of act – people or things.

Table 6.1 gives a list of some services with their assigned attribute types and Table 6.2 shows how these may be used to group the services under the various classifications.

It is apparent that services are part of almost all organizations and not confined to the service sector. What is clear is that the service classifications and different attributes must be considered in any service design process.

(The authors are grateful to the contribution made by John Dotchin to this section of Chapter 6.)

Table 6.1 A classification of selected services

Service	Labour intensity	Contact	Interaction	Customization	Nature	Recipient of act
Accountant	High	Low	High	Adapt	Intangible	Things
Architect	High	Low	High	Adapt	Intangible	Things
Bank	Low	Low	Low	Fixed	Intangible	Things
Beautician	High	High	High	Adapt	Tangible	People
Bus service	Low	High	Low	Choice	Tangible	People
Cafeteria	Low	High	High	Choice	Tangible	People
Cleaning firm	High	Low	Low	Fixed	Tangible	Things
Clinic	Low	High	High	Adapt	Tangible	People
Coach service	Low	High	Low	Choice	Tangible	People
College	High	High	Low	Fixed	Intangible	People
Courier firm	High	Low	Low	Adapt	Tangible	Things
Dental practice	High	High	High	Adapt	Tangible	People
Driving school	High	High	High	Adapt	Intangible	People
Equipment hire	Low	Low	Low	Choice	Tangible	Things
Finance consultant	High	Low	High	Adapt	Intangible	Things
Hairdresser	High	High	High	Adapt	Tangible	People
Hotel	High	High	Low	Choice	Tangible	People
Leisure centre	Low	High	High	Choice	Tangible	People
Maintenance	Low	Low	Low	Choice	Tangible	Things
Nursery	High	Low	Low	Fixed	Tangible	People
Optician	High	High	High	Adapt	Tangible	People
Postal service	Low	Low	Low	Adapt	Tangible	Things
Rail service	Low	High	Low	Choice	Tangible	People
Repair firm	Low	Low	Low	Adapt	Tangible	Things
Restaurant	High	High	Low	Choice	Tangible	People
Service station	Low	High	High	Choice	Tangible	People
Solicitors	High	Low	High	Adapt	Intangible	Things
Sports coaching	High	High	High	Adapt	Intangible	People
Take-away	High	Low	Low	Choice	Tangible	People
Veterinary service	High	Low	High	Adapt	Tangible	Things

Table 6.2 Grouping of similar services

Service factories	Service shops	Mass services	Professional services	Personal services
Bank	Cafeteria	Bus service	Accountant	Beautician
Cleaning firm	Clinic	Coach service	Architect	Dental practice
Equipment hire	Leisure centre	College	Finance consultant	Driving school
Maintenance	Service station	Courier firm	Solicitors	Hairdresser
Postal service		Hotel	Veterinary practice	Optician
Repair firm		Nursery		Sports coaching
		Rail service		
		Restaurant		
		Take-away		

CHAPTER 6 – HIGHLIGHTS

- There must be a synergistic relationship between marketing, design and operations for long-term success.

- The traditional product/service development process used in many industries leads to barriers between functions.

- Changing the traditional approach to an integrated iterative one requires each element of the design process to be carried out in the context of the others. Teamwork is essential.

- Research involves discovery, development concerns improvement, and design is the translation of requirement into the reality of products or services.

- Design projects pass through the stages of conception, acceptance, execution, translation and pre-operational activities. These each have their own requirements for successful design and development to take place.

- Design activities must be controlled and the use of critical path analysis is often useful. This is particularly so in the sharing of resources when several design projects are underway.

- Design costs should be estimated at an early stage and a costing system established. Design effort is expensive and it is worth considering its purchase from research associations, government research organizations, educational establishments, private design organizations, or by licence to operate or manufacture.

- Design costs may be further reduced by the use of computers, specialization by designers, the design of families of products or services, and using libraries, information services and classification/coding schemes.

- In the transition of designs to operations, drawings, product specifications or service/process layouts may be used. A good change control system for these is essential.

- In the design of services, three distinct elements may be recognized in the service package: physical (facilitating goods), explicit service (sensual benefits) and implicit service (psychological benefits). Moreover, the characteristics of service delivery may be itemized as: intangibility; perishability; simultaneity; and heterogeneity.

- Services may be classified generally as service factory, service shop, mass service, professional service, and personal service. The following service attributes are important in designing services: labour intensity, contact interaction, customization, the nature of the service act, and the direct recipient of the act.

- Use of this framework allows services to be classified in the five groups.

Recommended reading

Bowen, D.E., Chase, R.B., Cummings, T.G., and associates, *Service Management Effectiveness*, Jossey Bass Pub., 1990

Provides an excellent framework for operations design and management in the service sector.

Heskett, J.L., Sasser, J.R. and Hart, C.W.L., *Service Breakthroughs*, The Free Press, 1990

This book discusses service firms, such as Aticorp, UPS and Marriott, and how they have changed the 'rules of the game' in their respective industries by consistently meeting or exceeding customer needs and expectations.

Lorenz, C., *The Design Dimension: Product Strategy and the Challenge of Global Marketing*, Basil Blackwell Ltd, 1986

Deals with the impact of good design upon competitiveness. Very well illustrated by case studies. Well worth reading as a stimulant.

O'Neal, C., and Bertrand, K., *Developing a Winning JIT Marketing Strategy*, Prentice-Hall, 1991

The book for industrial marketers on how to improve competitiveness in the global marketplace by implementing JIT practices (see Chapter 23).

Chapter 7

Product/Service: Variety and Value

Variety management

Within any organization, variety is inevitable. It will exist in the products made and the services offered, in the methods and procedures used, in the materials and documentation employed and in the organizational and operating techniques. Whilst some variety is desirable, as variety increases so organizational problems and costs will increase. Thus, for example, an increase in the number of materials stored will increase the storage room required, increase the difficulties of stock recording, increase the number or orders placed, and so on. As variety increases, controllability decreases. Control of variety is essential and the task of *reducing* variety with subsequent control of the remaining variety is one of the most fruitful tasks which can be undertaken by any organization.

An approach to variety control

Increase of variety is insidious; new parts, equipment, methods and procedures, and materials are often introduced for reasons valid only for a short time. Variety control is a matter for management as a whole and must become part of the tradition of the company. This is not to imply that no changes should ever take place, but that the widest possible view should be taken of all changes, and their *total* effect on the organization considered. As has been truly said, change is not necessarily progress. Equally truly, the job of the operations manager is to achieve the maximum result with the minimum effort.

Aims of a variety control programme

1. Minimum variety of products and services.
2. Minimum variety of parts.
3. Minimum variety of materials.
4. Minimum variety of processes.
5. Minimum variety of people/skills.

Whilst variety in the finished products or services offered can allow the organization to gain significant competitive advantage, the effect of this in terms of potential operational complexity must not be ignored. The management of the conversion or provision process should be orientated to recognize this variety, and variety controlled in the associated areas.

Variety control can be undertaken in three ways:

(a) simplification – 'the reduction of unnecessary variety';
(b) standardization – 'the control of necessary variety';
(c) specialization – the concentration of effort on undertakings where special knowledge is available;

all of which combine to reduce and control variety. A programme can start in any one place in an organization, or it can proceed on a number of fronts simultaneously. It is a continuing process and, though certain techniques will prevent the spread of variety in some fields, in all there must be a continual awareness of the dangers of uncontrolled diversity: habits must be formed which will build up safeguards.

The benefits of variety control

These can be considered under three main headings as follows:

In marketing

A wide variety of products or services reduces the 'selling' which can be done at any one time. Reduction of this variety must not be carried to such extremes that the genuine needs of the customer are not satisfied, but care must be taken to avoid those 'marginal' products or services which are so often provided in small quantities to suit (possibly irrational) customers' tastes and yet are not charged at prices high enough to recover their costs. The argument is often put up that this 'special' will bring with it a flood of other work, yet all too often the sprat catches no mackerel. A wide diversity of products or services is often characteristic of a young company, a declining one, or one which has no need to control costs. Fierce competition brings with it a reduction in the number of products and a consequent intensification of selling effort.

In cases where an after-sales service must be provided, the more concentrated the output the better the service can be and, since the number of spare parts which must be kept is reduced, the less the cost of the service. This can be a very potent selling factor and can often 'clinch' a sale, as well as building up the goodwill which brings with it repeated orders.

In design

The fewer the designs, the greater the productivity of the technical departments. It is frequently found that a part will be designed which could be identical to, or is replaceable by, an existing part. This wastes not only design effort but subsequent production, production control and operating effort. Often minor modifications to an existing part will render it useful for a number of functions other than that for which it was first designed. At first this might appear to impose restrictions upon the designer which might inhibit his creative ability, yet in fact it will release him from the drudgery of detailed designing. No designer calls for special screws, nuts, wire diameters, sheet metal thickness – standardization is accepted here, yet the variety of products which can be made from these items is infinite.

Concentration upon a limited field allows a designer to build up a body of knowledge which will permit him to answer questions within that field very much more rapidly than if his interests ranged over a wide area. This again does not produce stagnation, since the concentration brings with it a deepening of knowledge and a more fundamental understanding of the problems within that field of limited study. This is generally recognized, so that there are now no individual designers responsible for, say, the complete design of an aeroplane; there are design teams, each member of which specializes upon a few aspects.

In operations

If one part can be used in place of two, operating runs will be longer, and ancillary time (setting, breaking down) will be reduced, both absolutely and when 'spread'. Fewer production aids will be required, and there will be a higher utilization of special equipment. Variety reduction generally will reduce stocks by the reduction in the number of different items held, and by the lower minimum (insurance) stocks resulting from the merging of parts, and stores space will be more fully utilized. The cost of stock control and stocktakings will be correspondingly reduced. The larger quantities and the fewer products or services produced simplify the production control problem and ease the difficulties of the buyer in that he has fewer orders to place, and those he does place are for larger quantities.

Standardization in methods and procedures permits higher levels of efficiency to be achieved. The techniques of method study provide a framework for examining the rationale behind differences between work methods.

The success of fast food operations derives largely from the very small variety of products offered.

Benefits of variety control

1. Intensification of selling effect.
2. Better after-sales service.
3. Greater technical productivity.
4. Better understanding of technical problems.
5. Larger runs.
6. Less ancillary time.
7. Fewer operations aids.
8. Higher equipment utilization.
9. Reduction in total stocks.
10. Greater use of stores space.
11. Easier stock control.
12. Quicker stocktaking.
13. Simplification of production control.
14. Reduction in buying effort.

Variety control in the finished product or service

When considering variety control in the final product or service, two aspects of the range offered to the market must be investigated simultaneously:

1. How much income does each item/or service produce?
2. How much contribution does each item or service generate?
    Where,

Contribution = Selling price − Direct costs

To illustrate the need for both aspects to be investigated, consider this simplified and somewhat exaggerated example:

Item	Income produced £	Contribution £
A	6,210	700
B	2,415	607
C	8,895	513
D	778	350
E	585	233
F	346	117
G	97	− 23
H	391	− 47
I	204	− 59
K	1,142	− 82
	21,063	2,250 − 211
		=2,309

If these are ranked in order of (a) income and (b) contribution, the following results will be obtained:

(a) Rank by income:

		Income	
Rank	*Product*	*£*	*% of total*
1	C	8,895	42.2
2	A	6,210	29.5
3	B	2,415	11.4
4	K	1,142	5.4
5	D	778	3.7
6	E	585	2.8
7	H	391	1.9
8	F	346	1.6
9	J	204	1.0
10	G	97	0.5
		21,063	100.0

(b) Rank by contribution:

		Contribution	
Rank	Product	£	% of total
1	A	700	30.3
2	B	607	26.3
3	C	513	22.2
4	D	350	15.2
5	E	233	10.0
6	F	117	5.0
7	G	– 23	–1.0
8	H	– 47	–2.0
9	J	– 59	–2.5
10	K	– 82	–3.5
		2,520 –211	109.0–9.0
		=2,309	=100.0

Clearly a better picture is obtained by a graphical presentation of the results of the above analysis. This is illustrated in the case of the contribution in Fig.7.1.

Alternative forms of this representation can be found in Appendix 1, where Pareto analysis is introduced.

To consider either income or contribution in the absence of the other could readily lead to incorrect conclusions: for example, product K, which is ranked fourth by

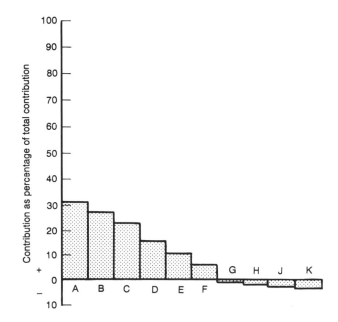

Fig. 7.1   Products ranked by contribution

income, actually makes a loss, and product A, which produces most contribution, does not produce most income. It is not unusual to find that it is most easy to sell that product which is severely under-priced.

One common approach to variety control at this stage is to consider first the items, ranked by income, and to subject all low-income items to a very close scrutiny. It may be that some of these have not yet achieved sales maturity, or they may have prestige value. In the absence of any such good commercial reasons these low-income items should be considered as prime candidates for abandonment.

The second analysis – that of contribution for each item – is most usefully considered after the income for each item has been examined. Of the items remaining after the pruning already suggested has been carried out, it may well be found that the contribution provided by some products is either low or negative, and items F, G, H, J and K should again be subjected to a very close scrutiny to determine whether sales can be increased, or whether a cost-reduction programme should be initiated.

The income–contribution chart

Another approach, which virtually enables the above two stages to be coalesced, is to plot an income–contribution chart. In this the abscissae are the income ranks, and the ordinates the contribution ranks. Thus, product A has an income rank of 2, and a contribution rank of 1, and A is represented by the point (2,1); see Table 7.1. All the points are plotted on the income–contribution chart (Fig.7.2): ideally, volume and contribution ranks should correspond, giving a straight line at 45° to either axis. Points lying *above* this line should be tested as follows:

(a)   Can costs be reduced?
(b)   Can prices be increased?

while points lying *below* this line should be tested:

(a)   Can sales volume be increased?

Table 7.1 Income contribution ranks

Product	Rank by income	Rank by contribution
A	2	1
B	3	2
C	1	3
D	5	4
E	6	5
F	8	6
G	10	7
H	7	8
J	9	9
K	4	10

Neither of the above approaches in itself can determine the action which must be taken, but they can provide excellent guidance. Both, of course, demand good recording and costing procedures. Where there is a large number of items or services provided, the procedure described may become unwieldy and costly. In this sort of situation, initial consideration of only the high-income, high-contribution items (the 'A' items in both sets of ranking – see Appendix 1) is recommended.

One large firm of manufacturing chemists reduced its product range from 1,500 to 221. This was done by:

(a) eliminating all products whose sales were less than 0.01 per cent of total annual turnover;
(b) Examination of all products whose gross profit was below a certain level;
(c) Detailed consideration of the sales trends of each remaining product.

To assist their customers, whose goodwill might have been jeopardized by the abandoning of certain products, they negotiated the transfer of orders for discontinued lines to other firms in the same field who were still making these lines. This drastic reduction of range was accompanied by a reduction in the total number of orders received, but the size of the orders received increased, and there was, in fact, an expansion in total turnover.

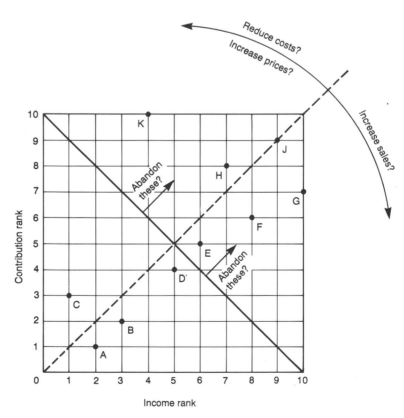

Fig. 7.2 Income–contribution chart

Making the customers' specification is a much more difficult task, since each customer will require a different product. Here the marketing department can proceed in two ways:

1. Set up a range of stock items which can be offered to the customer in place of the customer's own design. If a substantial saving in price or excellence in delivery can be shown, the customer will often be prepared to forego some of his individuality.
2. If the above is not possible, try to guide the customer into preparing designs which employ parts which are already designed and for which equipment and instructions already exist. If these do not affect either the appearance or the performance of the product into which they are incorporated, there is a good chance that the customer will accept them, particularly if other advantages accrue.

It is often possible to identify a common 'core' and to customize to the customer's requirements from this. Examples include the variety of 'go-faster' stripes to customize cars, which are cheaper than complete freedom in choice of colour; and trousers with the bottoms of the legs unfinished, so that they can be tailored to the customer's exact size.

Variety control in the inputs and materials

Wherever items are purchases from outside suppliers, they should be appropriately and adequately defined. This will be done either by drawings made internally, and covered by a logical numbering system, or specifications laying down the salient factors concerning the item. Such specifications must, wherever possible, be industry-approved – for example, those issued by the British Standards Institution. Use of such specifications will not only ensure that items are to a uniform and known standard but also that the goods concerned are most likely to be made in quantity by a number of manufacturers, thus being cheaper and more readily available than specially designed parts. Should any doubt be felt on this score, the reader is advised to purchase first a quantity of screws to a British Standard specification and then the same quantity of a similar screw to a special design.

Variety in raw material will lead not only to complexity in the raw material stores themselves but also to possible variation in the subsequent product. This in turn will be felt throughout the whole operation, causing variations in equipment and processes. This is particularly significant in flow production, where the effects of variation can be very serious, but it must not be ignored in batch production, where variations do not make themselves felt so immediately.

Many products are built up from a number of parts and, if the final product or service cannot be standardized, yet it may be possible to standardize some of the parts. This can usually be done most easily in the unseen or invisible components – for example, interlinings and pockets in men's wear – but in order to be able to do it at all it is necessary to identify readily any component. Even a relatively small company will have a large range of parts – almost certainly over 2,000 if the company is well established.

Should a new part or constituent appear to be necessary, there must be some simple way of discovering whether one which is acceptable already exists. This can be attained by using mechanical sorting devices, and small needlesort cards are available. Even better, of course, is a computer. Most micros now have ample capacity for this purpose. However, when the storage and sorting of numbers is carried out, a very effective technique which simplifies the work of the designer/stock controller/operations manager is to number all drawings and documents in such a way that the number itself identifies the part or constituents.

A discussion of the desirable properties of an effective coding system appears elsewhere and there is no doubt that the long-term benefits of a good coding system will considerably outweigh its installation costs. Care must be taken to ensure that the system is fitted to the user organization: an unnecessarily complex scheme can be expensive, and the simpler the scheme the better. However, *ample provision must be made for expansion*: the costs and inconvenience of changing from one scheme to another can be high.

Variety control in the conversion process

Throughout any organization there will inevitably be a number of similar processes, procedures and systems. At the very least there will be processes which, while not being similar in themselves, produce similar results. It may be possible to modify some or all of these and create a single process which will perform all that is required at an acceptable level of efficiency. This may apparently increase the *unit* cost of some processes, but it will reduce the *total* costs to the organization. The reduction in the variety of methods used will result in a greater flexibility of human resources, a higher possible utilization of equipment, and a simplification of the organizational task. Thus, if two different documents are processed in the same way, the preparation and organization of the resources required can often be substantially reduced. Similarly, if one piece of equipment can be used in place of two, the maintenance problem is considerably eased. The gains in this field are likely to be greater in small-scale rather than large-scale operation.

Just as an analysis of finished products is likely to show that the bulk of income is derived from a comparatively small part of the product range, so an analysis of operating processes is likely to show that, of the total capability, an extremely small part produces the bulk of the workload. Thus, in an investigation of manufacturing in 25 German companies (Opitz), it was found that 80 per cent of all turned jobs had diameters of less than 200 mm despite the fact that the permissible turning diameters of the machine tools were greatly in excess of 200 mm. Similarly, while nearly all turning machines have facilities for thread cutting, only 25 per cent of the jobs examined used these facilities. Later work by PERA (Production Engineering Research Association) in the UK has produced similar results, and these *component statistics* indicate that considerable savings can be achieved both by reducing the variety and complexity of equipment being used and by grouping together components with common technological needs so that groups of components can be produced in one batch, rather than in several separate batches. This gives rise to an organizational system known as 'group technology', which is more fully discussed later.

> **Steps towards a variety control programme**
>
> 1. Use industry-agreed standards if possible.
> 2. Use company-agreed standards if possible.
> 3. Standardize raw materials.
> 4. Standardize parts.
> 5. Simplify identification of materials and parts.
> 6. Standardize methods, procedures and systems.
> 7. Standardize routes.
> 8. Standardize plant and equipment.

Control of value

Value analysis is a cost-reduction and control technique which operates by attacking the basic design of the product or service, rather than – as is done in work study – by improving the way in which the product is made or the service offered. In an ideal world, where all designs were as economical, simple and elegant as possible, value analysis would have no place; or, it could be argued, it would be carried out at the conception and design of the product or service. In the present, imperfect world in which most managers find themselves, value analysis can provide a disciplined way of attacking cost.

Value analysis is 'an organized procedure for the efficient identification of unnecessary cost . . . by analysis of function . . .', *function* being 'that property of the product or service which makes it work or sell'. The essence of value analysis, therefore, is first to identify the function of the product and then to examine alternative ways in which this function can be achieved, finally choosing that which involves least cost. To do this, a routine has been evolved which, if followed, is likely to produce acceptable results.

The identification of function

The first, and most important, step in value analysis is to make a formal statement of the function of the product or service; in itself this is valuable and often surprisingly difficult. Most investigations of problems start with questions. The work study engineer asks 'What is the purpose of this operation?', the marketing manager 'What shall we sell?' and the value analyst 'What does it *do*?'

It is important that the question of function should be answered explicitly and in writing. One authority suggests that the answer should be recorded in two words, a verb and a noun; for example:

'gives light' for a lamp;
'supports weight' for a beam;
'transmits force' for a shaft;
'transfers cash' for a cheque.

This isolation of function is a 'process of deletion'. For any statement of function the question can be asked: 'What can be discarded without diminishing the statement?' and steadily, redundant words, ideas, concepts are jettisoned until the most economical statement is obtained.

Rarely is there only one function; there are usually several, and all need to be identified and stated. Of the various functions, one is usually of more importance than the others, and this, the *primary* function, is examined first.

Value

Value may be equated with *price*, which is that which 'must be given, done, sacrificed . . . to obtain a thing', and any product or service will have several different values:

(a) *Exchange value*, the price a purchaser will offer. This, the conventional purchase price, is the sum of two parts: the value due to usefulness and the value which ownership itself bestows. These are often referred to as:

(b) *Use value*, the price the purchaser will offer in order to ensure that the purpose (or function) is achieved.

(c) *Esteem value*, the price which is offered beyond the use value.

$$\text{Exchange value} = \text{Use value} + \text{Esteem value}$$

The exchange value is set by the market and is influenced by the usefulness and esteem in which the product is held. In purchasing it is useful to try to express these values in monetary terms, in order to assess their acceptability. Thus, consider two items, A and B, carrying out different tasks, both of which can be purchased for the same price (£100). By comparing these with others and with the tasks which have to be carried out, valuations can be made:

'It is worth £60 to get function A completed.'
'It is worth £10 to get function B completed.'

	A	B
Exchange value	£100	£100
Use value	£ 60	£ 10
Esteem value	£ 40	£ 90

Thus, the questions which now can be posed are:

'Is A desired so much that £40 must be paid in excess of its usefulness?'
'Is B desired so much that £90 must be paid in excess of its usefulness?

Of course, use value is a subjective judgement, but it is one which most people make ('I reckon that is worth . . .' is a common enough remark) and by setting it down in numerical terms, a measure – albeit an imprecise one – is provided. In some cases, when design work is being carried out, the use value is determined effectively by the target cost, which should appear as part of the design specification.

When an organization produces something for its own use – for example, for incorporation into a marketable product, or for marketing as a complete entity – a fourth value can be recognized:

(d)   *Cost value* (sometimes called the *cost price* or *intrinsic value*), the sum of all the costs incurred in providing the product.

The difference between the cost value and the exchange value is the profit, and in most situations it is the profit which must be increased; the task of the value analyst may be said to be that of decreasing the cost value while maintaining or increasing the use and esteem values.

Carrying out a value analysis exercise

Value analysis may be applied to any product or any procedure, but some exercises are likely to be more rewarding than others. In general, multi-component hardware will generate savings more readily and quickly than single-component products or administrative procedures, although startling results have been recorded on the value analysis of a single pin, and on the analysis of an organization. Clearly, the product or procedure to be analysed must be one in which worthwhile savings are possible.

The value analysis team

Many – possibly most – of the successes of value analysis derive from the fact that a problem is attacked by a number of people simultaneously. Whether these people should constitute a permanent team, or be called together, is open to discussion. Probably the best solution is to have a *small* permanent core of experienced people who co-opt as many of their colleagues as seems desirable. Certainly those immediately concerned *must* be present, and where purchased parts are concerned, a representative from the supplier will attend. It will always be found useful to invite intelligent 'laymen' to join, 'laymen' in this context comprising those who have no special case to plead or cause to defend. The size of the team is important – too large and it will become unwieldy and impossible to convene, too small and it will be too inward-looking. A membership between six and ten appears satisfactory.

A structured approach

Gage has laid down a 12-step process for a conducting value analysis exercise. Whilst the focus within these is largely on manufacturing, it will be appreciated that, with suitable elimination and modification, they can be applied in any environment.

1. *Select the product to be analysed*. Here the problem is to identify the product or service which will give the greatest return for the costs incurred in the analysis itself. Rules are obviously impossible to lay down, but the following indicate situations likely to produce worthwhile results:
    (a)   a multiplicity of components;
    (b)   a large forecast usage;
    (c)   a small difference between use value and cost value;
    (d)   considerable market competition;
    (e)   a long-designed product;
    (f)   the generation of considerable documentation;
    (g)   the creation of organizational complexity.
2. *Extract the cost of the product*. The cost required here is the marginal or out-of-pocket cost. An absorption cost would involve decisions on the apportioning of

overheads which could easily distort any apparent cost savings. The calculation of marginal costs is not always easy, and it is here that companies first experience difficulties in value analysis. At this stage, details of individual components are not required.

3. *Record the number of parts.* In general, the larger the number of parts, the greater the chance of cost reduction.
4. *Record all the functions.* This forces consideration of the purpose of the product or service. Many serve more than one purpose and all the functions should be stated here, preferably in verb–noun form.
5. *Record the number required currently, and in the foreseeable future.* This gives magnitude to the effort which can be expended, and the costs incurred in the analysis.

These five questions are 'fact-finding' – they firmly establish the bases upon which all further work is created.

6. *Determine the primary function.* Whilst a number of functions may be present simultaneously, it is not possible to consider them all at the same time – some order of priority must be established. This is done by reconsidering the list prepared in step 4 and deciding which would be the primary function in the view of the purchaser/user of the product.
7. *List all other ways of achieving the primary function.* It is here that value analysis requires the presence of a number of people, the value analysis team. Ideas are obtained by means of a 'creativity' or 'brainstorming' session at which ideas are generated and advanced by means of a free flow of ideas. It involves a relaxed atmosphere with an absence of criticism and a desire to contribute something by all present. The purpose of the leader is to stimulate these contributions and to create the freedom of thought and behaviour which is essential. Judgements on ideas are withheld until a later date – the more outrageous the idea, the more welcome it should be, both for itself and as a stimulant.

   Many UK managers reject the idea of brainstorming, since the thought of 'making an ass of myself' is anathema to them. Care must be taken, therefore, in setting up and running the session to see that no criticisms of any ideas are made, and that when the sifting of ideas is carried out later, it is done on objective grounds. Follet's Law of the Situation ('. . . accept the orders given by the situation') is as valid in value analysis as in other areas of management.
8. *Assign costs to all the alternatives.* To avoid losing the momentum of the brainstorming session, costs must be assigned to the various alternatives as rapidly as possible, but it is better not to try to assign these costs during brainstorming or the free flow of ideas will be dammed. It is probably desirable to adjourn the VA meeting and reconvene it later when the costs are available. To avoid too much delay, 'order of magnitude' costs are acceptable.
9. *Examine the three cheapest alternatives.* Steps 7 and 8 allow the three cheapest alternatives to be selected and examined for feasibility and performance. The design of the new product will begin to emerge at this stage.
10. *Decide which idea should be developed further.* From step 9 and the examination carried out there, a decision is taken upon which idea should be developed further.
11. *See what other functions need to be incorporated.* Re-examination of step 4 will

show which other functions have not already been incorporated in the suggestions in step 10.

The above steps may produce a complete solution, or it may be that further detailed work needs to be carried out to finalize the new design. Here checklists of ideas may usefully be produced. The precise list will depend on the organization, but the common feature is the question:

'Does its use contribute value?'

Every addition, whether it be an extra component, tolerance, hole, bend, document, form . . . should be examined against this question. Equally useful is the inverse:

'Can anything be removed without degrading the product?'

While the 'new' product is being developed, the value analysis team can undertake the final step.

12. *Ensure that the new design is accepted.* Conservatism, the principle of 'worry-minimization' and sheer inertia will all combine to resist new ideas. To forestall this, the VA team should consider the ways in which the new idea can be 'sold'. This will almost certainly require

   (a) a model,

   and statements of:

   (b) anticipated savings,
   (c) anticipated capital expenditure,
   (d) improvements in value,

   and a proposed plan in terms of:

   (e) critical path analysis network.

The above 12 steps are incorporated in Gage's twelve questions, shown in the box.

Gage's 12 value analysis questions

1. What is it?
2. What does it cost?
3. How many parts?
4. What does it do?
5. How many functions are required?
6. Which is the primary function?
7. What else will it do?
8. What will *that* cost?
9. Which three of the alternative ways of doing the job show the largest difference between 'cost' and 'use value'?
10. Which ideas are to be developed?
11. What other functions and specification features must be incorporated?
12. What is needed to sell the ideas and forestall 'road-blocks'?

Value engineering

The application of VA techniques – and particularly those concerned with the isolation of function – to the design stages of a product or a system is clearly most desirable. Greater savings, though probably less identifiable, can be made, although for 'one-off' and short-run tasks, only prior-value studies are possible. The term *value engineering* is often reserved for this cost-prevention exercise.

CHAPTER 7 – HIGHLIGHTS

- A variety control programme aims to reduce variety in: products and services; materials; parts; processes; people/skills.
- There are three approaches to variety control: simplification; standardization; and specialization.
- Benefits from variety control occur in: marketing, design, and operations.
- Variety control can be applied to the finished product or service, to inputs and materials and to the conversion process.
- To plot an income-contribution chart, for each item income rank is plotted on the abscissa and contribution rank on the ordinate; the chart indicates those items for potential elimination, and those items for cost reduction, price increase or sales volume increase.
- Function is defined as that property of the product which makes it work or sell: it is expressed as a noun plus a verb.
- The exchange value, the price a purchaser will offer, is made up of two parts, the use value (the price offered to ensure the purpose is achieved) and the esteem value (the price which is offered beyond the use value).
- Value analysis is an organized procedure for the efficient identification of unnecessary cost, by analysis of function.
- A structured approach to value analysis, may be carried out by a team who identify the function of the product or service; examine different ways in which this function can be achieved; and choose that which involves least cost.
- Value engineering is the application of value analysis techniques at the design stage of a product or service.

Recommended reading

Fowler, T. C., *Value Analysis in Design*, Van Nostrand Reinhold, 1990

This claims to be a detailed guide to performing modern value analysis, with 36 case histories from the author's experience.

Juran, J.M., *Managerial Breakthrough*, McGraw-Hill, 1965

Though over 20 years old, this book is well worth reading. Dr Juran shows how an A-B-C (Pareto) analysis can be applied to a wide variety of managerial problems.

Miles, L.D., *Techniques of Value Analysis and Engineering*, McGraw-Hill, 1972

This is the first text on value analysis. Written by the 'originator' of VA, it is stimulating and useful if a little dated.

Chapter 8

Quality

This chapter discusses the general issues concerned with the management of quality, the policy and systems that are required. Chapters 20 and 21 deal with the techniques used in the actual control of quality.

Defining quality

The reputation attached to an organization for the quality of its products and services is accepted as a key to its success and the future of its employees. To prosper in today's economic climate, any organization and its suppliers must be dedicated to never-ending improvement, and more efficient ways to obtain products or services that consistently meet customers' needs must constantly be sought. The consumer is no longer required to make a choice between price and quality, and competitiveness in quality is not only central to profitability, but crucial to business survival. In today's tough and challenging business environment, the development and implementation of a comprehensive quality policy is not merely desirable – it is essential.

Quality is often used to signify 'excellence' of a product or service – we talk about 'Rolls-Royce quality' and 'top quality'. In some engineering companies, the word may be used to indicate that a piece of metal conforms to certain physical dimension characteristics, often set down in the form of a particularly 'tight' specification. If we are to define quality in a way which is useful in its management, then we must recognize the need to include in the assessment of quality, the true requirements of the 'customer'.

Quality, then, is simply meeting the customer requirements, and this has been expressed in many ways by others:

'fitness for purpose or use' – Juran.

'the totality of features and characteristics of a product or service that bear on its ability to satisfy stated or implied needs' – BS4778, 1987 (ISO 8402, 1986) *Quality Vocabulary: Part 1. International Terms*.

'the total composite product and service characteristics of marketing, engineering, manufacture, and maintenance through which the product and service in use will meet the expectation by the customer' – Feigenbaum.

There is another word that we should define properly – 'reliability'. 'Why do you buy a Volkswagen car?' 'Quality and reliability' comes back the answer. The two are used synonymously, often in a totally confused way. Clearly, part of the acceptability of a product or service will depend on its ability to function satisfactorily over a period of time, and this aspect of performance is given the name 'reliability'. It is the ability of the product or service to continue to meet the customer requirements. Reliability ranks with quality in importance, since it is a key factor in many purchasing decisions where alternatives are being considered. Many of the general management issues related to achieving product or service quality are also applicable to reliability, but this topic is covered specifically in Chapter 9.

Our definition of quality requires that both the needs of the customer and his/her *perceived needs* are explored. Frequently, a choice of product or service is made upon apparently irrational grounds; identical offerings, presented in different ways, will sell in vastly different quantities, and will have different qualities ascribed to them. The detergent which sells better in a blue box than a red one, the bank account which has a higher status because of the leather chequebook wallet, are well known. Similarly, a quality judgement is often related to the price paid without any regard to the discernible properties being purchased. The reasons for a purchase may be difficult to identify, yet their reality must not be denied.

The quality of products and services is important not only for users but also for suppliers. For manufacturers, quality deficiencies result in additional costs for inspection, testing, scrap, re-work, and the handling of complaints and warranty claims. In the so-called service industries, errors, checking, enquiries and complaints account for losses in efficiency and productivity. Repeat sales and future market share will also be affected, with significant effects on profitability and survival. Quality must, therefore, be taken into account throughout all the areas of marketing, design, purchasing, production or operations, and distribution. It must be controlled in all these functions, and their activities co-ordinated to achieve a balanced corporate quality performance. Quality performance will not just happen; effective leadership and teamwork is the only sure recipe for success. Real understanding and commitment by senior management, together with explicit quality policies, lead to an improvement throughout the entire organization, which in turn generates a momentum for the improvement of products, services and performance.

Achieving quality relies upon consideration of both the external environment and the internal resources: the identification of the customer's requirements must be matched by the ability to produce a product or generate a service which will be recognized as satisfying the needs. In the event of a conflict between these two determinants, the intended market segment may have to be changed, or the internal resources may have to be re-examined. A word of warning; the customer's perception of quality changes with time and any organization's attitude to quality must change with this perception. The skills and attitudes of the producer are also subject to change, and failure to monitor such changes will inevitably lead to dissatisfied customers. Quality, like all other corporate matters, must be reviewed continually in the light of current circumstances.

A traditional approach to many transformation processes is to depend on 'production' to make the product and 'quality control' to inspect it and divert that output which does not meet the requirements. This is a strategy of *detection* and is wasteful because it allows time and materials to be invested in products which are not always saleable. This post-operation/production inspection is expensive, unreliable and uneconomical.

It is much more effective to avoid waste by not producing unsaleable output in the first place – to adopt a strategy of *prevention*. The prevention strategy sounds sensible and obvious to most people. It is often captured in slogans such as 'Quality – right first time'. This type of campaigning is, however, not enough on its own. What is required is an understanding of the elements of a systematic control system which is designed for the prevention of products or services which do not conform to requirements. Management must be dedicated to the on-going improvement of quality, not simply a one-step improvement to an acceptable plateau.

A *quality policy* then requires top management to:

(a) establish an 'organization' for quality;
(b) identify the customer's needs and perception of needs;
(c) assess the ability of the organization to meet these needs;
(d) ensure that supplied materials and services reliably meet the required standards of performance and efficiency;
(e) concentrate on the prevention rather than detection philosophy;
(f) educate and train for quality improvement;
(g) review the quality management systems to maintain progress.

The quality policy must be publicized and understood at all levels of the organization.

Design and conformance

We have defined quality as the degree of satisfaction of customer needs. So the quality of a motor car, or washing machine, or a banking service is the extent to which it meets the requirements of the customer. Before any discussion on quality can take place, therefore, it is necessary to be clear about the purpose of the product, in other words what those customer's requirements are. The customer may be internal or external to the organization and his/her satisfaction must be the first and most important ingredient in any plan for success.

The quality of any product or service has two distinct but interrelated aspects:

(a) quality of design, and
(b) quality of conformance to design.

Quality of design

This is a measure of how well the product or service is designed to meet the customer requirements. If the quality of design is low, the product/service will not satisfy the requirements.

The most important feature of the design, with regard to the achievement of the required product quality, is the *specification*. This describes and defines the product or service and should be a comprehensive statement of all aspects of it which must be present to meet customer requirements.

The stipulation of the correct specification is vital in the purchase of materials and services for use in the transformation process. All too frequently, the terms 'as previously supplied' or 'as agreed with your representative' are to be found on purchasing orders for suppliers. The importance of obtaining quality inputs cannot be over-emphasized and this cannot be achieved without adequate specifications.

A specification may be expressed in terms of the maximum amount of tolerable variation on a measurement, the degree of finish on a surface, the smoothness of movement of a mechanical device, a particular chemical property, the number of times the phone rings before it must be answered, and so on. There is a variety of ways in which specifications may be stated and the ingenuity of man must be constrained in order to control the number of forms of specifications present in any organization.

Quality of conformance to design

This is the extent to which the product or service achieves the quality of design. What the customer actually receives should conform to the design, and direct production or operating costs are tied firmly to the level of conformance achieved. Quality cannot be inspected into a product or service; the customer satisfaction must be designed into the whole system. The conformance check then makes sure that things go according to plan. A high level of final product inspection or checking of work is often indicative of attempts to inspect in quality, an activity which will achieve mostly spiralling costs and decreasing viability.

The area of conformance to design is largely concerned with the performance of the *process*, which transforms a set of inputs, including actions, methods and operations, into desired outputs – products, information, services, etc. In each area or function of an organization there will be many processes taking place, and the output from one is often the input to another. Clearly it is essential to have an effective *system* to manage each process. The recording and analysis of data play a significant role in this aspect of quality and it is here that the tools of 'statistical process control' (SPC), described in Chapters 19 and 20, must be applied effectively.

The costs of quality

Manufacturing a product or generating a service which meets the customer requirements must be management in a cost-efficient manner, so that the long-term effect of quality costs on the business is a desirable one. These costs are a true measure of the quality effort. A competitive product based on a balance between quality and cost factors is the principal goal of responsible POM. This objective is best accomplished with the aid of competent analysis of the costs of quality.

The analysis of quality costs is a significant management tool which provides:

(a)   a method of assessing the overall effectiveness of the management of quality;
(b)   a means of determining problem areas and action priorities.

The costs of quality are no different from any other costs in that, like the cost of maintenance, design, sales, production/operations management, information and other activities, they can be budgeted, measured and analysed.

Having specified the quality of design, POM has the task of achieving a service or product which matches it. This comprises activities which will incur costs that may be separated into the categories of failure costs, appraisal costs and prevention costs. Failure costs can be further split into those resulting from internal and external failure.

Internal failure costs

These costs occur when products fail to reach designed quality standards and are detected before transfer to the consumer takes place. Internal failure includes:

Scrap – defective product which cannot be repaired, used or sold.

Re-work or *rectification* – the correction of defective output or errors to meet the required specifications.

Re-inspection – the re-examination of output which has been rectified.

Downgrading – product which is usable but does not meet specifications and may be sold as 'second quality' at a low price.

Waste – the activities associated with doing unnecessary work or holding stocks as the result of errors, poor organization, the wrong materials, etc.

Failure analysis – the activities required to establish the causes of internal product failure.

External failure costs

These costs occur when products or services fail to reach design quality standards and are not detected until after transfer to the consumer. External failure includes:

Repair and *servicing* – either of returned products or those in the field.

Warranty claims – failed products which are replaced under guarantee.

Complaints – all work associated with servicing of customers' complaints.

Returns – the handling and investigation of rejected products and services, including any transport costs.

Liability – the result of product liability litigation and other claims, which may include change of contract.

Loss of goodwill – the impact on reputation and image which impinges directly on future prospects for sales.

External and internal failures produce the *costs of getting it wrong*.

Appraisal costs

These costs are associated with the evaluation of purchased materials, processes, intermediates, products and services, to assure conformance with the specifications. Appraisal includes:

Verification – of incoming material, process set-up, first-offs, running processes, intermediates, final products and services, and includes product/service performance appraisal against agreed specifications.

Quality audits – to check that the quality system is functioning satisfactorily.

Inspection equipment – the calibration and maintenance of any equipment used in appraisal activities.

Vendor rating – the assessment and approval of suppliers of all products and services.

Appraisal activities result in the *costs of checking it is right*.

Prevention costs

These are associated with the design, implementation and maintenance of the quality system. Prevention costs are planned and are incurred prior to production. Prevention includes:

Product/service requirements – the determination of quality requirements and the setting of corresponding specifications for incoming materials, processes, intermediates, finished products and services.

Quality planning – the creation of quality, reliability, production/operation supervision, verification and other special plans (e.g. trials) required to achieve the quality objective.

Quality assurance – the creation and maintenance of the overall quality system.

Appraisal equipment – the design, development and/or purchase of equipment for use in appraisal.

Training – the development, preparation and maintenance of quality training programmes for operators, supervisors and managers.

Miscellaneous – clerical, travel, supply, shipping, communications and other general management activities associated with quality.

Resources devoted to prevention give rise to the *costs of making it right first time*.

The costs of quality

1. Internal costs
2. External failure costs
3. Appraisal costs
4. Prevention costs

The relationship between the so-called direct costs of prevention, appraisal, and failure, and the ability of the organization to meet the customer requirements is shown in Fig 8.1.

Where the ability to match a quality acceptable to the customer is low, the total direct quality costs are high, the failure costs predominating. As ability is improved by modest investment in prevention and possibly appraisal, the failure costs drop, initially very steeply.

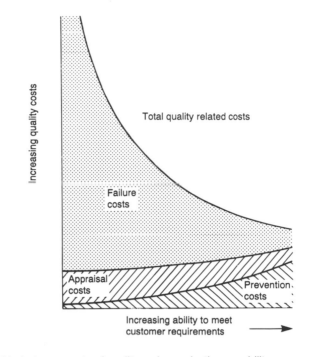

Fig. 8.1   Relationship between costs of quality and organization capability

It is possible to envisage the combination of the costs of failure declining, appraisal declining less rapidly, and prevention increasing, leading to a minimum or 'optimum' in the total costs. Such a minimum does not exist because, as it is approached, the requirements change and become more exacting.

Total direct quality costs, and their division between the categories of prevention, appraisal, internal failure and external failure, vary considerably from industry to industry and from plant to plant. The work of Juran, one of the so called 'gurus' of quality, has suggested that total quality costs in manufacturing average 10 per cent of sales turnover. Another famous writer on quality, Feigenbaum, has introduced the idea that in the average organization there exists a 'hidden plant', amounting to approximately one-tenth of productive capacity. This is devoted to producing scrap, re-work, correcting errors, replacing defective goods/services and so on. Thus, a direct link exists between quality and productivity, and there is no better way to improve productivity than to convert this hidden plant to truly productive use. A systematic approach to the control of quality provides an important way to accomplish this.

Management responsibility and the quality system

'Quality is everyone's business' is an often-quoted cliche, but 'Everything is everyone's business', and so quality often becomes 'Nobody's business'. The responsibility for quality begins with the determination of the customer's quality requirements and continues until the product or service is accepted by a satisfied customer. The management functions identifiable within this process, together with their duties (some of which are shared activities and, therefore, appear under several functions), are as follows:

Senior management

(a) A clear understanding of quality.
(b) A commitment to a defined quality policy.
(c) To ensure that the correct quality systems and attitudes pervade the organization.
(d) To support and encourage the never-ending improvement.

Marketing

(a) Determination of customer requirements.
(b) A knowledge of the competitors' operating levels.
(c) Setting of product and service specifications.
(d) Analysis of customer complaints, sales staff reports, warranty claims and product liability cases.
(e) Downgrading of products/services.

Research and development/design/management services

(a) Setting of appropriate specifications (including bought-out materials, processes and products/services).
(b) Pre-production/operation and prototype trials.
(c) Design and specification of equipment used for verification.
(d) Analysis of some re-work/rectification problems.
(e) Downgrading of products/services.
(f) Analysis of complaints and warranty claims.

Production or operations management

(a) Agreement of specifications.
(b) Pre-production/operations and prototype trials.
(c) Training of operations and associated personnel, including supervisors, foremen, etc.
(d) Special handling and storage during production/operation.
(e) Supervision and control of quality at all stages.
(f) Line or process control.
(g) Finished product/service control.
(h) Analysis of scrapped, re-worked, rectified, replaced and downgraded products/services.

Purchasing

(a) Vendor-supplier selection rating and approval.
(b) Procuring of materials and services of the required quality.

After-sales and technical service

(a) Product/service specification and performance evaluation.
(b) Pre-production/operation and prototype evaluations.
(c) Analysis of customer complaints and claims.

Stores, transport and distribution

(a) Special handling and storage.
(b) Receiving and checking of supplies.
(c) Checking and despatch of finished or replacement products or services.
(d) Receiving, checking and sorting of returned products for replacement or repair.

Quality assurance

(a) Quality planning.
(b) Quality advice and expertise.
(c) Training of personnel.
(d) Provision of purchased supplies, processes and finished products/service appraisal methodology.
(e) Analysis of customer complaints, warranty claims and product/service liability cases.

Where responsibility for quality lies

1. Senior management.
2. Marketing.
3. R & D/Design/Management services.
4. POM.
5. Purchasing.
6. After-sales/Technical service.
7. Stores/Transport/Distribution.
8. Quality assurance.

A quality assurance system, based on the fact that all functions share responsibility for quality, provides an effective method of acquiring and maintaining desired quality standards. A quality assurance department should not assume direct responsibility for quality but should support, advise and audit the work of the other functions, in much the same way as a financial auditor performs his duty without assuming responsibility for the profitability of the company.

The actual control of quality during operations must rest squarely on the shoulders of POM, who must ensure that all the appropriate concepts and techniques are applied to this task. Organizationally, this means that staff who actually control quality are within the POM function – those who do the work day in, day out. This requires a good-quality system to help manage the processes.

A quality system may be defined as an assembly of components, such as the organizational structure, responsibilities, procedures, processes and resources for implementing quality management. The quality system must be documented, i.e. using the procedures and paperwork referred to in Chapter 1. This usually takes the form of a quality manual, the sections of which cover such matters as:

(a) who should be responsible for the functions affecting quality;
(b) once installed, how the system should be audited and reviewed to remain effective;
(c) the planning considerations involved in setting up the quality system.
(d) the documented work instructions required;
(e) the records that will be required;
(f) how problems may be identified and corrected;
(g) which design functions need to be controlled;
(h) the sort of system required for the control of documentation and changes;
(i) the control of verification equipment required;
(j) the control of purchased materials and services;
(k) the controls required during production or operations;
(l) the requirements at final inspection;
(m) any sampling procedures which should be used;
(n) the control of non-conforming materials or services;
(o) the identification of inspection status of materials in the production process;
(p) the procedures required to protect and preserve product or service quality;
(q) the need for training.

The reader is referred to the International Standard, ISO 9000 series (UK dual-numbered Standard BS5750) for detailed recommendations in setting up a quality system. Some general information and advice is also given in *Total Quality Management* by Oakland (Butterworth-Heinemann, Oxford, 1989) and *Quality Improvement through Standards* by Dale and Oakland (Stanley Thornes, London, 1991).

The control of quality is a managerial function in which the quality of materials, processes, skills and products is controlled for the purpose of preventing defective output. To meet this responsibility, organizations must use every device practicable to prevent, detect and correct errors that occur in the steps of production. This implies that, to achieve the control of quality, the variables which may affect quality and which can result from the actions of people, the nature of materials, and the performance of machines, must all be controlled. Technologies and market conditions vary between different industries and markets, but the basic concept of quality management and the financial implications are of general validity. The objective should be to produce goods and services which conform to the requirements of the customer. The way to accomplish this is to use a systematic approach in the operating departments of marketing, design, production or operations, quality assurance, purchasing, sales and others – nobody should be exempt. The systematic approach to quality is not a separate science or a unique theory, rather a set of valuable tools which becomes an integral part of the 'total' quality approach.

Teamwork for quality improvement

Quality circles and quality improvement/corrective action teams

It is claimed that quality circles (QCs) originated in the early 1960s in Japan with the purpose of improving the quality of Japanese products. They have certainly become one of the most publicized aspects of that country's approach to quality.

It is very easy to regard quality circles as the magic ointment to be rubbed on the affected spot, and unfortunately many managers in the west see them as a panacea which will cure all ills. There are no panaceas but, given the right sort of introduction, commitment by top management, and the environment in which to operate, quality circles can produce the motivation to achieve quality improvements at operator level.

In essence a quality circle can be easily defined:

'A *quality circle* is a group of employees who meet *voluntarily* at frequent and regular intervals to discuss problems encountered in their work with a view to discovering solutions to these problems, these being installed with, where necessary, managerial support.'

Successful installation and continuation of any quality improvement team requires that all concerned, and particularly *management*, should examine the concept from the three fundamental aspects of production/operations management: the social, the technical and the managerial.

Social aspects of quality teams

Quality improvement teams can only operate successfully if there is *commitment* on all sides. No interested person from the working group or involved in the process should be excluded, although effective teams seem to contain 7–10 members. Participation in discussions should be free and ideas, however wild, should be encouraged and discussed.

The social purpose of quality improvement teams and circles is to provide the powerful motivation of allowing people to take some part in deciding their own actions and futures. A financial budget is a strong motivating force *if those who are held responsible take part in its preparation*, and the quality team should bring with it a similar motivation. A good, well-trained and sympathetic leader will see it as an essential part of his task to develop the abilities of each member of the team. Since the leader is usually the group or process supervisor, he or she benefits directly by considerable assistance in solving nagging problems.

Technical aspects of quality teams

There is available a wide range of invaluable techniques which may be used in quality improvement. These include:

(a)   process flow charting;
(b)   brainstorming;
(c)   cause and effect analysis;
(d)   data gathering and histograms;
(e)   Pareto or A–B–C analysis;
(f)   scatter diagrams; and
(g)   control charts

and before any quality improvement activity can begin, the team must have some knowledge of the above. The techniques listed are not exclusive to quality teams and find application in most fields of management. None of them requires a high initial level of education, even control charting is capable of being understood at all levels if properly explained. Outside assistance in training may, however, be desirable.

Managerial aspects of quality teams

Quality improvement, like any other activity, will not be successful unless there is complete managerial commitment and support. The quickest way to kill the motivation of a team is to ignore a proposal arising from it. If the team leader has been properly trained, only feasible solutions will be proposed and these should be implemented as rapidly as possible. This requires an open-mindedness on the part of managers which some find difficult. It must be realized that the real 'experts' on performing a task are those people who do it day after day.

Aspects of quality teams

Social
Technical
Managerial

Total quality management

Errors have a way of multiplying and errors in one part of an operation create problems elsewhere, leading to more errors, more problems and so on. Most people in business then spend a large proportion of their time correcting errors, looking for things, checking why things are late, rectifying, re-doing, apologising to customers, etc.

Total Quality Management (TQM) is a way of managing to improve the effectiveness, flexibility and competitiveness of a business as a whole. It involves whole companies getting organized in each department, each activity, and each person, at each level. For an organization to be truly effective, every single part of it must work properly together, because every person and every activity affects and in turn is affected by others. It is in this way that Japanese companies have become so competitive and so successful.

TQM is also a method of removing waste, by involving everyone in improving the way things are done. TQM must be applied throughout an organization so that people from different departments, with different priorities and abilities, communicate with and help each other. The methods are equally useful in finance, sales, marketing, design, accounts, research, development, purchasing, personnel, computer services, distribution and production/operations.

Some of the most exciting applications of TQM have materialized from departments which could see little relevance when first introduced to the concepts. Following training, many examples from different departments of organizations show the use of the techniques. Sales staff have monitored and increased successful sales calls, office staff have used TQM methods to prevent errors in word-processing and improve inputting to computers, customer services have monitored and reduced complaints, and distribution staff have controlled lateness and disruption in deliveries.

It is worthy of mention that the first point of contact for some outside customers is the telephone operator, the security people at the gate, or the person in reception. Equally, the paperwork and support services, such as invoicing and sales literature publications, must match the needs of the 'customer'. Clearly TQM cannot be restricted to the 'production' or 'operational' areas without losing great opportunities to gain maximum benefit.

The organization which believes that the traditional quality control techniques, and the way they have always been used, will result in total quality is wrong. Employing more inspectors, tightening up standards, developing correction, repair and re-work teams does not promote quality. Traditionally, quality has been regarded as the responsibility of the 'QC' department, and still it has not been recognized in some organizations that many quality problems originate in the service or administration areas.

In addition to culture and communication issues, there are three major components of TQM:

1. A documented quality management system.
2. Statistical process control (SPC) (see Chapters 19 and 20).
3. Teamwork for quality improvement.

These are complementary in many ways and they share the same requirement for an uncompromising *commitment* to quality. This must start with the most senior management and flow down through the organization. Having said that, either SPC or the quality system, or both, may be used as a spearhead to drive TQM through an organization. The attention to many aspects of an organization's operations – from purchasing through to distribution, from data recording to control chart plotting – which are required for the successful introduction of a good-quality system, or the implementation of SPC, will have a 'Hawthorn effect' concentrating everyone's attention on the customer/supplier interface, both inside and outside the organization.

Much of industry and the service sector would benefit from the improvements in quality brought about by the approach represented in Fig. 8.2. This will ensure the implementation of the management commitment represented in the quality policy, and provide the environment and information base on which teamwork thrives.

A systematic, structured approach to the launch of quality improvement through a balanced introduction of a quality system, SPC and teamwork will provide a powerful spearhead with which to improve capability, and thereby market share. The importance of the use of SPC and improvements in quality management

Fig. 8.2   The TQM model

systems cannot be over-emphasized. With increases in automation and the use of flexible manufacturing systems (FMS), optimized production technology (OPT) and the adoption of just-in-time (JIT) the requirement for a total approach to quality is paramount.

A complete treatment of TQM is available in *Total Quality Management* by John Oakland (Butterworth-Heinemann, Oxford, 1989).

CHAPTER 8 – HIGHLIGHTS

- An organization's reputation for quality is the key to its success. This is linked to a never-ending improvement philosophy.
- Quality is simply meeting the customer requirements. This requires that both the needs and the *perceived needs* of the customer are explored. These needs change with time.
- The identification of customer requirements must be matched by the capability of the producing organization.
- The 'detection' strategy of post-production/operation inspection of errors and faults is wasteful. It must be replaced by the 'prevention' of failure – controlling the inputs to processes.
- A quality policy is required, which must be publicized and understood at all levels of the organization.
- There are two basic aspects of quality – design and conformance. Quality of design is a measure of how well a product or service is designed to meet customer requirements. Quality of conformance is the extent to which it achieves the design quality.

- Analysis of quality costs is a significant management tool. These costs comprise internal and external failure costs, appraisal costs and prevention costs. As ability to meet requirements improves, the failure costs fall sharply.
- The various management functions each have responsibilities for quality. A quality assurance system, based on these shared responsibilities, provides an effective method of acquiring and maintaining desired standards.
- The international standard ISO 9000 series (BS5750) gives detailed recommendations for setting up a quality system.
- Teamwork is essential for quality improvement. Quality circles have been successful in Japan and other countries in harnessing the expertise of the whole workforce. Quality circles and quality improvement or corrective action teams can be considered under social, technical and managerial aspects.
- Total Quality Management (TQM) is a method of removing waste, errors, scrap, etc., by involving everyone in improving the way things are done. TQM must be applied throughout an organization so that people in the various departments can treat each other as internal customers and suppliers and set about meeting requirements.
- TQM requires commitment from all staff, a culture of right-first-time, good communications, and three major components – documented quality systems, statistical process control (SPC) methods (Chapters 19 and 20), and teamwork for improvement.

Recommended reading

British Standards Institution, *Quality Systems*, BS5750, 1987 (ISO 9000 Series)

The international standard for quality management systems.

Crosby, P.B., *Quality is Free*, McGraw-Hill, 1979

Getting dated, but a very readable book in which the author uses real case histories to illustrate points. The style is very American.

Dale, B., and Oakland, J.S., *Quality Improvement through Standards*, Stanley Thornes, 1991

A detailed look at the various British Standards which can be used in quality management.

Dale, B.G. and Plunkett, J.J., *Quality Costing*, Chapman & Hall, 1991

A crucial factor in the process of continuous quality improvement in the collection and use of quality related cost information. This book provides useful guidance on the subject.

Feigenbaum, A.V., *Total Quality Control*, 3rd edn, McGraw-Hill, 1983

The first author to coin the term *total* quality. This provides a comprehensive guide to the language and meaning of quality.

Garvin, D.A., *Managing Quality*, The Free Press, 1988

An American author addressing the reasons why the 'growing mythology about quality has not produced the expected revolution in US quality performance'. Includes an excellent review of quality history (in the US) and analysis of what the Japanese have done.

Juran, J.M., *Juran on Leadership for Quality, an Executive Handbook*, The Free Press, 1989

Still the doyen of quality management, Juran provides top level managers with specific field-tested methods they need to successfully lead in the quest for superior quality.

Murphy, J.A., *Quality in Practice*, Gill and MacMillan, 1986

Written by the Chief Executive of the Irish Quality Control Association for the 'working manager'. It is a practical book covering the organizational behavioural and managerial aspects of quality.

Oakland, J.S., *Total Quality Management*, Butterworth-Heinemann Professional Publishing, 1989

A best-seller in the field of TQM.

Price, F., *Right Every Time*, Gower, 1990

A guide, from a UK point of view, to Deming's approach to quality.

Rothery, B., *ISO 9000*, Gower, 1991

This practical book guides the reader through the maze of repercussions when ISO 9000 is adopted.

Townsend, P.L., *Commit to Quality*, Wiley, 1986

A blend of traditional ideas and techniques offered to the manager to improve competitiveness and employee morale.

Zeithaml, V.A., Parasuraman, A. and Berry, L.L., *Delivering Service Quality*, The Free Press, 1990

Building on seven years of research, the authors have constructed a model for service quality which balances the customer's *perceptions* of the value of a particular service with the *need* for that service.

Chapter 9

Reliability

Defining reliability

Quality is a property which may change with the age of the product or service. Clearly, part of the acceptability of a product will depend on its ability to function satisfactorily over a period of time. This aspect of performance has been given the name 'reliability':

Reliability is the ability to continue to be fit for the purpose or function.

Reliability ranks with quality in importance, since it is a key factor in many purchasing decisions where alternatives are being compared. Many of the general management issues related to achieving quality, which were discussed in Chapter 8, are also applicable to reliability. It is not proposed that these should be repeated here, but the critical requirements of:

(a)   a company policy on reliability and
(b)   top management commitment

cannot be over-emphasized.

Clearly, every product or service will eventually fail, although in some cases the possibility is small enough for it to be effectively immortal. With pressures to reduce cost and the increasing complexity, the probability of a product or service failing within the user's anticipation of its working life is likely to be finite. As reliability is such an important aspect of competitiveness, there is a need to *design reliability* into products and services. Unfortunately, the testing of a design to assess its reliability is often difficult, sometimes impossible, and the 'designer' must invest in any insurance which is practicable. Some methods of attempting to assure reliability are:

1.   Use proven designs.
2.   Use the simplest possible design – the fewer the components and the simpler their designs, the lower the total probability of failure.
3.   Use components of known or likely high probability of survival; it is usually easier to carry out reliability tests by over-stressing components of a product or service than by over-stressing the complete product or service.
4.   Employ redundant parts where there is a likelihood of failure. It may be that a component or part of a system must be used which has a finite probability of

failure (*F*). Placing two of these parts in parallel will reduce the probability of *both* failing to F^2. Three in parallel will *all* fail with a probability of F^3, and so on. Clearly the costs of redundancy must be weighted against the value of reliability.

5. Design to 'fail-safe'.
6. Specify proven operations/methods.

The designer and reliability

1.   Use proven designs.
2.   Use simple designs.
3.   Use high-reliability components.
4.   Use redundancy.
5.   Use 'fail-safe' methods.
6.   Use proven operations.

Failure

In the discussion of reliability, it is important to be clear about what is meant by failure. When a product, system or component no longer performs its required function, it is said to have failed. This definition assumes that the required function is known exactly. A motor car could be described as either working perfectly or broken down completely, but there could be something in between. It may, for example, achieve a higher fuel consumption than when new. Whether the latter is regarded as failure depends entirely on what is defined as the required function and this in turn may depend on the use of the product or service.

To assist in the definition of failure, it may be useful to consider the various types and causes.

Types of failure

Total failure – results in a complete lack of ability of the product or service to perform the required function.
Partial failure – the item does not work, or the service is not provided, as well as expected, but it has not completely failed.
Gradual failure – takes place progressively over a period of time and perhaps could be anticipated by some kind of examination.
Sudden failure – occurs very quickly and is not easily predicted by investigation or examination.

Causes of failure

Clearly there are many causes of product/or service system failure, but two main general ones are common:

Weakness – is inherent in the product or service itself and, when subject to the normal stresses of use, results in one of the types of failure described above. Weakness is usually introduced by poor or wrong design, materials, processes or operation.

Misuse – represents the application of stresses which are outside the usual capability of the product or service system

Failure mode, effect and criticality analysis (FMECA)

It is possible to analyse products and services to determine possible modes of failure and their effects on the performance of the product or operation of the service system. Failure mode and effect analysis (FMEA) is the study of potential failures to determine their effects. If the results of an FMEA are ranked in order of seriousness, then the word *criticality* is added to give FMECA.

The primary objective of an FMECA is to determine the features of service or product design, and production/operations which are critical to the various modes of failure. It uses all the available experience and expertise from marketing, design, technology, purchasing production, distribution, service, etc., to identify the importance levels or criticality of potential problems and stimulate action which will reduce these levels. FMECA should be a major consideration at the design stage of a product or service.

The elements of a complete analysis are:

1. *Failure mode*. The anticipated conditions of operation are used as the background to study the most probable failure mode, location and mechanism of the product or system and its components.
2. *Failure effect*. The potential failures are studied to determine their probable effects on the performance of the whole produce/service and the effects of the various components on each other.
3. *Failure criticality*. The potential failures in the various parts of the product or service system are examined to determine the severity of each failure effect in terms of lowering of performance, safety hazard, total loss of function, etc.

FMECA may be applied at any stage of design, development, operations or use but, since its main aim is to prevent failure, it is most suitably applied at the design stage to identify and eliminate causes. With more complex product or service systems, it may be appropriate to consider these as smaller units or sub-systems, each one being the subject of a separate FMECA.

Special FMECA pro-formas are available (for example, see Fig. 9.1 p. 117) which sets out the steps of the analysis as follows:

1. Identify the product or system components.
2. List all possible failure modes of each component.
3. Set down the effects that each mode of failure would have on the overall function of the product or system.
4. List all the possible causes of each failure mode.
5. Assess numerically the failure modes on a scale from 1 to 10. Experience and

reliability data should be used, together with judgement, to determine the values, on a 1–10 scale, for:

P = the probability of each failure mode occurring (1 = low, 10 = high)
S = the seriousness or criticality of the failure (1 = low, 10 = high)
D = the difficulty of detecting the failure before the product or service is used by the consumer (1 = easy, 10 = difficult)

					Rating					
Value	*1*	*2*	*3*	*4*	*5*	*6*	*7*	*8*	*9*	*10*
P	Low chance of occurrence				$\rightarrow$		Almost certain to occur			
S	Not serious, minor nuisance				$\rightarrow$		Total failure, safety hazard			
D	Easily detected				$\rightarrow$		Unlikely to be detected			

6. Calculate the products of the ratings, $C = P \times S \times D$, known as the criticality index, for each failure mode. This indicates the relative priority of each mode in the failure prevention activities.
7. Indicate briefly the corrective action required and, if possible, which department is responsible and the expected completion date.

When the criticality index has been calculated, the failure may be ranked accordingly. It is usually advisable, therefore, to determine the value of C for each failure mode before completing the last columns. In this way, the action required against each item can be judged in the light of the ranked severity and the resources available.

FMECA

1. Identify components.
2. List failure modes.
3. List failure effects.
4. List causes of failure modes.
5. Assess failure modes P, S, D.
6. Calculate criticality index, $C = P \times S \times D$ and rank failure modes.
7. Indicate corrective action.

Measures of reliability

For the purposes of illustrating some of the more common measures of reliability in current use, a 'life-table' for 150 door locks operated over 30 units of time has been set out in Table 9.1. Note that in practice a much larger number of items would be likely to be tested if valid results were required.

Clearly, all measures of reliability are time-dependent.

The reliability, $R(t)$, of a product is the probability that it will be still functioning at time t. This may be calculated as follows:

(1) Component	(2) Failure mode	(3) Effect of failure	(4) Cause of failure	(5) P	(5) S	(5) D	(6) C	(7) Corrective action
System unit	System will not 'boot' up	Loss of power completed functional failure	Incorrect system program; poor connection	3	10	9	270	Determine failure definition
Monitor	Incorrect colours	Green/amber colours not available	Incorrect colour graphic display card	2	2	2	12	Investigate display card and replace
Disk drive	Disks cannot be read	Loss of data	Incorrect installation; cavitation	4	8	10	320	Install disk drives correctly
Keyboard	Keyboard locks	All keys disabled: data cannot be transmitted	Assembly adjustment; poor connection	4	2	5	40	Full keyboard test and examination of system detail
Printer	Wrong printer details entered	Unable to print files	Incorrect printer details entered	6	3	3	54	Printer specification detail to be examined
Hard disk	Wear – fracture	Loss of storage performance	Dirty disk – drive mechanism	3	5	2	30	Adjust running track/replace disk
Optional expansion card	Functional failure of expansion card	Additional facility not available	Expansion card not connected properly	7	1	8	56	Change procedure for hardening and grinding; to be re-assessed after tests

Product – Personal Computer   Sub-system – Microprocessor   P Probability of occurrence   S Severity of failure   D Difficulty of detection   C Criticality index $- P \times S \times D$ FMECA No. X206   Date

Fig 9.1 Failure mode, effect and critically analysis (FMECA), applied to a personal computer.

$$R(t) = \frac{\text{Number surviving at time } t}{\text{Number existing at } t = 0}$$

The other side of this coin is $F(t)$, the so-called cumulative distribution of failure:

$$F(t) = 1 - R(t)$$

$$\text{or } F(t) = \frac{\text{Cumulative number of failures by time } t}{\text{Number existing at } t = 0}$$

There are two other similar measures of reliability in use: the *probability density function of failure*, $f(t)$:

$$f(t) = \frac{\text{Number failing in unit time at time } t}{\text{Number existing at } t = 0}$$

and the failure of hazard rate, $\lambda(t)$:

$$\lambda(t) = \frac{\text{Number failing in unit time at time } t}{\text{Number surviving at time } t}$$

In Table 9.1 for the time period 10–11, in which 60 units were functioning at the beginning and 57 were functioning at the end of the period:

Table 9.1 'Life-table' for 150 door locks

Operating period (time units)	Number operating at start of period (units)
0 – 1	150
1 – 2	123
2 – 3	109
3 – 4	99
4 – 5	91
5 – 6	84
6 – 7	78
7 – 8	74
8 – 9	69
9 – 10	65
10 – 11	60
11 – 12	57
12 – 13	54
13 – 14	51
14 – 15	49
15 – 16	47
16 – 17	44
17 – 18	42
18 – 19	40
19 – 20	38
20 – 21	35
21 – 22	32
22 – 23	29
23 – 24	26
24 – 25	24
25 – 26	22
26 – 27	20
27 – 28	17
28 – 29	15
29 – 30	13

Number existing at $t = 0$	150
Number surviving at $t = 10$	60
Number surviving at $t = 11$	57
Cumulative number of failures at $t = 11$	93 (150 - 57)
Number failing in unit time at $t = 11$	3

Hence, at time t,

Reliability function $\qquad R(11) = \dfrac{57}{150} = 0.380$

Cumulative distribution function of failure $F(11) = 1 - 0.380$ or $\dfrac{93}{150} = 0.620$

Probability density function of failure. $f(11) = \dfrac{3}{150} = 0.02$

Failure or hazard rate $\lambda(11) = \dfrac{3}{57} = 0.053$

The values for $R(t)$, $F(t)$ and $\lambda(t)$ for the 30 test periods under consideration are shown in Table 9.2 and represented graphically in Figs 9.2 and 9.3.

The curve produced by plotting $F(t)$ is clearly an integration of the probability density function of failure $f(t)$. The curve derived from the $R(t)$ plot is a mirror image of the $F(t)$ plot. The curve from the plot of failure or hazard rate λ (t) is known as the 'bath-tub curve' from its shape, and it is extremely useful in the analysis of product reliability. This shape is characteristic of the failure-rate curve of many well-designed components, including the human body (Fig. 9.4).

Table 9.2 Calculations of $R(t)$, $F(t)$, $f(t)$ and $\lambda(t)$ for 150 door locks

Time elapsed since start of operations (time units)	Number still operating at time t (Q_t units)	Number failing during the period between t and $(t + 1)$ $Q_t - Q_t+1$	Reliability $R(t) = Q_t/Q_o$
0	150	27	1.000
1	123	14	0.820
2	109	10	0.727
3	99	8	0.660
4	91	7	0.607
5	84	6	0.560
6	78	4	0.520
7	74	5	0.493
8	69	4	0.460
9	65	5	0.433
10	60	3	0.400
11	57	3	0.380
12	54	3	0.360
13	51	2	0.340
14	49	2	0.327
15	47	3	0.313
16	44	2	0.293
17	42	2	0.280
18	40	2	0.267
19	38	3	0.253
20	35	3	0.233
21	32	3	0.213
22	29	3	0.193
23	26	2	0.173
24	24	2	0.160
25	22	2	0.147
26	20	3	0.133
27	17	2	0.113
28	15	2	0.100
29	13	2	0.087
30	11	–	0.073

Cumulative distribution function of failure, $F(t)$ $(Q_0 - Q_t)/Q_0$	Probability density function of failure $f(t) =$ $(Q_t - Q_{t+1})/Q_0$	Failure or hazard, $(t) = (Q_t - Q_{t+1})Q_t$
0.000	0.180	0.180
0.180	0.093	0.114
0.273	0.067	0.092
0.340	0.053	0.081
0.393	0.047	0.077
0.440	0.040	0.071
0.480	0.027	0.051
0.507	0.033	0.068
0.640	0.027	0.058
0.567	0.033	0.077
0.600	0.020	0.050
0.620	0.020	0.053
0.640	0.020	0.056
0.660	0.013	0.039
0.673	0.013	0.041
0.687	0.020	0.064
0.707	0.013	0.045
0.720	0.013	0.048
0.733	0.013	0.050
0.747	0.020	0.079
0.767	0.020	0.086
0.787	0.020	0.094
0.807	0.020	0.103
0.827	0.013	0.083
0.840	0.013	0.083
0.853	0.013	0.091
0.867	0.020	0.150
0.887	0.013	0.118
0.900	0.013	0.133
0.913	0.013	0.154
0.927	–	–

The bath-tub curve

The bath-tub curve is usually considered to be made up of three distinct parts:

(a)   the 'infant' or early failure phase, when the failure rate decreases rapidly;
(b)   the 'adult' or 'useful life' phase, when the failure rate is almost constant;
(c)   the 'wear-out' phase, when the failure rate increases.

Clearly, it is desirable that the initial phase should be as short as possible, and to this end manufacturers may 'load' or 'burn-in' their products before sending them to the user, so that the consumer meets the product at the beginning of its 'adult' or 'useful' life. The constant value of the failure rate, which pertains during most of the useful life of the product, is the value usually implied when reference is made

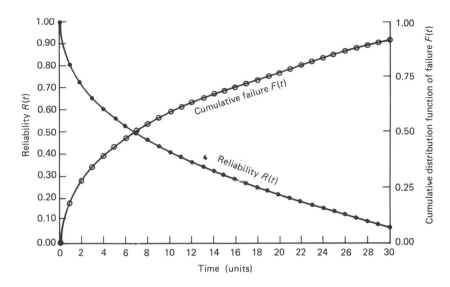

Fig. 9.2 Curves for reliability and cumulative distribution function of failure

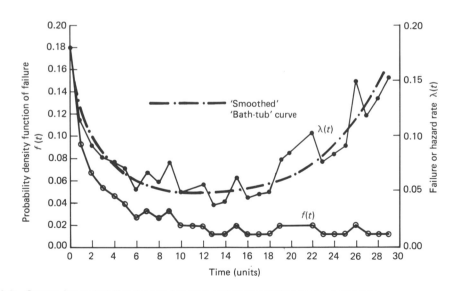

Fig. 9.3 Curves for probability density function of failure and failure or hazard rate

to 'the failure rate of the component'. When the failure rate has increased to a value twice that during the constant failure rate period, the 'wear-out' phase is said to start. Knowledge of when this begins is vital if warranty or guarantee periods are to be determined on the basis of the product reliability.

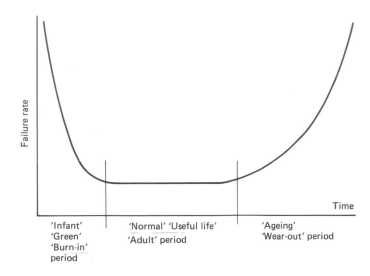

Fig. 9.4   The bath-tub curve

During this period the reciprocal of the constant failure rate, $1/2(t)$ is known as the mean time between failures (MTBF):

$$\text{MTBF} = \frac{\text{Evaluation time period}}{\text{Number of failures in the time period}}$$

For example, during the time period 10–20 in Table 9.1:

$$\text{MTBF} = \frac{10 \text{ time units}}{25 \text{ failures}} = 0.4 \text{ time unit}$$

and a component can be expected to fail, on average, every 0.4 time units in this phase, i.e. we can expect 2.5 failures in every time unit.

Generalized expression for the reliability function

During the 'useful life' phase, the reliability function is effectively in an exponential form, but this does not hold during the early failure and wear-out stages. A more generalized expression due to Weibull may be used for the whole life of the product, when:

$$R(t) = \exp\left[-\left(\frac{t - \gamma}{\alpha}\right)^{\beta}\right]$$

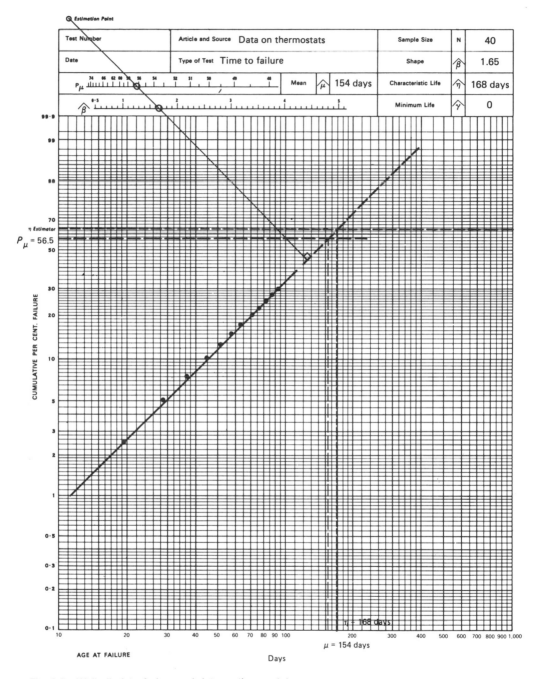

Fig. 9.5 Weibull plot of observed data on thermostats

where α is the 'scaling' parameter, β is the 'shaping' parameter and γ is the 'locating' parameter. By choosing appropriate values of α, β and γ the whole bath-tub curve may be regarded as a series of Weibull frequency distribution curves where

β < 1 during the early failure period;
β = 1 during the useful life or constant rate period;   .
β > 1 during the wear-out period.

The estimation of the three Weibull parameters, α, β, γ, is carried out easily by means of Weibull probability graph paper. In order to use this paper, the age at failure must be plotted against the cumulative percentage of failures at that time. An example of such a plot is shown in Fig. 9.5, from which the parameters can be found as follows.

The *locating parameter*, γ, has a value of zero. If γ is not zero, then a straight line will not be obtained.

The *shaping parameter*, β is found by drawing a perpendicular from the 'estimation point' to the plotted Weibull line. Where they intersect, the β scale gives the estimate of β. In this example, β = 1.65, indicating that the sample is in the 'wear-out' phase.

The *scaling parameter*, α, is replaced by the *characteristic life parameter*, η, that is the time at which 63.2 per cent of the units are expected to have failed [$F(t) = 0.632$]. This is found by reading the age on the horizontal scale at which 63.2 per cent of the items have failed. In this example, the 'η estimator' line gives the characteristic life as 168 days.

A further useful parameter can be obtained from the Weibull plot. The perpendicular from the estimation point to the Weibull plot also intersects a scale labelled P_μ. The value of P_μ so obtained is the percentage of items which have failed by a time equal to the mean life, μ (or the 'mean time to failure', MTTF). In this example, $P_\mu = 56.5$ and from the Weibull plot this indicates that the mean life of the items is 154 days. The MTTF should be the average life of the entire sample, if all units were allowed to go to failure. In the example, the test was terminated after 93 days when only 30 per cent of the units had failed. The excellent straight-line plot allows us to extrapolate to 154 days as the mean life. This will be true only if there is no change in the mode of failure.

Not all failure data are adequately represented by a single Weibull distribution and it is sometimes necessary to transform the data in order to use this type of analysis.

System reliability

Systems, including *managerial and computer systems*, can be considered to be of two kinds:

1. *Series systems* where two or more components operate in series (Fig. 9.6).

Fig. 9.6   A series system

The characteristics of this situation are:

(a) if either component fails, the system itself fails;
(b) the effective reliability of the system between points A and B is

$$R_{AB} = R_1 R_2$$

where R_1 and R_2 are the reliabilities of the two components or, more generally:

$$R_{Total} = R_1 R_2 \ldots R_N$$

Since R, by definition, is less that 1, then the total reliability of a series system is always less than the reliability of each component. For example, if

$$R_1 = 0.95 \text{ and } R_2 = 0.90, R_{AB} = 0.95 \times 0.90 = 0.855$$

2. *Parallel systems* where two or more components operate in parallel (Fig. 9.7).

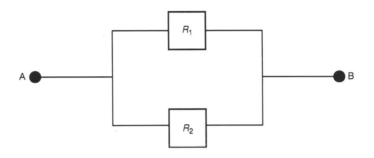

Fig. 9.7   A parallel system

The characteristics of this situation are:
(a) if either component fails, the system continues to operate, albeit at a reduced performance,
(b) the effective reliability of the system between points A and B is:

$$R_{AB} = 1 - (1 - R_1)(1 - R_2)$$

or, more generally:

$$R_{Total} = 1 - (1 - R_1)(1 - R_2)(1 - R_3) \ldots (1 - R_N)$$

Here the total system reliability is greater than the reliability of each component. As before, if $R_1 = 0.95$ and $R_2 = 0.90$:

$$R_{AB} = 1 - (1-0.95)(1 - 0.90)$$
$$= 0.995$$

In managerial terms, this means that the combined reliability of two control systems acting in parallel is greater than that of either system, and the greater the number of systems, the greater the total reliability. Thus, a cost control and a stock control system acting in parallel will be more effective than either system acting singly.

A final word

Reliability, like all other properties of products and services, will not just happen: it must be designed and built in using systematic methods and techniques. These include establishing a quantified reliability specification, techniques for failure prediction, testing, data collection and analysis. Reliability can be influenced by everyone involved in the producing organization from marketing right through to delivery and after-sales service, and those outside it concerned with the supply of goods and services.

CHAPTER 9 – HIGHLIGHTS

- Reliability is the ability to continue to be fit for the purpose or function, i.e. to meet the customer requirements, over time.

- Reliability is related to quality and ranks with it as a key factor in many purchasing decisions. Many of the general quality management issues and concepts also apply to reliability. Like quality it requires a company policy and top management commitment.

- There is a need to design reliability into products and services. Some ideas for doing this are to use proven simple designs, high-reliability components, redundancy, fail-safe methods, and proven operations.

- Failure, when a product, system, or component no longer performs the required function, exists in various types – total, partial, gradual, and sudden. Common causes of failure include weakness and misuse.

- Failure mode, effect and criticality analysis (FMECA) is the study of potential failures to determine their effects, with ranking in terms of seriousness. The study elements of an FMECA are failure mode, failure effect, and failure criticality. Special FMECA proformas are available and the technique follows a systematic stepwise procedure.

- Measures of reliability include: reliability, $R_{(t)}$; failure, $F_{(t)}$; probability of failure, $f_{(t)}$; and failure or hazard rate, $\lambda_{(t)}$.

- The curve from the plot of failure or hazard rate, $\lambda_{(t)}$ with time is known as the 'bath-tub' curve, from its shape. It is made up of three parts: early failure, useful life, and wear-out phases.

- A generalized expression – the Weibull distribution – may be used to describe the whole 'life' of a product.

- Systems of all types may be considered to be either in series or in parallel. The latter are generally more reliable than the former.

Recommended reading

Basu, A.P., *Reliability and Quality Control*, Elsevier, 1986

Covers the general principles of quality reliability, showing the relationship between them and how managerial activity affects both.

Dhillon, B.S. and Reiche, H., *Reliability and Maintainability Management*, Van Nostrand Reinhold, 1985

Some 288 pages of reasonably straightforward advice on the managerial aspects of reliability. Well illustrated.

Lloyd, D.K. and Lipow, M., *Reliability: Management, Methods and Mathematics*, 3rd edn, American Society of Quality Control, 1990

At times a mathematical approach, but it does give a clear indication of the methods required to manage reliability.

Smith, D.J., *Reliability and Maintainability in Perspective*, Macmillan, 1985

Practical, contractual, commercial and software aspects of reliability covered in detail.

Chapter 10

Product, Service, Operations and Competitive Strategies

Distinctive competences

Within any successful organization there is a series of distinctive competences (DCs) which enable it to compete effectively. These are the tasks that it does or 'products' which it makes better than, or at least as well as, the major competition. It is important that the organization formally recognizes this and works at maintaining these DCs, developing them further in a structured and a systematic manner. They are influenced by many factors, some directly within the organization's control, and others less so or outside it all together.

The workforce is one of the principal assets of an organization, and its skills are frequently a significant factor. In order to maintain the DCs it is necessary to retain staff, to develop new staff's expertise in the existing skills, and to retrain existing staff as new skills become 'available' and appropriate. Thus within a consultancy specializing in writing computer software, in order to expand and develop it is necessary not only to recruit new programmers, but also to make sure that the existing programmers are competent in the latest versions of a particular language, or 'learn' a new language if this will enable them to exploit the capability of the system hardware more effectively in software development.

Equipment, plant, buildings – in fact the physical resources – can also lead to or contribute to DCs. Clearly these are linked to the skills of those operating or using them. Thus the computer programmer might need the latest hardware to exploit fully the systems which he/she is developing. Technology development can have a very significant effect here. Consider those retail outlets which now offer colour photographic development and printing based on the latest processing technology with a one-hour turnround.

The work processes themselves can lead to DCs, in terms of the way that they are actually organized and carried out. Consider the craftsman-like input into the manufacture and assembly of a specialized sports car.

Finally, the programmes or timetables for the management of the conversion or manufacturing process can also have a significant contribution to the achievement of these DCs, in terms of speed or accuracy of delivery of the product or service. Consider the planning required to enable SNCF to state that the Orient Express will arrive at Paris Est at 2037 and leave at 2100.

It is clearly crucial that any organization effectively 'monitors' its DCs. The environment is dynamic in all its aspects – the market, technology, skills and processes – and these are constantly changing, some at a very rapid rate. It is important that the organization develops in line. An organization should audit its activities to ensure that it is aware of the impact of its DCs on the market, and that it does not lose its position through change. Equally this provides the framework for developing new commercial opportunities. Clearly POM plays a crucial role in this process as operations provide, or are responsible for, many of the key inputs.

Some factors contributing to distinctive competences

1. Product/service:
   (a) specific functions;
   (b) special services.
2. People:
   (a) skills;
   (b) training.
3. Plant/equipment:
   (a) specific functions/operations;
   (b) technology.
4. Programmes/plans:
   (a) speed or accuracy of delivery;
   (b) speed or accuracy of provision.
5. Processes:
   (a) specific ways of organizing work.

Wickham Skinner developed the idea of the 'focused factory'. He noted that a factory which concentrated on a narrow range of products for a particular market sector or segment will generally out-perform the more traditional plant with a wider range of activities and markets. This focus enables the conversion process to be efficiently and effectively orientated towards the achievement of the organization's objectives, without the conflict which frequently follows the incompatible multiple objectives of a traditional plant with its extended variety. This conflict can manifest itself in attempts to deliver to short lead times products or services with high levels of customization at lowest cost and high resource utilizations. Although the concept of a 'focused factory' was introduced in a manufacturing environment, it is clearly valid in 'service' situations.

The analysis and evaluation of alternatives

As part of the developmental process it is important not only to identify alternative opportunities but also to analyse these formally and evaluate them. This depends crucially on data availability. Clearly this has important implications for some of the other functions within the organization, which will be responsible for 'collecting' these data. A problem here might be that whilst these other areas also require data for their own role in the evaluation process, they might be needed in a different format from that required by production/operations for its role. An organization which operates a rapid exchange service for tyre replacement ('your new tyre fitted within 15 minutes') may decide to extend its range of activities and offer the same service for exhausts. It may be found that the skills in exhaust fitting are quite different from those of tyre changing, and moreover there is a much wider range of exhaust parts than tyre sizes. It might therefore not be possible to offer the same level of service which the tyre customers had come to expect ('you always have my tyre size in stock, but I have to wait while you order the replacement silencer box'). Whilst the marketing function can determine the need and likely demand for the service, POM is concerned about the operations implications of providing the service, in terms of skills, materials, delivery and so on.

It is important that all decision making on new commercial opportunities be based on the firmest possible foundations and wherever possible this underpinned by the best available data. There are a number of quantitative techniques which can support this process, even in situations where a degree of uncertainty exists. One class of approach is mathematical programming, a technique which relies on building a mathematical model of the decision-making process with decision variables, constraints and an objective. An algorithm or a set of rules is used to determine the best decision subject to the constraints. Examples of decisions appropriate for this are where to locate a factory, or what is the best product mix; this methodology is described in a later chapter. A second approach is based on decision trees. These involve looking at the possible outcomes in a decision-making process and associating probabilities, resource usages, costs and potential benefits with each. Some plant investment decisions, with a range of possible outcomes, can be analysed using this method. Another approach is based on simulation (or what is sometimes known as 'what if' analysis). A model, normally computer-based, is built of the situation and the results of making various decisions can be predicted. For example, the impact of purchasing various types of new equipment on throughput, stock levels, customer service and so on, might be estimated.

Other functional interfaces in strategic decision making

Strategic decisions should not be made in a vacuum, and the implications of such decisions on all the functional areas within the organization must be fully investigated wherever possible.

Research and development (or its equivalent in 'services' – new product development) is responsible for generating new ideas for products or services likely to appeal to the market. The marketing department needs to establish the consumer 'requirements', which requires close liaison with R&D. At the same time it is important that the production or operations implications are examined in terms of the organization's ability to produce the product or deliver the service. This links to the facilities required – equipment, plant, technology (the engineering function in manufacturing). In services this frequently includes information technology (IT) equipment. The personnel function will have information about the workforce skills, and is likely to have responsibility for training, development and recruitment where necessary.

It is important that equipment is appropriate and can support operations, decisions over new purchases should be clearly linked to developing existing and new DCs. There is an obvious link here into accounting/finance in order to evaluate correctly the economic implications as well as the operational aspects. When the equipment involves IT, then the rapid growth and development in this area can make the timing of these decisions crucial. It is only necessary to look at the growth of computer power and the decline in hardware costs to verify this. The rapid introduction of EPOS (Electronic Point Of Sale) systems and bar-code readers in supermarkets demonstrates the advantages to be gained by much more rapid 'throughput' of customers. A further development of this could be the integral system within the shopping trolley which records items as they are loaded. Trollies could only be released when the appropriate 'bank card' had been wiped through the system, debiting automatically the customer's account. Whilst this virtually eliminates waiting at checkouts, the current costs of such systems (and possibly the state of technology) preclude their use at present.

Clearly all of this must be completed in a sound financial environment in terms of income and expenditure.

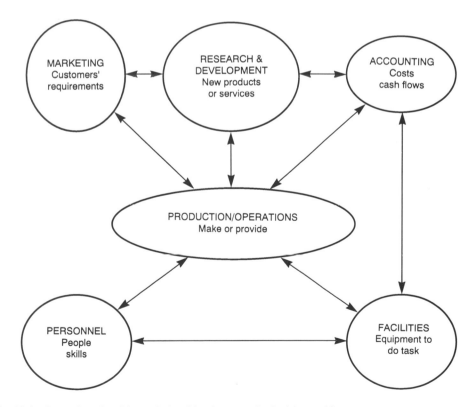

Fig. 10.1 Some functional interrelationships in strategic decision making

It is important that this process takes place in a structured and planned manner (Fig. 10.1), building on the existing DCs of the organization, and identifying specific markets. Clearly this requires close co-operation between the different functions, to the extent that the boundaries begin to disappear as all are working towards the common goal of the organization. This is frequently achieved through multi-function project teams.

The product/service life cycle

A concept frequently introduced in marketing is that of the product life cycle, and many authors have produced variations on this theme. Figure 10.2 illustrates a possible form for this.

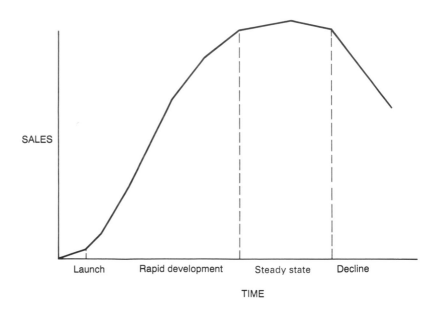

Fig. 10.2   Form of the product life cycle

There are several clear stages. The introductory stage is while the new product or service is being launched on to the market. During this period volumes are likely to be low and this can have significant implications for operations in terms of the organization of the manufacture of the product or the provision of the service. As the product/service succeeds in the market place, volumes will increase. This can put strains on the way the manufacturing system or service delivery system is organized. Frequently it can mean a change in the methods and possibly new, different, equipment. As demand/sales levels off a period of stability is reached, and it might be necessary to start to think about the introduction of a replacement or new product/service which will be launched in order to compensate for the loss of revenue when the existing product/service reaches the decline. Whilst it is easy to discuss these concepts and the planning necessary on this abstract model, it is far more difficult to forecast the move from one stage to another in order to be able to manage changes to operations and plan R&D and replacement launches.

Some of the aspects of a structured approach to the evaluation of operations implications of each stage and the transition from stage to stage are illustrated in the matrix in Fig. 10.3. Hence, for example, in going from launch to rapid development it is necessary to look at the implication for the 'people' in terms of available skills and training.

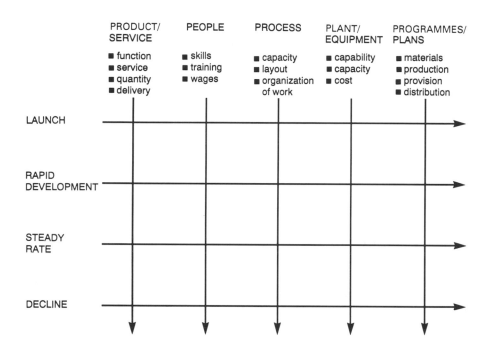

Fig. 10.3   Evaluation of the operational implications of the different stages in the product life cycle

POM as a strategic competitive weapon

It should be clear from the earlier discussion that sound POM practice is central to an organization's ability to compete successfully. It is just as important to consider the implications for POM of strategic decisions as it is for the other functional areas. Indeed, the identification and development of DCs depends crucially on sound POM and, using the structured approach, POM can be seen as a competitive strategic weapon.

CHAPTER 10 – HIGHLIGHTS

- Distinctive competences of an organization are those tasks which it does or those products which it produces better or at least as well as the major competition.

- Factors contributing to distinctive competences are product/service (specific functions or services); people (skills and training); plant/equipment (specific operations and technology); programmes/plans (speed and accuracy of delivery or provision); processes (specific ways of doing work).

- There is a need for a structured audit.

- A focused factory is a factory concentrating on a narrow range of products for a particular market sector. This 'specialization' allows effective and efficient organization of the conversion process towards achieving the organization's objectives.

- Analysis and evaluation of alternatives should take into account the importance of relevant data and use of quantitative techniques, e.g. mathematical programming, decision trees, simulation.

- The functional interfaces are: marketing (customer requirements); research and development (new products or services); personnel (people, skills); accounting (costs, cash flows); facilities (equipment, technology).

- The product/service life cycle goes through the following stages: launch; rapid development; steady state; decline.

- There is a need to examine implications for POM in movement from one stage in product life cycle to next.

Recommended reading

Hayes, R. and Wheelwright, S.C., *Restoring our Competitive Edge, Competing through Manufacturing*, Wiley, 1984

A comprehensive, well referenced text with an American perspective.

Hill, T., *Manufacturing Strategy, the Strategic Management of the Manufacturing Function*, Macmillan, 1985

One of the few texts on manufacturing strategy written from a UK perspective, well worth reading.

Hill, T., *Manufacturing Strategy: Text and Cases*, Irwin, 1989

A comprehensive coverage of the topic, including 20 detailed case studies.

Skinner, W., *Manufacturing in the Corporate Strategy*, Wiley 1978

A definitive text in which the author develops his approach which is based on analysing corporate strategic needs and showing what managers can and must do in order to make manufacturing more of a corporate weapon. A number of chapters are adaptations of his articles in the *Harvard Business Review*, including a detailed presentation of his concept of the 'focused factory'.

Skinner, W., *Manufacturing, the Formidable Competitive Weapon*, Wiley, 1985

Well worth reading.

Voss, C.A. (ed.), *Manufacturing Strategy: Process and Content*, Chapman & Hall, 1991

An interesting collection of 12 papers, which, after an initial overview by leading authorities in the area, covers (i) strategy formulation and implementation, (ii) the global context of manufacturing strategy, (iii) tools, frameworks and approaches associated with analysis and implementation of manufacturing strategy, and (iv) current and future needs in research.

The Plant or Facilities

One of an organization's main assets is its plant or facilities. This section focuses on those issues which contribute to the effective management of these. Location, design and layout are examined, and approaches for selection and maintenance are presented.

Chapter 11

Location and Design of the Plant or Facilities

The supply–distribution system

One of the key features of a transformation system is the efficiency with which the output is transferred to the recipients. Any consideration of this will include the determination of where to place the plant or operational facility, and how much transportation of the inputs and outputs will be required. The way in which the inputs are obtained and the outputs distributed has an effect on:

(a) the total cost of the product or service;
(b) the number of customers that can be reached;
(c) the location of the organization and its units;
(d) the design of the plant or operational facilities.

An efficient supply–distribution system will reduce costs and lead to a more effective service in the form of quicker deliveries and less stock-outs. The type of output involved is clearly a major factor in the determination of the best distribution system. The plant producing artefacts can be located near to the consumer, or so that products must be transported. Services, such as those provided by hotels, golf courses, churches, schools, hospitals and hair salons, are either expensive, difficult or even impossible to transport and these organizations usually perform the service in the recipients' vicinity. There are other examples of services of such rarity, fame or excellence that consumers transport themselves to the location of the facility, e.g. Disneyland, London and New York theatres and the Mayo Clinic in Switzerland.

The supply, receipt, storage and movement of materials, people, equipment and finished goods or services affect not only the number and location of units to be established, but also the design of the transformation facilities. All the potentially available plant must be considered as part of the whole supply–distribution system to devise the best strategy for obtaining the right inputs and desired outputs. Plant flexibility, efficiency, effectiveness, capacity, lead times, and so on, will be determined by plant design, and constantly changing environments may require repeated re-designs if forecasting methods do not allow the establishment of stable facilities for the foreseeable future. The advancements in computers and robotics, and the shortages of certain materials and energy sources also must be carefully examined by the operations management team engaged in facilities location and design.

Location strategy

It is difficult to set down rules whereby the problem of facilities location can be programmed but there are a number of factors which should be considered. It is worth differentiating between the problems of *location* and of *site*: the *location* is the general area, and the *site* is the place chosen within the location. The decision on siting thus probably proceeds in two stages: in the first, the general area is chosen; and then a detailed survey of that area is carried out to find possible sites. The final decision is made by taking into account more detailed requirements.

The following are some of the factors which will influence the choice of location.

1. *Proximity to market*. Organizations may choose to locate facilities close to their market, not merely to minimize transportation costs, but to provide a better service. The closer the plant or facilities are to the consumer, the easier it is to provide just-in-time delivery, to respond to changes in demand and to react to field or service problems. The choice of market proximity is clearly restricted for those providing a pure service, which is not easily transported. Customer-based services such as retail stores, health care, theatres and restaurants clearly must be located close to the market.

2. *Integration with other parts of the organization*. If the new plant or facility is one of a number owned or operated by a single organization or group, it should be so situated that its work can be integrated with that of the associated units. This will require that the group should be considered as an entity, not as a number of independent units (see also the later section single and multiple facility locations).

3. *Availability of labour and skills*. Labour may be more readily available in some cases than in others. Certain geographical areas have traditional skills but it is very rare that a location can be found which has appropriately skilled and unskilled labour, both readily available, in the desired proportions or quantities. The choice often has to be made between a location where skilled people exist, but are not readily available, and one where there is a supply of unskilled labour. Of course, new skills can be taught, processes simplified and/or made less exacting, and key personnel moved.

4. *Availability of amenities*. A location which provides good external amenities – housing, shops, community services, communication systems – is often more attractive than one which is more remote. One important amenity in this connection is good *personnel* transport – buses and trains – and some companies find this so vital that they provide special company transport facilities.

5. *Availability of transport*. It is important that good transport facilities are readily available. There are five basic modes of physical transportation; air, road, rail, water and pipeline. Goods intended largely for export may indicate a location near a seaport or a large airport, but the choice of transport method, and therefore location, will clearly depend on relative costs, convenience and suitability. Mail-order businesses, delivery services, and operations like Disney World tend to make location decisions based very much on entry to a good transportation network.

6. *Availability of inputs*. Good transport facilities will enable goods and services to be obtained and delivered readily, but a location near main suppliers will help to reduce cost and permit staff to meet suppliers easily to discuss quality, technical

or delivery problems. Any purchaser who has tried to improve the delivery performance of an inaccessible supplier will bear witness to the considerable difficulties involved. Important supplies that are expensive or difficult to obtain by transport should be readily available in the locality.

7. *Availability of services.* There are six main services which need to be considered:

(a) gas;
(b) electricity;
(c) water;
(d) drainage;
(e) disposal of waste;
(f) communications.

Certain industries use considerable quantities of water, e.g. food preparation, laundries, chemicals, metal plating, etc.; others use a great deal of electricity, e.g. steel and smelting processes. An assessment must be made of the requirements for these, for as far ahead as possible. Under-estimating the needs of any of the services can prove to be extremely costly and inconvenient. Financial services often require rapid communications throughout the world. Hence, large banks often locate in large, well-developed cities with excellent telecommunication networks.

8. *Suitability of land and climate.* The geology of the area needs to be considered, together with the climatic conditions (humidity, temperature and atmosphere). Modern building techniques are such that almost all disadvantages of terrain and climate can be overcome but the cost of so doing may be high and a different locality could avoid these initial costs. Clearly, services based on ocean resorts, ski resorts and other outdoor health pursuits present severe geographical or environmental constraints on location.

9. *Regional regulations.* It is important to check at an early stage that the proposed location does not infringe any local regulations. A study must be made of the appropriate by-laws and of any special regulations concerning the disposal of effluents, hiring, etc.

10. *Room for expansion.* It is most unwise to build to the limit of any site unless the long-range forecast indicates very definitely that the initial building will never be required to increase in size. This is a most unlikely circumstance and adequate room for genuine expansion should be allowed.

11. *Safety requirements.* Some production units may present, or may be believed to present, potential dangers to the surrounding neighbourhood; for example, nuclear power stations, chemical and explosives factories are often considered dangerous. Location of such plants in remote areas may be desirable.

12. *Site cost.* As a first charge, the site cost is important, although it is necessary to prevent immediate benefit from jeopardizing long-term plans.

13. *Political, cultural and economic situation.* The political situation in potential locations should be considered. Even if other considerations demand a particular site, knowledge of the political, cultural and local prejudice (e.g. restriction of women or foreign workers) or economic difficulties can assist in taking decisions. For some service organizations, such as insurance companies, gambling casinos and private educational institutions, the 'business climate' of an area or city may be a major factor in site location.

14. *Special grants, regional taxes and import/export barriers.* Certain government and local authorities often offer special grants, low-interest loans, low rental or taxes and other inducements in the hope of attracting certain industries to particular locations. As these are often areas with large reservoirs of labour or natural resources, such offers can be most attractive. Location of facilities in foreign countries to avoid exportation difficulties is now well accepted, and some Japanese companies have used this method successfully throughout the world.

Factors influencing the choice of location

1. Proximity to market.
2. Integration with the organization.
3. Availability of labour and skills.
4. Availability of amenities.
5. Availability of transport.
6. Availability of inputs.
7. Availability of services.
8. Suitability of land and climate.
9. Regional regulations.
10. Room for expansion.
11. Safety requirements.
12. Site cost.
13. Political, cultural and economic situation.
14. Special grants, regional taxes and import/export barriers.

Location evaluation methods

In most location problems there are some 'mandatory' factors which must be fulfilled. Thus an oil refinery *must* have excellent main services, in particular fresh water. Once these key factors are identified, the location problem ceases to be open and becomes a choice from a number of sites. Here, an *evaluation* technique, based on ranking the various weighted factors, can be helpful. There are a number of methods, but the principles are similar:

1. Examine the various factors and assign to them weights representing their importance to the situation being changed. The least important factor may be given a weighting of 1 and all other factors then expressed as multiples of this, as whole numbers. It may be that a rather coarse scale is produced, but time should not be wasted striving after unnecessary accuracy and precision; a crude indicator is all that is required.
2. Each of the locations is examined and 'ranked' for each factor, this ranking being carried out factor by factor, not location by location.
3. Each ranking is then multiplied by the appropriate weighting factor and the scores totalled for each possible location. These totals indicate the desirability of the possible locations compared with each other.

Factor	Weight	A rank	A	B rank	B	C rank	C	D rank	D	E rank	E
Proximity	6	3	18	3	18	2	12	5	30	1	6
Integration	0	–	0	–	0	–	0	–	0	–	0
Labour	9	1	9	5	45	4	36	2	18	3	27
Amenities	6	1	6	2	12	4	24	5	30	3	18
Transport	4	5	20	4	16	3	12	2	8	1	4
Inputs	4	4	16	1	4	2	8	3	12	5	20
Services	5	1	5	2	10	2	10	5	25	4	20
Land and climate	2	4	8	2	4	5	10	3	6	1	2
Regional regulations	8	5	40	2	16	4	32	3	24	1	8
Expansion	2	3	6	4	8	2	4	5	10	1	2
Safety	0	–	0	–	0	–	0	–	0	–	0
Cost	1	5	5	1	1	2	2	3	3	4	4
Politics/ culture	0	–	0	–	0	–	0	–	0	–	0
Special grants etc.	2	2	4	1	2	5	10	4	8	3	6
TOTALS			137		136		160		174		117

Possible location: A, B, C, D, E

Fig. 11.1 Assessment of possible plant location
(*Note*: It must be emphasized that this is a hypothetical example: the weights assigned to each factor must not be taken to be recommendations of any kind)

The results for *a hypothetical* case are shown in Fig.11.1. The matrix form is convenient: the rank is placed in the left-hand side of the cell, above the diagonal, while the result of multiplying the ranking by the weight is placed in the right-hand side, below the diagonal. The total score is the sum of these right-hand entries.

The problem of selecting a location is characterized by numerous factors with complex interrelationships, which can be evaluated only qualitatively. Moreover, the information required to make the decisions is often incomplete and the prediction of future conditions difficult. Various techniques developed to solve parts of the total problem include linear programming, and heuristic and simulation models based on a particular aim, such as minimizing transport costs.

Linear programming (LP) may be helpful after an initial screening phase has narrowed down the feasible alternative sites to a small number. The remaining candidates are then evaluated, one at a time, to identify the one that provides the best overall system performance. Most frequently, overall transportation cost is the criterion used for performance evaluation. A special type of linear programming called the *transportation method* (see Chapter 29) has been found to be used in plant location. The most common example of this type of problem is that where a plant or facility 'feeds' a number of units or, inversely, where a producing or operating unit is 'fed' from a number of sources – and the site location must be chosen to give a minimum total transportation cost. If the cost of transportation is directly proportional, both to the distance travelled and to the number of units, then mathematical equations can be produced relating the source to the distance between the 'feeder' and the 'fed'. The equations may then be solved to give the location which will minimize total transport costs, and this location is then accepted as the recommended site for the plant or facility. In any but the most trivial of examples, the manipulations are tedious to perform manually and a computer is generally used for this purpose. Many standard programs are available and readily adaptable to specific situations.

Single and multiple facility locations

Multiple facility location decisions differ in some important aspects from single facility locations. For example, a new competitor to the recreational organizers of 'Centre Parks' could lay out a plan for locations all over Europe taking into account many factors. When Centre Parks adds a new location, however, consideration must be given to its present locations and the specific recreations offered at each one. Banks, TV companies, hotel chains and motor-car dealerships are some examples of organizations which all face multiple location decision problems.

Plant or facilities location and transport or distribution decisions are obviously very interdependent, and for large companies, supplying many products or services from multi-site locations to thousands of customers, the problems are staggering in their complexity. The most effective planning systems are those that tackle the complete location and distribution problem. Owing to recent technological advances, the use of micro-processors, computers and containerization, comprehensive computerized planning and distribution systems are available to aid production/operations managers determine the following factors related to distribution centres:

(a)   number;
(b)   location;
(c)   size;
(d)   allocation by customers;
(e)   allocation by manufacturing or service centres;
(f)   quantities involved;
(g)   modes of transport.

Other questions (for example, what savings will be derived from improving the system?) should also be answered. To determine these answers and factors, large quantities of data are required to be obtained and manipulated and this will require considerable effort. The benefits of a good system are, however, so great that the effort is worthwhile.

One of the most powerful applications of computerized location and distribution planning systems is the simulation of the potential changes in the environment and policies, controllable or otherwise, and the study of their effects. This provides information for the decision maker about the combinatorial effects of changes in such fundamental matters as:

(a)   the market and demand structure;
(b)   plant capacity (expansion and contraction);
(c)   products, services and their mix;
(d)   prices;
(e)   material costs;
(f)   fuel or energy availability and costs;
(g)   resource availability, including labour;
(h)   modes and organization of transportation;
(i)   the number of distribution centres;
(j)   the weather.

Factors in the design of plant or facilities

The detailed design of plant or facilities should be undertaken by an operations management team, including an architect, working within a brief which indicates:

1.   Accommodation required, both immediate and potential.
2.   Latest possible completion date.
3.   Life of the plant or facilities.
4.   Proposed site.
5.   Maximum cost.

All the above should derive explicitly from the long-term plans for the organization; if they are not so derived, then it could well follow that the 'immediately useful' plant could, in the long term, be a useless embarrassment to the company. It should be noted that it is unlikely that the brief will be finalized at the first attempt: management is unlikely to be able to estimate the cost of new facilities unless very recent and comparable experience is to hand. The factors which should be considered include the following.

1.   *Size* Identification with, and commitment to, a place of work are powerful productivity-increasing forces. The larger the unit, the more difficult it is to rally these forces – everybody, at some time, has experienced with distress the 'small cog in a large machine' feeling. Generally, the smaller the unit the better, and it is often better, considering the *total situation*, to create a number of small discrete units rather than one large one. Economies of scale here are often illusory.
2.   *Number of floors.* A problem requiring very early resolution concerns the number of floors. The choice between a single- and a multiple-storey building, unless it is resolved by the circumstances of the site, is difficult to make.
3.   *Access.* Free movement of goods in and out of the unit is as important as

free movement within the building. It will, therefore, be necessary to know the anticipated frequency and weight of all movement between the unit and its environment, and it is most important to try to forecast these for as long ahead as possible. The availability of car parking space for staff and customers may also be a very important consideration.

4. *Services*. An essential estimate required before detailed design begins is the type and quantity of power and other supplies to be used. Gas, water, electricity and compressed air may need to be freely available, and ample provision made for computer terminal points, telephones, public address, burglar and fire-alarm systems. Fire prevention and control systems – fireproof doors, sprinkler systems, hoses, fire escapes – are invariably best 'built-in' rather than applied as afterthoughts.

5. *Headroom required*. Many modern production techniques require the use of overhead movement, suspended plant and storage above head-height; in fact, a plant can often be considered to be formed in two layers, one from the floor upwards and one from the ceiling downwards. Inadequate headroom cannot easily be remedied after the building is complete and it is unwise to curtail the distance between floor and ceiling too severely.

6. *Loads to be carried*. The loads developed in a work area arise not only from the immediate equipment itself, but also from the storage of materials. If a floor is the ceiling of a lower storey it may also be required to carry the weight of any suspended conveyors, tools, trunking or similar fixtures.

7. *Lighting*. There may be special requirements on lighting which must considered; for example, colour-matching processes are most easily carried out in daylight, whilst some photographic processes require a complete absence of light. Wherever possible, it seems desirable to provide natural lighting with a sight of the outside world.

8. *Heating and ventilation*. These require to be treated at the start of the design: costs of heating often form a substantial part of total running costs, and every effort should be made to conserve, and distribute usefully, heat and fresh air. Insulation, draught screens, warm-air blankets and heating ducts are best installed during construction, and not later when their installation can be costly, unsightly and disruptive. This is particularly true if it is necessary to incorporate air-cleaning, humidifying or drying plant within the ventilation system, and location of noxious processes should be determined early in order that outlet flues may be well clear of any fresh-air intake points, and of any locations where the effluent itself might be harmful.

9. *Disposal of waste*. The social consequences of uncontrolled waste disposal are rapidly and sadly becoming apparent, and all waste products and effluents must be readily dispersed without damage or inconvenience. Reference must be made to local regulations here, since there may be restrictions on emissions, the use of rivers as receivers of waste water, or other special regulations. Specialist advice on these matters is usually available from government sources.

10. *Special process requirements*. If possible, any special process requirement should be known at the outset. Typical examples of such requirements are:

   (a) need for particularly close temperature control, for example in calibration or measuring departments;

(b) need for stable floors, for example in laboratories, where transferred vibrations can upset accurate readings and cause considerable waste of time and effort;

(c) need for special security measures, e.g. in noisy, dangerous or secret processes, or when dealing with large sums of cash;

(d) need for special lighting requirements;

(e) need for any special amenities.

Factors affecting the design of plant or premises

1. Size.
2. Number of floors.
3. Access.
4. Services.
5. Headroom required.
6. Loads to be carried.
7. Lighting.
8. Heating and ventilation.
9. Disposal of waste.
10. Special process requirements.

CHAPTER 11 – HIGHLIGHTS

- The efficiency with which the outputs of any transformation system are transferred to the recipients is one of its key features. One of the major contributors to this is the location of the plant or facilities.

- The form of the supply and distribution systems will have an effect on the product/service cost, the number of customers reached, the location of facilities and their design. Clearly, the type of output affects the choice of system.

- Problems of choice of location (general area) must be distinguished from problems of actual site choice.

- The following factors will influence the choice of location: proximity to market; integration with other parts of the organization; availability of labour/skills; amenities; transport; inputs and services; suitability of land; climate; political, cultural and economic situation; regional regulations; taxes; special grants; import and export barriers; site cost; room for expansion; and safety requirements.

- In most location problems there are some mandatory factors to be fulfilled. These often lead to a choice between a number of possible sites, when an evaluation technique is useful.

- There are various evaluation techniques but most involve an examination of the various factors (usually with importance weighting attached), ranking of the locations for each factor, multiplication of the weighting/ ranking scores, and consideration of the various possible locations using these results.

- Most location decisions are complex and benefit from a systematic approach such as *linear programming* (LP). This technique is usually based on minimizing a 'cost' category, such as *transportation* through solving equations. Many standard LP computer programs are available.

- Multiple facility location decisions differ from those involving a single facility. The factors which must be considered include: number; location; size; allocation by customers, and by manufacturing or service centres; quantities involved; and modes of transport. This often requires large volumes of data to be analysed and the use of computers is essential. They can also be used to simulate and study changes in the environment and their effects.

- The detailed design of facilities should be undertaken by a professional team, working to a brief which indicates: accommodation required; latest completion date; life of the facilities; proposed site; and maximum cost. These should all derive from the long-term plans for the organization.

- In the facilities design brief, the following factors should be considered: size; number of floors; access (including car-parking) services; headroom; loads; lighting; heating and ventilation; waste disposal; and any special process requirements.

Recommended reading

Domschke, W. and Drexl, A., *Location and Layout Planning*; (Lecture Notes in Economics and Mathematical Systems Series), Springer-Verlag, 1985

For those who wish to become involved in the detailed modelling approach to planning the location and layout of the plant.

Love, R.F. *et al., Facilities Location: Models and Methods*, Elsevier, 1986

The book is a comprehensive work dealing specifically with location decisions. It should be consulted by those with such decisions to make.

Konz, S., *Facility Design*, Wiley, 1985

The title misleads, as the text deals with aspects of plant location, layout and design.

Murdick, R.G., Render, B. and Russell, R.S., *Service Operations Management*, Allyn and Bacon, 1990

This book contains an excellent chapter on service location analysis, which it is claimed differs in many ways from industrial location analysis. The reason given is that manufacturing costs tend to vary substantially between locations, whereas in service firms costs vary little within a region.

Peters, M.S. and Timmerhans, K., *Plant Design and Economics for Chemical Engineers*, 3rd edn (Chem. Eng. Ser.), McGraw-Hill, 1980

Clearly a specialist's book, which is useful for all production management personnel in process industries.

Chapter 12

Layout of the Facilities

Strategic issues of layout

The word 'layout' is here used to indicate the physical disposition of the facilities or plant and of the various parts of the plant. Thus the layout will encompass both the location of equipment within a small department, and the disposition of departments upon a site.

Layout will affect the organization of the facilities, the technology whereby the task is carried out, and the flow of work through the unit. The velocity with which work flows through a unit is one of the determinants of survival of that unit, and the layout problem is thus one of fundamental importance to any organization. It is necessary, therefore, to ensure that the policy decisions concerning organization, method and work flow are made *before* the facilities are laid out rather than to trying to fit organization, method and work flow to the layout. This is a particularly important area of POM responsibility since here we are dealing with the capital equipment of the organization which, in general, is difficult to relocate once it has been put into position. Every practising manager must know of situations where a piece of equipment or an operation is in an extremely inconvenient position but, because of the difficulty in moving it, the organization has to tolerate gross inefficiency. The layout must express policy and not determine it.

Types of layout

Broadly, facilities can be laid out in two ways, either to try to serve the needs of the product or service (product layout) or to serve the needs of the process (process layout). Often organizations start, when very small, with a service or product layout and, as it increases in size, they tend to move towards a process layout in the belief that such a layout will make better use of the physical resources. The choice of a product or process layout is so bound up with organizational decisions that discussion of them is left to Chapter 15, 'Production/operating systems design'.

Criteria for a good layout

Whilst the techniques employed in making a layout are normal work-study or industrial engineering techniques, the process is a creative one which cannot be set down with any finality, and one in which experience plays a very great part. Furthermore, it is not possible to define a 'good' layout with any precision. However, there are certain criteria which may be satisfied by a layout, and these are discussed below.

1. *Maximum flexibility*. A good layout will be one which can be rapidly modified to meet changing circumstances. In this context, particular attention should be paid to the supply of services, which should be ample and of easy access. These can usually be provided much more simply and cheaply at the outset of a layout, and failure to do so can often prevent very necessary modifications to unsatisfactory, outdated or inadequate layouts.

2. *Maximum co-ordination*. Entry into, and disposal from, any department or functional area should be in such a manner that it is most convenient to the issuing or receiving departments. Layout requires to be considered as a whole and not parochially.

3. *Maximum use of volume*. Facilities should be considered as cubic devices and maximum use made of the volume available: cables, pipelines and conveyors can be run above head-height and used as moving work-in-progress stores, or tools and equipment can be suspended from the ceiling. This principle is particularly useful in stores, where goods can be stacked at considerable heights without inconvenience, especially if modern lifting devices are used. In offices, racking and ducting can be installed to minimize use of floor space.

4. *Maximum visibility*. All the people and materials should be readily observable at all times: there should be no 'hiding places' into which goods or information can get mislaid. This criterion is sometimes difficult to fulfil, particularly when an existing facility is taken over. It is also a principle which is strongly resisted, and special offices, stores, cupboards and enclosures are often requested, not because of their utility but because they form a symbol of office or status. Every piece of partitioning or screening should be scrutinized most carefully, as it introduces undesirable segregation and reduces effective floor space. Definite lines of travel should be provided and, if necessary, clearly marked. No gangways, passages or corridors should ever be used for storage purposes, even temporarily.

5. *Maximum accessibility*. All servicing and maintenance points should be readily accessible. For example, equipment should not be placed against a wall in such a manner that necessary maintenance cannot easily be carried out. The maintenance under these circumstances is likely to be skimped – at best it will occupy an excessive time. If it is impossible to avoid obscuring a service point, then the equipment concerned should be capable of being moved – it should not be a permanent installation.

6. *Minimum distance*. All movements should be both necessary and direct. Handling work adds to cost but does not increase value; consequently any unnecessary or circuitous movements should be avoided. It is a common failing for material, including paper, to be moved from a work station to a temporary storage place while waiting finally to pass to the next storage point. This intermediate rest-place

is often unnecessary and unplanned, being used only because an empty space appears convenient, or because the process flow is not properly planned.

7. *Minimum handling*. The best handling of material and information is no handling, but where it is unavoidable it should be reduced to a minimum by the use of whatever devices are most appropriate. Any material being worked on should be kept at working height, and never have to be placed on the floor if it is to be lifted later.

8. *Minimum discomfort*. Draughts, poor lighting, excessive sunlight, heat, noise, vibrations and smells should be minimized and if possible counteracted. Apparently trivial discomforts often generate troubles greatly out of proportion to the discomfort itself. Attention paid to the lighting and general decoration and furniture can be rewarding without being costly. Professional advice on the recommended intensity of lighting for various tasks can be obtained, and most manufacturers of lighting equipment will provide useful suggestions on this subject. The Health and Safety at Work Act (1974), and the various regulations associated with it, are relevant here and specific requirements are often laid down (see Chapter 32).

9. *Inherent safety*. All layouts should be inherently safe, and no person should be exposed to danger. Care must be taken not only of the persons operating any equipment but also of the customers and any 'passers-by'. This is both a statutory and a moral requirement, and great attention should be paid to it. Adequate medical facilities and services must also be provided, and these must satisfy the requirements of the Health and Safety Executive. Fire is an ever-present hazard and much useful advice can be obtained from the local fire service and often from insurance companies.

10. *Maximum security*. Safeguards against fire, moisture, theft and general deterioration should be provided, as far as possible in the original layout rather than in later accretions of cages, doors and barriers.

11. *Efficient process flow*. Work flow and any transport flow should not cross. Every effort must be made to ensure that paper or material flows in one direction only, and a layout which does not conform to this will result in considerable difficulties, if not downright chaos. The use of gravitational force in certain types of processing can lead to great savings in energy and time. The inefficient pumping of materials round chemical plants, for example, often results from insufficient attention paid to the alignment of certain equipment at the layout stage.

12. *Identification*. Wherever possible, working groups should be provided with their 'own' working space. The need for a defined 'territory' seems basic to many animals including the human being, and provision of a space with which a person can identify can often enhance morale and provide a very real feeling of cohesion.

Advantages of a good layout

A layout satisfying the conditions below will have the following advantages over one which does not:

1. The overall process time and cost will be minimized by reducing unnecessary handling and movement, and by generally increasing the effectiveness of all work processes.

Some criteria for a good layout

1. Maximum flexibility.
2. Maximum co-ordination.
3. Maximum use of volume.
4. Maximum visibility.
5. Maximum accessibility.
6. Minimum distance.
7. Minimum handling.
8. Minimum discomfort.
9. Inherent safety.
10. Maximum security.
11. Efficient process flow.
12. Identification.

---

2. Supervision and control will be simplified by the elimination of 'hidden corners' in which both information and material can be misplaced.
3. Changes in the programmes will be most readily accommodated.
4. Total output from a given facility will be as high as possible by making the maximum effective use of available space and resources.
5. A feeling of unity among employees will be encouraged by avoiding unnecessary segregation.
6. Quality of the products or service will be sustained by safer and more effective methods of operation.

Planning the layout

The following information should be available before a layout can be planned.

1. The company organizational structure.
2. The type of production/operating system to be employed.
3. The type and quantity of people involved.
4. A dimensional plan of the space to be laid out. Whilst it is not essential to have accurate scale drawings of the areas, it is usually essential to have an accurate knowledge of dimensions. Thickness of buttresses and skirting boards, and dimensions of protrusions on walls (switchboxes, fuseboards, etc.) are sometimes overlooked yet may be significant in any environment. The availability of existing supplies and the locations of existing offices, toilets and permanent structures must also be indicated.
5. The volume of work to be produced from the space, both immediately and in the foreseeable future.
6. The operations to be undertaken, their descriptions, sequence and standard times. Note must be taken of any dangerous, noisy, dust- or smoke-producing, or otherwise special, operations.

7. The equipment needed to carry out the operations and any special requirements it imposes, such as particularly strong floors, maintenance facilities and safety devices.
8. The number of movements of material from one work centre to another during a representative working period. This may be expressed either in absolute terms or as a ratio of the number of moves between centres to the minimum number of moves between the 'least used' work centres. This information is conveniently represented on a 'travel chart' (see Fig. 12.1).
9. Any 'dead', 'ageing', 'stabilizing' or other process storage time.
10. The volume of material or buffer stocks required at each work station.
11. The volume of main stores and finished-goods stores required. This depends not only on the type of product/service but also upon the supply and dispersal situations. Any special storage facilities should also be noted.
12. The lines of communication and fire exits required.
13. Any special requirements – burglar alarming, for example – imposed by the local authority or by the insurer.
14. Any special inspection requirements.
15. Any special geographical requirements which must be met, e.g. the specific location of a distribution centre.
16. Any spare facilities or equipment which will need to be stored in the space under consideration.

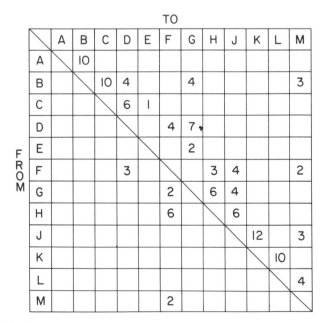

TO

FROM

	A	B	C	D	E	F	G	H	J	K	L	M
A		10										
B			10	4			4					3
C				6	1							
D						4	7					
E							2					
F				3				3	4			2
G						2		6	4			
H						6			6			
J										12		3
K											10	
L												4
M						2						

Fig. 12.1 Travel chart

Process layouts

There are probably two levels at which layouts are required. In one, the various *departments* have to be sited, and in the other the items of equipment within a department need to be located.

Departmental location: operations sequence analysis

It has been pointed out earlier that there are a number of different, and sometimes conflicting, requirements which should be satisfied when preparing a good layout. Since it is usually impossible to resolve the conflicts between these different requirements, it is often convenient when planning process layout to accept a single criterion – that of minimum travel costs – as the starting point for planning:

$$\text{Minimum cost} = \sum_{i=1}^{n} \sum_{j=1}^{n} x_{ij} \, C_{ij}$$

where
n	=	total number of work centres or departments;
i, j	=	individual departments;
x_{ij}	=	number of units, loads, or people moved between departments i and j;
C_{ij}	=	cost to make one movement between departments i and j (this may be conveniently represented as a distance rather than a worked-out cost).

If the movements between departments are known or estimated, the method of *sequence analysis* may be employed to produce a 'proximity' statement which may then be imposed on the plan of the physical structure. This is probably best illustrated by a simple example.

Twelve 'organisation units' A,B,C . . . M have been identified, and the number of movements between units discovered, either by direct observation or by analysing the appropriate documents. If no data exist, then estimates of such movements must be made, and it is convenient to express these as a proportion of the movements on the least-used route. Thus, in the example, it is estimated that the smallest number of movements in unit time is from department C to department E. Movements to and from the other departments are given as proportions of the 'from C to E' movement (Fig. 12.1).

Examination of this chart shows that on some routes (for example D–F) traffic is required to flow each way (3 units from F to D, 4 units from D to F). Such two-way traffic inevitably causes difficulties; the existing organization and technology should be examined to see if such traffic can be removed. This will mean inspecting the emptier half of the travel chart – in this case, the half lying beneath the diagonal – to see if any re-routeing can take place which will empty the cells and give a one-way flow.

For the purpose of reducing traffic between departments, a movement *from* department X *to* department Y is effectively the same as a movement *to* department X *from* department Y. The travel chart is therefore converted to a 'journeys between' chart: Fig. 12.2.

This can now be transformed into a 'journeys between' *network*, which has the form of a conventional critical path analysis (CPA) network (see Chapter 28) (Fig. 12.3) with the duration time value being replaced by a statement of number of journeys. A forward and backward pass will then identify the most heavily loaded path or paths (in CPA terms, the *critical path*). Clearly, departments on this path should be placed as close to each other as physically possible, a 'head' department on the critical path being adjacent to its 'tail' department, so that in the example, departments A–B–C–D–F–H–J–K–M–N should be as close together as possible in the sequence stated.

JOURNEYS BETWEEN

	A	B	C	D	E	F	G	H	J	K	L	M
A		10										
B			10	4			4					3
C				6	1							
D						7	7					
E							2					
F							2	9	4			4
G								6	4			
H									6			
J										12		3
K											10	
L												4
M												

Fig. 12.2   'Journeys between' chart

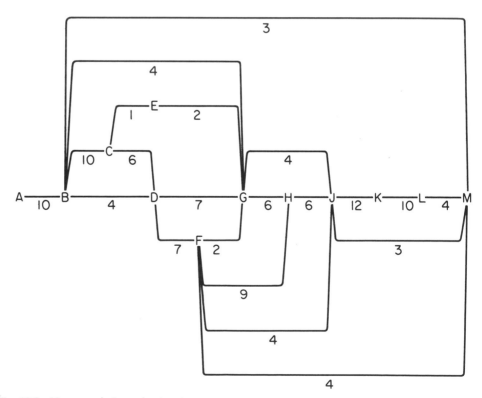

Fig. 12.3   'Journeys between' network

The area required for, and if necessary the shape of, each department are determined and templates representing these areas are prepared, a square shape being initially used if no other shape is mandatory. These templates are then placed upon an appropriately scaled representation of the total area being planned, and moved in accordance with the results of the 'journeys between' network. As with any other layout technique, no unique solution will emerge, and considerable attention must be given to the actual physical conditions.

Layout of work areas

The departments having been located, the equipment within the departments must be laid out. Such a layout is not a task for which a general technique is available. If the technological routes are reasonably constant and the 'journeys between' fairly predictable, then the operations sequence analysis method may be applied.

However, the process tends to be largely one of trial and error, of laying out, modifying and laying out again. It is desirable, therefore, that a layout should first be planned not on the space itself but upon models. These models can take one of two forms:

1. Two-dimensional models which consist, in the simplest form, of a plan upon which is laid cut-out representations of the space required by the various items of equipment. It is convenient to make these cut-outs of stiff card or a colour different from that of the plan itself. It is often found helpful to use the same colour for similar types of equipment, and gangways can also be represented by coloured strips of card.
2. Three-dimensional models, which are built up from scale models of the equipment to be used, and of the operators using them. These models can either be represented by simple blocks of wood, or they can be castings purchased from a company specializing in making such models. Three-dimensional layouts tend to be expensive, and are therefore not used in simple cases. On the other hand, in a complex or large layout the three-dimensional model has such substantial advantages that it is wise to consider its use. Among the advantages are clarity, vividness, demonstration of the need for or use of headroom, and an ability to photograph and transmit elsewhere (e.g. to customers, suppliers and trainees) the proposed new layout. Like any other work-study solution, the idea must be 'sold' to the user, and a three-dimensional model is useful here.

When the type of model to be used has been decided, the operation sequence should be re-examined. It is usually found that there are one or two 'key' operations whose positions are fixed by external requirements.

The planning sequence then continues as follows:

1. Locate the 'key' operations on the plan.
2. Locate main passageways or corridors: it is usually better if these are parallel to the main walls rather than running diagonally across a floor space. It is also usually more convenient if these start and finish at outside or connecting doorways, and they must be adequate for the collection and delivery of material.
3. Locate the remaining work areas to allow work, material or people to flow naturally between key operations. At this stage it is not necessary to locate

equipment in detail but to fix areas occupied by various types of equipment, i.e. departmental or sectional areas.

4. Locate minor passageways.
5. Locate equipment in detail within departments or sections.
6. Complete the layout by locating all subsidiary equipment – rubbish bins, telephones, etc.
7. Test the layout against the principles stated above. A string diagram (i.e. the representation of the route of material or people by a piece of string or cotton – see Chapter 17) is often helpful in establishing the distance of travel.
8. When satisfied with the layout itself, view the actual space, if possible. Visualize the installed proposed layout, walk over the proposed passageways and check the installation. It is often found that time spent here can often be handsomely repaid by discovering features not apparent on drawings and models.
9. Check the final layout against the organization's general policies and specifications.

Layout of work stations

1. Prepare model(s).
2. Study operation sequence.
3. Choose 'key' operations.
4. Locate 'key' operations.
5. Locate main passageways.
6. Locate remaining work areas.
7. Locate minor passageways.
8. Plan individual areas in detail.
9. Locate subsidiary equipment.
10. Test completed layout against principles of good layout.
11. View area to verify layout.
12. Check against policy.

Product layouts

The design of flow lines to produce specific products or services is a complex subject which requires the collaboration of technologists, engineers, designers, managers and social scientists. Consideration will be given in Chapter 15 to the factors which should be considered before designing the operations/production system, and the discussion here concerns line balancing – the attempt to balance the various work stations on a line in time.

There are three basic types of flow lines:

(a) *single model* on which only one product or service is produced;
(b) *mixed model* on which more than one product/service is produced simultaneously;
(c) *multi-model* involving flow production in batches of different products/services, which are produced on the same line.

Before introducing the techniques of line balancing, it is necessary to define some terms.

The *demand* is the required rate of operation or production, in units (Q) per unit time (T).

A *work element* is a distinct part of a process, often identified for convenience of observation and measurement. E_i is the work content associated with element i.

A *work station* is a position on a flow line at which certain work elements are performed. N is the number of work stations.

Total work content is the sum of the standard times for all the work elements, i.e. $\Sigma^{ki}=1 =1E_i$, where k is the number of elements.

The *cycle time* (C) is the time available at each station for the performance of the work allocated to it. C is obtained from the demand: $C = T/Q$.

The *service time* (S_j) is the time required to complete the work assigned to the station j. C must be greater than S_j, otherwise the demand will not be met. $\Sigma\, S_j = \Sigma\, E_i$.

The *balance delay* (D_j) at a particular station j is the difference between the cycle time (C) and service time (S_j). $D_j = C - S_j$. For a whole line, $D = \Sigma D_j = NC - \Sigma\, S_j$.

The *balancing loss* (L_j) at a particular station j is the balance delay (D_j) represented as a percentage of the cycle time (C):

$$L_j = \frac{D_j}{C} \times 100\% = \frac{C-S_j}{C} \times 100\%$$

For a whole line, the average balance loss, L is given by:

$$L = \frac{D}{NC} \times 100\% = \frac{NC - \Sigma S_j}{NC} \times 100\%$$

Precedence constraints are derived from technological relationships between the work elements and affect the order in which they can be carried out. They are usually represented in a precedence diagram.

Zoning constraints either preclude the grouping of certain work elements at the same station (negative) or necessitate the allocation of certain elements to the same work station (positive).

Given the desired output rate of a product, the work elements and their work contents, and other constraints, the objective of line balancing is to allocate work elements to work stations to:

(a) minimize the number of work stations;
(b) conform to the constraints;
(c) minimize the balancing loss;
(d) spread the loss evenly between stations.

Line balancing method

The method is best explained using an example. The forecasts for the likely demand of the AMBLER product indicate that annual sales will be 10,000 units. The product is made up from 16 work elements (Table 12.1):

Table 12.1 Work elements in the AMBLER project

Element	Work content (min)	Precedes
A	3.6	E
B	2.5	F
C	2.7	G
D	2.6	H,J
E	1.6	K
F	1.4	K
G	2.4	L
H	3.3	M
J	1.7	N
K	3.4	S
L	2.8	P
M	1.9	R
N	2.4	R
P	3.6	S
R	2.8	S
S	1.3	M

The technical considerations dictate that elements E and F must not be processed together, neither must elements H and L. If the normal working week is 35 hours and 44 weeks constitute the normal year, the design of work stations may be achieved by the following stepwise process.

Step 1: Draw the precedence diagram
The technological relationships in the production of this product may be as represented in Fig. 12.4, which is similar to an activity-on-node network.

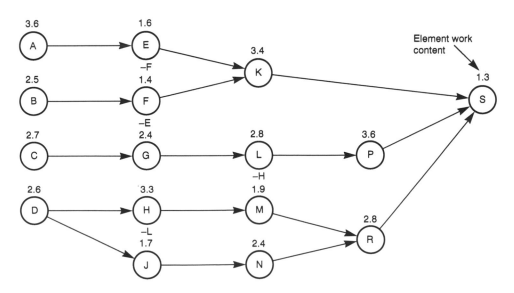

Fig. 12.4   Precedence diagram for the AMBLER product

Step 2: Calculate the cycle time and the minimum number of work stations (N min)

Demand	=	10,000 per year
Time unit	=	1 minute
1 year	=	44 × 35 × 60 = 92,400 minutes
Therefore, Q	=	10,000/92,400 per minute
Cycle time, C	=	92,400/10,000 minutes
	=	9.2 minutes
Total work content		$= \Sigma E_i = E_A + E - E_C \dots E_S$
	=	3.6 + 2.5 + 2.7 ... 1.3
	=	40 minutes

$$N_{min} = \frac{\text{Total work content}}{\text{Cycle time}} = \frac{\Sigma E_i}{9.2}$$

$$= 4.3$$

i.e. N_{min} = 5 (next - higher integer)

Step 3: Calculate and rank positional weights (RPW)

The RPW technique is a rapid heuristic method which provides acceptable solutions to the line balancing problem. The positional weight (PW) of an element x may be calculated, using the precedence diagram, by summing the work content values of all elements along all connected paths from the product to the element x. For example, the PW of element D in Fig. 12.4 may be calculated:

$$\begin{aligned} PW(D) &= E_D + E_H + E_M + E_J + E_N + E_R + E_S \\ &= 2.6 + 3.3 + 1.9 + 1.7 + 2.4 + 2.8 + 1.3 = 16.0 \end{aligned}$$

The remainder of the positional weights have been calculated in this way, and are shown on Fig. 12.5.

The work elements are then ranked in order of decreasing PW, which is a measure of the 'size' of an element and its position in the processing sequence. The rank position weights (RPWs) provide the order in which elements are considered for allocation to work stations.

Step 4: Allocate work elements to work stations

To attempt to design a flow line which has the calculated minimum number of work stations (i.e. 5), provides a cycle time of 9.2 minutes, and contradicts neither the precedence nor the zoning constraints, the elements are allocated to work stations in order of decreasing RPW as follows

Element D, with highest PW, is allocated first to station 1. This is acceptable since D is not preceded by any other element, there is spare time available in station 1, and there are no zoning constraints (see Table 12.2). Element C is the next to be allocated, with the second highest PW, no precedence or zoning constraints violated, and sufficient unassigned cycle time to accommodate it. Work station 1 is completed by the allocation of element G, the third highest PW. The same procedure is repeated for the remaining work stations, elements being allocated by RPW, unless cycle time, precedence or zoning constraints prevent this.

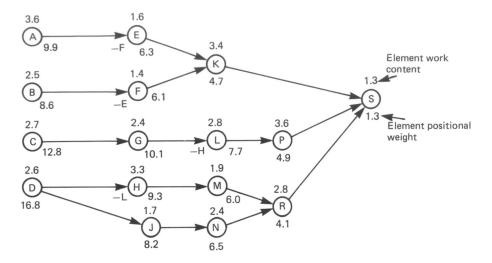

Fig. 12.5   Positional weights (PW) for the AMBLER product

Table 12.2 Allocation of work elements for cycle time of 9.2 min

Work station (WS)	Element i (zone constraint)	PW	Preceded by	Element work content, E_j	Cumulative service time S_j	Available time, $C-S_j$
1	D	16.0	–	2.6	2.6	6.6
	C	12.8	–	2.7	5.3	3.9
	G	10.1	C	2.4	7.7	1.5
2	A	9.9	–	3.6	3.6	5.6
	H(−L)	9.3	D	3.3	6.9	2.3
	J	8.2	D	1.7	8.6	0.6
3	B	8.6	–	2.5	2.5	6.7
	L(−H)	7.7	G	2.8	5.3	3.9
	N	6.5	J	2.4	7.7	1.5
	F(−E)	6.1	B	1.4	9.1	0.1
4	E(−F)	6.3	A	1.6	1.6	7.6
	M	6.0	H	1.9	3.5	5.7
	P	4.9	L	3.6	7.1	2.1
5	K	4.7	E,F	3.4	3.4	5.8
	R	4.1	M,N	2.8	6.2	3.0
	S	1.3	K,P,R	1.3	7.5	1.7

Step 5: Calculate balance delay and balancing loss for the line

It is very rare that a perfect balance can be achieved in the design of flow lines: the cycle time (C) will not equal service time (S_j) in all work stations. In the example of the AMBLER product, the allocation has produced the situation shown in Fig. 12.6,

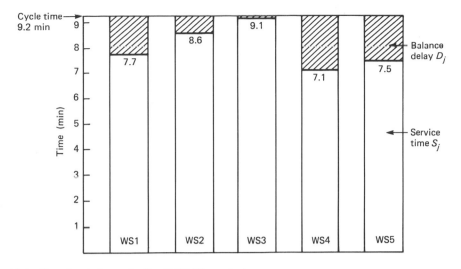

Fig. 12.6   Flow line balance for the AMBLER product

in which neither the work station times are balanced nor is the maximum work station time equal to the desired cycle time. The balance delay for this line may be calculated:

$$D = NC - \Sigma S_j = (5 \times 9.2) - 40 = 6.0 \text{ minutes}$$

and the balancing loss is:

$$L = \frac{NC - \Sigma S_j}{NC} \times 100\% = \frac{6.0}{5 \times 9.2} \times 100\% = 13.0\%$$

This represents a significant under-utilization of resources, which may not be apparent to the casual observer because a worker may well perform the allocated work operations in the available time; in other words, the work will expand to fill the cycle time. The cycle time could be reduced to 9.1 minutes (highest S_j) with a corresponding increase in output to:

$$\frac{44 \times 35 \times 60}{9.1} = 10.154 \text{ units}$$

and a reduction of balancing loss to:

$$L = \frac{(5 \times 9.1) - 40}{5 \times 9.1} \times 100 = 12.1\%$$

It may, then, be desirable to increase output to minimize balancing loss, and the procedure becomes one of seeking a balance for the initial cycle time (C), followed by achieving the best balance and minimizing the cycle time for the same number of work stations.

> **Steps in line balancing method**
>
> 1. Draw precedence diagram.
> 2. Calculate cycle time (C) and minimum number of work stations (N_{min}).
> 3. Calculate rank positional weights (RPWs).
> 4. Allocate work elements to work stations.
> 5. Calculate balance delay (D) and balancing loss (L).

Installation of a layout

Once a new layout has been finalized, it must be put into practice. This involves two separate and distinct steps:

(a)   planning the way in which the new installation is to be carried out;
(b)   supervising while the plan is carried out.

The planning technique known as critical path analysis (see Chapter 28) is ideally suited for both these tasks. Every manager in every type of organization will have seen the newly constructed 'wall' which has had to be demolished to allow entry of a new piece of equipment. Time spent in planning is invariably time well spent.

The use of the computer in preparing a layout

The co-existence of a large number of criteria makes the definition of an 'optimum' layout virtually impossible. Furthermore, the writing of a computer program for plant layout becomes a task of some considerable difficulty *unless some very drastic simplifications are made.*

At the time of writing there are four well-known computer programs available to assist in the preparation of a layout. The oldest and most widely discussed is CRAFT (Computerized Relative Allocation of Facilities Technique) which was written in 1963/1964 by Armour, Buffa and Vollman: it adopts as the criterion to be minimized that of total handling cost. CORELAP (Computerized Relationship Layout Planning), ALDEP (Automated Layout Design Program) and RMA Comp 1 (Richard Mather and Associates) all adopt some form of proximity criterion, attempting to assemble the resources being planned in such a way as to ensure that those items which need to be near each other are in fact so placed.

The choice of program depends upon the user's objectives and the particular layout problem being studied. It is important for the user to understand the features of the program under consideration, and its limitations. Some experienced plant designers argue that a computer cannot really understand the complexities of the task. One manager, however, experienced a different sort of use for the ALDEP routine. He found that his computer-printed proposals for re-layout were seldom corrected or amended by his superior, but when he presented hand sketches or drawings, his boss had a tendency to change and alter things regularly. The computer can clearly offer a powerful psychic influence! It is clear that the plant layout specialist understands the problem better than a computer assistant, but it makes sense to use the data-handling facilities of the micro-processor to aid the decision-making process.

Another aspect which has been observed is the computer's ability frequently to propose unusual or creative solutions, which would normally be rejected at an early stage by manual methods. It is wise for the operations manager, charged with a layout problem, to allow the computer to offer help, but not to be led blindly to an unwise decision or be mesmerized by computer technology.

CHAPTER 12 – HIGHLIGHTS

- Facilities layout encompasses the location of equipment within a department and the disposition of departments on a site.
- Layout affects the organization of the facilities, the technology involved, and the flow of work. Policy decisions affecting these should be made *before* laying out the facilities.
- There are two types of facilities layout: product and process. Criteria for a good layout include *maximum* flexibility, co-ordination, use of volume, visibility, security, safety and accessibility; *minimum* distance, handling and discomfort; efficient process flow, and identification.
- Certain information is required before a layout can be planned, including the organizational structure, the type of production/operating system to be employed, the type and number of people, a dimensional plan of the area, the volume of work, the operations, the type of equipment, (including spares), the number of material movements, and details about stocks and storage areas.
- In the location of departments, operations sequence analysis may be employed to produce a statement of ideal proximity. This involves the use of travel and 'journeys between' charts and networks.
- The layout of actual work areas tends to be largely one of trial and error. Here the use of two- and three-dimensional models is useful.
- The design of flow lines for product layouts is a complex subject which involves technologists, engineers, designers, managers and social scientists, who must all work together.
- There are three basic types of flow lines: single, mixed, and multi-models.
- The objective of line balancing is to allocate work elements to the minimum number work of stations in order to minimize and spread the 'balancing loss', and yet conform to all the constraints.
- A simple line balancing method involves the drawing of a precedence diagram to show the technological relationships, the calculation of the cycle time, minimum number of work stations, and the 'rank positional weights' (RPWs), and the allocation of work elements to work stations. The balance delay and balancing loss for the line may then be calculated.

- The installation of a new layout involves both planning the way in which the new installation is to be carried out, and supervising while the plan is implemented.
- There are currently several computer programs available to assist in the preparation of a layout, including CRAFT, CORELAP, ALDEP, and RMA Comp 1. The choice of program depends on the user's objectives. These must be used with care, bearing in mind that *decisions* about layout must be taken by the management, not by the computer.

Recommended reading

Apple, J.M., *Plant Layout and Materials Handling*, 3rd edn, Wiley, 1977

A very comprehensive, practical book, well illustrated – particularly in the materials handling/warehousing area.

Domschke, W. and Drexl, A., *Location and Layout Planning*, Springer-Verlag, 1985

See comments at the end of Chapter 11.

Sule, D.E., *Manufacturing Facilities – Location, Planning, and Design,* PWS–Kent, 1988

Intended as a textbook for facility planning and design courses in industrial engineering and business curricula. It places some emphasis on the use of computers in facility planning analysis.

Tompkins, J.A. and Moore, J.M., *Computer Aided Layout – A User's Guide*, American Institution of Industrial Engineers, 1980

This text pulls together a comparison of five of the leading computer programs or routines available for the development and selection of layouts. Still extremely useful for those who need to study this subject in depth.

Chapter 13

Equipment Selection

Operations managers often initiate proposals for the purchase of equipment, such as production and office machinery, computers, software, cars and trucks. The reasons for its purchase include the following.

1. New equipment is required for the production of new products or services.
2. Increased sales volumes demand an expansion of the available capacity.
3. Existing equipment has become obsolete and/or changes in technology are required to maintain competitiveness.
4. Existing equipment has entered the wear-out phase of its life and must be replaced.

When it has been decided to purchase equipment, a survey should be carried out. This is conveniently done in two stages; firstly a *use analysis* (or technological sifting) will reduce the range of possible equipment to manageable proportions and, secondly, a *cost* (or economic) *analysis* will determine, if necessary, which of a number of equally acceptable technical alternatives is the most economical.

The purchase of any piece of equipment must eventually be justified on economic grounds, and its cost recovered from the selling price of the goods made or the services offered. Other criteria may be taken into consideration – for example, prestige – but in general these will be of marginal importance, and of significance principally when deciding between a number of possible pieces of equipment all of similar cost.

A forecast of potential use must be made. If this forecast is *robust*, i.e. likely to be achieved, then a predisposition to purchase will follow. If the forecast is weak, and unlikely to be achieved, then a more cautious (risk-averse) decision might be to sub-contract the work.

Choice of technology

The following considerations concern the technical specification of equipment.

1. *Capacity*. The capacity of the equipment needs to be ample for the purpose envisaged during the foreseeable future, and in this context reference must be

made to the long-term forecast, particularly when the cost is heavy. Whilst it is foolish to purchase a piece of equipment which will soon be overloaded, it is almost certainly unnecessarily expensive to purchase one of a very much higher capacity than will ever be required unless there are other determining factors.

2. *Compatibility*. Whenever possible, new equipment should be of a type similar to or identical with the existing equipment. The resultant simplification in the provisioning of spare parts, in maintenance, in operator training, in setting and preparation, and in loading, are enormous. In the purchase of computer software, for example, compatibility with the existing hardware, operating system and other software is vital.

3. *Availability of associated equipment*. Much of the new, highly complex equipment now available can only be fully utilized if a wide range of associated equipment is employed, and the availability of this can often dictate choice. This is particularly true of computers and computer-controlled equipment which is of minimal value without its associated 'software'.

4. *Reliability and after-service*. Equipment breakdown can be costly and can also jeopardize service of delivery dates; hence its reliability is very important. Reference to other users, if possible, is often very helpful here. The availability of a good after-sales service should be investigated.

5. *Ease of maintenance*. Maintenance costs need always to be as low as practicable, and equipment which is difficult to service will not only have a high maintenance cost, it will also provide an inducement to carry out maintenance inadequately.

6. *Ease of learning to use*. The speed with which new equipment can be utilized depends on how easy it is to learn how to use it. This applies particularly to computers and software, where the quality of the supporting documentation and training will greatly influence the learning period.

7. *Ease of preparation*. Ancillary time (setting up, stripping down, cleaning) is expensive and reduces the running time of the equipment, so its ease of preparation should be considered.

8. *Safety*. Plant and equipment need to be safe and, though it is very rare to find unsafe equipment on the market today, this aspect repays study. Accidents are costly in a lowering of output, in deterioration of morale and in bad staff relations. The onus of preventing them is firmly on the employer and management, both in law and in common humanity.

9. *Ease of installation*. This point can be easily overlooked; when it may then be found, on installation, that access doors are too low, or permissible floor loading exceeded, by the new equipment.

10. *Delivery*. The delivery situation needs to be investigated to see that the needs of the organization can be matched by the delivery promised. An investigation into the reliability of the supplier in this respect is worth making.

11. *State of development*. Newly designed equipment is sometimes marketed before the design has been entirely finalized or stabilized. Guarantees on this are highly desirable, although it must be recognized that no guarantee can compensate for the loss of goodwill attendant upon broken delivery or service promises.

12. *Effect on existing organization*. Some new equipment, when installed, will demand changes in the existing organization. Thus, a robotic machine tool, for example, will require that considerable managerial re-thinking takes place. Pre-planning is vital and this is often centralized in the production/operations planning

department. Automated equipment of any type concentrates the planning into action *before* the work commences. If the need for this planning is not accepted, then the benefits of the equipment will not be realized. Equally, the effects of computers and computer-operated systems being installed without consideration of their impact upon the existing organization can be disastrous.

From an examination of suppliers' catalogues, visits to showrooms and other plant, discussion with colleagues and other interested people, a short-list of equipment will be drawn up using considerations similar to the above. A useful device for carrying out further sifting is a matrix, similar to that described in Chapter 11, where the choice of location was discussed. The resulting list must then be subjected to a cost analysis to choose between the various items listed.

Purchasing equipment is similar to buying a car; we would like it to be big and fast enough for our needs, handle well, be tried and tested, well-equipped (particularly with safety features), reliable and easy to service, and within our price bracket. It also helps to judge its suitability if we can take it for a test drive.

Use factors affecting choice of equipment

1. Capacity.
2. Compatibility.
3. Availability of associated equipment.
4. Reliability and after-service.
5. Ease of maintenance.
6. Ease of learning to use.
7. Ease of preparation.
8. Safety.
9. Ease of installation.
10. Delivery.
11. State of development.
12. Effect on existing organization.

Economic appraisal concepts

There are a number of ways of carrying out an economic analysis, and it must be understood that whatever technique is used it must be consistently applied to all equipment. An economic analysis is more useful in distinguishing between different items of equipment than in setting an accurate figure on its absolute cost.

The aim of an economic analysis is to appraise the *cost of producing* from a given piece of equipment, not just the cost of the plant itself. This can be considered to be made up of two parts:

(a) the standing cost, which is the cost incurred by the equipment installed and ready for use but not being operated;
(b) the running cost, which sets down the cost of running the equipment in order to generate the required products or service.

The standing cost

In the calculation of standing cost, executive decisions have to be made: notably, what depreciation should be considered, what is the expected return on invested capital, what allowance should be made for taxes, insurance and rates, and what rent is charged to the floor space occupied (see Chapter 4). These, together with the purchase price, are summed to give an average annual standing cost. The above discussion implies that the equipment is being *purchased outright*. There are, of course, other ways of obtaining equipment, for example:

1. *Hire purchase*. Contracts can be negotiated for long periods (up to 10 years) with the interest tied to the bank rate. In some cases, payments can fluctuate with a known seasonal variation in output.
2. *Leasing*. Here the user never actually *owns* the equipment leased, it being argued that the *use* of the equipment is more important than its *ownership*.
3. *Hiring*. Effectively, this is leasing, but usually a maintenance contract is implied or required.

All these methods should be considered as they may well have substantial tax and cash flow advantages over outright purchase. In these cases, of course, the annual charges are the standing charges discussed above.

The running cost

To calculate the average running cost, a knowledge of the average annual total output is required. For equipment producing for stock, this is a comparatively simple piece of information derivable from the sales forecast. For equipment used to produce entirely to customers' orders or service requirements, the details of output required cannot be forecast in such detail. The most satisfactory approximation is obtained by forecasting the anticipated average output and using this forecast as the basis of the calculations. From the figure of expected output, the cost of power and supplies, the direct cost of operation/production, the cost of ancillary labour and the cost of upkeep and maintenance are calculated, and then added together to give the average annual running cost. It must be remembered that any material costs may vary with the type of equipment, since different models may require material to be presented in different ways, and so may generate different waste.

The annual cost is the sum of the standing and running costs, and it is calculated for each piece of equipment on the short-list. The life cycle cost (LCC) is then the sum of the annual costs over the whole life of the equipment. Obviously, the final decision will depend on the results of both the use and the economic analyses.

Depreciation and obsolescence

Once a piece of equipment has been installed it will, in general, immediately start to lose value. This arises from two main causes, namely:

(a) *depreciation*, which may be defined as the diminution in the intrinsic value of an asset due to use and/or the lapse of time, and is a result of normal usage, bad handling, bad maintenance, accidents, or wear due to disease or chemical action;

(b) *obsolescence*, which is the loss in the intrinsic value of an asset due to its supersession, and is a result of a reduction in market for the product or service for which the equipment is intended, a change in design of the type of equipment, or a change in legislation.

The purchase of a piece of equipment involves an expense which, if the organizations to continue independently in being, must be recovered from the proceeds of running the organization. The usual way of recovering this expense is by a charge in the profit and loss account against the profits before arriving at the net profit, and of showing the loss of value of the equipment by reducing the value of the asset in the balance sheet. This reduction in value is known as the *depreciation* suffered by the equipment.

Recovery can be effected in a number of different ways. Ideally, of course, the total cost of the equipment should be recovered when its 'life' has been spent. Since it is extremely difficult to predict the life of some equipment, arbitrary methods of writing down depreciation are adopted as policy. These may vary from organization to organization but should always remain constant within an organization. Depreciation of equipment was discussed in detail in Chapter 4.

The 'life' of equipment

It is helpful to recognize that equipment may have several different 'life-spans':

1. *The physical life*. This is the length of time over which the equipment can be usefully and *economically* used. It depends upon a number of factors including the maintenance carried out and the use to which the equipment is put, and it is usually determined by the maintenance and breakdown costs, which become excessive at the end of physical life.
2. *The technological life*. This is the length of time elapsing before the new equipment becomes available which makes the existing model obsolete.
3. *The product, service, or market life*. This is set by the product which is made or the service offered, by the equipment no longer being required. This may be very much shorter than the physical life and the equipment be in excellent physical condition. Whilst normal market conditions will force recognition of the product or service life, there is a danger of equipment in large groups of companies being worked beyond the product/service life, since they are perforce being sold to captive purchasers within the group.
4. *The 'book' life*. This is the time during which the equipment is depreciated to a nominal value. This is often calculated on the basis of minimizing tax, rather than any other consideration.
5. *The economic life*. This is the shortest of the first three lives. If it can coincide with the book life, then there may be some agreement between the book-keeping and the financial considerations.

The 'lives' of plant

1. Physical.
2. Technological.
3. Product.
4. Book.
5. Economic.

Methods of economic appraisal

A 'use' or technological survey may reveal that for a project there are a number of equally acceptable pieces of equipment: the choice between them must then be resolved on cost or economic grounds. There are a number of methods used to carry out this resolution, and they are illustrated in Chapter 4.

It must be emphasized that the techniques described in Chapter 4, and their variants, are methods of judging the desirability of alternative capital expenditure decisions – they permit comparison of one project with another, or one project with a standard set for use in the company. They do not readily form the basis of costing systems, and they should not be used as such.

It is invaluable to check the actual results from an investment against the forecast results. This will test the assumptions upon which the forecasts have been made and help in the preparation of future plants.

Computer-integrated operations

The ideal situation for computer-integrated manufacturing (CIM) operations is the creation and design of new products on a computer, the conversion of those designs into operations instructions, and the actual production using the instructions.

The main structure of CIM is thus given by computer-aided design and computer-aided manufacturing (CAD/CAM). CAD hardware and software capabilities have progressed rapidly in recent years, enabling the designer to create design drawings and specifications without a drawing-board, and to do it better. Using CAD, products, services and their components can be created, their dimensions changed, and features checked without the need for expensive prototypes. In the packaging industry alone, this had led to enormous savings in time and money.

CAM is rather more ambitious than CAD, if it is used in its broadest sense of taking the CAD-generated design and following it through to the finished product.

The most notable improvement in computer equipment over the past ten years has been in the area of price performance. The user has also benefited through lower software licence fees. System standards are now further simplifying application development and the availability of these tools is allowing developers to consider and deliver applications which could not even have been thought of just a few years ago. These new tools and more powerful computers will be useless, however, unless they are applied to solve user problems, and this is particularly true early in the design stage of the process.

With the fantastic increase in computer performance and equally amazing reductions in storage costs, we are in an age where we have the capacity increasingly to store additional knowledge more cheaply. Up until recently, the cost and performance of computer resources made it prohibitive to capture the extent of information required to solve some engineering and operational problems. The progression towards the capabilities we know today can be seen in the CAD databases. It is the application of the newly available computer tools and resources which allow for such dramatic increases in the amount of knowledge which can be stored and interacted with in a database. Similarly, knowledge has been captured in the application of software which accesses these databases. Today's advanced programming tools make such capturing of knowledge not only possible, but expected.

Knowledge can also be captured in computer models and accessed through expert system technology. The ability to store specialized knowledge easily and make it available widely throughout an organization is one of the most exciting prospects of the application of this technology. For years, many companies have faced the challenge of integrating the design and operations functions – even establishing communication. In today's more competitive market place, design for producibility or operability has become a necessity. Expert systems are helping here.

With constant demands for new, better products and services delivered more quickly, equipment is under increased pressure to speed designs to market, without sacrificing quality or cost, but rather improving on each. Today's modern tools – embodied in new 'work-stations', which are often 'personal mainframes', new software development tools, and powerful new engineering application software – should force us all to re-evaluate what is expected of our equipment. We expect faster, better decisions, with greater concern for quality and safety. This must be combined with equal pressure to reduce costs, integrate new materials, and solve new design problems. Fortunately the new tools can provide the help we need in these areas.

The challenges are to harness these new tools. Systems exist today so that they can be applied to improve all kinds of outputs at reduced costs. It will be the strategic application of these tools which will have the broadest impact on products and services, their performance, their costs, and the overall success of the organization.

CHAPTER 13 – HIGHLIGHTS

- Reasons for acquisition of equipment include: new products/services required; expansion of capacity; changes in technology; equipment in wear-out phase.

- An equipment survey should be carried out before purchase. This is in two phases: a use or technology sifting; and a cost or economic analysis. The latter must eventually justify the purchase. A forecast of potential use must also be made. The more robust this is, the less risk is involved in the decision.

- In the technological survey of equipment the following should be considered: its capacity; compatibility; availability; reliability; after-sales service; ease of maintenance, installation, learning to use and preparation; safety; delivery and state of development; and its effect on the existing organization. A matrix analysis (similar to plant location) may be useful.

- There are a number of ways of carrying out economic appraisal of equipment. Its aim should be to determine the *cost of producing*, which is in two parts – the standing cost and the running cost.

- There are several alternatives to outright purchase of equipment – hire purchase, leasing, or hiring. Possible tax and/or cash flow advantages may be derived from these methods.

- The average annual equipment running costs require knowledge of the average annual total output expected. Good forecasts are essential here. The sum of the standing (or purchase) costs and running costs give the annual cost for each piece of equipment under consideration.

- The life cycle cost (LCC) is the sum of the annual costs over the life of the equipment.

- Depreciation and obsolescence cause loss of equipment value. This expense must be recovered from the proceeds of the organization. The depreciation suffered by the equipment is usually charged in the profit and loss account, and reduces the value of the assets in the balance sheet.

- Equipment may have several 'life spans': physical life; technological life; product/service or market life; book life; and economic life.

- The number of equally acceptable pieces of equipment suggested by the use/technological survey must be resolved on cost or economic grounds. The methods are described in Chapter 4. It is worthy of note that these are *not* costing systems, but are methods of judging alternative capital expenditure decisions. The actual results from an investment decision should be checked against the forecast results as soon as possible.

- Computer-integrated manufacturing (CIM) is the creation, design and production of new products using computers. CIM comprises computer-aided design (CAD) and computer-aided manufacturing (CAM).

- CAD allows new design features to be checked out without the need for expensive prototypes. CAM is more ambitious in that it follows the process through to finished product manufacture. The new powerful computer-based tools must be used, however, to solve user problems.

- CAD databases and software now allow vast amounts of knowledge to be sorted and interacted with. Expert system technology helps to design for producibility or operability, with faster, better decisions, integration of new materials, greater concern for safety and quality, and reductions in costs. This will be of strategic importance for future successful organizations.

Recommended reading

Clark, J., *et al., Capital Budgeting*, Prentice-Hall, 1984

A well-illustrated exposition on the planning and control of capital expenditures.

Holt, R.N., *Capital Budgeting*, Ivy Soft, 1986

A short but excellent discussion of the salient features of the subject.

Kaufman, M., *Capital Budgeting Handbook*, Dow Jones–Irwin, 1985

A fairly comprehensive statement of the subject with an international perspective.

Mott, G., *Investment Appraisal*, Pan Books, 1987

Short, inexpensive, simple to read. Includes discussions on DCF and life cycle costing. Very useful.

White, J.A., *Production Handbook*, 4th edn, Wiley, 1986

Provides some information which may help in the technical assessment of equipment.

Chapter 14

Maintenance of the Facilities and Equipment

Maintenance policies

Maintenance of facilities and equipment in good working order is essential to achieve specified levels of quality and reliability, and efficient working – the best equipment will not work satisfactorily unless it is cared for, and the cost of a breakdown in the system can be very high, not only in financial terms but also in poor staff morale and bad relations with customers. The workforce and the materials must also be 'maintained', through training, motivation, health care and even entertainment for the people, and proper storage and handling of materials.

The objectives of maintenance are:

1. To enable product or service quality and customer satisfaction to be achieved through correctly adjusted, serviced and operated equipment.
2. To maximize the useful life of the equipment.
3. To keep equipment safe and prevent the development of safety hazards.
4. To minimize the total production or operating costs directly attributable to equipment service and repair.
5. To minimize the frequency and severity of interruptions to operating processes.
6. To maximize production/operation capacity from the given equipment resources.

Within the context of maintenance, failure is defined as an inability to produce work in the appropriate manner rather than an inability to produce any work (see Chapter 9). Thus a piece of plant which deteriorates and consequently produces work of too low a quality or at too high a cost is said to fail. Work carried out before failure is said to be overhaul, or preventive maintenance work, whilst that carried out after failure is emergency, breakdown or recovery work (Fig. 14.1). It is worth noting that work can sometimes actually proceed while a plant has 'failed' but continues to produce: for example, some types of overhauls may be carried out at a power station while electricity is still being generated, albeit at an enhanced cost.

It has been pointed out by Chase and Aquilano that the maintenance system exists within and as a part of the operating system as a whole. Inevitably the needs of the sub-system may appear to conflict with the needs of the system itself. For example, frequent overhauls may reduce costs by avoiding expensive breakdowns or replacements. Unfortunately, the more frequently the overhaul the lower the

Fig. 14.1   The time of failure

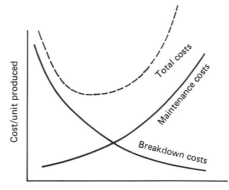

Fig. 14.2   Derivation of total cost of maintenance policy
(*Note*: The *total* cost curve is the sum of the other two)

availability of the plant, equipment, so that direct production costs will increase (Fig. 14.2). Clearly it is the total cost which must be examined in order to discover the most satisfactory maintenance policy. As in other areas of management, this 'most satisfactory' policy is unlikely to occur by chance. Data must be systematically gathered and analysed. The costs associated with equipment failure and the costs of overhaul work are compared and a maintenance plan prepared, which offers a satisfactory match of costs and equipment availability. In this sense, *all* maintenance work should be *planned*.

Historically, the term 'planned maintenance' has been misguidedly restricted solely to the overhaul work: this is better described as *preventive*. There are many cases where the best policy is to allow the equipment to fail before carrying out maintenance work. Such work is undoubtedly 'planned' even though the timing of the work is uncertain.

There are then broadly two types of maintenance policy:

1.   Repair or replacement due to equipment failure.
2.   Preventive maintenance.

The first type is an emergency-based policy, in which the plant or equipment is operated until it fails and then it is maintained. Formal preventive maintenance may take four different forms:

(a) Time-based, which means doing maintenance at regular intervals, e.g. every two months. It is easy to monitor time and this form is used when deterioration is likely to be time- rather than usage-dependent, or when usage cannot easily be measured.

(b) Work-based, i.e. maintenance after a set number of operating hours of volume of work produced, e.g. every 40,000 photocopies. Usage can be more difficult than time to monitor and some form of 'auto-counting' of output should be used, if possible.

(c) Opportunity-based, where repair or replacement takes place when the equipment or system is available, e.g. during a holiday closure. This can extend the interval between maintenance to an unacceptable level, but it may be suitable for equipment which has intermittently heavy use.

(d) Condition-based, which often relies on planned inspection to reveal when maintenance is prudent, e.g. replacement of a brake pad when it has worn to 2 mm thickness. This is dependent on monitoring equipment condition which can be difficult, and out of the question if a time-consuming strip-down precedes any examination or inspection.

These various types of policy often operate together, overlap or coincide. For example, time-based and work-based maintenance will coincide if the rate of work is constant; condition-based replacement may occur during a time-, work- or opportunity-based maintenance activity.

The need for data

Choice between the various policies needs to be made on objective grounds if possible; this underlines the need for good data collection and analysis.

It is not easy to try to discover the actual time taken and the work involved when carrying out a maintenance task, particularly when the plant is large and/or complex and the maintenance work carried out far from simple. Rational policies, however, need to be based on data, and the need for the collection and analysis of reliability and maintenance information cannot be over-emphasized. Furthermore, it is invaluable to feed particular problems and difficulties back to the designer or supplier of equipment, since it may be possible to reduce overhaul times on new equipment.

The collection of costs over the life of a piece of equipment, and the use of these costs to project costs over the life of new equipment, is known as life cycle costing. Basically, the question to be asked is: *How does the cost of maintaining compare with the cost of not maintaining?* This is not always an easy question to answer, and some policies, particularly preventive maintenance policies, are often taken 'on trust'.

Total preventive maintenance (TPM)

Well-designed preventive maintenance plans can reduce the incidence of emergency maintenance. In the production of standardized product design along flow lines, where there is little if any work-in-progress between adjacent operations, an equipment breakdown at one operation will quickly cause all other downstream operations to come to a standstill. This situation can arise just as easily in the supply of cheeseburgers in a 'burger-bar' and the preparation of letters of credit in a bank as in the assembly of motor cars. An extensive preventive maintenance programme is essential to reduce the frequency and severity of work flow interruption in these situations.

In automated production environments, again not restricted to manufacturing, preventive maintenance programmes must be part of the POM policy. Where automated equipment operates continuously, without the need for operatives, human intervention will be required in the form of a maintenance unit to keep the equipment lubricated, adjusted and generally operating in good condition. As automation increases throughout various types of operation, there will be a need to move to smaller production workforces and larger maintenance crews. Hence, some of the production operatives replaced by robotics and computer-aided systems will require retraining to provide the necessary increase in maintenance staff.

Because of the increasing introduction of just-in-time (JIT) methods, in which in-process stocks and batch sizes are reduced to very low levels, the near-absence of work-in-progress will focus attention on equipment and system failure. JIT demands perfect equipment maintenance, since breakdowns cannot be tolerated. It is not sufficient to speed up repairs to minimize down-time: breakdowns must be eliminated through an effective prevention strategy.

Where operatives are employed in production, this strategy requires their total involvement. They must be given the responsibility for preventing equipment failure by conducting checks, inspecting, lubricating and adjusting their own equipment with meticulous attention to detail. Just as in the achievement of quality of conformance, operators must be given the tools to do this, and this means providing the appropriate training to be able to detect, find and eliminate potential causes of trouble before they manifest themselves in a system failure.

The maintenance unit

Duties

Many of the activities associated with effective preventive maintenance require particular knowledge and training, meaning that maintenance is a specialized service. In order to take advantage of the benefits of specialization, all direct maintenance should be carried out by one unit under a maintenance manager, who may be responsible for duties other than the maintenance of equipment. Since the production operations unit employs the bulk of the physical assets of an organization, it will be found to be most satisfactory if the maintenance department is part of the production/operations manager's responsibility. Separation between POM and maintenance inevitably leads to frustration and dysfunction.

The duties of the maintenance unit include the care of plant, buildings and equipment, the installation of new equipment, and the supervision of new building. Typical sections of the maintenance department are:

1. *The equipment fitters*, who install, maintain and repair all mechanical equipment.
2. *The electricians*, who install, maintain and repair all electrical equipment, including power plants and all communications equipment. A vital sub-section is the group of electronic specialists who look after the increasingly important control systems so prevalent in today's automated world. Although the actual maintenance of some of these may be in the hands of the owners of the equipment – for example, the telephone company or the local suppliers of electricity – all dealings with the owners should be through the maintenance department, so that individual complaints or comments should be made first to the appropriate maintenance supervisor(s)
3. *The builders*, which include any carpenters, bricklayers, plumbers or painters. Included in the responsibility of this section may be the provision and upkeep of all fire-fighting equipment (hoses, extinguishers, sprays, sprinklers), unless a separate department exists only for this purpose, and the care and control of the heating and ventilating plant.
4. *General labourers*, who will carry out the moving of material and equipment. These will usually include a 'heavy gang' equipped for and capable of manhandling bulky and heavy loads.
5. *Cleaners*, who will be responsible for all cleaning and sweeping, including the care of toilets and wash-places.
6. *Sub-contractors*, who are necessary to maintain specialist equipment, e.g. telephones, computers and office equipment.

Rules governing maintenance work

In order that there should be some control over the work of maintenance, three rules should be enforced:

1. All requests for formal maintenance work must be made (preferably in writing) to one central control point. No work should be carried out without the knowledge and approval of the maintenance supervision at that point. Lack of strict adherence to this rule will result in a wasteful use of skilled staff and an inability to keep to any schedule of essential work.
2. Maintenance stores must be as carefully controlled as any other of the company's stores, as the absence of a vital part can lead to an expensive plant shut-down. On the other hand, excessive stocks can tie up valuable capital.
3. Records of all work carried out, including a statement of materials required, should be kept, as these may assist in setting rational maintenance, replacement and depreciation policies. They are part of the essential database referred to earlier.

Planning the programme

A routine maintenance programme can be set up as follows:

1. List all work which is required to be carried out by external authorities:

(a) The washing and/or the painting of all inside walls, partitions, ceilings and staircases.

(b) The thorough examination, followed if necessary by an overhaul and accompanied by a written report issued by a competent person, of all lifts, lifting equipment, cranes, hoists, boilers, weighing machines, large computers, postal and insurance franking machines, etc.

2. List, with the frequency required, all work deemed desirable by the appropriate manager. This will include the overhaul and servicing of all machines and items of plant, including office equipment, computers and any company cars or other transport. The frequency of maintenance may need to be set initially by the 'best guess' or manufacturer's recommendations but thereafter it should be verified against records kept of performance and breakdown.

3. Prepare standard documentation and instructions covering the maintenance required on each item listed. These instructions should be *in detail* and should avoid the 'overhaul as necessary' type of instruction. The purpose to which the equipment is put should be considered when deciding the scale of the maintenance required, as identical pieces of plant being used for different purposes may well need entirely different levels of maintenance. In setting up these standard instructions, CPA can be invaluable in examining and determining the methods and in instructing the staff on all types of maintenance, from short-duration overhauls, with individual activities of only a few minutes, to very lengthy plant shut-downs.

4. Prepare a plan of work covering at least 12 months, in such a way that no maintenance section is in any way overloaded. This is very conveniently done on a Gantt chart, or one of the equivalent computerized planning programs for the control of maintenance work which are commercially available.

5. From the plan, issue instructions to the appropriate staff when necessary, requiring them to carry out work, and record on the plan when the work has been done.

6. Carry out post-maintenance audits to verify the times allowed for various tasks and to provide information for future policy making.

To ensure that all items of equipment are included, it is desirable to number them and then to make a plant register. At the outset, this must be prepared from a physical inventory which is then checked against the organization's asset register. Thereafter it should be kept up-to-date by an information system that reports every piece of equipment purchased, replaced or removed.

The effectiveness of a maintenance policy and programme should be judged not on the vigour with which emergency repairs are carried out but on the freedom from such emergencies.

Maintenance in operation

Maintenance staff will need to make decisions about whether to repair or replace items, components or parts of equipment and when to carry out scheduled maintenance. Reliability data can be a useful aid, and many clues will come from the bath-tub

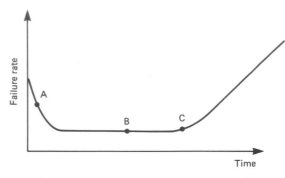

Fig. 14.3   Failure rate or bath-tub curve — typical of many products and systems

curve (Fig. 14.3 – see Chapter 9), which will be of use to the maintenance manager for:

(a)   *diagnosis* of the causes of equipment failure problems;
(b)   *prescription* of solutions to these problems.

As mentioned in Chapter 9, Weibull analysis of the reliability data enables maintenance staff to glean even more information. In particular, the slope of the Weibull plot (β) is of great assistance in selecting an appropriate maintenance policy.

Point A: Early failures ($\beta < 1$)

Figure 14.3 shows the following characteristic points. These are associated with a running-in period and may be due to sub-standard components of the product or service, or excessive stresses induced by incorrect installation or adjustment. As the weak parts are replaced by non-defective parts, the trouble should die away. Total system replacement at point A is not recommended since this will return the bath-tub curve to its start-point and the early failure period will recommence. Improvements in failure rate can be made by better design and careful running-in and adjustments during commissioning. Should the hazard rate curve have the appearance of Fig. 14.4, a high initial failure rate, followed by a low and very long constant failure rate period – a characteristic typical of many electronic components – then scheduled replacement every 1,000 hours of service may result in 30 per cent failures in the first 24 hours! Replacement here, after the initial 'burn-in' period, is pointless.

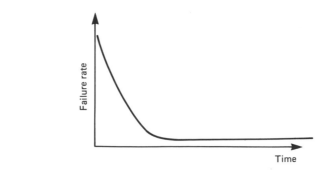

Fig. 14.4   Failure rate curve with extended random failure period

Point B: Constant failure probability (β ≃ 1)

Random failures occur due to various possible combinations of circumstances. To reduce the level of failure rate in this period, it is necessary to examine the design and operation of the equipment. Emergency maintenance is required for the remaining random breakdowns since system replacement will re-introduce early failures.

Point C: Wear-out failures (β > 1)

The equipment, having survived the chance failure period, will encounter an increased failure rate associated with wear-out. At this stage, the relationship between age and failure rate can be predicted, it should be well defined, and the preventive maintenance may be quantified.

One important parameter to be determined is the interval between the preventive maintenance actions. If a time-based system is being considered, let this interval be T. The fraction of items which may be expected to survive until this time is the reliability, $R(T)$. This should be available from maintenance records. The fraction which fails, and hence requires emergency or breakdown maintenance before preventive maintenance is due, will be $1 - R(T)$. The average or expected life of the items *if all are allowed to operate until breakdown* can be evaluated numerically, e.g. by computer package, by graphing and counting squares to measure the area under the curve, or by a 'finite difference' method, using

$$E(T) = \sum_{t=0}^{T} R(t)\Delta t$$

An example should illustrate the methods to be employed.

Ten identical pieces of equipment were installed during an annual shut-down. Their performance had been monitored over the previous 50 weeks and the times noted at which failure of the items necessitated their replacement. One item was still functioning at the end of the year (Table 14.1).

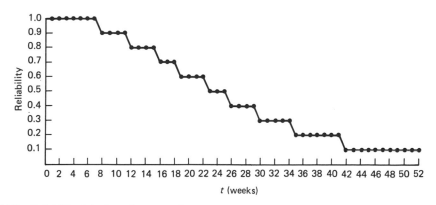

Fig. 14.5   Reliability data from the example

The reliability vs time data are plotted in Fig. 14.5. The average or expected life to failure of the ten items cannot be obtained directly as one is still functioning. If the company were considering a preventive maintenance policy (PMP), for the items, involving maintenance every T weeks, then $E(T)$ can be calculated by measuring the area under the curve for the period 0–T (Table 14.2).

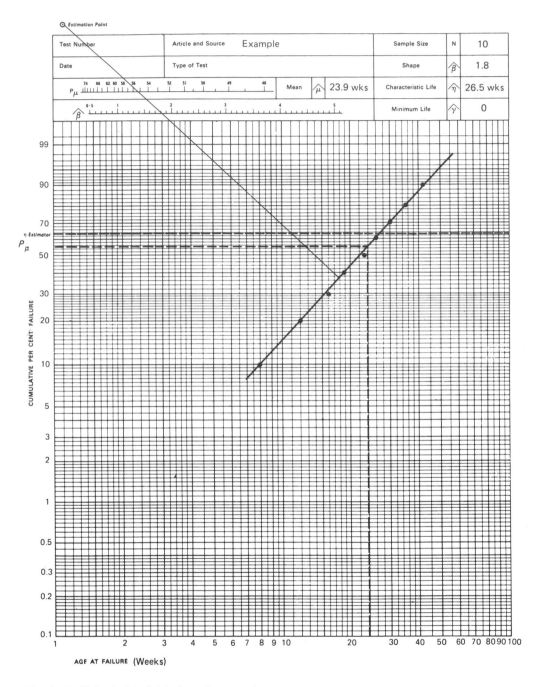

Fig. 14.6   Weibull plot of data from the example

Table 14.1

Time (weeks)	8	12	16	19	23	26	30	35	42
Cumulative failures	1	2	3	4	5	6	7	8	9
Reliability $R(t)$	0.9	0.8	0.7	0.6	0.5	0.4	0.3	0.2	0.1

Table 14.2

T(weeks)	4	8	12	16	20	24	28	32	36	40	44	48
E(T)	4	7.95	11.50	14.65	17.30	19.55	21.30	22.65	23.70	24.50	25.05	25.45

Table 14.3

T (weeks)	4	8	12	16	20	24	28	32	36	40	44	48
E(T)	3.96	7.75	11.15	14.15	16.69	18.77	20.39	21.60	22.47	23.06	23.44	23.68

However, a PMP should only be considered if the equipment is in the wear-out phase of the bath-tub curve, i.e. has a Weibull parameter $\beta > 1$. The Weibull plot of the data is shown in Fig. 14.6. This shows that $\beta = 1.8$ and hence a PMP should be considered. The average life to failure of all ten items may be obtained as described in Chapter 9, and is 23.9 weeks. Why is this less than the expected life if the items are replaced at say, 40 or 44 weeks? The explanation lies in the overall sample size of only ten items and the random nature of the failures. A more accurate estimate of $E(T)$ would be obtained if a smooth curve were drawn through the points (Fig. 14.7) or observed reliability values were replaced by values from the Weibull curve (Table 14.3).

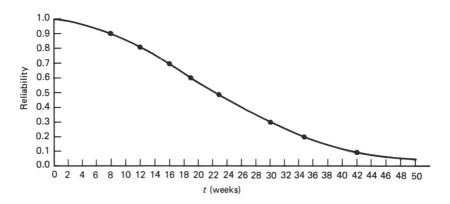

Fig. 14.7   Reliability curve from the example

These values are now consistent with the Weibull value for expected life. A rather less tedious method of calculation uses the equation $E(T) = \Sigma R(t) \triangle t$.

So far, analysis of the reliability data has yielded an expected life. $E(T)$, the fraction of items to be repaired due to breakdown, $1 - R(T)$, and the fraction to be overhauled due to the PMP, $R(T)$. In unit time, $1/E(T)$ items would be expected to receive attention; e.g. if $E(T)$ is 6 months then, on average, 1/6 of the items would be maintained each month. $R(T)/E(T)$ of those would be preventive maintenances and $[1 - R(T)/E(T)]$ would be due to breakdown. It is now necessary to look at the costs involved in order to choose the optimum value of the maintenance interval, T.

If the item survives until the planned time, let the cost of the preventive maintenance action be C_M. Any item failing in service will almost certainly incur a greater expense, e.g. loss of production, programme interruption, damage to work-in-progress, cost of assembling an emergency repair team, etc. Let this cost be C_F. In the simplest case, both C_F and C_M will be constant. The cost per unit time incurred by items failing will be $C_F [1 - R(T)]/E(T)$, i.e. the cost per failure multiplied by the number of such failures. Similarly, the cost of the preventive maintenances will be $C_M R(T)/E(T)$ and the average cost of all maintenance action per unit time $K(T)$ is therefore:

$$K(T) = \left\{ C_F \left[1 - R(T) \right] + C_M R(T) \right\} / E(T)$$

$$= \frac{C_F}{E(T)} \left[1 - R(T) \left(1 - \frac{C_M}{C_F} \right) \right]$$

The optimum policy is that which gives the lowest value of $K(T)$ and the problem posed is that of finding the value of T which achieves this. Usually, K_T is plotted against T to find the minimum value.

Suppose that the items in the above example are submerged bearings in a fermentation vessel. Since they operate in a mildly abrasive environment, they are liable to failure and the maintenance work is to replace them. The fermentation takes 5 days and the vessels are then available for 2 days for cleaning, maintenance, sterilization and re-charging. If the bearing is replaced during this turn-round period, the cost is £400. If, however, it breaks down in service, an additional cost of £600 is incurred for items such as additional cleaning and preparatory work. A further £5,000 is attributed to loss of profits, etc.

Thus C_F = £6,000, C_M = £400 and hence C_M/C_F = 1/15.

$$K(T) = \frac{6,000}{E(T)} \left[1 - R(T) \left(1 - \frac{1}{15} \right) \right] = \frac{6,000}{E(T)} \left[1 - \frac{14 R(T)}{15} \right]$$

Values of $R(T)$ are obtained from the Weibull plot (Fig. 14.6) and $E(T)$ from Table 14.3. The calculations are summarized in Table 14.4.

Further calculations of $T = 6$ and $T = 10$ confirm that the minimum cost occurs after 8 weeks and the average cost is £116.9 per week per bearing.

By comparison, if the bearings are replaced only on failure, then the average life is 23.9 weeks, cost is £6,000 and average weekly cost is £251.

The ratio C_M/C_F clearly has a considerable influence on the optimum interval. In general, the smaller the value of C_M/C_F, the more likely is a PMP to be a viable proposition.

Table 14.4

T	$R(T)$	$\dfrac{14}{15} R(T)$	$1 - \dfrac{14}{15} R(T)$	$E(T)$	$\dfrac{6{,}000}{E(T)}$	$K(T)$
4	0.97	0.905	0.095	3.96	1,515.2	143.9
8	0.91	0.849	0.151	7.75	774.2	116.9
12	0.81	0.756	0.244	11.15	538.1	131.2
16	0.69	0.644	0.356	14.15	424.0	150.9

The above model contains limiting assumptions such as: repair restores equipment to 'as new' condition, costs are constant, etc. These restrictions may be relaxed and more complex models developed.

When equipment or systems are designed, produced and assembled so that they run in a trouble-free manner, and can be easily rectified when necessary, they are said to have high *maintainability*. This can be quantified by the mean time to repair (MTTR). The measure of reliability introduced in Chapter 9, the mean time before failure (MTBF), can be combined with the MTTR to give an overall measure of an equipment's *availability*:

$$\text{Availability} = \frac{\text{MTBF}}{\text{MTBF} + \text{MTTR}} \times 100$$

For example, a word-processor work-station which has a mean time between failures of 800 hours and a mean time to repair of 3 work days ($3 \times 8 = 24$ h) has an availability of:

$$\frac{800}{800 + 24} \times 100 = 97.1\%$$

If the reliability can be improved and/or the repair time reduced, the availability will increase.

Repair and replacement

The repair limit

Repair – the replacement of defective, damaged or worn parts – is clearly part of preventive maintenance. However, when the costs of repairing are substantial and unforeseen, it is necessary to consider whether it is more economical to replace the equipment rather than to repair it. One simple method whereby this problem is not overlooked – or resolved by default – is to set a repair limit. If the estimated cost of the repair exceeds the repair limit, the piece of plant or equipment is considered for replacement. This emphasizes the need for adequate records to be kept for items such as cost of repair. Without these it is difficult to use the repair limit theorem. Easily obtainable, low-cost items are probably replaced automatically, whilst high-cost or items that are difficult to obtain are referred to a replacement committee. The value set upon the repair limit is likely to be a complex function, depending upon age, availability of replacement, possible loss of output and resale value. Repair limits should not be set 'once-for-all' – they need to be regularly reviewed.

Replacement due to failure

Group replacement

When it is necessary to maintain a group of items in working order, it is sometimes more economical to replace the group as a whole, even if some of the items are still functioning satisfactorily, than to replace each item as it fails. Such a situation may arise when the cost of replacement of an item as an individual is greater than the cost of replacement when it is replaced as one of a group. This is so well exemplified by the problem of replacing electric light bulbs that it is frequently referred to in the literature as *the light bulb problem*. The method of treating this problem is best demonstrated by an example.

The light-bulb problem

Assume that past records reveal that, out of 100 new light bulbs, on average:

    80 survive for at least 1 month;
    40 survive for at least 2 months;
    10 survive for at least 3 months;
     0 survive for more than 4 months.

Furthermore, it is found that the cost of replacing a light bulb is made up of two parts:

(a) the cost of bringing the electrician, his mate and his equipment to the site – this cost is £50:
(b) the cost of replacing a light bulb once the electrician is available – this cost is 40p.

Thus the replacement cost is calculated as follows:

For a group of n bulbs	£$(50 + 0.4n)$
For an individual bulb	£50.4
For n bulbs replaced individually	£$(50.4 \times n)$

The problem can now be stated as follows: Should each bulb be replaced as an individual when it fails, or should the whole group of bulbs be replaced after some interval of time?

For the sake of arithmetical simplicity, it will be assumed that there is a total of 100 bulbs at the site, although this restriction is not necessary.

Average bulb life

From the available data it can be seen that, on average, out of 100 bulbs initially good:

By the end of month 1, 20 lamps will have failed;
By the end of month 2, a further 40 lamps will have failed;

By the end of month 3, a further 30 lamps will have failed;
By the end of month 4, a further 10 lamps will have failed.

Hence, there are, on average:

$$
\begin{array}{ll}
10 \text{ lamps with a life of 4 months, that is a life of 40 lamp-months} \\
+30 \text{ lamps with a life of 3 months, that is a life of 90 lamp-months} \\
+40 \text{ lamps with a life of 2 months, that is a life of 80 lamp-months} \\
+20 \text{ lamps with a life of 1 month, that is a life of 20 lamp-months} \\
\hline
100 \text{ lamps thus have a total life of} 230 \text{ lamp-months}
\end{array}
$$

That is, the average bulb life is 2.3 months.

Individual replacement

Replacing each bulb singly as it fails would entail replacing 100 bulbs in 2.3 months at a cost of:

$$£(100 \times 50.4)$$

that is, an average monthly cost of:

$$\frac{£100 \times 50.4}{2.3} = £2.191 \text{ per month}$$

Group replacement

As it is necessary to keep the total quantity of working bulbs constant at 100, group replacement will involve (a) replacing defectives as they occur, and (b) replacing 100 bulbs at fixed intervals of time. To examine this situation it is therefore necessary to calculate the rate at which individual replacements are necessary. This can be done analytically, but the underlying processes are probably most clearly shown by a failure tree.

At the beginning of month 1, there are 100 bulbs working satisfactorily, but by the end of that month, only 80 of the original bulbs are functioning: this is shown by the horizontal branch:

$$100^{0.8} \text{———— S ———— } 80$$

where the transfixed S indicates survival, and the elevated 0.8 indicates the survival rate. In order to keep the number of bulbs constant, the 'dead' 20 bulbs must have been replaced, and this is shown by a diagonal line:

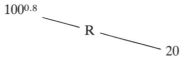

so that at the beginning of the next month the 100 bulbs are made up from 80 'originals' and 20 'replacements'. By the end of the month, the 80 originals will have dropped to 40 originals (a survival rate of 0.5) and 40 replacements. Of the 20 bulbs replaced at the end of month 1, 0.8×20, that is 16, will have survived, and 4 will have needed to be replaced. At the end of month 3, 10 'originals' will

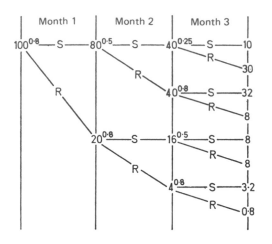

Fig. 14.8   Replacement free for the first three months

have survived, and 30 will have been replaced: of the 40 replaced during month 2, 32 will have survived and 8 will have been replaced, and so on (see Fig. 14.8). In drawing a replacement tree of this sort, it must be remembered that replacements initially represent 'original' bulbs, and hence survive on average at the rate shown in the initial data, namely:

Out of 100 bulbs:
   80 survive for at least 1 month;
   40 survive for at least 2 months;
   10 survive for at least 3 months;
    0 survive for more than 4 months.

A complete survival tree for 5 months is shown in Fig. 14.9. From this it is possible to calculate the number of bulbs replaced on average from an original group of 100 new bulbs:

20 replaced in month 1
44 replaced in month 2
46.8 replaced in month 3
42.96 replaced in month 4
42.512 replaced in month 5

It is now possible to deduce the total cost of replacing the group each month, every two, three, four . . . months, etc.:

1. *Group replacement at end of month 1*. There will be 20 bulbs replaced as individuals at a cost of:

$$£(20 \times 50.4) = £1,008$$

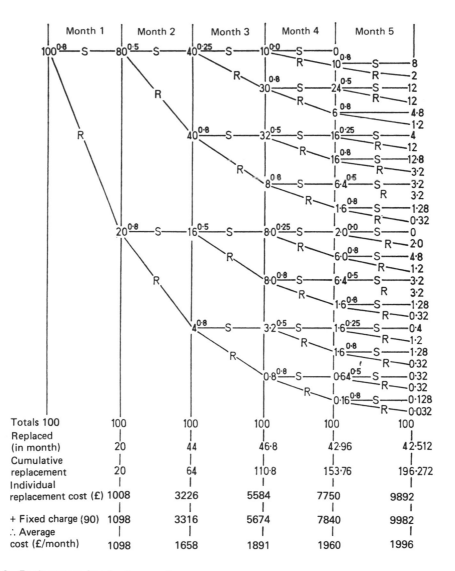

Fig. 14.9 Replacement free for five months

plus 100 bulbs replaced as a group at the end of the month at a cost of:

£(50 + 0.4 × 100) = £90

2. *Group replacement at end of month 2*. There will be (20 + 44) bulbs replaced as individuals at a cost of:

£(64 × 50.4) = £3,225.6
     say   £3.226

plus 100 bulbs replaced as a group at the end of the period at a cost of £90;

∴ Total replacement cost = £3.316

∴ Average monthly replacement cost $= £\dfrac{3,316}{2}$

$= £1,658$

Similarly, the average monthly costs of group replacement at the ends of 3, 4, 5 months can be calculated to be £1,891, £1,960 and £1,996 respectively.

Comparing these amounts with the average monthly cost of individual replacement – £2.191 per month – it will be seen that the most economic policy will be to group-replace at the end of each month.

Failure which can be tolerated

The above situation implies that failure brings with it penalties so large that replacement must be carried out upon or before failure. In some situations the costs incurred by failure are such that inactivity, both of equipment and of the maintenance department, can be tolerated until some convenient time has elapsed, for example until a specific number of items are not working or until a shift has ended.

In this case, it is necessary to balance the costs due to inaction against the costs of replacement. Here again, it is necessary that information concerning failure frequency rates and replacement costs are available, as well as the costs due to inactivity. The necessary criterion then is that the cost attributable to inactivity during time T must be less than the cost of replacement at time T.

Knowing the various failure parameters. the above conditions enable the optimum replacement time to be calculated.

Replacement due to deterioration

Inevitably, all equipment deteriorates with time, although in some cases the time span may be extremely long. To decide whether equipment should be replaced is a problem similar to that considered under the heading 'Capital expenditure budgets – depreciation and DCF' (Chapter 4). Here one of the pieces of equipment being considered is the existing plant, and it is this which is compared with the alternative equipment/plant available. Clearly the various factors ('installed price', 'indirect charges', 'maintenance charge' . . .) refer to the values applicable at the time when the appraisal is being made, not the initial values which were relevant when the plant or equipment was first installed.

Aspects of modern maintenance

Technology is increasingly complex, with electronics, robotics and computer control now influencing every walk of life. These have clearly led to many changes in maintenance activities. Special and continuous training programmes are required to provide the necessary knowledge, understanding and skills to service the increasingly specialized equipment and to keep up with the developments in the field. Specialist organizations have developed to provide maintenance services on a sub-contract basis, and transport vehicles, computers, office equipment and medical support systems are often serviced by outside companies. The specialized technical knowledge and skills are frequently more economical to acquire on a call-in fee basis than an in-house team.

The advances in technology have enabled the development of systems which reduce the cost of maintenance while improving operational performance. These are usually computer-based devices which enable the detection of faults before severe difficulties, and even damage, occur. For example, sensing devices may be installed to monitor factors such as vibration, local temperatures, pressures, consumption of lubricants, changes in electrical resistance, composition of products from a chemical plant, etc. Changes in such factors often indicate changes in the condition of equipment and can give timely warning of approaching failure. This approach has been called *predictive maintenance* and can usefully be coupled to a preventive maintenance policy. Computers can, of course, be used in the actual maintenance for:

(a) planning maintenance;
(b) financial control of maintenance;
(c) spare part inventory control;
(d) reliability and failure data collection and analysis;
(e) operational research models applied to maintenance, e.g. queuing theory and simulation.

Modern maintenance management is far more than repairing and servicing equipment. The perspective of maintenance must be broadened to the long-range performance aspects of the complete customer service system. Failure of any component in that system can cause total disaster, and the viability of the whole organization is dependent on effective maintenance policies and operations.

The authors are grateful for the contribution made by J. Geoff Marsland during the writing of this chapter.

CHAPTER 14 – HIGHLIGHTS

- The objectives of maintenance are to enable product or service quality, maximum and safe use of equipment at maximum capacity, and a minimal total operating cost through few interruptions.

- With regard to maintenance, failure of equipment is an inability to produce in an appropriate manner. Work done before failure is overhaul or preventive maintenance, whereas work carried out after failure is emergency, breakdown or recovery.

- The maintenance system exists within and is part of the whole operating system. There is some conflict between frequency of overhall and total maintenance/breakdown costs, and the 'most satisfactory' policy must be found. Data are important in these decisions, so that all maintenance can be planned.

- There are broadly two types of maintenance policy: repair or replacement due to failure, and preventive maintenance. The latter may take four different forms: time-based, work-based, opportunity-based, and condition-based. The various types often overlap, but the choice between them must be made using good data.

- In certain flow-type production situations, breakdowns can bring the operation to a standstill. In highly automated environments preventive maintenance must be part of the POM policy. Operators may need to be given some responsibility for preventing equipment failure.
- In some fields, maintenance is a specialist service, and comes under the direction of one manager, preferably within the POM area. Duties include care of plant, buildings, and equipment, installation of new equipment and new building supervision. Typical sections include: fitters; electricians; builders; general labourers; cleaners; sub-contractors.
- Maintenance rules include: all requests for formal maintenance should be made (in writing) to one central point of control; maintenance stores must be carefully controlled; records should be kept of all work carried out.
- A routine maintenance programme should include: lists of work to be carried out by external and internal authorities; standard documentation and instructions for carrying out the work; a plan of work covering at least 12 months; initiation instructions to start and carry out work; records of work done; post-maintenance audits. An inventory or plant register should also exist.
- Reliability data should be used in the diagnosis of causes of equipment failure, and in the prescription of solutions. Weibull analysis is of great assistance in selecting an appropriate maintenance policy. Depending on the slope of the plot (β), problems can be identified as being due to early failures, constant failure probability, or wear-out failures.
- Maintainability can be measured by the mean time to repair (MTTR) and the mean time before failure (MTBF). These give rise to a measure of availability.
- A repair cost limit may be set, beyond which the equipment is not repaired but replaced. This depends on age, availability of replacements, possible loss of output, and resale value. With a group of items, it is sometimes more economical to replace the group as a whole, even if some items function satisfactorily. The light-bulb type case may be used to solve this problem.
- The increased use of more complex technology has led to many changes in maintenance activities. Special knowledge and training are required to service increasingly specialized equipment and keep up with developments. The advances have enabled the reduction in costs of maintenance through predictive systems, often coupled to a preventive maintenance policy.

Recommended reading

Borsenik, F.D., *Management of Maintenance and Engineering Systems in Hospitality Industries*, 3rd edn, Wiley, 1991

A specialist but none the less, useful work, recently updated to reflect current thinking and approaches in the area.

Corder, G.G., *Maintenance: Techniques and Outlook*, 3rd edn, British Council of Productivity Association, 1980

Its title describes the text admirably. It remains a practical and useful book.

Cordero, S.T., *Maintenance Management Handbook*, Fairmont Press, 1987

A comprehensive work covering the subject fully.

Kelly, A. and Harris, M.J., *Management of Industrial Maintenance*, Butterworth, 1983

Answers the needs of industry in defining the maintenance management function and making sense of failure statistics and fault diagnosis. Well illustrated with practical examples.

SECTION 4

The Processes

It is crucial that the way work is organized is subjected to a systematic study, in order that the correct process for this may be established, the best method for the individual tasks be identified, and satisfactory achievement be monitored.

This section presents and evaluates the various approaches to work organization: job, batch, flow and group working. Work Study/Organization and Methods is developed as a means for determining the best use to be made of materials, personnel and equipment in performing a task, and also for establishing the 'work content' of that task. The various techniques of Statistical Process Control (SPC) are illustrated as a means for monitoring and controlling quality.

Chapter 15

Production/Operating Systems Design

The organization and flow of work

There are a number of ways in which the conversion process can be organized, in terms of the manner in which the tasks are 'handled'. The main methods of handling are job, batch, flow and group. This chapter examines these in the context of *any* organization, whilst the next chapter focuses on aspects peculiar to manufacturing.

It is important to recognize that these approaches to organizing the conversion process are not necessarily associated with any particular volume of tasks. Depending upon the circumstances, the same task can be undertaken by any of the above approaches. It is equally important to realize that the approach adopted dictates to a large extent the layout of the equipment. This chapter will attempt to indicate the main features of each of the methods.

Each approach exhibits distinct characteristics and requires different conditions for its effective inception and working. The particular circumstances at any time must be carefully considered before a decision is taken as to the method to be used. Frequently, the decision reached depends on the development of the company concerned. Many organizations start on a job basis; proceed, as volume increases, to batch methods, in part at least; and finally manage to flow-produce all or some of the products concerned.

It must be said that it is rare to find in any unit that only one approach is used; in a radio factory for example, the final assembly of the receiver might well be organized to use flow methods, while the manufacture of the raw chassis is carried out under batch conditions and the manufacture of the jigs, tools and fixtures proceeds under job conditions.

The job approach

Job, 'one-off', project, or 'make complete' are descriptions given to the organization whereby the complete task is handled by a single worker or group of workers. The hairdresser who cuts, washes and perms the customer's hair, the tailor who makes the entire suit, the construction of a bridge, installation of capital plant in a factory, and ship-building are all examples of tasks which are organized using the job approach. These illustrations range from the small scale, usually associated with low technology, through to the large scale, often relying on higher technology, for which the term 'project' is sometimes reserved.

Low-technology job

When the technology for the job is low, the organization is extremely simple as skills and processing equipment are readily obtainable. Thus a bespoke tailor with a small clientele will:

(a)   measure the client;
(b)   cut the cloth;
(c)   cut the lining;
(d)   tack the cloth together for a 'fitting';
(e)   try the tacked garment on the customer;
(f)   alter the garment as required;
(g)   make buttonholes;
(h)   fit all closures;
(i)   press the finished garment;
(j)   parcel up the garment.

The organization required for the above tasks is simple. The tailor will need to have multiple skills, and the equipment needed will be available whenever required – utilization of equipment is unimportant.

Consider a hairdresser with four customers each requiring their hair to be cut, washed, dried, permed and set. As service on each customer is completed, the entire process is repeated on the next. Clearly the hairdresser must be capable of carrying out each stage, and while one stage is being carried out (say, washing), the other stages/equipment (for example, drying – hairdrier) remain unused. Considering the individual customer, work is being completed rapidly – viewed as a product, value is being added rapidly and continuously (see Fig 15.1). It is possible to have four

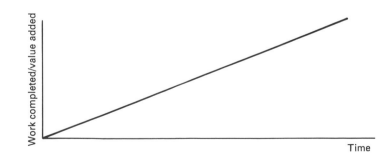

Fig. 15.1   Increase in work completed/value added for a single task organized using the job approach

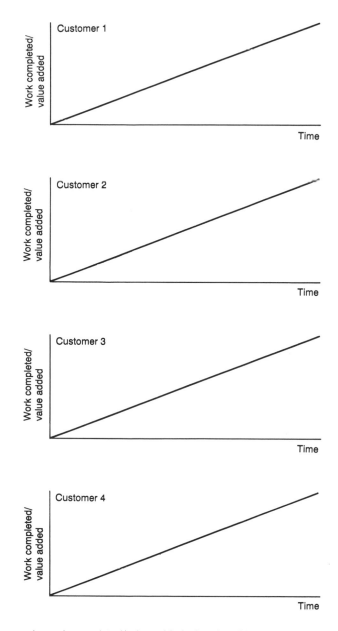

Fig. 15.2   Increase in work completed/value added when four identical tasks are organized using the job approach

hairdressers to handle the four customers simultaneously, provided each has the required facilities. In this situation work is completed/value is added to each customer continuously and in parallel, as in Fig. 15.2. Clearly, in addition, each hairdresser can react to and take account of each customer's specific requirement. A characteristic of the job approach is the ease with which variety/customization of the task can be handled.

Characteristics of organization using the job approach, for low-technology tasks

1. Organization simple.
2. Multiple worker skills.
3. Work completed/value added rapidly.
4. Easy to handle variety.
5. Easy to handle customization.
6. Low equipment utilization.

High-technology jobs

As technology increases, managerial problems also increase, unless the labour force and other resources are dispersed at the end of each task – something which happens, for example, when a film is made by an independent producer. If continuity of employment and resources is required, transfer between tasks will create difficulties. This gives rise to a 'matrix' organization.

Consider a task (task 1) for which a supervisor (M1) is responsible. The technology of the task calls for it to pass through stages A,B,C and D and technological

			Task		
			1	2	3
Skill	*Skill supervisor*	*Task supervisor* →	M1	M2	M3
A	SA		A1	A2	A3
B	SB		B1	B2	B3
C	SC		C1	C2	C3
D	SD		D1	D2	D3

Fig. 15.3   Matrix organization

complexity and cost require that the working group be made up of a number of different skill groups (sub-groups A1, B1, C1, . . .). To allow skills and other costly resources to be employed continuously, the organization as a whole deals with a number of tasks and at the time of examining the situation each task has its own supervisor and its complement of skill groups.

A member of sub-group A1 has thus a dual responsibility – to *task supervisor* M1 for work on task M1 and to *skill supervisor* SA for his skill performance. However, once sub-group A1 has completed its work on task 1 it will be available for work elsewhere. Assuming that task 10, say, requires the 'A' skill, then if the unoccupied sub-group A1 is of the correct size, it may be transferred to task 10. However, if the group size is incorrect, sub-group A1 will be changed, and if several tasks require skill 'A', then there will be competition for sub-group A1.

An individual with an 'A' skill will thus find that he not only has a dual responsibility, but that his responsibility and relationships are continually changing as sub-groups are formed and re-formed. Equally, physical resources may pass from task to task and from sub-group to sub-group. These shifting responsibility and communication networks are extremely difficult to control, and in very large situations control disappears altogether. The essential features of project control appear to be:

1. Clear definition of *objective*.
2. Agreement of *quantifiable* results at specified periods of time.
3. A management committee which is *empowered* to take decisions concerning the needs of jobs, labour and other resources.

An illustration of this matrix organization can be found in some business schools, where the tasks refer to the different activities/programmes: undergraduate, postgraduate, post experience, research . . ., each with its manager; and the skill groups correspond to the subjects: finance, marketing, production/operations, . . . each with its subject head.

Batch methods

As companies grow and volumes increase, it is not unusual to see the conversion process organized so that batch methods can be used. Such methods require that the work for any task is divided into parts or operations, and that each operation is completed throughout the whole batch before the next operation is undertaken. This technique is probably the most commonly used method for organizing manufacture, typical examples being the production of electronic instruments, transformers and so on. By its use, some degree of specialization of labour is possible, and capital investment is kept low, although the organization and planning required to ensure freedom from idle and waste time is considerable. It is in batch methods that the production control department can produce most benefits, and these can often be spectacular, but it is also in batch methods that it will be found most difficult to organize the effective working of a production control department.

Aims of batch methods

1.   Concentrate skills.
2.   Obtain high equipment utilization.

In order to clarify the difference between job and batch, consider five identical tasks to be carried out by a number of workers. Using job methods, the workers would be divided into five groups, and each group would be responsible for one entire task. (With the earlier example, each hairdresser dealt entirely with one customer.) Using batch methods, the work content of each task would be broken down into a number of elements not necessarily of equal work content, and the workers would be divided into groups. The first group would complete the first operation on all five tasks, passing the batch as a whole on to the next group, and so on until the tasks were complete. In general, the batch is not passed on from one worker or group to the next until all work is completed on that operation: transferring part-batches can often lead to considerable organizational difficulties. (With the earlier example, one person would cut, another wash and a third dry, and so on. The first worker would cut, one after the other, the hair of the five customers; when this was completed on all five, the 'batch' of five customers would be passed to the next worker where the process would be repeated for washing, and so on.)

It should be noted that, using batch methods to handle the five tasks described above, four tasks are always waiting, no work being carried out on them. Referring to Fig. 15.4, and considering the situation with regard to the first of the five tasks,

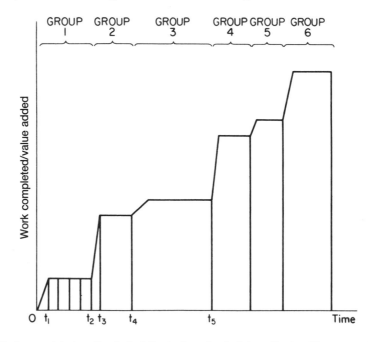

Fig. 15.4   Work completed on the first of five tasks using batch methods with no organizational delays between operations

work will be carried out on this during time t_1. This task will wait until time t_2 while work is being carried out on the other four tasks. Work will then re-start on this first task during time t_2–t_3, when it will again rest until t_4, and so on. In fact, the total waiting time of any one task in a batch of n tasks totals $100(n-1)/n$ per cent of the total batch task time.

In addition to the waiting period indicated above, the organizational difficulties of batch methods may well generate other idle times. Where numbers of batches are passing through the same processing stages, and competing for resources, it is usual to move a batch from a worker or process into a 'queue' or 'work-in progress' store, to wait (queue) there for the next worker or process to become available. This is characteristic of batch methods, where the work completed on the task increases irregularly and results in a substantial queue or work-in-progress. The sequencing of batches from different tasks to reduce this source of queueing time is one of the most difficult problems encountered in the management of an operations unit, and however successfully it is solved, there will inevitably be some element of queueing brought about by this competition for resources. Thus, in batch methods, there is an idle period for each unit in the batch, while work is proceeding on other members of the batch, and another idle period while the whole batch is in the between-process queue. This results in the time between the origination of work on a batch and its eventual completion being much greater than the total work content of the batch, sometimes startlingly so.

The effect of the considerable time lag between starting the task with the investment of resources to complete it, and the subsequent cash inflow from the customer, can be very serious in terms of the investment of capital which is tied up in the part-completed tasks. On the other hand, the queues of tasks awaiting further work permits the operations section to absorb shocks and changes, thus building in some elements of flexibility, and it assists in making more effective use of the various limited resources. This balancing of investment in queues of part-complete tasks and utilization of resources is a continuing problem, and one to which there is rarely a simple unique answer.

Batch methods and functional layout

The observation concerning the irregularity of the manner in which work is completed on a task is a great simplification. Another, and much more serious, delay period is created by the layout of equipment and workers in a so-called functional or process layout system. In this system, which is by far the most common within organizations in both the UK and US, equipment is grouped together according to the function which is carried out. Thus all drills will be together, as will all mills, presses, lathes and so on. This is most commonly met with in jobbing production, and again may be found in non-manufacturing activities. Provision of typing from a typing pool is a form of process layout, whilst in design departments it is often found necessary to divide the designers into specialist teams, each team dealing with all the problems of a similar type.

To examine the functional layout problem in more detail, consider a task which has to go through six operations to be completed. This could be a document being handled in a clerical environment (a mortgage application) or the manufacture of a product. First it has to go through process A, and on to process B before returning ('backpassing') to process A for further work to be completed on it. It goes from here to process C, then process D, and before completion requires process B to be carried out on it. This 'technological' or 'processing' route is summarized as:

Operation	Process required
1st	A
2nd	B
3rd	A
4th	C
5th	D
6th	B

In a functional layout, all of the resources (workers and equipment) to carry out process A are grouped together, as are those for process B, and so on. Figure 15.5 illustrates the situation where each process has six workers/equipment (A, . . ., A6 and so on), each of which can handle a particular task.

For the task illustrated above, it enters the system and is handled by any unoccupied 'resource' which can carry out process A, say A2. When this is complete, it should pass directly to process B. However, due to the presence of other tasks, none of these resources is available, so the task has to queue. This can be simply in a pile of work waiting in front of process B, or in a 'proper' work-in-progress stores, depending on the environment. Here for convenience it is referred to as S1.

When one of the process B resources, say B2, becomes free, the task is taken from S1 to B2. Having been completed here it should pass directly back to process A, but again the presence of other tasks forces queueing in, say, S1. Eventually A5 becomes free, and the task passes to it for the third operation. Again storing is necessary before, say, C4 is available, and this processing–storing–processing sequence is repeated until eventually the finished task enters the receiving store.

This complex process flow has the following effects.

1. It causes the task to be in the unit, though not being worked on, for a time *very considerably longer* than the time represented by the work content. A throughput time of less than five times the work content is rarely achieved.
2. It creates an organizational problem of very high complexity. The single task discussed is but one of a number of tasks, each following similar but not identical routes. An attempt to display the total task work flow in a small unit of six tasks, four processes each with six resources is given in Fig. 15.5. This itself is a gross over-simplification: in reality, 100 tasks and 500 'resources' (equipment/workers) for 50 processes would not be unusual.
3. It presents very difficult control problems, since each task must be tracked through each resource. This will often present data-collection and processing problems which are so great that the control task is abandoned and all action is taken on an 'emergency' or 'fire-fighting' basis.

The advantages claimed for functional layout are:

1. Flexibility: task-processing sequences and priorities can be readily changed.
2. Utilization of equipment can be high.

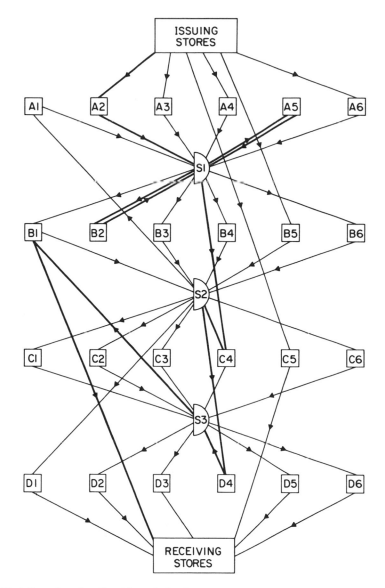

Fig. 15.5 Work flows in a functional layout situation

3. Since workers will tend to concentrate on a single process, their skills in this process can be considerable.
4. Supervision of a group all carrying out the same, or a similar function, will create a considerable depth of knowledge concerning those processes.
5. The non-availability of a single resource for a process does not stop processing, since others are available.

Characteristics of batch methods

1. Organizationally difficult.
2. Use of specialized skills.
3. Possibility of high equipment utilization.
4. Probability of poor work flow.
5. Value added slowly/work completed slowly.

Flow methods

Batch methods are characterized by the irregularity in the way the work is carried out on a particular task, or the increase in the value added to the material involved. Batch becomes flow when the rest/idle/queueing period mentioned earlier is eliminated. Flow has been defined as a method of organization such that the task is worked on continuously, or alternatively as a system whereby the processing of material is continuous and progressive.

Aims of flow production

1. Improved work/material flow.
2. Reduced skills.
3. Added value/completed work faster.

Flow methods, therefore, mean that as the work on a task at a particular stage is complete, it must be passed directly to the next stage for processing without waiting for the remaining tasks in the 'batch' and, when it arrives at the next stage, work must start immediately on the next process. In order for the flow to be smooth, the times that the task requires to be spent on each stage must be of equal length, and there should be no movement off the flow line. For example, inspection should be physically located within the flow line, and be subject to the same time constraints as the other processes. Furthermore, since the whole system is balanced, any fault or error at a particular stage affects not only that stage but also all other stages in the flow line. Thus a fault or error occurring at one stage on a line which cannot be resolved within the cycle time of the line will result in that stage being held up. This in turn causes all previous stages to be held up and all subsequent stages to run out of work. Thus the flow line must be considered as a single entity and not be allowed to break down at any point.

Figure 15.6 shows a batch of three identical tasks which require three processes, and compares this with the first three tasks if the work were organized using flow methods. Note that flow methods require that the work involved in the three processes is 'divided up' in such a way that a task is worked on by each stage for the *same amount of time*. In this case the situation is illustrated when there are five stages.

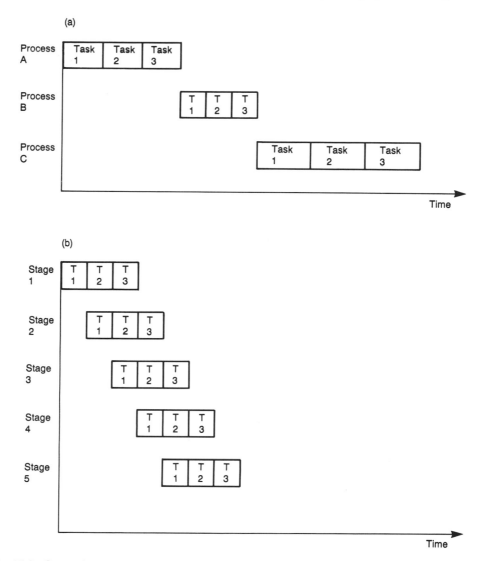

Fig. 15.6 Comparison of batch and flow methods. (a) batch; (b) flow

In order that flow methods can operate satisfactorily, a number of requirements must be met.

1. *There must be substantially constant demand.* Should demand be spasmodic there will be a build-up of finished work which can give rise to storage difficulties. Alternatively, if production is caused to fluctuate along with demand, then the setting-up and balancing of the flow line will need to be carried out frequently, giving an excessive high total cost. In some organizations with widely varying demands, a levelling-out can be achieved by making for stock during the 'flat' periods, the stock supplementing the current operations during 'peak' periods.

The price paid for this organizational simplification is, of course, the cost of holding the completed products. Some tasks, e.g. hairdressing, processing cheques, insurance claims, cannot, however, be 'made to stock'.

2. *The product or task must be standardized.* A flow line is inherently inflexible and cannot accommodate variations in the work required. A quasi-variety is achieved by varying finishes, decorations and other small items.

3. *Materials must be to specification and delivered to time.* Due to the inflexibility mentioned above, the flow line cannot accept the variations in material which can be incorporated if batch or job methods are being used. Furthermore, if material is not available when it is required, the effect is very serious, since the whole line will be frozen.

4. *All operations comprising the task must be defined.* In order that the line will maintain its balance, all operations must remain constant. This can only be done if the operations are recorded in detail.

5. *Work must conform to quality standards.* Using job or batch methods, variations in quality/errors at one stage can be compensated for by extra work elsewhere: with flow methods this cannot happen, since each stage has a defined operation, with a pre-set allowed time.

6. *The correct plant and equipment must be provided at each stage.* Lack of correct apparatus will unbalance a line, causing weaknesses throughout the whole sequence. This can result in a severe under-utilization of equipment; should a work-station/stage require a piece of equipment for only a part of the operation time, this equipment must be provided *and its under-utilization accepted.* Attempts to share equipment between stages will, in general, destroy the flow of work. In circumstances where the equipment required is extremely costly and its under-utilization cannot be tolerated, the flow line may have to be 'broken' at this point and batch methods substituted.

7. *Maintenance must be by anticipation, not default.* If equipment breaks down at any one stage, the whole line is halted. To avoid this a programme of preventive maintenance must be in force.

8. *Inspection must be 'in line' with operations.* Unless the inspection stage is balanced with the rest of the operations a dislocation of the flow will inevitably take place.

9. *All stages must be balanced.* If the requirement that the tasks do not queue is to be fulfilled, then the time taken at each stage must be the same, i.e. the line must be 'balanced'. This can lead to an inefficiency due to an inability to balance stages. For example, assume that a task/product with a work content of 8 man-hours has to be carried out/made at a rate of 300 a week, with a normal working week of 35 hours.

$$\text{Total weekly work content} = 300 \times 8 \text{ man-hours}$$

Hence,

$$\text{Number of operators/stages required} = \frac{300 \times 8}{35} = 68.6$$

$$\text{Time for each operation} = \frac{8}{68.6} \times 60 \text{ minutes}$$
$$= 7 \text{ minutes}$$

This is the cycle time.

Clearly it is not possible to obtain 68.6 operators – 69 must be used. To meet the required output, then, a flow line with at least 69 stages needs to be set up, the work content of each stage being 7 minutes. At best, therefore, there will be a loss due to the employment of the extra 0.4 operator needed to make up a whole number. In addition, it may be found that one stage has a work content of only 4 minutes and that it cannot be compounded with any other stage. Under these circumstances, this stage and another congruent stage will have idle times of 3 and 4 minutes respectively. These losses are 'synchronizing' losses, and the only way of avoiding them would be to increase the rate of output – something which presumably would not be acceptable to the marketing department. In the situation when an element cannot be reduced to the required stage time – for example, a machine-controlled operation is 10 minutes – then resources must be increased so that the effective operation time becomes less than the stage time. This can lead to an under-utilization of resources.

The achievement of the above requires considerable planning *before* operations commence, particularly in assuring that the correct material is delivered on time, and that the operations are equal in duration. Common examples where flow methods are used are the manufacture of motor cars, watches or domestic radio receivers.

It must be noted that flow methods are not necessarily used for large-scale production. For example, one firm found it profitable to flow-produce three large items of equipment a day, a task which they had previously undertaken by batch production methods. The following advantages can be derived from the effective institution of flow techniques:

1. The direct labour content will be reduced, since the comprehensive pre-planning which is necessary will often produce economies in time.
2. Assuming the product/task is initially 'designed' correctly, the reproducibility, and hence the accuracy and precision, are high.
3. Since inspection is 'in line', deviations from standard are rapidly picked up.
4. Since there is no rest period between operations, work-in-progress is at a minimum.
5. Again, since there is no waiting period, the provision of work-in-progress stores is unnecessary, and the total storage space required is significantly reduced.
6. Handling is reduced.
7. Control (including operations, budgetary, quality and supervisory control) is simplified, the flow line being virtually self-controlling.
8. Any weakness in materials or methods is immediately highlighted.
9. Material requirements can be planned more accurately.
10. Investment in materials and resources used for a task can be more rapidly translated into income from sales.

One possible problem which may arise, particularly in high-volume flow, is that the constant repetition of a short time-cycle task may induce boredom and frustration and consequent low morale. In turn, this may give rise to lateness, absenteeism, poor quality and, in extreme cases, positive disruption of the flow line to break monotony.

Requirements for flow methods

1. Substantially constant demand.
2. Standardized product/task.
3. Materials to specification and to time.
4. Operations must be defined.
5. Work must be to quality standards.
6. Correct plant and equipment must be provided.
7. Maintenance by anticipation, not default.
8. Inspection 'in line' with operations.
9. Stages must be balanced.

Line balancing in flow methods

In practice, the setting up of a flow line involves two associated problems:

(a) the minimizing of synchronizing loss;
(b) the maximizing of resource utilization.

Where a product/task is complex, there are certainly a large number of possible sequences in which the operations can be carried out, and the choice of sequence will affect both of the above problems. The choosing of a sequence gives rise to the class of problems known as *line balancing*, a wholly logical solution to which has yet to be found, although several heuristic methods are available. This is discussed further in Chapter 12.

The group approach

Batch production, linked to functional or process layout, and flow production, linked to product layout, can be thought of as extremes in terms of flexibility and the types of layout associated with the method of organizing work. The group approach, sometimes referred to as Group Technology (GT) or Cellular Manufacturing, can be thought of as an attempt to capitalize on the benefits of both batch and flow. Essentially, this involves seeking similarities, rather than looking for differences. Similar tasks/jobs/products are identified and formed into *families* and the resources required for these are formed into *groups or cells*. Benefits from this approach include such elements as easier planning of work, reductions in preparatory time, and better social relationships. The approach can be viewed from three principal standpoints: technical, social and managerial.

Technical implications

Much of the original work on group technology, as its title suggested, was carried out in a manufacturing context, although the concept extends naturally to many situations where work is being organized. A principal focus was on reducing set-up or preparation times. A number of approaches to the identification of similar products/components/tasks have been suggested. A first involves an examination of the requirement of each task in terms of the different processes – *production flow analysis*. A second starts with an analysis of the design characteristics of products – here a comprehensive coding and classification system is desirable. An abstract concept – the 'composite task or product', combining all the features of the tasks or products in the family – helps establish the processing requirements of the entire family. These have been largely developed in the context of manufacturing and will be explored in more detail in the next chapter.

Social implications

While engineers were considering the problems of reducing set-up time, sociologists were suggesting that many of the current problems of industry were attributable to the 'de-humanization' of work. This resulted from working in highly structured environments, such as the batch production functional layout shop, where it is essential to attempt to plan and control the total working day of each individual, or working on long flow lines with short cycle times where operators repeat the same simple task very many times during the working day. Experimental evidence was adduced to support the suggestion that a 'humanization' of work should take place, where jobs were 'enriched', and operators given much more freedom to choose their own methods and tempo of working. Such suggestions clearly require alteration in the magnitude of the working group. Small-group working with considerable operator autonomy, therefore, seemed the next necessary advance in industrial effectiveness.

This 'sociological' suggestion coincides with the needs of group working and the two streams of thought complement each other. The needs of group technology from a technical sense coincide with the needs for small-group working in a 'sociological' sense.

Managerial implications

Despite the advent of the computer, with its ability to handle vast quantities of data, the production/operations function can require more information than can be handled if the organization is to proceed in a conventional manner. Many managements have attempted to create large 'control' systems whereby detailed reports on the day-to-day, and sometimes hour-to-hour, working of each operator, and location of each job/task, are recorded. These systems invariably have collapsed, not merely under the mass of information but also because of the difficulty of obtaining up-to-date information from the operating point.

Provided that a sensible balance has been struck between load and capacity in a planning period, group working reduces this problem in two ways:

1. Planning the work flow requires only that work be planned into and out of a cell. *It is not necessary to plan the work through each resource within the cell.*
2. Monitoring the behaviour of the cell will effectively monitor the behaviour of all the people within the cell.

This delegation of authority 'to the coalface' is a difficult, sometimes traumatic, step for some managements to take. It requires that authority for detailed working be placed at the work point itself and many managers find this unacceptable. However, if an attempt is made to operate a group system while at the same time planning work in detail on to each resource within each cell, organizational conflicts will rise which will destroy the effectiveness of the cell and of the production effort itself.

Characteristics of a group or cell

It has been suggested by those with extensive experience in the field that an effective group has seven characteristics. These are:

1. *The team*. Groups contain a specified team of workers who work solely or generally in the group.
2. *Products/tasks*. Groups produce or carry out a specified 'family', or set, of products or tasks. In an assembly department these products will be assemblies. In a machine shop the products will be machined parts. In an insurance office the tasks could relate to the different types of policy.
3. *Facilities*. Groups are equipped with a specified set of machines and/or other equipment, which is used solely or generally in the group.
4. *Group layout*. The facilities are laid out together in one area reserved for the group.
5. *Target*. The workers in the group share a common product/task output target. This target output or 'list order' is given to the group at the beginning of each period for completion by the end of the period.
6. *Independence*. The groups should, as far as possible, be independent of each other. They should be able to vary their work pace if they so wish during a period. Once they have received materials and tasks, their achievement should not depend on the services of other groups.
7. *Size*. The groups should be limited to restrict the numbers of workers per group. Groups of 6–15 workers have been widely recommended. Larger groups up to 35 workers may be necessary for 'technological' reasons in some cases. Such larger groups have been found to work efficiently in practice.

Choice of family

The composition of the family of tasks/products which are allocated to a group is largely determined by the resources available within the organization: too large a family will require a large amount of resources in the group; too small a family may result in duplication of equipment. Four aspects of the group likely to result from a family should be examined:

1. What load will the family generate?
2. What capacities and capabilities would be needed?
3. Is it possible to set up the group for the family?
4. Is the necessary equipment available or obtainable?

It should be noted that it is unlikely that all the resources, especially equipment in a group are equally loaded – some degree of under-utilization is probably inevitable.

Ideally the family should be so chosen that it is economical to set up the group once and then leave it thus set up indefinitely. This is not always practicable, and a group may accommodate two or more related families whose tasks differ significantly from each other. Note that the group should carry out *all* operations on a family in order to achieve the benefits of reduced handling and reduced synchronization loss.

Benefits from group working

The following benefits are usually claimed for group working.

1. Reduced unit preparation time.
2. Improved learning, resulting in lower processing times.
3. Improved labour efficiency resulting from standardization and simplification.
4. Improvement in the effective use of equipment.
5. Lower handling times due to reduction in transport distances.
6. Simplification in planning procedures.
7. Need for buffer (inter-stage) storage reduced with consequent reductions in:
    (a) stocks;
    (b) work-in-progress (WIP);
    (c) storage space.
8. Throughput times reduced.
9. Simpler management.
10. Improved social relationships.

Associated concepts

Continuous operations

This term usually refers to operations which continue for 24 hours a day, seven days a week, throughout the year. Clearly, this must be a flow process, and it usually implies a very high-volume, very capital-intensive situation, e.g. oil refining or sheet-glass making.

Jobbing

The term *jobbing* is usually used to imply operations carried out only against customers' orders, and not for stock. It does not indicate any particular method of organizing the work.

Mass production

In common usage the term mass production is often loosely understood to imply a particular type of production. In fact, mass production is nothing more than production on a large scale, and as such can be under either job, batch or flow methods. The greater volume of mass production will usually result in a reduced unit direct labour cost, since a greater total expenditure on production aids and service functions will produce increases in productivity without an increase in unit indirect costs. Thus, if a number of small factories all producing identical articles coalesce into one large unit producing the same total quantity of the same articles, it is possible to increase considerably the effort on work study, tooling, plant, inspection and production control beyond that in any of the individual factories. The total cost could then be lower than the sum of the costs in all the individual factories – although flexibility may be lost, inertia may be increased and morale may suffer.

It is sometimes assumed also that during mass production quality will of necessity suffer. This is not so: it is not correct to equate mass production with *low* quality but generally with *uniform* quality; this quality level depends on managerial policy and not on the scale of production.

Another equally invalid assumption is that increased production *necessarily* leads to increased profits. This is not always so: increased production may lead to reduced *manufacturing* costs, but the total net return to the enterprise may be diminished by the need to reduce selling prices or increase promotional expenses in order to sustain the volume of production.

Batch processing

In some environments, a group of 'products' are 'treated' simultaneously: 20 door panels might go through a heat-treatment process together after being painted, 120 students might all attend the same lecture. Clearly this is constrained by the capacity of the resource (oven, lecture theatre). There are similarities as well as differences between this and the batch approach to organizing work.

CHAPTER 15 – HIGHLIGHTS

- In the job approach, the complete task is handled by a single worker or group of workers.
- The characteristics of the job approach are: it is organizationally simple; multiple worker skills are required; work is completed or value is added rapidly; it is easy to handle variety; it is easy to handle customization; equipment utilization is low.
- In the batch method, work on the task is divided into parts or operations, and work is completed on all items in the batch before it is passed on to the next operation.
- The aims of batch processing are concentration of skills and high equipment utilization.

- The characteristics of batch methods arc: it is organizationally difficult; specialized skills are required; there is a possibility of high equipment utilization; there is a probability of poor work flow; value is added or work is completed slowly.

- The advantages of a functional layout are flexibility, high utilization, specialization of skills, specialized supervision and it is insensitive to breakdowns.

- Using flow methods, work on a task is carried out in stages; when work on one stage is complete it is passed immediately to the next stage where work starts at once. Thus the task should be worked on for the same length of time at each stage.

- Requirements for flow are: substantially constant demand; a standardized product; materials to specification and on time; operations defined; work to quality standards; correct equipment provided; maintenance by anticipation; inspection 'in line' with operations.

- The advantages of flow are: economies in time due to pre-planning; high reproducibility; deviations from standard are rapidly identified; minimum work-in-progress; total storage requirements reduced; handling is reduced; control is simplified; a more accurate assessment of material requirements is possible; investment is rapidly translated into income.

- The group approach involves a search for similarities. Similar products/ tasks are formed into *families* to be processed by appropriate *groups* of resources.

- There are three perspectives of group working: technical, social and managerial.

- The characteristics of a group are: the team, specific products or tasks, appropriate facilities, a group layout of facilities, a realistic group target, independence from other groups and size (preferably 6–15)

- The benefits from group working are: reduced preparation time; improved learning, and reduced processing times; improved efficiency from standardization; improvements in effective use of equipment; reduced handling; simplified planning; reductions in WIP and storage space; reduced throughput times; simpler management; and improved social relationships.

Recommended reading

Burbidge, J., *The Introduction of Group Technology*, Heinemann, 1975

A practical book written by one of the great pioneers of GT. As with all Burbidge's work, the writing is lucid and helpful. The serious worker will find it well worth seeking out papers on GT by this author.

Gallagher, C.C. and Wright, W.A., *Group Technology and Manufacturing*. E. Horwood, 1986

A modern, comprehensive and well-referenced text.

Chapter 16

Manufacturing Systems Design

The organization of manufacturing operations

It is probably fair to say that in manufacturing more attention is likely to be paid to the organization of the production system, than to the equivalent system in a service environment. Factors which influence this choice of organization include the required skill levels of the workforce and the dependency on specific equipment. In service operations with high levels of contact with the customer (e.g. health care, hairdressing), the presence of the customer in the system can have a significant impact. The customer can add a large element of uncertainty in specifying and changing requirements. This can have an impact on the possibilities available in terms of organizing the work. The chosen method is less likely to fit within the standard categories, and more likely to be a hybrid. The patient interacts with the doctor during preliminary diagnosis, feeding in symptoms which in part determine the tests to be performed. The 'process time' is difficult to determine beforehand, so 'flow' methods would be difficult to use in this case. However, having been through this stage, the requirements for subsequent stages (e.g. X-ray, blood testing) might be known with more accuracy, and if 'decoupled' from this first stage, could be planned more tightly – flow methods possibly being appropriate.

Generally the customer is not 'present' during manufacturing operations, even when 'job' methods are being used with high levels of customization. The system is more manageable and easier to plan, and once the specification has been agreed manufacture and delivery can go ahead, largely without any further interaction with the customer.

Technology, possibly, has a larger role to play in manufacturing, to be discussed in a later section, although its place in services is becoming more significant. Automatic Teller Machines (ATM) are now commonplace in financial institutions, and Electronic Point of Sale (EPOS) systems are widely used in retailing. This also can have a significant impact on the way work is organized.

Job, batch and flow production methods

These methods of organizing production can generally be more readily identified within a manufacturing environment, with the movement from job through batch to flow frequently being associated with stages in the product life cycle or/and increasing volume. This ease of identification is linked to the higher 'visibility' of the product (as compared with a service) and possibly the greater use of equipment, linked to layout. Process layout is associated with batch, and product layout with flow.

Flow production methods (with high levels of automation) are frequently associated with car assembly plants, and often with the manufacture of the components which feed these plants. However, in both of these environments batch and group methods have been used effectively. It is dangerous to think in generalities. Most methods of organizing production can be used in any particular environment. The appropriate method depends on a number of considerations, including some of the characteristics of the environment itself.

Group technology

Although the concept of group working can be adopted in non-manufacturing or service environments, the origins are in manufacturing. One major stimulus to move to Group Technology (GT) was that by grouping products into families and providing cells to produce these families with significantly reduced set-up times. Current thinking in terms of other approaches to set-up time reduction have reduced the impact of this. However, there are a number of other significant benefits including those associated with the 'human' aspects of working; for example possibilities for job enrichment and greater autonomy within the groups.

The key to the successful use of GT is the identification of the *families* of products/components and the establishment of the *cells* of machines to produce these. In a small organization it is possible that this may be done 'by eye'. However there are a number of ways that the families and cells can be set up in a more formalized and structured manner.

Coding and classification

A sound coding and classification scheme can provide a robust basis for forming together similar components or products. Indeed, the benefits of such a scheme are much broader than simply in the implementation of GT, it can be used to assist standardization as part of a variety management programme, and is essential for computer applications for identification purposes.

To be of use in GT, the scheme must be related to the manufacturing or design features of the item. It would be of little use trying to exploit a system based on 'sequential allocation' (the next new item manufactured or stocked is allocated the next available code in sequence) or based on the location in the finished-product store. The code will need to embody within it information concerning such factors as shape, size (dimensions), materials and processes required. It can then be a relatively simple sorting process to group similar items by one or more of these parameters. Indeed, if additionally associated with each item are data on the workload generated and forecast volumes, then the implied total load on each cell can be calculated. This is clearly an ideal computer application, and standard packages can be utilized.

Composite component

Once a family has been identified, a *composite component* may be conceptualized, one which contains all of the features of all members of the family (see Figs 16.1 and 16.2).

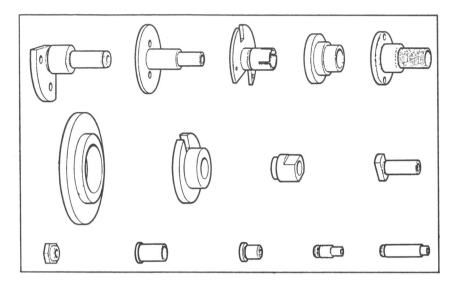

Fig. 16.1   A typical GT family (*The Production Engineer*, February 1970)

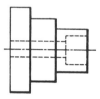

Fig. 16.2   The composite component derived from the family

Although this component may have neither physical form nor physical expression, the concept itself is found to be an extremely useful one in later work. The available machines are then surveyed to find which group can best be put together to produce the family, and this group of machines is then physically moved together to form a 'cell' or 'group'. The group is set up to make the family and the actual parts then produced by leaving out those operations not appropriate to the particular part being made, the effect of this grouping being to reduce total set-up time.

Production flow analysis

While coding systems use the physical characteristics of the products to form families, PFA uses the *method of manufacture* as the point of departure for classification. The route cards are examined and progressively sorted into sets, the common factor in each set being the processor on which successive operations are carried out. Thus, the complete set of route cards is first sorted into *first operations sets* (sets A, B, C . . .) one of which (set A) will be the set of routes on which the first operations will be carried out on processor A. Set A is then sorted again into sets, these being determined by the second operation (sets AB, AC, AD . . .). Set AB, the set which has its first operation on processor A and its second operation on processor B, is again sorted by the *third operation* (sets ABC, ABD, ABE . . .) then by the fourth operation (sets ABCD, ABCE . . ., ABDE, ABDF . . ., ABEF, ABEG . . .) and so on.

From this sorting, groups will emerge with common processing characteristics. Very small sets are examined to see if routes can be changed in order to move these small-set jobs into other larger sets. The larger sets are examined to see if they present adequate loads to the processors within the set, and again modifications are made to routes to balance loads where necessary. It may also be desirable to combine or to split sets to provide appropriate loading.

This system may appear tedious, but it will be found to be simpler in practice than in precept. Where very large numbers of route cards are involved, a sample can be taken to form the families, and it has been suggested that a manual analysis is readily possible with 2,000 route cards, so that a sample of 2,000 from 10,000 would be quite feasible. Clearly, of course, the sample must be a random one.

Group technology and just-in-time

Organization into a 'family' and 'group' will not only offer the ability to reduce ancillary time, it will also simplify material flow, increasing the velocity of the material through the system when compared with batch production under functional layout. It has been suggested that functional layout is likely to create queues of work as jobs compete for resources, and control problems as it is necessary to monitor each job through each processor. In GT, queueing is reduced since cells are balanced to handle the foreseeable market demand, and control is provided by monitoring the *entry to* and *exit from* the cell.

For example, a product has six operations and a technical route as follows:

Operation	Processor
1	A
2	B
3	A
4	C
5	D
6	B

If this is a member of a family, the other members will have similar technical routes. Demand for the whole family may justify the group comprising the following processors:

Processors	Number
A	2
B	2
C	1
D	2

The cell could then be set out *according to the technical needs of the family* (see Fig 16.3).

The material for the product then enters the cell, flows through it, the members of the family not necessarily taking the same route, and leaves. The only monitoring necessary *from outside the cell* is to observe the times of entry and exit. The control of flow *within the cell* is provided internally by the group leader or the group itself.

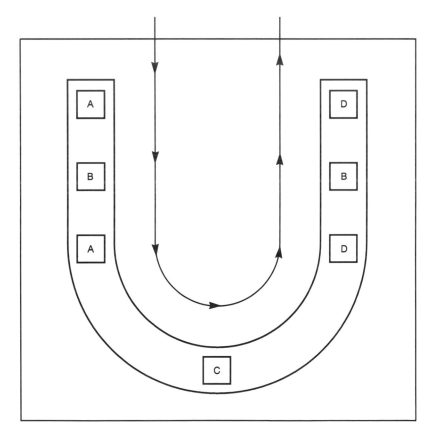

Fig. 16.3   U-shaped cell showing one-item flow

There is an increasing trend for cells to be laid out in a U-formation (see Fig. 16.3), which contrasts with the linear layout of a flow line. This offers advantages of flexibility of manning, since it is easier to move staff around to balance the work-load. Linked to job training and multi-skilling, this offers the workforce a higher level of job satisfaction and improvements in morale. The U shape also offers high levels of visibility to cell members to see work flows and identify and cope with problems by anticipation. Indeed, as will be seen in a later chapter, the use of GT, and in particular U-shaped cells, is advocated in the implementation of the just-in-time (JIT) philosophy – the instantaneous satisfaction of the customer's demand with zero waste.

Flexible manufacturing systems (FMS)

The application of automation and computer control to a GT cell results in what is sometimes known as a flexible manufacturing system.

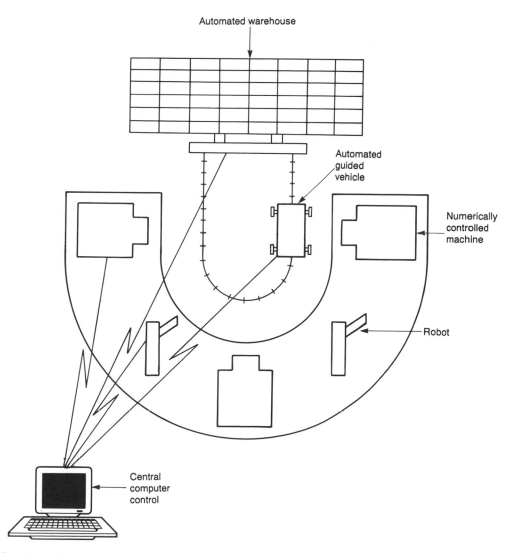

Fig. 16.4   Schematic representation of a flexible manufacturing system

A flexible manufacturing system (FMS) can be considered to be a GT cell with the following facilities:

(a)   computer-controlled machines which have the ability to carry out *their own set-ups* upon instructions from the computer;

(b)   equipment which can move the workpiece from machine to machine at the correct time and in the correct posture, again at the behest of a computer (automated guided vehicles, robots);

(c)   a computer which will link together the machines and material handling equipment.

The consequence of the above is that the cell becomes very much more flexible (it is claimed that one such system can handle in excess of 40 different workpieces in random order) and the need for human intervention is reduced, ideally to zero. There will, clearly, still be the same needs as a conventional GT cell, namely the ability to identify a family (although the FMS family can be larger than the GT family) and to design an appropriate cell to handle the family. Since human labour can disappear altogether from the cell, longer operating hours are very much more readily achievable.

There is one very substantial difference between GT and FMS, namely that FMS involves *very substantial capital investment*. The consequence of this, of course, is that the installation of an FMS is not a matter to be undertaken lightly. It requires a very thorough study of the anticipated market for at least the next five years and a thorough understanding of the objectives of the company. Those who have tried to install FMS without a substantial pre-planning of this sort have found that it has turned into a white elephant which is an embarrassment to everybody as well as being a financial burden.

Very significant benefits have been reported by users, including reduced product cost through higher equipment utilization, reduced set-up and scrap levels, increased market competitiveness through ability to change mixes and volumes rapidly and to customize, and improved quality through high levels of consistency and constant monitoring.

Against this must be balanced the substantial capital costs mentioned above, the hardware and software maintenance costs and the need to ensure that the FMS does not simply move the bottleneck to a later non-automated part of the process.

CHAPTER 16 – HIGHLIGHTS

- In Group Technology (GT), groups or cells of machines are formed to process families of similar products.
- Identification of groups/families is facilitated by: coding and classification according to design aspects of the items; the concept of the composite component, an amalgam of the features of the entire family; and production flow analysis (PFA) which classifies by similar processing requirements.
- U-shaped cells/groups offer advantages of flexibility in terms of role changing, and greater viability, and are often implemented as part of a Just-in-Time (JIT) programme.

- Flexible manufacturing systems (FMS) comprise: a number of work stations consisting of computer numerically controlled machines; automated materials handling, with robots, automated guided vehicles, and an automated storage and retrieval system; a central computer providing supervisor control.
- Features of FMS include the ability to handle variety while reducing lead times and inventories; production of specialist designs to meet exact market needs; rapid response to changes in product, demand, and production requirements; more consistent product quality; high initial capital investment; high hardware and software maintenance costs.

Recommended reading

Ayres, R.U., *Computer Integrated Manufacturing*, Volume 1, Chapman & Hall, 1991

The first of a four volume series, this volume focuses on an overview of the current situation with regard to CIM technologies, together with forecasts of future developments.

Hunt V., *Computer Integrated Manufacturing Handbook*, Chapman & Hall, 1989

A comprehensive introduction to CIM for the specialist and layperson.

Institution of Production Engineers, *Management Guide to Flexible Manufacturing*, 1986

An excellent introduction to FMS. Discusses philosophy rather than technology.

Chapter 17

Method Study

Work study

Work study is 'a *management service* based on those techniques, particularly method study and work measurement, which are used in the examination of human work in all its contexts, and which lead to the systematic investigation of all the resources and factors which affect the efficiency and economy of the situation being reviewed, in order to effect improvement'.

This definition indicates clearly where present-day work study differs from earlier job improvement schemes: a systematic discipline has been set up, providing a framework in which to work. Regrettably, work study has been endowed with a glamour which leads newcomers to believe that it is a panacea for all the ills which arise in production/operations. This, of course, is not so: it is one of a number of equally important management tools and cannot replace good management, although it may indicate areas requiring investigation.

Traditionally, work study is associated with 'shop-floor' or direct labour. When applied to indirect work, the term 'organization and methods' (normally abbreviated to O & M) is used. The techniques of the O & M man are exactly those of the work study practitioner, but applied to clerical and administrative procedures, and in non-manufacturing environments.

In a Joint Industrial Training Board report on *Training for Work Study Practice*, the following excellent statement occurs:

Work study attains its benefits through, firstly, investigation of the current situation, examining especially any apparent weaknesses (for example, poor performance by an operating team or machine or the high cost of a job): this diagnosis is followed by the determination and introduction of appropriate improvements in operating methods. The investigation and review will cover operating methods, selection of type of equipment, usage of equipment, layout, supply and usage of materials, availability of ancillary services, e.g. materials handling, organization of work, effectiveness of planning procedures and progress control, and the potential effect of the investigation on overall cost and profitability.

By virtue of its far-reaching nature, the inception of work study must be undertaken most carefully. For example, in examining the procedures for handling and processing documents, investigations may show that a significant cause of inefficiency is the time the computer takes to process the information. This might appear to be a criticism of the software developed by the data-processing department, which in turn may be revealed to be conditioned by the general financial policy of the company, limiting the size and power of computer purchased. Thus, what may start as a simple improvement of method programme may call into question the action of a number of senior executives. Such a situation could well cause considerable resentment and in some cases active opposition. An equally difficult situation is the employment of a work study practitioner in a department without adequate managerial support, so that any suggestions or improvements are not implemented. This results in bitterness on the part of the work study practitioner and work study itself being brought into disrepute.

At the outset of any work study programme, therefore, it is vital that all concerned should understand the principles, techniques and limitations of work study. As with any facet of management, success depends upon the co-operation of the people concerned, and positive steps must be taken to obtain the goodwill of those whose work is to be studied. *Secrecy, or the appearance of secrecy, must be avoided at all costs*. The ideal situation is one where work study is not considered as a separate entity but as an integral part of all activities. It is highly desirable that all levels of management down to shop-floor/office supervisor level appreciate the scope and limitations of work study. Indeed some of the techniques can be used effectively by management without the need for excessively long training periods to become proficient.

Work study has two closely related facets: *method study*, an examination of the ways of doing work, and *work measurement*, which is the assessment of the time which a job should take. Both are carried out systematically and follow very similar patterns.

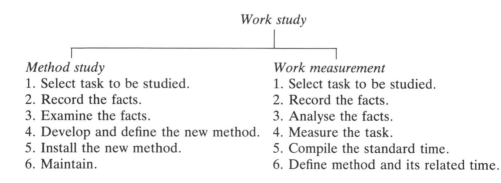

Work study

Method study
1. Select task to be studied.
2. Record the facts.
3. Examine the facts.
4. Develop and define the new method.
5. Install the new method.
6. Maintain.

Work measurement
1. Select task to be studied.
2. Record the facts.
3. Analyse the facts.
4. Measure the task.
5. Compile the standard time.
6. Define method and its related time.

Method study: the systematic approach

Select

The selection of the task to be studied is a *managerial* responsibility. The attitude 'go and have a look around the production floor or office and find something to deal with' is irresponsible and not likely to produce long-term benefits. As with any other operations activity, a method study – and its subsequent implementation – will cost money, and an estimate of the likely costs should be made before starting. Should these costs exceed probable savings, then the study should only be carried out *if there are other valid, identifiable reasons*, for example the need to improve safety. Some indications of the possible need for a method study are:

(a) *bottlenecks* generating long queues of work-in-progress, long delivery times, or unbalanced work flow;
(b) *idle equipment or people* giving rise to an under-utilization of resources;
(c) *inconsistent earnings*, where the earnings are tied to work completed;
(d) *poor or inconsistent quality* or high error rates, which may arise from poor or inappropriate working methods, procedures or conditions.

An injury of any kind may be caused by a poor method of working. It is sensible to method study *every* job at which an accident has occurred.

A critical path analysis of a project will show where effort must be applied to reduce total project time. Activity sampling (to be described in the next chapter) and Pareto analysis (Appendix 1) are also two techniques which can be used to help select the task to be studied.

It is unwise to carry out a study on a job where there is any form of industrial unrest – the *motives for the study will be suspect*. Once a task has been chosen, all involved – however remotely – should be informed, and the reasons for the choice and the desired outcome should be explained. Even quite innocent studies can take on a sinister appearance if the reasons for them are not known and understood.

Record

Once the task is agreed, the study will start by the practitioner concerned *recording the facts* by direct visual observation. This recording requires to be carried out extremely carefully, since important factors may be overlooked or ignored. *All* facts require recording, preferably at the time and place of occurrence. A number of different recording methods are available, and that which is used must be appropriate to the circumstances.

Process charts

These are 'charts in which a sequence of events is portrayed diagrammatically by means of a set of *process chart symbols* . . .' Their purpose is to provide an unambiguous, succinct record of a process so that it may be examined, analysed and – desirably – improved, usually away from the workplace.

Five symbols have been generally agreed and are in current use. These are illustrated in Fig.17.1.

It is useful to differentiate between two types of operation:

(a) '*do*' operations where work is actually performed on the material or equipment, resulting in an increase in added value;
(b) '*ancillary*' operations where material or equipment is prepared, cleaned down, or put away.

○   Operation: '. . . usually the part, material, product or document . . . is modified or changed.'

⇨   Transport: '. . . movement of workers, materials or equipment from place to place' without otherwise furthering the process.

▽   Permanent Storage: '. . . a controlled storage . . .'

D   Delay or Temporary Storage: '. . . a delay . . . for example, work waiting between consecutive operations or . . . temporarily laid aside.'

☐   Inspection: 'Inspection . . . for quality and/or . . . quantity.'

Figure 17.1   Charting Symbols

Cross-hatching may be used to emphasize the 'do' operation, as in Fig.17.2.

Distances are recorded to the left of the transport symbol, and brief descriptions are written on the right of the symbol.

These symbols, combined in a process chart, give a rapid picture of a process, showing clearly where it is worked on, where it is transported and so on. The care with which this recording is done will largely determine the final success of the study.

There are basically two types of process chart, differing in the level of detail recorded:

(a) *Outline process chart.* In this, the overall picture of the sequence of events and of the introduction of materials in a process is given by recording operations and inspections, using only two symbols (the circle and the square) of the five available.

(b) *Flow process chart.* This provides considerably more detail than the outline process chart, and all five symbols are used. Flow process charts refer either to the *man* (or machine/equipment), i.e. to the activities performed by the man, or to the *material* (the activities carried out upon the material) and not normally to both simultaneously. Pre-printed forms are often prepared within larger organizations.

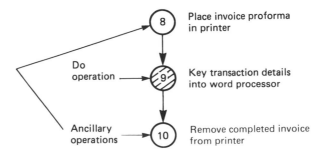

Fig. 17.2   Emphasizing 'do' operations by hatching

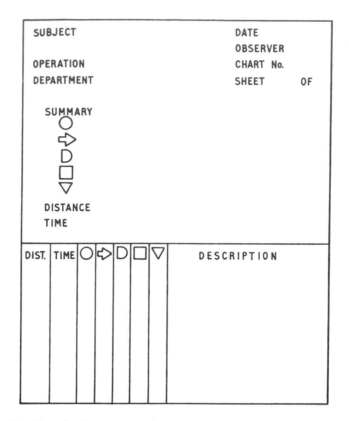

Fig. 17.3 Pre-printed form for flow process chart

Time-scaled charts

These are charts where two or more activities which are proceeding concurrently or simultaneously are shown on a common time scale. Again, there are broadly two sets of time-scaled charts, differing in the level of detail:

(c) *Multiple activity chart.* This chart, which may be considered to be a vertical Gantt chart, is used to show the time relationships between two or more workers, machines or materials. Essentially, a vertical column is erected for each, and the work performed is recorded as shading within the column. Time is recorded on the left and a brief description of the activities on the right. From the chart, the ratio of working to non-working time can be determined, and an attempt at balancing can be made.

(d) *Simultaneous movement chart* (SIMO chart). In this the movements of two or more parts of a worker's body are recorded. The movements are generally of very short duration – of the order of milliseconds – and the preparation of a SIMO chart usually requires a frame-by-frame analysis of a cine film or video tape of the work being studied. The elements of work may be recorded by *therblig symbols*, which were first used by Gilbreth, hence the name – therblig is Gilbreth spelt backwards (almost!). There are now 17 therbligs covering such elements as grasp, hold, unavoidable delay. There are a number of varieties of SIMO charts which do not use therblig symbols, but employ one or other of the *predetermined motion time systems* (PMTS) codes. These codes usually carry with them time values for the performance of the individual elements being recorded, and the PMTS charts are most frequently prepared as a means of work measurement. These are discussed in more detail in Chapter 18. Whilst SIMO charts can enable imbalances to be detected, they are difficult to prepare, and likely to be expensive both in time and equipment. They are used only if very great justification can be demonstrated.

Movement charts

When movement is to be recorded, one or other of the movement charts is employed:

(e) *Travel chart.* In complex situations it is sometimes confusing to try to use a flow diagram, and a travel chart (see Fig. 17.4) can be used. In this, the number of movements made over a period of time can be recorded. Movement is always assumed to start with the left-hand row title and move to the column headings, so that movements from department 7 to department 4 and from department 2 to department 16 are as shown by the two crosses. By adding up the crosses in the rows, the 'movements out' can be found, while summing the columns gives 'movements in'.

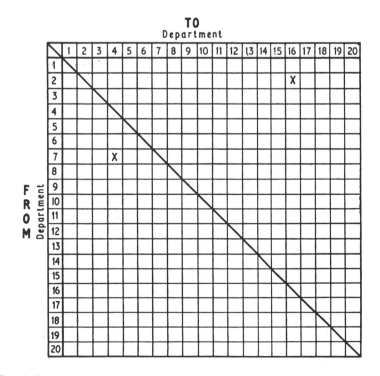

Fig. 17.4 Travel chart

(f) *Flow diagram*. This displays the workplace and the locations of the various activities, drawn to scale. The five standard symbols are used, and the diagrams again refer to worker, material or machines/equipment. Effectively, it can be considered to be a flow process chart drawn upon a scale drawing of the workplace.

(g) *String diagram*. Here again a scale drawing is used which is mounted upon a wooden panel. A preliminary survey identifies the locations of terminal points, and a fine string is wound between these pins to represent movement, supplementary pins being inserted where directions of movement change. The advantage of string over pencil marks on a piece of paper is that repeated journeys over common paths can be shown without risk of obliteration or confusion. Unwinding and measuring the strings will enable the distances moved to be discovered. The string diagram will display vividly faults in a layout which cause bottlenecks, back or cross-tracking or other movement difficulties.

Examine and develop

The examination and analysis of the facts and the development of a new method can, and in general should, be carried out away from the place where the task is being performed. It is not easy to separate the development from the analysis, and for this reason these two are considered together.

In order to ensure that a new method is developed, there are two essentials:

(a)   an open mind, and
(b)   a systematic approach,

and within particular organizations, a 'laundry list' of possible alternative procedures, methods and materials may be found useful. The open mind is largely a matter of experience and climate within the organization: recriminations about past decisions, and investigations into past reasons and behaviour serve little purpose and invariably generate ill-feeling. The systematic approach can be assisted by the questioning technique.

The questioning technique
The activities in a process are subjected to an interrogation which follows a fixed pattern. It may be thought that 'delays' and 'transportations' should be attacked first, but this is not so: an 'operation' which is eliminated may well cause a 'delay' or a 'transportation' to disappear. Similarly, a modification to a 'do' operation may remove the need for an 'ancillary' operation. Hence *attack 'do' operations first*.

1. *Purpose*:	What is being done?	3. *Sequence*:	When is it done?
	Why is it being done?		Why then?
	What else could be done?		When else could it be done?
	What should be done?		
2. *Place*:	Where is it being done?		When should it be done?
	Why there?	4. *Person*:	Who does it?
	Where else could it be done?		Why that person?
			Who else might do it?
	Where should it be done?		Who should do it?

5. *Means*:   How is it done?
               Why that way?
               How else can it be done?
               How should it be done?

These questions are asked in the *above order*: if the purpose is dislodged, all other questions are meaningless. If the place is changed, then the sequence, person and means may be altered. If, on the other hand, the means is questioned *first*, then a great deal of effort may be expended in analysing and improving a method which is later found to serve no useful purpose.

From the above recording and analysing, a picture of a new method will begin to emerge. This is a difficult step to systematize, and the speed with which a new method is proposed will depend on the experience, background and ingenuity of the practitioner concerned. Nevertheless, the more closely is the job examined and analysed, the easier it will be to *develop the new method*. Moreover, the first two questions of each of the five sets can be thought of as forming the 'examine' phase, while the second two comprise the 'develop' stage. The technique of 'brainstorming' can sometimes help with this. It may be that the new method or procedure requires 'technical support' from areas away from the competences of the practitioner, for example the development of more efficient software. In this case the assistance of a systems expert will be required. The 'best' solution need not be the most complex. A faster printer might provide the requirement improvement instead of a 'larger' computer.

The new method should be recorded in the same way as the existing one, the two compared, and a summary of the advantages made, along with the cost of the new installation. Any new method must, of course, be inherently safe.

Install

The new method, once approved by the work study practitioner, and the expenditure (if any) authorized by the appropriate person, requires to be *installed*. A process layout must be written and the technique 'sold', first to the supervisor and the management, and then to the workers concerned. Without goodwill the new method may well fail – no system or method is any better than the persons operating it. Many a good idea has fallen down because the worker concerned has not accepted it. In 'selling' the idea, the work study practitioner must first 'sell' himself: this does not mean that he must be offensively 'hearty' or friendly, but he must be respected and trusted by the workers. During the course of a study, the practitioner will have much information thrust upon him and he must not abuse the confidence placed in him by disclosing information intended for his ears alone. Once the idea is accepted, the worker must be trained in it by precept and example, and a habit of good working developed. Training is not considered complete until the productivity expected is achieved.

Maintain

Inevitably, habits of work different from those desired by the work study practitioner will develop unless the method/procedures are *maintained*. This may require continual visits from the practitioner concerned, but it is better if this is done by the worker's immediate supervisor. For this to be possible, the method must be written down clearly and concisely and thoroughly understood by the supervisor. If variations in the procedures then arise he can either correct them or, of they appear desirable, submit them to the work study department for incorporation into the process layout.

Methods improvement and materials handling

The movement of material and documentation from one place to another is found within every organization, and its study – materials handling – is sometimes considered to be a separate discipline. It is, in fact, one aspect of work study, and any materials-handling problem must be solved by normal work study techniques. This section will introduce some of the considerations specific to materials handling. Inevitably, much of this is more relevant to manufacturing than to non-manufacturing, although there are some common points.

Costs of materials handling

The costs of materials handling are often difficult to identify: however, it seems likely that in many factories, *at least* one-quarter of the final cost is attributable to the handling of the materials. It is suggested that every manager should cause an investigation to be carried out on the handling costs within his organization. The results would certainly be illuminating and probably alarming. Ignorance of the magnitude of the costs of materials handling is certainly one reason why so little attention is paid to this important subject. It is frequently found that improvements in materials handling provide the quickest and cheapest ways of improving profitability, although attention to this matter should always be given in the initial design and layout of the operating unit.

Unlike many other operations, the movement of materials adds to the cost of the product or service, while leaving its value unchanged. It is therefore important first to *reduce the need* for the handling, and second to *reduce the cost* for that handling which is inevitable. Any materials-handling problem must thus start with the layout of the department (the criterion of minimum distance – 'all movements will be both necessary and direct' – must be applied), and with the design of the product or service, which should be such that, during the various stages of provision, no unnecessary material is transported. This latter aspect coincides with the view that the most economical design is that which requires least material and documentation to be removed. It is often said that the best materials handling is no materials handling.

Aids to good materials handling

Accepting that there is an inescapable need for some handling, attention should be given to:

(a) *Correct identification of material and documentation.* The cost and frustration of trying to identify anonymous material and documentation is high.

(b) *Correct packing of material and documentation.* Easily damaged material requires careful handling and this in itself is costly. While the use of NCR (no carbon required) paper permits multi-part documentation to be prepared more efficiently, it must be handled carefully if the copies are to be kept legible and unmarked.

(c) *Capacity of equipment.* To try to economize by purchasing light or near-capacity equipment is frequently a false economy since it may result in multiple loads being required, rather than single loads.

(d) *Size of load.* Always move the largest possible loads, again to avoid multiple handling.

(e) *Weight of container.* The heavier the load, the more difficult it is to move. Effort should be expended in moving the material, rather than the container – hence, use the lightest possible container.

Check-list when handling material

1. Identification of material.
2. Method of packing.
3. Capacity of equipment.
4. Size of load.
5. Weight of container.

The reduction of cost of residual movement can be considered under the following four headings.

Use of manpower

The use of manpower for moving material is so flexible that it tends to be extravagant. The following rules apply:

1. Do not use productive operators for moving material: use labourers or messengers.
2. Do not move material in small quantities: the use of a full wheelbarrow or sack-truck is easier and cheaper than the movement of single items.
3. Do not require loads to be manually raised above shoulder-height or set upon the floor. Keep the loads at working height.

Use of gravity

Gravity is always present, and can provide a cheap and reliable source of motive power. Slides, chutes, roller conveyors and ball tables will all assist in the easy movement of material, and roller conveyors can be assembled in very many ways, incorporating junctions, branches, gates and traps of all kinds.

Use of power

Gravity conveyors are limited in that they will work only on a downward incline and they are not suitable for moving certain types of goods – for example, powders and liquids – without subsidiary containers. For any movement on the level or uphill, therefore, powered conveyors are necessary. The addition of power often permits operations to be carried out by the conveyor system itself, and many multi-stage plants are machines linked by conveyors, or conveyors with machines added to them. The power is not only available to carry out the work; it can also control the flow, and precise timing of movements is possible.

Use of packaged loads

Conveyors in general can be used for the continuous movement of goods, and the conveyor itself can be allowed to run whether it is carrying material or not. An alternative method of moving material is by means of devices which convey discrete loads. These have been widely developed and are particularly useful in the storage rather than in the processing of material. They include hoists and cranes, manually and physically propelled trucks and fork-lift trucks.

The environment and efficiency

The effectiveness with which work is carried out is conditioned not only by *method* but also by *environment*. Indeed, it is artificial to separate these factors since they are clearly interdependent, and the only justification which can be offered here is that of practical convenience. A further simplification will be introduced, namely that of considering only the *physical environment* and ignoring the more subtle and probably more important psychological aspects of work.

The study of man in his working situation is known in the UK as *ergonomics*, from the Greek word for work, or, in the USA, as *human engineering*. While the intuitive use of ergonomic concepts is not new, the codification and classification of knowledge received a very considerable impetus from the demands of the armed forces during the Second World War. Regrettably, however, much of the material currently available is either not used or ignored by the designers of machines and equipment, so that it is still not uncommon to find controls so placed that they cannot be conveniently operated, or adjustments which can only be carried out by three-armed midgets.

Man and his dimensions

It is a matter of common observation that man, like all other products of man, is variable. As a consequence, equipment for general use should either be capable of simple and rapid adjustment (for example, the typist's chair) or it should be so designed that it will cater for the majority of persons likely to use it (for example, the access door to a workroom). To be able to ensure that one or other of these conditions is met, it is necessary to know something of the significant dimensions of the human body and how they vary across the population being examined.

There are various anthropometric tables available; whilst useful, they must be treated with care as the information set out in them may depend upon many factors, including gender, geographical origin, age and occupation. Thus, the figures obtained from a study of, say, recruits to the City of London police force are not likely to be of immediate application when designing equipment for, say, use by drivers of the Paris Metro.

If a table of dimensions is available from a population which differs from that which is required, then all dimensions can be multiplied by the ratio of the mean height of the initial population to that of the required population. Possibly more useful than the sample tables of human dimensions are the recommendations for equipment dimensions published by the British Standards Institution.

Man at the workplace

Without suggesting that the psychological circumstances of work are not of very great importance, man can also be regarded as a machine with well-known physical requirements. These requirements are frequently ignored, and the ability of man to function in unsuitable situations is quite remarkable. However, to ignore them will inevitably result in stress and discomfort, and therefore any such action should be *as a result of a positive decision* and not as a result of apathy or drift.

Man's physical requirements at the workplace have been, and are still, the subject of considerable research. The results of this research and much experience are summarized here.

1. *Sit rather than stand.* Unless there is some overwhelming reason not to, work should be carried out seated. Even when work demands that the operator stands, then a comfortable seat should be provided for use whenever the work cycle permits.
2. *Permit a change in position.* The workplace should not be so designed that the working posture cannot be changed. A fixed position is invariably tiring, and should be avoided.
3. *Aim for a natural working position.* Any working position which involves an unnatural posture – a twisted trunk or an extended arm position, for example – will create undue fatigue.
4. *Keep movements symmetrical.* Balanced movements are not only less tiring, they are also more easily controlled.
5. *Ensure adequate working space.* A confined space is not only psychologically distressing, it may increase physical fatigue by causing muscles to be tensed in an effort to avoid the constrictions.
6. *Ensure the working area is at a comfortable height.* The correct height of a working area will depend on the nature of the work.
7. *Use mechanical devices to hold work.* The use of the hands to hold work is generally unnecessary and always tiring. Jigs and/or fixtures can usually be designed to remove the need for the hands to act as clamps. For example, document holders should be provided for operators keying data into a VDU.
8. *Support arms.* Support can often be usefully provided for elbows, forearms and hands. These should be upholstered, adjustable, generous in size and robust.
9. *Support feet.* Feet should, if possible, be placed firmly and comfortably upon the floor. If this is not possible, a robust footrest should be provided. A single bar or an upturned transit box is generally not satisfactory.

Man as a machine

1. Sit rather than stand.
2. Permit a change in posture.
3. Aim for a natural working position.
4. Keep movements symmetrical.
5. Ensure adequate working space.
6. Ensure comfortable working height.
7. Use mechanical devices to hold work.
8. Support arms.
9. Support feet.

Man and the machine

Man is essentially a tool-using animal, and the earliest tools, often extensions of their users, were built for an individual's personal use and modified to have the correct 'heft' and 'feel'. Today, tools tend to be much more complex, and the working power tends to be provided from sources outside the user. This results in a loss of direct contact between the operator and the workpiece, so that he/she will need to receive information concerning the work and transform this into action by operating some form of control. Care must be taken, therefore, to ensure that the operation of the machine does not become so complex that it is an end in itself and either the work or the operator suffers.

Information

All information provided should be *pertinent, adequate, timely* and *accurate*. Broadly, there are three ways of presenting information: by sound, by vision and by touch.

1. *Sound*. Sound signals are extremely useful for alarm and warning purposes, and are most effective if used intermittently.
2. *Sight*. Measurements, except in very special circumstances, are usually displayed visually. Such displays may be *continuous*, where a pointer moves over a scale, or *digital* where a set of digits is displayed.
3. *Touch* (*controls*). Controls operate by touch, and serve both to communicate information and to operate the machine. The types of controls include cranks, handwheels, knobs, levers, pedals, push-buttons and joysticks.

Layout of displays and controls

If poorly used, a display or control can lose much of its effectiveness. Whilst man is extremely adaptable and capable of considerable accommodation, it is wasteful to require him to stretch, bend or otherwise contort himself if this can be avoided by sensible layout of the control and display devices. The 'Cranfield Man' was created by researchers at Cranfield Institute of Technology to use the control of a lathe in current use – he was required to be $4\frac{1}{2}$ ft tall, 2 ft across the shoulders and have an 8-ft arm span! Regrettably, he is still not yet 'dead'.

Controls should be located so that they are easily handled by the operator. When it is necessary to mount a large number of controls, locate the 'fine' ones as near to the operator as possible and the 'coarse' ones further away. Try to fit the control devices to the scale of the work: a delicate knob for light work, a more robust one for heavier work.

A display should, if possible, be located near, or in relation to, its control device. Where a number of displays are required, try to:

(a) group them according to purpose;
(b) differentiate them by colour and/or position.

Wherever possible, try to standardize upon the direction of travel of pointers or scales, and try to alight the 'key' points of the display so that they are all in the same direction.

Similarly, standardization in computer software usage is important. For example, the field in which the date is entered should always be the same, as should be its format. Designers should avoid requiring data in a format convenient to the computer (such as 930213 for 13 February 1993) which is likely to be confusing for the user.

In the final analysis, a good design is one which 'feels' right, where the hands of the operator fall naturally upon the controls and the eyes fall easily upon the displays. Such an integration is neither easily described nor easily achieved, and however much care is taken in the design stage, testing by *operators possessing skills comparable with those for which the machine is designed* is most desirable.

Man and the working environment

Lighting

Good lighting is important: it assists in the efficient performance of work, it allows people to move easily and safely, and it creates and displays the character of the item being illuminated.

Glare and contrast

The overall effectiveness of a lighting system will depend not only on its intensity, but also upon the glare and contrast generated. Glare is said to occur when the intensity of light is such that it does not contribute to useful seeing, and may arise either directly, when it is caused by the primary light source, or indirectly, when it is generated by reflections from surfaces of some kind.

Contrast exists when *differences* in brightness occur, and frequently the existence of adequate contrast can enormously improve the modelling of the task being illuminated.

Climate

The 'climate' of work, as used here, is affected by:

(a) air temperature;
(b) air movement;
(c) air pollution;
(d) the relative humidity of air.

General recommendations for levels of the above factors are clearly impossible since the type of work being carried out will affect the requirements. It must be remembered that the climatic factors are invariably better and more cheaply dealt with at the initial design stage of the building; therefore any special requirements concerning climate should be made known to the designing architect. As the use of any building is likely to change throughout its life, provision should be made for the modification and control of environmental factors.

Fortunately, the human body has a high adaptability to climatic conditions, and frequently all that is required is to provide adequate means of heating. If more comprehensive control is needed, it is possible to provide it by means of complete air-conditioned plants.

Noise

Noise, which is best described as any unwanted sound, will not merely cause annoyance, it may also affect efficiency by inducing stress and it may mask communications.

It is worth noting that too little noise can be almost as great a problem as excessive noise. One of the authors recalls that when engaged upon the design of acoustic devices, he found that working in an acoustically 'dead' room produced feelings of fear which were extraordinarily distressing and which must have affected his work adversely.

The control of indirect labour

Traditionally, work study is associated with 'shop-floor' or direct labour; however, the costs associated with so-called 'indirect' labour are often as high or *very much higher* than the direct labour costs. To control these costs, work study has been applied to indirect labour. The application of work study in the office is frequently referred to as organization and methods (O & M).

Recording methods

Whilst many O & M officers use the standard work study symbols in Fig. 17.1, some workers have added special symbols of their own devising, a procedure to be deplored. The increasing use of information technology (IT) and the consequent need to analyse data flow systems has brought about a genuine need to produce a set of flow chart symbols for data processing. The British Standard Specification *Data Processing Problem Definition and Analysis, Part 1: Flow Chart Symbols* (BS4058, 1966) embodies these symbols – some 30 in all – and gives some recommendations upon the conventions to be used in drawing data flow charts. It must be recognized that these charts record the flow of *data* rather than the activities of men or machines, and they thus serve purposes quite different from work study charts.

An example of method study in an office environment

A large insurance broker's office is staffed by a manager and seven assistants. A variety of business is handled for individuals and for companies, covering motor vehicles, travel, building and generally all classes of risks.

An existing client's motor insurance has fallen due for renewal. He feels that the renewal premium is too high and calls into the office to see if he can get cheaper cover with an alternative insurance company. One of the assistants comes to the counter to handle his query. Figure 17.5 shows the layout of the broker's office. He retrieves the

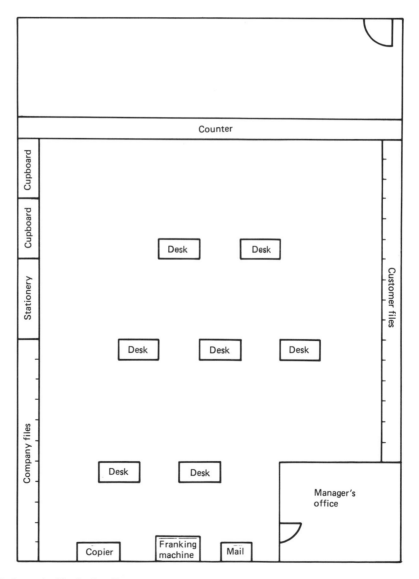

Fig. 17.5   Layout of broker's office

	○	⇨	D	□	▽
Walk to counter to answer query		●			
Take customer details	●				
Walk to customer filing cabinets		●			
Delay while search for file			●		
Retrieve file	●				
Walk to counter with file		●			
Confirm correct file has been retrieved				●	
Establish details of insurance companies to consult	●				
Walk to company filing cabinets		●			
Delay while search for required files			●		
Retrieve files	●				
Walk to counter with files		●			
Calculate premiums for selected companies	●				
Select company for insurance cover	●				
Fill in proposed form	●				
Walk to desk		●			
Retrieve cover note and receipt booklets from drawer	●				
Return to counter		●			
Fill in cover note and complete receipt	●				
Take cheque for payment to manager		●			
Verify signature, amount, date etc.				●	
Return to counter		●			
Hand over cover note, receipt	●				
Return paperwork to customer's file	●				
Walk to customer filing cabinet		●			
Return customer's file to cabinet					●
Walk to company filing cabinet		●			
Return company files to appropriate cabinets					●
Return to desk		●			
Return cover note and receipt booklets to drawer					●

Fig. 17.6   Flow process chart

client's file, consults scales charged by other insurance companies and, with the client, selects alternative cover which offers better value for money. The client writes out a cheque and is given a receipt and a cover note as proof of the insurance cover until the policy and certificate are prepared by the company. The assistant returns the files and documentation and goes back to his desk.

This and similar operations are carried out many times each day. No one questions

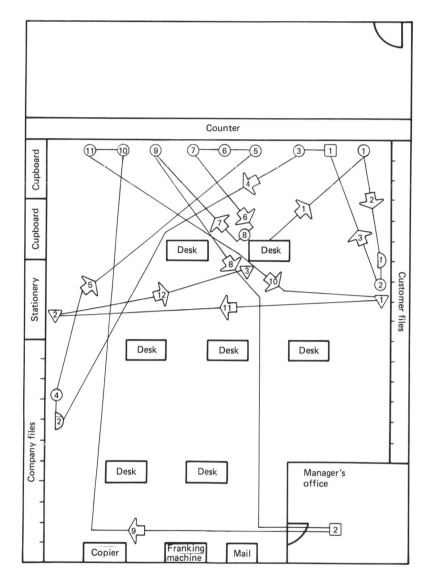

Fig. 17.7 Flow diagram

how efficiently they are being carried out. Indeed, it is difficult to establish this from the brief description above. The techniques of method study provide the tools to examine this situation. Charting techniques can be used to record and present the existing method. Specifically, a flow process chart (Fig. 17.6) presents the detail of the individual activities. This is complemented by a flow diagram (Fig. 17.7) which is simply the plan of the broker's office, showing the activities and the sequence in which they take place. This diagram immediately gives the impression of inefficiency. However, it should be stressed that the casual observer would not see the detail in this diagram from observing the office. What would be seen would be a certain amount of activity, without time appearing to be deliberately wasted. There would be no lines drawn on the floor showing all movements!

Together the chart and the diagram can be used as the basis for examining the existing method and developing the improved method. The diagram indicates where inefficiency might lie, the chart provides the detail necessary to examine critically the activities involved. The questioning technique provides a structure for this. Some immediate questions are:

1.   Why is it necessary for the manager to authorize cheques?
2.   Why are the files spread out?
3.   Why is it necessary to collect the receipt book from the assistant's desk?

These and other issues can be analysed using the framework of questions relating to purpose, place, sequence, person and means. It is left as an exercise for the reader to complete this process, and to present the appropriate flow diagram and flow process chart for the improved method. Readers may arrive at different charts depending on the interpretation of the situation. It should be noted that for illustrative purposes only the chart and diagram refer to both man and material simultaneously.

CHAPTER 17 – HIGHLIGHTS

- Method study is a systematic examination of the way of doing a task and the determination of the best method.
- The systematic approach includes the stages: select the task to be studied, (criteria include bottlenecks, idle resources, poor quality); record the existing method (use charting techniques: flow process, flow diagram); examine the record (use of questioning technique); develop and define the improved method (use the questioning technique and charting techniques); install the improved method; and maintain the new method.
- Causes of high materials handling costs may be ignorance of costs, poor equipment layout, poor stores layout, excessive manual effort, and inadequate/inappropriate equipment.
- Good materials handling requires attention to identification of material, method of packing, capacity of equipment, size of load, and weight of container.
- Some guidelines for man at the workplace: sit rather than stand; permit a change in posture; aim for a natural working position; keep movements symmetrical; ensure adequate working space; ensure comfortable working height; use mechanical devices to hold work; support arms and feet.
- Consider the advantages of presenting information by sound, sight and touch ('controls').
- The working environment is influenced by lighting, glare and contrast, climate and noise.

Recommended reading

Barnes, R., *Motion and Time Study*, Wiley, 1980

A thorough discussion of work study by one of the most respected US workers in this field. The comprehensive text includes detailed material on PMTS. Liberally illustrated.

British Standards Institution, *Glossary of Terms Used in Work Study and Organization and Methods (O & M)* (BS3138)

Not merely a glossary of terms, it includes explanations of how various terms (such as standard time, performance control) are derived. Now expanded to include material on payment by results and performance indices.

Currie, R.M. (revised by Faraday, J.E.), *Work Study*, Pitman, 1986

An invaluable introduction to work study, giving a comprehensive treatment to both method study and work measurement.

Doty, L.A., *Work Methods and Measurement for Management*, Delmar, 1989

This American text includes material on value engineering, motivation and safety, as well as method study and work measurement.

International Labour Office, *Introduction to Work Study*, 1979

A valuable introduction, and reference text.

Niebel, B.W., *Motion and Time Study*, Irwin, 1988

Another basic American text on the subject.

Chapter 18

Work Measurement

The need to measure work

Work measurement techniques are intended to reveal the work content of a task. In order that different tasks may be compared, the work content is always measured in the same units, those of *time*. The time taken to complete any job is considered to be the time which a qualified worker – that is, one who has the necessary physical and mental attributes and has acquired the necessary skill – would take if working without over-exertion throughout a normal period while applying him/herself to the job.

Uses of work measurement data

Frequently it is assumed that the principal use of work measurement data is in establishing the basis for financial incentive schemes. How could the production planner's schedule work if he did not know how long it was expected to take? How could management establish manning levels for flow lines without knowledge of the work content of the product the line is being set up to produce? There are, in fact, many other uses for work measurement data, some of which are discussed in later chapters. For convenience they are presented below:

1. Scheduling and loading.
2. Line balancing and establishing manning levels.
3. Efficiency comparisons.
4. Comparison of alternative methods.
5. Basis for budgetary and cost control systems.
6. Estimating future costs and loads.
7. Financial incentive schemes.

Methods of work measurement

There are a number of different techniques for work measurement, which can be categorized as either *direct*, where actual observations are made of workers, comprising time study and activity sampling, and *indirect*, comprising synthetic timing, predetermined motion time systems (PMTS) and analytic estimating. The best known and probably the most widely used of all of these is time study.

Time study

An operator is observed to carry out a given task in six minutes. This is known as the *observed* time and takes no account either of any allowances or of the ability of the operator – it is just the time which the operator being observed took while actually working, from the moment of starting to the moment of finishing. In order that ability and effort can be compensated for, the operator is *rated*, i.e. mentally compared by the observer with a qualified operator working at standard performance.

An observer is thus required to have a very clear concept of the rate at which a worker who possesses the necessary physical and mental attributes, and the required skill, would satisfactorily carry out the task under observation safely, accurately, at the correct speed and without undue strain. Having this concept, the observer then must assess the worker being studied against this criterion. It is clearly an extremely difficult task, since it involves the comparison of a number of different yet dependent features of the subject's work with those of the 'qualified worker'. For example, the subject may be working at the right speed, yet at a lower level of precision or in a less safe manner. Alternatively, the precision achieved may be much higher than necessary, yet the quantity produced may be too low. All the factors concerning the work being carried out must be assessed and integrated into a single rating figure, and this should be done while the task is actually being carried out. Moreover, the task may involve a number of different operations which involve different levels of effort. For this reason, and to permit a more accurate study, it is normal to split the task into a number of *elements*, each clearly distinguished from the next by a *break point*. Each element making up the task is then separately timed and rated. So the observed time of six minutes for the task may in fact be shown:

Element	Observed time (min)	Rating
1	1.70	135
2	3.10	90
3	1.20	80

In this illustration it is assumed that on the first element, if the operator has been working one-third as hard again as a qualified operator, he would have been rated at 133. In practice, rating is never assessed in increments smaller than 5 units, so the figure of 133 would normally be recorded as 135. The time which a qualified operator would have taken – known as the basic time – is

$$1.70 \times \frac{135}{100} \text{ minutes, that is } 2.30 \text{ minutes}$$

In practice, it is unusual to establish the basic time simply from a single observation of the task. Normally it will be timed and rated through a number of cycles, and an average basic time calculated for each element. The basic time for the task is then taken as the sum of these: in the illustration assume this is 6.05 minutes. The usual guidelines for the number of cycles to be timed suggest at least 50 for short-cycle jobs, and 20–30 for long-cycle jobs. Strictly, since a sample of work is being observed, the larger the number of cycles in the sample, the better the accuracy of the estimated basic time. It is, in theory, possible to establish statistically the number of cycles to be timed and rated.

The rating is essentially a matter of proper training and considerable experience on the part of the observing work-study practitioner, and obtaining consistency in rating both between different practitioners at the same time and the same practitioner at different times is extremely difficult, and is a matter to which much attention has been paid. A common technique for obtaining consistency is by means of *rating films/videos*. In these, the same operations are performed at various ratings. The work study practitioner views these, rates the operations, and then compares his rating with that given by the film/video. He then views the same operation performed as before but in a different sequence, and again rates the operations. This is repeated until consistency is obtained. The whole process is repeated after a convenient interval of time – say one month. By means such as these, some considerable degree of consistency is obtained, and it is claimed that ratings can be consistent to ± 5 per cent – a very necessary requirement if an accurate measurement of work content is required.

There are a number of different *rating scales*, just as there are different temperature scales. These differ by the value put on, and the derivation of, the fixed point – the *standard rating* point. This rating corresponds to the average rate at which qualified workers will naturally work, providing that they are properly educated, equipped and motivated. Probably the earliest rating scale is that which assumes that the unmotivated worker (the so-called 'day worker', one who is paid at 'day-rate' and does not earn any financial incentive) works at a 60 rating, and that the motivated worker will work one-third as hard again, that is at an 80 rating. The standard rating on this '60/80' scale is thus 80. Other scales which are 'pegged' to the 'unmotivated' worker are the 75/100 and 100/133 scales.

The British Standard rating, for reasons which are cogently argued in BS3138, 'pegs' the rating scale to the performance of the motivated worker, and gives a value of 100 to the standard rating point, making no assumption about the rating of the 'unmotivated' worker. This recommendation has been rapidly accepted by UK practitioners, and it is now becoming rare to find rating scales other than the BS one in British companies. It is used in this chapter.

During a day the operator will need to relax in order to overcome fatigue – whether mental or physical, real or imaginary – and to attend to various personal needs such as drinking a cup of tea or going to the lavatory. These factors are taken into account by adding to the basic time a relaxation allowance which has been previously agreed within the organization for each type of work and each circumstance. Within the organization being discussed, let us assume that the relaxation allowance for the task in question is $12\frac{1}{2}$ per cent. The relaxation allowance would thus be:

$$6.05 \times \frac{12.5}{100} \text{ minutes, that is } 0.76 \text{ minutes}$$

Under some circumstances there may be small irregularities in work – for example, due to small quantities of defective material – for which some allowance should be made. This is done by adding an allowance – a *contingency allowance* for extra work – which in the example might be $2\frac{1}{2}$ per cent:

$$6.05 \times \frac{2.5}{100} \text{ minutes, that is 0.15 minutes}$$

The work content of the task is then defined as:

Basic time
+ Relaxation allowance
+ Contingency allowance for extra work

= 6.05 + 0.76 + 0.15 minutes, that is 6.96 minutes

This represents the working time for the task being studied throughout the 'attended time'. There are, however, allowances which may have to be made for non-working time before it is possible to calculate the daily output. These allowances arise out of the process itself: for example, there may be a dead period while a machine is slowing down, or there may be idle time due to an overlapping in two machines required for the same task. These are known as 'process allowances for unoccupied time' and 'interference time'. Once these are added to the work content, the average operation time is obtained. This is the *standard time* and is:

Work content
+ Contingency allowance for delay
+ Unoccupied time allowance
+ Interference allowance

Assuming the last three factors are 3 per cent, 2 per cent and 1 per cent respectively, in the example:

Standard time = 6.96 + 0.21 + 0.14 + 0.07 minutes
= 7.38 minutes

so that if the task were carried out 100 times consecutively it would take 100×7.38 minutes, not $100 \times$ observed time. The task is said to contain 7.38 standard minutes of work and if, in fact, the actual time taken for 100 repetitions was 680 minutes it would be said that 738 standard minutes were produced in 680 minutes.

Most financial incentive schemes require yet another time, the *allowed time*. This is the time which, if fully used, will earn for the operator no bonus or premium. Any time less than the allowed time generates a *time saved*, and it is very common to gear bonus earnings to this time saved (see Chapter 31). The *allowed time* is derived from the *standard time* by the addition of a *policy allowance*, the magnitude of which depends upon a managerial policy concerning the acceptable level of earnings of the grade of operator concerned. The relations of these various times to each other are shown in Fig. 18.1.

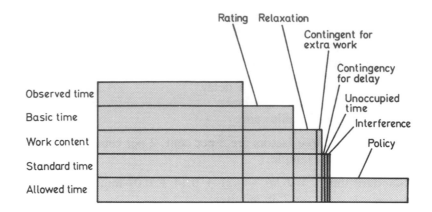

Fig. 18.1   Extending the observed time into the allowed time

---

Steps in time study

1. Confirm the 'best' method is being used.
2. Break the task down into elements.
3. Time and rate the elements through a number (20–50) of cycles of the task.
4. Calculate the basic times of each element in each cycle.
5. Calculate the average basic time for each element and, by summing, the basic time for the task.
6. Add allowances to the basic time to arrive at work content.
7. Add further allowances to give standard time and, if required, the allowed time.

It can be seen that time study is a direct observational technique in which an experienced work-study practitioner watches a worker, times what is being done, and 'rates' the work. Unfortunately it is viewed with great suspicion by some operators who remember the days of rate-cutting, where the usual reason for using a stopwatch was either to set a rate (that is, a bonus price) or to cut it. On the other hand, it is a completely intelligible technique which can be understood with the minimum of explanation, unlike some other techniques which are so esoteric that they smack of black magic.

Much suspicion will be removed if a clear explanation is given to the person being timed of the reason for the timing, if it is carried out in a perfectly open manner and if the operator has been given ample time to settle into an orderly rhythm of work carried out in accordance with a method laid down by a proper method study. No attempt should be made to carry out a time study if the work is not capable of being done correctly – for example, if the correct equipment or the required material is not to hand.

Activity sampling

The British Standard definition of this is:

a technique in which a number of successive observations are made over a period time of one or a group of machines, processes or workers. Each observation records what is happening at that instant, and the percentage of observations recorded for a particular activity or delay is a measure of the percentage of time during which that activity or delay occurs.

The technique was developed by a statistician (L.C. Tippett) who was attempting to establish utilization figures for some textile looms in the 1920s. Clearly, to have carried out the large number of time studies (forming a 'production study') required would have been prohibitively expensive. Essentially, he made a large number of random observations of the looms, noting the state of each (working, under repair, being set up, and so on) on each occasion. This formed the basis of calculating the percentages of time that the looms spent in each of these states. Since the process is only being observed at random points in time rather than continuously, a sample of the activity is obtained and, as such, there is likely to be an element of inaccuracy in the estimates. As the number of observations increases, the accuracy improves. In fact, from an examination of the underlying statistics it is possible to measure the accuracy of the estimate, provided the number of observations made to arrive at it is known.

An exercise would start with discussions with the workers, explaining to them the observation process and the reasons for the study. This would be followed by an examination of the process, establishing the activities to be identified. A preliminary study is normally carried out to confirm that the set of activities identified is complete, and to generate some preliminary results in order to establish the number of observations required in the full study. This preliminary study would normally cover 100–200 observations made at random points during a representative period of time, and could involve the design of a proforma on which to record the data. After the study it is possible to determine the number of observations in the full study using the formula (Appendix 2):

$$N = \frac{4P(100 - P)}{L^2} \text{ (for 95 per cent confidence)}$$

where N = Number of observations;
  P = Percentage occurrence of desired activity;
  L = Required percentage accuracy.

Suppose this preliminary study indicated that 35 per cent of the time is spent on productive work, and in the full study it is felt that an accuracy of 2 per cent is desirable (that is, they want to be reasonably confident that the actual value lies between 33 and 37 per cent, assuming the study confirms the value of 35 per cent), then the formula implies:

$$N = \frac{4 \times 35 \times (100 - 35)}{2 \times 2} = 2{,}275 \text{ observations}$$

If the work centre concerned has five operators, this implies 455 tours of the centre in the full study. It is now possible to plan the main study with the 455 tours covering a representative period of time.

Having carried out the full study, it is possible to use the above formula, suitably re-arranged:

$$L = \sqrt{\frac{4P(100 - P)}{N}}$$

to establish the actual accuracy in the percentage occurrence of each activity.

Stages in use of activity sampling

1. Examination of the process to be sampled:
   (a) consultation with operators;
   (b) identification of activities.
2. Preliminary study:
   (a) random observations (100–200);
   (b) design of proforma for data collection;
   (c) confirmation of activities;
   (d) establishment of number of observations in full study for desired accuracy.
3. Full study:
   (a) random observations over a representative period;
   (b) calculation of percentage occurrence of activities;
   (c) calculation accuracies of percentage occurrences.

The technique of activity sampling, although quite simple, is very powerful. It can be used in a variety of ways, in a variety of environments, both manufacturing and non-manufacturing. Whilst it can be used to indicate areas which are worthy of further analysis by, for example, method study techniques, it can also be used to establish time standards themselves. While time study requires training and experience before a practitioner can employ it effectively, activity sampling can be used to advantage with much less training. For this and other reasons, the practical considerations in applying it are covered in detail in a later section.

Synthetic timing

Within any organization, the same elements of work will recur even if the jobs themselves differ. If the work-study department comprehensively record the methods for the individual elements making up each job that is studied, together with the composition of the elemental times, this can be used as the basis for the standard times for new jobs. The appropriate elements are identified and the time for the new job established by adding the previously assessed times for these.

Many organizations will build up books of tables of these times, entering new elements as they are discovered. In some cases it is possible to reduce the figures to simple charts. A good classification system for the retrieval of the data is essential, and the master file, carrying the original data, must be carefully preserved. The loss of a set of synthetic data can be extremely serious.

Since working conditions, traditions and work patterns differ from place to place, *it is most unwise to try to transfer synthetic or analytical estimating data from one company to another.*

Analytical estimating

Usage of this technique normally results from incomplete synthetic data. The time required for the task is built up from synthetic data where possible, but supplemented where such data are not available for particular elements by estimates based on the best available knowledge and experience. These estimates are frequently provided by those with an intimate knowledge of the processes and product involved, for example the production engineer.

Predetermined motion time systems (PMTS)

In the above techniques (synthesis and analytical estimating), work is broken into course elements appropriate to the organization and situation in which the technique is being used. A predetermined motion time system (PMTS) breaks the work down into sets of basic human motions and, by combining these, any task can be synthesized. A number of such systems are available, probably the most widely used being method-time measurement (MTM) in one or other of its forms.

Original MTM (MTM-1) identifies basic motion categories, examples of which are:

Reach,
Move,
Apply pressure,
Grasp,
Position,
Release,
Disengage.

For each of these, tables are available giving the time for each motion under various conditions of distance, difficulty or load. The unit of time measurement is a TMU (time measurement unit) where

$$1 \text{ TMU} = 0.00001 \text{ hours} = 0.036 \text{ seconds}$$

and all times are 'levelled', that is they are the times taken by an 'average' operator, so that the need for rating vanishes. Thus, MTM-1 shows that to reach to a fixed location over a distance of 20 cm is R20A would take 7.8 TMUs while to reach over the same distance to a very small object is R20D would take 11.4 TMUs.

Table 18.1 The nine categories of MTM-X

Category	Description	Code
1. Get	Reach to and grasp an object	GE (easy)
		GD (difficult)
2. Put	Move and position an object	PE (easy)
		PD (difficult)
3. Regrasp	Shift the grasp on an object	R
4. Handle weight	Apply force to move an object	HW
5. Apply pressure	Apply force where no movement is involved	A
6. Eye action	Eye focus and eye travel	E
7. Step	A pace in walking	S
8. Bend down	Bend the trunk	BD
9. Arise from bend	Straighten the trunk	AB

Considerable world-wide experience over many years shows that MTM-1 is capable of giving highly accurate results. It is, however, tedious and time-consuming in its use, and it has been claimed that to analyse 4 minutes can take as long as 10 hours. In the 1960s a second-generation system, MTM-2, was produced that is much faster to handle and which has an accuracy comparable with MTM-1, particularly where the total aggregated time is greater than 1 minute. The simplification has been achieved by reducing the number of alternative conditions and ignoring movements which occur very infrequently in practice.

A later development is MTM-X, which has nine categories, shown in Table 18.1. There are three distance codes: N is for near distance (less than 15 centimetres), F is for far, and X is for variable. These simplifications enable the standards to be summarized on a small card (Fig. 18.2).

Despite the enormous simplification in MTM-X compared with the original sets of tables, experience and training are needed in judging complexities. *No attempt should be made to use MTM-X or any other PMTS system without appropriate instructions.*

Unlike synthesis or analytical estimating, the basic data for PMTS can be transferred, not only from company to company, but from one part of the world to another.

	MTM-X			
	GE	GD	PE	PD
N	8	17	5	19
F	16	25	14	28
X	13	20	9	22

R	HW	A	E	S	BD	AB
6	5	14	7	18	29	32

WARNING: Do not attempt to use this data unless you have been trained and qualified under a scheme approved by the MTM Association

Figure 18.2 Summary of MTM–X standards

Most PMTS data are derived from large-scale studies of elemental movements, the time for an element being taken as the *average* of all the studies. Times, therefore, are said to be *levelled*. However, the studies themselves do not include any ratings of the operators and since it cannot be assumed that all operators were 'standard' operators working 'at standard', a PMTS time does not equal a 'BS hundred rating' time. In 1969 it was stated, and it was subsequently repeated to one of the authors, that

$$MTM \ 100 \ = \ BSI \ 83$$

That is, that if an MTM study generates a time of, say, 20 seconds, this will be equivalent to a BS hundred time of

$$\frac{20 \times 83}{100} \text{ seconds}$$

$$= 16.6 \text{ seconds}$$

The advantages of the three synthesizing techniques are:

1. Short-run tasks can be work measured.
2. Rating, the most difficult part of a time study, is not necessary.
3. The results obtained are consistent. This is particularly important in small batch production where there are too few repetitions carried out for an accurate time study.
4. A reasonable estimate of work content can be obtained before the task is actually carried out. This is particularly true of synthesis and analytical estimating which are therefore usable in pre-production and estimating work.

Techniques of work measurement

1. Direct:
   (a) time study;
   (b) activity sampling.
2. Indirect:
   (a) synthetic timing;
   (b) analytical estimating;
   (c) predetermined motion time systems (PMTS).

The computer and work study

As would be expected, the computer has made its greatest contribution to work study in the area of work measurement. In time study the elemental times and ratings for a job must be recorded both accurately and clearly, without this recording distracting the work-study practitioner from his task of observing. The advent of digital stopwatches has improved accuracy. However, clarity is still important when the observed times and ratings have to be extended to derive the standard time for the task. Indeed, some practitioners claim to spend more time on analysis and administration than on observing work. In large departments where clerks are employed to carry out the analysis, clarity of recording is even more crucial. Microcomputers are now available for this process, at a range of prices offering a variety of facilities. These range from special programs for portable general-purpose computers to specially developed microcomputers built-in to hand-held study boards. These can easily be set up to analyse a particular task. All that is required is the input of the rating and an indication that the break point has been reached. The internal clock automatically records the time this occurs. This establishes the integrity of the time data. Depending on the equipment, the data can be dumped on to some local storage medium (for example, cassette) for later analysis, or the analysis can be carried out on the spot. This subsequent analysis can frequently be carried out using standard microcomputers (for example IBM PCs), and programs/software are available for a number of different routines, including building up a database of standard element times. It has been claimed that the use of such systems can save over 80 per cent of work-study analysis time. Moreover, it appears that, typically, analysis and observation might take equal lengths of time.

The purpose-designed microcomputers are normally also capable of handling activity sampling. All the basic calculations relating to accuracy, and so on, can be carried out, and various report summaries produced.

The reader interested in finding out more about these types of system is referred to the advertising pages of journals and magazines concerned with work study, management services and production engineering. Most vendors provide comprehensive documentation indicating the scope of the systems.

Computer databases of element times can easily be set up using such systems. For companies with a geographically widely spread organization, a single database can be built up and accessed from a variety of locations: this contributes significantly to consistency and efficiency. As an alternative to a company building up its own database, these can be obtained ready-constructed together with the necessary software. It is claimed that, for comparison, the following times are required to prepare a time standard of 45 minutes:

8 hours using conventional work study;
40 minutes using synthesis;
12 minutes using a computer system.

In setting up a computerized database to handle machine-shop standard times, it is claimed that the synthetic system took 10 weeks compared with an estimated 3 man-years of stopwatch studies. The system cost the equivalent of $1\frac{1}{2}$ years' salary of a work-study officer.

Clearly this is based on only one instance. Comparisons depend on local circumstances, environmental problems, and so on.

Clerical work measurement

Work measurement in non-manufacturing environments presents – *or is often said to present* – problems of such magnitude and complexity that its use is severely limited. These problems when examined seem to be:

1. *The creative nature of the task.* It is argued that many office workers are involved in creative tasks, and '. . . it's impossible to time thinking'. Upon examination, however, it will be found that the creative content is frequently such a small proportion of the whole that it can be absorbed within an associated physical activity.
2. *The irregularity of the work.* It is true that the work of, say, a secretary may be highly irregular. Thus in the middle of typing a letter she may be required to stop and take dictation, make coffee, welcome a visitor, answer the telephone . . . . Frequently, it will be found that much of the irregularity is entirely unnecessary, arising principally from the lack of organization, and lack of discipline of the supervisor.
3. *Prejudice.* The belief that the office worker is necessarily superior to other employees dies hard and this belief often carries with it the concept that they must not be subjected to such 'indignities' of the shop-floor as the measurement of work. Fortunately, more sensible attitudes are replacing these prejudices, but it is obviously vital that the warning against secret work measurement must be heeded. Knowledge is the greatest enemy of prejudice, and any attempt at clerical work measurement must be preceded by full and comprehensive discussion on the purpose of the measurement.

Clearly it is not usually possible or *useful* to measure indirect work as accurately as highly repetitive, large-volume machining work. However, it will often be found that high accuracy is not necessary.

Methods of clerical work measurement

All the techniques of work measurement are available, but it is found in practice that time study – the use of the stopwatch – is rarely satisfactory, partly because of the difficulties of rating and partly because of prejudice. Activity sampling is widely used for department studies, while there are a wide range of proprietary PMTS available. These include:

> Master Clerical Data (MCD)
> Clerical Standard Data (CSD)
> Universal Office Controls (UOC)
> Clerical Milli-Minute Data (Clerical MMD)
> Office Staffing Standards (OSS)
> Basic Work Data

All these appear to have been developed from MTM.

Mulligan clerical standards are said to be directly derived from micromotion studies of clerical work.

Usually and desirably associated with the measurement of indirect labour is some form of control system. These systems, like the PMTS above, often have proprietary names, and are often sold as complete packages by consultants. At one time the 'package' implied a particular type of work-measurement technique, but most practitioners now use whichever technique is most appropriate. Among the best-known names in this field are variable factor programming (VFP) and group capacity assessment (GCA).

An exercise in the application of activity sampling

A small section within the payment services group of a bank handles two major types of transaction: bankers' payments and drafts. Each of these has three processes carried out on it: logging (preparation of a record showing its status and so on): typing (preparation of the basic documentation); and VDU (input of the basic accounting information concerning the transaction into the computer via a visual display unit). The intention is to study the section to establish how the five assistants spend their time. After discussion and consultation with the assistants, it is decided to carry out an activity sampling exercise. Further discussions take place with the section relating to the objectives of the study and it is agreed that the section head will carry out a preliminary study over a typical two-day period. Random-number tables are used to generate the random times when each tour of observation will be made. Activities are identified, the proforma designed and the study takes place as planned. The results are presented in Fig 18.3.

The proforma for the data collection can take a number of different designs. That illustrated has a high level of detail, and analysis can be quite time-consuming. The work patterns of each assistant can be identified. This might be undesirable (the assistants might find it threatening and refuse to co-operate). The initials of the five assistants could be replaced by the codes of the activities, and tally marks used to indicate the number of times each activity is observed on each tour. This guarantees anonymity but at the expense of loss of information.

It is possible to conclude from the analysis in Fig. 18.3 that miscellaneous activity (MA) should be further sub-divided since it occurs relatively frequently (33 per cent of time), and further examination of this non-productive time could lead to improvements in efficiency. In the full study, this subdivision could be

(a)   transaction-related MA (e.g. filing),
(b)   non-transaction-related MA (e.g. meetings, training),
(c)   personal (e.g. toilet, coffee break),
(d)   waiting for work,

and so on. For ease of presentation, in this illustration the single activity MA will be retained.

It is now possible to consider the number of observations to be made in the full study. To do this, the activity with the largest percentage occurrence (DT) will be considered (in practice, MA would be further sub-divided). If the objective of the exercise is simply to establish the current situation, accuracy of 5 per cent in 27 per cent occurrence of DT might be acceptable (i.e. it is necessary to be 95 per cent confident that the actual percentage occurrence is between 22 and 32 per cent). If the values are to be used for operations planning and control, 3 per cent accuracy might be adequate (24–30 per cent). If the values are to be used for detailed costings, 1 per cent accuracy might be necessary (26–28 per cent).

Activity sampling study							Sheet: **1**

Preliminary

SUBJECT: Payment Services Bankers Payments and Drafts section

STUDY DURATION: 2 days

DATE: 25/02/87 - 26/02/87

TAKEN BY: A.P.M

Activities:

Code	Description	Code	Description
PL	Logging Bankers Payments	DT	Typing Drafts
PT	Typing Bankers Payments	DV	VDU on Drafts
PV	VDU on Bankers Payments	MA	Miscellaneous activity
OL	Logging Drafts		

Round Number	Random Time	Assistant: AB	CF	DJ	HS	BT
1	9.14	PT	DT	DV	MA	DV
2	9.23	PL	MA	PT	DT	DT
3	9.37	DT	PT	DT	PT	MA
4	9.51	DL	DV	MA	MA	DT
5	10.01	MA	DT	MA	DT	DL
6	10.17	DT	MA	DT	MA	DV
7	10.24	MA	PL	MA	MA	DT
8	10.41	DV	PT	DV	PT	MA
9	10.51	PT	MA	DL	PV	DT
10	11.02	MA	DL	DT	MA	MA
11	11.19	DT	MA	MA	MA	PL
12	11.43	DL	DT	PT	DT	MA
13	11.53	MA	MA	DT	MA	PV
14	13.04	DT	PT	PL	MA	DT
15	13.21	PT	DL	DV	DT	PT
16	13.43	MA	PV	DL	PT	DT
17	13.56	PT	MA	MA	MA	MA
18	14.09	MA	DV	PT	DL	DT
19	14.49	PV	DT	DT	MA	MA
20	15.19	DT	MA	MA	DT	DV
21	15.37	MA	PL	MA	MA	DT
22	16.02	DV	MA	DT	DT	MA
23	16.39	DT	PT	MA	DV	DT
24	9.23	DV	DT	DV	PT	DV
25	9.32	PT	MA	MA	MA	PT

Round Number	Random Time	Assistant: AB	CF	DJ	HS	BT
26	9.47	MA	DT	DT	MA	MA
27	10.03	DT	DV	MA	PL	DT
28	10.19	DV	MA	PT	DT	MA
29	10.32	MA	PT	MA	MA	PT
30	10.49	MA	MA	DT	DV	MA
31	11.17	PL	DT	MA	DT	DL
32	11.25	DT	MA	PL	MA	DV
33	11.47	DV	DV	DT	MA	PT
34	13.17	DL	PT	MA	DL	MA
35	13.39	DT	DT	DL	DT	DV
36	13.52	PT	DT	DT	DV	MA
37	14.23	MA	MA	DT	PT	PL
38	14.52	DT	DT	PT	DT	DT
39	15.13	MA	DL	DV	DV	PT
40	15.29	DV	DV	PT	DT	DT

ANALYSIS

ACTIVITY	NO.	%
PL	9	4.5
PT	28	14
PV	4	2
OL	13	6.5
DT	54	27
DV	26	13
MA	66	33

Fig. 18.3   Preliminary study

Clearly, if the largest percentage occurrence had been much less than 27 per cent, the values of 5, 3 and 1 per cent for the accuracies would need to be revised downward. The derivation of the formulae involved and a discussion of an alternative measure of the accuracy is given in Appendix 2.

In this example, a value of 2 per cent will be taken for the required accuracy. Using the formula presented earlier gives:

$$N = \frac{4 \times 27 \times (100 - 27)}{2 \times 2} = 1{,}971, \text{ say } 2{,}000 \text{ observations}$$

This will involve making around 400 tours over a representative period of time. It is worth noting that the results of the preliminary study are not included in this. During this earlier period, workers are becoming accustomed to being observed and not necessarily behaving totally normally. Again, random numbers are used to establish when the tours should be made. The results of this are shown in Fig. 18.4.

These results give a clear picture of how the assistants spend their time. If potential tasks for method study exercises were being sought, obviously those on which the assistants spend significant percentages of their time are potential targets. However, these data can be used in a much broader context, provided additional information is collected during the period of the study.

Suppose a record is kept of the attendance of the assistants during the period of the study and the number of documents handled. It is then possible to estimate the 'standard times' for the transactions. In fact, all five assistants were working 7 hours

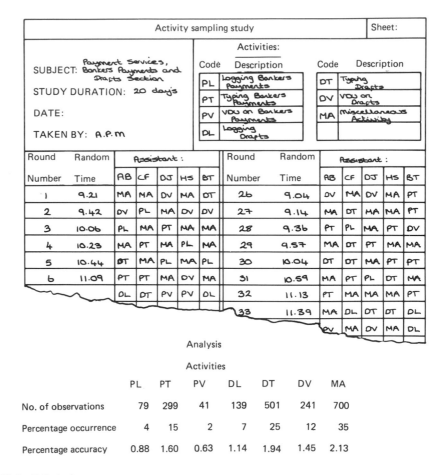

Fig. 18.4   Full study

Table 18.2 Allocation of 42,000 minutes across tasks

				Activity			
	PL	PT	PV	DL	DT	DV	MA
Percentage occurrence	4	15	2	7	25	12	35
Total time (min)	1,680	6,300	840	2,940	10,500	5,040	14,700
No. of transactions	422	422	422	1,123	1,123	1,123	
Time per transaction (min)	3.98	14.92	1.99	2.62	9.35	4.49	

per day for the 20 days of the study, and 422 bankers' payments and 1,123 drafts were handled. The steps in allocating the 42,000 minutes across the activities are shown in Table 18.2.

However, it is not possible to use these transaction times as they stand, since no attempt has been made to handle the time for miscellaneous activity. If this had been associated with specific transactions, it could be added in directly. However, in the absence of any further detail, this time is allocated in proportion to the transaction time, as follows:

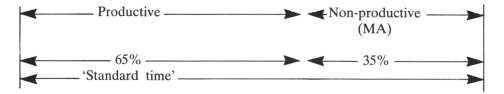

Hence the factor for non-productive allowance is 35/65 = 0.54. The time for each transaction is multiplied by 1.54 to estimate the standard times. These are shown in Table 18.3 in minutes. They can now be used for all the purposes discussed earlier: transaction costing, manpower planning, and so on.

Table 18.3 Standard times (min) corrected for non-productive activity

	Logging	Typing	VDU	Total
Bankers' payments	6.13	22.98	3.06	32.17
Drafts	4.03	14.40	6.91	25.34

CHAPTER 18 – HIGHLIGHTS

- Work measurement is carried out to establish the work content of a task.
- Uses of work measurement data include: scheduling and loading; line balancing and establishing manning levels; efficiency comparisons; comparison of alternative methods; basis for budgetary and cost control systems; estimating future costs and loads; financial incentive schemes.
- Methods of work measurement are either direct (time study, activity sampling), or indirect (synthetic timing, analytical estimating, predetermined motion time systems (PMTS)).
- Allowed-time calculation is based on the equation

Basic time   = Observed time × Rating/100
Work content   = Basic time
                      + Relaxation allowance
                      + Contingency allowance for extra work
Standard time   = Work content
                      + Contingency allowance for delay
                      + Unoccupied time allowance
                      + Interference allowance
Allowed time   = Standard time + Policy

Recommended reading

Anderson, R.G., *Organisation and Methods*, Macdonald and Evans, 1983

A useful handbook covering non-manufacturing aspects of work study, including clerical work measurement.

Oliver, S., *O & M for First Line Managers*, Edward Arnold, 1975

Written for the first line manager, recognizing that he/she is in the front line of O & M activities.

Whitmore, D.A., *Work Measurement*, Institute of Management Services, 1987

This definitive text has recently been revised to include discussion of the contribution of microcomputers in reducing the time spent on data collection and analysis in work measurement.

See also Recommended reading for Chapter 17.

Chapter 19

Controlling Quality through Measurement

In Chapter 8, the corporate implications of a positive quality policy and TQM were indicated. In this chapter, the methods whereby that policy is achieved are discussed. In general, the control of quality is achieved by some form of 'inspection', but it is the point and type of inspection that is critical to the attainment of conformance with requirements.

Traditional approaches to quality control

The task of inspection is taken by many to be the passive one of sorting out the good from the bad, when it should be an active device to prevent non-conformance.

When human inspection is used to sift out the result of quality problems, it is frequently found that every item, or element of a service, is examined in an attempt to stop defects reaching or being seen by the customer. In this type of monotonous, repetitive inspection procedure, '100 per cent inspection' generally turns out to be something less than 100 per cent. Monotonous tasks cause people to behave in a certain manner and to stop thinking about the job in hand. Research has shown that, typically, 15 per cent of the defectives or errors present are missed during so-called 100 per cent inspection.

Clearly, any control system based on *detection* of poor quality by post-operation/ production inspection is unreliable, costly, wasteful and uneconomical. It must be replaced by a different strategy altogether – that of *prevention* – and the inspection must be used to check the *system and process* of transformation, not the product. This leads to a 'how-am-I-doing?' type of check on the process, which should be carried out by the production operatives, not a separate 'QC police force' dedicated to detection and rejection.

A systematic approach

In any quality improvement process, data will form the basis for decisions and actions, and a thorough data-recording system is essential. If the symptoms of defective output are identified and recorded, it will be possible to determine what percentage can be attributed to any symptom, and the probable result will be that the bulk of the rejections derive from a few of the symptoms (see Fig. 19.1). To improve conformance quality, therefore, the major symptoms (A, B, C in Fig. 19.1) should be attacked first. An analysis of data to identify the major problems is known as *Pareto analysis* after the Italian economist (see Appendix 1). Without an analysis of this sort, it is much too easy to devote resources to removing symptom I, perhaps, because its cause is immediately apparent.

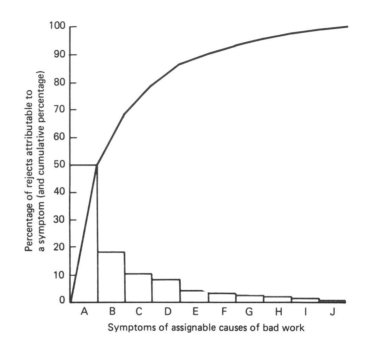

Fig. 19.1   Symptoms of assignable causes of bad work

Of course, any one symptom may be the result of a number of possible causes, and a series of investigations may have to be carried out to determine the effects of the possible causes.

A useful way of mapping the inputs which affect quality is the *cause and effect diagram*, also known as the Ishikawa diagram (after its originator) or the fishbone diagram (after its appearance) (Fig. 19.2). The effect being investigated is shown at the end of a horizontal arrow. Potential causes are then shown as labelled arrows entering the main cause arrow. Each arrow may have other arrows entering it as the principal factors or causes are reduced to their sub-causes, and sub-sub-causes, by *brainstorming*. The process is continued until all the conceivable causes have been included.

The proportion of non-conforming output attributable to each cause is then measured or estimated, and a simple Pareto analysis identifies the major causes which are most worth investigating. Cause–effect and Pareto diagrams together provide a most effective means of tackling problems and presenting quality improvement plans or the results of quality improvement programmes.

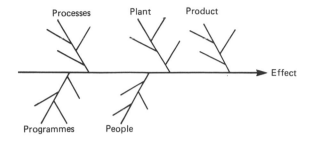

Fig. 19.2   The cause and effect, Ishikawa, or fishbone diagram

Statistical process control (SPC)

Since the responsibility for output lies with the producing department, the responsibility for achieving the appropriate quality in the transformation process must also lie with production/operations. To fulfil this responsibility, staff must be provided with the tools necessary to:

(a)   know whether or not the process is capable of meeting the requirements;
(b)   know whether or not the process is meeting the requirements at any point in time;
(c)   make a correct adjustment to the process when it is not meeting the requirements.

Statistical process control (SPC) methods, backed by management commitment and good organization, provide objective methods of process quality control in any transformation process, whether this is in the manufacture of artefacts or the provision of services. A systematic study of a process provides knowledge of the process capability and the sources of non-conforming outputs. This information can then be fed back quickly to the design and/or technology functions. Knowledge of the current state of a process also enables a more balanced judgement of equipment, both with regard to the tasks within its capability and its rational utilization.

SPC procedures exist because there is variation in the characteristics of articles and services. The inherent variability in every transformation process causes the output from it to vary over a period of time. If this variability is considerable, it is impossible to predict the value of a characteristic of any single item or at any point in time. Using statistical methods, however, it is possible to take meagre knowledge of the output and turn it into meaningful statements which may then be used to describe the process itself. Hence, statistically based process-control procedures are designed to divert attention from individual pieces of data and focus it on the process as a whole. SPC techniques may be used to measure the degree of conformance of purchased materials, services, processes and products to previously agreed specifications. In essence, SPC techniques select a representative, simple, random sample from the 'population', or the process input/output. From an analysis of the sample it is possible to make decisions regarding the current performance of the processor, and its inputs or outputs.

Types of quality data

Numerical information on quality will arise either from:

(a)   counting; or
(b)   measurement.

Data which arise from counting can only occur at definite points or in 'discrete' jumps. There can only be 0, 1, 2, etc., errors in a typed page; there cannot be 3.89 errors. The number of imperfections on a polished surface, the number of defects in a length of cloth, the acceptability or unacceptability of the lining of a drum are discrete data and are called *attributes*. As there is only a two-way classification to consider, attributes give rise to discrete data, which necessarily vary in jumps.

Data which arise from measurement can occur anywhere at all on a continuous scale and are called *variable* data. The weight of a capsule, the diameter of a piston, the tensile strength of a piece of rod, the time taken to process an insurance claim, are all variables, the measurement of which produces continuous data.

Causes of process variability

At the basis of the theory of process control is a differentiation of the causes of variation in quality during production. Certain variations in the quality of products or services belong to the category of chance or random variations, about which little may be done, other than to revise the process. This type of variation is the sum of the effects of a complex interaction of 'random' or 'common' causes, each of which is slight. When random variation alone exists, no major part of it may be traced to a single cause. The set of random causes which produces variation in the quality of a manufactured product may include draughts, atmospheric temperature changes, passing traffic or machine vibrations, electrical fluctuations and changes in operator physical and emotional conditions. This is analogous to the set of forces which cause a coin to turn up heads or tails when tossed. When only random variations are present in a process, the process is considered to be *in statistical control*. There is also variation in test equipment and test procedures, whether used to measure a physical dimension, an electronic or a chemical characteristic, or any other property. The inherent variation in testing contributes to the overall process variability and is always an important factor. In a similar way, processes whose output is not an artefact will be subject to random causes of variation: the weather, traffic problems, electricity supply, operator performance, etc.

Causes of variation which are large in magnitude and readily identified are classified as 'assignable' or 'special' causes. For the most part, these consist of differences among plant, equipment, processes, operators, materials and other miscellaneous factors. When an assignable cause of variation is present, process variability will be excessive and the process is classified as *out of control* or beyond the expected random variations.

Control charts

A control chart is a form of traffic signal, the operation of which is based on evidence from the small samples taken at random during a process. A green light is given when the process should be allowed to run. All too often, processes are 'adjusted' on the basis of a single measurement, a practice which can make a process much more variable than it is already. The equivalent of an amber light appears when trouble is possibly imminent. The red light shows that there is practically no doubt that the process has wandered and that it must be stopped and corrected to prevent production of defective material or the operation of an unsound process.

Clearly, such a scheme can be introduced only when the process is 'in control'. Since the samples taken are usually small, typically less than 10 in number, there are risks of errors, but these are small, calculated risks and not blind ones. The risk calculations are based on various frequency distributions.

These charts should be easy to understand and interpret. They can become, with experience, sensitive diagnostic tools which can be used by operators and first-line supervision to prevent defective output being produced. Time and effort spent to explain the working of the charts to all concerned are never wasted.

There are different types of control charts for variables and attributes data. The most frequently used charts for variables are mean and range charts which are used together. Number-defective or *np* charts and proportion-defective or *p* charts are the most common ones in use for attributes. Others found in use are moving average and range charts, number of defects (*c* and *u*) charts, and cumulative sum (cusum) charts. The latter offer very powerful management tools for the detection of trends or changes in attributes and variable data.

The range of type and use of control charts is now very wide, and within the present text it is not possible to indicate more than the basic principles underlying them. *Statistical Process Control*, 2nd edition, by John Oakland and Roy Followell, Heinemann, Oxford (1990), provides a comprehensive text on the subject.

Process control using measured data (variables)

When dealing with products or services having properties which are measured on a continuous scale, it is important to realize that no two measurements made will be exactly alike. The variation may be quite large and easily noticeable, such as in lengths of pieces of steel sawn by hand. When variations are very small, it may appear that each element of the output is identical. This is in fact due to the limitations of measurement, and 'instruments' with greater precision will show differences.

Process capability

In sampling a continuous variable, e.g. the length of a piece of steel or the time of arrival of delivery, the main assumption on which the statistical analysis is based is that the variable – say, the length or time – will be *normally distributed*, i.e. it will be bell-shaped.

For example, measurements of the length of 1,000 steel sheets were found to give the *frequency distribution* in Table 19.1. These values are shown as a *histogram* in Fig. 19.3; its shape and general symmetry indicate that a normal or Gaussian distribution (Fig. 19.4) conveniently describes the variation in the lengths.

Table 19.1 Frequency distribution for length of 1,000 steel sheets

Steel sheet length, rounded to nearest 0.05 mm (mm)	*Number of sheets*
60.10	1
60.15	6
60.20	12
60.25	18
60.30	85
60.35	214
60.40	339
60.45	201
60.50	75
60.55	33
60.60	10
60.65	4
60.70	2
	1,000

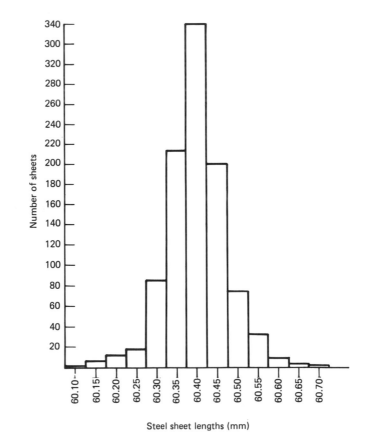

Fig. 19.3   Frequency distribution of steel sheet lengths

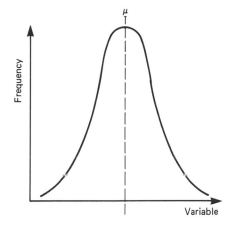

Fig. 19.4   The normal distribution of a continuous variable

The measure of 'central tendency' most frequently used is the *mean* or *average* μ of the process data. The measure of spread of values from the process is given by the *standard deviation* σ which is calculated by adding together all the squares of the differences between the measured values and the mean value, dividing the resultant sum by the total number (N) of observations, and then taking the square root of the result, i.e.

$$\sigma = \sqrt{\frac{\Sigma (x - \mu)^2}{N}}$$

A simpler method of estimating σ is usually used in SPC.

A process whose average is equal to the nominal or target value is said to be *accurate*. One which has a relatively small spread is said to be *precise*; the smaller the value of σ, the higher the precision. A specification related to variables, therefore, requires a statement on *both* accuracy and precision. Often 'high quality' is associated with high accuracy and high precision, whereas the true requirements may not necessarily imply such a combination.

Suppose the target length of the sheet steel cutting process was 60.4 mm, and that the process was being operated with a mean value μ = 60.4 mm, and a standard deviation σ = 0.1 mm, then from a knowledge of the bell-shaped curve and the properties of the normal distribution the following facts would emerge:

68.3 per cent of the sheets produced are within ± 0.1 mm of the average (μ ± σ).
95.4 per cent of the sheets are within average ± 0.2 mm (μ ± 2σ).
99.7 per cent are within average ± 0.3 mm (μ ± 3σ) (Fig. 19.5).

Controlling the process to achieve the target value, with little and reducing variation, is the aim of never-ending improvement. It is clearly essential that any tolerance zone exceeds the spread of the distribution, to avoid the production of defectives. If tolerances have been set for the sheets of steel at 60.4 ± 0.4 mm, then

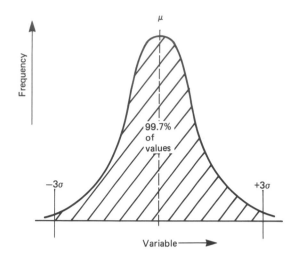

Fig. 19.5   The proportion of output contained in ($\mu \pm \sigma$)

very few will fall outside them (Fig. 19.6(a)). Conversely, if the spread of the process exceeds the specified tolerance of 60.4 ± 0.2 mm, as in Fig. 19.6(b), then there will inevitably be reject material.

The relationship between process variability and specified tolerances, known as the *process capability*, may be formalized using the standard deviation, σ, of the process. In order to produce within the specified requirements, the distance between the upper specification limit (USL) and the lower specification limit (LSL), i.e. USL − LSL, must be greater than the width of the base of the process bell, i.e. 6σ.

When a process is in statistical control, i.e. only random causes of variation are present, a *process capability index* may be calculated to relate the actual performance

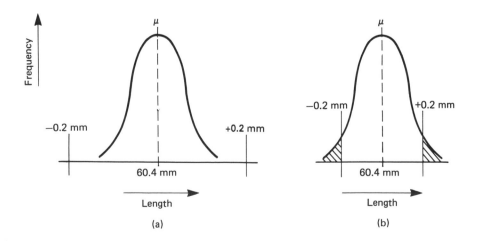

Fig. 19.6   The relationship between tolerances and process variability

of the process to its specified requirements. The simplest index is Cp, which quantifies the spread of the process relative to the specification limits:

$$Cp = \frac{USL - LSL}{6\sigma}$$

A second index, Cpk, quantifies both the spread and the setting of the process:

$$Cpk = \text{minimum of } \frac{USL - \bar{X}}{3\sigma} \quad \text{or} \quad \frac{\bar{X} - LSL}{3\sigma}$$

Values for Cp and Cpk greater than 1 indicate that three process standard deviations (3σ) either side of the mean are contained within the specification or tolerance band. To operate a process safely inside the required limits, the values of Cp and Cpk must approach 2. Clearly, when Cp or Cpk is less than 1, the process is incapable of achieving the requirements.

Control charts for variables

The standard deviation (σ) of a process distribution is one measure of variation. As the sample size in SPC is usually less than or equal to 10, a more convenient measure of spread is the sample range: the difference between the largest and smallest values in the sample. To control the plant or process it is necessary to check the current state of the average and spread of the distribution, and this may be achieved with the aid of mean and range charts.

If lengths of sheet steel are measured, it is clear that occasionally one will be found which is towards one end of the tail of the process distribution. This, if examined on its own, may lead to the wrong conclusion that the cutting process requires adjustment. If, however, a sample of five pieces is taken, it is extremely unlikely that all five lengths will lie towards one extreme end of the distribution, unless the process has changed. The average or mean length of five pieces will, therefore, provide a much more reliable indicator of the setting of the process. Moreover, the range of the sample will give an indication of the spread of the results from the process.

Capability and control

A series of, say, 20 samples of size five ($n = 5$) are taken from a process over a period of time, when no adjustments to the process have been made, say one sample every 15 minutes. Table 19.2 shows the individual lengths of 20 samples of five sheets of steel taken in such a way. The mean ($\bar{X}$) and range (R) of each group of five results are calculated and the grand mean of means (process mean, $\bar{\bar{X}}$) is determined, together with the mean of the sample ranges ($\bar{R}$). The results are as follows:

Table 19.2 Individual lengths, means and ranges of 20 samples of five steel sheets

Sample number	Length (mm) Piece 1	Piece 2	Piece 3	Piece 4	Piece 5	Sample mean (mm)	Sample range (mm)
1	60.45	60.46	60.52	60.55	60.55	60.51	0.10
2	60.45	60.55	60.59	60.55	60.52	60.53	0.14
3	60.49	60.49	60.58	60.49	60.54	60.52	0.09
4	60.43	60.43	60.44	60.47	60.51	60.46	0.08
5	60.47	60.50	60.48	60.50	60.44	60.48	0.06
6	60.61	60.58	60.53	60.42	60.46	60.52	0.19
7	60.48	60.56	60.57	60.50	60.43	60.51	0.14
8	60.49	60.49	60.55	60.57	60.54	60.53	0.08
9	60.45	60.47	60.53	60.51	60.46	60.48	0.08
10	60.51	60.43	60.51	60.44	60.49	60.48	0.08
11	60.48	60.50	60.52	60.58	60.49	60.51	0.10
12	60.48	60.56	60.47	60.51	60.54	60.51	0.09
13	60.48	60.54	60.58	60.57	60.54	60.54	0.10
14	60.57	60.49	60.43	60.51	60.49	60.50	0.14
15	60.47	60.47	60.51	60.48	60.43	60.47	0.08
16	60.49	60.41	60.53	60.52	60.54	60.50	0.13
17	60.43	60.48	60.54	60.47	60.48	60.48	0.11
18	60.57	60.47	60.52	60.52	60.53	60.52	0.10
19	60.48	60.42	60.50	60.49	60.48	60.47	0.08
20	60.55	60.52	60.52	60.47	60.55	60.52	0.08

$$\text{Process mean,} \quad \bar{\bar{X}} = 60.5 \text{ mm}$$
$$\text{Mean range,} \quad \bar{R} = 0.10 \text{ mm}$$

Mean charts

The means of samples taken from a stable process will vary with each one taken, but the variation will not be as great as for single pieces. Comparison of the two frequency diagrams of Fig. 19.7 shows that the spread of the sample means is much less than the spread of the individual sheet lengths.

In setting up a mean chart where samples of a given size (n) are taken at intervals from the process over a period when it is thought to be under control, the sample mean is recorded on a control chart. Providing that the sample size is $n = 4$ or more, then the mean values will be normally distributed even if the original population itself is not truly normal. This is known as the Central Limits Theorem. The standard deviation of the sample means, called the *standard error* to avoid confusion with the standard deviation of the parent population, is smaller than the parent standard deviation:

$$\text{Standard error of the sample means} = \frac{\sigma}{\sqrt{n}}$$

where σ is the standard deviation of the parent population.

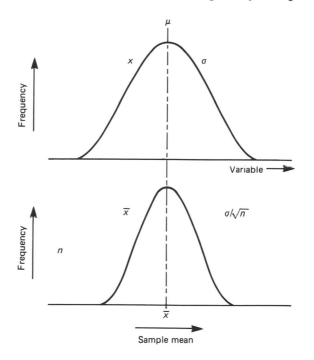

Fig. 19.7 What happens when samples of size *n* are taken and the means are plotted

Figure 19.8 shows the principle of the control chart for sample mean. If the process is running in control, it can be expected that almost all the means of successive samples will lie between the upper and lower action lines. These are set at a distance equal to $3\sigma/\sqrt{n}$ either side of the process mean:

$$\text{Upper action line (UAL)} = \bar{\bar{X}} + 3\sigma/\sqrt{n}$$
$$\text{Lower action line (LAL)} = \bar{\bar{X}} - 3\sigma/\sqrt{n}$$

The chance of a mean falling outside either of these lines is *c.* 1.5 in 1,000, unless the process has altered. If a point does fall outside, this indicates the presence of an assignable cause and the process should be investigated or the setting appropriately adjusted.

Figure 19.8 also shows warning limits which have been set at $2\sigma/\sqrt{n}$ away from the process mean:

$$\text{Upper warning line (UWL)} = \bar{\bar{X}} + 2\sigma/\sqrt{n}$$
$$\text{Lower warning line (WAL)} = \bar{\bar{X}} - 2\sigma/\sqrt{n}$$

The chance of a sample mean plotting outside either of these limits is *c.* 1 in 40, i.e. it is expected to happen once in every 40 samples. When it does happen, however, there are grounds for suspicion and the usual procedure is to take another sample immediately, before making a definite decision about the setting of the process.

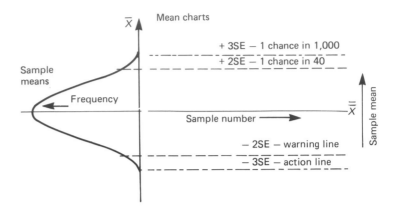

Fig. 19.8 The principle of the mean chart

Two successive sample means outside one of the warning lines indicates that action to investigate or adjust the process should be taken immediately.

In SPC for variables, the sample size is usually less than 12, and it becomes possible to use the alternative measure of spread of the process – the mean range of samples, R. Use may then be made of Hartley's conversion constant (d_n) for estimating the process standard deviation:

$$\sigma = \frac{\bar{R}}{d_n}$$

where d_n is obtained from Table 19.3.

Table 19.3 Hartley's constants d_n for sample size $n = 2$–10

Sample size	(n)	2	3	4	5	6	7	8	9	10
	d_n	1.13	1.69	2.06	2.33	2.53	2.70	2.85	2.97	3.0

Using the data already indicated,

Process mean, $\bar{\bar{X}} = 60.50$ mm,
Mean range, $\bar{R} = 0.10$ mm,
Sample size, $n = 5$,
Hartley's constant, $d_n = 2.33$:

Estimate of process standard deviation, $\sigma = \dfrac{\bar{R}}{d_n} = \dfrac{0.10}{2.33} = 0.043$

Hence,

$$\text{Mean chart action lines} = \bar{\bar{X}} \pm 3\sigma/\sqrt{n}$$
$$= 60.50 \pm \left(3 \times 0.043/\sqrt{5}\right)$$
$$\therefore \text{UAL} = 60.56 \quad \text{LAL} = 60.44$$
$$\text{Mean chart warning lines} = \bar{\bar{X}} \pm 2\sigma/\sqrt{n}$$
$$= 60.5 \pm \left(2 \times 0.043/\sqrt{5}\right)$$
$$\therefore \text{UWL} = 60.54 \quad \text{LWL} = 60.46$$

Alternative method of calculating mean chart limits

The action lines are at $\bar{\bar{X}} \pm 3\sigma/\sqrt{n}$. Substituting $\sigma = \bar{R}/d_n$, the limits become:

$$\text{Action lines at } \bar{\bar{X}} \pm \frac{3}{d_n \sqrt{n}} \bar{R}$$

As 3, d_n and n are all constants for the same sample size, they may be replaced with just one constant, $A_2 = 3/d_n \sqrt{n}$.

The action lines for the mean chart become:

$$\bar{\bar{X}} \pm A_2 \bar{R}$$

The warning lines may be similarly calculated from:

$$\bar{\bar{X}} \pm \frac{2}{3} A_2 \bar{R}$$

The constants A_2 and $2A_2/3$ for sample sizes $n = 2\text{--}12$ are listed in Table 19.4.

Table 19.4 Constants for use in the calculation of mean chart control limits

	Sample size (n)										
	2	3	4	5	6	7	8	9	10	11	12
A_2	1.88	1.02	0.73	0.58	0.48	0.42	0.37	0.34	0.31	0.29	0.27
$2A_2/3$	1.25	0.68	0.49	0.39	0.32	0.28	0.25	0.23	0.21	0.19	0.18

Applying these constants to the example data, the control limits may now be calculated directly from the values of X and R:

$$n = 5 \quad A_2 = 0.58 \quad 2A_2/3 = 0.39$$
$$\text{Action lines at } \bar{\bar{X}} \pm A_2 \bar{R} = 60.50 \pm (0.58 \times 0.10)$$
$$\therefore \text{UAL} = 60.56 \quad \text{LAL} = 60.44$$
$$\text{Warning lines at } \bar{\bar{X}} \pm 2A_2 \bar{R}/3 = 60.50 \pm (0.39 \times 0.10)$$
$$\text{UAL} = 60.54 \quad \text{LAL} = 60.46$$

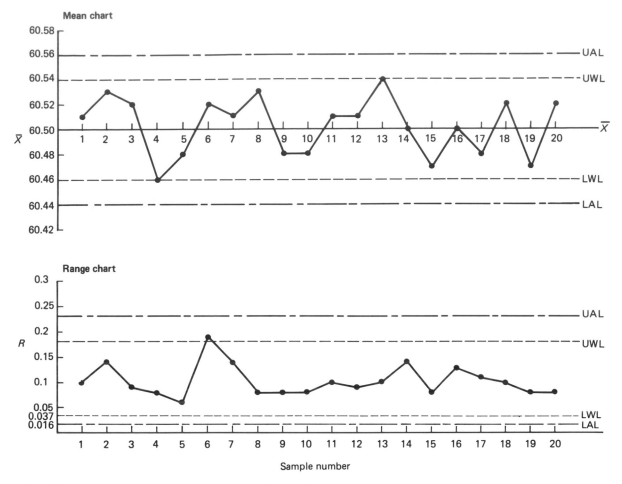

Fig. 19.9   Mean and range charts for steel sheets (Table 19.2, *n* = 5)

Figure 19.9 shows the mean values of the samples of five steel sheets, given in Table 19.2, plotted on a mean chart.

Range charts

A process is only in control when both the accuracy (mean) and precision (spread) are in control. A separate chart for control of process variability is required, and the sample standard deviation could be plotted. More conveniently, the ranges of samples are plotted on a range chart which is very similar to the mean chart, the difference between the highest and lowest values in the sample being plotted and compared with predetermined limits. The development of a more serious fault than incorrect setting can lead to the situation illustrated in Fig. 19.10, where the process collapses from form A to form B, for example due to failure of a part of the process. The ranges of the samples from B will have higher values than ranges in samples taken from A. If a range chart (Fig. 19.9) is plotted in conjunction with the mean chart, similar action and warning lines can be drawn to indicate trouble.

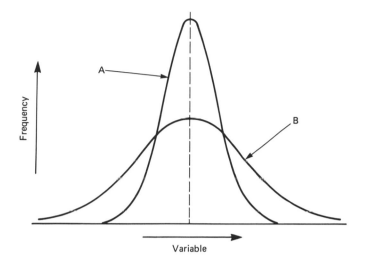

Fig. 19.10   Increase in spread of a process

The range control chart limits are asymmetrical about the mean range since the distribution of sample ranges is a positively skewed distribution. Table 19.5 provides four constants, $D'_{0.001}$, $D'_{0.025}$, $D'_{0.975}$ and $D'_{0.999}$, which may be used to calculate the control limits:

UAL at $D'_{0.001}$ $\bar{R}$,
UWL at $D'_{0.025}$ $\bar{R}$,
LWL at $D'_{0.975}$ $\bar{R}$,
LAL at $D'_{0.999}$ $\bar{R}$.

For the example data under consideration, the sample size is 5 and the constants are:

Action $D'_{0.001}$ = 2.34 $D'_{0.999}$= 0.16
Warning $D'_{0.025}$= 1.81 $D'_{0.975}$= 0.37

As the mean range, $\bar{R}$, is 0.19 mm, the control limits are:

$$
\begin{aligned}
\text{UAL} &= 2.34 \times 0.10 = 0.234\ \text{mm} \\
\text{UWL} &= 1.81 \times 0.10 = 0.181\ \text{mm} \\
\text{LWL} &= 0.37 \times 0.10 = 0.037\ \text{mm} \\
\text{LAL} &= 0.16 \times 0.10 = 0.016\ \text{mm}
\end{aligned}
$$

Stepwise procedure

The statistical concepts behind control charts for variables may seem a little complex, but the steps in setting up the charts for mean and range are very simple:

1.   Select 20 or so random samples of size n ($n \leqslant 12$).
2.   Measure the variable for each of the sample items.

Table 19.5 Constants used in the calculation of range chart control limits

Sample size (n)	Lower action $D'_{0.999}$	Lower warning $D'_{0.975}$	Upper warning $D'_{0.025}$	Upper action $D'_{0.001}$
2	0.00	0.04	2.81	4.12
3	0.04	0.18	2.17	2.98
4	0.10	0.29	1.93	2.57
5	0.16	0.37	1.81	2.34
6	0.21	0.42	1.72	2.21
7	0.25	0.46	1.66	2.11
8	0.29	0.50	1.62	2.04
9	0.32	0.52	1.58	1.99
10	0.35	0.54	1.56	1.93
11	0.38	0.56	0.53	1.91
12	0.40	0.58	1.51	1.87

3. Calculate each sample mean ($\bar{X}$) and range (R).
4. Calculate the grand or process mean, $\bar{\bar{X}}$, and the mean range, $\bar{R}$.
5. Look up the values of A_2, $2A_2/3$, $D'_{0.001}$, $D'_{0.025}$, $D'_{0.975}$, $D'_{0.999}$.
6. Calculate action and warning lines for the mean and range charts, following the simple formulae given above.

Process 'in control'

At the beginning of the section on setting up control charts for variables, it was stated that samples should be taken from the process when it is believed that the process is under control. Before the charts are used to control the process, the initial data are plotted on the mean and range charts to confirm that the distribution of the individual items was stable.

A process is 'in statistical control' when all the variations have been shown to arise from random or common causes and are non-attributable to assignable or special causes. The randomness of the variations may be shown by the plotted mean and range charts when there are:

(a) no mean or range values lying outside the action limits;
(b) no more than about 1 in 40 values lying between the warning and action limits;
(c) no incidences of two consecutive mean or range values lying in the same warning zone (chance of c. 1 in 1600);
(d) no runs of more than six sample means or ranges which lie either above or below the average control chart line;
(e) no trends of more than six values of mean or range which are continuously either rising or falling.

The initial example data under consideration, plotted on the mean and range charts in Fig. 19.9, clearly demonstrate that this process is in control, since all the above requirements are met. If the process examined in this way is not in statistical control, the assignable causes must be identified and eliminated. The process may then be re-examined to test for stability.

Having demonstrated that only random causes of variation are present, the next task is to compare the precision of the process with the required specification tolerances. Calculation of the process capability indices Cp and Cpk allows this to be done quickly and quantitatively. In the example, if the requirement was to produce a product within the range 60.20 (LSL) to 60.60 (USL), with the process standard deviation $\sigma = 0.043$ and process mean $\bar{\bar{X}} \times 60.50$:

$$Cp = \frac{USL - LSL}{6\sigma} = \frac{60.6 - 60.2}{6 \times 0.043} = 1.55$$

$$Cpk = \frac{USL - \bar{\bar{X}}}{3\sigma} = \frac{60.6 - 60.5}{3 \times 0.043} = 0.78$$

The Cp value of 1.55 indicates that the process spread is capable of producing an output within the specified tolerance, but the Cpk value (being greater than 1) suggests that the setting of the process is incorrect. In the case of sheets of steel, this will probably require only a simple adjustment to the process.

Controlling the process

When the process is shown to be in control, then the mean and range charts may be used to make decisions about the state of the process during production. For example, Fig. 19.11 shows mean and range charts for the next 23 samples taken from the steel sheet cutting process. The process is well under control, i.e. within the action lines, until sample 8, when the mean reaches the upper warning line – a repeat sample is required here. Sample 9 shows a mean plotted above the upper action line and corrective action must be taken. This action brings the process back into control but only until sample 11, where the sample mean is again in the warning zone – another sample should be taken immediately, rather than wait for the next sampling period. This sample (12) gives a mean above the action line: corrective action forthwith. But the action appears to be in the wrong direction, and the response results in over-correction with sample mean 14 well below the lower action line. The process continues to drift upwards out of control between samples 15 and 19, at which point the range goes out of control, indicating a serious malfunctioning of the process. The process clearly requires investigation to establish the assignable causes of change in the variability. This situation would not have been identified as quickly in the absence of the process control charts; this simple example illustrates the power of the charts in both quality control and in early warning of equipment trouble.

It will be noted that 'action' and 'repeat' samples have been marked on the control charts. In addition, any alterations in materials, the process, operators or any other technical changes should be recorded on the charts when they take place. This practice is extremely useful in helping to track down causes of shifts in mean or variability.

Comments about the implementation of SPC methods are given in Chapter 20.

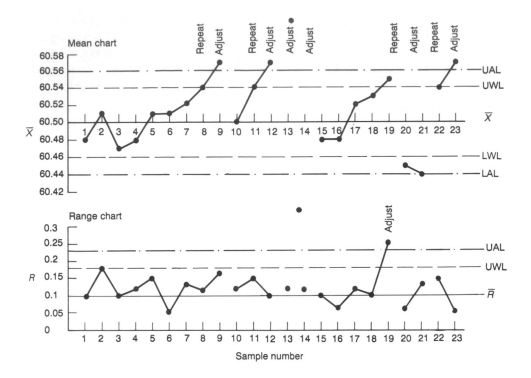

Fig. 19.11 Mean and ranges for next 23 samples of steel sheets ($n = 5$)

CHAPTER 19 – HIGHLIGHTS

- Inspection should not be a passive device to detect bad quality, but an active one to prevent non-conformance. Repetitive 100 per cent human inspection is time-consuming, costly, and ineffective in the control of quality.

- Data form the basis for decisions and actions, and a good recording system is essential. *Pareto analysis* then provides a useful method of narrowing down problems to target valuable resources.

- *Cause–effect diagrams may be used to present the results of brainstorming* of problems. These provide the information skeletons for quality improvement projects.

- Statistical process control (SPC) methods may be used to obtain knowledge of process capabilities and maintain control. SPC techniques examine the variation in the characteristics of articles, services and processes, using representative samples.

- Quality data arise from either counting or measurement. Data from the former occur in discrete jumps and are called *attributes*. Measurement on a continuous scale gives rise to *variable* data.

- There are basically two types of causes of variation – random and assignable causes. Each random, common or chance cause of variation is relatively slight and follows no particular pattern. Assignable or special causes of variation are larger in magnitude and are traceable to a specific event, person, machine, material, etc.

- When only random causes of variation are present, the process is said to be 'in control'. The presence of assignable causes results in the process being 'out of control'.

- A control chart is a form of traffic signal for a process. It helps the process 'operator' to distinguish between the presence of random and assignable causes of variation. Hence, the control chart can be a powerful diagnostic tool.

- There are different types of control chart for variable and attributes data.

- Using the normal distribution as an approximation, predictions can be made about the capability of a process to meet a set of specified requirements.

- A process whose average or mean (μ) is equal to the nominal or target value is said to be *accurate*. One which has a relatively small spread is *precise*. Spread is measured by the standard deviation (σ),

- Controlling a process to achieve the target value with little and reducing variation is the aim of never-ending improvement.

- The relationship between process variability and specified tolerances may be quantified using process capability indices, *Cp* and *Cpk*.

- Sample mean ($\bar{X}$) and range (R) charts may be used to monitor and control process accuracy and precision respectively. The charts carry action and warning limits.

- The stepwise procedure for using $\bar{X}$ and R charts to check the state of control and monitor the process is very simple to operate. There is a set of rules to help check that the process is initially in a state of control, and to make decisions as the process is run.

Recommended reading

British Standards Institution, *Quality Management Systems – Quality Control*, BSI Handbook 24, 1985

Contains eight standards related to quality control: BS2564 *Control Charts*; BS5309 *Sampling Chemicals*; BS5700 *Guide Process to Control*; BS5701 *Number Defective Charts*; BS 5703 *Cusum Techniques*; BS6000 and BS6001 *Acceptance Sampling for Attributes*; BS6002 *Acceptance Sampling for Variables*.

Caplan, R.H., *A Practical Approach to Quality Control*, 4th edn, Business Books, 1982

A very sound introduction to the subject.

Grant, E.L. and Leavenworth, R.S., *Statistical Quality Control*, 5th edn, McGraw-Hill, 1979

A very thorough discussion of the statistics of quality control.

Juran, J.M. (ed.), *Quality Control Handbook*, 3rd edn, McGraw-Hill, 1974

A comprehensive work which discusses quality control from particular industrial points of view. Probably on the shelves of most quality professionals.

Oakland, J.S. and Followell, R.F., *Statistical Process Control*, 2nd edn, Butterworth-Heinemann, 1990

One author has a biased view of this book. It attempts to provide a practical, non-mathematical guide to SPC, using real-life examples and data, drawn from a wide variety of industries, including the service sector. The other two authors have been convinced that it does!

Owen, M., *SPC and Continuous Improvements*, IFS Publications, 1989

This book covers the essential elements of SPC techniques in a practical way by making use of company experiences.

Price, F., *Right First Time*, Gower, 1984

A very readable book on SPC, aimed at senior managers as well as quality control specialists. It treats the subject in a novel way, but gets the message over very simply.

Wetherill, G.B., and Brown, D.W., *Statistical Process Control, Theory and Practice*, Chapman & Hall, 1991

This book provides a rather mathematical treatment of SPC – very useful to the SPC expert.

Chapter 20

Controlling Quality through Counting

Process control using attributes (counted data)

In the case of attributes, e.g. colour, general appearance, surface finish, absenteeism, when it is not possible to measure a product except in terms of 'good' or 'bad', present or absent, the control process is effectively that of determining which one out of two possible decisions is appropriate. When this two-way decision involves the classification of whole items or units as defective, the sampling process is governed by the laws of the *binomial distribution*.

If the proportion of the output which is not acceptable (the 'fraction defective') is p, and the 'fraction non-defective' is q (or $1-p$), clearly $p + q = 1$, and when a large number of samples, each of size n, is taken then the average number of defectives which will be found is np. If only one sample is taken, then the probability of finding $0, 1, 2, 3 \ldots$ defectives in any sample is given by the successive terms in the expansion of $(p + q)^n$, That is:

$$\text{Probability of 0 defectives} \ = \ p^0 q^n = q^n$$

$$\text{Probability of 1 defective} \ = \ np^1 q^{n-1}$$

$$\text{Probability of 2 defectives} \ = \ \frac{n(n-1)}{1 \times 2} p^2 q^{n-2}$$

$$\text{Generally, the probability of } x \text{ defectives} \ = \ \frac{n!}{x!\,(n-x)!} p^x q^{n-x}$$

$$= \ _nC_x p^x (1-p)^{n-x}$$

The average number of defectives obtained over a large number of samples is called the *expected number defective* and is given by:

Expected number defective $= np$

The standard deviation for the number of defectives in samples of size n, fraction defective p, fraction non-defective q, is:

$$\text{Standard deviation} = \sqrt{npq}$$

$$= \sqrt{\left[np\,(1-p) \right]}$$

Thus, if the fraction defective is 0.1 (that is, 10 in 100) and the sample size is 20, then the expected number defective will be:

$$20 \times 0.1 = 2$$

and the standard deviation will be:

$$\sqrt{(20 \times 0.1 \times 0.9)} = 1.34$$

The probability of a single sample containing:

0 defectives will be	$(0.9)^{20}$	= 0.122
1 defective	$20 \times (0.9)^{19} \times (0.1)$	= 0.270
2 defectives	$\dfrac{20 \times 19}{1 \times 2}(0.9)^{18} \times (0.1)^2$	= 0.285
3 defectives	$\dfrac{20 \times 19 \times 18}{1 \times 2 \times 3}(0.9)^{17} \times (0.1)^3$	= 0.190
4 defectives		= 0.090
5 defectives		= 0.032
6 defectives		= 0.009
7 defectives		= 0.002
8 defectives		= 0.001

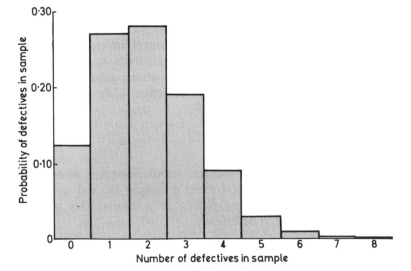

Fig. 20.1   Probabilities of a single sample containing a given number of defectives ($n = 20$, $p = 0.1$)

These probabilities, which have been represented graphically in Fig. 20.1, may also be found by reference to the many sets of statistical tables available.

If, from a population which previously had the above characteristics, i.e. $p = 0.1$, a sample of 20 items is taken and seven of these are found to be defective, then it can be said that the likelihood of this happening is so small (2 in 1,000) that it is extremely likely that the process producing the population has changed.

Number-defective (*np*) charts

The control chart for *number-defective* or *np* charts operates in a similar way to that for variables with warning and action lines. These lines are again set by reference to the average and standard deviation of the number of defectives in the samples, although in the case of the binomial distribution the $\pm 2\sigma$ and $\pm 3\sigma$ values do not present constant risk levels as in the control by variables case. However, to simplify matters, the action lines for the *np* chart may be calculated in the standard manner:

$$\text{Upper action line (UAL)} = np + 3\sqrt{[np(1 - p)]}$$
$$\text{Lower action line (LAL)} = np - 3\sqrt{[np(1 - p)]}$$

Similarly, the warning lines may be set at:

$$\text{Upper warning line (UWL)} = np + 2\sqrt{[np(1 - p)]}$$
$$\text{Lower warning line (LWL)} = np - 2\sqrt{[np(1 - p)]}$$

For the process producing 10 per cent defectives ($p = 0.1$), with a sample size $n = 20$:

Action lines $= (20 \times 0.1) \pm 3\sqrt{(20 \times 0.1 \times 0.9)}$
UAL $= 6.02$, i.e. just above 6   LAL $= -2.02$ (omit)
Warning lines $= (20 \times 0.1) \pm 2\sqrt{(20 \times 0.1 \times 0.9)}$
UWL $= 4.68$, i.e. between 4 and 5   LWL $= -0.68$ (omit)

A negative value for the lower lines indicates that they should be omitted and the finding of zero defectives in the sample is not an indication that the process has improved. For the upper control limits, although it is not possible to find fractions of defectives in attribute sampling, ambiguity is avoided by drawing the lines between whole numbers. Figure 20.2 shows a control chart for number defective (*np*) for the situation considered above, i.e. $n = 20$, $p = 0.1$.

Proportion defective (*p*) charts

In some situations it is not convenient to take samples of constant size and so the *proportion* of defectives in a sample is used as the quality indicator. In these

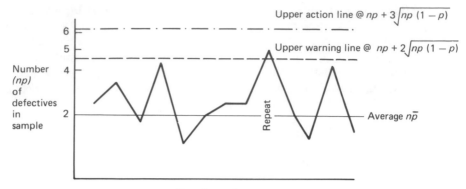

Fig. 20.2   An *np* chart for number defective in a sample of size *n* = 20, when proportion defective (*p*) = 0.1

proportion defective or *p* charts, the warning and action limits are calculated as follows:

Action lines at $\quad p \pm 3\sqrt{[p(1-p)/n]}$

Warning lines at $\quad p \pm 2\sqrt{[p(1-p)/n]}$

When samples of varying sizes are used to plot *p* charts, the control lines change and unique limits should be calculated for each sample size. For practical purposes, however, an average sample size (*n*) may be used in the calculations and the limits obtained are acceptable when individual sample sizes vary from *n* by no more than ±*n*/4. For sample sizes outside this range, separate control limits must be calculated.

Control charts for number of defects (*c*)

The control charts for attributes considered so far have applied to *whole defectives*. There are situations, however, where the number of defects or errors in the product or service is being counted. In these cases the binomial distribution does not apply because there are no values of *n* or *q* for the expression $(p + q)^n$. The *Poisson distribution* describes the results obtained from counting defects, and gives the following equation for finding the probability (*P*) of observing *x* defects in a unit:

$$P(x) = e^{-c}(c^{-x}/x!)$$

where   e=exponential constant, 2.7183;

$\qquad$ c=average number of defects per unit being produced by the process.

As with the binomial distribution, it is not necessary to calculate probabilities in this way, since statistical tables containing this information have been compiled.

The standard deviation of a Poisson distribution is very simply the square root of the process average:

$$\sigma = \sqrt{c}$$

and the action and warning lines for a c chart may be calculated in the usual simplified form:

Action lines at $c \pm 3\sqrt{c}$;
Warning lines at $c \pm 2\sqrt{c}$.

Lower action and warning lines on attribute charts

It is sometimes useful to insert lower warning and action limits on attribute charts. If points appear below the lower action limit, there is only a slight chance of this happening unless there has been a significant improvement in the process. In this case, it would be worthwhile investigating the cause of such a change, to discover how the improvement could be made permanent. The only other reason for a point plotting below the action limit would be inaccurate inspection or defectives being passed as good.

Cusum charts

The cusum (cumulative sum) chart is a graph which takes a little longer to draw than the conventional control chart, but which gives much more information. It is particularly useful for plotting the evolution of processes because it presents data in a way that enables the eye to separate true trends and changes from a background of random variation. Cusum charts can detect small changes in data very quickly and may be used for the control of variables and attributes. In essence, a reference or 'target value' is subtracted from each successive sample observation and the result accumulated. Values of this cumulative sum are plotted and 'trend lines' may be drawn on the resulting graphs. If a trend line is approximately horizontal, the value of the variable is about the same as the target value. An overall slope downwards shows a value less than the target, and if the slope is upwards it is greater.

Figure 20.3 shows a comparison of an *np* chart and a cusum chart which have been plotted using the same data – defectives in samples of 100 polyurethane foam products. The change, which is immediately obvious on the cusum chart, is difficult to detect on the conventional control chart.

Acceptance sampling

The techniques dealt with so far in this chapter and in Chapter 19 are directed towards process control activities. However, there may be a need in manufacturing

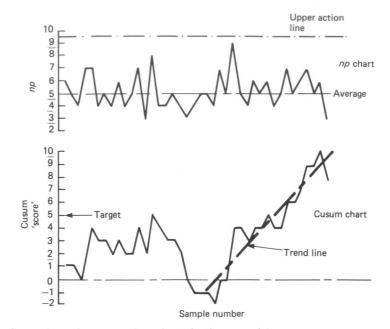

Fig. 20.3 Comparison of cusum and *np* charts for the same data

to carry out a further final check on a batch of finished products, before it reaches the consumer. Alternatively, material or services may be purchased without being able to ensure that the appropriate process control activities are taking place in the supply chain. In these situations, some form of inspection for acceptance or *product control* may be appropriate.

Such an inspection system should be concerned primarily with making sure that the product which passes the inspection point is of the appropriate quality. For this to be possible, it must be quite clear what is required. There are two aspects to a product specification with regard to inspection for acceptance, and there must be specific information on both of these if sensible decisions are to be made. The specification must contain a statement of what constitutes non-conformance. This is an extremely complex issue and demands careful thought before any inspection process gets under way. The various techniques of acceptance inspection will not resolve the problem of an ill-conceived definition of non-conformance. Nor can they cope with the absence of one. Unfortunately, the latter situation exists in far too many organizations, where high levels of expenditure on inspection or checking result in frustration and conflict. Sometimes, in cases of subjective assessment, it is necessary to provide samples of acceptable and unacceptable material to aid the decision process.

In addition to the requirement for a definition of non-conformance, there is a need to stipulate, quite categorically, the quantity or proportion which is allowed if a batch of product is to be considered satisfactory. This is known as the *acceptable quality level* (AQL); it may depend very much on the end use of the product or service and often leads to the classification of defects. For example, it may be considered that there are critical, major and minor defects which demand different quantification if customer satisfaction is to be ensured. In the production of aircraft there are obviously different requirements from those found in the manufacture of cast-iron manhole covers. Similarly, in the assembly of a piece of furniture, one fault, such as a deep scratch on a polished surface, may cause great distress, whereas other, slight, imperfections will pass unnoticed by many purchasers. These factors must be considered in the design of the inspection system. Sometimes it is necessary to design different schemes for different fault classifications to operate in parallel.

One hundred per cent inspection is a time-consuming, costly and unreliable method of product control. There are, of course, some situations in which this method is deemed to be an essential part of product control: the aerospace industry relies very heavily on this approach. Wherever it can, the system should move away from human inspection towards automated methods. This is not always possible or economical and some form of human involvement will always be required. In these cases, and where life-or-death consequences prevail, the only answer is to perform 100 per cent human inspection several times.

Acceptance sampling procedures, if they are applied correctly, will allow the quantification and limitation of risks of making incorrect decisions. In many cases, a properly designed and effectively administered sampling scheme is the most economical and practical way of making acceptance decisions. In cases of destructive testing, some form of sampling is the only acceptable alternative.

In deciding which type of scheme to use, it is first necessary to examine the nature of the quality characteristics which will be employed in the inspection process. Will the product quality be presented in the form of attribute data or variables? There are methods of acceptance sampling for both. Where only attribute data are available there is no choice, but when variables can be measured, two general approaches may be employed: either use acceptance sampling by variables, or convert the variable data into attribute form and use acceptance sampling by attributes. The advantages associated with using variables are similar to those found in process control: increased sensitivity and smaller sample sizes. The disadvantages concern the extra costs of obtaining the measured data and performing the necessary calculations; in some situations these may be considerable. The principles of acceptance sampling will be explained here with attributes, since these are the most frequently used plans. The methods used for variable data are generally very similar and the reader is referred to 'Further reading' at the end of this chapter for the details of acceptance sampling for variables.

Acceptance sampling techniques are used to decide whether to accept or reject a batch of items based on random sample(s). If a decision is taken to accept, then the remainder of the batch is accepted without further inspection. It must be clear that such a procedure gives no guarantee of the actual quality of the batch; it simply provides a decision-making process.

If a decision to reject the batch is taken, the remainder may be sentenced in several possible ways, depending upon the use of the product and any associated technological or economic factors. A rejected batch may be destined for:

(a) 100 per cent screening to rectify or replace all defectives;
(b) further inspection;
(c) use for lower-quality requirements;
(d) return to supplier;
(e) acceptance at discounted price; etc.

Operating characteristics

A characteristic of the mechanism of all sampling plans is that they are associated with risks. There are basically two types of risk derived from the sample or samples not being representative of the whole consignment, batch or production run. There is a risk that a decision may be taken to reject a batch which should have been accepted, i.e. of acceptable quality. This is referred to by statisticians as a *type I error*. Another term, which is more meaningful perhaps, is *producer's risk*. The *type II error* or *consumer's risk* is associated with the acceptance of goods the quality of which is unacceptable.

The efficiency of any sampling plan as a detector of acceptable and unacceptable batches is shown by means of its *operating characteristics* (OC) *curve*. This curve, which should be known for every sampling plan used, is derived by plotting:

The chance (or probability)   versus   The quality offered for
of a batch being accepted   inspection (usually measured
                                            in percentage defective)

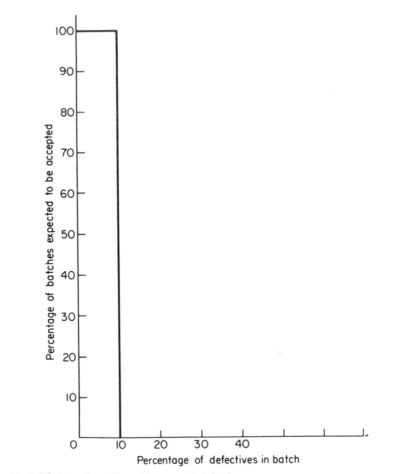

Fig. 20.4   Ideal OC curve for AQL = 10 per cent defectives

Single sampling plans

The simplest type of acceptance sampling scheme is one where a single sample (size *n*) is taken from the batch (size *N*) and the whole batch is accepted if the number of defectives found in the sample is equal to, or less than, the acceptance number (*c*). Ideally, the scheme should operate so that *all* batches which have an actual percentage of non-conformance equal to or less than the AQL are accepted on the basis of the single sample, and *all* batches which have an actual percentage greater than the AQL are rejected by the sample. The OC curve of this 'ideal' plan is shown in Fig. 20.4.

In practice, no scheme will offer this perfect discrimination. The OC of most sampling plans follows the curved lines of Fig. 20.5, which shows the consumer's risk at the *lot tolerance percentage defective* (LTPD) – the percentage of defectives which is unacceptable to the recipient.

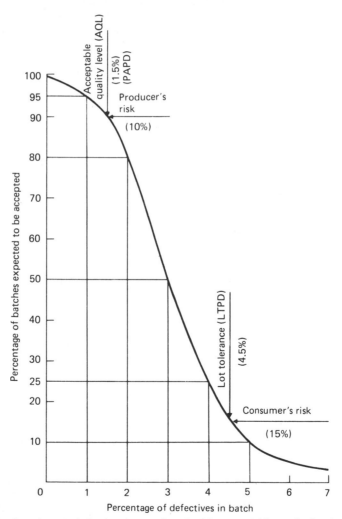

Fig. 20.5 Operating characteristic showing producer's risk, acceptable quality level, consumer's risk and lot tolerance

At a different point on the curve is the producer's risk. This coincides with the *process average percentage defective* (PAPD) – the average percentage of defectives being produced by the process when it is considered to be running at a level which is acceptable. This usually coincides with the AQL, the maximum percentage defective that can be considered to be acceptable by the consumer.

It is useful to consider, in general terms, the effect of the sample size (n) and acceptance number (c) on the discriminatory power of sampling plans. The two parameters n and c may be varied independently. If this is done, the following will be observed:

n The OC curve of a single sample plan becomes more rectangular, that is more discriminatory, as the sample size increases. This is shown very well in the comparison of the two schemes in Fig. 20.6. The ratio of n to c is the same in each case, but the higher sample size gives much better discrimination between good and bad batches. There is an inspection cost penalty for this, of course.

c Lowering the acceptance number lowers the OC curve. Figure 20.7 shows this in the curves for single plans of common sample size with varying c. The scheme with zero acceptance has no inflection in the operating characteristic – the curve is completely concave. This is a feature of all schemes with $c = 0$. What this means, of course, is that $c = 0$ schemes are very poor discriminators. In some organizations, however, it is believed that a plan which rejects batches when a single defect is found is a strong plan. It is evident, from the OC curves, that such schemes will not guarantee defective-free batches, although many bad lots will be rejected. More importantly, many good lots with low defective rates, which are considered to be economically acceptable, will also be rejected. If these are then subjected to 100 per cent screening, then the total inspection costs will increase too.

Operation of acceptance sampling plans

It must be fully understood by all who operate acceptance sampling schemes that the individual samples do not give any information about the quality of the remainder of the batch; they simply offer a decision rule – accept or reject (or submit to 100 per

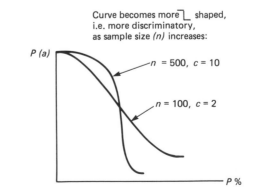

Fig. 20.6 Variation in OC curves with n

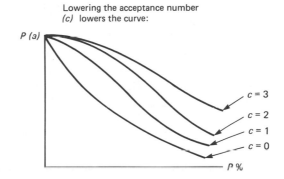

Fig. 20.7   Variation in OC curves with c

cent screening and rectification). It is quite clear, however, that in the operation of a scheme on a series of batches, over a period of time substantial amounts of data will be accumulated. Following the methods introduced earlier in this chapter, these data should be recorded in a systematic way so that additional use may be made of them. It should not go unnoticed, for example, that the proportion of batches being sentenced to 100 per cent screening or returned to a supplier has increased from 5 to 10 per cent. Indeed, when such an increase in rejection rate does occur, the OC curve should be consulted for an indication of the quality level of the input to the scheme, and all batches which have been accepted recently should be quarantined until further investigations take place. A most useful practice is to record the numbers of defectives found in each sample, together with the accept/reject decision. If these data are used to plot a number of defectives (np) chart, or a cusum chart, trends or sustained changes in the proportion of defectives present will be detected.

In addition to the single sampling scheme for attributes discussed above, there are in common use double, multiple and sequential schemes and acceptance sampling plans for variables. Standard tables, containing plotted OC curves, are available for assisting in the choice of appropriate sampling schemes for attributes and variables. In the UK, these are British Standards BS6000, BS6001 and BS6002, which have their equivalents throughout Europe, USA and the rest of the world.

SPC and the quality system

For successful SPC there must be an uncompromising commitment to quality, which must start with the most senior management and flow down through the organization. It is essential to set down a *quality policy* for implementation through a *documented management system*. Careful consideration must be given to this system as it forms the backbone of the quality skeleton. The objective of the system is to cause improvement of products and services through reduction of variation in the processes. The focus of the whole workforce from top to bottom should be on the processes, not the outputs. This approach makes it possible to control variation and, more importantly, to prevent non-conforming products and services, whilst steadily tightening standards.

The impact of a good quality management system, such as one which meets the requirements of the international standard ISO 9000 series (see Chapter 8) is that of gradually reducing process variability to achieve continuous or never-ending improvement. The requirement to set down defined procedures for all aspects of an organization's operations, and to stick to them, will reduce the variations introduced by the numerous different ways often employed for doing things. Go into any factory without a good quality system and ask to see the operators' 'black book' of plant operation and settings. Of course, each shift has a different black-book, each with slightly different settings and ways of operating the process. Is it any different in office work or for salespeople in the field? Do not be fooled by the perceived simplicity of a process into believing that there is only one way of operating it. There is an infinite variety of ways of carrying out the simplest of tasks: the authors recall seeing various course participants finding 14 different methods for converting A4 size paper into A5 size (half A4) in a simulation of a production task. The ingenuity of human beings needs to be controlled if these causes of variation are not to multiply together to render processes completely incapable of consistency or repeatability.

The role of the quality system, then, is to define and control process procedures and methods. Continual system audit and review will ensure that procedures are either followed or corrected, thus eliminating assignable or special causes of variation in materials, methods, equipment, information, etc., to ensure a 'could we do this job with more consistency?' approach (Fig. 20.8)

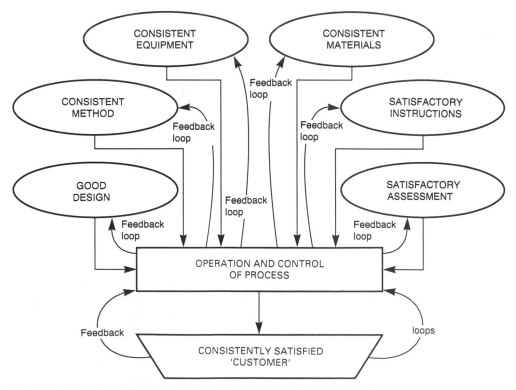

Fig. 20.8   The systematic approach to quality management

For measurements to be used for quality improvement, they must be accepted by the people involved with the process being measured. The simple self-measurement and plotting, or the 'how-am-I-doing?' chart, will gain far more ground in this respect than a policing type of observation and reporting system which is imposed on the process and those who operate it. Similarly, results should not be used to illustrate how bad one operator or group is, unless their performance is 100 per cent under their own control. The emphasis in measuring and displaying data must always be on the assistance that can be given to correct a problem or remove obstacles preventing the process from meeting its requirements first time, every time.

The implementation of SPC

One of the first steps in any implementation programme must be the provision of education and training for:

Managers,
Supervisors,
Operators and
Staff.

The courses, teaching methods, and materials used for this purpose must be very carefully selected, for much harm can be done by the insensitive teaching of 'statistics', which many people find indigestible. It is possible to learn and apply excellent methods of process control without becoming immersed in heavy theoretical studies.

For the successful introduction of SPC, the training must have follow-up, which can take many forms. Ideally, an in-house expert can provide the lead through the design of implementation programmes. The most satisfactory strategy is to start small and learn through a bank of knowledge and experience. Techniques should be introduced alongside existing methods of quality control (if they do exist), which allows comparisons to be made between the new and old methods. When confidence has been built upon the results of the comparisons, the statistical techniques can take over the control of the process. Improvements in one or two areas of the organization's operations, using this approach, will quickly establish SPC as a reliable tool for control of all processes.

Sometimes it is necessary to obtain help from outside sources – the prophet is rarely accepted in his own land – and many organizations can offer valuable assistance. Ideally, the people providing the initial training should also be involved in the follow-up activities, which should include 'workshop days' when specific process control and implementation problems are discussed.

The emphasis which must be placed on never-ending improvement has important implications for the way in which process control charts are applied. They should not be used purely for control, but as an aid in the reduction of variability by those at the point of operation capable of observing and removing assignable causes of variation. They can be used effectively in the identification and gradual elimination of random causes of variation. In this way the process of continuous improvement may be charted, and adjustments made to the control charts in use to reflect the improvements. This is described in detail in *Statistical Process Control*, 2nd edn by John Oakland and Roy Followell (Butterworth-Heinemann, Oxford, 1990).

Often in process control situations, action signals are given when the assignable cause results in a desirable event, such as the reduction of an impurity level, a decrease in error rate, or an increase in order intake. Clearly, assignable or special causes which result in deterioration of the process must be investigated and eliminated, but those that result in improvements must also be sought out and managed so that they become part of the process operation. Significant variation between batches of material, or between operators, or differences between suppliers, are frequent causes of action signals on control charts. The continuous improvement philosophy demands that these are all investigated and the results used to take another step on the long ladder to perfection. Action signals and assignable or special causes of variation should stimulate enthusiasm for solving a problem or understanding an improvement, rather than gloom and despondency.

The costs of introducing good methods of process control will be grossly outweighed by the savings which accrue. The inevitable reduction in waste, re-work and rectification costs, together with the increases in resource utilization and capacity, will directly repay the investment. The increased confidence and efficiency that derive from greater process knowledge will permeate the whole organization from design, office and purchasing staff through to sales and marketing. Moreover, the introduction of good process control methods will act as a 'spearhead' to draw through the organization many of the requirements for total quality management.

CHAPTER 20 – HIGHLIGHTS

- Process control using counted or attribute data often involves the classification of whole items or units as defective. These are governed by the laws of the binomial distribution.

- The control chart for number defective (np) operates in a similar way to $\overline{X}$ and R charts. It carries action and warning limits.

- Other control charts for attribute data include proportion defective (p charts) and number of defects (c charts). Defects follow the Poisson distribution.

- Cumulative sum (cusum) charts are useful for detecting slight changes and trends.

- Acceptance sampling may be used for product control to decide whether to accept or reject a batch of items, based on random sample(s). Such schemes require a statement of what constitutes non-conformance, and the proportion of non-conformance allowed. The latter is known as the acceptable quality level (AQL).

- Defects and defectives may be classified as critical, major and minor.

- Using acceptance samples gives rise to risks.

- Acceptance sampling allows the quantification and limitation of risks of making incorrect decisions from inspection data. Choice of schemes is determined by the type of product quality characterization presented.

- The risk of rejecting a 'good' batch is called a *type I error*, or the *producer's risk*. The *type II error* or *consumer's risk* is associated with the acceptance of 'bad' batches, The efficiency of any scheme, in terms of these risks, is shown by means of its *operating characteristic* (OC) curve.

- The process average percentage defective (PAPD) usually coincides with the AQL. The lot tolerance percentage defective (LTPD) is the level which is unacceptable to the recipient.

- Single sampling plans are the simplest schemes. A sample of n items is taken from a batch of size N, which is accepted if less than or equal to the acceptance number c of defectives are found.

- Acceptance sampling plans simply offer a decision rule – accept or reject the batch. Data from the operation of such schemes should be accumulated and used to improve the process.

- For effective SPC implementation, there must be a quality policy and a documented quality system. The impact of the latter is the gradual reduction of variation, through the definition, documentation, and control of processes.

- The implementation of SPC requires good training and follow-up. Sometimes outside help is required. Control charts if used correctly lead to never-ending improvement throughout an organization.

Recommended reading

See Recommended reading for Chapter 19.

SECTION 5

The Programmes or Resource Plans

All organizations must produce plans by which the operations are to be 'managed'. This section focuses on various aspects of this planning process. It covers aspects which could be considered to be an integral part of resource management, for example inventory management; special techniques appropriate in certain situations like linear programming; through to what might be thought of as support technologies, for example forecasting.

Chapter 21

Operations Control:
An Introduction

The nature of production/operations control

Every organization produces – or should produce – a 'hierarchy' of plans to enable it to fulfil its corporate purpose. These plans differ from each other in the level of detail at which they operate, and detail is in itself a reflection of the time-span covered by the plan. The largest time-span is exhibited by the overall company policy as determined by the board of directors. Consistent with this, but spanning a shorter period of time, is the marketing forecast which identifies and quantifies the products or services to be provided over the foreseeable future. It is important that these forecasts can be expressed in a form that reflects the resources required (for a building society, this forecast might be to handle 100,000 home loans) rather than in financial terms (to lend £2,500 million). The group within the organization whose responsibility includes examining the resource implications of this forecast is normally called the production control or operations control department (POCD). From the forecast, this department prepares a production plan or schedule which in turn generates a workload which is finally translated into action by first line management (see Fig. 21.1). It should be noted that the preparation of a set of plans is an iterative process since it may well be found that an inability to achieve a plan at one level may cause a change in the plans at higher levels. Equally, plans must 'interlock' and be acceptable

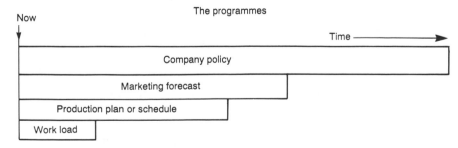

Fig. 21.1   Hierarchy of plans

to and agreed with all concerned. Thus a sales forecast must agree with the board's objectives and be compatible with the production/operations department's abilities.

The POCD is thus one of the planning departments within an organization and, indeed, some writers include planning in its title. In the present text, however, production/operations planning will be reserved for that function which concerns itself with the determination of the method or procedures to be followed, and the production/operations control will be understood to comprise *all* the control functions, namely:

1. Plan.
2. Publish.
3. Measure.
4. Compare.
5. Report.
6. Correct.

In essence, the POCD should be able at *all times* to answer two basic and apparently simple questions:

1. Can a particular set of tasks be undertaken and, if so, when?
2. How far have the tasks in hand proceeded?

In trying to provide these answers, POCD must attempt to organize the most effective use of human resources, materials and equipment. A major responsibility of the POCD is likely to include the generation of written instructions, and as a result it is often considered to be the paperwork-producing department. This is particularly true for manufacturing organizations. It is frequently perceived as being a low-level clerical responsibility, indeed one that can be largely handled by a computer. As such it is much maligned and its duties misunderstood. This misunderstanding is as frequently found at high as at low levels, with the result that appropriate staff status and facilities are not provided, duties consequently being ill-performed.

The qualities required of those responsible for production/operations control are no less exacting than those required of, for example, a cost accountant or chief designer, yet it is often found that the staff employed is this area are not adequately trained or experienced to carry out the duties satisfactorily. Working in this area needs a clear brain, capable of dealing with a large number of problems simultaneously, a thorough knowledge of processes, procedures and efficient office organization techniques, an appreciation of the importance of controlling costs, an awareness of the scope and limitations of using computers, and an understanding of mathematical methods and – more important – mathematical reasoning. Moreover, communications skills are also important since decisions in a number of other areas – for example, marketing and purchasing – can have a significant effect on the POCD. In addition, decisions made by the POCD can also influence these in other areas. The person responsible must be able to manage these interfaces effectively.

Many of the weaknesses of organizations – for example, excessive material stocks, failure to achieve processing targets, idle time – can be directly attributable to inferior or non-existent production/operations control, whilst really effective production/operations control can achieve increases in output and efficiency far more spectacular and at a far lower cost than any other management technique. Furthermore, no other activity can show effective results in the absence of good production/operations control. Every work study practitioner or O & M officer must, at some time, have suffered the bitter disappointment of seeing his improved procedures made ineffectual by the absence of material due to poor production/operations control. In any plan for improving efficiency or reducing losses throughout an enterprise, the organization of a really efficient POCD must come very high in priority: certainly no incentive scheme will work without an effective POCD.

The marketing interface

Broadly, there are two possible ways by which a company can derive its income:

(a) by *receiving* orders from customers, and subsequently completing work to fulfil these orders:
(b) by *obtaining* orders from customers, these orders being filled from work completed *before* their receipt.

Thus a restaurant may prepare each meal to each customer's specific requirements. Alternatively, the meal may be ready prepared and cooked, and kept hot prior to a customer's arrival (the principle behind 'fast food'). Some operations are such that the second option is not feasible. For example, a management consultancy cannot generally provide its service by work generated before receipt of the request for assistance: that is, 'storage' of the service is not possible.

Much of the task of production/operations control is concerned with *future* action and, therefore, the more accurately the future can be predicted, the better the chance of making effective plans. An order-receiving policy will inevitably produce greater uncertainty than an order-obtaining policy, which will carry with it greater risk. The marketing department will need to forecast future requirements, and bear responsibility for overprovision if the forecasts are incorrect.

The decision to change from 'order receiving' to 'order obtaining' is an extremely important one, whose effects, whilst felt throughout the organization, are of paramount concern to the department responsible for providing the product or service and to POCD. The value of good market research and sales promotion must not be under-estimated, and failure to align marketing with provision will result, at best, in chaos, and at worst, in failure.

Some of the functions of the POCD are more appropriate in a manufacturing context. In the remainder of this chapter it will be assumed that this type of environment will be considered, although an attempt will be made to indicate the relevance of these concepts where appropriate in non-manufacturing situations.

The functions of production/operations control

Scheduling resources

At the time of issuing a marketing forecast (in the case of making for stock), or at the time of acknowledging the receipt of an order (in the case of making to customer's order), marketing will issue an instruction which will authorize the manufacture of a product or group of products. This order is the starting point for all POCD activities concerned with actual manufacture, although POCD should already have assisted marketing in fixing the delivery date shown on the works order.

From the works order a production plan (or programme) is prepared, which involved assessing labour, equipment and material requirements and availability, and thence laying down the dates by which major functions must be complete. This production plan will be issued to the resources control section, wherein the availability of both human resources and equipment is verified, detailed programmes are prepared and the various departments have work allocated to them in as much detail as is useful. At the same time, a copy of the production plan will be passed to the *material control* section, which will check material availability, putting in train whatever action is necessary. The production plan will need to be revised whenever any change in any conditions (demand, materials, facilities etc.) takes place.

Material control

Material control is the reverse of the coin of which facilities control is the obverse. Since the number of items of information is so very much greater in the case of material than in that of labour and equipment, the same techniques are not necessarily appropriate. In general, the task of the material controller can be said to be that of assessing the need for material, and then taking appropriate action to see that this need is met. This subject is discussed in Chapter 26.

The consequences of unavailable materials can be extremely costly. Consider the Building Society about to increase its interest rates. A formal notice has to be sent to each borrower, but a shortage of envelopes (the requirement for which might be hundreds of thousands) can delay the issue of this notice and result in consequential loss of interest due to the society.

Despatch and progress

At the appropriate time, manufacture is actually initiated by the *despatch* section, which collects together all relevant documents, verifies the detailed availability of labour, materials, tools, equipment and production aids, and issues authorizing documents. Throughout the whole of this time, and during the subsequent manufacture, the *progress* section will observe performance, verifying that the requirements of the production plan are being fulfilled. Any deviations from this schedule are brought to the notice of the appropriate manager and any necessary modification to schedule made in order to overcome the results of these deviations. Should the final delivery date appear to be endangered, it is unquestionably the responsibility of the production/operations control department to inform the sales department in order that, if deemed desirable, the customer can be advised.

Avoidance of this simple courtesy will inevitably lead to a severe deterioration in customer relations, which in turn will eventually be reflected in the intake of orders. It will also result in a deterioration in relationships between the marketing and production/operations groups, which in the extreme can threaten the very existence of

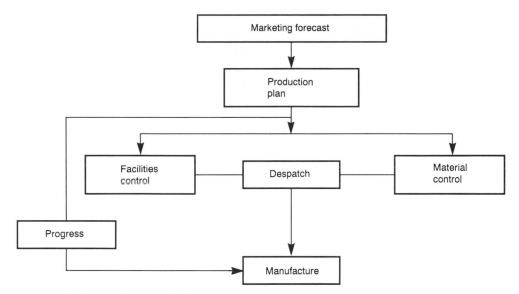

Fig. 21.2   Outline of the production/operations control department

the enterprise. A delivery date should be considered sacrosanct and every endeavour made to maintain it, but if it proves quite impossible so to do, the customer should be informed, and this information can only originate from the production/operations control department. The despatch and progress tasks are discussed further in Chapter 25.

In non-manufacturing or service operations a similar role to that of despatch exists: the receptionist or 'despatcher'. The responsibilities of this individual involve assessing customer needs and priorities and allocating resources as appropriate. As examples, consider the receptionist at a GP's surgery or the 'despatcher' at a fire station. This idea has been further developed by Voss et al. in *Operations Management in Service Industries and the Public Sector* (Wiley, 1985). The total picture is shown in Fig. 21.2.

Parameters affecting the production/operations control function

The organization and flow of work

The way in which the conversion process is organized, the technological methods used, the location of equipment and the degree of specialization of the direct workforce, will affect the production/operations control function. Broadly, the smaller the organization, both in physical and organizational size, and the greater the flexibility of the workforce, the easier will be the task of the production/operations controller.

Indeed, if batch methods are being used, scheduling work will be an on-going activity, possibly consuming significant resources, with raw-material control involving forecasting usage through an examination of requirements for finished production. Contrast this with the situation where flow production methods are being used, when scheduling will be largely 'pre-production' in setting up and balancing the line, and materials control is largely a matter of establishing that materials are available when required and to specification, being fed into the system at a regular rate.

Information and information flow

Production/operations control can only act upon the information that it receives. Regrettably, much of the information is weak:

(a)   standard processing or transaction or service times,
(b)   quantities of materials in store,
(c)   demand from customers, timing and quantities of customers' requirements,
(d)   availability of material from outside suppliers,
(e)   amount of work already completed, and
(f)   capacities of facilities

are all liable to be highly inaccurate. There is a considerable reluctance on the part of most members of an organization to pass over information concerning their own activities. This arises frequently because it is assumed that information is required for a punitive purpose – to form a 'do-it-yourself hangman's kit'. Management must make clear to all concerned that a free flow of information is in the best interests of everybody within the organization.

Short-term planning systems

The heart of the production/operations control functions is the short-term planning or scheduling function, which in essence establishes priorities with respect to some criterion measuring performance (for example, meeting customers' processing targets, achieving high labour/equipment utilization) for activities competing for limited resources (workers/equipment) over the near future (one week to one month). This is a difficult task to carry out and, sometimes with unfortunate consequences, can become a rich field for the mathematically inclined to plough. In the final analysis, the operation of any scheduling system will depend upon the ability of the workforce, administrators and first line supervisors to understand what is required by the system itself.

   Intelligibility, therefore, must be a prime concern: indeed, it is often better to sacrifice 'performance' in order to be able to produce a schedule which is understandable. It is also inevitable that priorities will change, and the scheduling method must be capable of accommodating change extremely rapidly.

The requirements of the conversion process

Since the production/operations controller is effectively planning a timetable for the movement of a task through a number of processes or procedures, the requirements of the task in relation to the conversion process must be well understood. Usually there will be several alternative ways in which a task can be carried out and it is frequently better to standardize on one particular method, for a substantial number of different tasks, than to try to obtain the 'best' from each process. One particularly difficult task to organize is that which prevents material flow taking place in one direction, for example where material leaves a work-station to return to the same work-station after other operations have been carried out, or indeed when a document returns to a section for further information to be added. Those responsible for setting methods and procedures should try to avoid this 'backpassing', or 'backtracking', and indeed should always consider the effects on production/operations control of their processing requirements. Any apparent loss in 'technological' efficiency may well be more than compensated for by the simplification of the production control task.

Stability of priorities

Every timetable or schedule is fundamentally a statement of priorities, and the more frequently priorities are changed, the more frequently will the timetabling need to be changed, it is a common experience for the 'Friday progress meeting'(!) to destroy all the priorities set at a previous meeting, and substitute new ones. This represents an impossible situation for the production/operations controller, who is left in the position of trying to run faster and faster in order to stay in the same position. Clearly, no priority statement can be considered as unchangeable: as circumstances change, so most priorities follow them. However, the common separation between the marketing function and the production/operations function can lead to priorities being set which are themselves unachievable, and a cynical definition of production/operations control is 'the art of trying to reconcile impossible requests with inadequate resources'. Whilst the production/operations department have the responsibility of trying to fulfil the needs of the market, so the marketing department have the responsibility of trying to produce robust forecasts for the production/operations people to act upon.

The myth of plant utilization

One of the most easily observed features of an operations unit is the presence of idle equipment and, under pressure from senior management, great efforts are often made to 'keep the machines/equipment working'. The effects of a 'utilization at any price' policy can be disastrous since excessive material and work-in-progress will result. A much more rational criterion is that of velocity of material flow – the more quickly material can be transformed into finished goods, the more rapidly can the initial investment be recovered. A healthy cash flow is an essential prerequisite for a healthy organization.

Parameters affecting production/operations control

1. Organization and flow of work.
2. Information and information flow.
3. Short-term planning system.
4. Requirements of the conversion process.
5. Stability of priorities.
6. The myth of plant utilization.

Production/operations control and the computer

The computer is able to store enormous quantities of information and carry out calculations very rapidly, in so-called 'real time', i.e. within such a time that information and analyses are available early enough to permit useful action to be taken. Furthermore, the computer will tirelessly repeat calculations for as long as it is required to do so: it will not, if properly instructed, generate mistakes either through fatigue or personal inaccuracy. These characteristics are clearly most valuable to the production/operations control function. Mini- and micro-computers make *real-time* access to programs and files a reality, and this speed, combined with distributed terminals, is transforming production/operations control in those environments where robust databases exist.

The application of the computer to the production/operations control function offers a significant challenge to the computer systems designer and analyst. This covers the data-processing aspects where, for example, it can be necessary to store and retrieve efficiently enormous quantities of information relating to the manufacturing methods for many hundreds or even thousands of tasks, each consisting of numerous operations on a variety of work centres with various machines. The analyst is faced with storing this information efficiently and in such a way that it can be retrieved and analysed in a number of different ways: the machines which are required by a certain task, the tasks which require certain materials, and so on. At the same time, the analyst can exploit the computer's arithmetic capability in such areas, assessing the requirements for common raw materials or components across a variety of tasks, all to be completed at different times, or evaluating the implications of processing a set of tasks in different orders of priority.

Computer manufacturers and computer software consultants have risen to this challenge and produced a wide variety of systems which cover all the functions (and more!) outlined earlier. These tend to be presented in a modular form so that a user (with the consultant's guidance) can build up a system which closely matches requirements. Alternatively (and normally at a significantly higher cost), it is possible to develop (or have developed) a system which perfectly matches requirements. There is the analogous comparison between the off-the-peg and bespoke suit. With bespoke, the system should be more flexible in that it should meet requirements exactly, involve less change to existing procedures, and be more capable of interfacing with computer applications in other functional areas.

Comparison between off-the-peg and bespoke software

1. Off-the-peg software:
   (a) speed of development and implementation;
   (b) cost;
   (c) preview before purchase.
2. Bespoke software:
   (a) flexibility;
   (b) less change required to procedures;
   (c) easier to interface and modify.

Detailed discussions of the role of the computer in the different functional areas of production/operations control will be deferred until the subsequent chapters in which those areas are covered.

CHAPTER 21 – HIGHLIGHTS

- Organizations produce hierarchies of plans at a variety of levels of detail: company policy; marketing forecast; production plan or schedule; workload.
- The Productions/Operations Control Department (POCD) is involved in the preparation of the production plan.
- The POCD must provide for the most effective use of human resources, materials and equipment.
- A company can operate on the basis of receiving orders or obtaining orders, and this choice can have a significant effect on POCD.
- The principal functions of the POCD include scheduling resources, materials control, and despatch and progress.
- The following factors affect POCD operations: organization and flow of work; information and information flow; the short-term planning system; the requirements of the conversion process; the stability of priorities; the myth of plant utilization.
- A computer contributes data-processing capability and arithmetic ability to the function.
- Its programs can be bespoke or off-the-shelf.

Recommended reading

Bertrand, J.W.M., Wortmann, J.C., Wijngaard, J., *Production Control: A Structural and Design Oriented Approach*, Elsevier, 1990

A comprehensive overview of the elements of good production control structure for the serious student, complemented by four case studies.

British Standards Institution, *Glossary of Production Planning and Control Terms* (BS5191), 1975

Defines some 150 terms commonly used in production control, as well as some terms concerning quality and costing. The section titles give an indication of the scope of the glossary: basic production characteristics; process and resource characteristics; production planning terms; load/capacity planning; stock planning; scheduling; general durations; operations durations; production control documentation; quality control terms; cost control terms. Invaluable in sorting out semantic difficulties and resolving arguments between colleagues.

Burbidge, J.L., *Production Planning*, Heinemann, 1971

An invaluable book written by a manager turned teacher. He keeps his feet well on the ground, and uses diagrams and descriptions rather than hiding behind mathematical analyses.

Corke, D.K., *Production Control in Engineering*, Edward Arnold, 1977

A useful, practical book written by a management consultant.

Fogarty, D., Blackstone, J. and Hoffmann, T., *Production and Inventory Management*, 2nd edn, Chapman & Hall, 1990

Designed to bridge the academic and professional worlds.

Silver, E.A. and Peterson, R., *Decision Systems for Inventory Management and Production Planning*, 2nd edn, Wiley, 1991

Presents a detailed discussion, of the major decisions in production planning, scheduling and inventory management facing organizations.

Tooley, D.F., *Production Control Systems and Records*, Gower, 1985

The contents of this text complement much of the material in this chapter.

Chapter 22

Forecasting

The importance of forecasting in production/operations control

Forecasting is clearly not one of the mainstream activities within the production/operations control function. Nevertheless there are a number of aspects of this function which rely on forecasts of one sort or another if they are to be carried out effectively. Most fundamental is the likely future demand for the products or services being provided by the enterprise. In addition, there are a number of other factors related directly to the management of the conversion process. These include being able to predict the requirements for materials of all types, the times to allow for procurement of these, likelihood and durations of equipment breakdown, absenteeism rates of workers, scrap or error rates, and so on. An ability to quantify these factors will clearly improve the quality of the decision making in the production/operations control area. This quantification can be based on 'guestimates' – think of a likely figure, and double it as a margin for error – or it can be soundly based, taking into account all available information and historical data. The purpose of this chapter is to introduce briefly some of the more basic methods of forecasting based on historical data.

The marketing interface

The basic input into the production/operations control function is the forecast by the marketing group of the requirements for the products or services being provided. Without this forecast, planning and control would be extremely difficult, if not impossible, to carry out effectively. A wide-ranging list of factors needs to be taken into account in producing this forecast. This includes: historical pattern of demand – whether there is a trend or seasonal effect; to what extent demand is influenced by economic considerations outside control (e.g. taxes); whether it is intended to try and influence demand directly (e.g. through advertising, price variation); and so on.

The basic difference between providing for specific customers' demands and satisfying demand from stock will also influence demand and attempts to forecast it. It is tempting to view all of these interdependent factors and abandon all attempts at a structured approach to forecasting demand. This is unwise; a structured approach should be used wherever possible to support the forecasting process. Moreover, techniques exist for monitoring forecasts, comparing these with actuals and detecting bias, leading to improved prediction.

The materials interface

Predicting material requirements is a subject which is central to the materials management function within production/operations control. However, not only is it necessary to forecast requirements, but also to estimate how long it will take to acquire (or convert) the materials. These two pieces of information are necessary inputs into any materials management system. The type of material (raw, work-in-progress and so on) in part indicates how it should be managed, which also establishes how its requirements should be determined. Again a structured approach to the forecasting puts subsequent analysis on a firmer basis. Care should be taken when examining historical requirement figures to establish future demand. Do these historical figures actually represent demand, or that part of demand which was satisfied? Is a record kept of occasions when items were required but not available?

Basic techniques

Moving averages

In Table 22.1 the usage of copier paper by the local office of a building society is presented. Suppose it is necessary to predict the requirement for paper in order to manage its procurement more effectively. The best estimate of the requirement for

Table 22.1 Reams of copier paper used per week over 24-week period

Week	Reams used	Week	Reams used
1	132	13	152
2	163	14	170
3	171	15	131
4	148	16	153
5	135	17	137
6	162	18	172
7	107	19	122
8	144	20	142
9	127	21	189
10	193	22	138
11	142	23	161
12	163	24	133

week 2, in week 1, is simply the requirement in week 1, i.e. 132. At the end of week 2, it is possible to estimate the requirement for week 3 as the average of the first two weeks' actual requirement, i.e. 147.5. The estimate for week 4, at the end of week 3, would then become 155.3, and so on until the end of week 24, when the estimate for the requirement for week 25 is the average of all the requirements to date. This has the disadvantage that as the process continues there are more and more data to store, and all are given equal weight in estimating the demand in the next period. It is possible to get round this by introducing the idea of a *moving average*, only including a fixed number of the most recent values. Considering a 5-point moving average, the forecast for week 6 is simply:

$$(132 + 163 + 171 + 148 + 135)/5 = 749/5 = 149.8$$

When the requirement for week 6 is known, it is possible to forecast the requirement for week 7 as the average of the five most recent values:

$$(163 + 171 + 148 + 135 + 162)/5 = 779/5 = 155.8$$

Alternatively, note that 132 was dropped and 162 was added, a gain of 30 to the total, or 30/5 = 6 to the average.

Table 22.2 Forecasts using 5-point and 11-point moving averages

Week	Reams used	Forecast reams used 5-point moving average	Forecast reams used 11-point moving average
1			
2			
3			
4			
5			
6	162	149.8	
7	107	155.8	
8	144	146.6	
9	127	139.2	
10	193	135.0	
11	142	146.6	
12	163	142.6	147.6
13	152	153.8	150.4
14	170	155.4	149.4
15	131	164.0	149.3
16	153	151.6	147.8
17	137	153.8	149.4
18	172	148.6	147.2
19	122	152.6	153.1
20	142	143.0	151.1
21	189	145.2	152.5
22	138	152.4	152.1
23	161	152.6	151.7
24	133	150.4	151.6
25	?	152.6	149.8

The remainder of the values, together with the forecasts based on an 11-point moving average, are presented in Table 22.2. Two possibilities exist in presenting these data. It could be argued that the average of the first five values should be shown at the centre, i.e. against week 3, and similarly with subsequent averages (indeed, this approach is followed in the more complex situation proposed in the final section of this chapter). However, since this value is being used as the forecast for week 6, it will be shown against week 6.

These results are shown plotted in Fig. 22.1 The difference between the 5-point and 11-point moving averages can be seen clearly. Both averages, as would be expected, damp down the random variation in the requirement. The 11-point average, because it involved an average over a larger number of values, will tend to be more 'stable', but equally will be slow to react to actual changes in level of requirement. The 5-point average, however, will respond more rapidly to actual changes, but is likely to be unduly influenced by random variations. The selection of the number of points in the average aims at achieving a compromise between these factors. It has been suggested for forecasting short periods ahead (four to five weeks) that the moving average could be over 10–15 values for weekly data, or over 3–5 values for monthly data.

A minor modification to this approach is to avoid giving equal weight to all values in the moving average. Suppose it was considered desirable to give more emphasis to

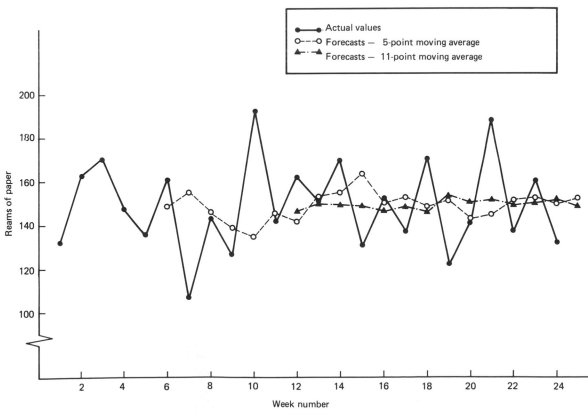

Fig. 22.1   Actual values compared with moving average forecast

more recent values. For the 5-point moving average example, it is possible to choose weights of:

$$0.4, \ 0.3, \ 0.2, \ 0.07 \ \text{and} \ 0.03$$

(note the weights sum to one, and contrast with 0.2, 0.2, 0.2, 0.2, 0.2, implied by the regular 5-point average). These weights give:

$$0.4 \ (135) + 0.3 \ (148) + 0.2 \ (171) + 0.07 \ (163) + 0.03 \ (132) = 147.97$$

as the forecast for week 6, and

$$0.4 \ (162) + 0.3 \ (135) + 0.2 \ (148) + 0.07 \ (171) + 0.03 \ (163) = 151.76$$

as the forecast for week 7, and so on.

However, with *weighted moving averages*, the user has to decide upon both the number of points in the average and the weights to apply.

Exponentially weighted moving averages

The previous approaches either gave each of a fixed number of most recent values equal weight or differential weights in arriving at an average. This approach uses all available historical data, with the weights applied to each getting smaller as the data get older.

The formula for this approach is:

Forecast for next period = Forecast for last period + α (actual for last period − forecast for last period)

where α is the smoothing constant, which must lie between 0 and 1. The above formula is a simplification of the basic formula which expresses the forecast as a weighted average of all the actual values to date, with the weights forming an exponential series.

Typical values for α lie between 0.1 and 0.2, with an interpretation similar to that placed on the number of points in the moving average. A small value of α results in slow reactions to sudden changes, whilst a large value can result in an over-reaction to random fluctuations.

Illustrating this method with the data from the previous example, it is necessary to obtain the *first* forecast before the formula can be applied. Initially, this is normally taken to be the straightforward arithmetic mean. The value of α used is 0.1. So:

Forecast for week 11 = Average of requirements for first 10 weeks (132 + 163 + 171 + 148 + 135 + 162 + 107 + 144 + 127 + 193)/10 = 148.2
Forecast for week 12 = 148.2 + 0.1 (142 − 148.2) = 147.6
Forecast for week 13 = 147.6 + 0.1 (163 − 147.6) = 149.1

Table 22.3 Forecasts using exponential smoothing $\alpha = 0.1$ and $\alpha = 0.2$

Week	Reams used	Forecast	
		$\alpha = 0.1$	$\alpha = 0.2$
12	163	147.6	147.0
13	152	149.1	150.2
14	170	149.4	150.5
15	131	151.5	154.4
16	153	149.4	149.7
17	137	149.8	150.4
18	172	148.5	147.7
19	122	150.9	152.6
20	142	148.0	146.5
21	189	147.4	145.6
22	138	151.5	154.3
23	161	150.2	151.0
24	133	151.3	153.0
25	?	149.4	149.0

and so on. The calculations are summarized, for both $\alpha = 0.1$ and $\alpha = 0.2$, in Table 22.3.

Again a better picture is obtained by presenting the results graphically: this is done in Fig. 22.2. It is possible to see the forecast using the higher value of α responding more rapidly to changes. Indeed, there is an extension to this approach which allows the value of α to vary depending on the size of the error: actual − forecast. (This is the

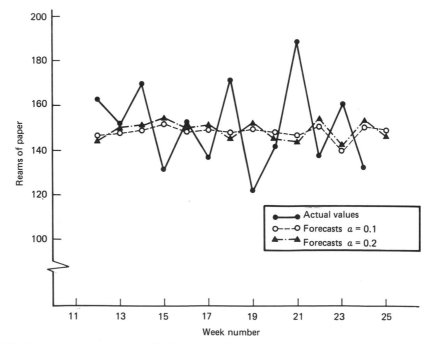

Fig. 22.2   Actual values compared with forecasts using exponential smoothing

final term in the formula for exponential smoothing.) If this error is large (indicating a change in level), then α needs to be large to allow the forecast to respond; when the error is small, α again is reduced in size. (This *adaptive smoothing* can offer potential if changes in level are anticipated.)

With exponential smoothing, fewer data elements need to be stored: latest forecast, latest actual, α compared with moving averages (say ten values). In the past this has had an impact on storage requirements for computer application. However, for all but the largest sets of items, this should not cause problems with current computer storage capabilities.

Other techniques

The previous approaches assumed that the level of requirement was relatively static and that there was random variation about this level. The current forecast at any time represents the most up-to-date estimate of that level. Thus the forecasts for weeks 25, 26, 27 . . . are all the same. Clearly the situation might arise where there is an increasing/decreasing trend in addition to random variation (see Fig. 22.3). The forecasting method needs to estimate this trend, and the one-period-ahead forecast will differ from the two- or three-period-ahead forecast. Both the methods described can be extended to handle this situation. With the moving average, this simply involves fitting a line to the points in the moving average. The extension to the exponential smoothing method is slightly more complex.

The second situation which might be encountered is seasonality: systematic peaks and troughs during particular weeks or months of the year (see Fig. 22.4). Here it is possible to expect requirements to be higher than average in quarter 2, and lower than average in quarter 3, and also subject to a generally increasing trend. Noticing that the seasonal effect follows a four-period (quarters) cycle, it is possible to take a

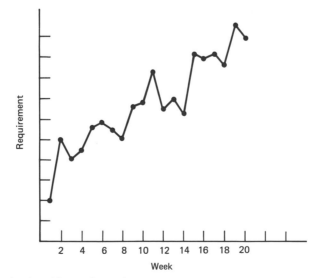

Fig. 22.3   Increasing trend in requirements

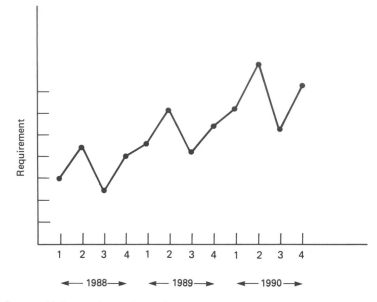

Fig. 22.4   Seasonal influence in requirements

four-quarter moving average to eliminate the seasonal effect and 'isolate' the trend. This is because each average will contain one 'high' value (quarter 2), one 'low' value (quarter 3) and two 'normal' values (quarters 1 and 4); first average: (q1 + q2 + q3 + q4)/4; second average: (q2 + q3 + q4 + q1)/4, and so on. These moving averages values are used to estimate the trend line. The seasonal adjustments can then be made by assessing how much above or below this trend the different quarters are. The forecast for a particular quarter involves extrapolating the trend to this quarter, and then making the appropriate seasonal adjustment.

A final technique which will be briefly discussed is one which can be used to monitor forecasts rather than to forecast itself. Essentially it involves cumulating the sum of the differences between the actual value and the forecast value each period. If the forecasts are systematically biased above or below the actual values, the differences will be predominantly negative or positive and the *cusum*, as this cumulative sum is called, will either get smaller and smaller, or larger and larger; otherwise the cusum will oscillate around zero. This is a very powerful technique which has application in a number of other areas, including statistical process control.

Estimating the error

It is important to recognize that forecasts are only predictions of future values, and as such are subject to possible *errors*. Indeed, it would be somewhat surprising if the forecasts were 'spot-on'. However, it can be of great use to the user of the forecasts if some estimate can be made of the likely error. This error can be measured by the *mean absolute deviation* (MAD), which is the mean of all of the errors (neglecting

Table 22.4 Calculation of MAD

Week	Reams used	Forecast	Error
12	163	147.0	13
13	152	150.2	1.8
14	170	150.5	19.5
15	131	154.4	22.6
16	153	149.7	3.3
17	137	150.4	13.4
18	172	147.7	24.3
19	122	152.6	30.6
20	142	146.5	4.5
21	189	145.6	43.4
22	138	154.3	16.3
23	161	151	10.0
24	133	153	20.0
		Total =	222.7
		MAD =	17.1

the sign – all considered positive). This calculation for the forecast using exponential smoothing (with $\alpha = 0.2$) is shown in Table 22.4.

If various assumptions are made about the underlying distributions (primarily concerning normality; see under Recommended reading at the end of the chapter), it is possible to estimate the standard deviation as follows:

Standard deviation = 1.25 × Mean absolute deviation

In the case of the example,

Standard deviation (SD) = 21.4

Subsequently statements can be made concerning confidence levels in a range of possible values for forecasts (based on 2 SD either side of the forecast for 95 per cent confidence and 3 SD for 99.7 per cent confidence).

Based on the earlier example, with the forecast of 149 as the requirement for week 25, it is possible to suggest 95 per cent confidence in the actual value lying between $149 - 2 \times 21.4$ and $149 + 2 \times 21.4$, i.e. in the range 106–192.

This chapter has only really scratched the surface of forecasting techniques. The interested reader is referred to any of the number of texts on forecasting for further details, particularly of those techniques mentioned in this final section.

CHAPTER 22 – HIGHLIGHTS

- Forecasting has an important role to play in POM. Typical applications include: future demand for products or services; material requirements; procurement times; durations of breakdowns, absenteeism; scrap or error rates.
- The two major interfaces with POM where forecasting is important are with marketing and materials.
- Two basic approaches are the n-point moving average: Forecast = Sum of the n most recent values; and exponential smoothing: Forecast = Last forecast + α × Last error, where Error = Actual − Forecast.
- Mean absolute error (MAD) measures the error:

$$\text{MAD} = \frac{\text{Sum of all errors (taken as positive)}}{\text{Number of errors}}$$

Recommended reading

Jarrett, J., *Business Forecasting Methods*, 2nd edn., Basil Blackwell, 1991

Uses cases and examples to demonstrate the advantages and limitations of the various forecasting techniques, and the importance of interpreting results.

Lancaster, G.A. and Lomas, R.A., *Forecasting for Sales and Materials Management*, Macmillan, 1985

This text is written to provide the non-specialist with a knowledge of forecasting, enabling him or her to apply such knowledge in a forecasting situation. Very readable.

Lewis, C.D., *Industrial and Business Forecasting Methods*, Butterworths, 1982

This book claims to present the 20 per cent of forecasting models available which are used in 80 per cent of practical forecasting applications.

Makridakis, S. and Wheelwright, S.C., *The Handbook of Forecasting – A Manager's Guide*, Wiley, 2nd edn, 1987

One of a number of texts on forecasting by these authors; here they edit contributions from some of the experts in the area. It is divided into four parts; role and application of forecasting in organizations, approaches to forecasting, forecasting challenges, and managing the forecasting function.

Saunders, J.A., Sharp, J.A. and Witt, S.F., *Practical Business Forecasting*, Gower, 1987

This book is intended for the manager who uses forecasts and for anyone involved in preparing them. It explains the reasoning behind the various forecasting techniques but avoids the mathematical and statistical detail.

Wheelwright, S.C. and Makridakis, S., *Forecasting Methods for Management*, Wiley, 5th edn, 1989

A very good reference text, recently thoroughly updated and revised.

Chapter 23

Capacity Management and Operations Scheduling

The meaning of capacity

The capacity of a unit is its ability to produce or do that which the consumer requires, and clearly there must be some match between *needs* characterized by market forecast and *abilities* characterized by capacity. A statement of capacity is rarely simple, and it is useful to distinguish between three different capacity levels:

Potential capacity is that which can be made available within the decision horizon of the most senior executive.

Immediate capacity is that which can be made available within the current budget period.

Effective capacity is that which is used within the current budget period.

The production/operations controller is generally concerned with the second and third of these levels, since he must deal with immediate, rather than long-term, problems. Furthermore, it should also be recognized that one of the objectives of the marketing department is to try to ensure that the effective and immediate capacities coincide. It should be noted that the more 'nearly effective' approaches 'immediate', the more rigid must the organization become: flexibility can only be achieved when immediate capacity is not fully used.

Constraints on immediate capacity

Immediate capacity is limited by:

(a) the plant/equipment size;
(b) availability of equipment;
(c) availability of manpower;
(d) availability of cash;
(e) financial policies;
(f) purchasing policy;
(g) sub-contracting policy;
(h) the technical demands of the tasks;
(i) the number of different tasks being undertaken.

For example, the capacity of a restaurant is limited by the size of the 'eating' area, or the number of tables.

Influences on effective capacity

Effective capacity can be influenced by:

(a) technical abilities in the pre-operations stages;
(b) organizational skills in the planning stages;
(c) purchasing skills;
(d) sub-contracting skills;
(e) maintenance policies and abilities;
(f) versatility of workforce;
(g) efficiency of workforce.

Differences between effective and immediate capacities

A great deal of work has been carried out on the utilization of equipment, i.e. the differences between effective and immediate capacity. Frequently these studies have involved the use of activity sampling to establish the proportion of time the equipment was being used productively, and to identify the reasons for and quantify the extent of non-productive time. These reasons range across preparation time, planned maintenance, emergency maintenance, idle (no planned work), idle (operator absent), and so on. The picture that emerges is that effective capacity is frequently less than 50 per cent of immediate capacity. While it is unlikely that these two capacities will ever coincide, it is clear that significant increases in capacity are possible, often by improved production/operations control. It is also clear that to measure capacity solely on the basis of available time is likely to give gross errors. Allowance must always be made for current local performance.

Capacity change

Within a production/operations environment, it seems probable that:

1. The ability of an individual to chance capacity is directly related to that individual's position in the organization's hierarchy.
2. The time necessary to implement a capacity increase is proportional to the magnitude of the increase.
3. The number of acceptable capacity changes which can be handled at any one time is finite.

Every programme implies a certain level of capacity and, if the above statements hold true, it is important that the implicit capacity decisions are made by an individual at the correct level in the organization. To present the production/operations controller with a programme which requires a capacity change greater than his hierarchical position will permit him to effect, can only result in frustration and the non-achievement of the programme. Similarly, if the need for a capacity change is recognized too late, it will not be achieved either, and failure must again result.

Capacity changes may be achieved in a number of ways and stages, ranging from a number of small incremental changes to a large step change depending on environmental constraints. If a university reached the limit of its physical teaching capacity, it could increase the hours of availability (from 9.00–5.00 to 8.00–7.00) or by constructing further buildings.

The measurement of capacity

Capacity, being the ability to produce work in a given time, must be measured in the units of work, i.e. resource-standard time units available in unit time. Thus a work centre with a capacity of 1,000 machine hours in a 40-hour week should be able to produce 1,000 standard hours of work *of the type appropriate to that work station* during a 40-hour week. To be able to calculate the volume of actual work, it is necessary to know:

(a)   The work content of the product;
(b)   the ancillary times involved in the production;
(c)   the effectiveness of the work station.

The measurement of capacity and the above factors is frequently undertaken by the production engineering department in manufacturing organizations, and it is useful to confirm these measurements by records of actual performance.

The above comments can also be interpreted in non-manufacturing contexts. Consider measuring the capacity of a small taxi firm which has four cars available from 9.00 to 5.00 five days per week. It could be argued that the capacity is $4 \times 5 \times 8$ hours per week (ignoring breaks). The work (or number of 'trips') will depend on the start and finish locations, traffic conditions, and so on.

As with load, it is not uncommon to find capacity quoted in terms of quantity of products made in unit time ('. . . 100 dozen pairs a day', '. . . 40 letters of credit per hour'). Such statements should be treated with great caution; changes in methods, procedures, materials, quantities etc. can result in changes in effective capacity. Unless the work unit is dedicated to a single product, it is safer always to refer to units of work rather than to units produced.

Finite or infinite capacity planning

In detailed planning, two conflicting constraints – time and capacity – have to be considered. If time is fixed, for example by the customer's required delivery date or transaction-processing cycle, then it is possible to accept time as the primary constraint and plan backwards to accommodate these times. However, this can be somewhat difficult in practice, since it is not generally possible to determine beforehand whether all of the tasks can be fitted in with the currently available capacity, and much time can be spent trying to solve an insoluble problem. Indeed, even after recognition that capacity needs to be temporarily increased, the extent of this increase and its timing still has to be established; clearly there are a variety of options open to the decision-maker, all with different cost implications.

Planning backwards to infinite capacity offers a partial solution to this problem. Many manufacturing and transaction-handling processes go through a number of stages in a sequential manner. If the plan is being prepared on a period-by-period basis (say week), then the backward plan can be prepared on the basis of one stage per period. This means that the final stage (operation) of the task is allocated to the period representing the delivery date, the penultimate task is allocated one period earlier, and so on. This produces a slightly more realistic plan of what might happen. This process indicates where overloads are likely to be and gives a far better picture of when and to what extent extra resources will be required. However, to confirm or propose revised delivery dates, a finite capacity plan must be developed. Generally, it is far simpler to produce a forward (rather than a backward) plan to finite capacity. For this, tasks are put into some priority order and, following this sequence, added to the plan in such a way that they are started as soon as possible at each stage, but only using as much resource as is available. Clearly, the criterion used for prioritizing the tasks will have a significant effect on the performance of the plan. This will be discussed in a later section.

Scheduling and loading

A schedule is a representation of the time necessary to carry out a task, and should take account of the technical requirements of the task, marketing forecast and available capacity. It is not simply a list of the operations required, since additionally it takes into account the technological relationships between these various operations.

Information requirements

The nature of a product may allow several operations in its manufacture to be carried out concurrently, whilst other operations may need to be completed before the next one can be started. A route or list of work to be done would not show this situation, whereas a schedule would take this into account (see Fig. 23.1). The graphical presentation of the bar chart for the schedule is essential for this clarity. With complex interdependencies between operations, use of a 'precedence diagram' (see Chapter 28) rather than a bar chart may be desirable.

Consider a metal-framed chair with a padded seat and back rest. Information related to this is presented in Table 23.1 and Fig. 23.1.

A *job schedule* shows the plan for the manufacture of a particular job. This is the work study input into production/operations control, indicating method and times in sufficient detail for the function to be adequately carried out. Once this schedule has been produced, it need not be changed unless there is a change in either the job (for example in the product being produced) or in the method of manufacture. A company which makes a range of products could draw up a number of schedules which are kept filed and used as the basis for production/operations control. These schedules would show elapsed time – the time between successive operations – rather than specific

---

Route for manufacture of batch of 10 type A chairs

	Operations	Time (units)
A	Cut metal frame	2
B	Weld frame	3
C	Paint frame	2
D	Cut wood for seat	2
E	Cut foam for seat	1
F	Cut pvc for seat	2
G	Make seat	2
H	Cut wood for back	1
I	Cut foam for back	2
J	Cut pvc for back	2
K	Make back	1
L	Assemble chair	3
M	Pack	2

Table 23.1   Route for chair manufacture

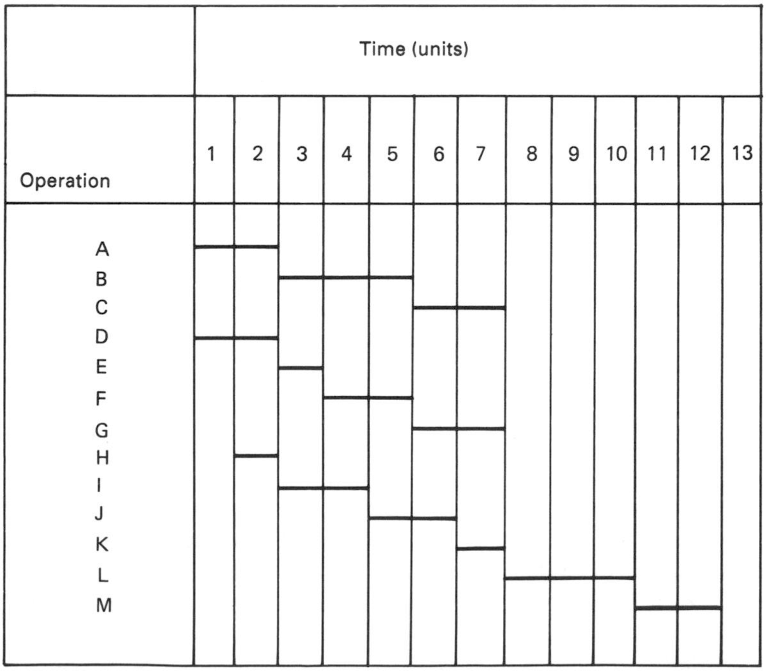

Fig. 23.1   Job schedule for chair

calendar dates. Once an order for a specific job is received, it is then possible to fix actual dates for the start and finish of each operation making up the job. When producing a schedule, it is important to record upon it:

1. The product to which it refers.
2. The quantity scheduled.
3. The labour used.

Similar information is required in the context of planning in service environments. The hospital administrator needs to know the resource requirement for a particular operation: days in the ward, time in the operating theatre (surgeon, theatre staff required); post-operative care, and so on. The college administrator needs information concerning all of the courses in producing room schedules.

Most organizations carry out a number of tasks simultaneously. It is necessary therefore to amalgamate a number of job schedules. This can only be done when the delivery dates for each job are known and the whole amalgamation will then specify the work to be carried out in each department throughout the period being planned. This process is called *scheduling* and the result known simply as the *schedule, production schedule* or *factory schedule* for the plant as a whole.

Optimum job conditions obtain when the various job schedules can be transferred on to the production schedule as they stand without modification, so that the job is finished just as it is required and each operation starts just as the operation(s) before it finish(es). However, this rarely happens in practice since a number of jobs will be 'competing' for the same resources, and it would require a number of operations on different jobs to be carried out simultaneously in the same department. This would result in the departments concerned at one time being required to carry out more work than is possible, but at other times being partially idle. The preparation of the production schedule will thus require attention to be paid to:

1. The dates upon which delivery of the finished products is due.
2. The job schedules for the appropriate tasks.
3. The capacities of the various sections or departments.
4. The efficiencies of the various sections or departments.
5. The planned maintenance schedule.
6. Planned holidays.
7. Anticipated sickness/absenteeism/casual holidays.
8. Existing commitments.
9. Availability of raw materials, components, packaging and so on.
10. External priorities set on the individual jobs.
11. Allowances for scrap or re-work.

Not all this information will necessarily be readily available within an organization. It may be necessary, therefore, to set up the systems to record the data and to carry out the required analysis. It is unwise simply to use figures which represent the 'desired' values. Suppose historical records indicate an absenteeism level of 20 per cent, and this is regarded as far too high. The temptation might be to use a value of, say, 5 per cent in calculations, hoping to force it down to this level. However, this will distort the picture produced by the schedule, producing results which are wrong. The correct course of action is to investigate the causes of the level being at its current value, and to tackle these.

It should be noted that whilst a schedule that completely occupies all work-stations at all times gives high utilization of resources, it is accompanied by considerable inflexibility. When the future is known with some security – for example, in an aggressive marketing situation where goods are mass-produced and suppliers well controlled – such scheduling may be possible and desirable. In the more usual batch-production conditions, some flexibility is extremely desirable, and this can be built in by deliberately underloading resources and/or by using sub-contractors. Clearly, such actions generate extra costs and these must be considered as the price which must be paid to be able to handle uncertainty.

The load and loading

Loading differs from scheduling only in terms of detail and time span. A schedule might programme the work for a department for a period of a month, whilst a load could be the timetable of work for an operator for a day or a week. Not infrequently the final loading – the hour-to-hour assignment of work to the individual operator – is carried out by the first line supervisor.

The *load* is the work assigned to a machine or operator, and *capacity* is the resource available to complete the available work during any convenient period of time. Both load and capacity should be measured in the same units to make comparison meaningful. When the load equals capacity, then the department, machine or operator is said to be *fully loaded*. If load is greater than capacity, the plant is *overloaded*; while if load is less than capacity, then the plant is *underloaded*. It is prudent when drawing up an initial schedule deliberately to *underload* capacity in order to provide some ability to react to change. It is suggested that a 70 per cent load is the maximum which should be aimed for in the first place.

The preparation of loading schedules for a process or worker is capable of providing substantial improvements in productivity. Ideally, every worker should know the tasks which have to be undertaken for as far ahead as is realistic, normally at least one working week. By so doing it will be possible:

1. To make maximum possible use of plant, equipment and personnel.
2. To establish and meet target dates.
3. To establish a case for new plant/equipment.
4. To improve worker morale.

It is frequently possible to express the load on a machine or process in a variety of ways:

(a) money (a machine is required to produce X per hour);
(b) weight (a machine is required to produce X tonnes per hour);
(c) length (a machine is required to produce X metres per hour);
(d) quantity (a process is required to handle X transactions per hour).

However, in the context of production/operations control, the only sensible measure of load which can be used directly and universally for comparisons is standard hours of work at a known rate of working.

It is folly to set a delivery date or target transaction processing time without due regard to the load, yet this is done so frequently that it could be said to be general practice. This will inevitably lead to costly usage of labour and broken delivery dates, and should be discouraged at all costs. Once capacity has been filled, it is possible to insert other work only at the cost of delaying existing commitments.

The problem of scheduling

The key to efficiency in a production/operations unit is the ability to schedule effectively, and yet *scheduling* is an exercise which is not resolvable in unique logical terms. Two barriers to efficient scheduling exist.

The difficulty in identifying the purpose for which scheduling is being undertaken Many criteria exist against which the soundness of a schedule can be judged; for example,

> minimum production costs, and
> minimum storage costs

are two possible criteria. It is easy to suggest that the schedule produced should achieve both. However, minimum production costs might imply long production runs of the same product before changing, in order to spread the set-up cost over a large number of units. This will lead to holding high stocks of items and inflated storage costs. There are many more criteria which can be stated and an attempt to satisfy them all can lead to a result which satisfies none. The criteria can be considered to fall under a number of headings: financial; marketing; production/operations. Some examples are listed below.

1. Financial:
    (a) minimum production/operations costs;
    (b) minimum storage costs;
    (c) minimum stock investment;
    (d) minimum cash outflow.
2. Marketing:
    (a) achieve delivery dates;
    (b) achieve transaction-processing targets;
    (c) minimize number of late jobs;
    (d) maximize customer satisfaction.
3. Production operations:
    (a) maximise labour utilization;
    (b) minimum set-up preparation times;
    (c) maximise equipment utilization.

It is tempting to suggest that these should be combined into a single financial measure. However, a number of intangible problems will still remain; for example, is it better to have one job two weeks late or two jobs each one week late? Should one traveller have to wait two hours for a taxi or should two travellers each have to wait one hour? The choice of criterion should be made after careful consideration of the aims of the organization.

The extremely large number of possible schedules

If there are N tasks to be processed in sequence through M processes, there are $(N!)^m$ possible schedules. This number can be reduced by requiring that the order of the jobs on the first process should be retained for all the other processes. This produces a so-called ordered schedule, and for N tasks there are a mere $N!$ possible schedules. Thus, for 20 tasks there would be 20! different schedules. It is left as an exercise for the reader to calculate how long it would take even the fastest of modern computers to generate and evaluate all these schedules and to print out the 'best'.

Reducing the scheduling problem

The problem, however difficult, must be solved, albeit in a most imperfect way. To simplify the task, there are a number of fairly obvious common-sense steps which can be undertaken:

1. Reduce the product/service range if possible. Many companies manufacture products or offer services which produce little income and less contribution. As can be seen above, reduction in variety gives a proportionally greater reduction in scheduling complexity.
2. Reduce the component range. Unnecessary variety in components is extremely costly.
3. Examine the available resources. Much equipment is needlessly complex, and uniformity in types of equipment can substantially ease the scheduling problem.
4. Carry out a job enlargement programme. To train staff to carry out a number of tasks rather than only one task will improve flexibility and morale.
5. Investigate the use of sub-contractors. The off-loading of peaks of work can sometimes be very rewarding in terms of the organizational simplification which results.
6. Separate out the 'big' tasks which consume a great deal of labour and 'small' tasks which consume little labour. To try to mix 'big' and 'small' work in the same work areas is usually very difficult, and a 'small order' section organized more informally than 'a large order' section will usually be quite effective.
7. Ensure close liaison between production/operations and marketing. Tension can often be relieved by dialogue with customers.
8. Reduce the size of the organizational units. The difficulty of scheduling – and, indeed, managing – increases considerably with size.
9. Increase the autonomy of work areas. Constraints are often imposed on the grounds that greater 'control' is obtained. Unless a good visible reason can be found for imposing a restriction, it is best left unimposed.
10. Once a forecast and a derived schedule have been prepared *and agreed*, they should only be changed for very compelling reasons. Discipline on all concerned must be accepted.

Simplifying the scheduling problem

1. Reduce the product range.
2. Reduce component range.
3. Examine available resources.
4. Enlarge all tasks where possible.
5. Use sub-contractors.
6. Separate 'big' and 'small' tasks.
7. Ensure close liaison with marketing.
8. Reduce size.
9. Increase autonomy.
10. Accept need for discipline.

Use of interstage stores

The virtual impossibility in batch production or processing of balancing the load on all stages results in gaps in the work available to a work area or section. To avoid the cost of this inactivity, it is common to find that sub-stores (interstage work-in-progress or buffer areas) are created between sections. These form 'pools' or 'reservoirs' from which succeeding stages can draw work and thus keep all stages at work. Whilst this avoids the 'idle time' cost of an unbalanced load, it substitutes for it the cost of holding the work-in-progress. Since this cost is difficult to identify and quantify, it is often ignored, yet it may well be that the idle-time costs, and the organizational costs to remove them, will in fact be less than the very high costs of holding stock. This area of cost creation may often repay investigation.

Scheduling rules

Whilst the above suggestions may simplify the scheduling task, they will not solve it, and the residual problem is still gigantic. To enable schedules to be constructed in practical circumstances, it is often useful to devise rules which can be used either to put tasks into priority order or simply to select the next task to be handled. These are sometimes referred to as *loading* or *dispatching* rules. Essentially they involve examining a particular characteristic of the tasks. Again these characteristics fall under the broad headings of financial, marketing and production/operations. Some of these are shown in Table 23.2.

Clearly the choice of loading rule should be linked to the criteria by which the schedule is measured. Some are easier to operate than others. If works order numbers are issued to tasks sequentially as they arrive, then scheduling by date of receipt simply involves selection of the task with the lowest works order number. This number would be stamped on the documentation accompanying the task. Equally, the delivery date would be recorded on this documentation so that loading by delivery date could also be easily accomplished. However, it may be felt that the amount of free time – the *slack* – is a better measure of the importance of a task. This involves

Table 23.2 Loading/despatching criteria

	Select/order according to
Financial	Highest value
	Highest contribution
Marketing	Earliest delivery date/shortest transaction processing cycle time.
	Least slack time
	Least slack time per operation
Production/Operations	Least set-up/preparation time
	Shortest processing time
	Earliest date of receipt

more effort: the work contents of the individual operations making up the task must be added together and subtracted from the delivery date. It is possible to go a step further and to argue that this slack time will be spent queueing before one or other of the processes, so that the measure should be the slack time divided by the number of operations. While the delivery date will normally be fixed throughout the processing of a task, the slack time per operation will change as the task is processed and needs to be repeatedly recalculated.

None of these rules will always produce the 'best' or 'optimum' schedule. However, they are fairly easy to operate and attractive to the user since they are based on common sense. They provide a consistency to scheduling which can reflect factors of importance to the organization.

Loading rules and the computer

Loading rules form the basis of the scheduling module of some computer software packages for production planning and control. When deciding which job to schedule next in producing the plan, the computer looks at the various characteristics of the tasks waiting. These characteristics include the factors listed above: value, delivery date, work content, external priority (importance of the customer). These are converted to a common scale (it is not possible to add directly a 'calendar date' to 'pounds value'), multiplied by weights specified by the user, and added together. This 'priority value' is used to select the next job. By specifying these 'weights', the user 'controls' the scheduling process.

Some special methods

Critical path analysis
One-off jobs can be dealt with by CPA (see Chapter 28). This is particularly suitable for tasks involving complex interdependencies between the individual operations making up the task. However, a multitude of such tasks produces a resource allocation problem just as intractable as the batch scheduling problem.

Johnson's two-processor algorithm

Where there are only two processes, they can be scheduled to minimize the total throughput time the makespan – by a procedure known by the name of its author: S.M. Johnson. This is easier to use than to derive, so an example will be presented. Consider a series of six jobs (A, B, . . . F) which all have to pass through two processes in the same order, i.e. first through process I, then through process II. Processing times (in units) are given below:

Job	A	B	C	D	E	F
Process I	1	6	5	5	3	6
Process II	2	4	6	4	2	7

A sequence table is constructed:

Sequence	1	2	3	4	5	6
Job						

The table of job times is scanned and the smallest time identified – in this case 1 (A:I). As this smallest time is on the first process, this job is put at the start of the sequence; had it been on the second process, the job would have been put at the end of the sequence. Having been scheduled, job A and its times are removed from consideration. Next smallest is 2 (E:II). Since this corresponds to the second process this job is put at the end of the sequence. As jobs are added into the sequence, their times are no longer considered; the sequence is built up inwards. At this point there is a tie: 4 corresponds to both (B:II) and (D:II), so there are two alternative solutions. The complete solutions can be built up and are shown below:

Sequence	1	2	3	4	5	6
Job	A	C	F	D	B	E
Job	A	C	F	B	D	E

Either of these schedules will minimize the total time taken to process all the jobs. However, in order to find this makespan it is necessary either to produce a table of start and finish times or to draw up a bar chart for the sequence. The use of this approach is rather limited, but could be useful in special circumstances, for example where two consecutive processes are very costly or combine to form a bottleneck. There are also two extensions: the first to ascertain three-process problems, and the second to develop a heuristic procedure (one which does not guarantee to obtain the best solution, just a good one) for the more general problem.

The branch and bound approach

A technique which shows great promise, and which is being increasingly used in scheduling batch production, is the branch and bound approach. The name derives from the ability to display the enumeration of the possible alternative schedules as a tree with many branches. To explore completely the totality of the feasible alternatives would require an examination of all branches; that is, with N jobs, $N!$ branches if only ordered schedules were considered. As previously pointed out, for anything but the very smallest problems this is impractical. However, it is possible to devise indicators (bounds) which show which branches are likely to produce good results and which are not. The branch which appears most promising is followed until a complete solution is obtained. At this stage a large number of other branches can be eliminated, since it can be shown that they cannot produce better solutions. The process continues by exploring other branches which do offer potential for improved solutions. The effectiveness of the approach depends on the method used for calculating the bounds (the 'tighter' these are, the more branches can be eliminated from the search) and the way branches are selected as 'promising' and further developed – branching (the better this is achieved the fewer the steps are necessary to arrive at a possibly improved solution). This process offers the further advantage that it can be terminated at any stage (before the optimum solution has been found) and the best solution found so far taken.

Line of balance

Line of balance (LoB), a special case of CPA, can be used in single batch situations, and is particularly useful when delivery rates are not linear with respect to time. Essentially, LoB consists of drawing a network for the production of a single unit and calculating the latest finish for all activities. If the delivery activity is taken as the last activity and a previous activity has to be finished four weeks previously, at week N say, the total quantity passed through the previous activity should be equal to the total quantity which should pass through delivery at week $N + 4$. This technique is covered in detail in Chapter 28.

CHAPTER 23 – HIGHLIGHTS

- *Capacity* is the ability to produce or to do that which the consumer requires: *potential capacity* is what can be made available within the decision horizon of the most senior executive; *immediate capacity* is that which can be made available within the current budget period; *effective capacity* is that which is used within the current budget period.

- Capacity should be measured by units of work rather than units produced.

- Planning can be carried forwards from when capacity first becomes available, or backwards from when a task is required to be complete.

- A job schedule provides the basic information concerning the method used for a task, and the times for the elements of work making up the task.

- A production schedule specifies the work to be completed during the planning period for each department. It takes account of: job schedules of the appropriate tasks; dates by which tasks should be completed; capacities and efficiencies of the sections/departments; planned holidays/maintenance and existing commitments; anticipated sickness/absenteeism/casual holidays; availability of all materials; external priorities for the tasks.

- Two key problems with scheduling are measurement of performance (financial; production/operations; marketing) and the large number of possible schedules.

- The scheduling problem may be reduced by reducing the product/service range; critically examining available resources; enlarging all tasks; subcontracting; separating big and small tasks; and increasing autonomy.

- Scheduling/loading rules should be used to ensure consistency: if financial considerations dominate, tasks could be selected by highest contribution; if marketing considerations dominate, tasks should be selected by earliest delivery date; if production/operations considerations dominate, tasks should be selected by least preparation time.

- Special methods that are available include: Critical Path Analysis for complex interdependencies; Johnson's approach for two processors, minimize makespan; Branch and bound for optimal solutions to larger problems.

Recommended reading

Baker, K.R., *An Introduction to Scheduling and Sequencing*, Wiley, 1974

A sound basic reference covering the models and methodologies in the scheduling field, a desirable prerequisite being some exposure to probability and statistics.

Bellman, R., Esogbue, A.O. and Nabeshima, I., *Mathematical Aspects of Scheduling and Applications*, Pergamon, 1982

A comprehensive text on scheduling theory, not for the mathematically weak, with detailed references and a variety of examples.

Goldratt, E.M. and Cox, J., *The Goal*, Gower, 1989

A revised version of the earlier text which introduced the concepts underpinning OPT. Now claims to cover MRP, JIT, SPC, . . . as well!

Chapter 24

Manufacturing Planning Case Study

Manufacture to stock versus manufacture to customer order

The previous chapter discussed the basic problem of scheduling and suggested that in a large number of cases it was not possible, or even desirable, to try to produce an ideal schedule. In practice, of course, it is essential to produce some feasible schedule, whether it is ideal or not. The problem is probably at its most acute in a batch production unit, and this chapter illustrates some guidelines which will help in the development of such a schedule. It must be stated unambiguously that the solution which is evolved is but one of many. It has the advantage of being workable – that is, it does not produce an overload before any work starts – but there may be many other equally good or 'better' solutions. For illustration, a manual method will be demonstrated for the development; a computer approach will be discussed later.

There are two main situations that occur.

1. Products are manufactured for *stock*, in which case it is possible to prepare the schedule and load at the beginning of the planning period: the 'marketing' situation.
2. Products are manufactured only against *customers' orders*, in which case it is necessary to schedule and load during the planning period: the 'selling' situation.

Frequently, of course, both the above will be found existing side by side in the same unit. Often it will be found convenient organizationally to separate the two into different units.

Illustration of planning manufacture for stock

Information requirements

The sales programme will be effectively in the form shown in Table 24.1.

From this, works orders authorizing production will be issued as shown in Fig. 24.1, and so on, covering all 14 jobs shown in the programme.

Table 24.1 Sales programme

Delivery by end of week	Product			
	A	*B*	*C*	*D*
1	20			20
2		10		
3			10	15
4	15	10		
5			20	10
6	10	10		
7			20	15
8	20			

Job number	1001
Product	A
Quantity	20
Delivery required	Week 1
Job number	1002
Product	B
Quantity	10
Delivery required	Week 2

Fig. 24.1 Works orders for the programme of Table 24.1

Table 24.2 Route and schedule of manufacture

	Job number		*1001*
	Product		*A*
	Quantity		*20*
Operation	*Department*	*Time*	*Number of operators*
1	D1	5 days	1
2	D2	6 days	1
3	D3	4 days	1
4	D4	5 days	1
5	D5	2 days	1

The production control department will then obtain from the planning department a route and schedule of manufacture for each product. Assuming that the manufacture is simple and that there is neither overlapping nor dead time, the route and the schedule will be identical and would take the form set out in Table 24.2 and, in all, 14 routes would be required which, when prepared, could be summarized as in Table 24.3.

From the production manager the production control department would obtain a statement of the capacity of each department (Table 24.4). These capacities represent the 'maximum theoretical' figures, which must be adjusted downwards to allow for

Table 24.3 The 14 manufacturing routes required

| Product | | Job | Work content (operator-days) in departments | | | | | Jobs completed |
Type	Qty	number	D.1	D.2	D.3	D.4	D.5	by end of week
A	20	1001	5	6	4	5	2	1
B	10	1002	10	10	10	10	10	2
C	10	1003	3	8	5	5	8	3
D	20	1004	12	24	32	20	12	1
A	15	1005	4	4	3	4	2	4
B	10	1006	10	10	10	10	10	4
D	15	1007	9	18	24	15	9	3
A	10	1008	3	3	2	3	1	6
B	10	1009	10	10	10	10	10	6
C	20	1010	5	15	10	10	15	5
D	10	1011	6	12	16	10	6	5
A	20	1012	5	6	4	5	2	8
C	20	1013	5	15	10	10	15	7
D	15	1014	9	18	24	15	9	7

Note: all fractions of an operator-day are rounded up to the next whole number for ease of calculation.

Table 24.4 Capacity of each department

Department	Weekly capacity (operator-days)
D1	12
D2	25
D3	33
D4	20
D5	12

sickness, absenteeism, casual holidays and so on. This adjustment (which can be made as a percentage) will be based on historical figures. In this example, it will be ignored for convenience.

From its own records, POCD would obtain statements of the existing loads, planned holiday periods and maintenance requirements

Existing load:

Department	Loaded until end of week
D1	46
D2	47
D3	48
D4	49
D5	49

Holidays:
All departments closed for weeks 50, 51.

Maintenance:
Department

D1
D2
D3   } All maintenance
D4   carried out
D5   in weeks 50, 51

The chart in Fig. 24.2 shows the initial situation in starting to plan work through the departments.

Backward schedule

Since delivery dates are specified, it is sensible *in this case* to start by scheduling from completion date backwards to the starting date. As mentioned in the previous chapter, it can be extremely difficult to attempt to schedule backwards and stay within the available capacity restrictions at least in part because of the number of different permutations of job orders. Indeed, it may not even be possible to fit all the jobs in before their delivery dates. Consequently, the first schedule is carried out to 'infinite capacity' – ignoring any restrictions on capacity – in order to indicate when and where conflicts are likely to occur so that action may be taken where possible to resolve these problems. In order to model the sequential nature of the production route, this schedule is prepared on the basis of one operation per week.

Before any scheduling takes place, POCD should correct the standard times given on the various route cards for any known or foreseeable department inefficiencies; for the purposes of this illustration, it is assumed that all work is carried out 'at standard' so no adjustment is therefore necessary. The resultant programme is shown in Fig. 24.3. It can be seen that this indicates that severe overloading might occur on a number of occasions.("INSERT FIGURE 24.3")

Overloading is quite unacceptable since it represents a task which is incapable of being fulfilled. There are a number of ways whereby an overload can be reduced, including:

(a) increasing available resources, either on a short-term basis by working overtime, or on a long-term basis by buying more plant and equipment or hiring more workers;
(b) sub-contracting the work producing the overload – this often results in shifting effort from the direct producing departments to the support departments, for example to the purchasing department;
(c) improving the manufacturing method to reduce work content;
(d) changing the product design, again to reduce work content or to permit the purchase of complete parts;
(e) negotiating a change in delivery date.

Forward schedule

In order to evaluate the effects of increasing the available resources or to establish

Week number

Dept	Capacity in operator days	Prod.	46	47	48	49	50	51	52
D1	12	A							
		B							
		C							
		D							
		Load	12						
D2	25	A							
		B							
		C							
		D							
		Load	25	25					
D3	33	A							
		B							
		C							
		D							
		Load	33	33	33				
D4	20	A							
		B							
		C							
		D							
		Load	20	20	20	20			
D5	12	A							
		B							
		C							
		D							
		Load	12	12	12	12			

Column 50–51: HOLIDAYS AND MAINTENANCE

Fig. 24.2 Initial blank programme

1	2	3	4	5	6	7	8	9

Week number

Dept	Capacity in operator days	Prod.	46	47	48	49	50	51	52
		A		1001 (5)					1005 (4)
		B			1002 (10)				1006 (10)
D1	12	C				1003 (3)			
		D		1004 (12)		1007 (9)			
		Load	12	17	10	12			14
		A			1001 (6)				
		B				1002 (10)			1003 (8)
D2	25	C							1007 (18)
		D			1004 (24)				
		Load	25	25	30	10			26
		A				1001 (4)			
		B							1002 (10)
D3	33	C							
		D				1004 (32)			
		Load	33	33	33	36			10
		A							1001 (5)
		B							
D4	20	C							
		D							1004 (20)
		Load	20	20	20	20			25
		A							
		B							
D5	12	C							
		D							
		Load	12	12	12	12			

HOLIDAYS AND MAINTENANCE

Fig. 24.3   Backward schedule to infinite capacity

1	2	3	4	5	6	7	8	9

1008
1009 (3)
(10)
1012
(5)

1010
1011 (5)
(6)
11

1013
1014 (5)
(9)
13
14
5

1005
1006 (4)
(10)
14

1008
1009 (3)
(10)

1010
1011 (15)
(12)
27

1013
1014 (15)
(18)
13
33

1012
(6)
6

1005
1006 (3)
(10)

1003
1007 (5)
(24)
29

1010
1011 (10)
(16)
13
26

1008
1009 (2)
(10)

1013
1014 (10)
(24)
12
34
4

1002
(10)
10

1005
1006 (4)
(10)

1003
1007 (5)
(15)
20
14

1010
1011 (10)
(10)

1008
1009 (3)
(10)
20
13

1013
1014 (10)
(15)
25

1012
(5)
5

1001
(2)

1002
(10)

1005
1006 (2)
(10)

1008
1009 (1)
(10)

1012
(2)

1004
(12)
14

1003
1007 (8)
(9)
10
17

1010
1011 (15)
(6)
12
21

1013
1014 (15)
(9)
11
24
2

Week number

Dept	Capacity in operator days	Prod.	46	47	48	49	50	51	52
D1	12	A			1001 (5)				
		B			1002 (10)				1006 (10)
		C							1003 (3)
		D		1004 (12)		1007 (9)			
	Load		12	12	12	12			12
D2	25	A				1001 (6)			
		B				1002 (10)			
		C							1003 (8)
		D			1004 (24)				1007 (18)
	Load		25	25	25	15			25
D3	33	A							1001 (4)
		B							1002 (10)
		C							
		D				1004 32			1007 (24)
	Load		33	33	33	32			23
D4	20	A							
		B							
		C							
		D							1004 (20)
	Load		20	20	20	20			20
D5	12	A							
		B							
		C							
		D							
	Load		12	12	12	12			

(Weeks 50–51 columns marked: HOLIDAYS AND MAINTENANCE)

Fig. 24.4 Forward schedule to finite capacity

1	2	3	4	5	6	7	8	9

Row block 1:
- 1005 (4)
- 1009 (10)
- 1008 (3)
- 1012 (5)
- 1010 (5)
- 1011 (6)
- 1013 (5)
- 1014 (9)
- 12 | 12 | 12 | 12

Row block 2:
- 1005 (4)
- 1006 (10)
- 1008 (3)
- 1009 (10)
- 1012 (6)
- 1010 (15)
- 1011 (12)
- 1013 (15)
- 1014 (18)
- 19 | 23 | 13 | 21 | 18

Row block 3:
- 1005 (3)
- 1006 (10)
- 1008 (2)
- 1009 (10)
- 1012 (4)
- 1003 (5)
- 1010 (10)
- 1011 (16)
- 1013 (10)
- 1014 (24)
- 33 | 13 | 25 | 4 | 33

Row block 4:
- 1001 (5)
- 1002 (10)
- 1005 (4)
- 1006 (10)
- 1008 (3)
- 1009 (10)
- 1012 (5)
- 1003 (5)
- 1010 (10)
- 1013 (10)
- 1007 (15)
- 1011 (10)
- 1014 (15)
- 20 | 20 | 20 | 20 | 11 | 20 | 4

Row block 5:
- 1001 (2)
- 1002 (10)
- 1005 (2)
- 1006 (10)
- 1008 (1)
- 1009 (10)
- 1003 (8)
- 1010 (15)
- 1014 (15)
- 1004 (12)
- 1007 (9)
- 1011 (6)
- 1011 ... 1014 (9)
- 12 | 12 | 12 | 12 | 12 | 12 | 12 | 12 | 12

what delivery dates can be achieved with the available resources, it is now necessary to produce a finite capacity schedule. It is easier to carry this out in a forward direction. However, it is first necessary to decide on the order in which the jobs are to be added into the schedule. Since delivery dates are involved, the order will be determined by these, with jobs with the highest work content having priority in the case of equal delivery dates. Hence the jobs will be scheduled as shown in Table 24.5.

The result of scheduling the jobs in this order is shown in Fig. 24.4. In producing this schedule it is assumed that the time necessary for transport between departments is negligible, and so a job can start in a subsequent department as soon as it has finished in its current department, provided capacity is available. Moreover, work has been loaded on to departments without any regard for the number of operators in them and the desirability of having several operators processing the same job. Clearly, local circumstances will determine the significance of these factors in practice. The lengths of the lines associated with each job are not intended to be proportional to its duration or work content; they are simply to give an indication of the week(s) in which it is planned. This programme satisfies the capacity constraints – no department is overloaded – but at the expense of missing some of the delivery dates (Table 24.6).

Clearly, these changes in delivery must be agreed with the customer who, in this case, is the marketing department. The schedule shows periods both when operators are waiting for work and when jobs are waiting to be processed. There is no guarantee that it is the best schedule in any sense; its appeal is simply that it was produced taking account of delivery dates and delivery was considered to be important. Had utilization been important, jobs of similar types could have been grouped together in order to improve 'efficiency'; for example, all As together (1001, 1005, 1008, 1012); then all Bs, and so on. This obviously disregards the delivery requirements. Equally, if it was felt necessary to attempt to achieve more of the delivery dates, then it would be possible to relax the rule which required that a job could only move on to the next department when it had finished in its current department, and consider 'splitting' jobs and sending ahead.

Table 24.5

Order	Job number	Delivery date (end of week)
1	1004	1
2	1001	1
3	1002	2
4	1007	3
5	1003	3
6	1006	4
7	1005	4
8	1010	5
9	1011	5
10	1009	6
11	1008	6
12	1014	7
13	1013	7
14	1012	8

Table 24.6

| | Delivery date (end of week) | |
Job number	Required	Planned
1001	1	2
1002	2	2
1003	3	4
1004	1	1
1005	4	5
1006	4	5
1007	3	3
1008	6	8
1009	6	7
1010	5	6
1011	5	7
1012	8	10
1013	7	10
1014	7	8

Figure 24.5 illustrates the effect of this on job 1002:10A, splitting it into two separate jobs of 5A.

Whilst splitting the job reduces the elapsed time for manufacture and thereby improves delivery potential, it produces a plan which, having gaps, offers less scope for high efficiencies. Moreover, by increasing the number of separate entities to plan and control, it adds to the organizational complexity. The load on each department can be read straight off the programme as shown. In turn, the load on individual machines/operators can be readily deduced.

Derived load

Consider department Dl. This has a total capacity of 12 operator-days each week, and this is made up of the work of two operators (Smith and Jones) for six days each week. Their programme of work, i.e their individual loads for weeks 47 to 52, is represented by Fig. 24.6.

Note: It must be emphasized again that the solution of Figs 24.4 and 24.6 is but one of many possible sets of solutions, and no claim is made that it is in any way 'the best'.

The authors consider that generally it is not necessary to break the load down to individual operators, and the actual allocation of work should be left to the first line supervisors, who will have the detailed local knowledge necessary for carrying out this task. Clearly this loading must be recognized as part of the supervisor's task, and time and facilities allowed to enable it to be carried out. If this is not the case, it will be found that much time is lost by operators waiting for a supervisor to find an appropriate job. This loss of time can sometimes assume alarming proportions, besides putting an unreasonable strain on the first line supervisor, and causing a great deal of ill-feeling among the direct operators, particularly if bonus payments are involved.

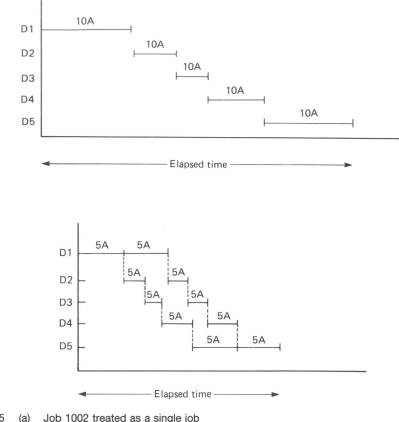

Fig. 24.5   (a)   Job 1002 treated as a single job
            (b)   Job 1002 treated as two jobs

Manufacturing against customers' orders

In the problem of manufacturing for stock, the tasks are known before the planning period is started, and time is available to adjust the programme with some precision. In the case of bespoke manufacture, this will be so only if the time-cycle of manufacture is long and the orders received well before production must start. Should the manufacturing cycle be short and deliveries rapid, alternative techniques may be necessary, particularly if the volume of orders is great. Scheduling and loading will not be so accurate, and it is wise under these circumstances to attempt to underload each department by at least 30 per cent in order that any inaccuracies or poor performances will not have too great an effect on the overall performance.

The sales programme will have been prepared in the form of the number of hours of work which it is anticipated will be received by the factory in the form of customers' orders. Under these circumstances it may be convenient to build up a load in diary form, the load increasing as orders arrive. It is clearly not possible to issue a manufacturing programme in detail at the outset of the planning period. The frequency with which a programme is issued will depend on the manufacturing

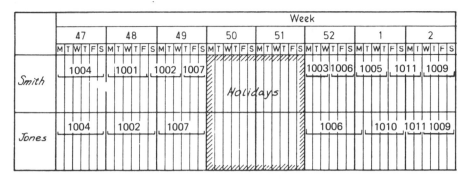

Fig. 24.6 Individual loads for Smith and Jones for weeks 47 to 52

time, the delivery time and the volume of orders, but a factory with a one-week manufacturing cycle and a short delivery should aim to issue a four-week programme each week. Thus, in week 1, a programme covering weeks 1, 2, 3 and 4 is issued. In week 2, the programme will cover weeks 2, 3, 4 and 5, and so on. The setting of delivery dates in this circumstance *must* be a matter for close consultation between the marketing department and the production control department and unilateral decisions by one or other department can only lead to eventual disaster.

Loading against customers' orders

In this case the loading operation becomes more difficult, since it is necessary to plan the detail, preparing a route for each order as it is received. Such a procedure is not, in itself, inherently difficult, becoming so only when the volume of work becomes great.

D1			D2			D3			D4			D5			
Total hours available 96			Total hours available 200			Total hours available 240			Total hours available 160			Total hours available 160			Week no. 28
Job no.	Hours	Total hours	Job no.	Hours	Total hours	Job no.	Hours	Total hours	Job no.	Hours	Total hours	Job no.	Hours	Total hours	
															30 June–6 July
2001	20		1984	44		1970	20		1940	24		1920	10		
2002	15	35	1986	50	94	1972	18	38	1942	30	54	1921	12	22	
2008	24	59	1987	20	114	1973	24	62	1943	15	69	1924	10	32	
2009	18	77	1990	30	144	1974	30	92	1946	16	85	1927	8	40	
2014	14	91	1992	32	176	1977	50	142	1950	25	110	1928	14	54	
			1993	30	206	1978	45	187	1953	20	130	1934	10	64	
						1981	35	222	1956	32	162	1936	8	72	
												1937	12	84	

Fig. 24.7 Diary form of loading

The route having been prepared, there are a number of methods whereby a load is built up. The simplest is a diary, where a series of sheets (see Fig. 24.7) is drawn up, one for each week; as orders are prepared and planned, work is loaded into the appropriate week. As with schedules, planning can be carried out either backwards or forwards.

An alternative method is to represent the load graphically on a bar chart of a type exactly similar to Figs 24.3 and 24.4. This will produce a much more striking effect than the diary: if there are a large number of orders, however, the chart becomes unmanageable and the detail too fine for easy reference. The chart does have the advantage that it can be used not only as a loading chart but also as a progress chart, and when used in this fashion it is known as a Gantt chart. Progress is shown on a Gantt chart by superimposing a line on the loading line, the length of which is proportional to the work done.

One disadvantage of a bar or Gantt chart drawn on paper is that it is inflexible, i.e. any modifications require alterations to, or complete redrawing of, the chart itself, which in a complex chart can be both costly and difficult besides being a substantial source of error. To try to avoid this a number of mechanical devices have been designed whereon the work is represented by a card, peg, tape or other device which is held on to a board. Changes are then made by moving the representational devices as required. The ingenuity of these planning boards and their very considerable flexibility command attention, and anyone wishing to install a loading system would be well advised to see all the boards now marketed.

Most computer-based scheduling systems provide the facility to draw a Gantt chart. This enables the calculations required in drawing up a chart like Fig. 24.4 to be carried out accurately and rapidly. Changes in the various parameters, e.g. different levels of overtime, can be assessed and different scenarios evaluated. However, the output from such packages is only as good as the data input. So, for example, the use of a computer will not in itself remove the problems associated with an inability to estimate job times accurately.

It must be remembered, however, that no system is any better than the people working it; no method, however good, can make up for inefficient operation on the part of staff. For this reason, if for no other, simplicity should be a primary requirement in any loading/progress system.

CHAPTER 24 – HIGHLIGHTS

- There are two main situations: either products are manufactured to stock, and it is possible to prepare the schedule and load at the beginning of the planning period; or products are only manufactured against customers' orders, and it is necessary to schedule and load during the planning period.

- To plan manufacture for stock, there are information requirements: a sales programme; routings and times; capacities, adjusted for efficiencies, holidays and sickness. A backward schedule to infinite capacity, with one operation per week, gives an overview of the situation and problem areas. A forward schedule to finite capacity can establish achievable delivery dates, there is a need to prioritize.

- To plan manufacture against customers' orders, there are similar information requirements to manufacture to stock. Use of a diary is recommended for flexibility.

Recommended reading

See Recommended reading for Chapter 23.

Chapter 25

Data Capture and Release

Preparing work for release

In any sequence of work a great deal of activity takes place prior to the commencement of the actual operations. This will include:

(a) preparing manufacturing drawings/statements of procedures;
(b) designing and making special production/operations aids;
(c) preparing job/operations layouts/routes;
(d) preparing material lists;
(e) purchasing and/or allocating material;
(f) preparing material requisitions;
(g) setting bonus rates and preparing bonus cards.

The actual activities will depend on the environment in which the transformation process is being carried out, and the type of transformation.

All this activity must be coordinated, and this is done most conveniently by the production/operations control department. Once all these preparations are complete, the actual transformation process can start, and the formal act of *releasing* the work is known as *despatching*. The despatch section will thus be seen to be the bridge between operations and pre-operations. When all functions are being carried out correctly and to time, the despatching function will be of least importance, and in large-scale flow production will become vestigial, being a routine clerical task. It is then often found convenient to merge the despatch function with the progress function, when they are both carried out by a single section.

A similar role exists in a number of service operations: the receptionist in a doctor's surgery, allocating patients and preparing their records; or the receptionist for a taxi company.

Responsibilities of the despatch section

This section will normally be responsible for the following duties.

1. Checking the availability of material and then taking appropriate action to have it transferred from the main stores to the point at which it is first needed.

2. Ensuring that all production/operations aids are ready when required and then having them issued to the appropriate departments.

3. Obtaining appropriate drawings/specifications/procedural instructions and material lists. These must be checked to confirm that they are the correct issue required.

4. Withdrawing job/operation tickets, bonus cards, operation layouts, route cards, material requisitions and any other necessary paperwork. These are issued to the appropriate supervisor.

5. Obtaining the inspection/checking schedules. This information is issued to the inspection/control department, along with advice that work is about to commence.

6. Informing the appropriate supervisors and the progress section that work is about to start.

7. At the conclusion, ensuring all process layouts, instructions and so on are returned to their correct location.

Issuing work

It is possible, particularly when using a computer, to schedule work and prepare it for launching far ahead of its required starting date. There is then a temptation for the despatcher to issue all the work that has been scheduled. However, this should generally be firmly resisted: only those jobs whose starting dates are imminent should be despatched. Should all jobs be issued, the supervisor will be presented with work which cannot be encompassed in the next planning period and will then have to make a choice among the work, which may well create the undesirable situation of completing work that is not required immediately and leaving undone work that is needed urgently.

Progress

Once work has started, it is necessary to check that it is proceeding according to plan. It might be considered *either* that this is unnecessary (since work is going as anticipated) *or* that it is a tacit admission of inefficiency (since work is not going as anticipated). On these grounds, it could be argued that if a car is being driven along a straight road it is not necessary to watch its progress. Just as the car will encounter irregularities in the road which, although slight, may accumulate to cause it to deviate from its intended route, so it will be found that there are many factors over which the production/operations manager has little or no control which can affect the operations. For example:

1. Materials may be delivered late.
2. Associated departments/sections may be behind in their own operations.
3. There may be excessive absenteeism, beyond that anticipated.
4. The customer may change his requirements.
5. Strikes or 'acts of God' can hold up processing.
6. Breakdowns may be greater than anticipated.

Furthermore, all plans are liable to be in error due to normal human failings; errors due to deliberate malevolence are rare, and are usually readily detected.

The receptionist allocating a taxi to take a passenger to town cannot anticipate the accident which will delay the taxi and prevent it from picking up the next passenger he/she has allocated to it in time for this passenger to catch a particular train.

The progress chaser

The comparison of performance with plan is the responsibility of the progress department. This is normally staffed by clerical workers (progress clerks) who record, collate and compare information, and by perambulatory staff known as *progress chasers* (in the USA 'expediters'). The chaser is responsible for seeing that any details which have been overlooked, or which have not proceeded according to plan, are put right. These details are often of such a nature that they can be resolved only by very detailed investigations, involving much walking and talking. In small organizations, these duties are often carried out by the first level supervisor, but in geographically large units there may be such time taken in going from one section to another that the supervisor is away from his/her own department an undesirably long time.

Product and process responsibilities

Chasers may either be responsible for processes (i.e. for drills, or for data input) or for products (i.e. for the progress of a single job from inception to completion). The process responsibility has two advantages: that the chaser becomes very familiar with each individual in his sphere of activity, knowing the strengths and weaknesses of each; and secondly, that he knows intimately the geographical disposition of the department, being able to identify immediately the places where items are most likely to be mislaid.

On the other hand, with highly complex manufactured products the effect of variations in production and design can be appreciated only by persons with design experience; as a result, product chasing is often necessary, the chaser being dignified by the name of *project engineer*. The project engineer has an overall view of a project, and can foresee and counteract the effects of weaknesses in any department upon the project as a whole. There is a tendency today to employ product and process chasers simultaneously.

It must be clearly understood, of course, that the chaser supplies an advisory service and has no authority over direct operations personnel. Informal arrangements may often arise whereby the chaser acts in the supervisor's place, but it must never happen that the responsibility for output, which is unquestionably the supervisor's, should devolve upon the chaser. The chaser should always discuss problems with the appropriate supervisor, never the operator. Should the results of these discussions be unsatisfactory, he should then move up the organizational structure to the person to whom he is next responsible.

The fundamental problems of progress

Ideally, the progress section should always be able to provide detailed information on the location and state of all the work which is in progress. This should be capable of being done from existing records supplemented by detailed knowledge obtained by the chaser at the point of work. This ideal can be very difficult to attain, even in quite small organizations, because of the complexity of the situation which arises from two fundamental problems:

1. *The problem of data capture.* The returning of information from an operations department to POCD is usually regarded by operators and supervisors as an unnecessary and irritating ritual, and is carried out with great reluctance and little accuracy. Furthermore, this information must be in a usable form: surprisingly enough, chasers themselves tend to record information in the most unsatisfactory way, often relying on memory and scraps of paper rather than written records.
2. *The problem of volume.* The information once obtained will be of great volume, yet much of it will excite little interest, since it will relate to work which is, in fact, proceeding satisfactorily. Hence it is necessary to sift and analyse the information obtained.

The receptionist in a doctor's surgery can be frustrated by the doctor calling for his next patient himself. She knows neither how long he will be with his current patient, nor even who the current patient is. This can make further 'planning' somewhat difficult.

Data capture

Information can be obtained from an operations department in a number of ways:

1. *Automatically.* If a process is linked to a machine or conveyor, mechanical, electrical or electronic counting and/or recording devices may be used. These can also be employed if it is possible to guarantee that all products pass a particular point.
2. *In the operator's work record.* The operator can be required to maintain a log, showing which operations, and how many of each, he/she has carried out. This can be done in very abbreviated form involving little writing, and is probably most satisfactory for repetitive work. It will sometimes require verifying by the supervisor.
3. *On a job card.* This is a variation of the work record, in that the operator is presented with a card specifying the work to be done. It is usually prepared in the POCD from the specified route for the work, and can form an authority for the operator to carry out the task specified. The operator will fill in the quantity of the operation carried out, his/her name and any other information required. The cards are collected daily and returned to the progress section for analysis. This technique is particularly useful in small batch production since the card itself can be used as part of the scheduling system and can instruct the operator in the task he/she is to carry out; it will thus relieve the supervisor of these duties.
4. *On detachable tickets.* If production is repetitive, a ticket can be prepared which

accompanies each item. Each ticket will bear the job number of the product, the serial number of the individual item (if applicable) and a list of the operations through which the product will pass. The ticket will be fixed to the product as part of the first operation and, as each operation is completed, the operator will sign the appropriate portion of the ticket and detach it, placing it in a box designated for that purpose. This box is emptied at least daily by the progress clerk, and the results prepared by analysing these tickets. For fast-moving work this can be very useful, since the operator is involved in very little work. A disadvantage is that the tear-off portions can become lost.

5. *By walk-and-count*. This is the most primitive method of all, and relies on the progress chaser's walking round his/her own sphere of activity and counting the work seen. It would be most unwise to rely solely on this method of collecting information, since it can be very tedious and inaccurate if carried out continuously.

The information obtained above is necessary for the production control department to carry out its duties. It must be pointed out, however, that the information is very similar to that required by the costing department and the wages department if an incentive bonus scheme is in use. If possible, the bonus cards should be used to provide progress information, since they will tend to be filled in promptly and accurately. Organizationally, the turn-round of information must be very rapid since both the progress and the bonus departments require it at the same time. Often these cards go first to the progress section which, after abstracting the required information, will pass them on to the bonus section.

Volume

The volume of information obtained is particularly great when items are being batch-produced. Job production clearly presents little difficulty in this respect, while flow production can be considered to be single-operation production, where again volume is not so difficult. Furthermore, flow production has the advantage that any difficulties are immediately brought to notice since they affect the whole system.

Batch production not only presents the most difficulty but also has the greatest need for feedback of information. Two methods for reducing the volume of data are suggested below:

1. *Key points*. In any processing sequence there will be found to be a number of key points arising from either the processing method itself or from the geographical layout of the department. Such key points are often found to be inspection or verification points. If information is obtained only at these points, then it will be possible to localize problems without pinpointing them. This type of short cut will reduce the volume of information considerably, though at the same time sacrificing some detail.

2. *Complete batch*. During manufacture it is found that there is a temptation to move each item of a batch on to the next location as soon as it has been processed. This is particularly so if the batch is 'urgent'. This can result in a batch being spread throughout the whole organization and, as a consequence, information will need to be obtained about each item. If, however, the batch is

kept complete, the volume of information is much reduced, since a single return will give all that is required. Moreover, this will also simplify other aspects of production administration, for example material issue and control, and loading. When batches are expected to move through departments at a regular rate, then colour coding can offer the potential of identifying deviations from this regular pattern.

The use of the computer

Computers can play a major role in the areas of despatch and progress as part of a production control system. If this system is being used to produce a schedule, covering both the resources (operators and facilities) and materials, then much of the information required by the despatcher is available from the system. The load calculations can be used as a guide to determine the timing of the work to release, and the system can actually be used to produce much of the documentation to accompany this release: job cards, route cards, material requisitions, and so on. Use of the computer can significantly improve the quality of this documentation, particularly in the areas relating to legibility and provision of adequate instructions. Indeed, this can go as far as the paperwork which ultimately reaches the customer.

Bar coding

The computer system can also provide the facilities to analyse the data on the progress of the work through the department. However, it is just as dependent as the clerical systems on accurate and timely feedback of these data. Early systems mimicked manual procedures, relying on keying into the computer once a day information from the job cards returned from completed work. The computer could process the data much faster, but still relied on the operator to fill in the card accurately and return it speedily on completion of the work. With the availability of systems offering on-line real-time access, it has become possible to allow the operator to feed

ISBN 0-273-03235-6

9 780273 032359

Fig. 25.1   A bar code

back directly to the computer information on completed work, and, if appropriate, to see details of the future load and outstanding work. In this way the computer should always have an accurate and up-to-date picture of the status of all work. Developments in data-capture devices have significantly improved this aspect. The *bar code* (Fig. 25.1) is having a significant impact here.

When producing documentation for the release of work, this can include a printed bar code which enables the computer subsequently to identify the job. An operator can then simply use a bar-code reader to feed back information quickly and accurately to the computer on the status of the job as it goes through different sections. Depending on circumstances, this information can be stored locally and part-processed before being fed back to the production planning system, or it can effectively be fed directly back. It is claimed that, using bar codes, data can be entered three times faster than by a skilled keypunch operator, and that whilst manual data entry using keyboards might generate one error every 300 characters, with high-quality bar codes the figure is one error in 300 million characters scanned. These, then, offer significant potential to the progress function to overcome the fundamental problems.

The codes themselves can be of considerable use in other areas, since they should uniquely identify the item. Instead of being allocated randomly they can encapsulate an abbreviated description of the principal 'parameters' of an item. Thus the first two digits could specify the principal material used in the manufacture, the next the processing requirements, the next the major dimensions. These codes then form the basis of a classification system which can be used in such areas as variety reduction (standardization) and the formation of group technology cells.

Presentation of progress information

The information collected by the progress department will provoke action only when it shows that some task is *not* proceeding according to plan. It is necessary therefore to present the information in such a manner that deviations from plan are made immediately and urgently observable. This is most easily done with the aid of charts or graphs, though the accountant's device of changing the colour of the figures can be used.

The type of graph chosen will depend upon the use to which the information is to be put. Broadly, however, charts may be considered as being of two types:

(a) individual charts, showing some single aspect of operations; and
(b) overall charts, showing the progress of interrelated functions.

Individual charts

If the output of a single operator, process or department is required to be scrutinized and compared with plan, it can be shown up very readily by means of a cumulative graph. For example, suppose that the planned and actual number of transactions handled by an office are as shown in Table 25.1.

Table 25.1 Number of planned transactions versus actual number

| | Transactions handled | | | |
| | Planned | | Achieved | |
Day	Daily	Cumulative	Daily	Cumulative
1	4		4	
2	5	9	4	8
3	6	15	7	15
4	7	22	8	23
5	8	30	9	32
6	8	38	8	40
7	8	46	7	47
8	8	54	8	55
9	8	62	7	62
10	8	70	7	69
11	9	79	8	77
12	10	89	8	85
13	11	100	8	93
14	12	112	9	102
15	13	125		
16	14	139		
17	13	152		
18	12	164		
19	11	175		
20	10	185		
I	II	III	IV	V

Examination of the daily numbers (columns II and IV) will not readily reveal the failure to meet the plan: the cumulative figures (columns III and V) do in fact show the failure, but if these figures are represented graphically, then the failure becomes more striking (see Fig. 25.2).

This can be readily understood at all levels, and is very simple to construct and interpret. Care is needed in the choice of scales, but no difficulty will be found after a little practice. This type of graph is ideal for representing output and, with experience, can be very versatile.

Overall-charts

When a number of interrelated functions have to be represented simultaneously, the single-line graph is inadequate. Two or three graphs can be drawn on the same axes – beyond this number, the graph becomes cluttered and difficult to interpret. Furthermore, the relationship between various features is difficult to represent. For this reason it is necessary to use some other visual representation, and the most common is the Gantt chart.

When scheduling, it was seen that the simplest method of planning a complex series of functions was to use a chart relating time with required performance. Thus, if operation A is required to start on the fifth day and finish on the fourteenth day of

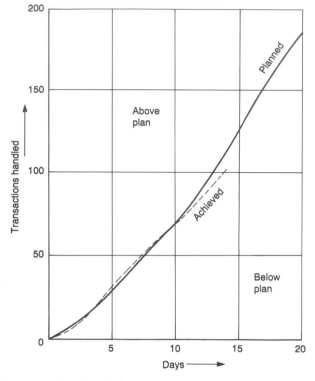

Fig. 25.2   Cumulative transactions handled

a sequence, while operation B starts on the ninth day and finishes on the twentieth of the same sequence, the chart should be as shown in Fig. 25.3(a). This shows clearly the interrelation between operations A and B as far as requirements go. The length of the bar represents time: if now it is also assumed to represent performance, the chart will be able to be used to show the relation between actual and planned. Assume that at the end of day 9 only 20 per cent of operation A were complete: this would be represented as in Fig. 25.3(b).

The length of the heavy bar represents performance, and it is only 20 per cent of the total length of line A. This shows clearly that operation A is lagging behind target, since after five days 50 per cent of the operation should have been completed. On the other hand, assume that at the end of day 11 operation A was 50 per cent complete while operation B was also 30 per cent complete. This would be represented as in Fig. 25.3(c).

The length of the operation B bar represents 30 per cent of the total length, and since only 25 per cent should have been completed by day 11, it extends beyond the cursor marks.

This simple device, of permitting length to represent both time and performance, is known as a Gantt chart and is widely used in very many applications. By a series of simple annotations, reasons for delays can also be represented, so that the chart can show a comprehensive picture of the state of a department. Most proprietary planning and progress boards are Gantt charts, performance being shown by coloured

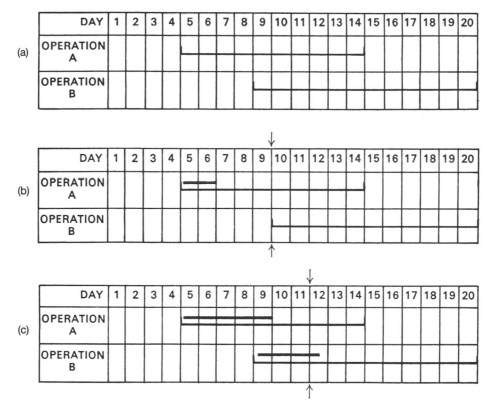

Fig. 25.3 Time–performance (Gantt) charts

markers, pegs, tapes or strings; few give information greater than the simple hand-drawn Gantt, although the use of colour may make the representation more vivid, but they often have the advantage of being able to be simply rearranged. Once a hand-drawn Gantt chart requires to be altered, it is necessary to re-draw it – a tedious operation.

Many computerized planning packages offer the option of Gantt chart-type output, and with graphics packages and printers these offer great scope for an up-to-date visual representation of status that is easy to interpret.

CHAPTER 25 – HIGHLIGHTS

- Despatching is the releasing of work so that the transformation process can start. A number of tasks must be completed in preparation of the commencement of the job including preparing procedure statements and material lists and requisitions.
- Progress chasing is monitoring the actual operations against planned operations.
- Problems in monitoring progress include capturing accurate data, and the volume of data.
- Methods for capturing data include: automatic counting or recording; the work record; the job card; detachable tickets; or 'walk-and-count'.
- The volume can be handled by monitoring at key points, or by moving items in batches.
- The role of computers lie in rapid processing of progress data and in data capture via bar codes.
- Progress information may be presented on individual charts (actual versus planned cumulative), or on overall charts (Gantt charts).

Recommended reading

See Recommended reading for Chapter 21.

Inventory Management

In most organizations the cost of material forms a substantial part of the final selling price of the product. Where the interval between receiving the purchased material and its transformation into profit by selling the completed product is short, then the cost of holding the material is likely to be insignificant. However, material is frequently stored either raw, partly finished or completely finished, and the costs associated with this can be high. There are a number of ways in which these costs can be calculated: it would seem reasonable to consider stock as an investment from which a return is expected. Since no return is forthcoming because the investment, being in materials, is being held like 'cash in biscuit tins under the bed', then these costs can be taken to include the 'loss' represented by failure to earn the expected return. Thus, if company policy requires that any investment should yield a return of 20 per cent of its value each year, then holding stock can be said to cost at least 20 per cent a year of the average value of the stock held. The cost of holding stocks worth £1,000,000 for one year will, therefore, be at least £200,000 when calculated on the above basis. If the money to purchase the stock has had to be borrowed, then the financing charges must be added to the cost.

However great the holding cost as a fraction of the value, it would be unimportant if the value of the stocks held were small. Unfortunately, this is all too frequently not the case. This can be confirmed by consulting any of the government statistics which summarize the various figures (including stock valuation) reported in company balance sheets. Indeed, these summaries are likely to under-estimate the true situation, since the valuations are frequently taken at one point in time, and it is not unknown for levels to be manipulated to present a more favourable picture.

The task of the materials control department

The materials control department is assumed to be required to maintain an adequate supply of correct material at the lowest total cost. The responsibilities include:

1. Determining the material requirements implied by the marketing forecast, and liaising with the purchasing department for their acquisition.

2. Receiving and storing the material, safely and in good condition, for its subsequent issue.
3. Issuing material upon receipt of appropriate authority.
4. Identifying surplus stock, and taking action to reduce it.

Buying/purchasing is a function which is not necessarily part of the task of materials control. Whilst it is on occasions claimed that the buyer should be a member of the materials control department, this is largely a matter of local organization and will depend upon, among other things, the value of the material compared with the selling price. For convenience, purchasing will be treated in a later chapter.

Types of materials

Various 'types' of materials may be managed and controlled by an organization:

1. *Raw materials and bought-in items*. These are 'processed' and value added to them to provide the required finished item.
2. *Work-in-progress*. These materials have been part-processed but are not yet in the form required by the customer.
3. *Finished products*.
4. *Service materials*, used in service and maintenance operations (e.g. cleaning fluid, light bulbs, printer ribbons).

Thus a pizza restaurant might hold stocks of tomatoes, cheese and flour which are eventually going to be used to make the pizzas and toppings. There may also be stocks of pizza bases (the dough having been prepared earlier) on to which a customer's specific requirement for topping can be added, and there may be stocks of 'standard' pizzas prepared for the 'take-out' market. There will be stocks of materials associated with running the restaurant, such as dish-washer powder.

Normally, the first and last type are the responsibility of the materials manager. Service materials can be regarded as 'indirect' in that their cost cannot be allocated, but must be apportioned and absorbed by 'cost centres'. Raw materials can be either 'indirect' or 'direct', in that their cost can be allocated.

The responsibility for the management of work-in-progress and finished products may be with the materials control department; equally, it could lie with some other section within the organization. Stocks of work-in-progress or finished products may result from inadequacies in the planning and control system, or from a deliberate policy to reduce the manufacturing time. The stocks of pizza bases enable diners to choose whatever pizza they require, but without having to wait for the entire pizza to be prepared and cooked.

In determining requirements, it is frequently necessary to forecast usage in the near future. There are various techniques available for this: some were presented in an earlier chapter.

Lead time

A term frequently used in materials management is 'lead time', which may be defined to be the interval between the perception and the fulfilment of a need. Two different but related variants are the procurement lead time and the manufacturing lead time. The former will be dealt with here; the latter will be discussed later. The procurement lead time is not necessarily the same as the delivery time, since it also includes the time required to place an order and the time to receive the goods into the appropriate store:

Procurement lead time		
Ordering time	Delivery time	Receiving time

The two components 'ordering' and 'receiving' can be substantial. It is frustrating but not uncommon for an operations manager to raise a purchase requisition and then to discover two weeks later that the purchase order has not been despatched. Equally, it is not unknown for a buyer to ring a supplier to enquire about an apparently late delivery, only to discover that it had arrived two weeks ago, but had not been cleared through 'goods inward inspection'.

The cost of this uncertainty in the lead time can be significant, not simply in terms of the annoyance, but because of the higher-than-necessary stock levels which are frequently maintained to allow for it. These first and last components are within the control of the organization and their careful management can reduce the uncertainty.

Approaches to materials control

Materials can be managed and controlled from two different, but related, perspectives. It is possible to examine the behaviour of the item itself in isolation – the independent demand situation, frequently advocated as the approach for finished products, or for service materials. Alternatively it is possible to examine the consequences of orders for finished products on an item (or items) – the dependent demand situation, suggested as appropriate for raw materials and work-in-progress.

The sheer volume of data to handle in materials management can present a daunting task, unless a computer is used, and even then it is not always appropriate to apply the same degree of control to all items. Pareto (or A–B–C) analysis can be used (based on the average value of the annual usage) to group the products. This can then provide a guide to the appropriate degree of control – tight, medium or loose (or free issue) (see Appendix 1) – to apply to each group. It is frequently found that by tightly controlling just 20 per cent of the products, it is possible to control 80 per cent of the value of the annual usage.

Material requirements planning (MRP) is one method of managing dependent demand items, and will be covered later in this chapter.

The independent demand situation

The trigger which causes the authorization of further purchases of stock, in this case, is the behaviour of the stock itself. Since this decision does not directly depend on the orders placed for finished goods, it is sometimes said to be an independent demand system. There are a number of procedures available, details of which can be found in the Recommended reading. Two of the more common systems will be outlined.

1. *The fixed order quantity or two-bin system.* With this, orders are placed when the level of stock has dropped to a previously determined level (the re-order level, or ROL). An order is placed for a (normally) fixed quantity (the re-order quantity or ROQ). The ROL is based on an analysis of the demand and procurement lead time, and it is chosen so that the replenishment order it triggers arrives just as the stock is expected to reach a minimum level. The ROQ is frequently based on economic considerations, one such approach being illustrated later in this section.

   Thus photocopier paper could be issued from two boxes, normally from the first box; when this is empty, sufficient to refill the box is ordered. While this is 'procured' the supply in the second box is used.

2. *The fixed re-order interval system.* With this, re-ordering takes place cyclically, i.e. an attempt is made to assess the usage and then re-order at fixed intervals of time. The quantity ordered can be either fixed or more usually calculated to bring the stock back to some predetermined maximum level. This cyclical ordering has the advantage that suppliers know well in advance when orders are going to be received; alternatively, if parts are made in the organization's own plant, the production control department can plan machine and labour loads at the beginning of the planning period. It also allows the purchasing department to plan its own work to the best advantage.

   Thus each week, sufficient paper to bring the level stocked up to, say 5,000 reams, might be ordered.

These approaches offer the opportunity of transforming aspects of materials management into a programmable structure which can be delegated or handled by a computer. They could be applied to the 50 per cent of products which often comprise 5 per cent of the annual value of usage (see Appendix 1), allowing attention to focus on the 20 per cent of products generating 80 per cent of the value of the annual usage.

Economic batch size (EBS)

The quantity to be ordered, whether from inside sources or outside suppliers, is dependent on a number of opposing factors. In any purchase or manufacture, there is an element of ancillary cost, either when plant is set up, cleaned or changed over, or when a purchase order is placed. This ancillary cost is spread over the number of items in the batch, and from this viewpoint the larger the batch size, the fewer batches are required per year and the lower the annual ancillary cost. However, with these larger batch sizes, higher average stock levels are held; this increases stockholding costs. The calculation of the most economical size of batch

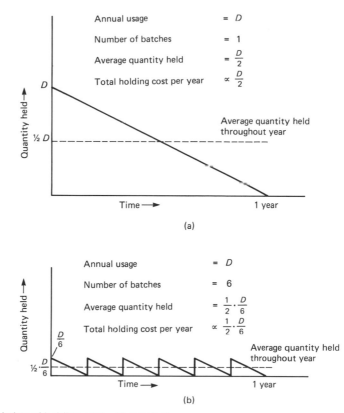

Fig. 26.1 Variation of holding cost with batch size

to manufacture is extremely difficult, involving, among other things, a knowledge of the costs attributable to unused capacity. The purchasing situation, however, is more tractable and the calculation can be usefully carried out.

While all the variations of the basic economic batch size formulation cannot be displayed here, the most commonly performed calculation illustrates the basic concepts. The ancillary cost is, in this case, the marginal cost of raising and servicing an order (the 'purchasing cost') and the simplifying assumption is made that (see Fig. 26.1) the product is used uniformly throughout the year. The annual requirement can be either bought in one batch, stocked and used from stores, or it can be bought as a number of batches (six are illustrated), stocked and again drawn from stores. In the first case the average quantity held throughout the year is higher than the average quantity held throughout the year in the second. Consequently, the annual holding cost in the first case is higher than in the second. Since the lead time and requirement are assumed to be constant, stockouts never occur, and there is no stockout cost, so the total annual cost is the sum of the annual holding cost, the annual ancillary cost and the annual purchase cost of the materials. The optimum batch quantity is where the total cost is a minimum, this being known as the economic batch quantity.

This result is illustrated in Fig. 26.2: as the batch size increases, the annual holding cost increases in proportion; whereas, if it is assumed that the ancillary

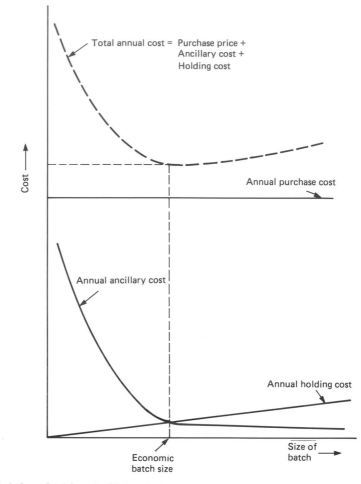

Fig. 26.2   Variation of total cost with batch size

cost is constant, independent of batch size, then the annual ancillary cost reduces as the batch quantity increases. The unit purchase cost is also assumed constant and independent of batch size, so the total annual cost is the sum of these three components, with the shape of the broken curve.

The accurate calculation of this economic batch size is difficult, and it has given rise to a number of alternative analyses. These difficulties arise from problems concerning the calculation of the holding cost, since this depends on a number of factors which are difficult to assess, such as the expected return on invested capital, cost of storekeeping, cost of material, wastage, depreciation, obsolescence, insurance, and a number of other factors of varying importance; and from the calculation of the ancillary cost.

The variation of total cost with batch size is illustrated numerically in the following example. As stated earlier, it is assumed that neither unit purchase cost nor ancillary cost varies with the batch size.

Assume:

Purchase price/cost	= £3 each
Annual holding cost	= 35% value of goods stocked
Purchasing cost for each batch	= £20
Annual usage	= 800

Number of batches	Batch size	Average annual quantity stored	Average value of stock	Total annual holding cost	Total annual purchasing cost	Total annual cost (carrying and purchasing cost)*
1	800	400	1,200	420	20	440
2	400	200	600	210	40	250
5	160	80	240	84	100	184
10	80	40	120	42	200	242
20	40	20	60	21	400	421

* For convenience, the fixed annual purchase cost (800 × £3) has been omitted.

The formula for the economic batch size (EBS) Q^* can be shown to be:

$$Q^* = \sqrt{\frac{2SD}{IC}}$$

where S = purchasing cost per batch;
D = annual usage;
I = annual holding cost as a fraction of the stock value;
C = unit price/cost of the item being purchased.

Using the values in the example:

S = £20
D = 800
I = 0.35
C = £3

$$Q^* = \sqrt{\frac{2 \times 20 \times 800}{0.35 \times 3}} = 174.6$$

Derivation of the simple EBS formula
Let the quantity ordered be Q. Then:

Number of orders placed per year	= D/Q
and Annual purchasing cost	= SD/Q
Average quantity held per year	= $Q/2$
∴ Annual holding cost	= $QCI/2$

Total annual variable cost, $T = \dfrac{SD}{Q} + QCI/2$

The EBS results from T being a minimum, which occurs when:

$$\frac{dT}{dQ} = 0, \text{ and } \frac{d^2T}{dQ^2} > 0$$

That is, when:

$$-\frac{SD}{Q^*} + \frac{CI}{2} = 0$$

or, rearranging, when:

$$Q^* = \sqrt{\frac{2SD}{CI}}$$

Note: In the above it is assumed that:
1. The unit purchase price is constant.
2. The usage is substantially constant.
3. It is not permitted to be out of stock.
4. Orders are fulfilled in one delivery.
5. Lead time is constant.

The sensitivity of the EBS
The EBS formula involves a square root and, as a consequence, there can be no guarantee that a 'sensible' result will be produced in relation to purchasing decisions. Indeed, in the earlier example, the formula gave a batch size of 174.6 items! In fact, the total cost curve is normally shallow round the optimum so no serious increase would arise from taking a value of 175. There will always be an element of uncertainty in the cost parameters. Instead of specifying a single value of the batch size, it is possible, after selecting an acceptable allowable percentage increase in minimum total variable cost, to calculate a range for the batch sizes which satisfy this. For the earlier example, if a 5 per cent increase is acceptable, any batch size in the range 127–239 will produce a cost within 5 per cent of the theoretical minimum.

The effect of price breaks on the EBS
It is not unusual for a supplier to offer to reduce the unit purchase price if a minimum quantity is purchased ('If you buy at 300 units at a time the price will drop to £2.95 each. . . .') The effect of this change in price – the 'price break' – can be seen by comparing the total cost at the EBS at the existing price level and the total cost at the price break level. The total cost curve of Fig. 26.2 then takes the form of Fig. 26.3.

It is also possible to turn the analysis round, and answer questions like 'What discount must be given on the price of £3 each to result in an order quantity of 500 being preferable to the calculated minimum cost value of 175?'

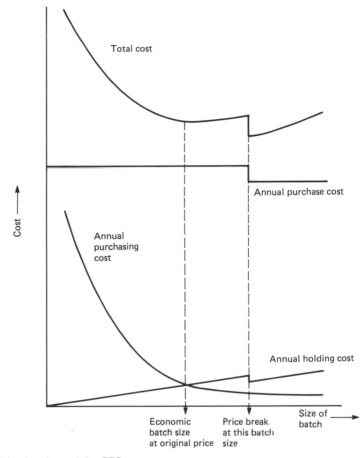

Fig. 26.3 Price breaks and the EBS

Insurance or safety stock

The above analysis assumes that the demand and lead time are known and substantially constant; in reality, both are likely to be subject to a mixture of random and predictable variation. In this case, the ROQ can still be estimated using the latest demand forecast as input into the EBS formula.

The ROL is dependent on the number of items expected to be required during the lead time, so in the 'constant' case this causes no problem. In the previous example, if the lead time is given as five weeks, then assuming 50 weeks per year, the ROL is $5 \times 16 = 80$, and the ROQ of 175 will arrive just as the last unit is used. However, if both the lead time and demand vary, the situation changes: the demand could be higher than anticipated, resulting in a stockout. In setting the ROL it is necessary to have safety stock, in addition to the expected demand in the expected lead time, to allow for this situation. This is shown in Fig. 26.4.

The choice of safety stock level can be related to the risk the manager is prepared to take of running out of stock. This can be viewed in the context of the various costs involved, some of which are outlined below.

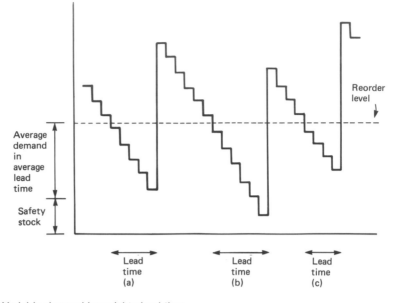

Fig. 26.4   Variable demand in variable lead time
  (a)   Average demand and average lead time
  (b)   Higher-than-average demand, longer-than-average lead time
  (c)   Lower-than-average demand, shorter-than-average lead time

1.   For finished products, the cost depends on whether the customer is prepared to wait or goes elsewhere for his requirement. It can involve loss of profit, lost goodwill.
2.   For raw materials, the cost depends on the consequences:
   (a)   running out of stock may result in idle workers and equipment; the cost could be proportional to the number of units short and the period of the shortage;
   (b)   production/operations may have to be replanned, a fixed cost largely independent of the number of items short and the period of the shortage;
   (c)   it may be necessary to buy from an alternative source at a premium price, incurring an additional cost proportional to the number of units short.

The use of safety stock increases the average stock level by this amount, having a consequential effect on the holding cost. If the uncertainty can be reduced, the situation can be improved. This can be achieved through a structured collection and analysis of data on demand and lead time, use of forecasting methods, and the tight management of those elements of the lead time which are within the control of the organization.

The dependent demand situation: material requirements planning (MRP)

The methods in the previous section can operate quite simply and satisfactorily when orders for finished goods are being received at a constant or at least smoothly and slowly varying rate, and this is reflected in the work-in-progress and raw materials requirements. However, when demand for the finished product is lumpy or erratic, then these methods may involve holding stocks of work-in-progress or raw materials for excessively long periods of time. Under these circumstances it can be desirable to use some form of control of purchasing and manufacturing which is derived from an examination of the orders received for the finished goods. One such form of control is known as material requirements planning or MRP, and since the control depends upon the order for the finished products, this procedure is said to be one of 'dependent demand'.

The approach is best illustrated with a short example concerning a small plant which makes furniture, specifically wooden-framed chairs and two-seat settees. The chair is shown in Fig. 26.5. The method of manufacture and materials for both products are very similar: wood (nominally 3 cm by 9 cm) is used to make two ends and two cross-pieces joining the ends. A frame to support the cushions is made from steel tube, rubber webbing and fabric which matches the cushions. Seat and back cushions are made from this fabric and foam chippings. Special patented fasteners are used in the final assembly.

Each seat cushion requires 0.60 m of fabric and 450 g of foam. Each back cushion requires 0.70 m of fabric and 550 g of foam. The chair has one of each type of cushion, the settee two. The end-pieces, which are common to both products, each

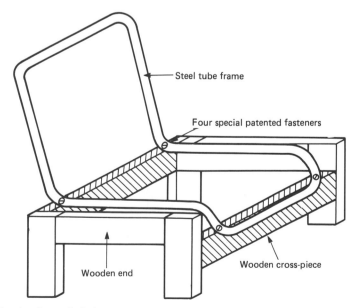

Fig. 26.5 Wooden-framed chair

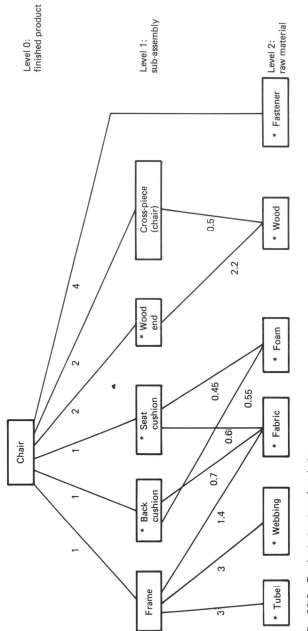

Fig. 26.6   Product structure for chair
Notes: *Indicates common item with settee. The number to the left of each link shows the number/quantity of the lower-level item needed in the manufacture of the higher-level item

require 2.20 m of wood, while the cross-piece for the chair is 0.50 m long, and for the settee 1.10 m long. The metal frame for the chair used 3.00 m of tube, 3.00 m of webbing and 1.40 m of fabric; for the settee the lengths are 6.00 m, 6.00 m and 2.80 m respectively. Four of the special fasteners are used in the assembly of the chair, six in the assembly of the settee.

The relationship between the finished product, its constituent parts and the raw materials can be shown in a product structure diagram, or bill of materials (BOM). This 'parts explosion' is shown in Fig. 26.6 for the chair. Level 0 traditionally refers to the finished product; in this example, there are only two other levels: level 1 – sub-assemblies; and level 2 – raw materials.

It is also necessary to have information relating to the current stock position with respect to all items. Included in this information are the various lead times, since if for example 500 m of wood are required in week 6, the materials manager must know that the procurement lead time is two weeks so that the order can be placed in week 4. This information is given in Fig. 26.7.

Item code	Item description	Unit of measure	Quantity on hand	Lead time	Safety stock
0–0000–01	Chair	each	25	1	20
0–0000–02	Settee	each	30	1	20
1–1200–01	Wood end	each	50	2	0
1–2000–02	Cross-piece – settee	each	65	1	0
1–1000–03	Cross-piece – chair	each	70	1	0
1–2000–04	Metal frame – settee	each	25	2	0
1–1000–05	Metal frame – chair	each	5	2	0
1–1200–06	Seat cushion	each	45	2	0
1–1200–07	Back cushion	each	45	2	0
2–4500–01	Webbing	metre	50	3	50
2–1230–02	Wood	metre	65	2	100
2–4567–03	Fabric	metre	95	3	50
2–6700–04	Foam	kilo	110	2	50
1–1200–08	Fastener	each	98	1	200
2–4500–05	Steel tube	metre	84	2	50

- An order for 100 metres of wood is due to arrive at the start of week 3
- An order for 500 fasteners is due to arrive at the start of week 2
- An order for 20 kilos of foam is due to arrive at the start of week 2

- Lead time is weeks to procure for raw materials (level 2)
- Lead time is weeks to manufacture/assemble for levels 1 and 0

Fig. 26.7 Stock status at week 1

It is currently week 1, and there are orders for 200 settees for week 8, 350 chairs for week 9, and 100 replacement seat cushions for week 7. These requirements are 'exploded' down through the bills of materials, and the implications for the sub-assemblies and raw materials assessed.

This process starts with the level 0 items; in general the gross requirements (GR) are taken, and the net requirements (NR) calculated taking account of the on-hand stock (OH), the orders due (OD) and the required safety stock (SS). The planned orders (PO) are then the NR offset by the lead time, known as 'time phasing'. The PO for the level 0 items provide the basis of the GR for the level 1 items, taking account of the product structure diagram, and the process repeats for all the level 1 items, cascading down the levels.

For chairs: GR = 350 (week 9)
NR = GR − OH − OD + SS = 350 − 25 + 20 = 345 (week 9)
Since the lead time is 1 week, PO = 345 (week 8)

For settees: GR = 200 (week 8)
NR = GR − OH − OD + SS = 200 − 30 + 20 = 190 (week 9)
Since the lead time is 1 week, PO = 190 (week 7)

Cascading down to the level 1 items, *all* should be considered, but for the purposes of this illustration only cushions will be considered. Both of the planned orders for settees and chairs will generate gross requirements for cushions. That resulting from settees is selected first since it is earlier in time.

For back cushions: 1. GR = 190 × 2 = 380 (week 7) (resulting from the PO for 190 settees in week 7, each settee requires 2 back cushions)
NR = GR − OH − OD + SS = 380 − 45 = 335 (week 7)
Since the lead time is 2 weeks, PO = 335 (week 5)
2. GR = 345 (week 8) (resulting from the PO for 345 chairs in week 8)
NR = GR − OH − OD + SS = 345 (week 8)
PO = 345 (week 6)

For seat cushions: 1. GR = 190 × 2 + 100 (week 7) (resulting from the PO for 190 settees in week 7, each settee requires 2 seat cushions, plus order for 100 replacements)
NR = GR − OH − OD + SS = 480 − 45 = 435 (week 7)
Since the lead time is 2 weeks, PO = 435 (week 5)
2. GR = 345 (week 8) (resulting from the PO for 345 chairs in week 8)
NR = GR − OH − OD + SS = 345 (week 8)
PO = 345 (week 6)

When all level 1 items have been analysed, it is possible to cascade down and consider all level 2 items. For the purposes of this illustration, only foam will be considered.

For foam:
1. GR = 335 × 0.55 + 435 × 0.45 = 380 (week 5) (resulting from the PO for 335 back cushions in week 5, each requiring 0.550 kg of foam, and PO for 435 seat cushions in week 5, each requiring 0.450 kg of foam).
NR = GR − OH − OD + SS = 380 − 110 − 20 + 50 = 300 (week 5)
Since the lead time is 2 weeks, PO = 300 (week 3)
2. GR = 345 × 0.55 + 345 × 0.45 = 345 (week 6) (resulting from PO for 345 back cushions in week 6 and PO for 345 seat cushions in week 6)
NR = GR − OH − OD + SS = 345 (week 6)
PO = 345 (week 4)

These calculations can be seen summarized in Fig. 26.8 each block being referred to as the 'material requirements plan' for the item concerned.

	Time period (week)								
	1	2	3	4	5	6	7	8	9
Chair (safety stock = 20)									
• on hand	25	25	25	25	25	25	25		
• orders due									
• gross requirement									350
• net requirement									345
• planned orders								345	
Settee (safety stock = 20)									
• on hand	30	30	30	30	30	30			
• orders due									
• gross requirement								200	
• net requirement								190	
• planned orders							190		
Back cushion									
• on hand	45	45	45	45					
• orders due									
• gross requirement							380	345	
• net requirement							335	345	
• planned orders					335	345			
Seat cushion									
• on hand	45	45	45	45					
• orders due									
• gross requirement							480	345	
• net requirement							435	345	
• planned orders					435	345			
Foam (safety stock = 50)									
• on hand	110	130							
• orders due		20							
• gross requirement					380	345			
• net requirement					300	345			
• planned orders			300	345					

Fig. 26.8 Partial MRP calculation

It is sometimes argued that safety stock need not be used in MRP. However, it is sometimes incorporated into the finished product stock levels to allow for uncertainty in the requirements. Scrap, re-work, uncertainty in manufacturing lead times and varying 'yields' are sometimes used to justify safety stocks of sub-assemblies. Uncertainties in procurement lead times and quantities are sometimes quoted as reasons for raw materials safety stocks.

The overall structure of an MRP system is presented in Fig. 26.9.

There are three major inputs:

1. The bill of materials (BOM – illustrated in Fig. 26.6) for all level 0 (finished) products; this must be kept up to date with any product specification changes.
2. Stock status information for all items (including lead times, illustrated in Fig. 26.7); this should be updated with all relevant stock transactions as they occur.
3. Master production schedule (MPS) requirements for all level 0 items, period-by-period over the planning horizon. This MPS will be made up of both firm orders and forecasts further into the future, for each time period and item (for example week-by-week for the next three months) rather than simply single requirements as in the earlier illustration. Since all procurement, manufacturing and assembly plans are based on this, it is imperative that it represents the best possible estimate of requirements.

In the illustrations presented above, the calculations were trivial. In practice, however, there may be many level 0 items, each having a product structure with hundreds of parts at levels 1, 2 and so on; these structures may have many common items. The plan may extend over a number of periods. The calculations cease to be trivial, and substantial computing facilities are required. Moreover, significant volumes of data need to be stored. The basic reports include the material requirements plans for each item, summaries of planned orders, stock status and the ability to trace materials back to the level 0 items in which these are used, and relate this to the net requirements. Many computer packages are available for MRP, running on a wide range of sizes of computer. These offer the user the ability to re-run the analysis as circumstances (requirements, manufacturing capacity, time)

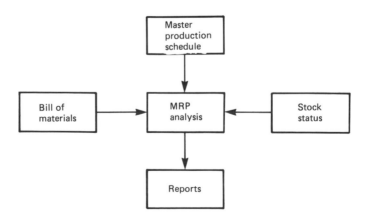

Fig. 26.9   MRP structure

change. In fact, if products are analysed into A–B–C categories on cost of usage, it can be possible to carry limited 'what if' MRP-type analysis rapidly for the 'A' items using a spreadsheet on a microcomputer.

The importance of accurate input data cannot be stressed enough. Sales forecasts forming the MPS must be as good as possible, inventory transactions must be routinely incorporated into the stock status data, and product changes must result in modifications to the product structure data. Many of the problems reported with the implementation of MRP have data inaccuracy as a contributory factor.

Manufacturing resources planning (MRP II)

The basic MRP procedures simply handle the materials aspects of production/operations control. No real account is taken of the resources available, apart from the inclusion of the manufacturing lead times in the analysis. Indeed, these are normally assumed to be constant, independent of the quantities being manufactured and other factors likely to influence them. MRP has been 'extended' in a number of directions. Rough-cut capacity planning is incorporated at the start, linking with the MPS. This can be used to evaluate the implications of the MPS for resources at the aggregate (department/section) level. There is no point in working with a MPS which places impossible demands on the manufacturing resources. This enables the MPS to be replanned or extra resources made available where necessary. The MRP is used to produce both detailed capacity plans and detailed materials plans, which in turn are implemented enabling shop-floor control and purchasing control to be carried out.

This enhancement, with MRP at its centre, forms the basis of manufacturing resources planning (MRP II). However, its application goes far in excess of simply materials management, so a detailed description will be deferred to a later chapter.

Materials management

Any effective inventory control system must have the appropriate procedures, documentation, information and organizational structure to support it.

Documentation

A stock control system will require a stock item file, which consists of the basic information on all items stocked with one record (or card in a manual system) for each item including basic information which falls into four categories:

(a) *General*:   Description
                   Code number
                   Unit of measure
                   Minimum level
                   Maximum level
                   Order quantity

(b) *Issues*:   Date
                      Works order number
                      Quantity issued
                      Balance
(c) *Purchases*:   Date of order
                      Purchase order number
                      Quantity ordered
                      Delivery date
                      Quantity delivered
                      Price
(d) *Allocation*:   Date allocated
                      Job number
                      Quantity
                      Date issued

The above list is not exhaustive and will have to be tailored to local circumstances. For example, some organizations may not use an allocation system, they 'earmark' stock for a particular job before actually issuing it to the job. Some types of items go into 'quarantine' on arrival in stock, only to be free for issue when some tests have been successfully completed. Sometimes it is necessary to be able to trace the materials issued to a job back to a particular delivery (lot-traceability). Stocks of some items may be held at several locations. Various different costing options may be required.

Each time a transaction occurs, it should be 'posted' against the appropriate areas (b), (c) or (d). Within a manual system (and possibly a computer system), this would require documentation for support:

1. *The materials (or stores) requisition.* This document authorizes issue of material, and should contain at least the following information:

   (a) material required, preferably with its code or part numbers;
   (b) quantity of material required;
   (c) originator's identification;
   (d) date of origin;
   (e) issuer's identification;
   (f) receiver's identification;
   (g) date issued;
   (h) quantity of material issued.

2. *Purchase requisition.* This is a request to the buyer to purchase material, and should bear the following minimum information:

   (a) material required with full specification;
   (b) quantity required;
   (c) date by which it is required;
   (d) estimated price;
   (e) originator's identification;
   (f) date of origin.

Under no circumstances should the entries be vague; thus the description 'as previously supplied' should not be used, nor should the date of requirement be 'as soon as possible'. Computer systems provide the discipline to require users to provide all the necessary information in an acceptable format.

Other documentation (reflecting various types of transaction) includes the following:

3. *A materials return or credit note*, which permits unused material to be returned from the manufacturing department to the stores.
4. *A materials transfer note*, which allows material to be transferred from one location to another or from one job to another.
5. *A scrap note*, which records the scrap generated and permits it to be handed in to the stores in exchange for good material.
6. *A shortage note*, which is issued from the stores to a requisitioner, informing him/her that material required is not available and citing the action being taken.

The stock record information can be held on a computer. If an integrated package is used, the production control module might access the stock item file to generate the materials requisitions, and the stock control module could produce the purchase requisitions. However, it is stressed that it is imperative that a detailed specification is produced for a potential computer application, identifying *all* the data to be stored and the transactions to be handled. Generally, manual systems are cheaper to modify after implementation than computer systems; moreover, the data are more 'visible' with a manual system. A very wide variety of 'off-the-shelf' computer packages are available for stock control.

Materials reduction programme

The stock valuation figure should include all stock except that which has been declared valueless and 'written off'. Often the so-called valuable stock includes much that is of little or no real worth notwithstanding the valuation placed upon it. Despite the lack of worth, the storage and 'annoyance' costs may be substantial, and any reduction in stock can have substantial real benefits, including reduction in holding costs and administrative and clerical effort, and increased availability of space.

The following steps can provide the foundation for a material reduction exercise.

1. Carry out an A–B–C analysis (see Appendix 1) of the value of stock held against the number of items of stock. Some computer-based stock management systems include the facility to carry out this analysis.
2. From the analysis, determine the A, B and C categories, the A items being those few which represent the bulk of the value, the C items being those many items of trivial value, and the B items being those of moderate value between A and C.
3. Examine the 'A' group to determine:
   (a) dead items – those which have not been used for two years;
   (b) slow-moving items – those which have been used in the last two years but have not moved in the last six months;
   (c) current items – those used within the last six months.

(*Note*: The definitions of these categories will vary from company to company and will depend upon the technology of the company concerned.)

4. Test the 'dead' items against the following:
   (a) Can they be used in place of current stock?
   (b) Can they be transferred into current stock?
   (c) Can a demand for them be predicted or stimulated?

If the answer to all the above is 'no', then the items should be written off and sold or given away. The arguments that they 'will come in useful one day' or 'we can't afford to get rid of them' are specious and must be resisted vigorously.

5. Repeat step 4 for slow-moving items.
6. Test the 'current' items against the following:
   (a) Is the

$$\text{Coverage} = \frac{\text{Units available}}{\text{Average units used}/\text{Unit time}}$$

   excessive? If so, then some part of the stock should be treated as 'dead' stock.
   (b) Can the unit price be reduced? Try (i) value analysis, (ii) work study of the manufacturing methods, (iii) alternative suppliers.
   (c) Can any item be made common with or interchangeable with other items? A good coding system is invaluable here.
   (d) Can the lead time for any item be reduced? The shorter the lead time (that is, the time between the decision to plan an order and its subsequent fulfilment), the lower the average value of stock which may be held. It may be that a supplier, hitherto discarded on price, may benefit the purchaser on grounds of a shorter, and more predictable, delivery.
   (e) Is the authority to purchase appropriately controlled? Item 'A' purchases are often better authorized only by senior members of the organization. The resulting inconvenience in getting such orders signed will, in itself, tend to discourage demands and purchases.
   (f) Is the stock-holding reviewed frequently enough? A perpetual inventory causing second stock checks of 'A' items can be of assistance here.
7. Repeat the above for 'B' items.
8. To try to carry out the above procedure for 'C' items is usually quite impossible, since the number of items is likely to be extremely large and the rewards obtained small. 'C' items, therefore, should be scrutinized only when stock cards are withdrawn for normal recording purposes. When step 7 above is completed, the whole process should be started again.

Storekeeping

Storekeeping is an important aspect of materials management and, for the purposes of this book, the storekeeper will be assumed to be responsible not only for the stores but also for the goods inwards or receiving role.

Responsibilities for goods inwards

All goods entering a unit should pass through a goods inwards section in order that their arrival should be recorded. The duties of this section include:

1. Recording the receipt of (or 'booking-in') all goods as they arrive.
2. Unpacking all goods and checking them against the originating order both for quantity and quality.
3. Returning all defective goods to the suppliers responsible. These should be covered by a reject note, giving the reason for the rejection.
4. Informing the purchasing and materials control departments of the receipt of all goods.
5. Returning all chargeable packing to the supplier.

Storekeeper's responsibilities

Organizationally, the responsibility for the stores may be in the hands of the accountant, the buyer or the materials controller. Furthermore, the duties of the storekeeper also vary greatly with the company concerned: in some organizations the storekeeper is virtually a materials controller, keeping comprehensive records and raising all purchase requisitions, whilst in others the storekeeper has no tasks beyond the receiving, storing and issuing of goods.

It is assumed here that the stores are part of the materials control department, and that the duties of the storekeepers are:

1. Receiving and storing in good order and condition all goods including raw materials, purchased parts and components, and partly manufactured items.
2. Issuing goods against authorized requisitions only. The storekeeper should never issue material (except for such items as have been declared 'free issue') without a requisition signed by a duly authorized person.
3. Collecting materials against sets of documents – order picking or 'kitting'. It is frequently convenient for the storekeeper to assemble together all of the materials required for the manufacture of the product specified in a particular works order.
4. Maintaining such records as may be required.
5. Carrying out any physical stocktaking as necessary.

Stores records

A knowledge of exactly what material is available is essential to the running of the production control department. This information is contained on the documentation mentioned earlier, in particular in the stock item file. It is crucial that this file be kept up-to-date, with transactions being posted as soon as is convenient after they occur. It is equally important that these records accurately reflect what is currently in stock.

Perpetual stocktaking

This is a means by which the physical stock (what is *actually* there) is compared with the theoretical stock (what the records say is there). It is easier to organize than the 'annual stock check' which entails stopping operations (normally over a weekend) and physically checking each stock item and comparing actual quantities with recorded quantities.

A perpetual inventory involves much less disorganization and is much simpler to organize than an annual stocktaking. Briefly, each day a number of items are checked so that by the year's end the whole stock will have been counted two or three times.

Each day a list can be presented to stores with details of those items to be checked. The storekeeper can return this with the quantities found in stock and the materials controller can then compare this with the record and investigate any discrepancies. The materials controller can prepare the lists in such a way that items requiring special care are more frequently checked.

CHAPTER 26 – HIGHLIGHTS

- The responsibilities of a materials control department include determining requirements; receiving and storing; issuing; and identifying surplus.
- Materials may be classified in four types: raw materials and bought-in items; work-in-progress; finished products; service materials.
- There are two approaches to materials control: independent demand, suitable for finished products and service materials; and dependent demand, for raw materials and work-in-progress.
- In the independent demand system, stock purchase may be initiated by deciding when to order, based on a re-order level (expected demand in expected lead time plus a safety stock); and by deciding how much to order, based on economic considerations, the economy batch size balancing holding and purchasing costs.
- In the dependent demand system; material requirements planning (MRP) involves determining raw material and work in progress requirement from an analysis of finished product forecast demand, and product structure data. The basic formula is

  $NR = GR - OH - OD + SS$ (PO is NR offset by lead time)
  NR = net requirements, OD = orders due,
  GR = gross requirements, SS = safety stock,
  OH = on-hand stock; PO = planned orders.

  The basic inputs are stock status (current stock positions of all items, including lead times); bill of materials (product structure relationships between products and raw materials); master production schedule (period-by-period demand for all finished products).
- Materials management documentation includes a stock item file (basic data for each item); a materials requisition (withdrawal of materials); a purchase requisition (for order placing/arrival); and miscellaneous, e.g. materials return, materials transfer, scrap and shortage notes.
- The materials reduction programme is a systematic procedure, based on a Pareto analysis by item-by-value of stock held, for identifying stock items which can be disposed of.
- Goods inward responsibilities include recording receipt; unpacking and checking; returning defective goods; informing other departments of receipt; and returning packaging.

- Storekeeper's responsibilities are receiving and storing; issuing materials; 'kitting' against works orders; maintaining appropriate records; and carrying out stock checks.
- In a perpetual stock check, each day a number of items have their physical stock checked against their theoretical (recorded) stock, and discrepancies are investigated. In an entire year, all items will have been checked several times.

Recommended reading

Barker, T., *Essentials of Materials Management*, McGraw-Hill, 1989

Discusses the practices and techniques of the topic from a practical perspective.

British Standards Institution, Guide to Stock Control (BS5729), 1981

A five-part guide covering the management of stock control, demand, assessment, replenishment of stock, data processing and storekeeping.

Crompton, H.K., *Supplies and Materials Management*, Macdonald and Evans, 1985

This book is intended for all staff involved in supplies and materials management. Its scope is wide, including purchasing provisioning, stock control, administration, properties of materials, handling.

Jessop, D. and Morrison, A., *Storage and Control of Stock*, Pitman, 1991

This text describes in detail stock control and storage from the elementary principles and simplest manual methods to the most sophisticated automated operations.

Leenders, M.R., Fearon, H.E. and England, W.B., *Purchasing and Materials Management*, 9th edn, Irwin, 1989

A comprehensive coverage of the purchasing/materials management functions in both profit and not-for-profit organizations.

Love, S.F., *Inventory Control*, McGraw-Hill, 1979

A comprehensive coverage of a variety of models with emphasis on those which are most readily applicable. Rather mathematical.

Orlicki, J., *Material Requirements Planning*, McGraw-Hill, 1975

The first authoritative treatment of time phased material requirements planning. Many examples and illustrations are used to show exactly how a MRP system works.

Tersine, R.J., *Principles of Inventory and Materials Management*, 3rd edn, North-Holland, 1988

A thorough coverage updated to take account of the latest developments.

Chapter 27

Manufacturing Planning and Control Systems

Manufacturing resources planning (MRP II)

The basic material requirements planning (MRP) system simply handles the materials aspects of production/operations control. No real account is taken of capacity implications. Clearly this is undesirable. MRP has been enhanced to take account of these and other factors; this has led to the development of a more sophisticated system: manufacturing resources planning (MRP II – since the initials are identical to those of material requirements planning). Initially the system is extended into *rough-cut capacity planning*. This takes the master production schedule (MPS) and looks at the resource implication at an aggregate level (department-by-department or section-by-section); there is no point in working with an MPS which is totally outside the capacity of the facilities. The MPS must be replanned or extra resources made available. Only when a satisfactory MPS has been derived is it worth proceeding with an analysis of the material and other requirements. Additionally there can be provision for the 'company plan' (with a larger timescale) to feed into the MPS, enabling a link to be made with the development of marketing strategy.

In addition to producing the detailed material plan, the system can produce detailed capacity plans provided it has the necessary job-routing data and so on. The implementation of these plans allows shop-floor and purchase control to be carried out. Performance monitoring and control can also be included in a number of dimensions including financial considerations. An essential element is the feedback of information concerning purchasing, manufacturing and so on. A simplified overview is shown in Fig. 27.1.

The system can now be thought of as a 'model' of the organization, which can be used for more than simply planning production. It is possible, because of the data/information retained within it, to evaluate the effects of decisions in a variety of different functional areas: financial factors and cash flow, marketing decisions and sales, engineering/research and development.

MRP II is essentially a computer system, and innumerable 'versions' can be purchased from different software and hardware suppliers and consultants. Moreover no two systems will be identical. Indeed, it could be argued that there is a continuum with 'simple' MRP at one end and 'full-scale' MRP II at the other. Most applications/systems fall between the extremes. It has been suggested by

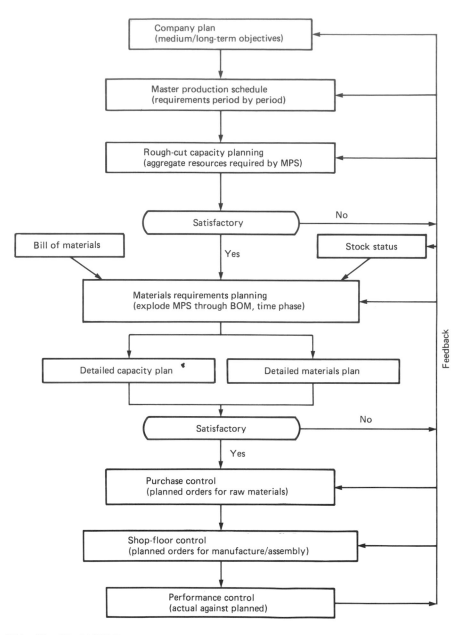

Fig. 27.1   Simplified MRP II

Table 27.1 Four classes of MRP/MRP II user

Class	Characteristics
D	MRP working in data-processing department only Poor inventory records Master schedule mismanaged Reliance on shortage lists for progressing
C	Used for inventory ordering, not scheduling Scheduling by shortage lists Overloaded master schedule
B	System includes capacity planning, shop-floor control Used to plan production, not manage the business Help still needed from shortage lists Inventory higher than necessary
A	Uses closed-loop MRP Integrates capacity planning, shop-floor control, vendor scheduling Used to plan sales, engineering, purchasing No shortage lists to over-ride schedules

Oliver Wight that MRP/MRP II implementations can be classified on a four-point scale, from A to D. Table 27.1 briefly describes these states.

Most organizations implementing MRP/MRP II are on the path from class D status to class A status. A difficulty faced is knowing, in a quantitative sense, where on the path the organization is, and what steps to take to effect improvements. A scoring system has been suggested in the Department of Trade and Industry's booklet *Managing into the '90s: Manufacturing Resource Planning*. A series of 25 questions are posed covering the four areas: (1) technical aspects of the system; (2) data integrity; (3) education; and (4) use of the system. Examples of these are:

1. *Technical:*
   (a) Time periods for master production schedule and material requirements plan are weeks or smaller?
   (b) Master production scheduling and material requirements planning are run weekly or more frequently?
2. *Data integrity:*
   (a) Inventory record accuracy 95 per cent or better?
   (b) Bill of material accuracy 98 per cent or better?
3. *Education:*
   (a) Initial education of at least 80 per cent of employees?
   (b) An on-going educational programme?
4. *Use of system:*
   (a) Shop delivery performance is 95 per cent or better?
   (b) Management *really* use MRP II to manage?

A score of 23+ implies class A, 20+ class B, 17+ class C, and less than 17, class D. Turning a 'no' into a 'yes' gives the user the route to improvement.

Benefits quoted for successful introduction of MRP II include reduced manufacturing lead times, reduced inventory levels (raw material, work-in-progress and finished products), and achievement of customer delivery dates.

Just-in-time (JIT)

Just-in-time (JIT) has been equated with an inventory control system which requires an organization's suppliers to provide raw material in small quantities, very frequently. It has also been represented as a planning and control system which uses cards to authorize the manufacture of small batches of components at various stages of the production process. Both of these can be regarded as elements of JIT, but here the view is taken that JIT is more than this; it is a basic philosophy, which applies equally to manufacturing and to non-manufacturing. This philosophy is about totally satisfying the customer's requirements, when these requirements arise, with no waste, i.e. no unnecessary use of materials, human or physical resources. It can be seen therefore that this philosophy applies equally to running a chemical plant, a hospital or a management consultancy. Clearly, as a concept it shares a great deal with total quality management (TQM). It is felt here to be far more important that the concepts are taken on board by an organization, than that detailed discussion takes place over whether what is being attempted is TQM or JIT.

There are a number of techniques which underpin JIT, some of which are more appropriate in manufacturing than in non-manufacturing. Equally, several apply to the planning and control function, as mentioned in the introduction – hence the inclusion of the topic in this chapter.

Total quality control

Any philosophy which includes perfectly satisfying a customer's requirements must have a strong element of quality control, and most definitions include this. Some aspects will be briefly mentioned here for completeness although they are covered in more detail in other chapters.

Organizations should have confidence in the materials which they obtain from their suppliers. They should not feel the need constantly to check the quality. Preventive maintenance plans should be prepared for all equipment, and statistical process control should be used to establish process capabilities and to detect changes in processes. Good housekeeping in the workplace ensures that workers have at hand the correct equipment and materials, and permits problems to be readily seen and steps taken to resolve them.

Enforced problem solving

In order to solve problems, they must be identified. In many organizations these problems are hidden by a high production cost which 'absorbs' their effects. It is possible to draw the analogy with a boat on a lake with the high water level hiding the rocks (Fig. 27.2). In attempting to reduce the production cost (frequently associated with high stocks – equated to reducing the water level), the problems can be seen, and identified, and therefore they can be tackled. Reducing stocks of raw materials may reveal there are problems with the quality of the supplier, or that the supplier does not deliver on time. Reducing work-in-progress may reveal high levels of scrap and re-work. Once identified, these problems can be tackled, The techniques and philosophy behind the teamwork of quality circles can be of assistance here.

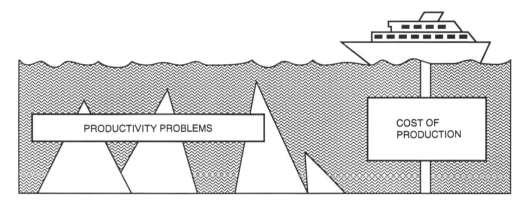

Fig. 27.2   Concealment of productivity problems

Batch production problems

Much manufacturing (and transaction processing – consider an insurance office handling claims) takes place in batches. Traditionally, production managers like large batches since these allow any set-up time to be shared throughout the entire batch. No-one wants to take an hour setting up a production line, to spend ten minutes manufacturing 100 litres of paint. How much better it is to manufacture 100,000 litres. This is the sort of philosophy behind the EBS formula of Chapter 26. Large batches cause many problems in terms of handling, stocking and space requirement.

An alternative perspective is to examine critically the set-up time, and to see if this can be reduced. Consider a production line used to put the filling into fruit pies, changing from blackcurrant to apple flavour. The line stops, the operator cleans the hopper which contains the blackcurrant filling, fetches the apple filling, fills the hopper with the apple filling and restarts the line. Clearly the concepts of method study can be used here, especially to record the existing method and develop an improved one.

The set-up or changeover time has two components: external, which does not require work to stop – this should be eliminated. The operator could fetch the apple filling *before* the line had completed filling the blackcurrant pies. The second component is internal; this does require work to stop, but it should be reduced. Instead of cleaning the hopper and filling it with apple filling, the apple filling should be stored in a second hopper which could be interchanged with the first and the first cleaned once the line had started again. In this way the set-up/changeover time has been reduced, allowing opportunities for greater flexibility through smaller manufacturing quantities.

A further problem associated with batch manufacture is the complexity it brings when associated with function layout. Large amounts of work-in-progress and significant efforts in scheduling are required if this combination is to be effective. Advocates of JIT propose the use of group technology layouts. Families of items with common processing requirements are identified, and groups of facilities to process these families are set up. The groups are semi-autonomous and responsible for their

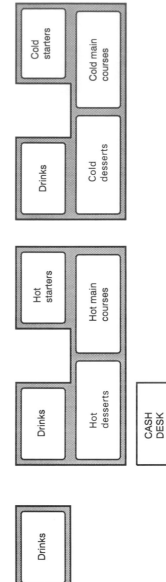

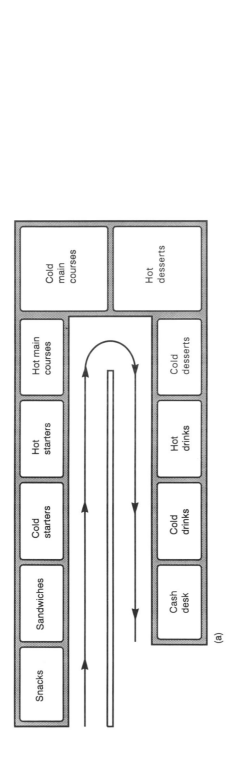

Fig. 27.3   Illustration of group layout
(a)   Traditional cafeteria layout
(b)   'Grouped' cafeteria layout

own management. This idea is described in more detail in Chapter 15, and illustrated in Figure 27.3, applied to a cafeteria.

Kanban systems

This system aims at a much tighter control of inventories. Frequently in manufacturing, utilization is seen as the principal goal; it is felt that operators and equipment must be kept working at all costs, ignoring the expense of interstage stores. The use of kanbans does not accept this, working on the principle that components should not be made until they are required, even if this results in operators stopping manufacture (and perhaps engaging in other activity like cleaning the work stations, quality circle work and so on). Indeed, this hold-up is not greeted with gloom; rather, advantage is gained from it since the bottleneck in the process has been identified. Management and operators can now work towards overcoming it. This might involve cross-training of operators, a critical examination of setting-up times and how these could be reduced, and so on. This forms part of the philosophy of enforced problem solving.

In fact, JIT has many similarities with flow line methods in that the whole process is balanced. The starting point is the schedule for the final assembly of the products. This is prepared and normally fixed for the planning horizon – say one month – and is used to derive the daily production rate. This is the only detailed plan produced. The size of the batch produced at any stage can be thought of as limited by the size of the container used to transport the items from one stage to the next. A simplification of the organization is shown in Fig. 27.4. A plant manufactures a variety of products by processing them through a number of work centres. Between each work centre is a store holding containers of components produced by the first work centre waiting to be processed by the next centre in the manufacture of one of the products.

The assembly schedules are derived from the detailed plan. A container of the final components needed in the assembly of the first product is withdrawn from the store after the final work centre in exchange for a card (kanban – Japanese for card). This card is the authorization to manufacture a replacement for the container of this component by the final work centre. To manufacture this final component, materials produced by the penultimate work centre are required, and a container is withdrawn from the store after this centre, again a kanban is issued to authorize replacement, and so on back down the chain to the initial raw material. A similar process applies to the second product, third product and so on. The assembly schedule thus 'pulls' production through the system. The schedule of work at any work centre is made up of the on-hand kanbans which have been pushed back down the system by the assembly schedules for the various final products. The order in which the kanbans have been received at any work centre determines the manufacturing sequence at that work centre, and if no kanbans are held, no manufacture must take place! Work-in-progress can be reduced and bottlenecks identified and eliminated by systematically reducing the number of components in a container. In this way the manufacturing system is balanced.

These kanbans can be used outside the strict manufacturing environment and they can be used to trigger replenishments from raw material suppliers, with the same stipulation that parts are not ordered to be received until required. Suppliers then become part of the system.

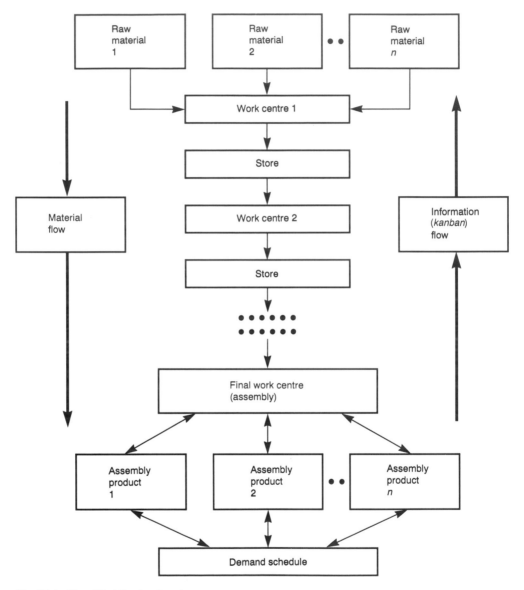

Fig. 27.4   Simplified 'kanban' system

Total Involvement

This can be viewed internally as well as externally. Everyone within the organization must be aware of the basic philosophy of JIT and of their role within its implementation. This applies to *all* areas not just manufacturing, since waste can be generated in all activities – consider the unnecessary copying of documents which takes place within the 'administration' functions of many organizations. There must be a commitment to the philosophy seen in top management's actions, and waste elimination should be tackled by cross-functional teams, who should be trained in the appropriate techniques.

This involvement can extend to suppliers, developing long-term relationships, breaking down traditional barriers. Co-operation in design and quality management systems can result in confident usage of raw materials, and knowledge that they are totally fit for their purpose. Co-operation in the preparation of production schedules and logistics can facilitate the extension of the kanban concept outside the organization. The mirror-image of these ideas can be extended to the organization's own customers.

Optimized production technology (OPT)

This approach has some similarities with the basic ideas behind using kanbans in JIT, but whereas the use of kanbans is essentially a manual approach, optimized production technology (OPT) normally requires software to support its application. In essence it is a philosophy which involves focusing attention on 'bottlenecks' in the production process. Underlying its application are a number of rules, which on occasion run contrary to 'established' practice in manufacturing planning. Some of these basic OPT rules are as follows:

1. Bottleneck or critical resources determine production for the entire system.
2. The level of utilization of non-critical resources should reflect the needs of the critical ones. So:
   – an hour lost at a bottleneck is an hour lost for the entire system;
   – an hour saved at a non-bottleneck has no real impact.
3. Bottlenecks determine both throughputs and inventories; why manufacture a component faster than a bottleneck can handle it?
4. The transfer batch size need not equal the process batch size.
5. The process batch size should not be fixed over all processes.
6. Schedules should be developed by looking at *all* constraints in parallel. Lead times are a consequence of schedules not predetermined.

Conventional practice might be to suggest large batches so that the set-up cost can be spread across more products (notwithstanding comments made earlier about set-up time reduction techniques). However, the OPT rules suggest that smaller batches could be manufactured at some non-bottleneck resources if as a consequence 'downstream' bottleneck resources can be 'fed' more effectively and their throughput increased. This can have implications for the accounting system, since the production manager might be 'penalized' for the implied inefficiency of the smaller batches, although the desired goal of higher throughput has been achieved.

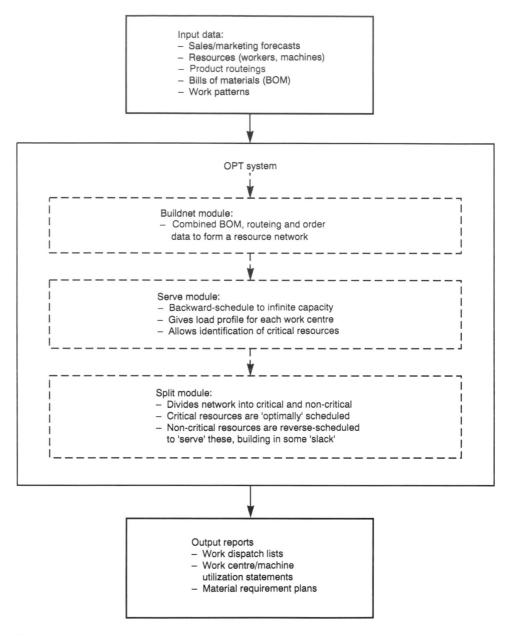

Fig. 27.5   Simplified outline of OPT

The basic principles behind OPT can and have been implemented within any manual or computer-based planning and control system. However, the largest number of actual applications have been supported by a software package. The basic outline is shown in Fig 27.5. The input data are similar to those required to support an MRP/MRP II system. Sales forecasts are taken and, with product routeing and bill of materials data, a resource network can be built up, incorporating information relating to work centres (the resources – workers and machines – required). The system carries out a complicated series of checks to try as far as possible to establish data accuracy. The system takes the marketing forecasts, and backward-schedules these orders from their required dates, carrying out this process to infinite capacity. This schedule is used to classify resources as *critical* or *non-critical*, based on utilization. The critical resources can be thought of as bottlenecks. The package then uses what is called a *proprietary algorithm*, to forward-schedule the orders optimally through the bottleneck resources. Finally, the orders are scheduled through the non-critical resources in such a way that the optimal schedule on the critical resources is not disturbed, and a buffer of safety capacity is included to allow for disruptions.

The heart of this approach is the *algorithm* which carries out the optimal scheduling of the critical resources. It has 'management parameters' which enable it to be fine-tuned to specific company objectives.

The benefits claimed include improvements in throughput, cash flow and efficiency, and reductions in inventory levels.

A comparison: MRP II, kanban, OPT

In reading the earlier sections it will have been noted that there have been significant similarities behind the concepts of MRP II, kanban and OPT. Each, for example, has as a theme the reduction of inventories. MRP II, and to a greater extent OPT, are planning techniques which require software support. MRP II *pushes* the requirements for finished products through the stages in the manufacturing process (represented by the bills of materials) and, taking account of lead times, generates planned orders for purchasing, manufacturing and assembly, if the requirements are to be met. The principles of bottleneck scheduling proposed by OPT can in theory be incorporated within the detailed capacity planning capability of the MRP II system. The kanban system is essentially a control and execution technique whereby a demand schedule (requirements) is used to manage assembly; when further components are required for this process these requirements are *pulled* from an earlier stage, generating a further requirement at that stage. This *pull* process repeats itself right through the manufacturing chain.

MRP II and OPT have high requirements in terms of the basic data to support the planning process, and systems to ensure the continued integrity of these data. They can handle a wide variety of products and components and complex environments, features which can cause difficulties for kanban systems without effective planning. *All* require good market forecasts, although kanban needs these to be relatively stable since the manufacturing process has been 'balanced'.

It has been suggested that for many situations a good combination is MRP II with OPT principles incorporated into capacity planning for the planning function, with kanban for execution and control.

Computer-integrated manufacture (CIM)

The organization has a number of opportunities for using computers within its operations. They can be used at the 'hard' end in the design process (Chapter 6) and in the manufacturing process (Chapter 16). This chapter has described how they can be used in the 'soft' end – the planning processes.

As the data for all these systems are pulled together and integrated and the software and procedures to support them consolidated, the total system moves towards computer-integrated manufacture. This is shown schematically in Fig. 27.6, in simplified form.

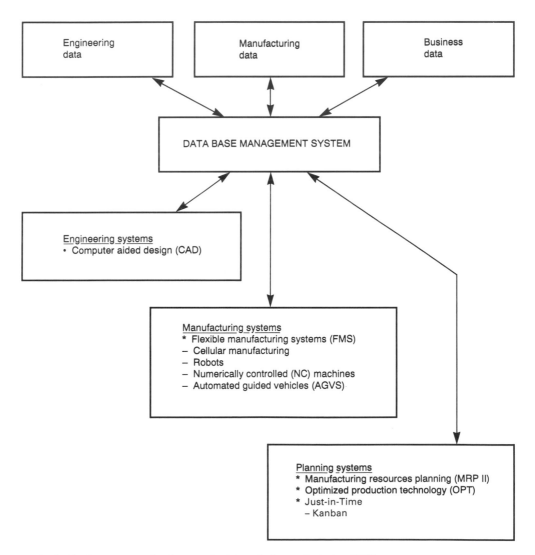

Fig. 27.6 Basic components of computer-integrated manufacturing (CIM)

World-class manufacturing

Increasingly, organizations are becoming aware of the need to be able to compete internationally if they are to survive, or at least grow. The phrase 'world-class manufacturer' has been coined for an organization which can compete in this market place. Stated simply, a world class manufacturer is 'one who can honestly say that it can compete with the best anywhere in the world'.

It should have the correct manufacturing capability to be able to satisfy totally the customers' requirements at the right price, delivered on time, and to operate profitably.

Few would dispute the sentiments of the above statements, However, the fundamental question concerns how world-class status may be achieved. The answer lies in some of the techniques/concepts introduced in this chapter, but more generally in the overall philosophy within this text: the adoption of sound production/operations management practice, supported by the appropriate concepts, and technologies. Figure 27.7 illustrates this. It is possible to argue over which 'box' a particular idea should appear in (is TQM *really* sound POM practice?). However, the really important issue is not this classification, but that the organization should consider all possible support, identify those which are appropriate to their environment, and then develop a sound action plan for the implementation.

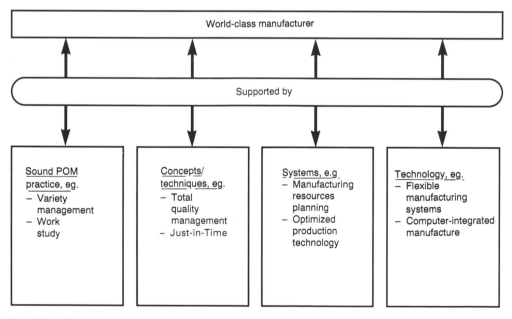

Fig. 27.7   Cornerstones of world-class manufacturing

CHAPTER 27 – HIGHLIGHTS

- Manufacturing resources planning (MRP II) is a computer-based decision support system for planning and controlling manufacturing operations. Marketing forecasts are used to develop feasible aggregate plans which are then developed into detail capacity and material plans. These detailed plans are monitored and feedback is used to manage materials, resources, finance and other functional aspects of the business.

- Just-in-Time (JIT) is the philosophy of totally satisfying the customer's requirement, when required, with no waste.

- JIT supportive techniques for waste elimination include: total quality control; enforced problem solving; batch size management; kanban systems; and total involvement (internal and external).

- Optimized production technology (OPT) is a planning system involving the identification of bottleneck resources, the 'optimal' scheduling of work through these, and the development of a plan for work through the remaining resources, to 'serve' the bottlenecks.

- Computer-integrated manufacture (CIM) is the integration of the computer applications and procedures to support manufacturing decision making, planning and control; it includes computer-aided design (CAD), flexible manufacturing systems (FMS), MRP II, OPT and JIT as appropriate.

- World-class manufacturing, 'the ability to compete with the best anywhere in the world', may be achieved through the application of sound POM practice and the appropriate techniques, systems and technologies.

Recommended reading

Gunn, T.G., *Manufacturing for Competitive Advantage, Becoming a World Class Manufacturer*, Harper Business, 1989

Puts world class manufacturing in perspective, and outlines the steps necessary to achieve it.

Landvater, D.V. and Gray, C.D, *MRPII Standard System*, Oliver Wight Publications, 1989

Very good on all aspects of MRP, including a much enhanced version of the MRP check-list.

Managing into the 90s: Just-in-Time; Manufacturing Resources Planning; Computer Integrated Manufacturing; Optimised Production Technology, Department of Trade and Industry, 1989

A very useful and informative series of four booklets, some of the material presented in this chapter draws on the structures underpinning the descriptions of JIT, MRP II, and OPT.

Schonberger, R., *World Class Manufacturing – the Lessons of Simplicity Applied*, Free Press, 1986

Schonberger, R., *World Class Manufacturing – Implementing JIT and TQM*, Free Press, 1987

Two basic reference texts by one of the earliest workers on WCM.

Schonberger, R., *Building a Chain of Customers*, Hutchinson, 1990

Develops the idea that linking the main business functions of marketing, production, finance and design can support the creation of a world-class company.

Umble, M.M., *Synchronous Manufacture: Principles of World Class Excellence*, Chapman & Hall, 1990

The first text to examine and explain the constantly evolving principles of synchronous manufacture.

Vollman, T.E., Berry, W.L. and Whybark, D.C., *Manufacturing Planning and Control Systems*, 2nd edn, Irwin, 1989

Covering the latest developments in this area (including JIT, OPT, MRP, MRP II), as well as the basic concepts. Recommended.

Chapter 28

Project Management

Project network techniques

The operations manager is frequently concerned with 'projects' with a definable start and finish such as:

maintenance;
installation of new plant or premises;
installation of new procedures;
laying or relaying out premises;
testing equipment or systems;
designing or modifying equipment.

For the planning and control of these and any other similar tasks, one of the project network techniques (PNTs) can be used.

Broadly, there are two forms which PNTs can take, one where activity is represented by a box or *node* (activity-on-node or AoN), the other where activity is represented by an *arrow* (activity-on-arrow or AoA). Within AoN two sub-divisions appear, depending upon the way in which the dependency of activities upon each other is shown. The original AoN form showed only a single type of dependency, but later a form emerged whereby multiple types of dependency could be represented. This latter form, *precedence diagramming*, is not susceptible to the very easy manual calculation of both single-dependency AoN and AoA, and it lay virtually dormant until cheap high-capacity microcomputers became available, since when it has grown in popularity. In this text single-dependency AoN, sometimes called the *method of potentials* (MoP), will be discussed more fully than either of the other two forms, since calculation does not depend upon immediate access to a computer. Translation to either of the other representations will not be found to be difficult.

The basic elements of MoP

Every project must have a definable start and finish to be susceptible to PNT planning. In AoN these two points in time are represented by rectangles (nodes), as are the constituent tasks in the project (the *activities*). The dependency of one activity upon another is shown by the way in which a *dependency arrow* links the two activities.

Consider, for example, the problem of moving one piece of equipment (X) to a new position, and installing in its place another piece of equipment (A). The first step is to define the starting and finishing situations:

Start: The project will be considered to start when the budget for removing and relocating X and A and obtaining any associated material handling material and tools has been agreed.

Finish: The project will be considered to be completed when X and A are in a position and ready to be used.

These definitions enable an elementary diagram to be drawn, as in Fig. 28.1.

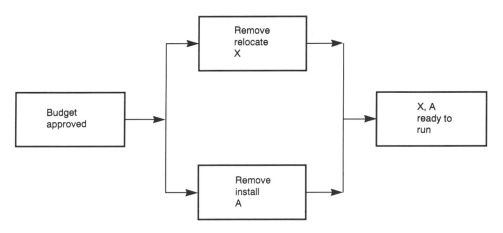

Fig. 28.1   Elementary network diagram

The 'Remove, relocate X' activity can be considered to comprise four activities:

    Clear site for X.
    Remove X.
    Re-install X.
    Test X.

Of these 'Clear site' must precede 'Remove X' since X must be placed somewhere once it is moved. Similarly, it can only be re-installed when removed, and testing must follow re-installation, so that the single node will break into a chain of four as in Fig. 28.2.

The 'Remove, install A' activity can be considered to comprise activities:

    Remove A.
    Install A.
    Test A.
    Obtain tools for A.
    Obtain associated material handling equipment.

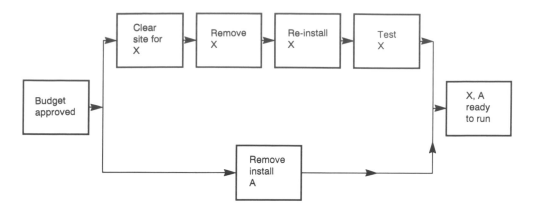

Fig. 28.2   More complex network diagram

Here again, 'Test', 'Install' and 'Remove' follow each other. However, the act of obtaining tools for A does not depend upon A at all – it can start as soon as the budget is approved, that is, at the *Start* node, but it must be completed before testing can start. The material handling equipment is similarly not dependent upon anything but budget approval (that is, *Start*), and does not influence testing or installation, the only requirement being that it must be available when A is ready to run – that is, by *Finish*, so the diagram develops as in Fig. 28.3.

A closer examination of this diagram indicates that A is installed without its site having been prepared, so an activity 'Prepare site for A' is missing. A is going to occupy the site previously used by X and so the activity 'Prepare site for A' depends upon X being removed, and it must be completed before A is installed. Once this is done, the rubbish generated by the preparation of the site for A can be carted away, and this activity, 'Cart rubbish' must be finished before the whole project can be considered to be complete. For ease of reference, each node is given a number or label.

Activity and dependency times

The diagram so far shows only the *logic* – the necessary technological requirements – of the project. To this must be added both the times required for each activity, these being set in the bottom left-hand box of the node, and the dependency times. A dependency time in MoP is the time which must elapse between the start of an activity and the start of an immediate successor. These are set as subscripts to the dependency arrows. In the present example the dependency times are the same as the duration times of the tail activities, but this need not necessarily be so: dependency times can be greater or smaller than the tail duration times if this is required by the project. It is sensible to start with 'Dependency time = Tail activity time' since this is the simplest managerial situation, and to modify it only if required by the time constraints of the project. Start and finish activities are generally assumed to have zero duration times.

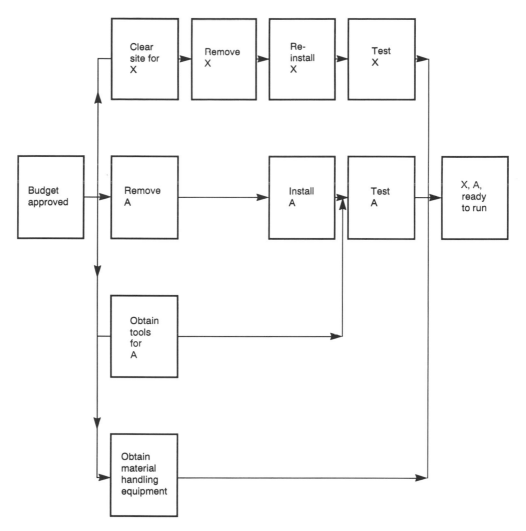

Fig. 28.3   Final network diagram

Analysis of the diagram

The total project time (TPT) is found by a *forward pass* where dependency times are added together from the *Start* node. The 'spare time' (float) available for any activity is then deduced from a *backward pass* where duration times are subtracted from the TPT at the *Finish* node.

The forward pass
The forward pass determines the earliest starting time (EST) for each activity. The present time (*now*) is taken as time 0 and this is entered in the top left-hand box of node 0. The earliest starting times of nodes 1, 7, 9 and 11 are therefore also time 0.

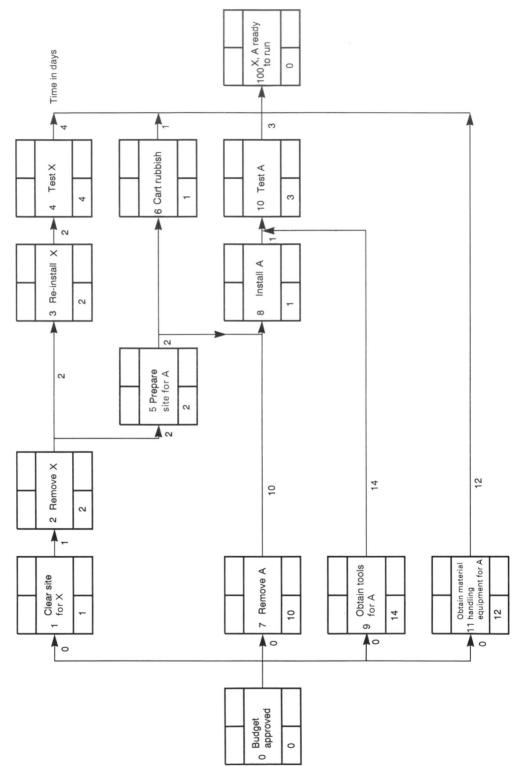

Fig. 28.4   Complete network diagram showing durations

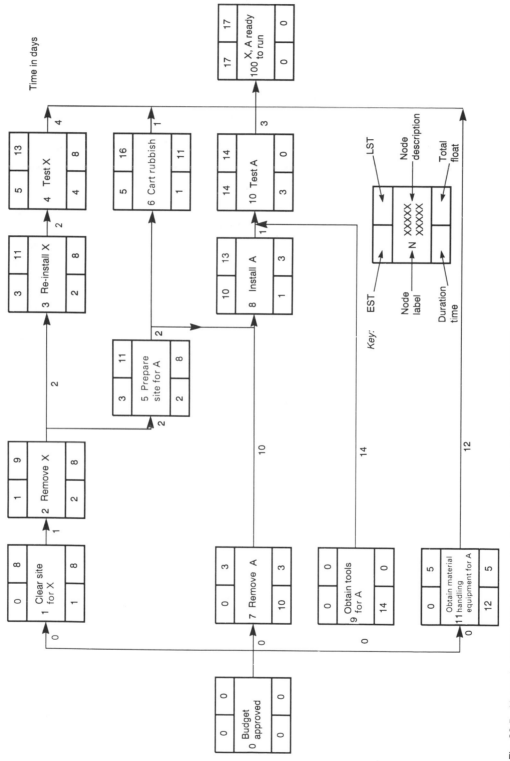

Fig. 28.5 Network diagram showing results of forward- and backward-pass calculations

(Note: This does not say that all these activities *must* start at time 0 but that they *can* start then.) Since the dependency time from node 1 to node 2 is one day, then EST for node 2 is day 1. Similarly, the ESTs for nodes 3 and 5 are day 3, and for nodes 4 and 6 they are day 5. Node 8 has two dependency arrows entering it, that from node 5 suggesting an EST of day 5 and that from node 7 suggesting an EST of day 10. Since node 8 cannot start until *both* entering dependencies are satisfied, the EST of node 8 must be the *larger* of the two values, day 10. This process is continued until node 100 is reached, which will thus have an EST of day 17, signifying that the TPT is 17 days.

The earliest finishing time (EFT) for any activity is readily obtained by adding the activity's duration time to its EST. Thus, the EFT of activity 5 is day 3 + 2 days = day 5. This is not recorded on the node since it is obtainable by inspection.

The backward pass

The backward pass directly determines the *latest starting time* (LST) for each activity. The LST for the *Finish* node is taken to be the same time as the EST for that node (in this example, day 17) and this is entered in the top right-hand box of the node. Note that this does not say that all the activities whose dependency arrows enter this node *must* finish at day 17, but that they may do so. Since the dependency time (the time which must elapse between the start of a node and the start of an immediate successor) between node 100 and node 4 is 4 days, then the LST for node 4 is day 13. Similarly the LSTs for nodes 6, 10 and 11 are days 16, 14 and 5. Moving backwards, nodes 3, 8 and 9 have LSTs of days 11, 13 and 0. Node 5 has two dependency arrows emerging from it, that from node 6 suggesting an LST of day 14, and that from node 8 suggesting an LST of day 11. Since the LST for node 5 must allow node 6 to finish by day 16 and node 8 by day 13, the smaller of the suggested LSTs for node 5 must be taken, i.e. day 11. Continuing this process, the LSTs for nodes 0, 1, 2 and 7 are found to be days 0, 8, 9 and 3 respectively.

The latest finishing time (LFT) for an activity is found by adding the activity's duration time to its LST. Thus, the LFT of activity 5 is day 11 + 2 days = day 13. This is not recorded on the node since it is obtainable by inspection.

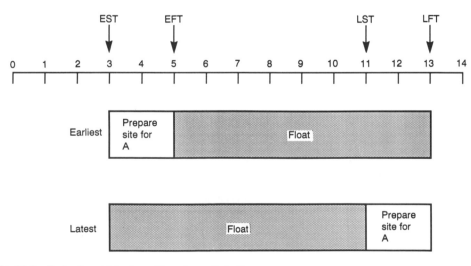

Fig. 28.6   Earliest and latest positions for activity 5

Float and the critical path

Examining again the network it will be seen that for some activities there is a difference between the earliest and latest starting times. For example, activity 5:

> Latest starting time (day) = 11
> Earliest starting time (day) = 3
> Difference = 8 days

This means that activity 5 can start any time between day 3 and day 11 without affecting the total project time, i.e. that activity 5 can 'float' by a total of 8 days: see Fig. 28.6.

On the other hand, for some activities there is no difference between their earliest and latest starting times. For example, activity 10;

> Latest starting time (day) = 14
> Earliest starting time (day) = 14
> Difference = 0

This means that this activity *must* start on day 14 and must not occupy more than its specified duration time (3 days), otherwise the total project time will be affected. The performance of activities which have no float are critical to the TPT and are known as *critical activities*, and the sequence of critical activities is known as the *critical path*. Float is recorded on the diagram in the bottom right-hand box of the node. The critical path is seen by the sequence of zero floats. The complete analysis can be tabulated as in Table 28.1.

In some situations the project is given a 'target' or 'acceptable' time, and in this case the backward pass will start with this target item. Under these circumstances the critical path may itself have float (*positive* float if the target time is greater than the final TPT, *negative* float if the target time is less than the final TPT). Criticality is measured by the size of the float:

> The critical path in a network is that
> path which has least float

Table 28.1

No.	Description	Duration	Start Early	Start Late	Finish Early	Finish Late	Float
1	Clear site for X	1	0	8	1	9	8
2	Remove X	2	1	9	3	11	8
3	Re-install X	2	3	11	5	13	8
4	Test X	4	5	13	9	17	8
5	Prepare site for A	2	3	11	5	13	8
6	Cart rubbish	1	5	16	6	17	11
7	Remove A	10	0	3	10	13	3
8	Install A	1	10	13	11	14	3
9	Tools for A	14	0	0	14	14	0
10	Test A	3	14	14	17	17	0
11	Obtain material handling equipment	12	0	5	12	17	5

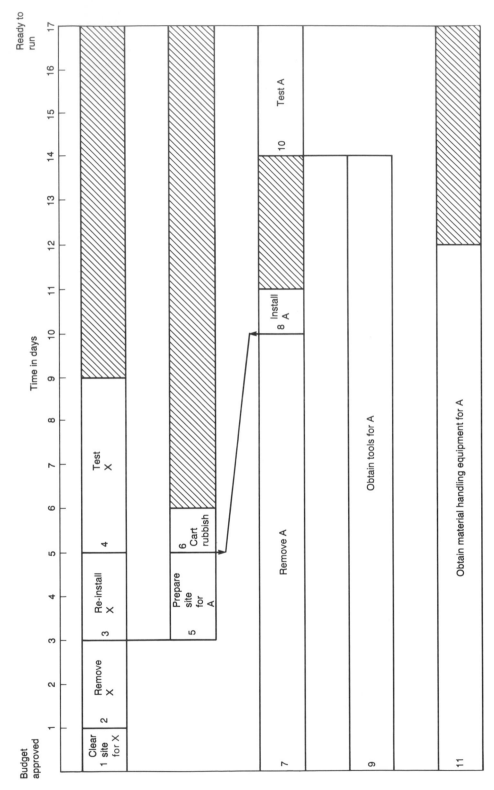

Fig. 28.7   Squared network

Reduction of total project time

The total project time can only be reduced by reducing the total length of the critical path. This can be done by using the critical examination technique of the work study engineer (Chapter 17) and/or by changing the logic, i.e. by changing some of the decisions inherent in the network. It must be remembered that if the reduction in the critical path is *greater than* the next-lowest value of float, a new critical path is created. Thus, if activity 9 is reduced by more than 3 units of time – to say 10 – then the sequence 0–7–8–10–100 forms a new critical path, the original one now becoming non-critical in part.

Representing the network as a bar chart

The network can be translated into a bar chart in a number of ways. One method is to 'square' the network, as in Fig 28.7; the similarity between this representation of the project and the original diagram is sufficiently great to make a description of the method of drawing unnecessary.

This bar chart representation is very useful in three ways:

(a) it illustrates the physical meaning of float;
(b) it is often more readily understood than the arrow diagram;
(c) it can be used to assist in the disposition of the various resources used in the project.

If a computer is used to draw the network, a 'cascade' diagram is likely to result (Fig. 28.8). Here each activity is allocated a single line and the activities are arranged

Node no.	Node description	0	1	2	3	4	5	6	7	8	9	10	11	12	13	14	15	16	17
1	Clear site for X	S	x	x	x	x	x	x	x	x									
2	Remove X		S	S	x	x	x	x	x	x	x	x							
3	Re-install A				S	S	x	x	x	x	x	x	x	x					
5	Prepare site for A				S	S	x	x	x	x	x	x	x	x					
6	Clear rubbish							S	x	x	x	x	x	x	x	x	x	x	x
4	Test X							S	S	S	S	x	x	x	x	x	x	x	x
7	Remove A	S	S	S	S	S	S	S	S	S	S	S	x	x	x				
8	Install A											S	x	x	x				
11	Obtain material handling equipment	S	S	S	S	S	S	S	S	S	S	S	S	S	x	x	x	x	x
9	Tools for A	C	C	C	C	C	C	C	C	C	C	C	C	C	C				
10	Test A																C	C	C

Fig. 28.8 Cascade chart in order of earliest finish
Key: S, schedule activity; C, critical activity; x, float

usually in order of their earliest finish. This diagram more nearly resembles a conventional Gantt chart and can be used to record progress very simply. Whilst the squared network can be derived directly from the basic network, the cascade network requires an analysis to be carried out first.

Resource allocation

In most situations, the resources available are limited, and it is obviously essential to see that the resources required are never greater than those available. Critical path analysis, while not resolving this situation uniquely, provides useful assistance in achieving an acceptable solution, since it shows which activities can be 'moved' without increasing the total project time, and also the effect of moving time-limiting activities. In the project so far considered, there are two 'removal' activities:

Activity 2: Remove X
Activity 7: Remove A

Assume that both of these are going to be carried out by the same gang, then, as drawn in Fig 28.7, *two* gangs are required during days 2 and 3, and if only *one* gang is available, then Fig 28.7 represents an impossible situation. However, it will be observed that both activities possess float (activity 2, 8 days; activity 7, 3 days), so that either can be moved. To start activity 2 after activity 7 has finished would increase the total project time by 1 day, but to start activity 7 after activity 2 has finished would use up float, but would not increase total time. Hence, the removal gang must carry out the sequence 'Remove X' then 'Remove A'. This would mean that the earliest and latest start and finish times would disappear – the activities concerned would be 'scheduled'. The analysis table would then appear as shown in Table 28.2.

This type of manipulation can be very difficult if there are a large number of activities and a large number of resources, as the number of possible 'moves' increases factorially with the number of activities. To allow a systematic procedure

Table 28.2

No.	Description	Duration	Start Early	Start Late	Finish Early	Finish Late	Float
1	Clear site for X	1	~~0~~ 0	~~9~~	~~1~~ 1	~~9~~ ~~8~~	0
2	Remove X	2	~~1~~ 1	~~8~~ ~~3~~ 3	~~3~~ 3	~~11~~ ~~8~~	0
3	Re-install X	2	3	11	5	13	8
4	Test X	4	5	13	9	17	8
5	Prepare site for A	2	3	11	5	13	8
6	Clear rubbish	1	5	16	6	17	11
7	Remove A	10	~~0~~ 3	~~3~~ ~~10~~ 13	~~10~~ 13	~~13~~ ~~3~~	0
8	Install A	1	~~10~~ 13	~~13~~ ~~11~~ 14	~~11~~ 14	~~14~~ ~~3~~	0
9	Tools for A	14	0	0	14	14	0
10	Test A	3	14	14	17	17	0
11	Obtain material handling equipment	12	0	5	12	17	0

to be followed, a set of decision rules must be generated. These rules, which will differ from organization to organization, will not necessarily produce a 'best' or 'optimum' solution, but they will tend to produce 'feasible' or 'workable' solutions in a reasonable time. It is probably more important to get a rapid solution than to strive for a 'best' solution, particularly as duration times are liable to change as the project proceeds. For all but the most trivial resource allocation problem, a computer is essential. There are very many good resource allocation programs available currently.

Control using PNT

Control upon the progress of a task can be exerted in basically two ways:

1. By using a derived bar chart and marking 'achievement' against plan. Many computer programs include this facility.
2. By inserting into the diagram the actual activity and dependency times and examining the effect on float. Again, this is very simply done with a computer.

Multi-dependency A-on-N diagramming (precedence diagramming)

As discussed above, the arrow used in A-on-N networking shows only one dependency, namely the interval between the start of one arrow and the start of the next. Some years ago IBM introduced another variation of A-on-N to which the name 'Precedence Diagramming' was given, whereby the location of the arrow signifies the type of dependency. This enables situations such as overlapping activities to be drawn easily, but manual calculation of a network becomes much more tedious. However, the advent of the microcomputer and its capability of handling complex situations has allowed multi-dependency A-on-N to become a very straightforward method of working. Essentially, there are three different dependencies:

1. *Start-to-start dependency*, which is the dependency used in single-dependency A-on-N (Fig. 28.9). Here, at least β days must elapse between the start of activity B and the start of activity A.

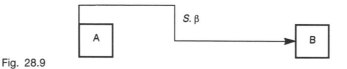

Fig. 28.9

2. *Finish-to-start dependency* (Fig. 28.10) Activity B may not start until at least α days after the finish of activity A.

Fig. 28.10

3. *Finish-to-finish dependency* (Fig. 28.11). Here, at least τ days must elapse between the completion of activity A and the completion of activity B.

Fig. 28.11

In an overlapping situation, these dependencies can be combined. If activity B may not start until at least α time units after the start of activity A, while at least τ time units are required for the completion of activity B after activity A is finished, this can be represented by Fig. 28.12. Float and the critical path have precisely the same significance as in single-dependency A-on-N.

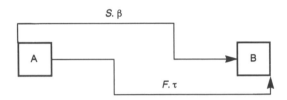

Fig. 28.12

Activity-on-arrow networking (critical path analysis, CPA)

Where AoN networking uses a node to represent an activity, AoA uses an arrow, dependency being shown by the relationship of one arrow to another. Arrows start and finish with circular nodes often known as events, but these serve mainly as devices in which to place identifying numbers. Thus, to represent the situation that A is *removed* from one place and *installed* in another, two arrows are required (see Fig. 28.13). The numbers in the circles provide a simple way of referring to the two activities. The subscript to the arrow denotes the duration time of the activity.

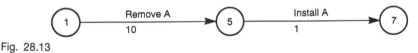

Fig. 28.13

The general rule in AoA is that an activity depends upon the activity(ies) from whose head event it emerges. This can lead to logical errors if an activity which does not require any time, a *dummy* activity (something which does not occur in AoN), is not used. If before installing A a site has to be *prepared*, then the diagram would appear as shown in Fig. 28.14.

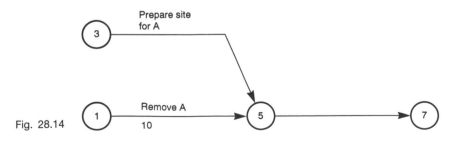

Fig. 28.14

If some rubbish which has arisen from the preparation of the site has to be *carted away*, then at first thought the diagram might appear to be Fig. 28.15.

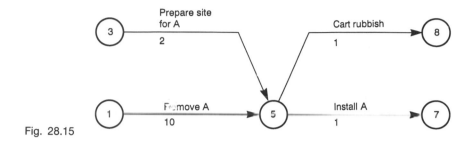

Fig. 28.15

However, this would show that 'cart rubbish' depends on 'preparing site' – which is true – and also on 'removing A', which is not true. To release this logical error, a dummy is inserted as shown in Fig. 28.16.

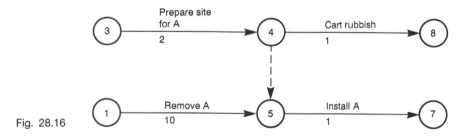

Fig. 28.16

A second use of the dummy is to ensure that two activities which have the same head and tail events have unique head and tail numbers; for example if a building society decides to change its mortgage rates, it is necessary to:

(a) prepare statements to members;
(b) obtain envelopes,
(c) post statements.

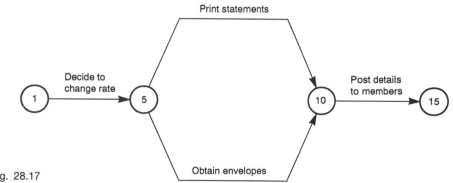

Fig. 28.17

At first sight this might create a network (Fig. 28.17). This then would result in two activities having the same head and tail numbers. This is resolved by inserting a dummy in one or other of the two activities (Fig. 28.18).

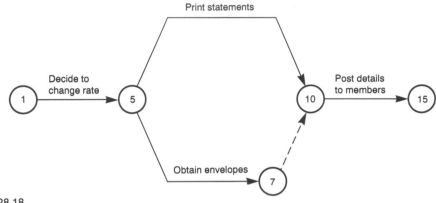

Fig. 28.18

Note: Some computer programs can tolerate this ambiguity.

The diagram is analysed substantially in the same way as an AoN diagram by a forward and a backward pass. In this case the forward pass given *the earliest starting time* of the activities emerging from the node, whilst the backward pass gives the *latest finishing time* of all activities entering the node. Remember always that dummies must enter the calculations, being given a duration time of zero. The AoA equivalent to Fig 28.4 is shown in Fig. 28.19.

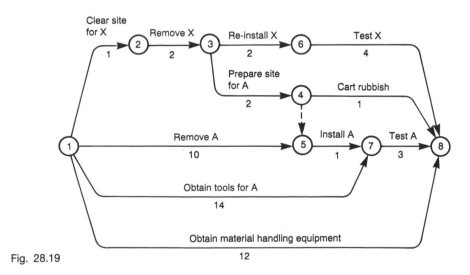

Fig. 28.19

The complete analysis of the diagram is, of course, the same as that of the AoN diagram (Table 28.3)

Table 28.3

SITUATION	C.P.A.	A-o-N.
Activity B depends on Activity A		
Activity C depends on Activities A and B		
Activities C and D depend on Activities A and B		
Activity C depends on Activity A; Activity D depends on Activities A and B		
Activity K depends on Activity A; Activity L depends on Activities A and B; Activity M depends on Activities A, B and C		

Table 28.3 *Contd*

SITUATION	C.P.A.	A-o-N.
Activity B, which must follow Activity A, may not start until D units of time have elapsed after the completion of A.	A 12 — Delay D — B 15	A 12 → 12+D → B 15
Activity B must not start until at least R units of time have elapsed after the start of activity A.	A 12 — R-12 — B 15	A 12 → R → B 15
The interval between the completion of A and the start of B must not exceed X. *Note:* This is Roy's 'Negative Constraint.'	NOT POSSIBLE	A 12, B 15; 12 and −(12+x)
Activity A and Activity W are both opening activities; Activity A may start at the beginning of the project; Activity W must not start until time T has elapsed after the start of the project.	A 12; Constraint T; W 20	Start 0 → A 12; T → W 20

Table 28.3 *Contd*

SITUATION	C.P.A.	A-o-N.
Activity B can start immediately Activity A is complete.		
Activity B can start immediately Activity A is complete and Activity C can start when part p of Activity A is complete.		
Activity B can start when part p of Activity A is complete; Activity C can start when part r of Activity B is complete; Activity B requires at least s.15 time to finish after the completion of A, and C requires at least v.18 to finish after the completion of B.		

Line of balance (LoB)

Historically, line of balance (LoB) was developed before project network techniques, and the two approaches are often considered to be separate but related techniques. Both are applied to jobs which are made up of a number of activities with complex interdependencies. The underlying model within LoB is normally taken to be the activity-on-arrow (AoA) representation of critical path analysis (CPA). It will be seen that if the original time-scaled stage–time diagram is abandoned, then LoB can be viewed as a quite conventional CPA system applied to a single-batch situation.

Where LoB can be used

Just as CPA is used to schedule and control a single job or project, LoB can be used to schedule and control a single batch (of the same job). The following requirements need to be satisfied:

(a) there must be identifiable stages in production at which managerial control can be exerted;
(b) the manufacturing times between these stages must be known;
(c) a delivery schedule must be available;
(d) resources can be varied as required.

Whilst it is possible to use LoB to control a number of separate batches, just as it is possible to use CPA to control a number of separate projects, the computational difficulties become great. It is, therefore, usual to use LoB in single-batch situations where the batch concerned is of some considerable importance to the organization. An estate of houses, a batch of computers, a batch of guided weapons, are examples of the type of work likely to be appropriate to LoB control.

An example of LoB

The applications of LoB will be illustrated by the following simplified example.

A sailing dinghy is manufactured as follows. The hull is bought in, materials to manufacture the interior fittings are purchased, these fittings are then made, and then fitted into the hull to make the basic shell. Materials to construct the mast, rigging and so on are purchased, this manufacture is carried out, and then the mast is assembled with the basic shell. Material for the sails is bought, the sails are made, and then fitted to the shell and mast to complete the manufacture of the dinghy. The final assembly stage can be considered to include the act of delivering the product to the customer.

Table 28.4

Week number no.	1	2	3	4	5	6	7	8	9	10	11	12	13
Quantity	2	4	8	12	10	18	20	22	18	10	8	2	2
												Total	= 136

The delivery schedule is shown in Table 28.4, with the first delivery in the week ending 1 January.

Step 1

Construct an activity-on-arrow diagram to show the logic and timing of the production. It will usually be found most convenient to start to draw this from the end (in this case, final assembly of the dinghy), and work towards the various opening activities. The network need not be closed at the start – multiple starts are quite permissible and useful here – and nodes need not necessarily be identified, although for convenience here letters are used. Duration times are those required for unit production: these times are maintained constant during production by variation of resources. The diagram is shown in Fig. 28.20.

Step 2

Carry out a reverse forward pass from time zero at the final node (K), i.e. assign to the final node a time 0, and then successively add duration times for each activity in order. This will give the set of figures marked against each node, 2 at J, 4 at I, 7 at H, and so on, shown in Fig. 28.21.

Node times

Whilst node times represent the latest possible finishing times for the various activities, it is probably more useful to consider these times in relation to the quantities which would pass through the head nodes at any given time. Consider,

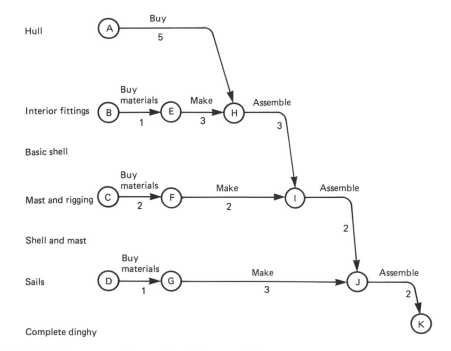

Fig. 28.20   Activity-on-arrow diagram for dinghy manufacture

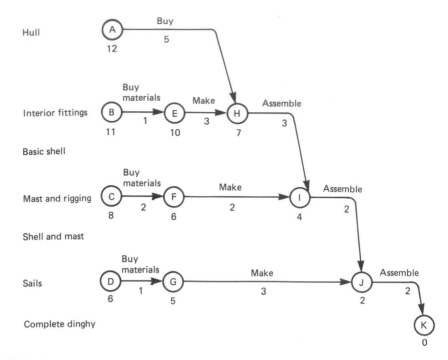

Fig. 28.21   Diagram showing node times

for example, the activity 'Buy materials for interior fitting'. Each kit of materials purchased and received will subsequently require three weeks to be made into the fittings, three weeks to be fitted into the hull to form the basic shell, two weeks to have the mast and rigging installed and two weeks to fix the sails and complete the dinghy:

3	+	3	+	2	+	2	= 10
(Make fittings)		(Basic shell)		(Shell + mast)		(Complete dinghy)	

Table 28.5

Activity	Equivalent week no.	Activity no.
Buy materials: interior fittings	10	1
Buy hull	7	2
Make interior fittings	7	3
Buy materials: mast and rigging	6	4
Buy materials: sails	5	5
Assemble basic shell	4	6
Make mast and rigging	4	7
Make sails	2	8
Assemble shell and mast	2	9
Complete assembly of dinghy	0	10

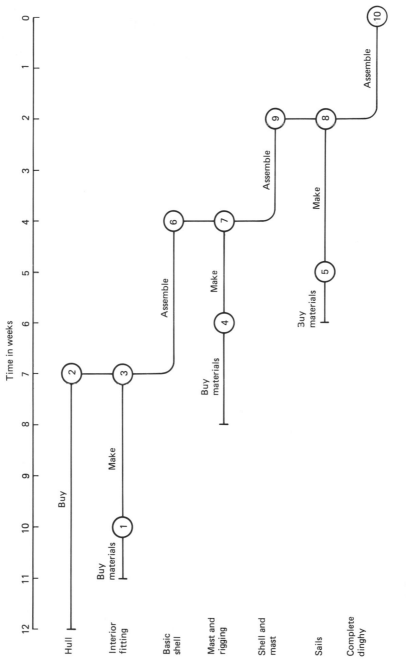

Fig. 28.22 LoB diagram

If the completion of the dinghy includes delivery to the customer, then the cumulative sets of materials purchased and received which should 'pass through' node E by time t is the cumulative quantity which should pass through node K (i.e. be delivered) by time $t + 10$. For example, two weeks after the start of delivery of complete dinghies to the customer, the total number of kits of materials for interior fittings purchased and received is equal to the cumulative number which should be delivered by week $10 + 2 =$ week 12, that is 134. This node time obtained by the reverse forward pass is called elsewhere the 'equivalent week number' for all the activities entering the node being considered.

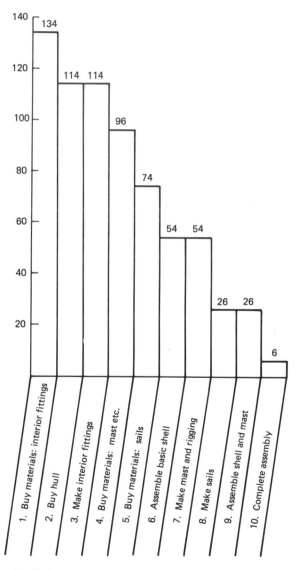

Fig. 28.23   Traditional LoB chart

Table 28.6

Date	Week number	Quantity	Cumulative quantity
9 October	−12		
16 October	−11		
23 October	−10		
30 October	− 9		
6 November	− 8		
13 November	− 7		
20 November	− 6		
27 November	− 5		
4 December	− 4		
11 December	− 3		
18 December	− 2		
25 December	− 1		
1 January	1	2	2
8 January	2	4	6
15 January	3	8	14
22 January	4	12	26
29 January	5	10	36
5 February	6	18	54
12 February	7	20	74
19 February	8	22	96
26 February	9	18	114
5 March	10	10	124
12 March	11	8	132
19 March	12	2	134
26 March	13	2	136

Table 28.7

	Volume of work completed is equivalent to volume delivered at week	Total units
Buy materials: interior fitting	2 + 10 = 12	134
Buy hull	2 + 7 = 9	114
Make interior fittings	2 + 7 = 9	114
Buy materials: mast and rigging	2 + 6 = 8	96
Buy materials: sails	2 + 5 = 7	74
Assemble basic shell	2 + 4 = 6	54
Make mast and rigging	2 + 4 = 6	54
Make sails	2 + 2 = 4	26
Assemble shell and mast	2 + 2 = 4	26
Complete assembly of dinghy	2 + 0 = 2	6

		Buy materials : interior fittings	Buy hull	Make interior fittings	Buy materials : mast etc.	Buy materials : sales	Assemble basic shell	Make mast and rigging	Make sails	Assemble shell and mast	Complete assembly
−12	9 Oct		S								
−11	16 Oct	S	C								
−10	23 Oct	2	C	S							
−9	30 Oct	6	C	C							
−8	6 Nov	14	C	C	S						
−7	13 Nov	26	2	2	C	S					
−6	20 Nov	36	6	6	2	C	S	S			
−5	27 Nov	54	14	14	6	2	C	C	S		
−4	4 Dec	74	26	26	14	6	2	2	C	S	
−3	11 Dec	96	36	36	26	14	6	6	C	C	
−2	18 Dec	114	54	54	36	26	14	14	2	2	S
−1	25 Dec	124	74	74	54	36	26	26	6	6	C
1	1 Jan	132	96	96	74	54	36	36	14	14	2
2	8 Jan	134	114	114	96	74	54	54	26	26	6
3	15 Jan	136	124	124	114	96	74	74	36	36	14
4	22 Jan		132	132	124	114	96	96	54	54	26
5	29 Jan		134	134	132	124	114	114	74	74	36
6	5 Feb		136	136	134	132	124	124	96	96	54
7	12 Feb				136	134	132	132	114	114	74
8	19 Feb					136	134	134	124	124	96
9	26 Feb						136	136	132	132	114
10	5 Mar								134	134	124
11	12 Mar								136	136	132
12	19 Mar										134
13	26 Mar										136

Fig. 28.24 LoB table for life of project

Step 3

Rank the activities in descending order of equivalent week number. This ranking (Table 28.5) gives the activity number – sometimes in LoB called the stage. This effectively provides the LoB diagram shown in Fig. 28.22, which can be built up by adding the activities in decreasing activity number, using Fig. 28.21.

Step 4

Prepare a calendar and accumulated delivery quantity table (Table 28.6).

Step 5

From Tables 28.5 and 28.6, deduce the quantity of each activity which should be completed by any particular date. For example:

It is now 8 January. How many of each activity should be completed?

Consider 'Make mast and rigging'. It is week 2. The quantity through 'Make mast and rigging' is equal to the quantity which can pass through the final stage in four weeks' time, that is, in week 2 + 4 = 6. From Table 28.6, this is a total of 54 units. A similar calculation can be performed for all activities (see Table 28.7).

This situation can be represented by the traditional LoB (Fig. 28.23).

A complete table for the whole 'life' of the batch can be drawn up if desired, and this is shown in Fig. 28.24. The S in the table indicates the latest date by which each chain of activities should *start*, this date being derived from the equivalent week numbers from the opening activities. The C in the table shows that the work must be *continued*.

Step 6

Record the actual progress upon either the LoB chart or the 'life' table. For example, suppose that at 8 January the achieved and planned results are those listed in Table 28.8. The chart is shown in Fig. 28.25 and the life table in Fig. 28.26.

Despite the over-fulfilment of the delivery schedule (15 delivered and only six required), it can be seen that a 'choking-off' of production will occur in weeks to come, because of under-fulfilment of some activities, and equally important there is some over-investment in work-in-progress on other activities. It may therefore be possible to transfer resources from the 'rich' activities to the 'poor' ones while

Table 28.8

		Achieved	*Planned*
1.	Buy materials: interior fittings	100	134
2.	Buy hull	100	114
3.	Make interior fittings	90	114
4.	Buy materials: mast and rigging	85	96
5.	Buy materials: sails	85	74
6.	Assemble basic shell	40	54
7.	Make mast and rigging	40	54
8.	Make sails	40	26
9.	Assemble shell and mast	15	26
10.	Complete assembly of dinghy	15	6

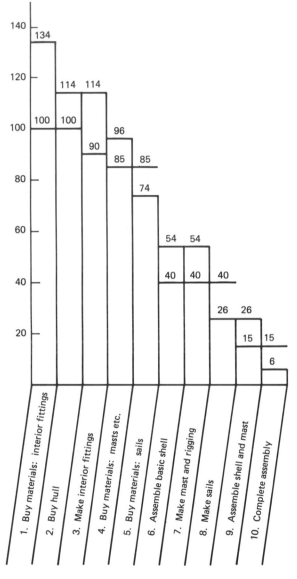

Fig. 28.25   Revised LoB chart

		Buy materials : interior fittings	Buy hull	Make interior fittings	Buy materials : mast etc.	Buy materials : sails	Assemble basic shell	Make mast and rigging	Make sails	Assemble shell and mast	Complete assembly
−12	9 Oct		S								
−11	16 Oct	S	C								
−10	23 Oct	2	C	S							
−9	30 Oct	6	C	C							
−8	6 Nov	14	C	C	S						
−7	13 Nov	26	2	2	C		S				
−6	20 Nov	36	6	6	2	S	C	S			
−5	27 Nov	54	14	14	6	2	C	C	S		
−4	4 Dec	74	26	26	14	6	2	2	C	S	
−3	11 Dec	96	36	36	26	14	6	6	C	C	
−2	18 Dec	114	54	54	36	26	14	14	2	2	S
−1	25 Dec	124	74	74	54	36	26	26	6	6	C
1	1 Jan	132	96	96	74	54	36	36	14	14	2
2	8 Jan	134	114	114	96	74	54	54	26	26	6
3	15 Jan	136	124	124	114	96	74	74	36	36	14
4	22 Jan		132	132	124	114	96	96	54	54	26
5	29 Jan		134	134	132	124	114	114	74	74	36
6	5 Feb		136	136	134	132	124	124	96	96	54
7	12 Feb				136	134	132	132	114	114	74
8	19 Feb					136	134	134	124	124	96
9	26 Feb						136	136	132	132	114
10	5 Mar								134	134	124
11	12 Mar								136	136	132
12	19 Mar										134
13	26 Mar										136

Fig. 28.26 Revised LoB table

preserving the delivery schedule: decisions here can only be taken in the light of local knowledge, and will require reference to both the activity-on-arrow diagram and the progress results.

CHAPTER 28 – HIGHLIGHTS

- Project network techniques (PNT) are used for planning and controlling projects made up of a large number of activities/tasks with complex interdependencies; the underlying model is a network.
- In activity-on-node (AoN) networks, the nodes in the network represent the activities.
- In activity-on-arrow (AoA) networks, the arrows in the network represent the activities.
- Analysis for AoN networks: a forward pass (summing activity times) is used to calculate the earliest start time (EST) of each activity; a backward pass (subtracting activity times) is made to calculate the latest start time (LST) of each activity.
- The critical path, those activities for which EST=LST, determines the project duration.
- The float is the difference between the EST and LST for an activity, and represents the possible increase in the activity's duration without extending the project.
- A bar chart representation shows the activities against a timescale; it can be used to identify and resolve resource problems.
- Multiple dependency can be used to represent start-to-start relations, finish-to-start relations and finish-to-finish relations.
- Line of balance (LoB) is used to control a single batch of the same product (e.g. an estate of houses).
- LoB requires identifiable stages in production at which managerial control can be exerted; manufacturing times between stages to be known; a delivery schedule; resources varied as required.
- Steps in application of LoB are:
  1. Construct an activity-on-arrow diagram to represent the logic in the tasks which make up the manufacture of the product.
  2. Carry out a 'reverse forward pass' starting at time zero with the final node, to calculate the equivalent week number.
  3. Rank the activities in descending order of equivalent week number, and prepare the LoB diagram – a time-scaled network.
  4. Prepare a calendar and accumulated delivery quantity table.
  5. From the calendar and LoB diagram prepare an LoB table showing the quantity of each activity which should be completed by each week number. For each week number this gives an LoB chart, and over the life of the project an LoB table.
  6. The progress of the project at any point in time can be recorded on the LoB chart and the LoB table.

Recommended reading

British Standards Institution, *Glossary of Terms Used in Project Network Techniques* (BSS4335)

Very useful. Aims to standardize the terminology and symbols used in PNT.

East, E. and Kirby, J., *A Guide to Computerised Project Scheduling*, Van Nostrand Reinhold, 1990

This text shows how to select and use the appropriate critical path program, and analyse the results generated by it.

Lockyer, K.G. and Gordon, J., *Critical Path Analysis and Other Project Network Techniques*, Pitman, 1991

A comprehensive and up-to-date text. Contains examples for the reader to work through.

Chapter 29

Resource Allocation – Linear Programming

This is a technique which can be used in a wide variety of decision-making situations in a number of different functional areas, including marketing, finance and distribution, in addition to production/operations management. A broad framework is one in which the manager is faced with decisions relating to the extent to which different activities are to be carried out. However, there are normally restrictions on the total extent to which these activities can be undertaken since, for example, they might be competing for limited resources. Overall it is necessary to establish the *actual extent* to which each activity is undertaken, while staying within the restrictions identified, and providing the most 'benefit'. The decisions are represented by variables, the restrictions by equations. If these relationships are linear, e.g. one unit generates £200 profit means three units generate £600 profit, one unit requires three hours of plant time in its manufacture means three units require nine hours, then the resulting decision-making problem can be represented as a *linear programme*.

An example of linear programming (LP)

A small multi-purpose plant is used to manufacture in batches two different herbicides: mosnok and daiseytox. These use different quantities of two active ingredients, CPA

Table 29.1

	Ingredients per batch (kg) CPA	DCP	Minimum no. of batches per week	Maximum no. of batches per week	Hours per batch	Profit per batch (£000s)
Mosnok	10	10	1	9	12	12
Daiseytox	5	17	1	9	12	8
Wt available per week	100	170				

432

and DCP, produced by other plants within the group. There is a limit on the availability of CPA and DCP. Moreover, the marketing section have established that there are both minimum and maximum numbers of batches of the herbicides required each week. The basic data are shown in Table 29.1.

The plant currently operates a full three shifts per day for six days per week ($6 \times 24 = 144$ hours).

The plant manager wants to know the number of batches of each herbicide to produce each week in order to maximize the total profit, while staying within the restrictions on availability of the active ingredients and the availability of the plant.

If x_1 and x_2 represent the numbers of batches of mosnok and daiseytox being produced each week, the limitations imposed by the minimum acceptable quantities and maximum required quantities can be expressed as:

$$x_1 \geq 1, x_1 \leq 9$$
$$x_2 \geq 1, x_2 \leq 9$$

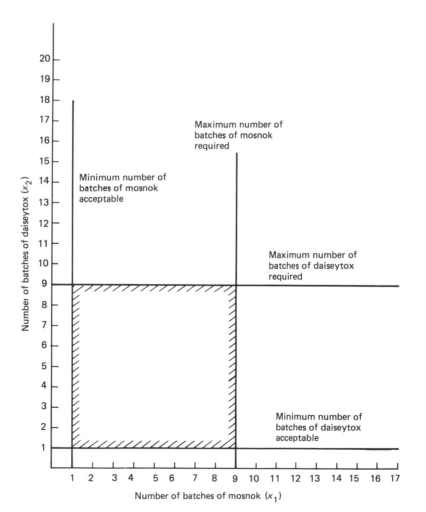

Fig. 29.1 Possible combinations satisfying the marketing restrictions

Since there are only two variables, this situation can be presented graphically. The straight lines $x_1 = 1$, $x_1 = 9$, $x_2 = 1$, $x_2 = 9$ are shown in Fig. 29.1; the area which they enclose shows the points which satisfy the minimum and maximum requirements. However, it is also necessary to take account of the other restrictions:

Availability of CPA:	$10x_1 + 5x_2 \leqslant 100$
Availability of DCP:	$10x_1 + 17x_2 \leqslant 170$
Plant availability:	$12x_1 + 12x_2 \leqslant 144$

The straight lines which come from these inequalities can be added to the graph drawn earlier, giving the feasible region of possible solutions shown in Fig. 29.2.

The full problem can now be stated as:

$$
\begin{array}{lrcl}
\text{Maximize} & 12x_1 + 8x_2 \\
\text{subject to} & x_1 & \geqslant & 1 \\
& x_2 & \geqslant & 1 \\
& x_1 & \leqslant & 9 \\
& x_2 & \leqslant & 9 \\
& 10x_1 + 5x_2 & \leqslant & 100 \\
& 10x_1 + 17x_2 & \leqslant & 170 \\
& 12x_1 + 12x_2 & \leqslant & 144
\end{array}
$$

Examining the objective function (as maximize $12x_1 + 8x_2$ is called), if the line $12x_1 + 8x_2 = 96$ is added to the graph, all points along this line correspond to solutions which give a profit 96. For this reason, this is sometimes called an *isoprofit* line. The line $12x_1 + 8x_2 = 120$ is parallel to this first line, further from the origin, and corresponding to a larger profit. To find the point corresponding to the solution with the *maximum* profit, it is necessary to 'push' these isoprofit lines out as far as possible, until the edge of the feasible region is reached. This is shown in Fig. 29.3.

The solution appears to lie at $x_1 = 8$, $x_2 = 4$. It can be seen that this lies at the intersection of the constraints corresponding to availability of CPA, and plant availability; consequently the value can be confirmed by solving the simultaneous equations:

$$
\begin{array}{l}
10x_1 + 5x_2 = 100 \\
12x_1 + 12x_2 = 144
\end{array}
$$

The profit is 128. There is unused DCP, since the point does not lie on the line $10x_1 + 17x_2 = 170$.

If the price per batch of daiseytox is increased by 4 and the costs remain the same, then the profit on each batch of daiseytox is increased to 12, and the objective becomes:

$$12x_1 + 12x_2$$

As these new isoprofit lines are 'pushed' out, instead of reaching a *corner* of the feasible region, they reach one complete edge, that part bounded by the *plant*

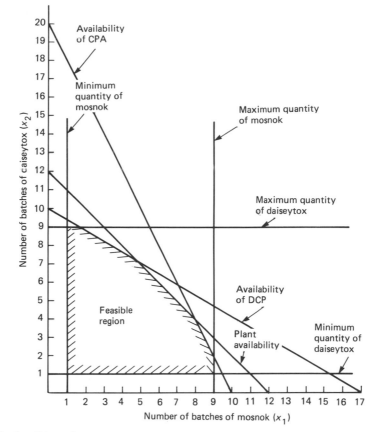

Fig. 29.2 The feasible region

availability constraint. This means that all points on this edge give the same maximum profit; these are known as *alternative optimal solutions*.

The R&D section develop a third herbicide which the plant can produce: cloverkil. An estimated minimum of two batches per week will be required, with a maximum of seven batches per week. Each batch requires 9 kg of CPA, 12 kg of DCP and 10 hours of plant time. The profit per batch is 10. If x_3 represents the number of batches of cloverkil produced per week, then this revised problem can be formulated as follows:

$$
\begin{array}{llll}
\text{Maximize} & 12x_1 + 8x_2 + 10x_3 & & \\
\text{subject to} & x_1 & \geqslant & 1 \\
& x_2 & \geqslant & 1 \\
& x_3 & \geqslant & 2 \\
& x_1 & \leqslant & 9 \\
& x_2 & \leqslant & 9 \\
& x_3 & \leqslant & 7 \\
& 10x_1 + 5x_2 + 9x_3 & \leqslant & 100 \\
& 10x_1 + 17x_2 + 12x_3 & \leqslant & 170 \\
& 12x_1 + 12x_2 + 10x_3 & \leqslant & 144 \\
\end{array}
$$

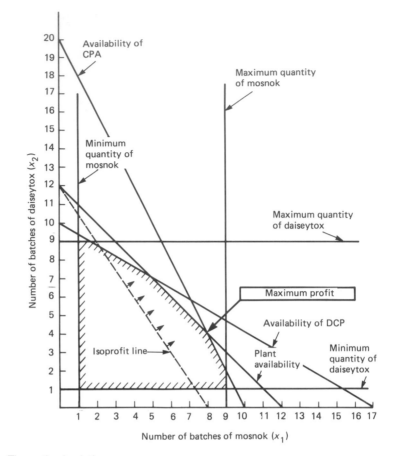

Fig. 29.3   The optimal solution

Clearly, since more than two variables are now involved, the graphical method cannot be adopted. However, there is another procedure, the *simplex method*, which can be used. Essentially the application of a set of rules results in the development of a series of solutions each satisfying the constraints, and each with a 'better' value of the objective function. This *iterative process* finishes when no further improvement is possible. The simplex method is the name given to this set of rules which is applied to the data to proceed from one solution to the next, and a criterion which establishes when no further improvement is possible. This procedure handles equalities rather than inequalities, so that additional variables need to be introduced. For 'less than' constraints, slack variables are added: so, for example, $x_1 \leqslant 9$ becomes $x_1 + s_1 = 9$, where s_1 represents the extent to which the maximum value of nine batches per week is not achieved. For 'greater than' constraints, surplus variables are added: so, for example, $x_1 \geqslant 1$ becomes $x_1 - t_1 = 1$, where t_1 represents the extent to which the minimum value of 1 is over-achieved. Further details of the application of the simplex method can be found in the Recommended reading at the end of the chapter. Clearly, any iterative procedure should be ideally suited to computer application, and this is discussed in a later section.

Extensions of linear programming

The basic model of LP can be extended in a number of directions. In the previous example it was chance that the result was a whole number of batches of each product each week. However, fractional values could have been interpreted: $x_2 = 31/3$, manufacture 10 batches of daiseytox every three weeks. However, this type of interpretation is not always possible. If the decisions are related to the numbers of different types of machine to be purchased, then clearly to talk of purchasing 31/3 machines is a nonsense. The basic LP solution procedure can be extended to the situation where the variables can only take whole-number values: this is known as *integer programming*.

Frequently the constant values within the LP are not known with certainty, and the decision maker would like to know the effect of changes in these values. For example, overtime could be worked on Sunday and increase the plant availability; however, will the extra profit cover the additional cost of this overtime? It is possible to increase the profit on one of the products, but will this justify an increase in the quantity produced? These and other 'what if' questions can be answered using *sensitivity analysis*. Indeed, it has been argued that this analysis is more use to the decision maker than the simple solution to the problem.

Other extensions include handling known forms of uncertainty, more than one objective, and non-linearities. Details of these and other extensions can be found in most texts on mathematical programming, the name given to all these techniques.

Linear programming and the computer

In practice, the vast majority of applications of LP rely on the use of a computer for the solution. Most computers support at least one LP package. Often the potential user is faced with a wide choice. Many of these packages can also handle the extensions outlined in the previous section. They automatically generate and interpret the slack and surplus variables required by the simplex procedure, can deal

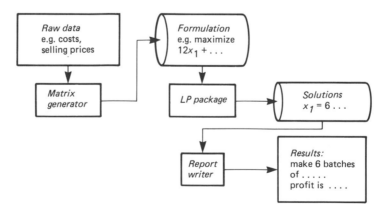

Fig. 29.4 Use of computer for IP

with integer variables and carry out sensitivity analysis. Packages on larger computers can solve problems with virtually any number of constraints and variables.

Frequently, considerable time can be spent setting up the formulation of the problem. The data come from a variety of sources for the constraints and objective – selling prices, different elements of costs and so on – requiring various calculations before forming the equations. Equally, having solved the linear programme, time is needed to interpret the solution in the context of the practical problem. Two computer programs, often supplied with LP packages, the matrix generator and report writer, can help with this. This use is shown in Fig. 29.4.

Applications of LP in POM

The successful use of LP comes not so much from the solution to the problem but more from the ability of the decision maker to formulate the problem as a linear programme in the first place. Problems arising in a variety of situations have been formulated to exploit the linear programme solution procedures. Some of the more general frameworks are outlined below.

Product mix (or resource allocation) problems

For example, a department in a hospital may be capable of carrying out various types of operation. Each type requires different levels of nursing and surgical support, bed occupancy and so on. The manager has to decide on the mix of operations to plan each week to stay within the availability of these resources while meeting the requirements of the patients. Another example was given in the worked example in the earlier section.

Blending problems

For example, to make an animal feedstuff with specific nutritive qualities, various combinations of basic food stocks may be used. This blending problem is to produce a solution at minimum cost.

Cutting problems

From a single product, for example, a reel of transformer steel, a number of products may be made by cutting the product. It is desirable to choose the combination which will generate the minimum waste.

Transportation problems

For example, a number of warehouses serve a number of retail outlets. The unit cost of each warehouse supplying each retail outlet is given. The objective is to establish the amount each warehouse should ship to each outlet in order to minimize the total cost while exceeding neither the availabilities at each warehouse nor the requirements of the outlets. The special structure of this formulation allows a simpler method than the simplex procedure to be used in the solution.

Assignment problems

For example, a number of tasks have to be allocated to a number of workers in an office. Because of their experience, backgrounds and so on, each worker has a different efficiency in completing each different task. The objective is to assign the tasks to workers in such a way the overall efficiency is maximized. This is the simplest of the LP routines.

CHAPTER 29 – HIGHLIGHTS

- The manager is often faced with: decisions over the levels at which to undertake various activities (these can be thought of as *variables*); limitations on the decisions caused by resource availability and other reasons (these define relationships between the variables, called *constraints*); an *objective* to achieve (e.g. maximum profit) – a further relationship between the variables. When the relationships are linear, the problem can be formulated as a linear programme (LP).

- The solution of a linear programme may be reached in two ways: two-variable problems can be solved graphically by drawing the straight lines representing the constraints and the objective; problems with three or more variables can be solved using the simplex procedure.

- A computer can be used with *matrix generator* software to set up the formulation from the raw data for input into the *LP package* (wide variety available); this outputs to the report writer, which takes the solution and interprets it in the context of the original problem.

- Extensions of LP include: integer programming, when some of the variables must take whole number values; sensitivity analysis for determining how the solution changes as the parameters within the problem change; uncertainty, non-linearities and multiple objectives.

- Standard problem formats for LP in POM include: product mix/resource allocation – determining level of activity, while staying within resource availability and maximizing profit; blending problems – mixing inputs with different features to form a composite with required characteristics at minimum cost; cutting problems – from a single base a number of products may be 'cut' and the objective is to determine the pattern which generates least waste; transportation problems – determining the amount each source should supply to each destination in order to minimize total cost, and staying within the availabilities of the sources and the requirements of the destinations; assignment problems – allocating tasks to workers for maximum efficiency.

Recommended reading

Hillier, E. and Lieberman, G., *Introduction to Mathematical Programming*, McGraw-Hill, 1990

Comprehensive coverage of all aspects of mathematical programming.

Hughes, A.J., and Grawiog, D.E., *Linear Programming: An Emphasis on Decision Making*, Addison-Wesley, 1973

A comprehensive treatment of linear programming, plus many of the extensions, with plenty of examples, from a practical standpoint.

Whitaker, D., *OR on a Micro*, Wiley, 1984

Includes a chapter on linear programming, and some of the special cases, together with a listing of a BASIC program for problem solving.

Wisniewski, M. and Dacre, T., *Mathematical Programming: Optimisation Models for Business and Management Decision-Making*, McGraw-Hill, 1990

Provides a conceptual understanding of the appropriate solution method, together with discussions of the practical implications.

Williams, H.P., *Model Building in Mathematical Programming*, 3rd edn, Wiley, 1990

A comprehensive text, not only covering linear programming but many of its extensions, but from a model building rather than an algorithmic approach, including twenty practical problems with discussions of associated formulations and solutions, recently extensively revised.

Zoutendijk, G., *Mathematical Programming Methods*, North-Holland, 1976

A thorough coverage of the algorithms for linear programming, and associated models.

Chapter 30

Purchasing

Purchasing objectives and policies

There are few organizations which are totally self-contained to the extent that their products and services are generated at one location from basic materials. Some materials or services are usually purchased from outside sources. The primary objective of purchasing is to obtain the correct equipment, materials, supplies and services in the right quantity, of the right quality, from the right origin, at the right time and cost. It has, however, a number of other duties, acting as the organization's window-on-the-world', providing information on any new products, processes, materials and services. Purchasing should also advise on probable prices, deliveries and performance of products under consideration by the research, design and development functions.

Since the 'total' cost of bought-in material or services may form a very large proportion of the final selling price of the organization's products or services, purchasing is an extremely important specialized function which should never be under-estimated. While the value of purchases varies from industry to industry, it averages 65 per cent of the turnover of all industries. Let us examine briefly the effects of good purchasing management on the profitability of a 'typical' manufacturing or service company with a turnover of £1,000,000 per annum and a profit of 10 per cent; the purchases account for £650,000 per annum. If a saving of 5 per cent can be achieved on the costs associated with purchasing by good management – price control, quality assurance, good transport methods, control of storage and stock holding, etc. – then the increase in profits will amount to £32,500, i.e. new profits of £132,500 or 13.3 per cent. If the same profit target of £132,500 is required, but no savings in purchasing are achieved, then the sales must rise to £1,325,000, an increase of 32.5 per cent. Such an increase in sales volume is often accompanied by either additional expenditure on sales and marketing effort or a cut in selling price, so the relationship is often not linear anyway.

Alternative means of generating savings or additional profits, such as increases in productivity, are often slow to be realized and the 'profits' may have to be shared. Savings in purchasing costs show immediately in the profit margin.

Although purchasing is clearly an important area of managerial activity, it is often neglected by both manufacturing and service industries. The separation of purchasing from selling has, however, been removed in many large retail organizations, which have recognized that the purchaser must be responsible for the whole 'product line' – its selection, quality, specification, delivery, price, acceptability and reliability. If any part of this chain is wrong, the purchasing function must resolve the problem. This concept is clearly very appropriate in retailing where transformation activities on the product itself, between purchase and sale, are small or zero, but it shows the need to include market information in the buying decision processes in all other industries.

Organizing purchasing

The inputs to purchasing appear from various sources, depending on the nature of the operation, but they include:

(a) *design* – from the concept to the product or service;
(b) *research and development* – of the processes used and the outputs produced;
(c) *production or operations* – detailed requirements of the transformation process, including data on waste, efficiencies and conformance with existing or planned facilities;
(d) *distribution* – either by the supplier or the customer, e.g. in retailing;
(e) *marketing* – future demands, feedback on quality, competitors and any other issue which affects purchasing;
(f) *finance* – terms of payment, creditors, invoice verification and payment, auditing of procedures, etc.;
(g) *legal services* – drawing-up and agreeing of contracts;
(h) *general management* – make or buy decisions.

The purchasing function, like any other in an organization, is ineffective if it exists in isolation. There is no ideal structure for the purchasing activity, since each organization will create unique demands, but there are basically two forms of orientation:

(a) centralization:
(b) decentralization.

Centralization and localization of purchasing

Within a single location, it is generally accepted that all purchasing should be carried out by one department. This avoids uneconomical small quantities, irritation of the vendors at having several contacts with the company, and the carrying out of a specialized function by non-specialists. In organizations with a number of sites, or with a number of autonomous divisions within the same site, the situation is not so straightforward. Buying can, under these circumstances, either be carried out at one central location for all units, however widely separated geographically, or by local buying departments.

Advantages of centralization
The advantages of centralized buying are:

1. A *consistent* buying policy.
2. *Maximum* purchasing power when conducting negotiations with vendors.
3. *Uniform* purchasing records and organization.

Advantages of decentralized buying
The advantages of decentralized buying are:

1. *Greater flexibility:* the centralized buyer for a number of sites or divisions will find it difficult to react rapidly to changes in the requirements of individual users.
2. *Close liaison:* a local buyer will be in closer contact with his/her own units and will be able to give greater assistance on the 'window-on-the-world' duties.
3. *Responsibility:* the senior executive who has control of purchasing for a location can be held responsible for the purchase of goods, and the site remains autonomous in this respect.

As is common with most organizational problems, the most usual situation, in widely spread organizations or groups of companies, is a compromise where both centralized and decentralized buying departments exist together. Each site or division has a separate purchasing department, while a centralized purchasing director or manager has the responsibility for co-ordinating the activities and directing the policies of the local buyers.

The organizational location of the purchaser will vary from one organization to another, but the most commonly found executives to whom purchasing is responsible are:

1. *The accountant*. It is argued that the buyer is spending the organization's money and, since the control of money is the responsibility of the accountant, then the buyer should report to the accountant. This arrangement will work best when the range of purchases is small and the source of supply limited as, for example, the polythene tubing used in polythene bag manufacture. In a company making complex equipment, particularly on a batch production basis, or in a multinational consultancy operation, this location is probably too remote from the point of operations to be effective.
2. *The managing director* or *the senior executive*. Where considerable quantities of material or services are being purchased, particularly of an expensive nature, it is often desirable for purchase negotiations to be carried out at as high a level as possible, since favourable terms can often only be negotiated directly with the chief executives of supplying companies. For this reason many CEOs or managing directors undertake the purchasing function themselves, or delegate it to some person directly responsible to them.
3. *The production operations manager* or *controller*. In many manufacturing or service situations, the need for resources to be flexible will often dictate that the buyer be part of the production manager's staff, either directly responsible to the production manager or to the production controller, possibly as head of the material control section, where he/she will undertake duties which include purchasing.

Make or buy decisions

The make or buy decision refers to the problem encountered by an organization when deciding whether a product or service should be purchased from outside sources or generated internally. The majority of make or buy decisions are made on the basis of price, but this is only one of a number of criteria which must be evaluated in this strategic decision. Other key points which must have influence are:

(a)   quality and how it is controlled;
(b)   continuity of supply;
(c)   technological and/or commercial knowledge and experience required.

The economics of production or operations probably comes last in this list, which places operational conditions higher than financial ones. Moreover, consideration of the 'non-cost' factors encourages longer-term contracts with suppliers to aid the achievement of production and quality levels and encourage investment in appropriate resources and new ideas. This results in excellent, mutually beneficial customer–supplier relationships developed over long periods, based on trust and the achievement of common objectives. The constant re-analysis of the make or buy decision in search of short-term advantage can destroy the relationship needed for long-term supply contracts having mutual profitability as their basic objectives. This does not say that the decision should be once and for all, for it clearly requires some periodic re-analysis to take into account changes in business and environmental conditions, and technology.

Most make or buy decisions are very complex, time-consuming and affect many parts of an organization. Senior management involvement is required in a number of the stages of this strategic decision. Problems may well be experienced in calculating accurate costs, and finding information on quality, supply and reliability, and technical know-how requirements, for each side of the equation.

Information inputs are required from both inside and outside the purchasing function, which clearly has a vital role to play. Informal and formal involvement of technical, financial (accounts) and production or operations control will always be necessary, together with a systematic approach based on careful weighing of the key factors – it is unlikely that one single factor, such as price, will be so conclusive as to dictate the obvious path to be taken.

It is interesting to note the changes in the provision of services by local authorities in the UK. There has been a re-think of the traditional approach of having a department with responsibility for all aspects of the service, including planning and specifying the service as well as delivering it on a day-to-day basis. In certain functions, work now has to be put out to compulsory competitive tender (CCT), rather than be awarded as of right to the authority's in-house workforce. In these functions, the management of service no longer relies directly on the management of people, but on the management of a purchasing contract with either the in-house organization or an external contractor.

Developments such as these have encouraged authorities to define two separate roles within each service; the *client* role and the *contractor* role, whether the service is provided by an internal group or by an external agency. The traditional service departments have, in many cases, been split into two separate sections reflecting the two main roles.

The purchasing system

The control of purchasing should be set out in a written 'purchasing manual' which:

(a) assigns responsibilities for and within the purchasing function;
(b) defines the manner in which suppliers are selected to ensure that they are continually capable of supplying the requirements in terms of material and services;
(c) indicates the appropriate purchasing documentation – written orders, specifications and certificates of conformity – required in any modern purchasing activity.

The purchase order

The purchase order is a contractual document which may well bind the originating organization to considerable expenditure. It is most important, therefore, that it should be clear and unambiguous. The following statements:

'Price to be agreed',
'Delivery as soon as possible',
'Of good quality',
'Of normal commercial quality',
'As previously supplied',
'As discussed with your Mr Jones',

and others of a similar nature should never be used, since they are too loose to be useful and can cause considerable difficulties later when delivery occurs of a quality other than that required, or at a date later than useful.

The purchase order should carry at least the following information:

1. Name and address of originating organization.
2. Name and address of receiving company.
3. Identifying number.
4. Quantity of produce or amount of service required.
5. A full description of the type, style, grade or other means of precise identification of the product or service.
6. The applicable issue of the product or service specification and any other relevant technical data (a reference to a published, current specification may be used).
7. Reference to any certification of conformity to requirements, which must accompany the delivered product.
8. Price agreed between purchaser and vendor.
9. Delivery agreed between purchaser and vendor.
10. Cost allocation – this for internal use.
11. Any delivery instructions.
12. Purchaser's signature and standing in the organization.
13. Purchaser's conditions of business.

The authority to sign purchase orders is usually restricted to one or two persons within the organization, and limitations may be imposed as to the amount of expenditure which may be incurred by a signatory: for example, some companies have a rule that orders of value greater than a certain amount must be sanctioned by the board.

Receiving inspection

Inspection on receipt of goods or services may be an essential component of the system of purchasing. The amount and extent of inspection performed on receipt varies, however, with the effectiveness of the suppliers' delivery and quality systems. It must be recognized that the conformance quality of supplied material or services can be controlled only at the point of their production. Inspection at receipt for acceptance or rejection is an inefficient and wasteful device, to be replaced, as soon as possible, by the use of receiving inspection to check that the necessary systems and procedures used by the supplier to control quality are in fact working effectively.

Futures

In some cases, orders at an agreed price are placed *now* for delivery *in the future*, the price being paid when the goods are delivered. This form of trading is most commonly met with in the commodity markets where foodstuffs and raw materials change hands. The advantage to the purchaser is the ensuring of supply of a vital product at a known price, while the vendor guarantees a sale, again at a known price. If either party forecasts the movement of the market incorrectly, then there will be a loss, but in exchange for some security. Purchasing futures differs from speculating, in that both goods/services and money change hands *in the future*.

Duties of a purchasing department

The usual duties that are assigned to a purchasing department are:

1. *Finding and approving suppliers.* In this context, suppliers must be taken to include both those who supply goods and those who supply services. This should be done not only by discussions with representatives and examination of catalogues and samples, but also by visits to the suppliers' premises. The technical approval of the vendor's product or service may be the responsibility of the quality or design departments, but the purchaser should be confident that the source of supply is stable, reliable and able to fulfil the demands made upon it. Visits to suppliers will not only help to give this assurance but will also allow the buyer to meet, in a direct manner, those people with whom he/she will be dealing and build up a spirit of goodwill between the two parties. Used with discretion, this goodwill can be of great value in times of difficulty.

   Purchasing managers should try wherever possible to assign quantitative values to the factors which are desirable in a supplier. There are a number of schemes such as *vendor rating*, which is discussed later.
2. *Purchasing at least total cost.* While the quality and quantity of goods or services may be specified elsewhere, the purchaser must purchase these at the most advantageous terms. He must be prepared to assist in or lead all discussion on

order quantities, and give advice on the imponderables – like anticipated service from the supplier – which can affect decisions on the choice of vendor.

Wherever possible, price should be fixed by competitive tender, if possible by comparison with a target purchase price. It has been pointed out earlier that the lowest purchase price may not necessarily be that which is least costly to the purchasing company, since it may attract other costs (rectification, sorting, progressing etc.) which increase the *total* cost of the purchased item. *Any unexpectedly low price should be treated with caution.*

A purchaser should obtain a list of satisfactory suppliers and should send out as many enquiries as convenient, requesting information on quality, delivery and price; these enquiries must be marked clearly FOR QUOTATION ONLY. Quotations should be examined for such items as delivery charges, discount structure (e.g. discounts for prompt payment), supplementary charges and any restrictions. The use of the learning curve as a negotiating tool is advocated by some, while the practice of incorporating a purchaser into a value analysis team is well established and very useful.

3. *Ensuring delivery of goods and services at the right time.* This will involve contacting suppliers before the due dates and seeking assurances that these dates will be maintained. A formal 'progress' system may be set up to do this, and a convenient method is to log all delivery requirements in diary form, perhaps raising an enquiry before the due date, following this up by a final enquiry just before the due date to confirm. It must be realized that deliveries which are too *early* may form a source of embarrassment, not only because payment may be demanded early, but because excessive space might be occupied. In some organizations the delivery date and, indeed, time of day may require to be specified to avoid congestion. It is not unknown for goods delivered early to be refused or delayed entry. This is particularly important, of course, in the food preparation service industries.

When progressing an order, care must be taken to avoid chasing that which has, in fact, already been supplied. This can only be done by maintaining a close liaison with the receiving department. A copy of the appropriate receipt documentation is usefully sent to purchasing to be recorded against the orders.

4. *Warning all concerned if deliveries are not going to be met.* If, as a result of the progressing action mentioned above, it is evident that a delivery date is not going to be met, the appropriate departments *must* be informed in order that work can, if necessary, and possible, be re-scheduled.

5. *Verifying invoices* presented by suppliers. This task is sometimes carried out by the purchasing department, sometimes by a 'customer service' department. It is necessary to check that the prices quoted on an invoice agree with those negotiated, and this can be done by a direct comparison with the purchase order if the price is quoted there. The absence of prices from purchase orders is to be avoided if possible, since it restricts the task of verification of invoices.

A further and more real need for verification of invoices arises from the problem of incorrect quantities invoiced or prices, perhaps caused by the return of defective material to the supplier. To help resolve this problem, a note of every 'rejection' should be passed to purchasing. The recording of these rejects will also help to build up a picture of the reliability of the supplier, and this may well affect the placing of future orders.

Note: The cost of verifying invoices can be extremely high, and in the case of low-value invoices, quite unjustified. It is as well to consider whether invoices below a fixed figure need to be verified.

6. *Organizing all discussions with suppliers*, both actual and potential. It will be found that departments, such as design, will need to meet suppliers and discuss problems with them and, while in many cases the only persons competent to carry out 'technical' discussions with suppliers are within the technical departments, these discussions should never take place without the knowledge of purchasing. This will avoid arrangements on delivery and price being made which do not accord with the company's purchasing policy. In some organizations, a firm rule is laid down that all correspondence with suppliers must be signed by purchasing even if it originated elsewhere. This may appear restrictive, but it can save much misunderstanding later on, often at a time when the 'technical' departments have relinquished all interest in the purchase.

7. *Speculative buying* is sometimes a duty of purchasing, and implies the purchase of goods, not from reasons of immediate need but because it appears that market conditions are particularly favourable. Thus, it may seem to the purchaser, from his intimate knowledge of the market, that a particular commodity is likely to become difficult to obtain or that its price is likely to rise sharply. Buying in the first case will guard against a hold-up, whilst in the second case it may permit material bought cheaply to be resold at a profit. Speculative buying is both difficult and potentially dangerous, and can result in a company carrying stocks which are difficult to clear.

8. *Advising on prices* for materials or services to be used in new markets or in modified designs. This activity can be of substantial value since it may help to decide major policy questions – for example, the feasibility of meeting a marketing requirement on price, or the likely cost of re-equipping a unit.

9. *Acting as a 'window-on-the-world'*. Purchasing brings continual contact with outside organizations, and this can prove a valuable channel of communication whereby news of novel processes, materials, services and equipments are brought to the notice of departments most concerned with these matters. In like manner, purchasing is often well placed to search out information, and experience of fending off persistent salesmen can avoid considerable waste of time.

Duties of purchasing

1. Finding and approving suppliers.
2. Purchasing at least total cost.
3. Ensuring delivery at the right time.
4. Warning of delays.
5. Verifying invoices.
6. Organizing all discussions with suppliers.
7. Speculative buying.
8. Advising on prices.
9. Acting as a 'window-on-the-world'.

Vendor rating

Vendor rating schemes are designed to assist the purchasing department to select the most appropriate supplier. Inevitably, some sort of ranking must always have been made, but the schemes should attempt to formalize the ranking technique and bring some objectivity to it. Basically, all schemes require that some quantitative data are obtained for each supplier on factors such as:

1. Quality.
2. Delivery.
3. Cost.
4. Service and reliability.

The importance of each of the above is not necessarily the same: for example, for many classes of goods, quality will be of much greater importance than cost. To account for these differences, the above factors may be weighted: for a hypothetical case, the weightings might be:

Factor	*Weight*
Quality	8
Delivery	6
Cost	4
Service and reliability	2

Suppliers are then 'scored' for these factors, each score being multiplied by the appropriate weight to give the final factor score. In the crudest possible scoring system, the purchaser may make a subjective assessment on a 1–5 scale, 5 being the 'excellent' score, 1 being the 'poor' score. The result might then appear as follows.

Supplier A *Factor*	*Weight*	*Score*	*Weighted score*
Quality	8	4	32
Delivery	6	4	24
Cost	4	5	20
Service and reliability	2	3	6
		Total	82

For a range of possible suppliers, this could be combined into a matrix as in Fig. 30.1.

Subjective scoring should, of course, be replaced by some objective method if possible. For example, the 'quality' score may be derived from a periodic assessment of the supplier's quality management system; the 'delivery' score from the number of late deliveries; the 'cost' score from ratio of the price quoted by a supplier to the target purchase price or the lowest obtainable price; and the 'service and reliability' score from a measurement of the number of 'progressing' calls which have to be made.

The purchaser, having placed an order with an approved supplier, is dependent upon that supplier to fulfil the delivery promises. While 'penalty' and 'break' clauses can be written into an order, they are often difficult to enforce, and by the time that

Factor	Weight	Possible Supplier			
		A	B	C	D
Quality	8	4 / 32	3 / 24	5 / 40	2 / 16
Delivery	6	4 / 24	5 / 30	2 / 12	3 / 18
Cost	4	5 / 20	2 / 8	2 / 8	5 / 20
Service	2	3 / 6	5 / 10	1 / 2	2 / 4
Totals		82	72	62	58

Fig. 30.1

it is known that the delivery will be late, it is often too late to renegotiate the order with a new supplier.

Just-in-Time (JIT) purchasing

Purchasing is an important feature of Just-in-Time (JIT) methods of inventory control. The development of long-term relationships with a few suppliers, rather than short-term ones with many, leads to the concept of *co-producers* in networks of trust providing dependable quality and delivery of goods and services. Each organization in the chain of supply is encouraged to extend JIT methods to its suppliers.

The requirements of JIT mean that suppliers are usually located near the purchaser's premises, delivering small quantities, often several times per day, to match the usage rate. Paperwork is kept to a minimum and standard quantities in standard containers are usual. The requirement for suppliers to be located near to the buying organization, which places those at some distance at a competitive disadvantage, causes lead times to be shorter and deliveries to be more reliable.

It can be argued that JIT purchasing and delivery is suitable mainly for assembly line operations and less so for certain process industries, but the reduction in the inventory and transport costs that it brings should encourage innovations to bring about its widespread adoption. Those committed to open competition and finding the lowest price will find most difficulty, as will those countries which, for geographical reasons. Suffer greater transport distances between customer and suppliers. Nevertheless, there must be a recognition of the need to develop closer relationships and to begin the dialogue – the sharing of information and problems – which leads to the product or service of the right quality being delivered in the right quantity at the right time.

CHAPTER 30 – HIGHLIGHTS

- The primary objective of purchasing is to obtain the correct equipment, materials, supplies and services in the right quantity, of the right quality, from the right origin, at the right time and cost.
- The inputs to purchasing come from various sources including design, research and development, production/operations, distribution, marketing, finance, legal services, and general management.

- There is no ideal structure for purchasing, but there are basically two forms of orientation; centralization and decentralization.
- The advantages of centralization include consistent policy, maximum purchasing power, and uniform purchasing. Advantages of decentralization include greater flexibility, closer liaison, and greater ownership or responsibility.
- The location of the purchaser varies but may be the accountant, the chief executive, or the production/operations manager.
- Make or buy decisions should be made on the basis of price, quality, continuity of supply, and technological and commercial knowledge/ experience.
- A written purchasing manual should exist and assign responsibilities, define how suppliers are selected, and refer to purchasing documentation, including specifications and purchase orders.
- The duties of a purchasing department include finding and approving suppliers, purchasing at least total cost, ensuring right-time deliveries, warning of delays, verifying invoices, organizing supplier discussions, speculative buying, advising on prices, and acting as 'a window-on-the-world'.
- Vendor rating schemes select the most appropriate suppliers by consideration of quality, delivery, cost, service and reliability.
- Purchasing is an important part of JIT methods. Partnerships and co-producers lead to trust and the development of close relationships and sharing information.

Recommended reading

Baily, P. and Farmer, D., *Purchasing – Principles and Management*, 6th edn, Pitman, 1990

Meets the needs of modern purchasing management. It is a clearly written practical guide, and contains a number of very useful references and suggestions for further reading.

Farmer, D. (ed.), *Purchasing Management Handbook*, Gower, 1985

A comprehensive work which should be in the hands of all those involved in the purchasing function.

Heinritz, S.F. and Farrell, P.V., *Purchasing: Principles and Application*, Prentice-Hall, 1986

An interesting book aimed at the generalist and offering an overview with useful practical guidance.

Heinritz, S.F., Farrell, P.V. and Smith, C.L., *Purchasing, Principles and Application*, 7th edn, Prentice-Hall, 1986

An excellent, wide-ranging American book. Well referenced. With case studies.

Leenders, M.R., *Purchasing and Materials Management*, 8th edn, Irwin, 1985

Remains the standard US text on this subject.

SECTION 6

The People

The people within the organization have an important role from the POM perspective. This section looks at the interface with personnel management, including payment by results systems, and explores the responsibilities for health and safety management.

Chapter 31

Production/Operations and Personnel Management

POM and the personnel policy

Personnel management can be considered to consist of two parts: one, the supervisory management exerted by the departmental head and his superiors in day-to-day relationships – the leadership exerted by the supervisor; and the other, the direction of the conditions of work of the employee. This chapter will be concerned only with the second aspect, which for convenience will be called *personnel management*.

Personnel management is generally accepted to cover the following activities:

1. Employment and manpower planning.
2. Education, training and development.
3. Industrial relations.
4. Health and safety and welfare.
5. Remuneration.

None of these can be said to be more important than others, although some are more neglected. It should be noted that, in general, the personnel administrator acts in an advisory capacity. This should not be taken to imply that the personnel function is any less important than any of the other support functions: indeed, there is no doubt that with the considerable growth in legislation and intervention by outside bodies, over the last decades the tasks of the personnel department have become extremely complex. Furthermore, behavioural scientists are daily revealing information concerning the nature of man and this, allied to the complexity of the task, requires that the personnel function can only be satisfactorily carried out by trained executives of a very high calibre.

Accepting that personnel management is an important feature of managerial activity, then, as in all other substantial matters, decisions should be made on the basis of a declared policy, not in an arbitrary manner. The importance of this cannot be over-emphasized: a location where anomalies or distinctions exist will develop internal stresses which can eventually seriously upset behaviour. Unless a policy has been carefully considered, anomalies will be extremely difficult to avoid. Equally, no organization can develop robustly unless the implications of technological and sociological developments and changes have been incorporated into its personnel policy. If the policy has been made public, then the translation of that policy into action is simplified, although it must be realized that the implementing of a personnel policy is made much more difficult if other aspects of management are weak. Goodwill and loyalty can and should be used to overcome difficulties, but they cannot be expected to make up for managerial inefficiencies.

The personnel manager must be actively involved in drawing up and determining this policy. He should be able, by training and inclination, to ensure that the needs of the employees as *people* should carry as much weight as the needs of the employers as an organization. As discussed elsewhere in a quite different context, all needs are utilitarian to their possessors, and the personnel function must not only advise, on matters such as the number of employees, their recruitment, selection, training and remuneration, but must also be in a position to comment upon human reactions to proposed action.

Employment and manpower planning

This aspect of personnel work covers the obtaining and selecting – in conjunction with departmental supervisors – of new staff, their introduction to the organization, and the checking of working conditions to ensure compliance with statutory rules and orders, local bye-laws, trade union agreements and any other appropriate regulations. It is interesting to consider that in many companies where the purchase of a piece of equipment will be the subject of much deliberation at board level, the recruitment of a new employee will be done on the basis of a five-minute interview, yet the cost of bringing the new employee to a fully useful working condition will be many times greater than the cost of the equipment. It is difficult to see why it should be considered that the choice of a new employee – possibly the most complex and unpredictable of organisms – is very much simpler than the choice of a new inert assembly of metal and plastic.

The personnel officer should try to ensure that:

1. The need for a new employee has been established.
2. The job has been adequately defined. Here he can assist by analysing in appropriate detail the *needs* of the job, and setting them down in a comprehensible manner.
3. Appropriate action is taken to locate likely staff. This may involve the use of Job Centres, advertising or direct 'head-hunting', or identifying appropriate internal staff. Properly kept records will show which channels are most effective in any particular circumstances.
4. Appropriate methods of selecting particular candidates are used. The range of tools here is very wide, from simple five-minute interviews to 'stress' interviews, from simple aptitude tests to complex psychological investigations. All of these, even the apparently simple interview, require skill in use, and trained personnel management should be able to advise on the techniques to be used and assist in the actual performance of the selection method.
5. Once an employee is engaged, he/she should be introduced to the work ('inducted') in such a manner that he/she understands clearly what is required, and what he/she can require of the organization.

6. When an employee leaves, the reasons for departure are investigated, not with a view to harassing the individual, but in order to resolve any problems. The costs of hiring are substantial, and if labour turnover can be reduced, real savings can be made.

Education, training and management development

All assets waste if untended, and this is probably more true of the human assets of an organization than any of the assets usually recorded on a balance sheet or financial report. Undoubtedly, there are everywhere human abilities which are untapped, and it is these which in the final analysis determine the success or failure of an enterprise. In a very dramatic way, professional football teams show how human development can be turned to financial benefit: a young player can be 'bought' for a few thousand pounds and, after appropriate training, be 'sold' for millions.

Throughout any work environment there is a continual need to educate and train at all levels. 'Sitting next to Nelly' is an inefficient way of learning, the student acquiring the bad habits along with the good. A positive training programme, based upon an analysis both of the needs of the job and of the individual, should be drawn up and implemented. Such programmes should encompass not only a training in manipulative skills but also in academic *and supervisory* skills, where appropriate. Whilst a leader may be born, by training he/she can be made more useful more rapidly. Moreover, if a potential supervisor can be withdrawn from immediate tasks for a training period, he/she can find time to think about the difficulties *and responsibilities* of the new post. This is as true at the operations manager level as at the lowest supervisor level of the organization. Too often a supervisor finds himself submerged in day-to-day problems without being able to consider more general issues, and if a training period does no more than allow a 'standing back' it will serve a very useful purpose, although it can often serve as a very positive motivating device. It should also be noted that in the UK *training in safety* is required by law: 'employers are to prepare written company safety policies and make them known' (see Chapter 32).

Not only should training be carried on *inside* an organization, but the broader extra mural training available at technical colleges, polytechnics and universities must be encouraged. Many organizations allow time off, with payment of fees and book allowances for such courses, believing that the long-term return will be substantial. External courses do have the added advantage over internal courses of allowing students from different companies and industries to exchange ideas – a most salutary experience when it is found that very few problems are special to any one organization. Considerable assistance, both financial and advisory, may be obtained from various training associations and boards.

The learning curve

It is well established that the time taken for an individual to carry out a task will depend upon, among other factors, the experience of the person, and that speed of performance and number of repetitions are related by a curve of the general shape

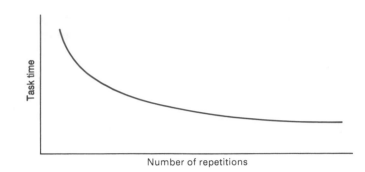

Fig. 31.1   Learning curve

of Fig. 31.1. This curve is the *learning curve* of the person for a particular task, and some observers claim to have detected noticeable learning even for short-cycle tasks after 1,000 or more repetitions. The slope of the curve at any point would seem to depend upon intelligence, motivation and age.

Organizations, which are groups of individuals, seem also to exhibit the same learning characteristics but *in a more predictable form*. The first observations of this phenomenon were by T. P. Wright in the US aircraft industry, and his findings have been repeated by many later workers. The learning curve for an organization is given by Wright's law:

> For any operation which is repeated, the mean time for the operation will decrease by a fixed fraction as the number of repetitions doubles.

Wright found that the reduction fraction was 0.8, so that an operation obeying Wright's law would have the curve of Fig. 31.2, which is plotted on normal Cartesian coordinates, or Fig. 31.3, which is plotted on log–log coordinates.

Later work in fields other than the aircraft industry suggests that the fraction is

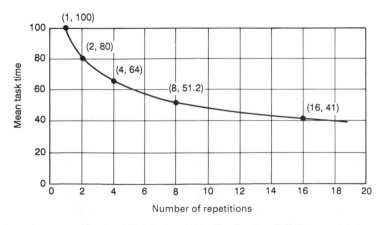

Fig. 31.2   Learning curve obeying Wright's law (reduction fraction 0.8) (linear scales)

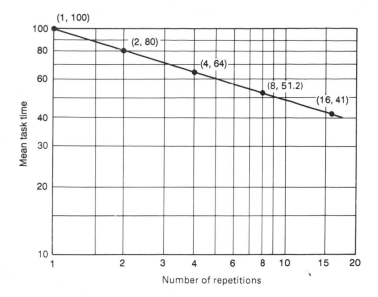

Fig. 31.3   Learning curve obeying Wright's law (reduction fraction 0.8) (logarithmic scales)

not necessarily 0.8 and that its value depends upon the proportion of labour which is man-controlled. The figures in Table 31.1 were given by Herschmann.

Appearance of the learning curve

The process of learning by an organization is no more automatic than the process of learning by an individual and, as with an individual, the most important factor appears to be motivation, which arises from a belief that something can be learnt and that it is desirable that it should be learnt. An organization which believes that it has no need or no room to improve is unlikely to demonstrate any marked learning.

   Apart from this apathy, there are other factors which will depress learning:

1. *Lack of continuity.* If a process is repeated, and then stopped, and then restarted after a time break, the mean time will increase immediately after the time break.
2. *Restrictions to output.* Some circumstances can give rise to deliberate restrictions in output – for example, the operation of some incentive schemes, the existence of some pricing policies, the belief or knowledge that work is coming to an end.

Table 31.1

Percentage of labour which is person-controlled	Reduction fraction
75	80
50	85
25	90

Factors affecting learning in an organization

1. Desire to improve.
2. Ability to improve.
3. Absence of time breaks.
4. Absence of restricting factors.

Industrial relations

The relationships between employer and employee can be difficult and delicate, frequently being dependent upon subtle intangibles and the ethos of the organization. Too often companies seek to simplify this situation by appointing an 'industrial relations officer' and expecting him/her to solve all problems. In truth, this relationship is not one which can be avoided. Good industrial relations stem from good personnel policies, and these *must be known and used by all managers at all levels*.

One author recalls a company where security of employment was extremely poor – as the founder of the company, a dynamic and forceful entrepreneur, would cheerfully and brutally dismiss 'offending' employees at all levels. This behaviour steadily hardened itself into a 'hire and fire' policy, as managers modelled themselves on the founder. The costs of this behaviour were substantial and in an attempt to reduce them, personnel officers were regularly employed – and as regularly were lost, as they tried to operate a personnel policy in conflict with this extant policy. Quality in industrial relations is like quality in the product or service: 'everybody's business'.

This having been said, it must also be recognized that the intervention of the state in matters concerning employment, and the activities of the trade unions, have made it necessary that at least one executive within the organization should specialize in industrial relations. The executive must be capable of representing the management of the company at any meetings which might take place with either trade unions, staff committees, shop stewards' committees or other negotiating bodies. This requires a thorough knowledge of all relevant agreements and local customs, and is not a matter which can be easily undertaken, since in some industries the various agreements are most complex and require great study. The situation in a multi-trades organization, where a number of trade unions are involved, is even more complex. In the UK the Department of Employment can help greatly in quoting the relevant agreements and advising on local customs.

Probably the most important feature of this work is that the personnel manager shall be *seen* to be scrupulously fair. He must present the company's point of view clearly and dispassionately and must not take issue on personal points. Goodwill in industrial negotiations is essential and any suspicion of underhandedness will result in a loss of confidence which will increase immeasurably the difficulties of later negotiations. Clearly, the organization's policy on industrial relations must be part of the overall personnel policy, and as such known to all.

Health and safety and welfare

There are a large number of statutory requirements concerning health and safety which must be observed, and these must be familiar to the personnel department who should bring to the notice of appropriate executives any breaches of these requirements. Good personnel records can be invaluable: poor 'sickness' figures may be an indication of dissatisfaction with work or the workplace.

Safety of the employee is not only a statutory requirement, it is a human obligation. Unfortunately, bad safety habits can spring up very easily and it is necessary to observe very closely all potentially dangerous activities. A climate of safety-consciousness must be built up by constant encouragement and propaganda; in many organizations a special safety officer is appointed whose sole responsibility is the safety of the employees. This function, if carried out thoroughly, can result in a prevention of lost time due to accidents and an avoidance of unnecessary suffering and hardship. Without adequate managerial backing, however, the safety officer will have great difficulty in performing the job and managements must realize that safety pays, if for no other reason than that injuries in the workplace lose more working time than any other cause. This matter is of such importance that it is discussed later in Chapter 32.

Under the general heading of welfare, personnel will usually help in organizing any special sickness benefit schemes, social and recreational facilities, and personal assistance to staff. The attention given to this aspect depends greatly upon the personnel policy, but it can be said that comparatively small expenditures in this field can produce substantial returns in staff loyalty and goodwill. Any personal assistance given, however, should be consistent: help given to one should not be arbitrarily withheld from others.

Remuneration

Decisions on wages and salary structures are the responsibility of the directors of the organization. However, it is in this area that the personnel manager must play a leading part in preparing the facts upon which any decisions are based. Fundamentally, the problems can be considered to be four in number:

1. The setting up of a logical structure appropriate to the organization, the technology and the environment.
2. The placing of employees within the structure.
3. The use of an incentive scheme.
4. The use of 'side' benefits, the provision of a company car, and private health schemes being two common additions to the salary 'package'.

The features of any salary package are very organization-specific. It is generally agreed, however, that in considering remuneration it is the total 'package' which must be identified. It must be emphasized that the personnel department can act only in an *advisory* capacity on these matters, but if it has built up sufficient goodwill it will be better placed than any other department to be of assistance.

Wage and salary structures

Within any one homogeneous department, it is relatively simple to set up an acceptable structure, but when comparisons are made between departments the problem becomes much more difficult. How, for example, should the wages of a senior laboratory assistant compare with those of a shorthand typist? Should a public transport worker draw more pay than a road digger? To try to achieve some parity between the pay of workers in dissimilar occupations within the same organization it is necessary to refer all jobs to a common base, i.e. to place all jobs in a recognized and agreed order of value. Once this has been done, this scale of values can be used as a basis upon which to build a wage structure. Whether, in fact, the scale of values is acceptable to the employer and the employee is a matter for local discussion. At least the setting-up of such a scale can help clarify managerial ideas on the relative worth of various tasks.

Job evaluation, grading or ranking

The setting of tasks in a scale of values is known as job evaluation, grading or ranking. The job evaluation is most commonly used, and consequently will be employed here. There are a large number of methods of job evaluation, and the choice of one or other must depend upon local circumstances. Reference should be made to the study and report entitled *Job Evaluation*, published by the International Labour Office.

In general, as a first step, all the jobs to be evaluated are considered and a list drawn up of the characteristics of the work which are considered to be important. These characteristics may vary between different types of work, but should be the same for similar occupations (that is, for jobs within a 'job-cluster'). It is probably unwise to list too many characteristics or the analysis will become unwieldy. Four main headings, which will cover the majority of occupations are commonly recognized, namely:

Skill.
Effort.
Responsibility.
Working conditions.

These main headings can then be subdivided into minor or derived characteristics according to the job-cluster concerned. For example, clerical work might be considered under the following headings:

Skill:	1. Mental.
	2. Manipulative.
Effort:	1. Mental.
	2. Physical.
Responsibility:	1. Financial.
	2. For subordinates.
	3. Personal.
Working conditions:	1. Surroundings.
	2. Monotony.
	3. Distractions.

Meanwhile in the same organization the analysis for a worker in a 'productive' department might be:

Skill:	1. Experience.
	2. Manipulative.
	3. Versatility.
Effort:	1. Physical.
	2. Aural.
Responsibility:	1. Quality of product.
	2. Safety of equipment.
Working conditions:	1. Surroundings.
	2. Noise.

For each group of jobs these characteristics are drawn up. The total value of the characteristics is then divided between the various constituents: characteristics of little importance are assigned low values, and those of greater importance high values.

Using these scales, a small committee, often of management and staff, will meet representatives of the various departments, explain the scales and the general idea to them, and invite them to assist in defining and grading the various tasks. These gradings must, of course, apply to the jobs, not to the individuals doing them, so that it is a comparison between, say, a copy typist, a telephonist, a clerical officer and a wages clerk, not between Miss A, Mr B, Mrs C and Mr D. The gradings throughout a department must be carried out by the same group of people in order that consistency is preserved, and it is useful to rate each characteristic of all jobs at once, rather than rate all the characteristics of each job at once. It is also desirable to include among the raters representatives of the people doing the various jobs in order that the less obvious features are not overlooked.

From this a series of definitions, along with a classification in order of value of the various jobs in a department, will be produced. This is done for all departments, and the various departmental classifications are integrated, usually by finding tasks of comparable value in each department.

Job evaluation can be useful, not only as a method of setting equitable salary rates but also as a means for identifying and defining jobs, thus simplifying the employment, movement and promotion of staff. As stated above, it is not a method of examining the relative effectiveness of various individuals and placing them within the structure: this is done by a merit rating of the individuals within a department and/or job.

The above refers to job evaluation for 'direct operations'. Schemes are available for setting up managerial job evaluations, for example the Hays/MSL scheme, which in the last few years has been extended to cover other workers and staff.

Merit rating

As with job evaluation, a careful study of the job is required, laying down the qualities required of the individuals expected to carry out the job concerned. These should cover only those characteristics which are likely to be of importance to carrying out the job; thus, in a work study engineer or a social worker, 'tact' is a very necessary quality, but in a research physicist or a refuse collector, it may be of little significance.

Ranking (or rating) is best carried out by at least two people with whom the group come into close contact. These rate all individuals separately and independently and then come together with a third person – for example, a personnel manager – to discuss the ratings and hence produce a consolidated rating. The method of rating is controversial: numerical systems (for example 1–10) are appealing, but it is the authors' experience that raters are loath to use either end of the scale, so that in fact a 1–10 scale becomes a 3–8 scale. A better way probably is by definition, e.g. outstanding, excellent, very good, good, very fair, fair, poor, bad, very bad. The rater then ticks the appropriate description, and at the joint discussion the descriptions are translated into numerical terms. In order to achieve consistency, one quality should be rated at a time for all staff being considered by any rater.

Merit ratings should be carried out at least half-yearly, and the results made known to the persons concerned. This will have the effect of informing all staff of their progress, and letting them know where they are failing and where they are most successful. The assessment will prevent any distortion occurring due to the exceptional happening: for example, if rating was carried out once only, and that just before pay increments were decided, a particularly serious mistake might colour the whole rating, giving an unreasonably poor result.

Payment by results (PBR)

One of the most common methods of attempting to increase effectiveness is by the setting-up of a payment by results (PBR) financial incentive, or bonus, scheme whereby the earnings of a person or group depend upon the results achieved. There is an increasing body of thought which holds that such schemes are not in themselves desirable and that any benefits which may appear to be derived arise, in fact, from the improvements in managerial methods necessary to run a PBR scheme. However, this matter is not in any way resolved and PBR schemes are found very commonly through industry, both in service and manufacturing.

Non-financial incentives

Within every organization there must be present a number of non-financial incentives, for example loyalty to the organization or to the supervisor, pride in the product or service, desire for praise or recognition, or a personal pride in the ability of a team to carry out a task better than any other group. Such 'emotional' incentives can act very forcibly, and a good leader or manager will always make the maximum possible use of them. Without such appeals, any organization will lose 'life', the atmosphere will become oppressive, and work will become nothing but drudgery.

Some organizations, however, offer tangible benefits as rewards for increases in effectiveness. Among these are:

(a) additional holidays;
(b) greater security;
(c) improved status;
(d) special working conditions.

The use of such incentives requires particular care on the part of the management to avoid any appearance of partiality, and it may be difficult to operate a comprehensive non-financial incentive scheme. The results are probably more long-term than the results of financial bonus schemes, and for this reason both types of scheme are often run side by side.

Financial incentives

It is the financial incentive that is most commonly thought of when PBR schemes are discussed. In these the earnings are related to effort, and such schemes are common at all levels. A chief executive's earnings can include a portion dependent upon the turnover or profitability of the company, a salesman can earn commission – a bonus on the orders he takes – and an operator can be paid on piece-work.

Installation of a PBR scheme

The installation of a PBR scheme must be the culmination of a great deal of preliminary work, all of which should be normal in a well-run organization. No scheme must be regarded as a substitute for good management, nor must it be considered the basis upon which good management is built. An insecurely founded scheme which is later withdrawn will create such persistent ill-will that subsequent well-conceived plans will have little chance of success.

The following must be investigated and put into operation before any incentive scheme is installed.

1. *Measurement*. Consistency in reward is essential. To achieve this, all rewards should be based upon some objective measure of the content of the job. Any work measurement programme will provide both the measurements and/or definition of the task measured. As a result, any subsequent discussions on rewards can refer back to the original conditions which applied at the time of setting the reward and so enable worthwhile comparisons to be made. In some organizations it may be necessary to obtain trade union agreement to carry out a work measurement programme, and this agreement may include a statement of the measurement technique which will be used.
2. *Effective operations management*. Under a PBR scheme, the idle time due to absence of material, of people, of capacity, of tools, or of techniques will result not only in frustration by the management but in loss of earnings by the people, which can lead to considerable ill-will and a high staff turnover.
3. *Effective quality management*. A reward is normally only paid for satisfactory work, and it is necessary that an acceptable quality system is in being.
4. *Sound salary structure*. To try to use a PBR scheme as a means of 'correcting' an unjust payment structure is to court disaster. Not only will the basic inequity remain, the obvious bias in the PBR scheme will create considerable distress.
5. *Training of administrative staff*. Whatever type of scheme is used, it will inevitably increase the burden upon the administrative staff, and in particular upon the salary or wages department. A very thorough training in the scheme must be given to the staff, who will need to be able to:

(a) carry out all the calculations; and

(b) appreciate all the details of permissible allowances.

Should this not be done, and should the scheme run into administrative difficulties at its inception, it may be discredited and fail.

6. *Consultation with employees*. Before any PBR scheme is installed, it is essential that those most directly concerned – those who are going to be paid under the scheme – should be consulted and any proposed scheme thoroughly explained, discussed and, if necessary, modified. This is not merely common courtesy; it prevents any misunderstandings and ill-feeling later on.

Points to be considered before installing a PBR scheme

1. Measurement.
2. Effective operations management.
3. Quality management.
4. Salary structure.
5. Administration.
6. Employee consultation.

CHAPTER 31 – HIGHLIGHTS

- Personnel management is concerned with employment and manpower planning, education, training and management development, industrial relations, health, safety and welfare, and remuneration.

- There should be a declared personnel policy, and the personnel manager should be actively involved in the determination.

- Personnel work includes obtaining and selecting new staff, introducing them, and checking their conditions of employment and work.

- There is a continual need to educate and train at all levels, using a positive training programme based on analyses of needs.

- The learning curve describes the speed with which a person or an organization learns to carry out a task or series of tasks. An important factor in this is motivation.

- There is a need for the organization to have some expertise in industrial relations. Fairness must be seen to be operating and goodwill is essential.

- The personnel department must be familiar with the large number of statutory requirements concerning health, safety and welfare. In addition, attention must be paid to other aspects of personnel, all derived from a consistent policy.

- Personnel management can play an important part in decision making on wages and salary structures. There must be a logical structure and the employees must be placed in it. The use of incentive schemes and side benefits must also be considered.

- Wage and salary comparisons between jobs and departments must be made from a common base. Job evaluation sets tasks in a scale of values and may be useful as a method of setting equitable salary rates and for identifying and defining jobs.
- A common method of attempting to increase effectiveness is by setting up a PBR financial incentive.
- Non-financial incentives given include extra holidays, security, status, and special working conditions.
- Before any incentive schemes are introduced, there must be good measurement, effective operations and quality management, a good salary structure and administration, and consultation with the employees.

Recommended reading

Friedman, B., *Effective Staff Incentives*, Kogan Page, 1990

A highly accessible and comprehensive manual that will provide every manager with an excellent understanding of this increasingly important subject.

Molander, C. (ed.), *Human Resource Management: a Practical Introduction*, Chartwell-Bratt, 1989

Several personnel management specialists at Bradford came together to produce this readable, valuable book.

Lorrington, D. and Hall, L., *Personnel Management*, Prentice-Hall, London, 1991

Written by two people with dissimilar backgrounds, one in industrial training, the other in organizational behaviour. Presents an overview of personnel management in the British situation.

Woods, M., *The New Manager*, and *The Aware Manager*, Element Books, 1988 & 1989 respectively

Guides to improving the skills of people management for newly appointed or for experienced managers.

Chapter 32

Health and Safety Management

Accidents

Every year fatalities occur and many injuries are still suffered by men and women as a direct result of accidents at work. Others suffer impairment brought about by health hazards with which they work. Clearly, there are humanitarian, legal and economic grounds for providing a safe place and system of work. To honour these obligations, it is necessary to implement an active programme of accident prevention. The preparation of a properly thought-out health and safety policy, together with continuous monitoring, can do much to reduce, if not eliminate, injuries and damage to health.

In order to formulate such policies and programmes it is necessary to define the word *accident*. Let us consider a case of four men tripping over the same obstacle. The first man trips and recovers his balance, the second falls and dirties his trousers, the third cuts his knee, the fourth fractures his skull on an adjacent table. Although the results differ widely and only two of the four men are hurt, these are identical accidents. It is the accident itself – the tripping – not the consequence of the accident which determines the need for investigation and corrective action.

A working definition of an accident then is:

> An *accident* is any unplanned, uncontrolled, unwanted, or undesirable event, or sudden mishap which interrupts an activity or function.

From this definition it should be clear that injury to people or damage to property is not an accident, but evidence to show that an accident has occurred. When considering some of the very large disasters resulting from industrial accidents, particularly those in the world's oil and chemical industries, it is difficult to avoid the emotion which demands retribution and corrective action. However, it must be recognized that similar *accidents* are happening all over the world every day, fortuitously without the same consequences. The call for investigative and preventative programmes in these cases is often less audible, but the need for their avoidance is just as important.

Everyone, from the senior executive to the youngest and newest entrants in the organization, has a part to play in creating and maintaining healthy and safe working conditions which have the principal objective of avoiding accidents, the consequences of which are pure chance. To achieve this, an effective safety policy must ensure that, just as with quality, 'everyone's concern' does not become 'nobody's business'.

The causes and effects of accidents

The effects of the most publicized industrial accidents are clear for all to see, but they may be classified for any accident under the headings:

I	*njury* – including disability, pain and suffering, etc.
D	*amage* – to equipment, buildings, markets, etc.
L	*oss* – of life, of earnings, of output, of 'image', of time, of profit.
E	*motion* – following injury, pain, death, etc.

The mnemonic constructed from the first letters of these headings may be used to emphasize that the inevitable discussion of the *effects* of accidents may be IDLE gossip in the business of accident *prevention*.

There are many statistics produced concerning the number of people who experience time off work, the number of deaths, or the value of lost production due to accidents at work. It is not proposed to repeat those here, but an interesting concept is Heinrich's pyramid of potential for accidents, which is derived from data on 'serious' and 'minor' injuries reported:

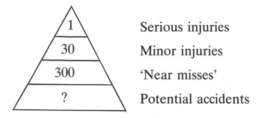

1	Serious injuries
30	Minor injuries
300	'Near misses'
?	Potential accidents

The potential for accidents which extrapolates from the known effects must be a concern for the POM function, and lead to an effective accident prevention programme being an essential part of its responsibilities.

The causes of accidents

Accidents don't just happen, they're caused is an often-used cliche which must be taken seriously if accidents are to be prevented. The use of excuses such as 'it was just a unique combination of circumstances', 'a risk we had to take', 'the result of human error', 'an unavoidable danger' as definitions of causes of accidents actually hinders their avoidance. What is required is a clear definition of an accident cause:

An *accident cause* is an uncontrolled hazard, without which there could be no accident.

It is possible to classify accident causes under the headings:

P	*lant*, e.g. a faulty stairway, electrical hazards.
E	*quipment*, e.g. a defective guard, incorrect equipment.
E	*nvironment*, e.g. high noise, insufficient light.
P	*eople*, e.g. careless, untrained, over-stressed.
S	*ystems* of work, e.g. poor procedures, bad housekeeping.

The mnemonic derived from the first letters of these headings may help to concentrate effort into finding the accident causes, which requires careful PEEPS at the workplace, training, systems of work, etc. The idea that a human being may present an 'uncontrolled hazard' may be foreign to some, but the responsibilities of the production or operations manager for training, supervision and motivation in safety consciousness cannot be abdicated.

Responsibilities and organization for safety

The establishment of positive safety policy objectives within an organization must be accompanied by the clear allocation of responsibilities within the management structure. It is generally accepted that the primary operational responsibility for ensuring safe working must rest with line management, and in particular there are two key areas which require attention:

1. *Senior executive level*. Direct responsibility for the general management of safety and health matters should be included in the duties of one of the senior executives in the same way that a director may be allocated overall responsibility for production, quality or marketing. In other words, safety and health should be treated like any other major managerial function, with a clear line of responsibility and command running up to an accountable individual at the top of the organization.
2. *First line supervision level*. The supervisor is 'on the spot' and in a position to know whether or not safety arrangements are working in practice; and his/her influence can be dramatic. The promotion of health and safety at work is first and foremost a matter of efficient management.

As with other areas such as quality and productivity, real progress in safety is impossible without the full co-operation and commitment of all employees. If they are to accept their full share of responsibility, however, they must be able to participate fully in the making and monitoring of arrangements for safety and health at their place of work. The appointment of safety representatives and committees is one way of increasing involvement and commitment. Some organizations have arrangements whereby all employees in a particular unit meet periodically for discussions about safety. This 'total involvement' approach stresses the need for the participation of every individual employee.

The safety adviser

Many organizations have realized the importance of the contribution which a qualified health and safety adviser can make to accident prevention. Smaller organizations may well feel that the cost of employing a full-time safety adviser is not justified, other than in certain very high-risk areas. In these cases, a member of the management team should be appointed to operate on a part-time basis, performing the safety advisory function in addition to his/her other duties. To obtain the best results from a safety adviser, he/she should be given sufficient authority to take necessary action to secure the implementation of the organization's safety policy, and must have the personality to be able to communicate the message to his/her colleagues or employees. Occasionally the safety adviser may require some guidance and help on specific technical safety matters.

The *role of the safety adviser* is to give advice to management on the:

(a)   establishment and review of *safety regulations* to meet the organization's requirements;
(b)   relevant *statutory/legislative requirements*;
(c)   *safety programmes* necessary;
(d)   existence of the correct *safety elements* in all job instructions;
(e)   *safety content* necessary in all training;
(f)   regular *inspection* of safety and housekeeping standards in all work areas.

Planning for safety

Systematic planning is a basic requirement for health and safety in all workplaces. For a safety plan to be effective, it must be part of a continuous review process which has as its objective zero accidents, through a strategy of never-ending improvement. The overall plan should include the basic elements set out in Fig. 32.1.

Some of the main points in the planning of safety are:

1.   *Plant*: the design, layout and inspection of plant and equipment, including heating, lighting, storage, disposal of waste.
2.   *Processes*: the design and monitoring of processes to reduce to a minimum the possibility of malfunction. Processes with high fire, toxic or explosion risks should be separated from less hazardous ones.
3.   *Workplace*: the establishment and maintenance of clean and orderly places of work, with clearly defined access ways and fire exits.
4.   *Facilities*: the provision and maintenance of adequate first-aid and medical facilities, and clean and hygienic wash and eating areas.
5.   *Procedures*: the preparation and practice of major emergency and first-aid procedures in the event of a serious hazard situation. These should be in the form of general plans and guides, rather than tremendous detail, but they should include specific managers' duties. Establishment of close liaison with the emergency services is essential here.
6.   *Training*: the provision of effective training for fire-fighting, rescue and first-aid crews.

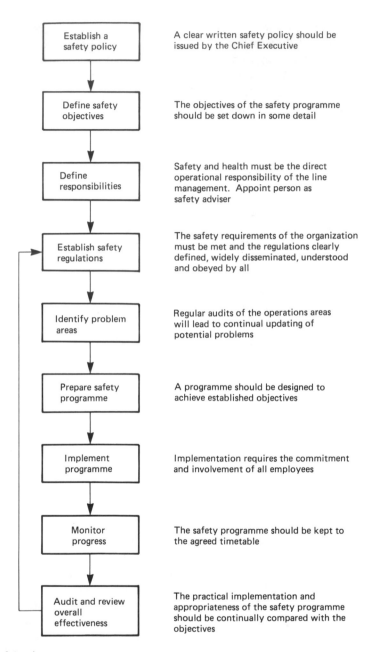

Establish a safety policy	A clear written safety policy should be issued by the Chief Executive
Define safety objectives	The objectives of the safety programme should be set down in some detail
Define responsibilities	Safety and health must be the direct operational responsibility of the line management. Appoint person as safety adviser
Establish safety regulations	The safety requirements of the organization must be met and the regulations clearly defined, widely disseminated, understood and obeyed by all
Identify problem areas	Regular audits of the operations areas will lead to continual updating of potential problems
Prepare safety programme	A programme should be designed to achieve established objectives
Implement programme	Implementation requires the commitment and involvement of all employees
Monitor progress	The safety programme should be kept to the agreed timetable
Audit and review overall effectiveness	The practical implementation and appropriateness of the safety programme should be continually compared with the objectives

Fig. 32.1   A safety plan

7. *Protection*: the provision of such protective clothing and equipment as may be necessary in the light of the processes operated. It is worth remembering, however, that priority should be given to prevention over protection

A safety management system

Accident prevention is the process of removing or controlling accident causes. There are three major elements in the accident prevention process:

1. Workplace inspection.
2. Accident or incident investigation and follow-up.
3. Safety training.

The first two have the same objectives: to find, record and report *possible* accident causes, and to recommend future corrective action.

Workplace inspections

There are basically six methods in general use:

1. *Safety audits and reviews* which subject each area of an organization's activity to a systematic critical examination. Every component of the total system is included, e.g. safety policy, attitudes, training, process, design features, plant construction and layout, operating procedures, emergency plans. Audits and reviews, as in the field of accountancy, aim to disclose the strengths and weaknesses and the main areas of vulnerability or risk.
2. *Safety survey* which is a detailed, in-depth examination of a narrower field of activity, e.g. major key areas revealed by safety audits, individual plants, procedures or specific problems common to an organization as a whole.
3. *Safety inspection* which takes the form of a routine scheduled inspection of a unit or department. The inspection should check maintenance standards, employee involvement, working practices, and that work is carried out in accordance with the procedures, etc.
4. *Safety tour* which is an unscheduled examination of a work area to ensure that, for example, the standards of housekeeping are acceptable, obvious hazards are removed, and that in general safety standards are observed.
5. *Safety sampling* which measures by random sampling, similar to activity sampling, the accident potential by counting safety defects. Trained observers perform short tours of specific locations by prescribed routes and record the number of defects seen. The results may be used to portray trends in the safety situation.
6. *Hazard and operability studies (HAZOP)* which are the application of a formal, critical examination to the process and technological intentions of new or existing facilities, or to assess the hazard potential of maloperation or malfunction of equipment and the consequential effects on the facility as a whole. There are similarities between HAZOP and FMECA studies (see Chapter 9).

The design of a workplace inspection system, combining all these elements, is represented in Fig. 32.2.

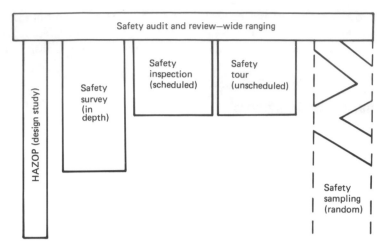

Fig. 32.2   A workplace inspection system

Accident or incident investigations and follow-up

The investigation of accidents and near-accidents can provide valuable accident prevention information. The method is based on:

Collecting data and information relating to the accident or incident.
Checking the validity of the evidence.
Selecting evidence relevant to the investigation aims.
Analysing the evidence without making assumptions or jumping to conclusions.

The results of the analysis are then used to:

Decide the most likely cause(s) of the accident or incident.
Notify immediately the person(s) able to take corrective action.
Record the findings and outcomes.
Report them to everyone concerned, to prevent a recurrence.

The investigation should not become an inquisition to apportion blame, but focus on the positive preventative aspects (Table 32.1).

Table 32.1 Types of follow-up to accidents and their effects

System type	Overall aim	General effects
Investigation	To prevent a similar accident	*Positive*: identification notification correction
Inquisition	To identify responsibility	*Negative*: blame claims defence

It is hoped that accidents are not normally investigated so frequently that the required skills are developed by experience, nor are these skills easily learned in a classroom. One suggested way to overcome this problem is the development of a programmed sequence of questions which form the skeleton of an accident investigation questionnaire. This can be set out using the PEEPS method to include:

Plant Equipment: Description, condition, guards, hazards, controls, access, etc.
Environment: Climatic, fumes, vapour, space, humidity, noise, etc.
People: Duties, information, supervision, instruction, training, protection, etc.
Systems: Procedures, instructions, monitoring, hazard warning, permits to enter, etc.

Safety training

It is generally believed that training is an important factor in improving safety performance. For training to be effective, however, it must be planned in a systematic and objective manner. Safety training must be continuous to meet not only changes in

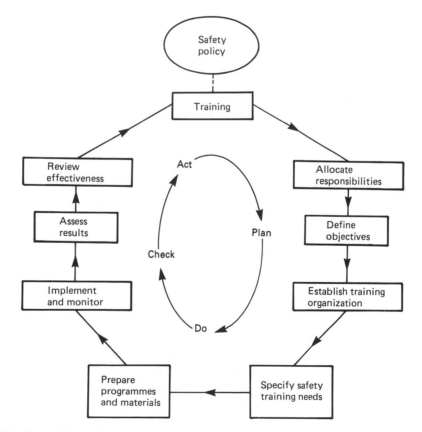

Fig. 32.3   The safety training cycle

technology, but also changes in the environment in which an organization operates, the structure of the organization and, perhaps most of all, the people involved.

Safety training activities can be considered in the form of a plan–do–check–act continuous improvement cycle (see Fig. 32.3), the elements of which are:

Ensure training is part of safety policy.
Allocate responsibilities for safety training.
Define training objectives.
Establish training organization.
Specify safety training needs.
Prepare training programmes and materials.
Implement and monitor training.
Assess the results.
Review the overall effectiveness.

The review process is essential for, even if the overall safety policy remains constant, there is a need to ensure that new safety training objectives are set, either to promote work changes or to raise the standards already achieved. The training organization should be similarly reviewed in the interests of continuous improvement.

Fire

Fires, like accidents, are rarely experienced by most individuals, but if a fire does occur it is likely to affect directly large numbers of people. The main causes of fire are electrical equipment, smoking, gas equipment, gas cutting and welding, oil and petrol equipment, rubbish burning, blowlamps and spontaneous combustion.

Organizing to prevent fire is, of course, the responsibility of management, and the following guidelines are useful:

1. Set up a fire prevention policy *and regularly review it*.
2. Establish clear lines of responsibilities for fire prevention.
3. Appoint a fire officer responsible to the top management.
4. Estimate the possible effects of a fire in losing buildings, plant, work-in-progress, workers, customers, plans and records.
5. Identify the fire risks, considering sources of ignition, combustible material and means whereby fire could spread.
6. Estimate the magnitudes of the risks to establish priorities.
7. Set up a fire protection drill for each site, department, or area.

As with general safety, there is a wealth of information available at little or no cost to assist in reducing the risk of fire. Each fire authority in the UK has a fire prevention officer who will be delighted to advise on any matter concerning fire hazards; the Fire Prevention Association (FPA) and HMSO publish many books and pamphlets dealing with all aspects of fire prevention and control.

Health and safety at work legislation

Health and safety legislation pervades most industrialized countries. The example of UK legislation will be used in this text, but similar approaches may be found in other countries. The aim of the Health and Safety at Work etc. Act 1974 is to provide the legislative framework to promote, stimulate and encourage safety awareness, effective safety organization and performance, and high standards of health and safety at work. It does this by various schemes designed to suit the particular industry or organization and by the accumulation of influences and pressures, operating at many different levels, in a variety of ways and from a number of directions. The Act's provisions do not supersede any of that large body of legislation generally referred to as the Factories Acts, but it produces a framework within which these and other Acts operate. Any summary of such a complex document must be inadequate, and the Act itself should be consulted where a detailed understanding is required.

Throughout the Act the phrase 'so far as is reasonably practicable' is used frequently to condition statements and provisions. The purpose of this is to recognize that technology is advancing and that which is 'reasonably practicable' in 1995 may be trivial in the year 2000. Thus, an organization's attitude to health and safety at work must be continually changing to take cognizance of changing capabilities.

The philosophy of the Act is embodied in three clauses:

1. It is the duty of every employer to ensure the health and safety at work of all employees.
2. It is the duty of every employer and every self-employed person to conduct his undertaking in such a way as to ensure that persons not in his employment . . . are not exposed to risks to their health and safety.
3. It is the duty of every employee while at work to take reasonable care for the health and safety of himself (herself) and of other persons . . . and to co-operate with his (her) employer on matters concerning safety.

To give substance to these matters, an employer is required specifically:

1. To prepare and distribute to all employees a written statement of general policy with respect to the health and safety at work of all employees, and of the means whereby this policy is to be carried out (where five or more people are employed). An example of an acceptable policy is given in Fig. 32.4.
2. Provide and maintain plant, systems, methods and places of work that are safe and without risks to health
3. Make arrangements for ensuring safety and absence of risks to health in connection with the use, handling, storage and transport of articles and substances.
4. Provide information, instruction, supervision and training to ensure health and safety at work of all employees.
5. Provide and maintain means of access and egress which are safe and without risks.
6. Consult with employees' representatives and committees on matters concerning health and safety. Regulations and codes of practice now exist concerning the appointment of safety representatives.
7. Establish safety committees if requested by safety representatives.
8. Ensure that information is given on safe use, instructions and hazards to all non-employees who may use plant and substances.

The Act concludes with a list of *criminal* offences which arise from failure to discharge any of the duties arising from it, or from contravention of sections of the Act or the requirements of an Inspector arising from the Act. The penalties include both fines and terms in prison and are clearly designed to make all at work take the Act very seriously indeed.

Company safety policy

The company's policy is to give the greatest importance to the safety of its employees. It is considered that this is a senior management responsibility which ranks with marketing, sales, design, production and accounting.

In the design, purchase, construction, operation and maintenance of all plant, equipment and facilities, it is the duty of management to do everything possible to prevent personal injuries.

It is also the duty of every employee to exercise personal responsibility and to do everything possible to prevent injury to themselves and others.

Fig. 32.4   A typical company safety policy

CHAPTER 32 – HIGHLIGHTS

- An accident is any unplanned, uncontrolled, unwanted or undesirable event, or sudden mishap, which interrupts an activity or function. Injury to people or damage to property is not an accident, but evidence to show that one has occurred.

- Everyone, from top to bottom of the organization, has responsibilities to avoid accidents. A safety policy is necessary to achieve this.

- The effects of accidents are generally injury, damage, loss, emotion – IDLE gossip in accident prevention. Potential accidents, extrapolated from known effects, can be many times greater in number than visible injuries and effects.

- An accident cause is an uncontrolled hazard, without which there could be no accident. Causes may be classified under the headings: plant; equipment; environment; people, and systems – PEEPS into the workplace are required to prevent or remove them.

- The primary responsibility for ensuring safe working must rest with line management and, in particular, the senior executives who are directly responsible for the general management of safety and health. This should be included in the specific duties of one of the executives.

- The supervisors at the first line level are in the best position to assess safety performance and their impact is dramatic. The full commitment, cooperation, and participation of all employees is essential. Safety advisers, representatives and committee appointments may be useful here.

- Safety and health must be systematically planned through a policy, objectives, definition of responsibilities, regulations, programmes and audit and review processes. These must take into account: plant; processes; the workplace; facilities; procedures; training; and any protection required.

- A system for managing safety should include the elements of workplace inspections, accident or incident investigations and follow-up, and safety training.

- Inspections include audits and reviews, surveys, tours, sampling, hazard and operability studies (IIAZOP).

- Investigations require the collection of data and the checking, selection and analysis of evidence – the results being used to decide causes, notify persons, record and report findings.

- Safety training must be systematic and follow the plan–do–check–act sequence of continuous improvement.

- Fire prevention is the responsibility of management, who must appoint a fire officer, estimate possible fire loss, identify and measure risks, and set up fire protection drills.

- Health and safety legislation sets duties upon employers and employees to conduct organizations and themselves in a safe manner. Specific requirements include the need for a published and written safety policy.

Recommended reading

A large number of useful Government publications are obtainable from the Health and Safety Executive (HSE). These set out facts and figures, and give guidance on how specific health and safety issues may be tackled.

Chandler, P., *An A–Z of Employment and Safety Law*, Kogan Page, 1981

An encyclopaedic text which contains much detailed information. The emphasis is on the practical application of the law, and the book summarizes the duties and obligations of employers and employees.

Dalton, A.J.P., *Health and Safety at Work for Industrial Managers and Supervisors*, Cassell, 1982

Possibly the most useful short text on the subject currently available. Well written with exercises in most chapters and suggested answers at the end of the book. Very usefully referenced. Thoroughly recommended.

Grimaldi, J. and Simons, H., *Safety Management*, 4th edn, Irwin, 1984

A handbook and a mine of useful information.

Pantry, S. (ed.), *Health and Safety: A Guide to Sources of Information*. Capital Planning Info, 1985

Useful for the health and safety officer.

Ritson, J., *Health and Safety at Work Act*, Ravenswood Publications, 1983

A down-to-earth practical guide to the health and safety legislation in the UK.

APPENDICES

1. A Worked Example of A–B–C or Pareto Analysis
2. Activity Sampling – Number of Observations Required
3. Representative Examination Questions
4. Short Cases in Production and Operations Management

Appendix 1

A Worked Example of A–B–C or Pareto Analysis

A–B–C or Pareto analysis is a systematic and structured approach to distinguishing between the 'vital' few and the 'trivial' many. The approach is best illustrated with an example.

Consider the problem faced by the administration manager at the head office of an insurance company. He is concerned about the large amount of documentation containing errors which has to be reprocessed. He classifies the types of errors into 25 categories (coded A–Z), e.g. post code omitted. Data are collected over

Table A1.1 Error types, frequencies and unit reprocessing costs

Error type	Frequency	Unit cost
A	398	13
B	256	53
C	673	2
D	45	67
E	364	498
F	297	12
G	10456	2
H	19	112
I	35	25
J	5361	2
K	498	6
L	1286	10
M	23	8
N	50	3
P	702	49
Q	97	3
R	1956	4
S	27	12
T	42	6
U	7684	3
V	196	2
W	78	4
X	501	70
Y	32	3
Z	3523	1

a representative period of time; these cover the number of errors of each type (frequency), together with estimates of the unit reprocessing cost, and are given in Table A1.1

Two analyses are possible: one based on frequency, and one based on total cost. That based on total cost will be illustrated. First it is necessary to calculate the total reprocessing cost for each type of error. Thus for type 'A' the total cost is 398 × £13 = £5174. The next step is to rank the types by decreasing total cost. This is shown as the first three columns of Table A1.2.

The grand total cost is £364,292, and it is possible to cumulate the total costs and to calculate the cumulative percentage of the total represented by each type of error in the ranked list. This is shown in the fourth and fifth columns in Table A1.2. The five types (E, X, P, U, G) contribute in total £294,704 to the grand total cost of £364,292 and this represents 80.90 per cent of the grand total. These five types represent 20 per cent of the total of 25 types. Figure A1.1 shows these results graphically, with the cumulative percentage of the range (each type represents 4 per cent) plotted against the cumulative percentage of total cost. For clarity the types are plotted in blocks of five. This indicates that five types of error (20 per cent) account for just over 80 per cent of the total reprocessing cost. These are the vital few on which attention should focus in order to reduce this cost significantly. This is not to say that the remaining 80 per cent should be ignored, but that resource should be used sparingly on these.

Table A1.2 Pareto analysis by total cost

Rank	Error type	Total cost	Cumulative total cost	Cumulative percentage	Percentage of range
1	E	181272	181272	49.76	4
2	X	35070	216342	59.39	8
3	P	34398	250740	68.83	12
4	U	23052	273792	75.16	16
5	G	20912	294704	80.90	20
6	B	13568	308272	84.62	24
7	L	12860	321132	88.15	28
8	J	10722	331854	91.10	32
9	R	7824	339678	93.24	36
10	A	5174	344852	94.66	40
11	F	3564	348416	95.64	44
12	Z	3523	351939	96.61	48
13	D	3015	354954	97.44	52
14	K	2988	357942	98.26	56
15	H	2128	360070	98.84	60
16	C	1346	361416	99.21	64
17	I	875	362291	99.45	68
18	V	392	362683	99.56	72
19	S	324	363007	99.65	76
20	W	312	363319	99.73	80
21	Q	291	363610	99.81	84
22	T	252	363862	99.88	88
23	M	184	364046	99.93	92
24	N	150	364196	99.97	96
25	Y	96	364292	100.00	100

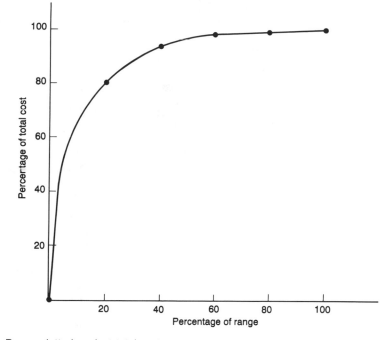

Fig. A1.1   Range plotted against total cost

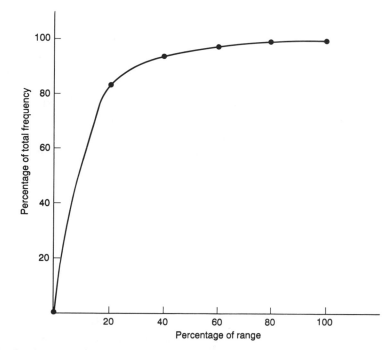

Fig. A1.2   Range plotted against total frequency

Table A1.3 Pareto analysis by frequency

Rank	Error type	Frequency	Cumulative frequency	Cumulative percentage	Percentage of range
1	G	10456	10456	30.22	4
2	U	7684	18140	52.43	8
3	J	5361	23501	67.92	12
4	Z	3523	27024	78.11	16
5	R	1956	28980	83.76	20
6	L	1286	30266	87.48	24
7	P	702	30968	89.51	28
8	C	673	31641	91.45	32
9	X	501	32142	92.90	36
10	K	498	32640	94.34	40
11	A	398	33038	95.49	44
12	E	364	33402	96.54	48
13	F	297	33699	97.40	52
14	B	256	33955	98.14	56
15	V	196	34151	98.71	60
16	Q	97	34248	98.99	64
17	W	78	34326	99.21	68
18	N	50	34376	99.36	72
19	D	45	34421	99.49	76
20	T	42	34463	99.61	80
21	I	35	34498	99.71	84
22	Y	32	34530	99.80	88
23	S	27	34557	99.88	92
24	M	23	34580	99.95	96
25	H	19	34599	100.00	100

It could be argued that frequency is also an important consideration; it represents the organization problems in handling the volume of reprocessing and the impression gained by the workforce of the 'quality' of the processing. Table A1.3 shows the basic calculations for frequency analysis.

The corresponding Pareto curve can be drawn (Fig. A1.2). The figures give a far more dramatic impression of the situation than the analysis tables, and are, therefore, a preferred representation for report purposes.

The 80/20 relationship illustrated is frequently found in practice, with 80 per cent of an effect being caused by 20 per cent of the types of causes. For this reason it is frequently referred to as the 80/20 law, although it is an empirical result.

Applications of A–B–C analysis

Operations control

In an organization undertaking a large number of tasks, an A–B–C analysis will often reveal that detailed control of a few orders will control the bulk of the organization's workload.

Material control

Analysis of annual usage commonly shows a concentration of value in a comparatively small number of items, so that if there are 10,000 items in stock at any one time, control of 20 per cent of these will in effect control 80 per cent of annual spending. This leads to a stock classification system whereby the first 'slice' is closely controlled, the next 'slice' (say from 20 per cent to 50 per cent of the ranked items) is controlled with less precision, and the remaining slice (from 50 per cent to 100 per cent of the ranked items) is controlled very loosely. These three 'slices' are often known as A items, B items and C items, and it is in the field of material control that the term *A–B–C analysis* was first used.

Variety reduction

This has been covered in Chapter 7. The Pareto analysis can be carried out by income and also by contribution. However, having carried out the A–B–C analysis, it is tempting to draw too many conclusions from it. For example, this could lead to the suggestion that all items after the first 50 per cent, ranked by contribution, be discontinued. This need not necessarily be justified, as some of the products may not have acquired any maturity in the market. Similarly, a high-income item may produce a very low contribution, and there may be a good case for discontinuing this item. The A–B–C analysis will help to put problems into perspective; it is a tool to *assist* decision making, not a 'go–no–go' gauge in itself.

Quality control

Assigning defectives to causes frequently demonstrates that the bulk of them originate from very few causes.

Maintenance

Calculation of time lost due to breakdown against assignable causes often assists in planning a maintenance programme.

Appendix 2

Activity Sampling – Number of Observations Required

N random observations of the proportionate occurrence of a statistic form a sample, size N, of mean proportionate occurrence π drawn from a population with a true proportionate occurrence P and a standard error:

$$SE = \sqrt{\frac{P(1 - P)}{N}}$$

In repeated sampling:

  67 per cent of the values of π lie between $P \pm 1$ SE.
  95 per cent of the values of π lie between $P \pm 2$ SE.
99.7 per cent of the values of π lie between $P \pm 3$ SE.

The inaccuracy resulting from taking π as an estimate of P may be expressed as L and for the 95 per cent (confidence) limits:

$$L \leq 2\,SE$$

That is:

$$L \leq 2\sqrt{\frac{P(1 - P)}{N}}$$

Thus, the number of observations N necessary to achieve an accuracy L at the 95 per cent confidence level is:

$$N \leq \frac{4P(1 - P)}{L^2} \qquad \text{where } P \text{ and } L \text{ are expressed as proportions}$$

or:

$$N \leq \frac{4P(100 - P)}{L^2} \qquad \text{where } P \text{ and } L \text{ are expressed as percentages}$$

If $P = 20$ per cent and $L = 3$ per cent (that is, the value of P lies between 17 and 23 per cent), then:

$$N = \frac{4 \times 20 \,(100 - 20)}{3 \times 3} = 711$$

Some typical values for this calculation are shown in Table A2.1.

Table A2.1

| | | \multicolumn{9}{c}{Percentage occurrence P} | | | | | | | | |
		10	15	20	25	30	35	40	45	50
L = Acceptable percentage accuracy.	1	3600	5100	6400	7500	8400	9100	9600	9900	10 000
	2	900	1275	1600	1875	2100	2275	2400	2475	2500
	3	400	567	711	833	933	1011	1066	1100	1111
	4	225	319	400	469	525	569	600	618	625
	5	144	204	256	300	336	364	384	396	400
	6	100	142	178	208	233	252	267	275	278
	7	73	104	130	153	171	186	196	202	204
	8	56	80	100	117	131	142	150	155	156
	9	44	63	79	93	104	112	119	122	123
	10	36	51	64	75	84	91	96	99	100

This calculation expresses the accuracy in absolute terms. It may be more convenient to express the accuracy in relative terms, as a proportion l of the proportion occurrence P.

This means $L = lP$ where l is the relative accuracy, so:

$$L = lp = 2\sqrt{\frac{P(1 - P)}{N}}$$

$$l^2 P^2 = \frac{4P(1 - P)}{N}$$

or

$$N = \frac{4P(1 - P)}{l^2 P^2} = \frac{4(1 - P)}{l^2 P}$$

where P and l are expressed as proportions.

Alternatively,

$$N = \frac{4(100 - P) \times 100^2}{l^2 P}$$

where P and l are expressed as percentages.

Suppose a factor occurs 25 per cent of the time ($P = 0.25$), and a relative accuracy in P of 10 per cent ($l = 0.10$) is acceptable (that is, it lies in the range $25 \pm 0.1 \times 25$ or between 22.5 and 27.5 per cent), then the number of observations required:

$$N = \frac{4 \times (1 - 0.25)}{(0.1)^2 \times 0.25} = 1200$$

or

$$N = \frac{4 \times (100 - 25) \times 100^2}{(10)^2 \times 25} = 1200$$

Appendix 3

Representative Examination Questions

As in the previous edition, the sources of questions have not been identified. The reasons for this are:

1. The authors have found that questions are quite widely used and that identification of source is difficult.
2. Many questions have had to be modified in order to provide sensible figures – inflation made the original figures appear nonsense.
3. Some questions which are still useful – a good examination question, like a good joke, never dies – were derived from institutions which no longer exist.

We would, nevertheless, like to thank all the authors of questions and hope that they will appreciate and accept our reasons.

Chapter 1   The production/operations function and the organization

1. Define 'operations management'.
    How will the actions of the marketing department affect the behaviour of the operations department?
2. What is to be sold is strictly the affair of marketing, while how it is to be produced is strictly the affair of operations.
    Comment on this statement, particularly with respect to providing satisfaction to the customer.
3. Operations management is necessarily a complex task. Suggest ways in which it can be simplified.
4. Discuss the definition: 'Operations management is the management of the transformation process'.
5. Describe a framework for understanding the operations function.

Chapter 2   Production/operations strategy

1. Why is good market research and forecasting an essential basis for good operations management?

2. From: The Marketing Manager
   To: The Operations Manager

   One of my reps. tells me that he can get an order – which could lead to substantial annual orders – for a product which would nicely fill up the spare capacity which you were telling me about. Moreover, the quality required is inferior to our present range so that you could transfer over any less satisfactory resources on to this job. Of course the profit margin is not so great as we would normally expect, but since your resources are not fully occupied, it would, nevertheless, be an increase in total profit. As the volumes both immediate and potential are substantial, I shall take no action until I hear from you. Details of the product are being passed to you by my rep. John Smith.'

   As an operations manager, what would be your response to this memorandum?
3. Discuss the proposition 'All objectives must be considered and optimized simultaneously'. Illustrate your answer with examples of your own choice.
4. 'Change is now the norm'. Discuss this statement with particular reference to the operational aspects and decision making of an organization.
5. How does the production/operations management strategy relate to the corporate policy. Suggest an approach for breaking down the task of setting POM strategy into handlable portions.

Chapter 3   Planning and controlling the operations

1. What issues must be considered in selecting the products and/or services to be offered by an organization? What role does marketing play in this process?
2. Preparing procedural manuals for production control is a bureaucratic waste of time. Discuss.
3. All successful planning systems appear to have a number of features in common. List and discuss these features.
4. Show the similarities between 'production control' and 'quality control'. What are the advantages of an explicitly designed control system over simple annual reports of performance.
5. Discuss together the propositions: 'Control is only possible if choice of action is present', and, 'It is always desirable to measure as precisely as possible'.

Chapter 4   Production/operations management and financial management

1. What is meant by the 'break-even' point? An organization whose fixed costs are £5,625.000 sells a single product for £31.25 each. The unit material cost is £9.375, while the other costs, assumed to be wholly variable, are £10.625 a unit. Graphically or otherwise, determine:

   (a) the break-even point;
   (b) the volume sold which will produce a profit of 10 per cent on the selling price;

(c) the effect on the break-even point of a reduction in material cost of 10 per cent.

2. What are the objectives which would influence you in setting up a system of budgetary control? Write short notes about the activities for which you would budget.

3. Standard costing allied to the employment of the break-even chart has particular value in the jobbing environment.

   (a) Give reasons why this should be the case.
   (b) Outline, for this situation, the method of allocative overheads.

4. Outline the scope and limitation of controlling capital expenditure through its budget.

5. Explain the principles of discounting cash flows. A new photocopying machine costs £5,400 to buy. The annual running cost and second-hand values vary with age as shown below:

Age (years)	1	2	3	4	5	6	7
Annual running cost (£)	700	780	880	1,000	1,150	1,300	1,500
Second-hand value (£)	4,400	3,600	2,900	2,400	2,000	1,700	1,500

Assuming discounting is not required, find the most economic age for placement in the following circumstances:

(a) a machine is required for an indefinite future;
(b) the current machine is now three years old and a machine is only required for five more years.

Chapter 5 Production/operations management in manufacturing and service environments

1. Describe the role of the customer in each of the following situations:

   (a) a supermarket;
   (b) a high street bank;
   (c) a dentists' surgery;
   (d) a fast food restaurant.

2. Using appropriate examples, compare and contrast inventory management in service and manufacturing environments.

3. Explain the role of the front office/back office operations in the following, and how this division can lead to increased efficiencies:

   (a) an insurance brokers' office.
   (b) a retail food store.
   (c) a restaurant.

4. Distinguish between manufacturing and operations environments and compare and contrast, using appropriate examples, the role of production/operations management in each.

5. 'The presence of the customer in service environment is both an asset and a liability.'
    Using examples of your own choice, discuss this statement.

Chapter 6   Marketing and product/service design

1. What principles should be considered in creating designs for economic operation? To what extent should the operations department be allowed to influence the design of a product or service?
2. List and explain the need for the information which should be written into a design specification.
3. List the principal stages in the design of a product or service and suggest a method of organizing the design work, indicating where the responsibility lies at each stage.
4. 'Thinking cannot be timed.' Discuss this remark with particular reference to the marketing and design work for a product or service.
5. 'The design department is the cradle of operating costs.' Discuss this statement and suggest the contribution that the design department could make towards minimizing such costs.

Chapter 7   Product/service: variety and value

1. The credit department of a large company involved in hiring equipment to a wide range of companies has a credit system whereby customers can submit queries to the department. The rental fee is not normally paid until the query has been resolved. This affects the cash flow of the company in addition to the costs associated with dealing with the query. In some cases, the invoice will be adjusted or a credit note issued; in other cases, no adjustment is needed. Typical examples in this latter class are (a) the customer's misunderstanding of the agreement, (b) the customer's misreading of the invoice itself, or (c) transfer of the equipment to another site, resulting in the invoice being wrongly addressed.

    Each query is given a code number identifying the type of query, the code numbers running from 01–17. 5561 queries were received over a three-month period, these being distributed amongst the codes as follows:

Nature of query	Credit code	Queries
Duplicated charges	01	274
Incorrect sales/rental tariff used	02	309
Trade-in credit to customers changing from competitor's product	03	1
Quality dispute – service	04	19
Quality dispute – machines	05	4
Incorrect invoice/credit note/invoice calculation	06	452

Incorrect allowance/discount	07	218
No proof of indebtedness to company	08	11
Non-cost adjustments (i.e no credit given)	09	3460
Machine discontinuation	10	304
Misrepresentation – waive minimum billing	11	11
Misrepresentation – non-standard terms	12	204
Delivery dispute – machines	13	117
Delivery dispute – consumables	14	10
Incorrect meter reading	15	138
Debt not worth pursuing	16	12
VAT adjustment	17	19

You are asked to look at ways of reducing the staff within the credit department. What initial action would you take? What additional benefits may accrue from the exercise?

2. (a) Explain how a company should undertake a comprehensive variety reduction exercise and describe the benefits which such an exercise might yield.

(b) Table 1 gives sales and cost data for a range of products. Which products should be considered as possible lines to discontinue?

Table 1

Product	Selling price (£)	Sales volume	Material cost (£)	Labour cost (£)	Overhead (£)
1	100	1000	20	20	50
2	50	200	10	10	26
3	71	400	30	20	36
4	3	9000	1	4	2
5	27	4000	5	5	14
6	61	500	12	10	30
7	22	400	4	2	10
8	16	300	3	1	10
9	107	200	22	20	80
10	20	1000	4	2	10

3. You are the Operations Director for an International Travel Agency operating from outlets in the major cities of Europe, covering both leisure and business travel.

Outline the areas where variety might cause management difficulties, and describe some of the approaches to controlling these situations.

4. Using examples of products and services of your choice, compare and contrast the use of value analysis in a non-manufacturing environment, such as a bank, with its application in a manufacturing company, such as a pharmaceutical manufacturer.

5. Describe the methods and techniques used in value analysis, and outline the structure of the value analysis team.

Chapter 8   Quality

1. Quality cannot be 'inspected' or checked into a product or service, nor can it be advertised in. Explain this statement with respect to the services offered by a hotel.
2. Explain the role played by the managing director of a manufacturing company in its quality assurance activities. What organizational features should exist for promoting and controlling quality?
3. Describe the various components of 'total quality related costs' and explain how they are inter-related. Discuss what action management may take to reduce these costs.
4. Quality is often said to be everyone's business, but what are the elements of an effective quality management system, and what are its detailed information requirements.
5. Explain the principles and operation of quality improvement teams. How can they help an organization, such as a bank, to improve its overall efficiency, within a total quality framework?

Chapter 9   Reliability

1. Explain what is meant by the reliability of a product. Indicate what influence the designer may have on reliability.
2. Discuss the various types and causes of failure and explain how 'failure mode, effect and criticality analysis' (FMECA) can be used to reduce the frequency of its occurrence.
3. Bruddersford Breweries have recently introduced a new 'party dispenser' pack, which basically consists of a re-fillable spherical container moulded in a cylindrical jacket. It is fitted with taps for filling and dispensing, and with a 'pressure' cartridge. The original batch, assembled for the test market, met with such a favourable response that the company was encouraged to start a large-scale production for the national market. The quality of the product, as monitored during production and by final inspection, seemed satisfactory. However, customers soon complained of various malfunctions, such as leaks, loss of pressure etc. How would you institute a reliability management programme to cure the problems and prevent their recurrence?
4. Oakman and Lockland Ltd operate a preventative maintenance programme in their polishing shop. Each machine is overhauled at six-monthly intervals. One set of items – the polishing brushes – are routinely replaced at this time, irrespective of their condition. An experiment has been carried out recently in which the performance of a batch of one hundred brushes was monitored. These brushes were only replaced at the overhaul if they were thought to be unsatisfactory.

    Brushes failing between overhauls are replaced immediately. The table below shows the number of brushes replaced each month. Draw the 'bath-tub' curve and explain how it could be used to design a maintenance policy for the brushes. What additional information might be required?

Months in service	1	2	3	4	5	6	7	8	9	10	11	12	13	14	15	16	17	18
Number failed in month	2	1	2	2	1	5	0	2	1	2	2	5	2	3	4	4	5	8

5. You have been appointed as a trainee production manager at the Backwoods plant of the Bruddersford Group. Your first assignment is to prepare a report on the 'Polykayoss' plant. One problem is that a key part of the transmission drive appears to be subject to frequent breakdowns with consequential production losses. You are able to find records of time to first breakdown of a batch of thirty components installed a year ago (see table below). Your supervisor is convinced that these failures are 'burn-in' failures. Is he correct?

1 period = 4 weeks   No. of components installed = 30

Period no.	1	2	3	4	5	6	7	8	9	10	11	12	13
Number suffering first breakdown	1	3	5	8	11	14	16	19	22	23	24	26	27

Chapter 10   Product, service, operations and competitive strategies

1. Using examples of your own choice describe how the various aspects of production/operations management change as a product/service moves from the rapid development stage of the product life cycle to maturity.
2. Explain the principles and rationale behind the concept of the 'focused factory', illustrating your discussion with practical examples.
3. Analyse what you consider might be the distinctive competences in the following organizations, identifying those aspects of production/operations management which contribute to the achievement of these competences:

   (a)   a fast-food restaurant;
   (b)   self-service grocery;
   (c)   pharmaceutical manufacturer;
   (d)   manufacturer of specialist sports cars.

4. Select an actual product or service and describe how it has developed through the various stages of its life cycle.
5. 'Sound production/operations management can be used to gain competitive advantage.'
   Discuss using examples of your own choice.

Chapter 11   Location and design of the plant or facilities

1. A rapidly expanding company, occupying rented premises extending to about 30,000 square feet on an industrial estate, is looking for a new site, about four times this size. List the factors to be considered in finding a suitable location.
2. Explain how various alternative sites, which have been identified by the company in Question 1, should be evaluated and a selection made.

3. How may the choice of location affect the activities of a non-manufacturing organization such as a management consultancy?
4. Explain the factors to be considered in the design of facilities using the example of a small hospital.
5. Discuss the factors which must be considered in the design of office premises for the head office of a large building society.

Chapter 12   Layout of the facilities

1. A decision has to be made to arrange the layout of a factory, either by grouping similar types of machines together in separate sections or by arranging them in sequence for line production.

    Give the factors you would consider in order to arrive at a decision and state the advantages and disadvantages of the sequential method of layout.
2. (a)   Discuss the different criteria which could be used to assess the layout of production facilities.
    (b)   List the information you would require to lay out equipment in an empty warehouse which is being converted to a manufacturing workshop.
    (c)   Describe the method of operations sequence analysis and show how each piece of information obtained would be used to complete the layout. How could a computer help in this process?
3. A Pareto analysis of work flow reveals that, of the total of 50 different items processed, 9 constitute more than three-quarters of the total number of movements. Materials for all jobs are requested from an issuing store and the jobs are finally delivered to a finished goods store. Details of these 9 items are as shown below:

Product type	1	2	3	4	5	6	7	8	9
Volume (in units) per unit time	5000	3000	7000	2000	1000	4000	5000	3000	800
Units per load moved	100	10	70	10	50	20	250	100	20

Operation no.	Work centre performing the operation								
1	A	F	F	A	A	B	D	G	A
2	B	G	G	B	C	C	A	H	B
3	C	H	H	C	B	A	D	K	C
4	D	J	J	D	D	H	C	J	D
5	E	K	G	K	A	J	B	H	E
6	K		K	E	K	K	J	J	F
7	A			C	H	C	K	B	G
8	F			G	J	D	G		H
9					K				J
10									K

The approximate areas of the work centres and stores are:

Work centre	A	B	C	D	E	F	G	H	J	K	*Issuing store*	*Receiving store*
Areas (m²)	100	120	80	60	90	60	105	130	100	120	210	250

It is required that all the above be accommodated within the following rectangular plan area:

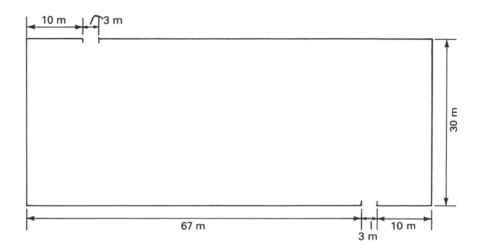

All aisles must be at least 3 metres wide.

(a) From the above, deduce the travel chart.
(b) From question a, deduce the journeys between chart.
(c) Suggest a possible schematic diagram.
(d) Draw a scaled plan area diagram showing the location of (i) all work centres, (ii) aisles, (iii) issuing and receiving stores.

4. The process involved in the manufacture of a product is as follows: It starts with the manufacture of four components, A, B, C, D. A, B and C are then used in the manufacture of sub-assembly E, which is then used with component D to make F. G is manufactured from F, and the finished product H, is manufactured from G. The times for these elements are given below:

Element	A	B	C	D	E	F	G	H
Time (min)	2.3	3.6	4.1	3.1	6.2	1.5	3.2	1.1

Output is set at 50 units per 8-hour day.

Draw the precedence diagram. Determine the minimum number of stages required if flow production methods are to be used. Suggest an allocation of elements to stages and discuss this allocation.

5. A product consisting of 17 work elements is to be produced down a flow production line. The work elements, their standard times and inter-relationships are given in the table below.

Work element	A	B	C	D	E	F	G	H	I	J	K	L	M	N	P	R	S
Work content (sec)	8	4	12	7	10	4	10	8	12	3	6	4	8	2	4	3	5
Preceded by	–	–	A	B,C	C	D,E	F	G,H	I	I	J	K	L	L,M	N		P

The technological zoning constraints are that elements A and E *must not* be carried out at the same work station and elements G and I *must* be carried out at the same work station.

If 120 products are required from the line per hour:

(a) Suggest a suitable assembly line allocation of work elements to work stations.
(b) What is the total balance delay and balance loss in the system you have designed?
(c) Can the balance delay and balance loss be reduced?

Chapter 13   Equipment selection

1. A small company is considering the purchase of a new lorry. List and discuss the factors which should be considered before making a recommendation, and indicate the components of a specification.
2. A plant engineer was considering the choice of purchasing one of two drilling machines, machine P and machine Q, both technically efficient and of the latest design. They both equally do the job sought in the factory.

   Machine P costs £50,000 to purchase, whereas machine Q costs £60,000 to purchase. Machine P is estimated to last 8 years with a salvage value of £10,000 at the end of this period. Machine Q is estimated to last 10 years with a salvage value of also £10,000 at the end of 10 years.

   Machine P is estimated to cost £6,000, £3,000 and £2,000 respectively in operating, power and maintenance expenses. Machine Q is estimated to cost £5,000, £2,000 and £1,000 respectively for operating, power and maintenance expenses.

   Assuming a current rate of interest or cost of capital at 10 per cent, which machine should the plant engineer choose?
3. Investment decisions for items of capital plant and equipment require consideration of numerous costs other than that of the item itself. What other costs are involved and how would an operations manager approach the task of selecting and justifying plant for a new project?
4. Explain the role of Computer Integrated Operations in the design and manufacture of products.
5. What is the aim of economic appraisal concepts and what are its component parts?

Chapter 14 Maintenance of the facilities and equipment

1. State the objectives of maintenance and explain the various types of maintenance policies available to an organization.
2. Explain what the term 'preventative maintenance' means as applied to a factory, and describe the features of such a system of maintenance.
3. Present the case for planned maintenance and outline the basic elements of a planned maintenance scheme. How has the approach to maintenance changed over recent years?
4. Show how data on reliability of plant may be used in maintenance decisions, indicating the changes in approach which may be required throughout the life of equipment in use.
5. (a)   What is meant by replacement theory?
   Discuss the main factors that require consideration in developing a replacement policy.
   (b)   A manager finds from past records that the costs per year of running an item of plant whose purchase price is £3000 are as given below:

Year	1	2	3	4	5	6	7	8
Running costs (£)	500	600	700	900	1150	1400	1700	2000
Resale price (£)	1500	750	375	185	100	100	100	100

How often should the plant be replaced?

Chapter 15 Production/operating systems design

1. A furniture manufacturer who produces mainly for stock is considering moving from batch production to flow methods for a range of 3 different sizes of coffee table. Describe the factors which should be taken into account in making this decision, and using figures of your choice, outline some of the analyses which will be required before any flow lines can be set up.
2. (a)   Describe the principal features of job, batch and flow methods.
   (b)   For each of the following environments, select an appropriate way of organizing the conversion process, explaining carefully your reasons:

   (i) a fish and chip shop;
   (ii) a management consultancy;
   (iii) a bespoke tailors;
   (iv) a car assembly plant.

3. Using examples of your own choice from both manufacturing and service environments, compare and contrast batch and flow methods.
4. Compare and contrast job, batch and flow methods; paying particular attention to (a) the ability to handle variety in products/service; (b) ability to handle changing volumes from period to period; (c) equipment utilization; (d) skill requirement of work-force; (e) materials management procedures and (f) scheduling.

5. For each of the following, compare and contrast two ways of organizing the conversion process:
    (i) a plant assembling car components;
    (ii) a fast food take-away;
    (iii) a small engineering plant;
    (iv) a garage repair/service facility;
    (v) an insurance brokers' office.

Chapter 16   Manufacturing systems design

1. You are the manager of the Claims Processing Department of a major insurance company. All classes of risk are covered including motor vehicles, domestic buildings, domestic contents, commercial contents. Your staff of 25 are currently organized by process, with one section responsible for putting together all of the documentation, another for client liaison – arranging surveys, visits, etc. – another for vetting the report and authorizing payment and so on.

    You are considering setting up semi-autonomous work groups. Explain how you would go about this, identifying any potential problems and outlining possible benefits.

2. In the 1970s one of the manufacturing plants of the Swedish Volvo car company introduced a form of group working. This demonstrated some quite spectacular benefits. US car manufacturers dismissed the approach, claiming it could not cope with the volumes produced by their plants, which were orders of magnitude larger. There is, however, some evidence now that they are re-thinking their original assessment.

    Compare and contrast flow production and group technology in the context of a plant assembling a popular make of car (e.g. Ford, Renault).

3. 'The major benefit of group technology (GT) is reduced set-up times. The Japanese have successfully developed approaches based on method study and production engineering for significantly reducing, if not almost eliminating, set-up times. Consequently GT has little to offer anymore!'
    Discuss.

4. The influence of technology, for example, flexible manufacturing systems, has and is having a significant impact on the ability of manufacturing industry to become more competitive. Technology, however, has no major role to play in the 'service sector'.
    Discuss.

5. 'Group technology is fine in principle, but it must result in under utilization of plant, which will inevitably lead to higher costs.'
    Discuss.

Chapter 17   Method study

1. 'Work study is seen by the work-force as a means whereby management can either get more work done for the same pay or the same work done for less pay.'

Discuss the above statement in the context of what you regard as the correct objectives for work study in production/operations management.

2. You have just been appointed the first O & M officer that a small building society has ever employed. Describe how you would go about selecting your first task for a method study exercise, and how you might go about this exercise.

3. (a) Many organizations neglect the area of materials handling, yet simple guide-lines and a structured approach to this can bring real benefits.

   Discuss, with examples.

   (b) While work study aims at improving productivity, the environment in which work is carried out can have a significant influence on efficiency.

   Discuss.

4. 'The principal objective of work study is to achieve higher productivity.'
   Using examples of your choice, discuss this statement with particular reference to the role of method study.

5. Explain what you understand by the following in the context of work study:

   (a) the questioning technique;
   (b) flow process charts;
   (c) flow diagrams.

Chapter 18 Work measurement

1. (a) A job consisting of four work elements is timed and rated through five cycles, the results of which are presented below:

	Element							
Cycle	*1*		*2*		*3*		*4*	
	OT	R	OT	R	OT	R	OT	R
1	1.54	100	3.10	100	2.21	95	4.12	100
2	1.68	90	3.31	95	2.10	100	4.27	95
3	1.41	110	2.91	105	2.07	105	3.90	105
4	1.21	130	2.21	140	1.62	130	3.10	135
5	1.45	105	2.98	105	2.01	105	4.21	95

OT = Observed time (in minutes).   R = Rating

What do you understand by observed time and the rating process?
Using figures of your own choice for the various allowances, use the above data to show how the allowed time is calculated, explaining carefully the steps involved.

   (b) Distinguish between (i) predetermined motion time systems; (ii) analytic estimating; (iii) synthetic timing.

2. You are the manager of the processing branch of the Western Trust Bank. You are becoming increasingly aware that staff within your branch appear to be 'wasting time'. Frequently, when passing through the work area, going either

from your office to the canteen or to your regular daily planning meetings with other managers, you notice groups of staff talking and apparently idle, while others are missing altogether.

When you ask your work area supervisor about this, he claims that the irregular patterns of work flow from the input branch cause the problems. The staff themselves claim that both the terminals and the central processor frequently break-down and some of the delay is caused by the switch to the standby system.

Describe how you would go about investigating the situation in your branch in a quantitative manner.

3. (a)   You are the manager of an insurance office. Explain what benefit you would expect from carrying out an activity sampling exercise, and describe in detail how you would carry out such an exercise.

   (b)   You have just carried out the preliminary study for an activity sampling exercise. This was based on 40 tours of observations of five clerks. The activity 'productive work' was observed on 139 occasions. Describe two different ways in which the accuracy could be expressed. Calculate these if the preliminary study results are used to estimate the percentage of time spent productively. Assume that 95 per cent confidence in the results is required. Determine the number of tours in the full study if an actual accuracy of 2 per cent in the final productive time percentage is required.

4. It is frequently suggested that activity sampling is simply an investigatory tool which is used primarily in a manufacturing environment to establish areas for further detailed analysis using other appropriate techniques such as method study.

   Use figures of your own choice to demonstrate that the above is a false impression and that activity sampling can be used in a much more sophisticated manner.

5. Write short notes on the following:

   (a) the rating process;   (d) basic time;
   (b) observed time;   (e) standard time;
   (c) allowances;   (f) allowed time.

Chapter 19   Controlling quality through measurement

1. How should the principles of quality control be applied in a non-manufacturing unit? Who is responsible for maintaining the quality of the 'output'? What role does 'inspection' play in the system?

2. You have inherited, unexpectedly, a small consultancy business which is both profitable and enjoys a full order book. You wish to be personally involved in this activity where the only areas of immediate concern are the high levels of paperwork errors and re-doing of administrative operations – costing together a sum equivalent to about 15 per cent of the company's total sales.

   Discuss your method of progressively picking up, analysing and solving this problem over a target period of 12 months. Illustrate any of the techniques you discuss.

3. (a) In quality control, what is meant by a process being 'in control'? When a process is not in control, what possible causes of variation should be considered? (b) Discuss the use of control charts for the control of both process and product variables. Indicate when these charts may not be used for *control* and, under these circumstances, how they may be used.

4. A panel is designed to fit an assembly, the process requiring a length of 100 mm ± 12 mm. An electrically driven saw is used and its output is examined by taking twenty samples of five panels over a period of 8 hours. The results of this investigation are given below in mm:

			Panel no.		
Sample no.	*1*	*2*	*3*	*4*	*5*
1	104	90	90	95	102
2	95	101	94	93	103
3	89	98	93	91	96
4	95	97	105	95	100
5	102	95	100	97	104
6	93	97	102	94	101
7	97	94	93	97	96
8	98	97	96	102	92
9	101	103	92	98	100
10	102	104	106	101	95
11	98	96	104	101	93
12	103	97	98	101	106
13	106	106	108	109	107
14	99	99	105	104	102
15	89	99	92	97	102
16	98	96	99	95	103
17	98	101	102	100	103
18	103	100	99	102	104
19	97	100	98	95	101
20	96	102	97	98	104

Using the appropriate control charts, analyse this data and comment on the state of the process and its capability to meet the requirements. (Hartley's constant $d_n = 2.33$)

5. Two identical reactors are used to produce a high-density polyethylene material. Process capability studies have been carried out by measuring the melt flow index (MFI) of the output. One-gramme samples are taken every 10 minutes and the MFI measured. The data is then grouped successively into fives and the following results have been produced over two shifts:

The requirements for the product are that it should possess a melt flow index of 138 ± 4 units.

Use the appropriate techniques to examine this data and discuss fully the state and capability of the individual reactor processes and any differences between them.

Explain all terms used to demonstrate your understanding of the methods used.

Discuss the implications for action by the process management, fully utilizing your analysis of the data.

	MFI values			
Sample no.	Reactor 1		Reactor 2	
	Mean	Range	Mean	Range
1	138.2	6	136.0	1
2	137.8	5	140.0	1
3	138.8	7	138.6	2
4	137.8	5	138.0	0
5	138.0	6	135.6	1
6	138.4	6	136.0	2
7	137.2	4	135.2	1
8	139.4	8	137.4	1
9	137.4	4	138.4	1
10	137.0	3	140.2	1
11	138.0	5	140.0	0
12	138.6	6	140.4	1
13	139.2	8	139.8	1
14	139.6	8	136.0	1
15	136.4	2	135.6	1
16	136.8	3	136.0	0
17	138.6	6	141.6	1
18	138.6	6	141.2	1
19	137.0	3	139.2	1
20	139.2	7	135.2	2

Chapter 20   Controlling quality through counting

1. A manufacturer of worsted cloth produces pieces of a constant length. Each piece is examined for defects. The minor defects (contaminating fibres, dirt) are repaired and the major defects (holes, slubs) are identified for the customer by tags attached to the cloth. A record of the number of minor and major defects is kept. The results over a period of one week are shown below.

Sample	1	2	3	4	5	6	7	8	9	10	11	12	13	14
Major defects	1	3	1	4	1	4	5	3	4	2	4	4	5	4
Minor defects	5	3	6	3	5	5	6	5	3	5	3	3	6	5

   Discuss two ways in which this data can be presented graphically and how it can be interpreted. Illustrate one of the methods by plotting the results for both the minor and major defects. Draw conclusions from your plots.

2. The following record shows the number of clerical errors found in a sample of 100 documents taken twice per day:

Sample no.	1	2	3	4	5	6	7	8	9	10	11	12	13	14	15
No. of errors	4	2	4	3	2	6	3	1	1	5	4	4	1	2	1

Sample no.	16	17	18	19	20	21	22	23	24	25	26	27	28
No. of errors	4	1	0	3	4	2	1	0	3	2	0	1	3

Sample no.	29	30	31	32	33	34	35	36	37	38	39	40
No. of errors	0	3	0	2	1	1	4	0	2	3	2	1

   Set up and plot the appropriate attribute chart and a cusum chart.

3. Identical oil seals were being produced on ten supposedly identical machines and the output was being mixed. However, one of ten machines was producing all defectives. The products were packed into cartons of 1000 seals and at this stage a random sample of 20 seals was taken and examined. The carton was passed if no defectives were found in the sample.

   Comment on the operation of this scheme, performing a complete analysis to support your conclusions. Explain all terms used.

   Explain how you would attempt to investigate and correct the problem of the faulty machine, indicating any methods, techniques and resources you might enlist for the task.

4. (a) Discuss the purpose of acceptance sampling, including in your answer a diagram showing the main features of an operating characteristic curve.
   (b) Explain briefly the following terms which are used in acceptance sampling: (i) producer's risk; (ii) consumer's risk; (iii) acceptable quality level (AQL).
   (c) Discuss how the technique of acceptance sampling may be applied in an accountancy function.

5. Batches of 500 electronic components are being inspected before despatch: the AQL is 1 per cent and a single sample plan is required to ensure a consumer's risk of 5 per cent for batches containing 8 per cent defectives. All defectives found during inspection will be replaced with good ones and all batches rejected by the scheme are to be rectified. Design a plan which will *minimize* the total inspection effort.

   If the average outgoing quality limit (AOQL) of the scheme must be 1.3 per cent or less, which single sample plan would you use?

Chapter 21 Operations control: an introduction

1. Describe the main functions of production/operations control, and compare and contrast their relative importance with different methods of organizing production/operations.
2. It has been argued that the success of an organization is determined by three factors:

   (a)   the price;
   (b)   the quality;
   (c)   the availability;

   of the product or service being provided.
   Describe how the production/operations control function contributes to this success.

3. Describe, in general terms, the contribution information technology might make to the production/operations control function, and suggest how this might develop over the next five years.

4. You are the production controller for a manufacturer of a standard range of office furniture. This range includes desks, chairs and cabinets. All your orders are for the wholesale market, against specific customer orders.

   Describe your principal responsibilities, and outline some of those factors likely to influence the way you discharge your responsibilities.

5. Compare and contrast the production control function in a manufacturing organization of your choice with operations control in a non-manufacturing organization of your choice.

Chapter 22   Forecasting

1. You are the operations manager of the input section of an international bank. The following table shows the transactions received for processing each week for the last 15 weeks:

Week	Transactions received	Week	Transactions received
1	1964	9	1884
2	1832	10	2046
3	1913	11	1756
4	1791	12	1816
5	1984	13	1882
6	1961	14	1781
7	1776	15	1914
8	1943		

   Show how a five-period moving average could be set up to forecast the transactions which might be received each week. How could the accuracy of these forecasts be measured? What would be the effect of changing to a ten-period moving average?

2. A small company manufactures a product used by the domestic leisure market. As might be expected, the demand for this product is highly seasonal. Describe why this is likely to cause problems for the production controller. Outline how a forecasting technique could be developed to predict the requirements.

3. The usage of a cleaning fluid used for pipelines in a chemical plant is shown below:

Week	Usage (litres)	Week	Usage (litres)
1	5109	8	5873
2	6323	9	6121
3	4821	10	5124
4	5425	11	5926
5	4234	12	4435
6	5513	13	5461
7	4719	14	4691

Show how exponential smoothing (with a smoothing constant $\alpha = 0.2$) can be used to forecast the requirement for cleaning fluid each week. How can the accuracy of these forecasts be measured. What would be the effect of changing the smoothing constant to $\alpha = 0.6$?

4. Compare and contrast moving averages and exponential smoothing as forecasting techniques, with particular reference to their use by the production/operations controller.

5. 'The production/operations manager has no use for forecasts. The nature of his responsibilities is such that he can only handle information and data which are certain.'
Discuss.

Chapter 23 Capacity management and operations scheduling

1. A printing services section has eight sets of documents to copy/collate and spiral bind. There is only one machine for each of these two processes, and the times required by each set on each machine are given below.

Document	Process (hours required) Copy/collate	Spiral bind
1	8	4
2	6	3
3	5	9
4	11	6
5	3	10
6	7	3
7	10	11
8	2	5

In what order should the documents be worked on if they should be all finished as soon as possible (minimize makespan)?. What is this makespan? Is the order unique? Outline the limitations of the method used.

2. You are the operations controller at the head office of a building society. All the society's different transactions are processed through the input section, and your responsibility includes the difficult task of scheduling work in this area.
Describe some of the steps you might consider taking to reduce the scale of this scheduling problem.

3. You are the Director of the Bruddersford Business School. You have just been informed that student numbers are to increase by 50 per cent over the next 5 years.
Describe and evaluate the alternative courses of action open to you to increase the physical capacity of the school.

4. (a) Describe the contribution work study makes to the production/operations control function.
   (b) Outline what you understand by and distinguish between the following

in the context of production/operations control: (i) job schedule; (ii) production schedule and (iii) load.
5. 'Infinite capacity scheduling, taking no account of load, is totally unrealistic and of no help to the planner.'
Discuss.

Chapter 24   Manufacturing planning case study

1. Three jobs require processing in a small machine shop with three machines A, B, C. Details are below:

Job	*Machine (duration – hours)*			*Value of job*	*Required for week no.*
	Operation 1	*Operation 2*	*Operation 3*		
1	A(20)	B(40)	C(30)	£4½K	24
2	A(60)	B(10)	C(20)	£6½K	25
3	A(30)	C(90)		£3½K	22

Describe in detail *three* criteria which could be used to determine the order in which the jobs could be scheduled. Use a bar chart to illustrate one of the schedules.

2. You are the production controller for a small manufacturing company using batch production methods. A standard range of products is made for the wholesale market against specific customer orders with specified delivery dates.

Describe your information requirement to plan and control production, indicating the relative importance and explaining how this information will be used.

3. You are the administrator of a small private hospital which does not accept 'emergency cases'. The hospital has a number of wards and operating theatres, a small pharmacy and a facility for diagnostic imaging.

You are responsible for the medium-term planning of both physical and human resources (physicians/surgeons, nurses, paramedics and so on).

Describe the basic data which you would need in order to proceed with this planning process. Outline how you might go about this planning process identifying the key activities.

4. A small manufacturing unit has four machines, A, B, C, D, which are used to manufacture a range of four standard hydraulic valves: HV1, HV2A, HV4, HV6HD. The standard times (standard minutes) on the machines for each valve are as follows:

Valve	*Machine – standard time*			
	A	*B*	*C*	*D*
HV1	150	80	120	210
HV2A	200	240	140	120
HV4	170	190	210	160
HV6HD	90	120	130	190

Currently, six jobs are waiting to be processed:

Job	Type	Required by end of week
1	10HV1	20
2	30HV2A	18
3	10HV4	17
4	10HV2A	19
5	30HV6HD	21
6	20HV1	22

The valves must be processed first by A, then B, then C and finally by D. All the valves for a particular job must be processed together, with the job only moving to the next machine when processing of all of the valves comprising a job is complete.

Use bar charts to compare the results of scheduling the jobs in order of:

(a) least total processing time;
(b) smallest total slack time.

5. Discuss the use of loading rules to schedule tasks and their relationship to performance measures.

Chapter 25 Data capture and release

1. A factory produces a range of ready-to-wear men's garments using batch production methods.

Outline the responsibilities of the despatch section, together with the information necessary to carry out these responsibilities.

2. 'The responsibility of the progress section is to check that operations are proceeding according to plan. Consequently the existence of such a section is an admission of lack of confidence in the planning function.'

Discuss.

3. The appropriate method for collecting progress data will depend in part on the method of manufacture being used.

Discuss the above statement, comparing the situation when job, batch, flow or group technology methods are being used. Outline some of the other factors which are likely to influence the decision.

4. 'The progress function is a fundamental part of production control in a manufacturing organization. However, it has no role in a non-manufacturing environment.'

Discuss this statement in the context of an example of a non-manufacturing organization of your choice.

5. 'The availability of cheap and widely available computers will resolve the two major problems facing the progress chaser.'

Discuss.

Chapter 26   Inventory management

1. A small company manufactures the trolleys used for carrying luggage and cases at airports, railway stations and ferry ports. They make two basic sizes, small and large, which are identical in design. This consists of a frame, made from square-section tube, cut and welded with special sockets welded to the bottom corners into which the four wheels are screwed. The handle is of circular-section tube, plastic covered, welded to and part of the frame. A special wire basket (common to both sizes) is bought-in complete and fixed in front of the handle with two special clips, stock status information is given below:

Item	Current stock	Lead time (weeks)	Unit of measure
Small trolley	10	2	unit
Large trolley	10	2	unit
Basket	20	2	unit
Basket clips	30	1	unit
Wheel	25	1	unit
Wheel socket	25	2	unit
Square-section tube	30	3	metre
Round-section tube	10	2	metre
Plastic cover	15	3	metre
Large frame	0	1	unit
Small frame	0	1	unit

The large trolley requires 14 metres of square-section tube and 1.5 metres of round section. The corresponding figures for the small trolley are 10 metres and 1 metre respectively. The length of plastic cover required is the same as the round-section tube.

The current requirements are for 100 large trolleys and 150 small trolleys in week 8.

Draw the bill of material for the trolleys. Produce the material requirement plans for all items.

2. The manager of a large insurance office is examining the purchasing policy for stationery. He starts with an envelope which is used extremely frequently – he estimates 10,000 per week – and costs 5p each. He estimates that the cost of placing an order is £50, independent of the order quantity, and that the cost of holding stock is approximately 35 per cent of the average value of the stock held.

Derive the economic order quantity for the envelope, and suggest how frequently it should be ordered.

The supplier offers to reduce the price to $4\frac{1}{2}$p each, if the whole year's requirement is ordered and paid for in advance. Should this offer be accepted?

Clearly outline all the assumptions made in the above analysis, and the consequences if these do not hold.

3. Distinguish between dependent demand and independent demand in the context of stock control, and describe methods appropriate for each.

4. You have just taken over the responsibility for a stores which is used to hold maintenance materials for the plant and buildings of a large factory complex.

There are over 20,000 different items in stock, with no formal methods currently being used for control. You suspect that the number of items stocked is excessive.

Describe some of the analyses you would carry out, and some of the methods you might use to manage the stores more effectively. Clearly indicate what data you will require.

5. (a) Write short notes on the following in the context of materials requirements planning (MRP):

    (i)   bill of materials;
    (ii)   safety stock;
    (iii) master production schedule;
    (iv)   stock status data;
    (v)   time phasing.

    (b) Explain why a company may wish to develop from materials requirements planning (MRP) to manufacturing resource planning (MRPII).

Chapter 27 Manufacturing planning and control systems

1. You are the Chief Executive officer of an organization of your choice. You plan to introduce Just-in-Time principles. Prepare notes for an appropriate briefing of your senior management team.

2. Explain what you understand by a 'world class manufacturer' and what steps might be taken to achieve this status.

    To what extent can this concept be extended to *any type* of organization, not simply those involved in manufacturing.

3. The basic principle behind optimized production technology (OPT) is to focus attention on scheduling bottle-necks. The commercialization of this concept is embodied in a software package aimed at manufacturing companies.

    Using an organization of your choice as an illustration, explore the suggestion that the principle is equally applicable in a service environment.

4. Describe the significance of the following in the context of a Just-in-Time programme:

    (i)   set-up time reduction;
    (ii)   enforced problem solving;
    (iii) Kanban systems;
    (iv)   group technology layouts.

5. Compare and contrast the following in the context of manufacturing planning and control:

    (i)   manufacturing resources planning (MRPII);
    (ii)   optimized production technology (OPT);
    (iii) Just-in-Time (JIT).

Chapter 28 Project management

1. An established company has decided to add a new product to its line. It will buy the product from a manufacturing concern, package it, and sell it to a number of distributors selected on a geographical basis. Market research has been done which has indicated the volume expected and size of sales force required. The following steps are to be planned:

Organize the sales office – hire the sales manager	*5 weeks*
Hire salesmen – the sales manager will recruit and hire the salesmen needed	*4 weeks*
Train salesmen – train the salesmen hired to sell the product to the distributors	*7 weeks*
Select advertising agency – the sales manager will select the agency best suited to promote the new product	*2 weeks*
Plan advertising campaign – the sales office and the advertising agency will jointly plan the advertising campaign to introduce the product to the public	*4 weeks*
Conduct advertising campaign – the advertising agency will conduct a 'watch for' campaign for potential customers to end at the time distributors receive their initial stocks	*10 weeks*
Design package – design the package most likely to 'sell', work to be done within the company on the basis of results of market research	*4 weeks*
Set-up packaging facilities – prepare to package the products when they are received from the manufacturer	*12 weeks*
Package initial stocks – package stock received from the manufacturer	*8 weeks*
Order stock from manufacturer – order the stock needed from the manufacturer on the basis of the volume indicated by the market research. The time given includes the lead time for delivery	*13 weeks*
Select distributors – the sales manager will select the distributors whom the salesmen will contact to make sales	*9 weeks*
Sell to the distributors – take orders for the new product from the distributors with delivery promised for introduction date. If orders exceed stock, assign stock on a quota basis	*6 weeks*
Ship stock to distributors – ship the packaged stock to the distributors as per their orders or quota	*6 weeks*

Questions:

(a) What is the earliest number of weeks in which we can introduce the product?
(b) If we hire trained salesmen and eliminate the training period of 7 weeks, can our product be introduced 7 weeks earlier?
(c) How long can we delay in selecting our advertising agency?
(d) What is the effect of a delay of (i) 1 week; (ii) 2 weeks; (iii) 3 weeks, in organizing the sales office?
(e) If the whole product launch operation is to be completed as rapidly as possible, what activities *must* have been completed by the end of week 16?
(f) What advantage, if any, would accrue if the selection of the advertising agency took place at the same time as the organizing of the sales office?

2. Within a small neighbourhood department store there are three sections in the shoe department:

    (a)   men's;
    (b)   women's;
    (c)   children's.

    There are three staff:

    (a)   a junior;
    (b)   a management trainee;
    (c)   a manager.

    The manager has to have a stock-take and he decides to do it as follows:

    (a)   The junior will remove stock, clean fixtures thoroughly and replace stock conveniently for stock-taking. She is not considered experienced enough to do more than this.
    (b)   The management trainee will then count and record the stock.
    (c)   The manager will sample check the trainee's stock-take.

    It is then decided to carry out the work section by section, starting with the men's section, following with the women's and finishing with the children's section. How long will this take? Considering only the activities:

Remove and clean men's stock	R_M	*2 hours*
Remove and clean women's stock	R_W	*8 hours*
Remove and clean children's stock	R_C	*2 hours*
Carry out men's stock-check	S_M	*4 hours*
Carry out women's stock-check	S_W	*8 hours*
Carry out children's stock-check	S_C	*6 hours*
Check men's stock-take	C_M	*3 hours*
Check women's stock-take	C_W	*8 hours*
Check children's stock-take	C_C	*2 hours*

3. The delivery schedule of components and the operation programme for the manufacture of three components are given below. Construct the line of balance for week 5. Indicate how you would use the line of balance to analyse production progress in the several different departments involved in the production system.

Week no.	0	1	2	3	4	5	6	7	8	9	10	11	12
Delivery required (units)	0	12	15	12	20	5	10	15	20	27	15	20	17

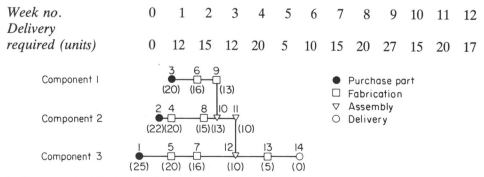

Fig. 1   Components delivery schedule

Figures in parentheses show the time in days that operations must be completed before delivery (e.g. operation 5 of components 3 must be completed 20 days before the delivery date).

4. Compare and contrast the use of critical path analysis with the use of line of balance.

5. Develop your own example to illustrate the use of line of balance, paying particular attention to the various steps involved in the analysis.

Chapter 29   Resource allocation – linear programming

1. A multi-purpose plant can be used to manufacture two products, A and B, from raw materials, Y and Z. The amounts of raw materials required, plant times and profits per batch are shown below:

Product	Profit per batch	Plant time per batch (hrs)	Units of raw material per batch	
			Y	Z
A	30	5	18	30
B	8	10	12	10

There are 216 units of raw material Y, and 300 units of raw material Z available per week. The plant is available for 150 hours per week.

Formulate, as a linear programme, the problem of establishing how many batches of each product to manufacture each week to give maximum total profit. Use the graphical method to solve this problem.

2. You are the operations director for a company which operates a number of multi-purpose plants at various different geographic locations.

Describe some of the areas where linear programming can help you with your decision making.

3. The following is a formulation of a product-mix problem facing a production manager:

Maximize $\qquad$ $30x_1 + 10x_2$
subject to $\qquad$ $10x_1 + 5x_2 \leqslant 50$
$\qquad$ $8x_1 + 8x_2 \leqslant 64$
$\qquad$ $16x_1 + 4x_2 \leqslant 64$

Explain the interpretation of the variables and constraints. Show how the graphical method can be used to solve the problem.

4. The basic linear programming model has a number of limitations when used to analyse certain operations management problems.

Describe some of these limitations and problems, and indicate how the model might be extended.

5. Linear programming has much to offer the operations manager as an aid to decision making.

Discuss this statement in the context of a non-manufacturing organization of your choice.

Chapter 30 Purchasing

1. What are the main objectives of efficient purchasing and what is the scope of the purchasing function within an organization?
2. Describe the work of the purchasing manager in a large hospital, explaining his relationships with other departments and with suppliers.
3. The board of directors of a large manufacturing company is to decide whether to centralize its purchasing activities. Discuss the advantages and disadvantages of such a move. Indicate the range of activities to be carried out by the senior purchasing executive if centralization goes ahead.
4. Explain how you would set up a system for purchasing. Draw up a list showing clearly all the information needed on a purchase order, justifying each entry.
5. A company is to establish a contract with a car-hire organization. Explain how a choice would be made between several different organizations offering this service.

Chapter 31 Production/operations and personnel management

1. Discuss the differences between, and the purposes of, job evaluation and merit rating. Describe how a job evaluation may be carried out.
2. 'The personnel manager holds the key to good relationships within a factory.' Examine this statement and state your reasons for agreeing with or dissenting from it.
3. Describe the operation of a scheme of merit rating, applicable to clerical and junior staff workers, with a view to rationalizing their salaries and assessing their worthiness of promotion. Discuss the likely reactions of the employees to such a scheme.
4. State a case justifying the establishment of a personnel department to a director who opposes this action on financial grounds.
5. State the principles which you consider must be observed when formulating a payment by results scheme.

Chapter 32 Health and safety management

1. Explain what you understand by the following terms in the context of health and safety at work:

    (a) an accident;
    (b) an accident cause;
    (c) an accident prevention programme.

2. Discuss the responsibilities for the safety of employees in a medium sized engineering manufacturing company. Indicate how you would organize and plan the health and safety programme.

3. Describe how you would set up an accident prevention programme for a potentially dangerous chemical production unit.
4. As the safety officer of a university, what steps would you take to communicate the 'message' of health and safety at work to the staff (academic and non-academic) and students?
5. Discuss the implications of legislation for health and safety, indicating the main components required. Give an outline of the essential contents of a company safety policy.

Appendix 4

Short Cases in Production and Operations Management

These cases are each intended to be covered in a teaching session lasting between 1 and 1½ hours, and have deliberately been kept short to permit this. Any necessary preparation or pre-reading can also be completed within this period.

Each case begins by referring the reader to the chapters to which it relates by the chapter number in the box. Each case starts with (i) a set of objectives, designed to introduce the reader to the broad issues covered by the case (without making the 'solution' or method of analysis obvious), and (ii) a list of specific issues to address, posing a set of focused questions with which to launch the case discussion session or alternatively to provide questions which the student should attempt to answer in a written submission. The case description follows (normally no longer than two pages), together with supplementary detailed information if appropriate. The accompanying *Lecturer's Guide* contains Debriefing Notes, which summarize what skills and knowledge the student should have gained in completing the case, and Tutor's Notes outlining what the authors consider to be the main issues to be extracted from the case analysis and, with quantitatively-based cases, some of the analyses which might be carried out.

The authors are grateful to colleagues who collaborated in developing and testing some of these cases and to students who have used them on Undergraduate, Postgraduate and Executive Development Programmes and have provided valuable feedback.

Case 1	Ch 1

THE PRODUCTION/OPERATIONS FUNCTION

Objectives

1 To 'break the ice' at any first Production/Operations Management seminar.
2 To explore the students' perceptions of the characteristics of the POM function.
3 To establish the similarities between traditional manufacturing units and other environments in which the concepts from production/operations management are appropriate.
4 To relate the problems in all these environments to the five Ps framework.

Specific issues to address

1 Describe any full-time, vacation, or Saturday job you have had.
2 Give your 'image' of the factory or service operation.
3 Discuss the characteristics of the operations of which you have experience.
4 Compare a 'typical factory' with a service operation, using the five Ps structure.

Case 2	Ch 6

THE POCKET CALCULATOR

Objectives

1 To practise writing a design specification for a commonly used article.
2 To realize the detail required in setting down a specification

Specific issues to address

1 Set down a design specification for a pocket calculator.

Description

Invite a team of students to set down a design specification for a pocket calculator (non-programmable).

Case 3	Ch 6, 8, 9, 13, 14 & 30

BRUDDERSFORD AUTOMATION LTD

Objectives

1 To examine the use of data and information in the make-or-buy decision.
2 To look at the changes which need to be managed in moving a product made in one country to another.
3 To evaluate the various aspects of quality in this case and to understand the impact of reliability considerations.

Specific issues to address

1 As Production Manager, would you recommend that your company should buy the seals from Germany for the DDC, or install equipment to make it within your own factory? Give reasons.
2 What problems do you envisage in 'anglicizing'?
3 Discuss, in the context of Bruddersford Automation Ltd, the proposition that inspection is a cost-sink, not a profit source.

Description

In the early 1900s Richard Ackroyd, son of a wealthy iron founder, became interested in the use of electricity in the home. He was, for his day, an outstandingly good electrical engineer and he designed some forms of household appliances which could be driven by electricity. One of his earliest designs was for a new vacuum cleaner which he eventually put into production. This sold well and was followed by such other devices as an electric door bell, an electric kettle and so on. The First World

War brought a substantial volume of work, so that the company, by the early 1920s, could be said to be extremely well-founded. The engineering excellence which had always gone into the products created for the 'Bruddersford Appliances Company Ltd' (BACL) a first-class reputation. Wartime and the need to produce had enabled it to purchase a number of sites all over the country and by the mid-1930s BACL was one of the largest suppliers of consumer durables in the electrical field. Its ability to innovate, however, was severely inhibited by the extremely firm control which Ackroyd exerted, and other more go-ahead companies soon became its equal in size. Once again, wartime enabled it to consolidate its position so that its decline in the market place was effectively halted and a consumer boom immediately after the Second World War kept it as a flourishing organization. However, the innate conservatism of the company, allied with its very diffuse production facilities, meant that the company was not in a position to compete satisfactorily with the attacks from both the USA and the Far East. Ackroyd died in 1965, and his place was taken by a succession of Chairmen, none of whom was able to restore the company's reputation.

Twenty years later BACL was being described in the financial press as 'the last of the dinosaurs'. One of the women's magazines, in discussing one of BACL's products, said '. . . Like so many of the goods from this house, this vacuum cleaner is positively fuddy duddy'. A Consumer Association report on the BACL product said that it was '. . . highly dangerous . . . should be withdrawn from the market on the grounds of poor quality . . .'

A few years ago a Shareholders' Meeting voted out the then Board of Directors and replaced it with a professional 'turn-round' team. This team set in train a substantial policy of disinvestment, selling off many of the factories which were non-profitable, out-of-date or otherwise not fitted to a new streamlined organization. The Board also decided to break the organization into a number of autonomous companies and one of these was to concentrate on the domestic side of the company's work. To signify this changed policy, this new organization was re-titled 'Bruddersford Automation Ltd' and the initials BAL were, wherever possible, to be incorporated into the company's products — thus BALFAN, BALVAC, BALPOLISHER and so on.

The senior executive of Bruddersford Automation Ltd in turn agreed with his Board a general policy which included the following:

1 There was to be a general re-design of all products in order to make them thoroughly up to date.
2 A quality improvement programme was to be put in hand in order to restore the prestige which the company had held in its very earliest days.
3 Wherever possible, and wherever cost-effective, parts for the products were to be purchased on the open market. This would allow concentration on the technical aspects of producing high-quality electrical goods rather than spending time on the design and manufacture of simple stampings and mouldings.
4 All projects were to be 'self-financing'.

As the first step in the modernization programme the Board had decided to manufacture and market under licence a domestic dry-cleaner, currently on sale in Germany. This looked rather like a large-sized washing machine and required considerable plumbing-in. It was, however, extremely simple to use and the Board felt that not merely would it give a new image to the company, it could also fill a gap in the market which had been created by the increasing costs of dry-cleaning at the local shop.

The following selected correspondence appeared within the organization and you are asked to comment upon it.

To: Production Director

From: DDC Project Investigator   **Date:** 15 May

I have just returned from Vacwerk where I have been examining the production of the DDC. Interestingly, they offer a two-year unconditional warranty on these machines! It is clear that, with the exception of one pair of parts, the whole equipment is well within our manufacturing ability, although we shall have to anglicize most of the components in order to allow them to be made on our machines. The novel components are the seals (one pair to each DDC) which have to operate at a much higher temperature than our present seals, and we have currently neither equipment nor experience to make these within our present establishment.

If we assume that the work on the DDC can be divided into manufacture of components and assembling of components, the total unit assembly work content for a DDC is about 10 man-hours. The present German production rate is 12,000 a year.

To: Production Director

From: Marketing Director   **Date:** 25 May

Domestic Dry Cleaner (DDC)

Our market research is not yet complete, but it seems likely that we shall expect sales of

       1,000 in year 1
       1,500 in year 2
       2,000 in year 3
       5,000 in year 4
     10,000 in year 5

Our selling price can be in the order of £1,950 and selling expenses are going to be very high, so that we shall look to you for a unit factory cost of about £900. We need an initial batch of 50 for demonstration purposes in six months time — say by 1 January next year.

To: Production Director

From: DDC Project Investigator   **Date:** 26 May

Seals for the DDC

On investigation I find that we can buy these complete from Germany at a price of £30 per pair. Alternatively a British-made machine can be purchased which will allow us to make these seals here. The costs will then be:

Machine + tooling (complete)	£100,000
Unit material cost	£4.30 per seal
Unit labour cost	£0.70 per seal

To: Production Director

From: Marketing Director   **Date:** 29 May

Figures recently to hand confirm our discussion over lunch the other day — 90 per cent of our products perform satisfactorily over our one-year warranty period. Incidentally, I was surprised to learn from Costing that a typical cost of a warranty repair is £500.

To: Marketing Director
    Production Director
    Financial Director

From: Managing Director   **Date:** 1 June

You will recall the decisions of the Board of 1 January this year:

1. We shall proceed with the manufacture and sale of a Domestic Dry Cleaner under licence from Vacwerk GmbH of Cologne and we shall accept the requirements that an unconditional warranty will hold for two years.

2. The Marketing and Production Directors will carry out appropriate investigations to allow a product plan to be financed in September this year.

I know your investigations have been ongoing for the last six months, and I am calling a meeting in my office on 10 June to discuss the situation concerning the DDC to date.

Case 4	Ch 7

POWELL ELECTRONICS

Objectives

1 To identify the effects of variety in many of its aspects on an organization's operations.

2 To understand the importance of managing variety in a structured and systematic manner.

3 To gain experience in the application of methods for variety management in a specific environment.

Specific issues to address

1 What are the immediate issues facing Powell, and their causes?

2 What steps should Powell take to improve the situation?

3 What specific recommendation for action do you make?

Description

A first-class degree in Electrical and Electronic Engineering enabled Gordon Powell to follow some research into microprocessor application at Bruddersford University. He obtained an excellent Ph.D. and became a member of staff, devoting a great deal of his time to electronic engineering research, focusing on novel application work.

During the course of his work he designed several instruments, parts of which were patented, and both he and the University derived some income from the use of these patents by a large industrial organization. During a meeting with the Managing Director of the organization which used his patents, it was suggested that a new company should be set up specifically to exploit Powell's technical ability.

(contd on p.526)

Cost Data

Code no.	Description	Unit selling price (£)	Quantity sold (units)	Total income (£)	Unit materials cost (£)	Unit labour cost (£)
001	Plug-in Module 1	4	260	1,040	3.1	1.0
002	Plug-in Module 2	8	2,030	16,240	1.7	0.8
003	SPA computer	1,000	16	16,000	3.8	10.2
004	RM oscilloscope	250	170	42,500	35.4	79.6
005	Power unit Type I	44	200	8,800	16.5	7.5
006	Power unit Type II	33	3,237	106,821	6.7	7.4
007	Power unit Type III	20	130	2,600	3.9	7.3
008	Pen recorder	80	80	6,400	10.2	1.1
009	Static switch unit	300	963	288,900	60.2	67.8
010	Digital voltmeter	162	700	113,400	112.5	23.8
011	Oscillator	117	100	11,700	26.7	35.3
012	Voltage regulator	20	600	12,000	2.0	2.3
013	Amplifier	52	400	20,800	16.9	35.1
014	Wave analyser	750	50	37,500	50.2	139.8
015	Drive unit	50	226	11,300	3.6	7.4
016	Plug board	9	7,105	63,945	1.25	5.0
017	Voltmeter A	80	485	38,800	32.5	20.0
018	Voltmeter B	55	430	23,650	3.7	6.3
019	Tunable amplifier	67	201	13,467	5.8	24.2
020	Chassis	12	1,200	14,400	4.1	1.9

INTERNAL CORRESPONDENCE

To: Gordon Powell   **Date:** 1 December

From: John Symes

Can you see your way clear to giving me more assistance? As you know I look after all our purchases and storage and with the large number of products we now have and the market we are handling, something like 4,000 different items of stock, I just cannot keep up with the paperwork, and I really haven't time to chase our suppliers in the way in which they should be chased.

INTERNAL CORRESPONDENCE

To: G. Powell, Managing Director   **Date:** 5 December

From: R. Hunt, Accountant

I must bring to your notice that we are running into a cash squeeze situation. At the moment we have invested a great deal of money in the design of new products which are not yet on the market, and are thus not generating any return and I do not wish to ask for another loan from Head Office. I think this is a matter of extreme urgency and would value a meeting of top executives with you to discuss this.

INTERNAL CORRESPONDENCE

To: G. Powell, Managing Director   **Date:** 21 November

From: J. Collins, Chief Inspector

I must bring to your attention the severe pressure my section is under. I haven't the manpower to carry out a thorough inspection of all finished products, and be responsible for repairs. It's only a matter of time before a calamity results.

INTERNAL CORRESPONDENCE

To: Gordon Powell   **Date:** 24 November

From: Fred Launder

I think it would be desirable if we could pay our salesmen some form of commission. As you know, the whole health of our company depends on our ability to sell and I really think we should offer special rewards to those people who sell most. I would like to suggest, therefore, that we set up a commission scheme for our salesmen, the commission being proportional to the volume of sales which they generate. If you will agree the principle I will work out the details.

As an engineer Powell was outstanding, although he was somewhat afraid that if he went into industry he would get 'bogged down' (his own expression) with administration. However, he was made an offer 'which he couldn't refuse' and he set up, with the assistance of the parent company, a small undertaking in a very agreeable spot on the slopes of the Pennines under the name 'Powell Electronics Ltd'. Broadly, this organization existed to design, manufacture and sell high-grade electronic equipment of all kinds. Powell's ability was quite outstanding and he was extremely prolific in bringing forward new ideas. Within a couple of years he had managed to put on the market a significant range of products. Selling and administration were not his interests, since he did not regard them as having any 'intellectual challenge'. However, he read in one of the management journals an article on 'Group Technology'. The concepts of the small autonomous unit seemed to him to be extremely appealing, and he thought that it would be desirable to investigate the possibility of setting up some sort of GT within his own organization.

As a first step he called for some figures concerning manufacturing costs from his Accountant. Much at the same time, he received four memoranda from associates which caused him some concern. One, from the Stock Controller/Purchasing Officer (John Symes), said that he was having enormous difficulty carrying out his job. A second, from his Accountant (Richard Hunt), pointed out that cash was becoming tight, and a third from his Chief Inspector, who was also in charge of repairs, said that he was overloaded and must have more staff. The fourth, from the Sales Manager (Fred Launder), asked for a new commission scheme for his salesmen.

Case 5	Ch 8

BRUDDERSFORD PLATING LTD
(from a case study entitled 'Executive Holloware' by Professor Kevan Scholes, Sheffield Business School)

Objectives

1 To examine the real causes behind quality problems in an organization.
2 To illustrate the high costs of failure.
3 To examine the factors influencing quality.
4 To distinguish important aspects of measurement and control.

Specific issues to address

As the Quality Assurance Manager, write a report to the Managing Director paying particular attention to the following:

1 Quality and its meaning at Bruddersford Plating.
2 Quality-related costs.
3 The factors which are influencing quality in the company.
4 The measurement of quality and the control systems you would introduce.

Description

'We must get to the bottom of this quality problem' said David Sloane, Managing Director of Bruddersford Plating, at one of his regular monthly meetings with senior managers. 'I've just seen some figures from Brian Matthews's accountants and it appears that it may be costing us more than £6,000 each month — and that's only reworking costs and customer returns; heaven only knows what the total cost might be. I've asked Ron Smith from Quality Assurance to look at this problem and report back to me by the end of July. I hope you'll all give him every assistance in sorting this one out.'

Quality had always been of importance to Bruddersford since many of their products were aimed at the top end of the market and commanded high prices. Their most important product line was gold-plated coffee pots retailing at anything from £400 upwards. Other products included gold-plated candelabra, small items of giftware (silver-plated), and tea-sets made from stainless steel and pewter. Bruddersford had been founded in 1953 in Bradford and began by manufacturing a wide range of tableware items. The company had gradually narrowed its range and had become one of the leading UK suppliers of top-quality tableware, as well as continuing to produce items for the less expensive end of the market. Turnover last year exceeded £12m although pre-tax profits of only £160,000 had been very disappointing compared with the company's profit performance over the previous 10 years. The Chairman's report for the year had sought to explain this poor profit situation.

'The results are, of course, a disappointment but are largely a result of production inefficiencies during this period of transferring our traditional craft methods to a batch production, light engineering, type system. We are confident that the new methods will give us the necessary competitive edge and help us return to, and exceed, our previous levels of profitability.'

Ron Smith, the Quality Assurance Manager, decided to approach his brief from the MD in two ways. Firstly, his department would undertake a quality survey on a sampling basis to assess the scale of the problem and, secondly, he would talk to people in the company who were either directly or indirectly concerned with quality. He decided to concentrate his efforts, in the first instance, on the gold-plated coffee pots, since they were by far the most important item made at Bruddersford.

Quality Control at Bruddersford
The Quality Assurance department's task was to ensure that goods leaving the factory were of the required quality. In addition, the department dealt with customer complaints. Internal quality assurance was performed on a batch sampling basis (10 per cent for most items) of goods leaving the final polishing process (see Table 1). In the case of coffee pots, they were inspected for both dimensional accuracy and surface finish (scratches and bruises). Batches rejected on a sampling basis were subjected to 100 per cent inspection and rejects either renovated or scrapped (depending on the nature of the defect). Certain items were subjected to 100 per cent inspection as a matter of course. The Quality Assurance department were, from time to time, involved in investigating quality problems arising during production, or with bought-in components (e.g. coffee-pot handles). The majority of these investigations arose as a result of complaints from the Buffing and Polishing Department about the number of scratched or bruised items they were having to deal with.

Ron Smith's Quality Survey
In addition to the records that were already available from final inspection and customer complaints, Ron decided to take a random sample of 100 coffee pots at various stages of the production system and assess their 'quality' in terms of

dimensional accuracy and surface condition. The results of his survey are shown in Table 2.

Having completed the survey, Ron decided to discuss his findings with Stephen Beesley, the new Production Director at Bruddersford. Beesley's reaction to the figures was as follows:

> 'Well, Ron, on the face of it, it looks as though I should have asked you to do a survey like this when I first arrived — there certainly seems to be a serious problem, particularly on scratching. I know that gold is not the easiest material to deal with but I'm surprised at the scale of the problem. What I find difficult to swallow is the fact that most of these scratches and bruises are being removed by reworking — so why did they get through the system in the first place? I think we'd both better have a word with Jim Broadhouse, the senior shop foreman.'

Knowing Jim's reluctance to speak too frankly when Stephen Beesley was around, Ron decided that he'd better have a chat with Jim by himself if he was going to get any useful information on the quality angle. He met Jim later that day in his office. Ron explained the results of his survey and asked for Jim's opinion:

> 'I don't doubt that your lads have done a good job, Ron,' said Jim, 'but you know the problems as well as I do. First of all, how do you decide what is a scratch and what is not a scratch? Even after 20 years I'm not sure how consistent I am on that one. Then, of course, there's Beesley breathing down my neck all the time about output — I mean he can't have it both ways, can he? What's more, the lads in the shop can't spend all day worrying about every little scratch — what would their pay-packet look like at the end of the week if they did? I think it'd be quite a good idea if you had a chat with Roy Kite in the Buffing Shop; he had a go at me only last week about this one!'

Ron decided to take up Jim Broadhouse's suggestion and managed to speak to Roy Kite a couple of days later. He told Roy he was particularly interested in his views on the scratching and bruising problems. Roy was only too willing to tell him!

> 'You probably know that I had a bit of a barney with Jim Broadhouse over this last week. It was about one batch of the coffee pots we got from assembly which were in a dreadful state. Apart from some deep scratches, half of them were bruised and should never have been let out of the shop. Jim seemed to feel I was being too fussy, but quite honestly if we've got to sort out rubbish like that we'll never earn a living wage — I don't think the chaps in assembly care any more. When I worked up there we used to do our own buffing and polishing and problems like this never arose, but with the new set-up, "The sooner we get them out and on the worksheet the better" seems to be the attitude. They don't seem to care if we send half of them back — it gives them more work to do.'

Ron decided that before he could put his report together he needed to see Ann Wilkinson, the Sales Director, and eventually Brian Matthews in Finance. He managed to see Ann the following week and he asked her about the customer complaints situation:

> 'Frankly, you probably know as much about this as I do since it's your people who investigate the complaints. As you know, most complaints come from the shops – very few from the public; although this may not be a fair picture as the shops may be passing on customer complaints. In the case of the gold-plated coffee pots, I'm sure that we're very often accepting responsibility for scratching that isn't our fault — but it's difficult to prove that, of course. The trouble is that they usually need to go back for buffing and then replating which must cost us a lot. One thing I find funny is that we've had very few

Table 1   Production Route for Gold-plated Coffee Pots

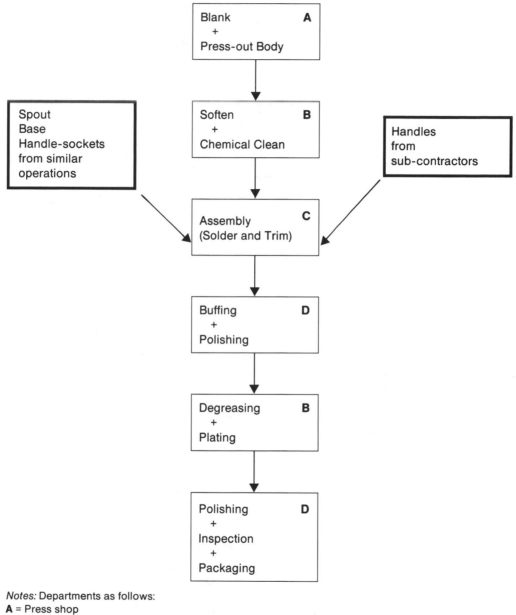

Notes: Departments as follows:
A = Press shop
B = Plating and softening
C = Assembly (Silversmiths, etc.)
D = Polishing

Source: Company records

Table 2   Quality Survey — Gold-Plated Coffee Pots

Stage of production process	Percentage sub-standard (Note 1)			
	Dimensional	Scratches	Bruises	Total (Note 2)
1. Leaving Press Shop (Bodies only)	2	24	6	28
2. Prior to assembly (all items)	2	32	6	32
3. Leaving assembly	0	30	8	32
4. Leaving Buffing and Polishing	0	20	1	20
5. Final inspection	0	5	1	5
6. Customer complaints (Note 3)	1	3	2	5

Notes:
1. Sample size = 100 in all cases except customer complaints.
2. Some teapots were rejected on more than one count.
3. Customer complaints per 100 dispatches (sample size 10,600).

Source: Ron Smith's survey

complaints about the new range — probably because they're fighting each other to get hold of them as they're selling like hot cakes apparently. The thing that worries me most at the moment is the backlog of work in the factory lengthening my delivery times.'

Ron met with Brian Matthews, the Finance Director, that afternoon and asked his opinion on the whole quality problem:

'I raised this with the MD because it's something that worried me for a long time', said Brian. 'The trouble, as I see it, is that we really don't know what's going on. For example, it's almost impossible to sort out reworking from normal work and even if you manage that, it's only guesswork as to the costs of reworking. I know that Stephen Beesley seems to think that a lot of the overtime in the Buffing Shop must be due to reworking and he'd like to cut it down.'

Following this chat, Ron decided it was about time he sat down and started work on his report if he was to meet the MD's deadline. The situation certainly didn't seem so straightforward as he'd assumed it might be!

Case 6	Ch 8, 19, 20 & 30

PURCHASE OF PINS

Objectives

1 To illustrate the use of statistical process control concepts in a purchasing environment.
2 To use process capability data in preparation for discussions with suppliers.
3 To practise process capability indices calculations and interpret the results.

Specific issues to address

1 How do you interpret the data on the pin measurements?
2 What percentage of pins would lie outside the specified range?
3 What options are open to both the customer and supplier?

Description

Steel pins are purchased in lot sizes of 10,000 and used in the manufacture of textile machinery. The agreed specification for the pin lengths is 30–32 mm. Following problems with the lengths of the pins, the supplier was persuaded to carry out a process capability study from which it was concluded that the process was in statistical control with a *Cpk* of 2.1 (sample size $n = 4$). The manufacturer further agreed to maintain control of the pin length using mean and range control charts, but was unwilling to supply the details of either the process capability study or the control charts. In addition, there were still occasional problems with both short and long pins. A random sample of 50 pins was taken from one delivered batch and the lengths measured. These gave a mean value of 31.2 mm and a standard deviation of 0.4 mm.

1. How do you interpret the batch results?
2. What percentage, if any, of this batch would lie outside the tolerance band?
3. What options are open to both the customer and the supplier?

Case 7	Ch 9

BRUDDERSFORD APPLIANCES PLC

Objectives

1 To introduce the concepts of reliability.
2 To understand the construction of a bath-tub curve.
3 To use the bath-tub curve in making decisions.

Specific issues to address

1 What would be the expected cost to Bruddersford Appliances if the recommended action is taken?

Description

Bruddersford Appliances plc manufacture equipment for the domestic market. One such machine has a production and distribution cost of £90. It is sold to the retailers for £140 and has a recommended retail price of £210. The company also offers a six-month warranty period. Records indicate that the average cost of a warranty claim is £50.

A competitor has just entered the market offering a superior machine retailing at £195 with an 18-month warranty period. Bruddersford are urgently developing an improved version which should be available in nine months' time. Various options to meet this competition and to retain a place in the market are being considered. One possibility, suggested after a market survey, is that the current sales of 4,000 per month can be maintained if the retail price is dropped to £165 and coupled with the extended warranty of 18 months. However, the retailers will insist on retaining their 50 per cent mark-up. If the existing model is to be withdrawn as soon as the new version is available, what would be the expected cost to the company if this action were taken?

A batch of 200 machines have been put through a simulated life-cycle test with the results shown in Tables 1 and 2.

Table 1

Age (months)	No. operational	Age (months)	No. operational
0	200	10	146
1	188	11	141
2	179	12	139
3	172	13	135
4	169	14	132
5	165	15	128
6	161	16	123
7	157	17	115
8	153	18	106
9	149	19	97

Table 2

λ = hazard rate = $\dfrac{N_t - N_{t+1}}{N_t}$ when N_t = no. operational at time t.

t	N_t	$N_t - N_{t+1}$	λ	t	N_t	$N_t - N_{t+1}$	λ
0	200	12	0.060	11	141	2	0.014
1	188	9	0.048	12	139	4	0.029
2	179	7	0.039	13	135	3	0.022
3	172	3	0.017	14	132	4	0.030
4	169	4	0.024	15	128	5	0.039
5	165	4	0.024	16	123	8	0.065
6	161	4	0.025	17	115	9	0.078
7	157	4	0.025	18	106	9	0.084
8	153	4	0.026	19	97		
9	149	3	0.020				
10	146	5	0.034				

Case 8	Ch 12

'BRUDBURGERS'

Objectives

1 To introduce the concepts of line balancing.
2 To allow students to perform a line balance and allocation of tasks with data.
3 To explain the difficulties and constraints associated with line balancing.

Specific issues to address

1 What is the smallest number of staff required to produce at the required rate?
2 What would happen if the average demand (a) fell to 380, or (b) rose to 580 Brudburgers?

Description

The Bruddersford Engineering Co. Sports and Social Club was planning a double celebration. Not only was this the 50th year of its existence but they had at last been able to extend the pavilion (and bar facilities). The Committee were planning a Gala to mark the occasion of the opening of the new building. Various events had been planned, including the finals of the inter-department cricket and bowls matches, children's races, etc.

Since the Board had made a modest grant towards the costs, and in the hope of attracting more members than usual, it had been agreed that no admission charge would be levied and that some at least of the refreshments would be provided free. A debate followed on just what food should be served. Eventually, after discussion, it was decided that a de-luxe hamburger, to be known as the 'Brudburger', would be the most acceptable to the majority of visitors. To keep within the budget, the committee decided that these delicacies would be produced by volunteers — after all, it was a Sunday, and hence the catering staff would otherwise have been on double-time.

The average attendance at the Annual Gala over the last five years was 160. However, they were reasonably confident that three times as many would be tempted by the free admission and snack. Entrance tickets would be issued and would entitle the holder to a free 'Brudburger'. Since the event was planned to last for seven hours, it would be impractical to prepare all the burgers in advance. Equally, sudden surges in demand would cause long queues. The tickets would therefore carry 'times' to ensure a reasonably steady demand.

Experiments were carried out to 'prove' the recipe and manufacturing method. Seven operations were identified and the chairman called for seven volunteers to staff the 'Brudburger' stall. However, a maintenance fitter on the committee, pointing out that assembly line jobs in the factory were 'balanced' in some way, suggested that if this were done, fewer people would be required.

List of operations and times

1.	Cook filling		0.35 minutes
2.	Toast bun		0.46 minutes
3.	Mix special sauce		0.48 minutes
4.	Place filling on bottom of bun		0.24 minutes
5.	Smother filling with sauce		0.26 minutes
6.	Place top on filling, sauce and bun		0.16 minutes
7.	Wrap bun, serve and collect ticket		0.40 minutes
		Total	2.35 minutes

Case 9	Ch 15 & 16

SEASIDE TRAILERS

Objectives

1 To examine the problems associated with batch and flow environments under seasonal conditions.
2 To evaluate flow production for this situation and discuss the relative merits of flow and batch production.
3 To examine the problems associated with the introduction of new products.
4 To learn how to recognize and use available data, to support decision making.

Specific issues to address

1 The appropriate style of manufacture for Seaside Trailers (using the data provided to support arguments).
2 The effects of varying demand on the decision.
3 The value of new products to the company product portfolio.

Description

John Oliver had left school at the age of 15 and had, since then, worked as a garage hand in a medium-sized garage in the centre of London. At the age of 45 Oliver found himself out of work as the garage closed down as the result of the construction of the M25. With his experience he could clearly obtain a job in another garage but he felt that he had had enough of 'working for other people', and he decided to set up on his own.

His hobby, which he had pursued throughout the whole of his married life, was camping. He was a very active member of the Camping Club of Great Britain and Ireland and took a prominent part in running, on a voluntary basis, a camp site near London. As his family had grown he had found it necessary to provide accommodation and comforts which could not easily be carried in the basic motor car which he owned, and he had therefore built for himself a small trailer. Essentially the trailer comprised a chassis which he bought from one of the specialist chassis manufacturers, to which he bolted some pre-formed angle-iron brackets, and to these in turn he screwed wood, thus forming a shallow box with an open top, sitting upon a spring chassis with a tow bar and appropriate electrical connections. This he had used for a number of years, and the interest in it was such that he had made several smaller trailers for other members of the Camping Club who camped with him on the same site.

At the time of his loss of job, therefore, he had already made about 20 trailers and although there were a number of similar products on the market, the price at which he sold his trailers, and the robustness of manufacture, were such that had he been able to make them, he could readily have sold many more. After much discussion amongst his friends in the camping fraternity he decided to take the plunge and set up a company specifically to manufacture such trailers. Having always wanted to get 'away from London' he decided to move to the South Coast; with the monies received from the sale of his London house, an *ex gratia* payment made by his employers, and his savings, he was able to buy a small house at the seaside, and further, to rent a disused church hall which he was going to turn into a small factory.

In his first year he advertised only in the journal of the Camping Club, an extremely modest and inexpensive form of advertising, but he succeeded in generating sufficient income to create for himself and his family an adequate, though not extravagant, living. He had been wise enough to employ a professional Accountant to deal with his financial affairs; this Accountant suggested that he should try to expand the business and employ other people. This he did, and over the course of years he managed to develop a more-than-adequate business which satisfied his personal needs for income and provided an interest and excitement for him. Some 10 years ago his company, 'Seaside Trailers Ltd', was turning out about 1,000 trailers a year. These were all made with very simple tools and he continued the practice of buying in as many pre-formed and pre-manufactured parts as possible. He had discovered that the trade was highly seasonal but he was able to increase his labour force during the non-holiday season by employing people who were usually engaged in the holiday trade. Many of these people, of course, had wives who ran 'Bed and Breakfast' establishments and were therefore quite used to dealing with a wide range of simple jobs involving elementary hand and machine tools. However, he had discovered that his health was failing and again, through his Accountant, he found a buyer for Seaside Trailers as a 'going concern'.

The purchaser of Seaside Trailers was a Finance Company which saw itself as a Holding Company, providing cash for 'on-going' organizations and deriving profit from them. The basic philosophy which they always followed was to take no active part in the management of the Company, beyond putting into it such managers as they felt would assist in deriving the appropriate return on their investment. This they did with Seaside Trailers: they appointed a Managing Director, Production Manager and Marketing Manager, and in order to retain Oliver's goodwill they appointed him Chairman of the Company. Over 10 years the Company continued Oliver's policy of simple manufacture of a basic trailer, which by this time had become effectively standardized; Oliver had continued to ensure that little or no departure was ever made from the original trailer which he had built some 25 years previously. The Marketing Manager had continually commented that his job was made more difficult by this very limited range of products but, as Oliver had pointed out, the Holding Company was receiving an adequate return on this investment, all employees were reasonably paid, and the Company had an adequate supply of cash in the bank, so that there was no need to 'seek trouble'.

Eventually Oliver's health gave out and he was replaced by a new Chairman, R. L. Donovan, who was a 'professional Chairman'. He was the senior partner in a medium-sized company of stock-brokers in London, and held a large number of Chairmanships in a very wide range of companies. After he had been in the post a year, he found the attached correspondence on file.

You are asked to consider the above situation with the appropriate memoranda.

1. Discuss the advantages and disadvantages of Seaside Trailers changing to flow production.
2. Outline the advantages and disadvantages from a *Production Manager's* point of view of actively seeking the new trailer from the 'Ministry of Defence'.

INTERNAL CORRESPONDENCE

To: Production Manager   **Date:** 2 June

From: Managing Director

Subject: (i) Flow production proposal
             (ii) Covered trailer for MoD

By coincidence the enclosed two pieces of correspondence arrived on my desk at much about the same time. Would you give me your opinion on the proposal from the Chairman? At this stage, do not undertake any substantial investigations, but list any information you would need to complete a cost analysis. I suggest you work on your estimated figure of 10 man-hours work content for either trailer. You will, of course, remember that we are very short of storage space, but doubtless we could rent some if necessary.

    As you see, George is riding his hobby horse again, but I do feel that in fact he has got a point. I don't think there is anything you need do about his letter until we see the drawings, but I thought I would like to give you as early a warning as possible.

INTERNAL CORRESPONDENCE

To: Managing Director   **Date:** 27 May

From: Chairman

Subject: Flow production proposal

One of the other companies of which I am Chairman has recently installed a flow production line, and it is clear that considerable benefits will accrue. Remembering that car manufacturers also have big flow lines, it occurred to me that we might use this system in producing our camping trailers. What are your views?

INTERNAL CORRESPONDENCE

To: Managing Director   **Date:** 25 May

From: Sales Manager

Subject: Covered Trailer for the MoD

As you know I have been re-establishing some of my contacts with old military friends, and I now have it on very good authority that in the very near future the Army will be inviting tenders for an initial supply of 150 covered trailers. These will be rather longer than our existing model, be fitted with a fibreglass top capable of easy removal, have a number of internal partitions and have an adjustable-height hitch. I have had a good look at our present model and I know that it is not capable of modification to meet this need, so that we shall have to design a new model.

I know you must be fed up with my continual moans that our product range is too restricted (only one model!). With minor modifications to the paintwork, this covered trailer will be extremely acceptable to the general public and I am confident that when we put it on the market it will give us a very competitive edge in the expanding leisure field.

I am getting a set of detailed drawings from my contact at the Ministry of Defence next week and I will let you have them immediately so that you can get work put in hand forthwith.

INTERNAL CORRESPONDENCE

To: Sales Manager   **Date:** 1 June

From: Managing Director

Subject: Covered Trailer for MoD

Thanks very much for your memorandum concerning this covered trailer. I shall await with interest the drawings.

INTERNAL CORRESPONDENCE

To: Chairman   **Date:** 1 June

From: Managing Director

Subject: Flow production proposal

I think that our problems are quite different from the car industry:

1. We are highly seasonal — our output/month is

Home:

J	F	M	A	M	J	J	A	S	O	N	D
200	500	2,000	1,000	800	400	200	400	100	50	100	200

Export:

J	F	M	A	M	J	J	A	S	O	N	D
700	1,000	400	200	100	300	200	200	300	450	300	400

Totals:

J	F	M	A	M	J	J	A	S	O	N	D
900	1,500	2,400	1,200	900	700	400	600	400	500	400	600

2. Our present batch production system does not involve any storage problems.

3. The Continental market will only accept a polyurethene finish, whereas we pride ourselves on providing a painted finish, to the customer's requirement, in the UK.

4. Our German agent demands excellent towing characteristics and we have to track-test, and if necessary specially modify, all trailers for this market.

5. We have established a good working tradition of temporarily increasing our labour force during our peak from the holiday industry workers. I would hesitate to upset these arrangements.

Of course, these are only preliminary thoughts, and I will investigate further and come back to you at a later date.

Case 10	**Ch 17 & 18**

HICKLING AND SONS

Objectives

1 To examine some of the misconceptions of the aims and usage of work study techniques.

2 To present a correct interpretation of the potential for work study in a specific environment, with particular reference to short-run jobs.

3 To develop an action plan to introduce and advance the effective and efficient use of method study and work measurement.

Specific issues to address

1 Describe the Managing Director's view of work study.
2 How does this opinion differ from the normally accepted view?
3 Assess the potential within Hickling and Sons for the application of method study and work measurement.
4 What actions should John Cherry take?

Description

Three months after his appointment as Chief Work Study Officer at Hickling and Sons (Tailors), John Cherry requested an interview with the Managing Director and owner, Charles Hickling.

'Glad to see you John, how are you settling down? Well, what do you think of our little Work Study section? It's going pretty well, isn't it? Of course, 30 years ago, when the place was a lot smaller, I did it myself. Do you know — some of those times I fixed then are still in use today!'

'Yes, Mr Hickling, so I have observed. What really worries me is that the take-home pay is all over the shop! The operators never know from one week to the next what their earnings will be! It's obvious to me that there's no relationship between allowed time and work content.'

'But you're making too much of this! When I used to do it, I took my stopwatch down to the shop floor, stood beside the girl, timed what she was doing, had a bit of a chat with her and fixed up a bonus there and then.'

'Well, that may have been alright during the 'sixties when you had plenty of long runs and money wasn't all that tight. But now we have a lot of small orders and the unions are that much stronger.'

'Yes! . . . But you'll never get a time for these short-run jobs — by the time you've got your stopwatch on to the job it's all over. All you can hope to do is to make a good guess at it. Look here, John, there are plenty of old stagers about the place with the experience to set a sensible time for any job you like to mention. As for unions, you can leave that side of the business to the Personnel Manager.'

'Look, I must be perfectly frank about this, Mr Hickling; I think that most of the times which are going out are useless and that's why we're in trouble. I think it's time we stopped guessing and looked into some of the other methods of fixing times. What's more, we've got to have a good look at the way jobs are being done and for this I need more resources in my department.'

'This is a great disappointment to me, John. I thought you came here to save money, not spend it.'

Case 11	Ch 17, 18 & 20

BRUDDERSFORD DEVELOPMENT CORPORATION

Objectives

1 To assess ways in which it is possible to establish how workers spend their time.
2 To examine the relationship between organization and methods, and operations planning/capacity planning.

3 To gain experience of applying appropriate O&M techniques and interpreting the results in a specific environment.

Specific issues to address

1 How can Jim Harvey investigate the statement made by the Administration Manager?
2 What data will he need for this investigation and how can this data be collected?
3 How can he determine the likely effects of the additional work generated by the takeover of the new company?

Description

The Order Processing Section of Bruddersford Development Corporation (BDC) handles all payments for goods and services provided for the Corporation nationwide. It consists of the following personnel:

Jim Harvey   Section Head

Terry Holliday
Tim Lee
Sue Carr   Order Processing Assistants
Harry Fenton
Pat Hulligan

The primary functions of the Section are:

(a) to handle invoice payments;
(b) to deal with written enquiries relating to the status of payments to suppliers;
(c) to set up accounts for new suppliers.

The activities involved in these functions are outlined below.

Invoice payments
The Section receives the supplier's original invoice document, authorized for payment.

1. A standard input form is prepared and coded from the invoice.
2. The data on this standard form is keyed into a nearby Visual Display Unit (VDU) connected to the central computer, and the data on the screen is validated.
3. The computer output is retrieved from the adjacent printer, checked, and prepared for dispatch to the supplier.

Enquiries
The enquiry form is received by the Section.

1. The status of the account is checked via a nearby VDU, rough notes are made on the back of the enquiry form.
2. A standard reply form is completed from the notes and dispatched to the originator of the request.

New accounts
A standard form is received from the New Accounts Clerk.

1. This is keyed into a nearby VDU, and screen-validated.
2. The confirmation output is retrieved, checked, and returned to the New Accounts Clerk.

BDC have just taken over a similar, but smaller, organization based in the north of England. In about two months' time Jim Harvey's Section will take over responsibility for the payments for this organization also. It is anticipated the procedures will be similar to current practice. Jim Harvey's immediate superior, the Manager of the Administration Department, has stated that he feels that 'the Order Processing Section has sufficient slack to handle the new work with existing staff'. Jim Harvey is not convinced!

Activity Sampling: Preliminary Study

Activity	No. of observations of each assistant carrying out each activity				
	TH	TL	SC	HF	PH
Invoice coding (IC)	6	6	8	5	5
Invoice input (II)	7	6	5	5	5
Invoice output (IO)	9	5	7	6	8
Enquiry input (EI)	6	5	7	6	5
Enquiry reply (ER)	8	7	6	8	7
New account input (AI)	4	4	4	5	3
New account output (AO)	3	2	2	1	2
Miscellaneous activity (MA)	7	15	11	14	15

Activity Sampling: Main Study

Activity	No. of observations of each assistant carrying out each activity				
	TH	TL	SC	HF	PH
Invoice coding (IC)	17	18	18	20	19
Invoice input (II)	16	18	17	17	17
Invoice output (IO)	24	22	21	20	22
Enquiry input (EI)	18	17	16	17	16
Enquiry reply (ER)	22	21	24	22	19
New account input (AI)	12	11	12	12	12
New account output (AO)	4	6	5	4	6
Miscellaneous activity (MA)	55	55	55	56	57

Case 12	Ch 19 & 20

CONTROLLING A LATHE OPERATION

Objectives

1 To set up control charts for the control of a variable.
2 To use the control charts to make decisions on the process.
3 To illustrate the power of mean and range charts in process control.

Specific issues to address

1 Use the information given to set up control charts for mean and range.
2 What is your reaction to the specification given? Would you consider any action necessary?
3 What is your interpretation of the operator's results?
4 Do you have any comments on the process and/or the operator?

Description

A component used as a part of a power transmission unit is manufactured using a lathe. Twenty samples, each of five components, are taken at half-hourly intervals. For the most critical dimension, the process mean $(\bar{X})$ is found to be 3.500 inches, with a normal distribution of the results about the mean, and a mean sample range $(\bar{R})$ of 0.0007 inch. The specified tolerance is 3.498–3.502 inches.

The following table shows the operator's results over the day. The measurements were taken using a comparator set to 3.500 inches and are shown in units of 0.001 inch. The means and ranges have been added to the results.

Record of results recorded from the lathe operation

Time	1	2	3	4	6	Mean	Range
7.30	0.2	0.5	0.4	0.3	0.2	0.32	0.3
7.35	0.2	0.1	0.3	0.2	0.2	0.20	0.2
8.00	0.2	−0.2	−0.3	−0.1	0.1	−0.06	0.5
8.30	−0.2	0.3	0.4	−0.2	−0.2	0.02	0.6
9.00	−0.3	0.1	−0.4	−0.6	−0.1	−0.26	0.7
9.05	−0.1	−0.5	−0.5	−0.2	−0.5	−0.36	0.4

MACHINE STOPPED — TOOL CLAMP READJUSTED

Time	1	2	3	4	6	Mean	Range
10.30	−0.2	−0.2	0.4	−0.6	−0.2	−0.16	1.0
11.00	0.6	0.2	−0.2	0.0	0.1	0.14	0.8
11.30	0.4	0.1	−0.2	0.5	0.3	0.22	0.7
12.00	0.3	−0.1	−0.3	0.2	0.0	0.02	0.6

LUNCH

Time	1	2	3	4	6	Mean	Range
12.45	−0.5	−0.1	0.6	0.2	0.3	0.10	1.1
13.15	0.3	0.4	−0.1	−0.2	0.0	0.08	0.6

RESET TOOL BY 0.15 inch

13.20	−0.6	0.2	−0.2	0.1	−0.2	−0.14	0.8
13.50	0.4	−0.1	−0.5	−0.1	−0.2	−0.10	0.9
14.20	0.0	−0.3	0.2	0.2	0.4	0.10	0.7

14.35   BATCH FINISHED — MACHINE RE-SET

16.35	1.3	1.7	2.1	1.4	1.6	1.62	0.8

Case 13	Ch 21, 23 & 24

BRANK'S GARAGE

Objectives

1 To introduce the importance of planning in operations.
2 To present the data required to permit scheduling.
3 To explore some of the techniques for preparing plans.
4 To develop various criteria for evaluating schedules.

Specific issues to address

1 Why does the situation described in the case occur? Consider specifically:
   (a) long lead times for short operation times;
   (b) apparent high cost.
2 Can operations be planned better, and if so, how should these plans be evaluated?

Description

Roger Curtis always had his car serviced at Brank's Garage. One evening he found himself at a social at his daughter's school in George Brank's company. As the evening wore on they became quite friendly.

'Look, George — there's something that's always puzzled me about your garage – and all other garages for that matter!'

'Go on? What's the problem?'

'Well, when I want my car serviced, I ring your service department, and they give me a date — usually about a week ahead.'

'Yes, that'd be about right — we're pretty full of work . . . we do a good job, you know!'

'Well, when I eventually get my car to you for a 12,000-mile service — not an engine change or anything like that, mark you — your Service Supervisor always tells me that it'll take the whole day — and it jolly well does. I put it in before 8.30 am and when I ring for it at about 5.00 pm, they always say that "it's just being finished" and when I get there about half an hour later I usually have to wait another ten minutes.'

'Yes, that's about normal I'd say.'

'Well, then — *I* can do that sort of service in a couple of hours, and you've got all the equipment *and* the skilled staff. Why do you have to take four times as long as me and charge the earth for it? After all, you're charging the poor motorist about £20 an hour — so you must be raking it in. How many men have you got? About a dozen — £2,000 a day, and I bet your wage bill's no more than £600 a day, so you're really on to a good thing!'

| Case 14 | Ch 25 |

'OH, THAT'S WHAT THE PATTERN SAYS'

Objectives

1 To introduce the need for the progress function in an organization.
2 To develop the responsibilities of the individuals carrying out this task.
3 To identify hurdles to successfully carrying out this task.
4 To propose approaches to overcome the inherent difficulties in the progress function.

Specific issues to address

1 How effectively is Mike carrying out his responsibilities as a Progress Chaser?
2 Why has the situation described in the case arisen?
3 How should the situation have been handled?
4 What recommendations would you make for changes to prevent recurrence?

Description

Mike O'Brien, Progress Chaser for the Making-Up Department, strolled casually along to the inspection area to check up on a batch of 50 overcoats which should have passed through inspection a couple of days earlier. To his dismay, he could not find them — and that important export order would be held up for them tomorrow! Hastily he looked in the work-in-progress store — again a blank. Finally he sorted through the bonus tickets in the works office. They'd never been made!

Realizing that extraordinary measures would have to be taken, Mike rapidly flicked through the tickets to find a similar job . . . and to his relief discovered a large batch of similar coats being made for S&M. Carefully he got out the two patterns — yes, they were effectively the same except that the S&M coat had five buttons. Going to the stores, Mike persuaded the storekeeper to issue him with the fabric, lining and trim 'I promise I'll let you have the paperwork before the day's out.'

Armed with these materials and the patterns, Mike found the seamstress who was making the coats for S&M. Exerting his considerable charm, he talked Mary into 'slipping in this special batch — I'll square up the bonus cards for sure!' and Mary made up the 50 coats. Continuing the good work, Mike got them wrapped up, and then with pride presented them to Inspection, where again he blarneyed his way to the head of the queue. Here his luck deserted him — the coats did not meet the export specification.

'It's no good, old boy, these export coats have special trim!'

'It can't be — they've been made exactly to the pattern!'

'Sorry — they're reject!'

Mike retraced his steps to Mary and told her the sad news.

'Well, I'll have to have a rectification ticket — I daren't do them again without one.'

Mike pleaded, but to no avail, and as he became more and more persistent, Mary became more stubborn. The foreman, attracted by the excitement, came to investigate. Mary explained tearfully what had happened and for her pains received a severe reprimand: '. . . and you don't take orders from anyone but me — is that clear?'

Having chastised Mary, the foreman turned to Mike.

'Mr O'Brien, we will continue this discussion in the Production Manager's office.'

The foreman strode away to the Production Manager, followed by a chastened Mike. The Production Manager heard out the foreman's complaint . . . 'going behind my back — giving my operators orders — upsetting good workers' . . . and then asked Mike for his comments. Mike explained, and when he had finished, the foreman broke in again with glee: 'That just shows what happens when these Progress Chasers do things without asking me. These export overcoats are a bit tricky — the machine has to be set up just right for the special trim, so I stayed behind a fortnight ago, and made up the coats myself. I re-set the machine afterwards so that Production wouldn't be upset, and I've got them in my office now, finished, wrapped and inspected!'

'But the trim's the same as for the S&M coats,' protested Mike.

'Oh, that's what the pattern says — but everybody knows that it's different – and I've got a complete batch of good coats to prove it!'

Case 15	**Ch 26**

BRUDDERSFORD BASKETS

Objectives

1 To examine materials management within a dependent demand environment.
2 To identify the data requirements to support a Material Requirements Planning (MRP) System.
3 To understand the MRP processing logic.
4 To be able to determine appropriate control parameters for an MRP system.

Specific issues to address

1 How should Bruddersford Baskets manage their materials?
2 Draw the bills of materials for the Baskets.
3 Produce the material requirements plan for all items.
4 Discuss the statements made by the Planner and by the Stock Controller.

Description

Bruddersford Baskets Ltd have a small production unit which specializes in manufacturing wire baskets for use in supermarkets. These baskets come in two sizes, small and large, and the basic design is identical.

Firstly, 5 mm gauge steel rod is bent and welded to make two rectangles, the larger forming the top and the smaller the base of the frame. Four additional lengths of rod are welded to join the corners of the top and bottom rectangles to make the complete frame. Lengths of 2 mm gauge rod are cut and bent, and spot-welded to the frame as a mesh to form the complete basket. Finally, two handles are cut from 5 mm gauge rod, part-covered with PVC tube, and fixed to the frame with four special clips.

The large basket requires 6 metres of 5 mm rod for the frame, 0.8 for the handle, 20 metres of 2 mm rod for the mesh, and 0.3 metre of PVC tube for the handle cover. The figures for the small basket are 4 and 0.7 metres of 5 mm rod, 14 metres of 2 mm rod and 0.3 metres of PVC tube.

The unit is experiencing great difficulties with its materials management. Frequently manufacture is being delayed because one or other of the raw materials is not available.

The Planner says it is because the ratio of 5 mm to 2 mm rod is different for the two sizes and the small size should be discontinued.

The Stock Controller says it is because so much wastage is left after cutting the rod.

The unit has just received a large order from a national supermarket chain for 100 large baskets per week and 200 small baskets per week for six weeks starting in six weeks' time.

Item	Unit of measure	Current stock	Lead time (weeks) (Note 3)
Large basket (Note 1)	each	150	2
Small basket	each	100	1
Large frame	each	50	2
Small frame	each	60	1
Large handle	each	100	1
Small handle	each	100	1
Special clips (Note 2)	each	20	2
5 mm rod	metre	200	3
2 mm rod	metre	50	3
PVC tube	metre	10	1

Notes:
1. 100 of the large basket stock has been allocated against an order for the S&M chain.
2. An order for 400 special clips is due to arrive next week.
3. Lead time: for finished products, this is the assembly time; for components it is the manufacturing time; and for 'raw materials' it is the procurement time.

Case 16	**Ch 27**

BRUDDERSFORD INSURANCE GROUP

Objectives

1 To examine the features of a Just-In-Time programme, in the context of a service organization.
2 To explore how the underlying concepts and techniques could be introduced.
3 To develop an action plan for the implementation.

Specific issues to address

A selection of recent internal correspondence is provided. This should be examined and assessed in order to:

1 Gain a picture of current operating practices.
2 Acquire an appreciation of the environment and culture of the organization into which JIT is to be introduced.
3 Identify areas for the application of the concepts which support JIT.

Description

Bruddersford Insurance Group (BIG) is a medium-sized insurance company handling risks associated with building structures, building contents, and cars. They market their contents and buildings policies under one company name, and their motor insurance under six company names targeted at different but overlapping market segments.

The General Manager is considering introducing the Just-In-Time philosophy. You have been employed as a consultant to carry out an initial feasibility study.

The following is a selection of recent internal correspondence. You hope that it will give you some background to the situation at BIG.

INTERNAL CORRESPONDENCE: BIG

To: Accounts Manager   **Date:** 1 July 1991

From: Purchasing Manager

Subject: Stationery Suppliers

I have just completed my annual review of stationery suppliers' prices. I am proposing that we open an account with the ACME Stationery Suppliers for all of our envelopes. Although this company have only just started trading, their prices for envelopes are cheaper than those of our current supplier: Ace Trading. We still stay with Ace for other items of office stationery and supplies; their prices have remained below the competition since we moved to them last year. The necessary data for input to the computer accounting system is below:

ACME Stationery Suppliers
Unit 6, Scar Top Industrial Estate,
BRUDDERSFORD, South Yorkshire SS23 5JD

Phone: 0908 562352   Contact: John Ackroyd
Account no: 43/981263
Product codes supplied: PE/1009, PE/1015, PE/1065, PE/1090, PE/1091, WE/1095, WE/1098, WE/1099, WE/1100

I should be grateful if this could be handled as a matter of urgency since envelope stocks are low and I anticipate placing an order in the very near future.

ref:memo 1

INTERNAL CORRESPONDENCE: BIG

To: Operations Manager   **Date:** 2 August 1991

From: Input Section Head

Subject: Data Errors

As you know we have had a number of problems with input errors in the creation of new customer files. Consequently, I am proposing that we employ a part-time VDU operator to verify all such documents. I should like your authorization to go ahead and advertise the post immediately.

ref:memo 2

INTERNAL CORRESPONDENCE: BIG

To: Operations Manager   **Date:** 5 August 1991

From: Systems Manager

Subject: Terminal Reliability

A number of members of your group have reported problems with the general enquiry facility whereby use of the 'control Q' keys in response to the company name for a motor insurance quotation produces a list of *all* companies' charges.

Due to excessive usage, some keyboards transmit a 'random' character when the 'control' key is used. I should be grateful therefore if you would instruct your group only to make enquiries on specific company names.

ref:memo 3

INTERNAL CORRESPONDENCE: BIG

To: Operations Manager   **Date:** 21 August 1991

From: Claims Section Head

Subject: Faulty Envelopes

Recently a number of clients have complained about correspondence arriving in unsealed envelopes. This is a serious matter since on occasions these envelopes have contained settlement cheques.

I have investigated the problem with my group, and feel that their handling is not causing the problem; the glue appears to come unstuck in transit.

ref:memo 4

INTERNAL CORRESPONDENCE: BIG

To: All Departmental Heads   **Date:** 7 August 1991

From: Administration Department

Subject: Client Files

There have been a number of occasions recently when it has not been possible to access client files — on some occasions they have already been in use, on others they have been mislaid or awaiting return to the originating department. This causes serious delays in handling clients' enquiries and claims, and has reflected badly on our image in the marketplace.

It has been decided to hold centrally a duplicate copy of all client files independently of originating department. As we already hold archive copies of the original proposal, this will simply involve copying all inward and outward correspondence to my department. I should be grateful if you would make the appropriate arrangements to carry this out.

ref:memo 5

INTERNAL CORRESPONDENCE: BIG

To: General Manager   **Date:** 5 August 1991

From: Operations Manager

Subject: Staffing

As you know my department consists of four main sections: New Business, Claims, Renewals, and Adjustments. Each carries out its processes across the entire range of risks: motor, contents and buildings. Within each section clerks specialize in one particular aspect of the process. Recently the level of claims has significantly increased and I should like to appoint a new clerk in this section, specializing in Client Enquiries.

ref:memo 6

INTERNAL CORRESPONDENCE: BIG

To: General Manager   **Date:** 9 August 1991

From: Systems Manager

Subject: New Laser Printer

As you know we have six separate companies dealing in motor insurance. Each has five basic documents sent out to clients. We spend significant amounts of time changing the printer from one set of pre-printed stationery to another. If we were to purchase one of the latest generation of laser printers, the increased print speed would enable us to increase significantly the output rate. I am preparing a cost estimate for your favourable consideration.

ref:memo 7

INTERNAL CORRESPONDENCE: BIG

To: Operations Manager   **Date:** 19 July 1991

From: Purchasing Manager

Subject: Printer Ribbons

You will recall that at the Departmental Heads' meeting last week the General Manager reported that expenditure on consumable items had risen by 75 per cent in comparison with the same period last year, and that he asked for a general review of expenditure under this heading. I have been examining my records and one of the items showing a considerable increase is printer ribbons. In order to effect economies in this area, I have to ask you to instruct your staff only to replace ribbons every six weeks, instead of every four weeks as is currently the practice.

ref:memo 8

INTERNAL CORRESPONDENCE: BIG

To: Accounts Manager   **Date:** 12 August 1991

From: Senior Accounts Clerk

Subject: Photocopier Account

As you know the warranty and maintenance contract provided 'free' for two years with our new copier expired last January. We agreed to use the supplier's call-out service when required rather than renew the contract. Their invoice summary is attached for settlement. Below I have itemized the calls we have had to make to them.

Date	Reason for call-out	Invoice no
21 Jan	Adjust paper feed	10981
3 Feb	Toner feed blockage	11092
23 Feb	Adjust paper feed	12009
16 Mar	Roller jam	12599
10 Apr	Overheating	11348
17 Apr	Adjust paper feed	12125
26 Apr	Adjust paper feed	14121
1 May	Dirty copies	15107
21 May	Adjust paper feed	15590
30 May	Transparency jam	16123
28 June	Adjust paper feed	16342
20 July	Adjust paper feed	17126

ref:memo 9

Case 17	**Ch 28**

BRUDDERSFORD UNIVERSITY NEW BUILDING

Objectives

1 To examine a situation in which project network techniques can be used to manage a complex set of activities.
2 To present the data required for the successful use of PNT.
3 To develop the use of PNT for planning, analysing, controlling and scheduling, and the investigation of each of these aspects in detail.

Specific issues to address

1 By drawing the network for the project, determine the earliest date at which the Grand Opening could be planned, and the critical activities.
2 Determine those periods when joiners will be required on site.
3 Assess the effects of delay in procuring the roof slates.
4 Examine the requirements for support workers.

Description

Over the last ten years there has been a substantial increase in activity at Bruddersford University Business School. Undergraduate courses in Business Studies have almost doubled in size and there has been a significant growth in the Part-Time Master's Degree in Business Administration. Facilities have been stretched to their limits (and beyond) and the University has set aside funds to support the development of a new teaching block, adjacent to the existing building in which the School is housed. While these funds are not sufficient to support the School's plans for this block, the Director is confident that the necessary extra can be found from contributions from local companies, organizations currently collaborating with the School and surpluses on Fee Income.

An outline plan for the building has been drawn up and the detailed planning is about to start. The project team has drawn up a list of the major activities, together with estimates of the durations of each. This is shown in Table 1 (following). The team has also started to examine the resource requirements. In addition to the specialist trades, there is a need for support workers, and the extent of this requirement is also assessed. Finally, the team has started to look at the interdependencies between the different activities. The detailed design must be complete before the planning application can be made, but work on clearing and preparing the site can start at once. Once planning approval has been received, all the necessary materials can be ordered. Once the steelwork has been erected, both the brickwork and the construction of the roof can start. When the roof is on and the brickwork complete, the exterior joinery, plumbing and electrical work can start; interior joinery must await completion of the exterior joinery. Once all the interior work is complete, decorating and furnishing can start in preparation for the Grand Opening.

The team are concerned about a number of issues. They need to know how the work will fit into the academic year, particularly in relation to vacations and the Grand Opening. The contractors have difficulty in obtaining skilled joiners, and would like a more accurate picture of when these would be needed. The support workers come from a pool shared across all active projects, so management need to see how the University requirement fits within the broader picture. The slates for the roof have to be imported from Germany to match the existing building, and there is a slight concern over the accuracy of the procurement time quoted.

Table 1   Activities, Durations and Resource Requirements

Activity		Estimated duration (days)	No. of support workers
A.	Detailed design	20	0
B.	Obtain planning permission	30	0
C.	Clear/prepare site	10	4
D.	Order/deliver steelwork	10	2
E.	Order/deliver bricks	5	1
F.	Order/deliver roofing materials	10	2
G.	Order/deliver joinery	8	2
H.	Order/deliver plumbing materials	5	1
I.	Order/deliver electrical equipment	10	1
J.	Erect steelwork	30	6
K.	Build brickwork	20	8
L.	Construct roof	10	3
M.	Complete exterior joinery	6	3
N.	Complete interior joinery	12	2
O.	Complete electrical installation	11	2
P.	Complete plumbing	15	1
Q.	Prepare for Grand Opening	20	5

Case 18	**Ch 29**

BRUDDERSFORD GENERAL ENGINEERING

Objectives

1 To examine the potential use of modelling in situations involving equipment choice.
2 To use appropriate solution procedures to solve the model.

3 To interpret the solution in its entirety in the context of the practical situation.

Specific issues to address

1 What decisions should be made in relation to the three different makes of machine?

2 What reassurances could you give the Production Manager in relation to your recommendations?

Description

Bruddersford General Engineering are in the process of re-equipping one of the job shops with new machines. There are currently three on the market which would be suitable, manufactured by 'Andex', 'Bonsall' and 'Chimtox'. These are all multipurpose machines, with very similar processing capabilities.

After discussions with the suppliers and visits to a number of sites to see the machines in action, it has been possible to put together some of the more crucial statistics comparing the three machines. Some of these are presented in Table 1 below.

Table 1   Comparison of the Andex, Bonsall and Chimtox machines

	Andex	Bonsall	Chimtox
Basic cost (£k)	10	16	20
No. of operators per machine	1	3	2
Maintenance per week (hours)	10	11	7
Output efficiency factor	0.4	0.5	0.6

Management feel that for the job shop to operate an effective service to customers, in terms of the number of orders which can be handled concurrently, and taking due account of the proposed layout, 12 machines in total should be purchased. However, there is a budget constraint of £200K. Currently 28 operators are employed and, while it might be possible to transfer some to other duties, further recruitment has been ruled out. The maintenance department can only offer the shop at most 116 hours of maintenance work per week.

Management are keen to reach a target output level from the unit, and after extensive consultations have come up with a comparable measure across all three machines — the output efficiency factor — and the target is a total weighted value of no less than 0.5.

Management are keen to keep costs to the minimum and, after advice from the suppliers, they estimate the hourly running costs for the Andex, Bonsall and Chimtox machines as £48, £50 and £56, respectively.

The Production Manager of the new workshop is rather concerned about all of the data involved. He claims that in the past figures have been presented with complete confidence, and subsequently estimates have in some cases been 'way out'.

Case 19	Ch 30

THE ICAM COMPANY LTD

Objectives

1 To examine the role of purchasing.
2 To consider the factors involved in centralizing purchasing in a group of companies.
3 To examine the relationship between technical production problems and purchasing.

Specific issues to address

1 What is the technical nature of the problem?
2 What factors must be considered when centralizing purchasing in a group of companies?
3 What should be the role of purchasing in an organization?

Description

The ICAM Company Ltd, recently taken over by the giant IPV Group, manufactures metal cabinets for the home market. The K.K.3 model accounts for approximately half of the output of ICAM and is scheduled for an output of 2,000 per week during the period April–August. The assembly line for K.K.3 has recently been semi-automated so that, at certain work stations, human operators have been entirely replaced by low-cost, computerized assembly tools. The modified line worked well for a day or two, then developed a bottleneck at a station where parts were riveted together, using an automatic riveter.

Charley Harrison, the Production Manager, recalling a discussion with a friend at a recent Institution meeting, immediately assumed that the rivets were at fault and rang Tom Levy, the Buyer, and said

'Look, Tom, you've got to get on to Carmyle Engineering about those rivets. Ask them what they're up to. We've never had trouble like this before.'

An hour later a furious Tom was in Charley's office, exclaiming:

'You won't believe this, but we don't get those rivets from Carmyles any more. I've just been down to the stores and they tell me that for the last month they've been delivered from Associated Fasteners in Walsall. This will be those types at Group HQ. They're really starting to push us around.'

Tom went on to explain that IPV had instituted a centralized buying policy and that he was no longer allowed to order direct from the suppliers. Instead, his purchase order, along with his recommendation as to the supplier, went directly to the Group Purchasing Office.

Charley was equally furious and phoned the Chief Buyer at Group Purchasing.

'Sorry, old boy,' he was told, 'but I'm afraid we've changed our supplier for those rivets. I know that Carmyle Engineering supplied you for years but, frankly, they were robbing you. We've found a company who will undercut them by 30 per cent, provided we buy in bulk. We've had no complaints from the other factories in the group and they've used stuff from Associated Fasteners for years. I'm afraid you'll have to get used to change.'

Charley was far from satisfied and decided he must see his Production Director in order to put him in the picture. He called Jack Simpson, a young Planning Engineer, into his office and quickly explained the position.

'I want you to spend a few days on this, Jack,' he said 'and give me a full report. Go where you like and ask what you like, but let me have the facts before I see the Director next Tuesday.'

Case 20	Ch 31 & 32

GEORGE FOREMAN

Objectives

1 To examine some of the problems typically faced in the implementation of Safety Policy.
2 To explore how good methods of communication might be used to address a potential safety problem.
3 To examine the roles of counselling and coaching in the prevention of accidents.

Specific issues to address

1 Faced with the problem described in the case, what would you as George Foreman do in the next week:
   (a) with the chargehands;
   (b) with the members of the department?
2 What new systems would you introduce to ensure compliance with good practice?
3 How would you gain the commitment to safe working from all employees without loss of morale, or resentment?

Description

As a result of the Health and Safety at Work Act (HASAWA) the Caustic Chemicals Company took a policy decision at Board level to increase the safety performance greatly throughout the whole company. This policy was expressed formally in a statement which came out under the Managing Director's own signature.

Great emphasis was placed in this statement on individual responsibility to eliminate unsafe acts and conditions at the workplace. The processes were inherently dangerous and, in the past, high standards of safety had been insisted upon in the processing departments; whereas previously there had been occasional lapses of good practice to which the chargehands had turned a blind eye, activities had since tightened up and very little change was necessary to ensure that all operatives adjusted to the letter, as well as the spirit, of company policy as now published.

In the Dispatch Department, however, the product appeared to be non-hazardous to most employees. It was all drummed off, or bagged in polythene, and they could not easily identify the material with being hazardous. They were always up against the clock when loading and unloading vehicles and although the departmental rules specified that protective clothing (issued free and consisting of a suit of overalls, over-wellingtons, plastic apron and goggles for use when handling particular chemicals), most workers 'did their own thing'. There was an array of different modes of dress and few complied with the proper scale of clothing deemed necessary. It was noticeable that the older hands generally conformed but the newer employees objected because they said that they couldn't see the need and anyway the company issue was too hot to work at the speed required.

Some years ago there had been a very unfortunate accident in the loading bay. While a 40-gallon drum was being loaded on the bed of a lorry, the forks of a fork-lift truck perforated the drum and the caustic contents sprayed over a loading hand with the result that he was permanently almost blinded (totally in one eye and with 50 per cent vision in the other).

The position in the shop is that the chargehands (of which there are two in a shop strength of 20) have allowed safety standards to find a differential level between individuals in the department. The older hands are resentful of the risks which they believe the younger members take — and which could involve the innocent equally.

George Foreman, a tough battler of a supervisor, has just transferred to overall responsibility for the Dispatch Area, as well as the General Factory Services (a compliant group of cleaners and service operators, etc.).

He has a remit from his manager to implement the company policy and rules 'to the letter'. He has had one meeting with the chargehands, telling them what he expected with regard to standards. They accepted what he said but no noticeable improvement has taken place over the last month.

Index